AF323595

Modeling Developing Countries' Policies in General Equilibrium

41 World Scientific Studies in International Economics

Modeling Developing Countries' Policies in General Equilibrium

Jaime de Melo

FERDI, France & University of Geneva, Switzerland

World Scientific

NEW JERSEY · LONDON · SINGAPORE · BEIJING · SHANGHAI · HONG KONG · TAIPEI · CHENNAI

Published by

World Scientific Publishing Co. Pte. Ltd.
5 Toh Tuck Link, Singapore 596224
USA office: 27 Warren Street, Suite 401-402, Hackensack, NJ 07601
UK office: 57 Shelton Street, Covent Garden, London WC2H 9HE

Library of Congress Cataloging-in-Publication Data
Modeling developing countries' policies in general equilibrium / Jaime de Melo.
    pages cm. -- (World scientific studies in international economics ; 41)
    ISBN 978-9814494809 (alk. paper)
    1. Developing countries--Economic policy. 2. Equilibrium (Economics) 3. Computable general
equilibrium models--Developing countries. I. De Melo, Jaime.
    HC59.7.M5347 2015
    338.9009172'4--dc23

                              2014040800

British Library Cataloguing-in-Publication Data
A catalogue record for this book is available from the British Library.

In-house Editor: Qi Xiao

Typeset by Stallion Press
Email: enquiries@stallionpress.com

Printed in Singapore

Credits

The author would like to thank the following publishers for granting permission to reprint respective chapters.

Reprinted with kind permission from Elsevier:

Chapter 1

Melo, Jaime de and Sherman Robinson. 1989. "Product Differentiation and the Treatment of Foreign Trade in Computable General Equilibrium Models of Small Economies", *Journal of International Economics*, 27(1–2), 47–67.

Chapter 4

Condon, Timothy, Vittorio Corbo and Jaime de Melo. 1985. "Productivity Growth, External Shocks and Capital Inflows in Chile: A General Equilibrium Analysis", *Journal of Policy Modeling*, 7(3), 379–405.

Chapter 5

Condon, Timothy, Vittorio Corbo and Jaime de Melo. 1990. "Exchange-Rate-Based Disinflation, Wage Rigidity and Capital Inflows: Tradeoffs for Chile: 1977–81", *Journal of Development Economics*, 32(1), 113–131.

Chapter 6

Bourguignon, François, William H. Branson and Jaime de Melo. 1992. "Adjustment and Income Distribution: A Micro-macro Model for Counterfactual Analysis", *Journal of Development Economics*, 38(1), 17–39.

Chapter 7

Melo, Jaime de. 1988. "Computable General Equilibrium Models for Trade Policy Analysis in Developing Countries: A Survey", *Journal of Policy Modeling*, 10(4), 469–503.

Chapter 9

Melo, Jaime de and Sherman Robinson. 1982. "Trade Adjustment Policies and Income Distribution in Three Archetype Developing Economies", *Journal of Development Economics*, 10(1), 67–92.

Chapter 11

Melo, Jaime de and Kemal Davis. 1977. "Modeling the Effects of Protection in a Dynamic Framework," *Journal of Development Economics*, 4(2), 149–172.

Chapter 21

Melo, Jaime de and David Tarr. 1996. "VERs under Imperfect Competition and Foreign Direct Investment: A Case Study of the US–Japan Auto VER", *Japan and the World Economy*, 8(1), 11–33.

Chapter 23

Melo, Jaime de, Julie Stanton and David Tarr. 1989. "Revenue Raising Taxes: General Equilibrium Evaluation of Alternative Taxation in US Petroleum Industries", *Journal of Policy Modeling*, 11(3), 425–449.

Reprinted with kind permission from Taylor & Francis Group:

Chapter 2

Melo, Jaime de and Sherman Robinson. 1992. "Productivity and Externalities: Models of Export-Led Growth", *The Journal of International Trade and Economic Development*, 1(1), 41–68.

Reprinted with kind permission from John Wiley & Sons:

Chapter 3

Dervis, Kemal, Jaime de Melo and Sherman Robinson. 1981. "A General Equilibrium Analysis of Foreign Exchange Shortages in a Developing Economy", *The Economic Journal*, 91(364), 891–906.

Chapter 16

Melo, Jaime de and David Roland-Holst. 1990. "An Evaluation of Neutral Trade Policy Incentives Under Increasing Returns to Scale," in Jamie de Melo and Andre Sapir, eds., *Trade Theory and Economic Reform: North, South and East: Essays in Honor of Béla Balassa*, 82–98.

Chapter 22

Melo, Jaime de and David Tarr. 1993. "Industrial Policy in the Presence of Wage Distortions: The Case of the US Auto and Steel Industries", *International Economic Review*, 34(4), 833–851.

Reprinted with kind permission from World Bank:

Chapter 8

Chenery, Hollis, Jeffrey Lewis, Jaime de Melo and Sherman Robinson. 1986. "Alternative Routes to Development", in Hollis Chenery, Sherman Robinson and Moshe Syrquin, eds., *Industrialization and Growth: A Comparative Analysis*. New York: Oxford University Press, 311–347.

Reprinted with kind permission from Oxford University Press:

Chapter 10

Bourguignon, François, Jaime de Melo and Akiko Suwa. 1991. "Distributional Effects of Adjustment Policies: Simulations for Archetype

Economies in Africa and Latin America", *The World Bank Economic Review*, 5(2), 339–366.

Chapter 12

Cadot, Olivier, Jaime de Melo and Marcelo Olarreaga. 2004. "Lobbying, Counterlobbying, and the Structure of Tariff Protection in Poor and Rich Countries", *The World Bank Economic Review*, 18(3), 345–366.

Chapter 19

Cadot, Olivier, Céline Carrère, Jaime de Melo and Alberto Portugal-Pérez. 2005. "Market Access and Welfare under Free Trade Agreements: Textiles under NAFTA", *The World Bank Economic Review*, 19(3), 379–405.

Reprinted with kind permission from Cambridge University Press:

Chapter 13

Faini, Riccardo, Jean-Marie Grether and Jaime de Melo. 1999. "Globalization and Migratory Pressures from Developing Countries: A Simulation Analysis", in Riccardo Faini, Jaime de Melo and Klaus Zimmerman, eds., *Migration: The Controversies and the Evidence*. London: Cambridge University Press, 190–220.

Reprinted with kind permission from MIT Press:

Chapter 14

Melo, Jaime de. 1977. "Distortions in the Factor Market: Some General Equilibrium Estimates", *The Review of Economics and Statistics*, 54(4), 398–405.

Chapter 15

Melo, Jaime de and Sherman Robinson. 1981. "Trade Policy and Resource Allocation in the Presence of Product Differentiation", *The Review of Economics and Statistics*, 63(2), 169–177.

Chapter 20

Melo, Jaime de and David Tarr. 1990. "Welfare Costs of US Quotas in Textiles, Steel and Autos", *The Review of Economics and Statistics*, 77(2), 489–497.

Reprinted with kind permission from University of Chicago Press:

Chapter 17

Melo, Jaime de and David Roland-Holst. 1991. "Industrial Organization and Trade Liberalization: Evidence from Korea," in Robert Baldwin, ed., *Empirical Studies of Commercial Policy*, Chicago: University of Chicago Press, 287–306.

Reprinted with kind permission from Springer Science + Business Media:

Chapter 18

Condon, Timothy and Jaime de Melo. 1991. "Industrial Organization Implications of QR Trade Regimes: Evidence and Welfare Costs", *Empirical Economics*, 16(1), 139–153.

About the Author

Jaime de Melo is Directeur Scientifique at the Fondation pour les Etudes et Recherches sur le Développement International (FERDI). He is also Emeritus Professor from the University of Geneva, where he taught from 1992 to 2012, a non-resident fellow at Brookings Institute, a CEPR fellow and a member of EU–GDN. He is an adjunct professor at the Bologna Center of the Johns Hopkins University and, since 2008, he also teaches at the Formation Universitaire à distance, Suisse. He is a founding member of the World Trade Institute. From 1972 to 1976 he worked at USAID and from 1976 to 1980 he taught at Georgetown University. From 1980 to 1993, he held several positions in the research department at the World Bank. He has consulted for the IMF, OECD, SECO, IGC, the EC Commission, and several governments. From 1986 to 1992, he was Professor Associé at Centre d'études et de Recherches sur le Développement International (CERDI) at the Université d'Auvergne. Since 2011, he is affiliated with FERDI. He has held several editorial positions and was Editor-in-Chief of *The World Bank Economic Review* (2005–2010). He holds degrees in Political Science (B.A. from Syracuse University, 1968), International Relations (M.A. from Johns Hopkins SAIS, 1970), and Economics (PhD from John Hopkins University, 1975). His publications are available at http://ideas.repec.org/e/pde173.html. His research interests focus on developing countries, particularly issues related to trade policy, migration, and the environment.

Preface and Acknowledgments

These two volumes *Modeling Developing Countries' Policies in General Equilibrium* and *Developing Countries in the World Economy* are a collection of mostly co-authored work at Universities and at the World Bank.

My years at the Research Department at the World Bank brought me a lot. The research department was instrumental in the development of general equilibrium modeling and the papers in *Modeling Developing Countries' Policies in General Equilibrium* owe a great deal to the atmosphere there. For anyone interested in developing countries, the World Bank was, and still largely remains, a place to be.

For the twenty years at the University of Geneva, I am thankful for the opportunity to enter into new collaborations and to start working on the political economy of trade and migration policies. Several papers in *Developing Countries in the World Economy* are the result of these collaborations.

But my longest and closest affiliation — almost thirty years — has been with CERDI, the premier department in France for studying development, especially problems on Africa, and now with FERDI, its closely affiliated think-Tank that has just celebrated its tenth anniversary. Lectures and seminars at CERDI were the source of collaborations and served as springboard for work in progress. And now, at FERDI we are involved in the debate and design of sustainable development strategies and on how to finance them in an inclusive way. Some of the challenges ahead are raised in the papers in *Developing Countries in the World Economy*.

All of the papers have previously been published in academic journals or in books. I thank the publishers for the permission to reprint them. I thank Bob Stern for inviting (and prodding) me to reflect and put these volumes together and the staff at World Scientific Publishing for seeing through the production process. I also owe a great debt to my family, Isabelle, Lea, Elissa and Ines for their patience and support.

Looking back, I have had the good fortune of engaging in these collaborations. Reflecting on them, I have mostly been on the receiving side in the exchange of ideas. I owe my co-authors a great debt and feel fortunate that many a collaboration has turned into a lasting friendship. I dedicate these volumes to them.

Geneva, January 2015

Contents

Credits   v

About the Author   xi

Preface and Acknowledgments   xiii

Introduction   1

Part I: Capturing Economy-Wide Linkages   19

Chapter 1   (with Sherman Robinson) Product
                 Differentiation and the Treatment
                 of Foreign Trade in Computable General
                 Equilibrium Models of Small Economies   21

                 Introduction
                 A Small-Country Model with Differentiated Trade
                 Terms-of-Trade and Transfers: A Graphical
                    Analysis
                 A Numerical Example
                 Conclusions
                 Appendix

Chapter 2   (with Sherman Robinson) Productivity
                 and Externalities: Models of Export-Led Growth 43

                 Introduction
                 Export-Led Growth: The Evidence
                 Externalities and Growth
                 A Model with an Export Externality

A Model with Import and Export Externalities
Illustrative Simulations of Export-Led Growth
    Industrialization
Conclusion
Appendix

Chapter 3   (with Kemal Dervis and
Sherman Robinson) A General
Equilibrium Analysis of Foreign Exchange
Shortages in a Developing Economy   71

Outline of the Model
Alternative Adjustments Mechanism to Foreign
    Payments Imbalances
Macroeconomic Effects of Alternative
    Adjustment Mechanisms
Resource Allocation Effects of Alternative
    Adjustment Mechanisms
Conclusion

Chapter 4   (with Timothy Condon and
Vittorio Corbo) Productivity Growth,
External Shocks and Capital Inflows
in Chile: A General Equilibrium Analysis   87

Introduction
The Record for 1977–82
A Multisector General Equilibrium Model of Chile

Chapter 5   (with Timothy Condon and
Vittorio Corbo) Exchange Rate-Based
Disinflation, Wage Rigidity and Capital
Inflows: Tradeoffs for Chile 1977–81   97

Introduction
Capital Inflows, the Real Exchange Rate
    and Investment: A One-Sector Analysis
Capital Inflows and the Real Exchange Rate:
    A Multisector Analysis

Capital Inflows, Disinflation and Employment
Conclusions
Appendix

Chapter 6   (with François Bourguignon and William Branson) Adjustment and Income Distribution: A Micro–Macro Model for Counterfactual Analysis   117

Introduction
Model Outline
A Numerical Application: Aggregations and Initial Conditions
Description of External Shock and Adjustment Packages
A Comparison of Alternative Adjustment Packages
Concluding Remarks
Appendix: Model Outline

Chapter 7   Computable General Equilibrium Models for Trade Policy Analysis in Developing Countries: A Survey   141

Introduction
A One-Sector Model
The Domestic Price System in Multi-sector Models
Applications to Trade Policy
Applications to Internal–External Balance and Growth
Applications to Intertemporal Issues
Conclusions

Part II: Archetype Economies   177

Chapter 8   (with Hollis Chenery, Jeffrey Lewis and Sherman Robinson) Alternative Routes to Development   179

Three Development Strategies
A Dynamic Computable General Equilibrium
   Model
Macroeconomics of Alternative Strategies
Prices, Incentives and Structural Change
Conclusions
Appendix A: Equations of the CGE Model
Appendix B: The Critical Parameters of the
   CGE Model

Chapter 9   (with Sherman Robinson) Trade
   Adjustment Policies and Income
   Distribution in Three Archetype
   Developing Economies   217

Introduction
External Shocks and Macroeconomic Adjustment
The Three Archetype Economies
The Macroeconomic Impact of an External
   Shock and Its Effect on the Distribution
   of Income
Class Conflict and Policy Choice
Conclusions
Appendix: The Equations of the Model

Chapter 10 (with François Bourguignon and
   Akiko Suwa) Distributional Effects
   of Adjustment Policies: Simulations
   for Archetype Economies in Africa
   and Latin America   243

Model Outline
Adjustment to an External Shock in the Two
   Archetype Economies
Distributional Effects of Alternative Adjustment
   Packages
Conclusion
Appendix

Chapter 11 (with Kemal Dervis) Modeling the Effects
of Protection in a Dynamic Framework   271

Introduction
A General Equilibrium Model of Trade and Growth
Static Costs, Dynamic Benefits and Imperfect
  Markets
The Quantitative Results
Specifying Explicit Savings Behavior
Conclusion
Appendix

Chapter 12 (with Olivier Cadot and
Marcelo Olarreaga) Lobbying,
Counterlobbying, and the Structure
of Tariff Protection in Poor and Rich Countries   295

Literature Background
Patterns of Tariff Protection in Developed
  and Developing Economies
Determinants of the Structure of Protection
Simulations: Endogenous Protection
  in Archetypal Rich and Poor Economies
Concluding Remarks
Appendix A: Derivation of the Efficiency
  and Political Effects
Appendix B: Equations and Calibration of the
  Simulation Model

Chapter 13 (with Riccardo Faini and
Jean-Marie Grether) Globalization and
Migratory Pressures from Developing
Countries: A Simulation Analysis   317

Introduction
A Ricardo–Viner Model of Migration

Decomposing the Effects of Globalization
on the Supply of Migrants for Two Archetype
Economies
Simulation Results
Sensitivity Analysis
Conclusions
Appendix

Part III: Costs of Protection from Trade Policy Regimes in Developing Countries   347

Chapter 14 Distortions in the Factor Market: Some
General Equilibrium Estimates   349

Introduction
Methodology
The Empirical Results
Conclusion
Appendix

Chapter 15 (with Sherman Robinson) Trade Policy
and Resource Allocation in the Presence
of Product Differentiation   357

Introduction
Product Differentiation and Domestic Prices:
    A Partial Equilibrium Analysis
Intermediate Products and Effective Protection
A General Equilibrium Analysis of Resource Pulls
Conclusions

Chapter 16 (with David Roland-Holst) An Evaluation
of Neutral Trade Policy Incentives under
Increasing Returns to Scale   367

Welfare Determinants of Trade Policy under
    Increasing Returns
Modeling Oligopolistic Domestic Markets

A Comparison of Trade Policies under Constant
and Increasing Returns to Scale

Evaluation of Protection in Sectors with Scale
Economies

Conclusion

Chapter 17 (with David Roland-Holst) Industrial
Organization and Trade Liberalization:
Evidence from Korea   385

Introduction

Trade Policies, Industrial Structure, and
Industrial Organization Policies in Korea

Modeling Imperfectly Competitive Domestic
Markets

Simulation Results

Conclusions

Chapter 18 (with Timothy Condon) Industrial
Organization Implications of QR Trade
Regimes: Evidence and Welfare Costs   405

Introduction

Profitability, and Firm Behavior in
Manufacturing under Different Trade
Regimes: Evidence and Modeling Issues

A Stylized CGE Model with QR and Industrial
Organization Focus

Illustrative Simulations of the Welfare Costs
of Protection under QR Trade Regimes

Conclusions

Appendix

Chapter 19 (with Olivier Cadot, Céline Carrère
and Alberto Portugal-Pérez) Market
Access and Welfare under Free Trade
Agreements: Textiles under NAFTA   421

Modeling Preference Pass-Through under Rules
  of Origin
Pass-Through Estimation and Results
NAFTA Welfare Effects for Mexican Producers:
  Some Simulations
Concluding Remarks
Supplementary Data

Part IV: Estimating the Costs of US Foreign Trade Policy   449

Chapter 20 (with David Tarr) Welfare Costs of US
Quotas in Textiles, Steel and Autos   451

Introduction
Model Outline
Elasticity and Premia Estimates
Welfare Cost Estimates
Employment
Conclusions

Chapter 21 (with David Tarr) VERs under Imperfect
Competition and Foreign Direct
Investment: A Case Study of the
US–Japan Auto VER   461

Introduction
The US Auto Industry during the
  US–Japan VER
Modeling and Auto Industry
Welfare Cost Estimates under CRTS
Welfare Cost Estimates under IRTS and
  International Capital Mobility
"Optimal" Interventions for the Auto Industry
Conclusions

Chapter 22 (with David Tarr) Industrial Policy in the
Presence of Wage Distortions: The Case
of the US Auto and Steel Industries   485

Introduction

Modeling Labor and Product Markets in Autos
and Steel

Costs of VERs under CRTS and No Wage
Distortions

Distortionary Costs of Protection with Labor
and Product Market Imperfections

"Optimal" Policies with Wage Distortions

Conclusions

Chapter 23 (with Julie Stanton and David Tarr)
Revenue-Raising Taxes: General
Equilibrium Evaluation of Alternative
Taxation in US Petroleum Industries   505

Introduction

The Model and the Elasticity Specification

Revenue and Welfare Effects of Proposed
Taxation of US Petroleum Industries

Efficient Taxation of US Petroleum Industries

Conclusions

Appendix: Elasticity Specification

Introduction

This volume collects papers written over the period 1975–1995 when I was active in general equilibrium modelling. At the time, applied (often called computable) general equilibrium (CGE) modeling was as much about solving models as it was about the study of the effects of policies on resource allocation and welfare. Two strands were developing independently. One, at Yale, pursued by Shoven and Whalley, used solution methods developed by Scarf (1973) to study the effects of taxation policies (fiscal and trade) on resource allocation in a world of perfect competition à la Arrow and Debreu. The objective was to quantify the efficiency effects of tax reforms in an economy-wide setting (Shoven and Whalley, 1992). The other strand was pursued at the World Bank's research department (Adelman and Robinson, 1978; Dervis *et al.*, 1982). There, emphasis was on the structural/dualistic features of developing economies (Chenery, 1979) and about reaching internal-external balance in the face of external and internal shocks. Quantifying the medium to long-run economy-wide effects of macro (exchange rate) and micro (mostly trade) policies on wages, prices, the distribution of income, patterns of industrialization and rural-urban linkages was to help inform World Bank lending activities.

While both strands were developing at the same time, in spite of using the word 'general equilibrium', they had a very different focus. Those in the Yale tradition had a firm micro-focus: they were largely concerned about extending the qualitative tax analysis developed in 2x2 general equilibrium models by Arnold Harberger and Harry Johnson to multiple sectors and factors, then to multiple countries. Those at the World Bank grew out of an earlier literature on multi-sector planning where prices were absent from the resource allocation process of a dualistic economy moving away from labor surplus. Developing countries' structural transformation was complicated by having to deal with the oil, terms-of-trade and external debt shocks of the 1970s. The papers collected here cover applications in both traditions.

Whether it was on simplex-based methods, or on tâtonnement processes and jacobian algorithms, much effort was expended in model calibration and in devising rapidly converging solutions to large systems of simultaneous non-linear equations. Frontier work on the development of solution techniques was also taking place at the World Bank with the GAMS high-level modelling system (Brooke *et al.*, 1988) that progressively replaced case-by-case often 'home-made' solution techniques. A big step forward, GAMS and its integrated palette of high-performance solvers contributed to the proliferation of CGE modelling.

The word count (see Figure 1) from the Google books Ngram Viewer for 'computable general equilibrium and applied general equilibrium' in economics books shows rising traction until around 1992 when it starts a slow decline. By then modelers were running out of new applications and on innovative models based on sufficiently accepted behavioral assumptions. Also attention turned towards micro-simulation tools — many embedded in CGE models — as multiple household and firm-level data sets became available to allow for more direct analysis of policies on firms and households (see the surveys in Dixon and Joergenson, 2013). The decline probably also reflects fatigue growing out of misuse and abuse of economy-wide general equilibrium applications.

All applications reported here are single-country models calibrated to a base year Social Accounting Matrix (SAM) assumed to reflect an equilibrium in the economy under the selected behavioral assumptions (often referred to as 'model closure'). All applications either have a trade focus, direct or indirect. Model closures contrasted include: perfect or imperfect competition; macro and/or micro equilibrium; externalities; distortions in goods or factor markets. Policy choices differ across applications. In many it is an invisible government, but in some it is lobbying activity (with or without

Figure 1: Word Count (Computable General Equilibrium + Applied General Equilibrium)/economics

Source: Google Ngram.

concern about overall efficiency). With few exceptions, all elasticities are taken off the shelf. No Monte Carlo simulation from distributions of parameter estimates, but quick and dirty sensitivity analysis with robustness focusing instead on alternative closure rules.

Part I: Capturing Economy-Wide Linkages

Papers in part I focus on key assumptions and on the scope covered by the models. Chapter 1, later called the 1-2-3 model (one country, two sectors, and three goods) presents the simplest open-economy trade model. It incorporates product differentiation on the import side (often called the Armington assumption) and on the export side (Constant Elasticity of Transformation (CET)). This formulation became the standard formulation for single-country models (except for the applications in chapters 11 and 14 where goods of different origin are assumed to be perfect substitutes). The paper also clarifies the homogeneity property of micro-focused perfect-competition CGEs and how the values of the 'exchange rate or conversion factor' depend on the choice of numéraire and shows how the equilibrium in the model is affected by a transfer and by a change in trade policy. As shown in the paper, the symmetric product differentiation assumption for imports and exports also accommodates the small-country assumption, a realistic assumption in many environments for the magnitudes involved in most trade policy reforms. The small-country assumption avoids searching for the trade policy that would maximize a country's welfare, an unrealistic endeavor in any case since, in a single country model, one cannot consider reactions by trade partners. Representation of the trade equilibrium by offer curves also shows that the formulation with product differentiation fits squarely in accepted trade theory.

Externalities are often introduced in CGEs. Chapter 2 extends the model of chapter 1 to incorporate the externality from exporting that has often been said to be the distinguishing characteristic between Import-Substitution Industrialization (ISI) and Export-Led Growth (ELG) strategies. It was motivated by the failure of the standard trade model to track reasonably well the development of the Korean economy where changes in the structure of the economy observed during the take-off stage could not be captured by the standard CGE model with product differentiation the import and export side (see the model presented in chapter 8 with the exogenous updating of trade shares between periods). The paper starts from the model in chapter 1 and adds learning-by-doing externalities from export activities to offer a possible explanation for the observed patterns of structural change in Korea during its first phase of industrialization into light-manufacturing during the period 1972–75. Then, a the rapid move of resources out of agriculture took place with a stable agricultural terms-of-trade index and a fall of nearly 40% in the price index of capital goods. This parsimonious model tracks well this period in Korea's ELG industrialization. As the mechanisms through which these Marshallian externalities might operate in an ELG strategy are not specified, the skeletal model is only a first step, though perhaps one to consider for aggregating firm-level estimates into an economy-wide framework.

The remaining chapters in part I move progressively towards incorporating macro mechanisms extending beyond (some might say departing) from the micro foundations underlying the applications to tax problems mentioned above. The extensions start with the modeling of alternative policies to adjust to an external shock coming from the combination of declining terms-of-trade, a rising service on external debt and the impossibility to borrow externally. This was the typical situation of the period of adjustment lending in the 1980s. Then, the World Bank, typically focusing on medium-term growth prospects, also had to address a closing of the expenditure-income gap. (Chapter 7 figure 2 shows the links between the current account, factor accumulation, the sectoral pattern of technical progress and the corresponding equilibrium real exchange rate.)

Chapter 3, written at a time when two-gap fix-price models were used to study foreign exchange shortages in developing countries, was motivated by a foreign exchange crisis in Turkey in the late 70s when the country had to effect an external transfer (captured in the model by adjustment to a reduction in external borrowing). The model was used to contrast adjustment by rationing (fix price or premium) with adjustment by a depreciation of the real exchange rate. Simulations showed the large changes in relative prices and ensuing income redistribution along with the extra costs in terms of lost GDP from adjusting by rationing foreign exchange rather than by a depreciation of the real exchange rate. In another application, after validation over the period 1973–77, the model was used to decompose the role of several real factors (differential in inflation rates, fall in remittances, higher OECD export prices, oil price rise and residual factors) in the equilibrium value of the real exchange rate. These are summarized in chapter 7, table 6.

Chapters 4 and 5 explore the consequences of a different episode that also ended up requiring a closing of the expenditure-income gap. In the late 1970s, Chile combined deep across-the-board structural reforms (see Melo, 2015, chapter 1) with a macro stabilization using the exchange rate as an anchor to reduce inflationary expectations. The policy package also included an opening of the capital account which was unusual in developing countries at the time. Restrictions on employment in the labor market were also lifted, but the authorities maintained wage indexation on past inflation in the labor market in the formal sector. Large capital inflows ensued.

Chapter 4 explores a puzzle about this episode and two views about the causes of the sharp 1982 recession. The puzzle related to the high growth rate during the 1977–81 reform period in spite of low investment rates. To investigate this, the model was used in the spirit of Total Factor Productivity (TFP) studies to arrive at a combined estimate of increased capacity utilization and TFP growth. Back-of-the envelope attributions to the reform-induced TFP growth were also carried out. In a second step, the model was used to contrast two views about the causes of the 1982 recession: external (a fall in the price of copper and higher interest rate on external debt service) versus internal (large capital flows combined with an exogenous real exchange rate resulting in a loss in external competitiveness). Insofar as the large capital inflows were induced by the fixing of the exchange rate, the simulations suggest that it was mostly domestic policies rather than external events that contributed to the crisis.

At the time, Chile was pursuing a policy to reduce inflation. A CGE model is not the first tool that comes to mind to study an episode of dis-inflation. In Chile, this period corresponded to one with high unemployment (over 10%) and important structural change resulting from the ongoing micro reforms. It was therefore necessary to take into account employment effects that would accompany the anti-inflationary policies. Chapter 5 does so by tacking an ad-hoc macro model to determine the price level which, in turn, was used to determine wages and employment in the manufacturing sector. Two ad-hoc extensions were added to the model. First, to account for the observed consumption splurge in durable goods purchases that occurred as the fixed exchange rate regime was losing credibility, domestic savings were related negatively to capital inflows (an ad-hoc short-cut to mimic forward-looking behavior in an economy in strong macroeconomic disequilibrium). Second, extraneous estimates from a three-asset portfolio model estimated from quarterly data were used to estimate the loss in reserves following from an expansion in the money supply. These estimates were then combined with a Phillips curve, also estimated from quarterly data to determine nominal wages. The outcome was a hybrid model with econometric estimates from quarterly data yearly data on sectoral employment. In this extended model, a reduction in capital inflows, reduces the price level, and attenuates wage increases. While the paper recognizes that the macro issues raised by the Chilean experience deserved a separate investigation, a skeleton multi-sector model would eventually be needed to trace the employment implications of a reduction in capital inflows.

Chapter 6 goes further. It presents a micro-macro 'maquette' addressed to the critique that the structural adjustment programs of the IMF and World Bank administered to countries did not focus on the welfare of the poor (see the critiques to the programs in the introduction). The joint participation of the two institutions meant that these packages had two components: demand management to stabilize the economy and structural adjustment to address supply-side effects of micro-focused reforms. The maquette links the short-run impact of macroeconomic policies that affect the distribution of income through inflation, the interest rate and other price changes with the medium to long-run distributional effects resulting incentive reforms. Portfolio shifts in response to asset price changes capture the often-heard criticism that structural adjustment packages worsened the distribution of income as owners of foreign-denominated assets gained from the devaluations that were part of the adjustment packages.

This maquette blends distributional shifts coming from relative price changes in multi-sector models with those coming from changes in asset prices captured in an IS–LM framework. Getting there required many debatable assumptions (no expectations, full adjustments in goods and asset markets within each period, no taking into account of rising external on expectations). How realistic and useful these shortcut assumptions are has to be left to the reader when comparing simulation results from alternative packages to an unquestionable adjustment facing developing countries at the time: effecting an external transfer. Simulations suggest that adjustment to an external shock (increase in the interest rate on the external debt and deterioration in the terms of trade) by an exchange rate depreciation dominates packages with contractionary monetary policy or fiscal contraction.

Chapter 7 surveys CGE contributions to the analysis of trade policy scenarios in developing countries. Among those not covered here are estimates of the extra costs of rent-seeking activities and the design of trade policies to raise revenue at least cost in environments with limited administrative capacity where some sectors cannot be taxed and where broad-based instruments like an income tax are not available. Trade policy strategies in the face of an external borrowing constraint represent another important application not covered in the applications here. The survey discusses the set-up of applications to optimal borrowing strategies which equate the real social discount rate with the real cost of foreign borrowing and the real rate of return on capital. Results from an application to a tariff reduction program in Thailand under a lending constraint are reported. They show that the loss in tariff revenue from a tariff reform could result in substantial negative welfare effects as a result of a reduction of foreign credit as the risk of debt repudiation increase following the reduction in tariff revenue.

Part II: Archetype Economies

Part II collects papers built around archetype economies. I was, and remain, a fan of archetype analysis in CGE modelling for two reasons. First, from the start, the reader is invited to accept that the estimates are orders of magnitude. Also, since archetype applications go to the essential structural features of the economy, they naturally push the modeler to experiment with different formulations. This approach, emphasizing mechanisms rather than numerical outcomes, is helpful in bringing forth a focus on orders of magnitude rather than on numerical results. Second, in developing countries especially, differences in structure can be significant and result in different outcomes for a same shock or a same policy response to a similar shock.

The 1970s and 1980s were also characterized by systemic shocks. These were identical across many countries (the oil price rise or the rise in interest rates to service the external debt were the same across countries) had differential effects because inherited structures were different: a typical Latin American economy was different from a typical African or from an East Asian economy. Under these — but also under other — conditions, simulations on archetype economies are instructive: they show not only that, as expected, different policy responses to an identical shock have different outcomes, but also that the same policy response has different outcomes across archetypes.

Chapter 8, written at the time when the merits of an industrialization strategy focusing on the domestic market were still debated, contrasts the development path of a representative country following an ELG strategy with one following an (ISI) strategy. The simulations suggest orders of magnitude of efficiency costs related to the bias in incentives under and ISI strategy and the lower capital accumulation from a given savings rate for the ISI strategy because of the higher relative price of capital goods under that strategy. The paper also reports on the marginal efficiency of capital inflows across strategies, an obvious improvement on those suggested by the earlier two-gap models.

Chapters 9 and 10 simulate the effects of external shocks on income distribution in archetype economies with income groups distinguished along three dimensions: sector of activity, source of income (capital or wages in chapter 9 augmented by the holding of assets in chapter 10) and within group variance.

In chapter 9, the emphasis is on distributional conflicts generated by the choice of adjustment policy (devaluation, premium rationing with or without fixed wages). Assuming that society is roughly partitioned into relevant power groups that evaluate correctly their fate ex-ante under each adjustment mechanism, simulation results are used to see how the political struggle between gainers and losers is reflected in the choice of adjustment policy under different weighing schemes: 'one person one vote'; 'one rupee one vote', and the 'elite' measured by the top 5% in the overall distribution of income. Policy rankings reported in table 9 show that rankings are invariant across archetypes and that devaluation is only selected under 'one person one vote' while premium rationing is selected under the 'elite' scheme.

Chapter 10 applies the maquette presented in chapter 7 for a Latin American and an African archetype. To bracket possibilities, closure rules are purposely orthogonal (flexible prices for Africa, mark-up pricing in the modern sector for Latin America; households and firms hold foreign assets and debt only in the Latin America archetype; downward wage rigidity in the Latin American archetype). Not surprisingly, the distributional consequences of a same adjustment policy are usually radically different across the two archetypes underscoring the importance of taking into account institutional and structural characteristics when drawing structural adjustment packages. In sum, 'one size does not fit all'.

Chapters 11 and 12 deal with two aspects of trade policy that benefit from being examined in general equilibrium In chapter 11, the infant-industry argument is re-examined in an extended setting more appropriate to the environment where protection was used to promote industrialization. In the standard discussion of the infant-industry argument, the static cost of protection are pitted against the dynamic gains of protecting sectors with presumably higher productivity growth in an otherwise Walrasian full-employment model and no other market frictions or market imperfections. To caricature that representation, the comparisons are between two industrialization strategies twenty to fifty years apart (the time it takes to industrialize) with silence over how the economy gets from here to there. In an economy in the early stages of industrialization, it is more likely that labor is either unemployed or available to the modern protected sector along a Harris–Todaro migration mechanism. As to investment, it could be perhaps be determined exogenously (by animal spirits!) or by a constant savings out of income or a constant savings out of profits. Finally, profit rates across sectors that guide the allocation of investment are unlikely to be equalized instantaneously as capital is reallocated across sectors through depreciation, the speed of reallocation a parameter varied across simulations. These descriptions amount to many market imperfections that can be usefully decomposed by simulations. The figures in the paper showing the ratio of utility levels under the protection and the laissez-faire industrialization strategies in a three-sector stylized model show quite different paths under rather small differences in assumptions.

Chapter 12 explores the view that the trade policy choices reflect a mixture of lobbying activity and concern about overall efficiency.

If this view is approximately correct, then can archetype economies approximate two stylized patterns in the data: (i) higher protection in low-income countries; (ii) a protection of manufacturing at the expense of agriculture in low-income countries and the opposite in high-income countries (see chapter 12, figure 1). The paper sets up a lobbying model with intermediate inputs leading to two predictions: (i) the net political power of final industries is greater than that of intermediate industries implying that, as observed in the data, there is tariff escalation by degree of processing: (ii) tariffs are higher in countries with sparse inter-industry linkages (i.e., developing countries) because there is less counter-lobbying activity. Simulations with archetypes representative of high and low-income economies reproduce the two predictions from the theoretical model that are observed in the data.

The rise of migratory pressures from South has raised the issue of appropriate measures by the North wishing to reduce them: direct measures (e.g., aid to increase income in the South) or indirect measures (e.g., a reduction in trade barriers on imports from the South). But again there is diversity in migratory pressures depending on country characteristics. Chapter 13 contrasts direct and indirect measures for two archetypes to show that trade and migration policies cannot be assessed separately.

Part III: Costs of Protection from Trade Policy Regimes in Developing Countries

Part III report on papers that examined the costs associated with developing-country trade policy regimes. At the time, Non-Tariff Barriers (NTBs) in the form of Quantitative Restrictions (QRs) on imports were pervasive leading to additional losses resulting from rent-seeking behavior. It was also often observed that firms were operating at an inefficient scale combined with market power coming from domestic markets sheltered by NTBs. Distortions in factor markets were also suggested as an important source of the misallocation of resources, with differentials in rural-urban wages far exceeding those that would result from differences in the costs of living (augmented by migration costs). Chapter 14, drawn from my Ph.D. thesis, revisits earlier partial equilibrium estimates of the costs of distortions in the labor market. Looking back 40 years, if the paper had merit at the time, it fell short on several counts including the specification of foreign trade.

Chapter 15 also revisits an earlier literature on Effective Rates of Protection (ERP) in a model where product differentiation solved the problem of excessive specialization in models where domestic and foreign traded products are perfect substitutes. Would a ranking of sectors by descending order of ERPs be a good predictor or resource pulls following a tariff reform? As explained and shown in the paper, taking into account changes in the prices of non-traded goods and other general equilibrium effects gives a different ranking of resource pulls than those predicted from a ranking of ERPs.

An influential paper by Richard Harris (1984) opened the way for the modeling of trade policy with scale economies and imperfect competition, an extension that lent itself well to the models with product differentiation. Assuming conveniently the small-country assumption, free trade would no longer be Pareto optimal as scale economies and imperfect competition result in a departure from marginal cost pricing. Maintaining the small country assumption through the CET while foreign firms are left out of the picture avoided specialization, but at the cost of giving a technological advantage to domestic firms that nonetheless eventually experience decreasing returns to scale in exporting activities. Also, even if the use of consistent conjectural variations to model imperfect competition may still be the best game in town, it falls short of characterizing satisfactorily behavior in oligopolistic markets.

Despite these trade-offs, these assumptions were adopted in the papers reported in chapters 16 to 18 (and 20 to 23). On the positive side, these shortcuts (and shortcomings!) allow for a decomposition of the welfare effects of protection under different behavioral assumptions into all the effects (except for product variety) identified in the trade literature under imperfect competition: scale economies, entry-exit and departure from marginal cost pricing.

Chapter 16, written for a festschrift presented to Béla Balassa, tested his recommendation of according temporary protection cum market neutrality with an across-the-board protection to domestic sales and exports for new industries. The paper decomposed the magnitude of the welfare effects into entry/exit, scale efficiency and, in some cases, the non-neutrality of incentives. The illustrative simulations suggested that policies achieving neutral incentives were superior to those creating non-neutral incentives.

Chapter 17 was inspired by Korea's development strategy between 1973 and 1979 during which Heavy and Chemical Industries (HCI) received four-fifths of all investments (usually at preferential rates) and protection from import competition. As documented in the paper, a very concentrated market structure emerged with especially high price-cost margins in the sectors shielded from import competition (see table 10.1). This led Korea to change its strategy and reduce protection to the HCI sectors. The model in chapter 17 is calibrated to these stylized facts and the welfare effects of trade liberalization are calculated under different model closures including one in which trade liberalization forces firms to price less collusively in the domestic market. Because agriculture was the most protected sector in Korea, in all cases, trade liberalization leads to a reallocation of resources away agriculture towards industry. In some cases, there is sufficient firm entry to result in a welfare loss. Without suggestion an active industrialization policy, the paper notes that the Korean industrial policy of favoring conglomerates (the 'jaebol'), and hence preventing entry, was consistent with exploiting scale economies but that it should be complemented by the discipline in domestic markets that would accompany competition from imports. Overall, however, under the ranges of alternatives considered, the gains from trade liberalization are greater under the more realistic scenarios assuming increasing returns to scale in the HCI sector.

Chapter 18 tries to put boundaries on the welfare costs of QR trade regimes by setting up a stylized model of a semi-industrial economy and computing the welfare costs of imposing a rationing of imports (20% reduction from free trade). Several assumptions about collusive behavior are envisaged, including the possibility that the extent of collusive behavior falls with firm entry to deter cheating.

Taken together, while incorporating important general equilibrium effects, these applications also reveal the limitations of what can be learnt with sector level data. Understanding firm entry/exit patterns into exporting activity and the drivers of increases in firm productivity (learning by exporting or, instead by self-selection of the most efficient firms in the distribution into exporting) are needed to better understand the links between trade policy and efficiency. The recent empirical trade literature with heterogeneous firms is a step in the right direction. At the same time, the range of outcomes illustrated in the papers here with models that ignore firm-heterogeneity suggests that it might still be difficult to generalize on the basis of these new findings that will, likely, continue to context-specific.

Chapter 19 deals with Rules of Origin (RoO), a new form of protection. With the worldwide fall in tariff protection, and the elimination of many NTBs, a new form of discriminatory trade restriction has come about. These are the origin requirements that must be satisfied by exporters to benefit from preferential market access. The rapidly growing number of preferential trading agreements (many between developed and developing countries) have resulted in Rules of Origin (RoO) that appear largely restrictive beyond those that would be needed to prevent trade deflection. Chapter 19 is a case study for Mexican exporters of Textiles and Apparel (T&A) to the US market where the average MFN tariff averaged 12% (Melo, 2015, chapters 11 and 15 describe these RoO and give further estimates of their costs). Here meeting origin required Mexican exporters to source textiles from the US (rather from the rest-of-the world). Pass-through estimates, based on HS-8 tariff line data, show that a third of the increase in the border price of final Mexican goods exported to the US goes to compensate for the higher cost of intermediates purchased from the US. Partial equilibrium calibrated simulations show that RoO approximately halved the gains to Mexican producers from preferential market access. So even in sectors like T&A where preferential margins are still substantial, RoO are a circuitous way of raising the profits of upstream industries in the developed-country partners by creating captive markets in the downstream final-goods producing sectors in the developing-country partner.

Part IV: Estimating the Costs of US Foreign Trade Policy

Part IV collects work about the US economy. It is included here to give examples of trade policy issues that can be investigated with more extensive data and knowledge about institutional details that should be taken into account when evaluating trade policies.

Chapters 20 to 23 report on extensions from a project with David Tarr seeking to estimate the relative costs of 'transparent' protection (i.e., tariffs) vs. the 'opaque' protection via Non-tariff Barriers (NTBs) in three sectors (Voluntary Export Restraints (VERs) in the auto sector and QRs in the steel and textile sectors). Melo and Tarr (1992) discuss data sources and key parameters at greater length than the papers here. With arguably reliable/plausible estimates of key elasticities and of the rents associated with NTBs, our efforts were directed at careful calibration under different assumptions about the functioning of the economy in the three protected sectors. This meant always starting from the same equilibrium under the different assumptions selected in: (i) goods markets — perfect vs. imperfect competition; (ii) factor markets — endogenous vs. exogenous labor supply and wage determination in the protected sectors; (iii) distribution of quota rents from the NTBs.

Chapter 20 assumes that all sectors in the US economy were operating under perfect competitions and so concentrates on the employment reallocation effect of removing protection in the three sectors under different assumptions about the distribution of rents. Subtracting the costs from workers having to search for new employment (on average for six years), with a discount rate of 7%, the benefit cost ratio of 65 of removing protection in these three sectors. The paper also shows that the welfare costs from QRs in the three sectors would be equivalent to a radial expansion of tariffs across sectors resulting in an average protection of 20% — a result that illustrated forcefully the economic costs of buying acquiescence from foreigners to restrict their exports to the US.

Chapter 21 models the US auto industry during the US–Japan VER (1981–84) recognizing that the industry operated under increasing returns to scale, and that profits were higher during the period of the VER. We also took into account that Japanese auto producers shared part of the rents with US auto dealers and that 'tariff-jumping' Foreign Direct Investment (FDI) by Japanese auto producers was also taking place. The case study produced under different assumptions about the functioning of the auto industry and capital mobility in response the VER. The case study shows that taking into account the endogenous determination of quota rents and the induced FDI reduced welfare costs by about 10%.

Chapter 22 contests a claim that tariff on sectors with wage distortions (the case of the US auto and steel sectors where wages were determined by labor unions) could be welfare improving if the tariff compensated sufficiently for the penalty coming from the wage distortion. Recognizing that the wage premium is endogenous because of the presence of labor unions, the paper shows that, contrarily to what was claimed, the wage premia in fact exacerbated the costs of protection.

Chapter 23 uses the model to estimate the welfare costs of alternative taxation of the petroleum industries debated at the time. The estimates show that raising a desired revenue by restricting taxes to refined petroleum imports (as desired by US petroleum refiners) would cost around 25 times more than if an excise tax was imposed on all petroleum products. The paper also gives estimates of the combination of excises taxes and import tariffs on the crude oil and petroleum products sectors that would raise a specified revenue at least welfare cost.

References

1. Adelman, Irma and Sherman Robinson (1978) *Income Distribution Policies in Developing Countries: A Case Study of Korea*, Stanford: Stanford University Press.

2. Brooke, Anthony, David Kendrick and Alexander Meeraus (1992) *GAMS 2.25: A User's Guide*, California: Brooks/Cole.

3. Chenery, Hollis (1979) *Structural Change and Development Policy*, London: Oxford University Press.

4. Dervis, Kemal, Jaime de Melo and Sherman Robinson (1982) *General Equilibrium Models for Development Policy*, London: Cambridge University Press.

5. Dixon, Peter and Dale Jorgenson, eds., (2013) *Handbook of Computable General Equilibrium Modeling*, UK: North-Holland, Elsevier.

6. Harris, Richard G. (1984) "Applied General Equilibrium Analysis of Small Open Economies with Scale Economies and Imperfect Competition", *American Economic Review*, 74(5), 1016–1032.

7. Melo, Jaime de (2015) *Developing Countries in the World Economy*, Singapore: World Scientific.

8. Melo, Jaime de, and David Tarr (1992) *A General Equilibrium Analysis of US Foreign Trade Policy*, Cambridge: MIT Press.

9. Scarf, Herbert (with the collaboration of Terje Hansen) (1973) *The Computation of Economic Equilibria*, New Haven: Yale University Press.

10. Shoven, John, and John Whalley (1992) *Applying General Equilibrium*, London: Cambridge University Press.

Part I:
Capturing Economy-Wide Linkages

Journal of International Economics 27 (1989) 47–67. North-Holland

PRODUCT DIFFERENTIATION AND THE TREATMENT OF FOREIGN TRADE IN COMPUTABLE GENERAL EQUILIBRIUM MODELS OF SMALL ECONOMIES

Jaime de MELO

Country Economics Department, The World Bank, Washington, D.C. 20433, USA

Sherman ROBINSON*

Department of Agricultural and Resource Economics, University of California, Berkeley, CA, USA

Received July 1986, revised version received November 1988

This paper examines the treatment of exports and imports, and external closure rules, adopted in recent single-country computable general equilibrium models of small economies. The paper presents a simple, one-sector analytic model which captures the major features of the multi-sector counterpart used in applied models. The paper derives graphical and algebraic solutions to the model and shows that, unlike some earlier external closures, this one gives rise to a well-behaved, price-taking economy. The model is also useful to illustrate the role of elasticities in popular trade-theoretic models that include traded and non-traded goods.

1. Introduction

In recent years, two classes of computable general equilibrium (CGE) trade models have been used to investigate external sector policies: single-country and multi-country trade models. The multi-country trade models [e.g. Deardorff and Stern (1986) and Whalley (1985)] have typically been concerned with resource allocation and welfare implications of tariff reductions such as those of the Tokyo round. The single-country models have been used to analyze a variety of external sector issues ranging from the impact of restrictions on foreign trade (e.g. tariffs and QRs, with or without rent

*We thank David Roland-Holst for help with derivations in the appendix, Taeho Bark, T. N. Srinivasan for discussions, a referee for very incisive comments, and Gabriel Castillo and Jackson Magargee for research and logistic support. The World Bank does not accept responsibility for the views expressed herein which are those of the authors and should not be attributed to the World Bank or to its affiliated organizations.

seeking) to the impact of changes in net foreign transfers or world prices on the equilibrium real exchange rate.[1]

For both types of models, the results from policy simulations depend on how export and import behavior are modelled. In a recent paper, Whalley and Yeung (1984) – henceforth WY – examine this issue for single country models using the term 'external closure' to refer to the various assumptions about export demand and import supply behavior. After noting that most applied models are quite disaggregated and separate traded and non-traded goods, they review three external closure rules in single-country models. for their first closure rule, WY choose a simple two commodity (import and export) formulation with no non-traded commodity to show that in these models, '...there is no currency exchange rate in the conventional use of the term as a financial magnitude determined from financial sector activity'.[2]

In the second of their three external closures, WY assert that the imposition of a zero trade balance condition in a two-good CGE model that incorporates product differentiation (i.e. the Armington assumption) with price-taking behavior for imports along with a downward-sloping foreign export demand curve with constant elasticity yields a model in which both domestic and foreign offer curves lie on top of one another.[3]

They are dissatisfied wih this specification and go on to propose a third external closure: a model with price-taking behavior and no product differentiation for tradables, plus the inclusion of non-tradables. In essence, this closure corresponds to a multi-sector version of the well-known dependent economy (Australian) trade-theoretical model. They show that, in this formulation, there is an exchange rate variable – or 'parameter', as they call it – that measures the relative price between composites of traded and non-traded goods. They show that, in this model, the foreign offer curve is a straight line, while the domestic offer curve has some elasticity (thereby following conventional trade theory). However, they feel that this price-taking assumption will be unpalatable in empirical models of large countries. More generally, they note that this model will not allow two-way trade, or cross hauling, which is widely observed in trade statistics at the aggregation levels used in all CGE models, and so is not a desirable specification.

---

[1]Dervis, de Melo and Robinson (1982) – henceforth DMR – review the theoretical specification of single-country trade models and present a number of applications analyzing the types of issues mentioned above. Robinson (1989) reviews recent models.

[2]Whalley and Yeung (1984, p. 126).

[3]WY also note that because export and import demand elasticities are not independent, the reduced forms for the export and import demand functions differ from the specification intended. Although econometricians do not typically incorporate the restrictions implied by balanced trade when they estimate export demand and import supply elasticities, the point that trade balance restrictions should be recognized in specifying combinations of export demand and import supply elasticities is correct and nicely made. For a general treatment in the n-commodity case see Jones and Berglas (1977).

J. de Melo and S. Robinson, Product differentiation   49

Several points about the WY analysis deserve comment. First, the role of the exchange rate in computable general equilibrium models has received attention for some time and we can find no case in which modelers interpret it as a 'financial variable'.[4] Second, the two-good model with both goods traded that WY use in their first discussion of external-sector closure does not represent well any of the applied CGE trade models, which invariably include some non-traded goods.[5] Third, an external closure using a price-taking formulation for all tradables in a model with perfect substitution will be unpalatable for stronger reasons than those mentioned by WY. If the price-taking formulation is not accompanied by some product differentiation, the model will generate extreme specialization whenever it is subjected to a policy simulation such as reduction in tariffs. The assumption of a downward-sloping foreign demand curve, while it will help (but not fix) the specialization problem, will lead to unrealistically strong terms-of-trade effects that will dominate the welfare results of policy changes in single-country models.[6]

The essence of the external-sector specification of most recent single-country CGE trade models can be captured by a simple one-sector model with symmetric product differentiation for imports and exports. This model embodies (and extends) well-understood results from neoclassical trade theory and provides a compact statement of the external closures found in most applied models. The model is also useful to illustrate the role of trade elasticities in the Australian (dependent economy) model with traded and non-traded goods. We show that the 'parameter' referred to by WY in the analysis of their third external closure still exists in this model. We indicate how its equilibrium value is influenced by the assumed values for trade substitution elasticities and by the choice of weights used as a proxy for the domestic price index in computations of real exchange rate indices.

With this framework, we provide a systematic exploration of the behavior of a small price-taking economy characterized by product differentiation on *both* the export and import sides. We argue that reasons for introducing product differentiation on the export side are the same as those for introducing product differentiation on the import side, namely that multi-sector models, even when they are disaggregated, do not disaggregate products sufficiently. This assumption has in fact been used by Dixon et al. (1982) and by Deardorff and Stern (1986). In Dixon et al. (1982) the justification is based on producers engaging in joint production, as in the

---

[4]See, for instance, DMR (ch. 6, sections 2 and 3) who discuss the role of the real exchange rate in general equilibrium models.

[5]WY do consider in eqs. (22)–(25) a formulation with one domestic good, but only for an exchange economy. As argued below, this formulation is not a simplified representation of a typical single-country CGE trade model.

[6]See DMR (ch. 6) for a discussion of specialization and chapter 7 for an alternative specification for export behavior. The empirical importance of terms-of-trade effects with downward-sloping foreign export demand curves is shown in chapter 9.

50   **J. de Melo and S. Robinson, Product differentiation**

original presentation by Powell and Gruen (1968). While plausible under certain circumstances, we think that a more general reason along the lines pointed out above is the more plausible rationale for introducing symmetric product differentiation. This said, it should be pointed out [see Anderson (1985)] that calculations of the costs of protection carried out in aggregate economy-wide models with product differentiation to overcome the problem of specialization may severely understate the costs of protection, at least with respect to partial liberalization. But our purpose here is to study the properties of economy-wide models, so this issue of bias in results from applied models can be left aside.

The remainder of the paper is organized as follows. In section 2 we present the model and use it in section 3 to show how equilibrium is affected by terms-of-trade shifts and by changes in net capital inflows, both common experiments in single-country models. The model is also useful for illustrating the role of elasticities in popular trade-theoretic models that include traded and non-traded goods. In section 4 we derive an expression for the elasticity of the domestic offer curve in our model with symmetric product differentiation and set up a numerical example. The expression and the numerical example show the role of initial conditions (i.e. openness to trade) and of values of trade substitution elasticities in determining the shape of the well-behaved domestic offer curve. We also illustrate the well-known fact that – once weights entering the relevant price indices are chosen – the equilibrium value of the real exchange rate (defined as the relative price of traded to non-traded goods) is indeed independent of the choice of numeraire.

2. A small-country model with differentiated trade

For most countries, and especially for developing countries, it is reasonable to assume that the country is 'small' on world markets and cannot affect its international terms of trade. However, it is also reasonable to assume that world prices in the tradable sectors do not dominate the domestic price system. We present below a simple analytic model which captures these stylized facts and discuss its theoretical structure.

We make the following assumptions: (1) domestically produced and imported goods are imperfect substitutes – the Armington assumption; (2) domestically produced goods sold on the domestic market are imperfect substitutes for goods sold on the export market; (3) the economy can purchase or sell unlimited quantities of imports and exports at constant world prices – the small-country assumption; (4) aggregate production is fixed; and (5) there is a balance of trade constraint.

2.1. Model equations

In table 1, eqs. (1) and (2) give the trade aggregation functions. In applied

J. de Melo and S. Robinson, Product differentiation   51

models, and in the numerical example of section 4, eq. (1) is a CES function, following Armington, and eq. (2) is a CET (constant elasticity of transformation) function.[7] For the analysis here, we only require that $F(\cdot)$ be convex to the origin, that $G(\cdot)$ be concave, and that both be homogeneous of degree one in their arguments. Given the assumption of fixed output, which is equivalent to assuming full employment, $G(\cdot)$ represents a production possibility frontier delineating the tradeoffs between exports and domestic supply.

Eqs. (3) and (4) translate foreign prices into domestic prices using a conversion factor, r, which we refer to as the 'nominal' exchange rate. It should be clear, but is worth repeating (as has been pointed out by DMR and WY) that this conversion factor, r, is not a financial exchange rate variable. Though often referred to as 'the' exchange rate, we refer to it as the 'nominal' exchange rate so as not to confuse it with the real exchange rate – the relative price of the domestic good in terms of the (fixed) traded goods – which is determined by the model. Indeed, the model could be written without reference to r – as is common in trade theory – by implicitly choosing it as numeraire. We use this approach below in subsection 2.2. However, since we wish to consider alternative choices of the numeraire, we maintain r in our formulation.[8]

We assume that producers maximize profits and that demanders minimize the cost of purchasing a given quantity of composite good Q.[9] These assumptions lead to eqs. (5)–(8). Eqs. (5) and (6) define composite good prices and are effectively dual cost functions. They are homogeneous of degree one in input prices. Eqs. (7) and (8) give the demand for imports and supply of exports arising from the first-order conditions.

Since only relative prices matter, the functions describing the model are homogeneous of degree zero in prices. To set the absolute price level, select r as numeraire. Eq. (9) gives the equilibrium condition for the balance of trade; that in foreign units (expressed in terms of the numeraire) the value of imports equals the value of exports plus $\bar{B}$. Finally, eq. (10) is the equilibrium condition for the supply and demand for the domestic good. Overall, the model has 10 equations and 10 endogenous variables: Q, M, D^d, D^s, E, P^m, P^e, P^d, P^q, and P^x. The homogeneity of eqs. (1) and (2) guarantees that the

---

[7]The CET formulation was first suggested by Powell and Gruen (1968). Though more elegant and easier to work with than the logistic supply curve proposed by DMR, it can be shown that the two specifications are empirically very close for local changes around equilibrium. De Melo and Robinson (1985) explore analytically in a partial equilibrium context, the implications of product differentiation on the domestic price system.

[8]Under appropriate numeraire selection, r becomes the real exchange rate, in which case it should be referred to as such.

[9]In fact, for the analysis here, we could assume that eq. (1) is a utility function which consumers seek to maximize.

52   *J. de Melo and S. Robinson, Product differentiation*

Table 1

A one-sector small-country model with differentiated trade.

(1)	$Q = F(M, D^d)$	Import aggregation function
(2)	$\bar{X} = G(E, D^s)$	Export transformation function
(3)	$p^m = r\bar{\pi}^m$	Import price
(4)	$p^e = r\bar{\pi}^e$	Export price
(5)	$p^q = f_1(p^m, p^d)$	Consumer price
(6)	$p^x = g_1(p^e, p^d)$	Producer price
(7)	$\dfrac{M}{D^d} = f_2(p^m, p^d)$	Import demand equation
(8)	$\dfrac{E}{D^s} = g_2(p^e, p^d)$	Export supply equation
(9)	$\bar{\pi}^m M - \bar{\pi}^e E = \bar{B}$	Balance of trade constraint
(10)	$D^d - D^s = 0$	Domestic demand–supply equilibrium

Notes:
M, E = imports, exports
D^d, D^s = demand and supply of the domestic good.
Q = composite consumer good
$\bar{X}$ = composite production
$\bar{\pi}^m$ = world price of imports
$\bar{\pi}^e$ = world price of exports
r = conversion factor; 'nominal' exchange rate
p^m = domestic price of imports, M
p^e = domestic price of exports, E
p^d = domestic price of domestic sales, D
p^q = domestic price of composite consumer good, Q
p^x = domestic price of composite output, X
$\bar{B}$ = exogenous balance of trade, or net foreign capital inflow (or outflow for negative $\bar{B}$)

system satisfies Walras' Law. This can be easily seen by writing out the aggregate income and expenditure equations

$P^x\bar{X} + r\bar{B},$ \qquad total income,

$P^x\bar{X} = P^e E + P^d D^s,$ \quad the value of production or GDP,

$P^q Q = P^m M + P^d D^d,$ \quad total expenditure or absorption.

Given the equilibrium conditions in eqs. (9) and (10), it follows that income always equals expenditure. The variable, $\bar{B}$, in eq. (9), denominated in foreign units, can be thought of as representing an increase (or decrease) in real income measured in terms of imports, given the fixed world price of imports.

2.2. A graphical presentation

This model is simple enough so that its properties can be shown

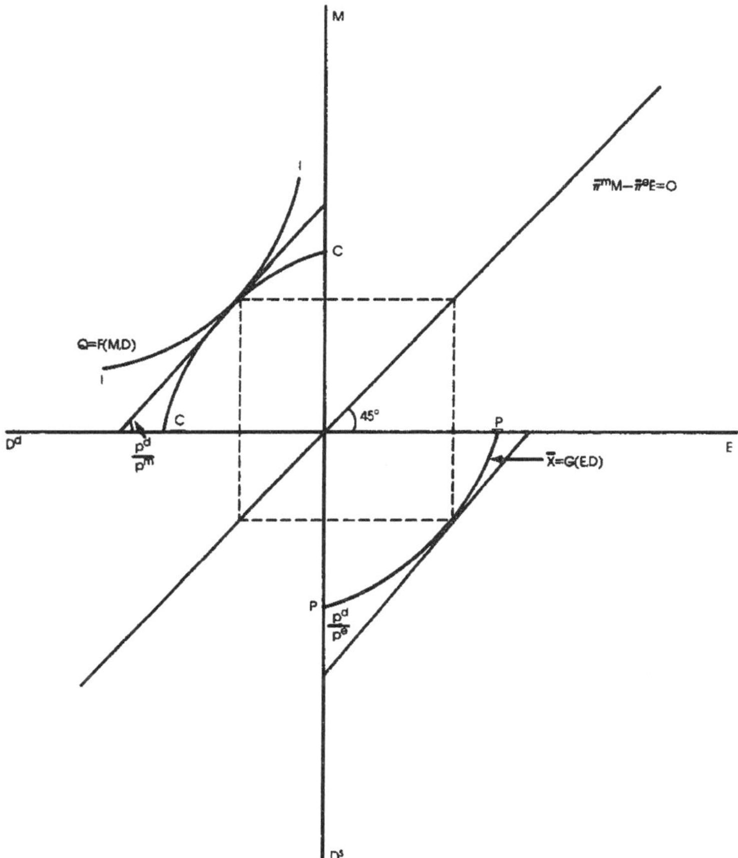

Fig. 1. Equilibrium in the small-country case.

graphically. Fig. 1 presents a four-quadrant diagram that captures the essential features. For convenience, choose units so that the exogenous world prices for both exports and imports equal one. Also, set r as numeraire and initially assume $\bar{B}=0$. In this case, the balance-of-trade equation defines the foreign offer curve and graphs as a 45° line in quadrant 1. The production possibility frontier, PP [eq. (2)], is graphed in quadrant 4. Quadrant 3 has a 45° line which simply indicates that domestic goods, D, which are supplied to the domestic market, are available for demand, defining equilibrium in the domestic goods market. The concave curve, CC, in quadrant 2 is the consumption possibility frontier, which is the locus of points that simultaneously satisfies the balance-of-trade constraint in quadrant 1 and the production possibility frontier in quadrant 4. Given our choice of units and the assumption that the balance of trade equals zero, the consumption possibility frontier in quadrant 2 is a mirror image of the production possibility frontier, *PP*, in quadrant 4.

In quadrant 2, the import aggregation function, equation 1, generates a series of 'iso-good' curves, *II*, analogous to indifference curves.[10] Equilibrium is achieved at the point of tangency with the consumption possibility frontier. At this point, the equilibrium price ratios, P^d/P^m and P^d/P^e, equal the slope of the tangents in quadrants 2 and 4, and are derived from the first-order conditions in eqs. (7) and (8).[11] Given our choice of units, the two ratios are equal, and the equilibrium value of P^d is the equilibrium value of the relative price of non-tradables to tradables. Thus, selecting r as numeraire is convenient since it allows us to interpret P^d as the real exchange rate. In this model, the foreign offer curve is the 45° line in the M, E quadrant in fig. 1. We derive in section 4 the elasticity of the domestic offer curve and show that it is a well-behaved curve which intersects the straight-line foreign offer curve.

Consider the limiting 'Ricardian' case corresponding to an infinitely elastic supply of exports. Then *PP* becomes a straight line, which in turn implies a straight-line consumption possibility curve. The real exchange rate is now fixed and, as in a Ricardian world, is determined by technology. Substitution possibilities in demand only determine the composition of production for domestic and for export sales.

Our graphical presentation can also be used to consider the closure criticized by WY; namely, a specification with product differentiation on the import side and with less than infinitely elastic foreign export demand. In this case, the model would include an extra equation, $\pi^e = [E/E_0]^{-1/\zeta}$, where $\zeta > 1$ is the constant price elasticity of foreign export demand and π^e is now endogenous. Now the foreign offer curve is given by:[12]

$$M = E_0^{1/\zeta} E^\alpha, \quad \alpha \equiv 1 - 1/\zeta, \quad 0 < \alpha < 1, \tag{2.1}$$

which is derived by substituting the above expression for π^e into the balance-of-trade constraint. This case is depicted in fig. 2, where E_0 is the equilibrium under the small country assumption (i.e. $\alpha = 1$). With market power, the foreign offer curve becomes OC, and the corresponding consumption possibility curve is C_0C_1 with new equilibrium at E_1. From the diagram,

---

[10]If we replace eq. (1) with an explicit utility function, the 'iso-goods' can be interpreted as indifference curves. Nothing changes in the analysis.

[11]This result can be derived from the maximization of (1) subject to (2) and (9) and is derived in the appendix.

[12]Note that for $0 < \zeta < 1$, the external constraint slopes downwards.

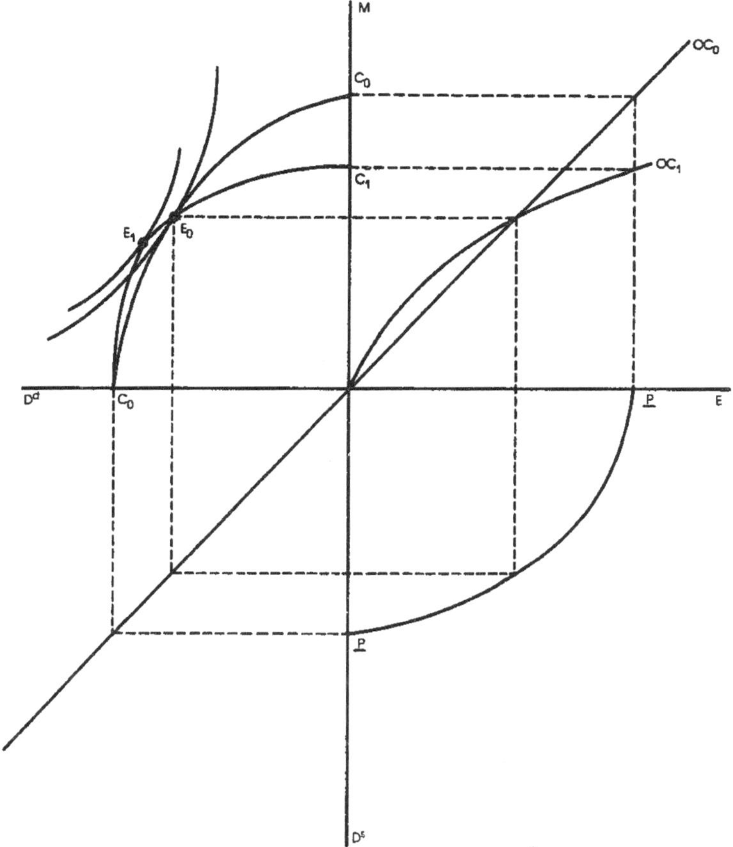

Note Foreign offer curve derived under the assumption of constant foreign demand elasticity > 1

Fig. 2. Equilibrium with constant foreign demand elasticity.

one can see that assuming market power leads to an optimum with less trade and a correspondingly lower real exchange rate.

Clearly this model, which is representative of many single-country CGE models, does not suffer from the problem of overlapping offer curves described by WY in their discussion of a similar model with constant price elasticities of foreign demand and import supply. As we have shown, the foreign offer curve in this model has the usual shape. As we analyze in some detail below, the shape of the domestic offer curve depends only on the parameters of the export transformation and import aggregation functions and also has the usual shape. Hence the two offer curves will intersect, but will certainly not coincide.

3. Terms-of-trade and transfers: A graphical analysis

Is the one-sector model with differentiated trade well behaved? We examine two typical experiments conducted with single-country models: a terms-of-trade shift and a change in foreign transfers.

3.1. Terms-of-trade change

Fig. 3 shows the effect on equilibrium of an improvement in the terms of trade $(TOT_0 \rightarrow TOT_1)$ corresponding to an increase in π^e, $d\pi^e > 0$. This terms-of-trade change shifts out the consumption possibility schedule to $C_0 C_1$. Will the economy supply a larger volume of exports at this improved terms of trade? The result depends on the shape of the domestic offer curve. As drawn in fig. 3, exports fall. The demand for the domestic good increases, which in turn implies that the domestic offer curve, FF, is inelastic.[13] Also note that the real exchange rate will appreciate. In the limiting 'Ricardian' case considered above, the real exchange appreciation will be equal to the change in terms of trade, i.e. $dp^d = d\bar{\pi}^e$.

3.2. An increase in foreign transfers

Fig. 4 shows the effect on equilibrium of an increase in foreign transfers. The effect of a transfer, $\bar{B}$, is an upward parallel shift of the external budget constraint to $O_1 O_1$ and the consumption possibility curve to $C_1 C_1$. Will the increase in transfers lead to a real exchange rate appreciation, as one would expect in a model where the domestic good is consumed? Yes, if the domestic good is not inferior in consumption, which is the case drawn in fig. 4 and is guaranteed for the CES function used in practice. Domestic consumption of D increases, exports fall, and imports rise.

The graphical apparatus developed here can also be used to examine the effects of a change in commercial policy. This is not done here since it does not lead to any new insights about the properties of the external closure under review. We conclude that the specified external closure gives rise to a well-defined real exchange rate whose variations to policy changes is in accord with the usual assumptions of neoclassical trade theory for small economies. The assumption of product differentiation thus leads to a much more realistic small-country model that can accommodate two-way trade

---

[13]We show below that the shape of the domestic offer curve depends on the two substitution elasticities and on trade shares.

J. de Melo and S. Robinson, Product differentiation 57

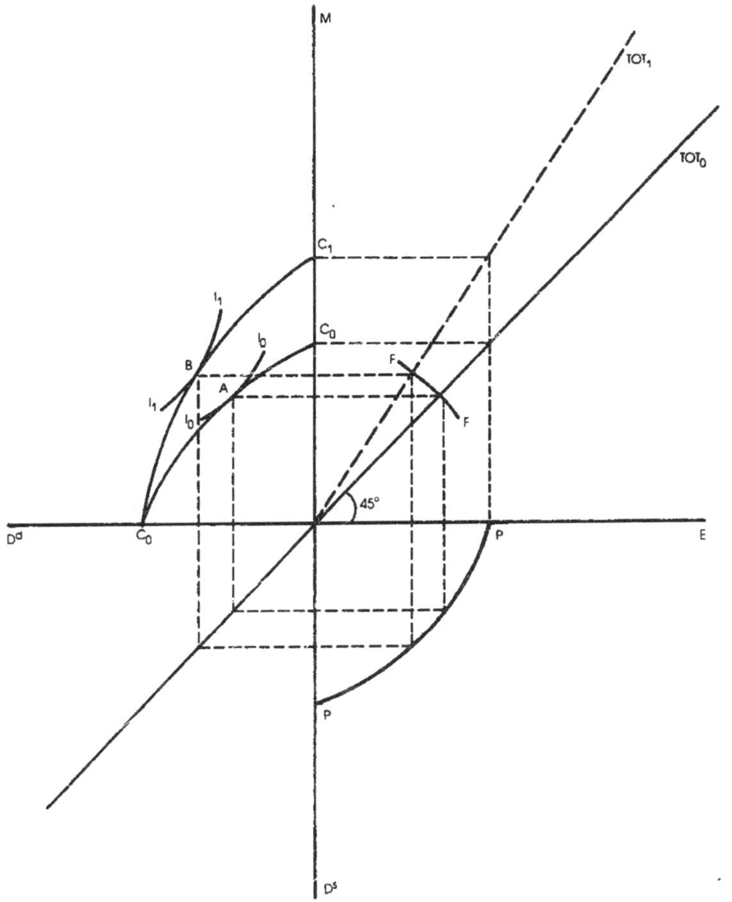

Fig. 3. Terms-of-trade improvement.

and a degree of autonomy in the domestic price system, but retains all the desirable features of the standard neoclassical model.

4. A numerical example

We conclude with a simple numerical example to show the influence of different parameter values on computed equilibria for an increase in transfers and a terms-of-trade change. Assume, as in typical applications, that the import aggregation function is CES and the export transformation is CET. Then eqs. (1) and (2) in table 1 are given by:

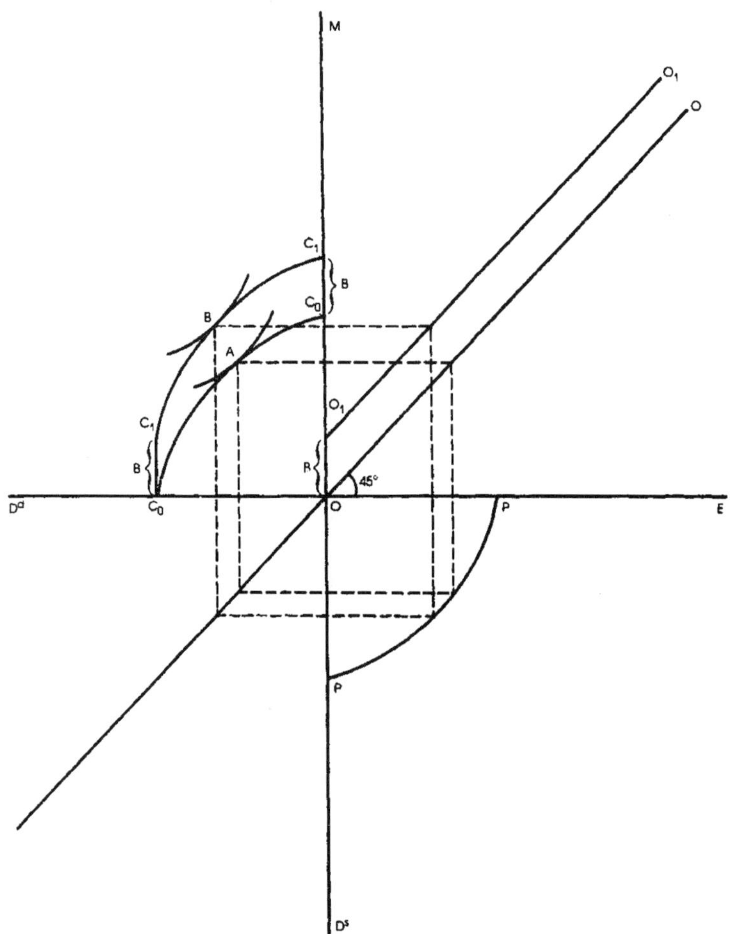

Fig. 4. An increase in foreign transfers.

$$Q = \bar{A}_1(\beta M^{-\rho} + (1-\beta)D^{-\rho})^{-1/\rho}, \qquad \sigma = \frac{1}{1+\rho}, \tag{4.1}$$

$$\bar{X} = \bar{A}_2(\alpha E^h + (1-\alpha)D^h)^{1/h}, \qquad \Omega = \frac{1}{h-1}, \tag{4.2}$$

where a bar denotes an exogenous variable and σ and Ω are elasticities of substitution and transformation, respectively. Following the calibration common in CGE models, we construct parameters for the CES and CET

J. de Melo and S. Robinson, Product differentiation   59

Table 2
Base solution values.

Transfer ($\bar{B}$)	Exports (E)	Imports (M)	Domestic demand (D)	GDP ($\bar{X}$)
0	25	25	75	100

Table 3
Welfare and real exchange rate calculations for an increase
in transfers.[a]

σ[b]	Ω[c]	Q	r/p^d	r	r/p^x
(1)	(2)	(3)	(4)	(5)	(6)
0.2	0.2	106.9	0.38	0.46	0.45
0.5	0.5	108.7	0.68	0.75	0.74
2	2	109.6	0.91	0.93	0.93
5	5	109.9	0.96	0.97	0.97
5	∞	110.0	1.00	1.00	1.00

[a]Transfer ($\bar{B}$) set equal to 10.
[b]Elasticity of substitution in CES [eq. (1), table 1, and eq. (4.1)].
[c]Elasticity of transformation in CET [eq. (2), table 2, and eq. (4.2)].

functions to produce the initial equilibrium formulated in table 2 such that all prices are unity, i.e. $\bar{\pi}^m = \bar{\pi}^e = r = P^x = P^m = P^e = 1$.[14]

Table 3 shows the effects on the welfare indicator, Q (column 3), and on the real exchange rate (column 4) of setting transfers equal to 10 – i.e. to 10 percent of initial GDP – under different values of the elasticities of import substitution and export transformation. Note that, in the limit, the increase in welfare is equal to the transfer itself. This result occurs when the marginal rate of transformation of production between sales to the domestic and export markets is infinite, i.e. in the Ricardian case discussed above. As expected, the required real exchange rate adjustment to absorb the transfer is an increasing function of the curvature of the CES and CET functions.

In this example, the numeraire is $p^q \equiv 1$. Had we selected another numeraire, such as fixing the value of the GDP deflator with base year quantity weights (i.e. to set $p^x \equiv 1$), then the equilibrium values of the 'nominal' exchange rate (or conversion factor) in column 5 would have been replaced by the values appearing in column 6. Likewise, with $p^d \equiv 1$ as numeraire, the equilibrium values for the 'nominal' exchange rate would have been given by the values in column 4. And, with $r \equiv 1$ as numeraire, the equilibrium value of p^d appearing in column 4 would have corresponded to

[14]The numeraire is $P^q \equiv 1$ and the solution is found by solving the maximization problem set in the appendix using the GAMS package developed by Arne Drud and Alex Meeraus.

the equilibrium value of the real exchange rate. Regardless of the choice of numeraire, the equilibrium values of the relative price indices appearing in columns 4 and 6 of table 3 remain unaltered.

In this one-sector model, there is no ambiguity with respect to the appropriate definition of the real exchange rate, r/p^d. In applied work. however, two problems arise. In multi-sector CGE applications, a choice must be made with respect to the weights entering the aggregator for the domestic price index. Even though the choice of weights will affect the computed values for the equilibrium real exchange rate, the equilibrating mechanism working through changes in the real exchange rate is the same, no matter what price is chosen as numeraire.

The other problem relates to the choice of weights used to proxy the domestic price index in computations of real exchange rate indices. Typically, the domestic price index is proxied by some published price index such as the CPI or the GDP deflator, both of which include traded goods. As shown by the values in the last two columns of table 3, when values of σ and Ω are low, the choice of proxy for the domestic price index makes a great deal of difference in the computed value of the real exchange rate. For example, with $\sigma = \Omega = 0.5$, the real exchange rate index with CPI (or GDP) weights used as proxy has a value of 0.75 (0.74) whereas the correct value is 0.68.

Finally, we come to the shape of the offer curve. It can be shown that the elasticity of the offer curve, ε^{oc}, is given by the following expression:[15]

$$\varepsilon^{oc} = -\frac{\alpha(\sigma+\Omega)+\lambda\sigma(\Omega+1)}{\Omega(1-\sigma)\lambda},\tag{4.3}$$

where

$$\lambda \equiv (1-\alpha)\left\{\frac{\alpha(1-\beta)}{(1-\alpha)\beta}\right\}^{\sigma(1+\Omega)/(\Omega+\sigma)}.$$

From expression (4.3), it is clear that the offer curve will be vertical ($\varepsilon^{oc} = \infty$) for $\sigma = 1$, positively sloping ($\varepsilon^{oc} > 1$) for $\sigma > 1$, and negatively sloping ($\varepsilon^{oc} < 0$) for $\sigma < 1$. For given values of Ω, ε^{oc} monotonically decreases for increasing values of σ (with discontinuity at $\sigma = 1$). For given values of σ, the curvature of the offer curve is less (ε^{oc} is lower), the higher is the value of Ω. Finally, for given values of σ and Ω, the value of ε^{oc} is larger, the more open is the economy.[16]

Figs. 5(a) and 5(b) trace the elasticity of the domestic offer curve for different values of σ, $\sigma \neq 1$. Negative values of ε^{oc} correspond to a backward-bending offer curve. In this case, the income effect of an improvement in the

---

[15]This result is derived in the appendix with $\pi^e = \pi^m = 1$ by choice of units.
[16]Openness is defined in the sense of high initial trade ($E/D, M/D$) shares.

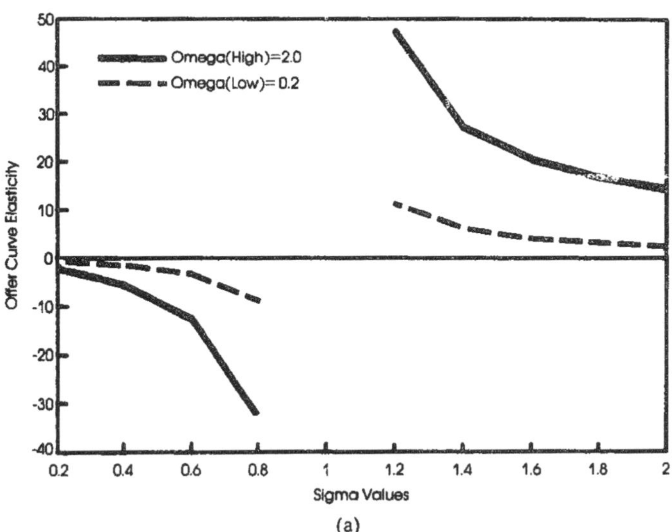

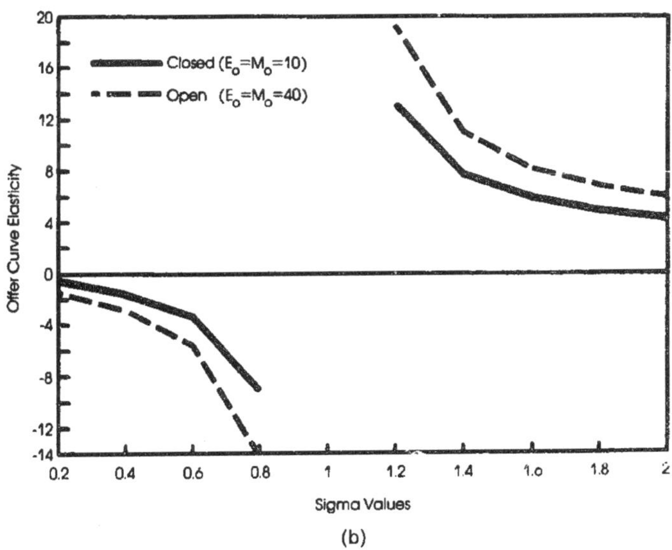

Fig. 5. Offer curve elasticity. (a) Medium economy ($E_0=M_0=25$). Offer curves with high and low omega. (b) Closed and open economy offer curves, with omega$=1$.

terms of trade dominates the substitution effect and less exports are supplied. Negative values of ε^{oc} imply that the real exchange rate must appreciate to ensure a greater supply to the domestic market (this is the case drawn in fig. 3). Raising the elasticity of export supply lowers the offer curve elasticity, which in the limit is unity. This result follows directly from the relation between the two elasticities along the external budget constraint. Increasing the degree of openness raises the offer curve elasticity, a result also found in standard trade-theoretic models.

Finally, fig. 6 traces the equilibrium values obtained from solving the model with the initial conditions in table 2 under a high and a low set of trade substitution elasticities. Fig. 6 draws the equilibrium values of the welfare indicator, the real exchange rate, and the import share in absorption for different values of the terms of trade. The arrows indicate the path of the variables as the terms of trade improve. As expected, welfare gains measured here in terms of absorption, Q, are larger for the higher set of trade substitution elasticities. The higher gain attributable to greater specialization appears as a much larger variation in the share of imports in absorption for the high value of σ. More importantly, fig. 6 confirms the critical role assumed by the value of σ in determining whether the real exchange rate will appreciate or depreciate when the terms of trade varies.

The two numeric [1] examples in fig. 6 could be construed to represent a developing country with a low import substitution elasticity and a developed country with a higher elasticity. For the developing country, adjusting to the deterioration in its terms of trade requires a real devaluation to generate increased exports required to pay for more expensive crucial imports. For the developed country, adjustment requires a real revaluation and a decline in the volume of foreign trade.

5. Conclusions

In this paper we have studied systematically the typical external closure of many single-country-applied general equilibrium trade models. We have shown that the standard assumption of product differentiation on the import side can be naturally extended to the export side. An external closure with symmetric product differentiation for imports and exports is theoretically well behaved and gives rise to normally shaped offer curves. We derive the elasticity of the domestic offer curve for a one-sector model and illustrate the model with a numerical example. The numerical example illustrates, under different trade substitution elasticities, the implications of the choice of weights used as a proxy for the domestic price index in computations of real exchange rate indices. The model is also useful to illustrate the role of foreign trade elasticities in the popular Australian model with traded and non-traded goods. In particular, we show the crucial role of trade substitution elasticities

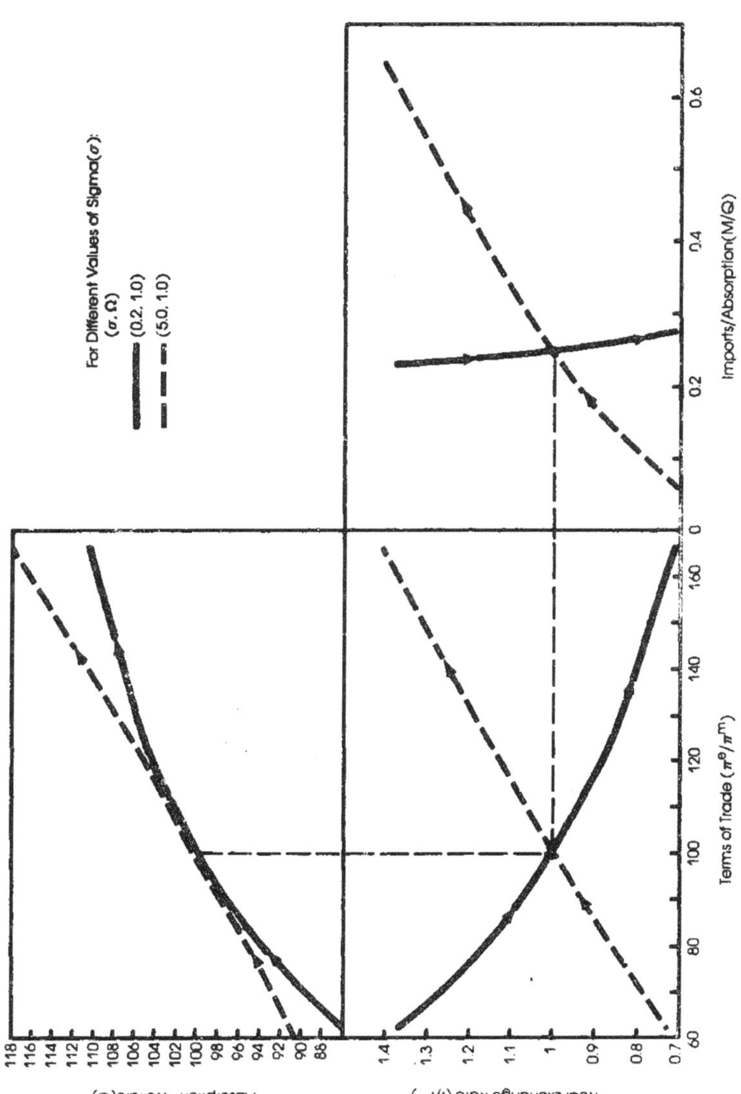

Fig. 6. Welfare, real exchange rate, and terms of trade.

64   *J. de Melo and S. Robinson, Product differentiation*

on the import side in determining the direction of change of the real exchange rate for terms-of-trade perturbations.

Appendix

A.1. Derivation of equilibrium conditions in fig. 1

To show that in equilibrium the MRS in consumption in quadrant 2 is equal to the MRT in production in quadrant 4, maximize (1) subject to (2) and (9) by setting the following Lagrangian:

$$L = Q - \lambda_x [\bar{X} - G(E, D)] - \lambda_b [\bar{B} - \bar{\pi}^m M + \bar{\pi}^e E]. \tag{A.1}$$

The first-order conditions are:

$$\frac{\partial L}{\partial D} = \frac{\partial Q}{\partial D} + \lambda_x \left[\frac{\partial G}{\partial D} \right] = 0, \tag{A.2}$$

$$\frac{\partial L}{\partial M} = \frac{\partial Q}{\partial M} + \lambda_b [\bar{\pi}^m] = 0, \tag{A.3}$$

$$\frac{\partial L}{\partial E} = \lambda_x \left[\frac{\partial G}{\partial E} \right] - \lambda_b \bar{\pi}^e = 0. \tag{A.4}$$

From (A.4):

$$\lambda_b = \lambda_x \frac{\partial \bar{G}}{\partial E} \bigg/ \bar{\pi}^e. \tag{A.5}$$

Substitute (A.5) into (A.3):

$$\frac{\partial Q}{\partial M} = -\bar{\pi}^m \lambda_x \frac{\partial G}{\partial E}. \tag{A.6}$$

Divide (A.6) into (A.2) to get:

$$\frac{\partial Q/\partial D}{\partial Q/\partial M} = \frac{\bar{\pi}^e}{\bar{\pi}^m} = \frac{\partial G/\partial D}{\partial G/\partial E}. \tag{A.7}$$

J. de Melo and S. Robinson, Product differentiation 65

Choose units so that $\bar{\pi}^e = \bar{\pi}^m = 1$. This establishes the condition asserted in the text, i.e.

$$\frac{\partial Q/\partial D}{\partial Q/\partial M} = \frac{p^d/p^q}{p^m/p^q} = \frac{\partial G/\partial D}{\partial G/\partial E} = \frac{p^d/p^x}{p^e/p^x}. \tag{A.8}$$

Therefore

$$\frac{p^d}{p^m} = \frac{p^d}{p^e}.$$

A.2. Derivation of elasticity of offer curve [eq. (4.3)][17]

We proceed in two steps. First, we derive the relation between M and E when MRS = MRT. In the second step we bring in the balance-of-trade constraint.

From (4.2) note that the CET defines a relation between E and D, i.e.

$$D(E, \bar{X}) = \left[\frac{\bar{X}^h}{(1-\alpha)\bar{A}_2^h} - \frac{\alpha}{(1-\alpha)} E^h \right]^{1/h}. \tag{A.9}$$

Using (A.9) in the FOC of the Lagrangian in (A.1) we have:

$$\frac{\partial L}{\partial M} = \frac{\partial Q}{\partial M} + \lambda_b \bar{\pi}^m = 0, \tag{A.10}$$

$$\frac{\partial L}{\partial E} = \frac{\partial Q}{\partial D} \frac{\partial D}{\partial E} - \lambda_b \bar{\pi}^e = 0. \tag{A.11}$$

Dividing (A.10) by (A.11) and rearranging gives:

$$\frac{\partial Q}{\partial M} = -\frac{\bar{\pi}^m}{\bar{\pi}^e} \frac{\partial Q}{\partial D} \cdot \frac{\partial D}{\partial E}. \tag{A.12}$$

The partial derivatives in (A.12) are obtained from differentiation of (4.1), (4.2), and (A.9):

$$\frac{\partial Q}{\partial M} = \beta \bar{A}_1 (\beta M^{-\rho} + (1-\beta)D^{-\rho})^{-(1+\rho)/\rho} M^{-(\rho+1)}, \tag{A.13}$$

$$\frac{\partial Q}{\partial D} = (1-\beta)\bar{A}_1 [\beta M^{-\rho} + (1-\beta)D^{-\rho}]^{-(1+\rho)/\rho} D^{-(\rho+1)}, \tag{A.14}$$

$$\frac{\partial D}{\partial E} = \frac{-\alpha}{1-\alpha} \left[\frac{\bar{X}^h}{\bar{A}_2^h(1-\alpha)} - \frac{\alpha}{(1-\alpha)} E^h \right]^{(1-h)/h} E^{h-1}. \tag{A.15}$$

[17]We thank David Roland-Holst for suggesting the approach followed in this derivation.

Substitution of (A.13), (A.14), and (A.15) into (A.12) yields, after manipulation, the following:

$$M = \left(\frac{\bar{\pi}^m}{\bar{\pi}^e} \frac{\alpha(1-\beta)}{(1-\alpha)\beta} \right)^{-1/(\rho+1)} \left[\frac{\bar{X}^h}{\bar{A}_2^h(1-\alpha)} - \frac{\alpha}{(1-\alpha)} E^h \right]^{(\rho+h)/(\rho+1)h} E^{-(h-1)/(\rho+1)}, \quad (A.16)$$

which gives the relation between M and E when MRS = MRT.

The second step involves taking into account the balance-of-trade constraint:

$$E = \frac{\bar{\pi}^m}{\bar{\pi}^e} M. \quad (A.17)$$

Substituting (A.16) into (A.17) and rearranging gives the required equilibrium relation betwen E and M:

$$E = \frac{\bar{X}}{\bar{A}_2} \left\{ \alpha + (1-\alpha) \left[\left(\frac{\bar{\pi}^e}{\bar{\pi}^m} \right)^{1-\sigma} \left(\frac{\alpha(1-\beta)}{(1-\alpha)\beta} \right)^{\sigma} \right]^{(\Omega+1)/(\Omega+\sigma)} \right\}^{\Omega/(1+\Omega)}. \quad (A.18)$$

To get an expression for the elasticity of the offer curve, ε^{oc}, note that the following relationships hold along an offer curve:

$$\varepsilon^{oc} = \frac{1}{\varepsilon_x^s} + 1, \qquad \varepsilon_x^s + \varepsilon_m^d = -1, \quad (A.19)$$

where

$$\varepsilon^{oc} \equiv \frac{d \log M}{d \log E}; \qquad \varepsilon_m^d \equiv \frac{d \log M}{\left(d \log \frac{\bar{\pi}^m}{\bar{\pi}^e} \right)}; \qquad \varepsilon_x^s \equiv \frac{d \log E}{\left(d \log \frac{\bar{\pi}^e}{\bar{\pi}^m} \right)}.$$

Log differentiation of (A.18) and some algebraic manipulation eventually yields:

$$\varepsilon_x^s = \frac{- \Omega(1-\alpha)(1-\sigma)\gamma^{\sigma(1+\Omega)/(\Omega+\sigma)}}{(\sigma+\Omega)\left\{ \alpha + (1-\alpha) \left[\left(\frac{\bar{\pi}^e}{\bar{\pi}^m} \right)^{(1-\sigma)\gamma\sigma} \right]^{(\Omega+1)/(\Omega+\sigma)} \right\}} \left(\frac{\bar{\pi}^e}{\bar{\pi}^m} \right)^{(1-\sigma)(1+\Omega)/(\Omega+\sigma)}, \quad (A.20)$$

where

J. de Melo and S. Robinson, Product differentiation   67

$$\gamma \equiv \frac{\alpha(1-\beta)}{(1-\alpha)\beta}.$$

By choice of units let $\bar{\pi}^e = \bar{\pi}^m = 1$. Then (A.20) simplifies to:

$$\varepsilon_x^s = \frac{-\Omega(1-\sigma)\lambda}{(\sigma+\Omega)(\alpha+\lambda)} \qquad\qquad (A.21)$$

where

$$\lambda \equiv (-\alpha)\gamma^{[\sigma(1+\Omega)/(\Omega+\sigma)]}.$$

Substitution of (A.21) into (A.19) yields eq. (4.3) in the text.

References

Anderson, J., 1985, The inefficiency of quotas: The cheese case, American Economic Review 75, 1, 178–190.

Armington, P., 1969, A theory of demand for products distinguished by place of production, IMF Staff Papers 16, 159–176.

Deardorff, A.V. and R.M. Stern, 1986, The Michigan model of world production and trade (MIT press, Cambridge, MA).

Dervis, K., J. de Melo and S. Robinson, 1982, General equilibrium models for development policy (Cambridge University Press, Cambridge, England).

Dixon, P. B., B. Parmenter, J. Sutton and D. P. Vincent, 1982, ORANI: A multisector model of the Australian economy (North-Holland, Amsterdam).

Jones, R.W. and E. Berglas, 1977, Import demand and export supply: An aggregation theorem, American Economic Review 67, 183–187.

Melo, J. de and S. Robinson, 1985, Product differentiation and trade dependence of the domestic price system in computable general equilibrium trade models, in: T. Peeters, et al., eds. International trade and exchange rates, 91–107 (North-Holland, Amsterdam).

Powell, A. and F. Gruen, 1968, The constant elasticity of transformation production frontier and linear supply system, International Economic Review 9, 315–328.

Robinson, S., 1989, Multisectoral models of developing countries: A survey, in: H.B. Chenery and T.N. Srinivasan, eds., Handbook of development economics (North-Holland, Amsterdam), forthcoming.

Whalley, J., 1985, Trade liberalization among major world trading areas (MIT Press, Cambridge, MA).

Whalley, J. and B. Yeung, 1984, External sector 'closing' rules in applied general equilibrium models, Journal of International Economics 16, 123–138.

Productivity and externalities: models of export-led growth

Jaime de Melo

The World Bank, University of Geneva, and CEPR

Sherman Robinson

University of California, Berkeley, USA

Abstract

In developing countries, successful export-led growth (ELG) industrialization has been associated with rapid structural change and productivity growth. There are major difficulties in explaining this performance using a standard neoclassical growth model. To develop a more satisfactory framework, we start from empirical and theoretical work with models incorporating externalities. We develop a simple analytical model with an export externality that captures the large increase in both total factor productivity and trade share associated with ELG. A second model is developed to decompose growth into various components: (i) factor accumulation, (ii) a factor reallocation effect from moving factors from low to high productivity sectors, (iii) an export externality effect arising from exporting light and heavy manufactures and (iv) an import externality effect arising from importing capital goods (heavy manufactures). The second model is implemented with data for an archetype semi-industrial country. In addition to accounting for the higher total factor productivity growth observed in countries pursuing ELG strategies, the model captures the patterns of structural change experienced by such countries better than simpler neoclassical models without disequilibrium features or externalities.

1. INTRODUCTION

The relationship between exports and growth is at the heart of much of the debate on the selection of a country's industrialization strategy. A central task in the area of trade policy is to identify the linkages through which trade policy promotes growth. Though seldom rigorously formulated, the export-led growth (ELG) strategy, contrasted with the import substitution industrialization (ISI) strategy, has often been cited as the main reason for observed differences in development patterns and performance among developing countries.

Even assuming the superior performance of ELG, there is still active debate about what exactly is the difference between ISI and ELG, and about the mechanisms through which policies followed under ELG strategies translate into higher growth. For some, it is the 'visible hand' involving an interventionist strategy of successfully 'picking winners' which is at the heart of ELG (Westphal, 1978; Westphal *et al.*, 1985). For others, it is the 'invisible hand' operating in markets with little government participation which explains its success (Balassa *et al.*, 1982; Little, 1982; Balassa, 1985; Krueger, 1985; Bhagwati, 1988). For the former, a judicious combination of selective infant industry protection, export promotion and intervention explains much of the success of ELG. For the latter, a relatively neutral set of incentives across activities, which promotes allocative efficiency, explains its superior performance.

These differences of interpretation aside, when pushed to provide an underlying theoretical model to explain the superiority of an ELG strategy, both camps invoke the loss of growth from the static distortionary costs due to excessive market interventions. These are the efficiency losses arising from distorted incentives in a neoclassical general equilibrium model. To these triangle losses, some would add the less easily conceptualized losses due to x-inefficiency and rent seeking or directly unproductive profit-seeking (DUP) activities. Pushed further, both camps, with varying enthusiasm, cite the still less easily conceptualized losses due to lower total factor productivity (TFP) growth over time and limited exploitation of economies of scale because of small markets. At this point, we have moved some distance from the static efficiency arguments in the neoclassical model. The interventionist school argues further that dynamic effects include mechanisms of 'technology transfer' from developed countries involving externalities that are missed in the static neoclassical model.

As argued in Section 3, the evidence suggests that these dynamic effects are crucial and must be an important part of any explanation of the relative performance of ELG and ISI. In Section 4, we propose a simple model incorporating externalities which captures one possible way of formalizing the link between exporting and higher growth. In Section 5, we go a step further and develop a more complete model in which externalities arise not only from exporting but also from the acquisition of technology embodied in imported capital equipment. In Section 6, we calibrate the model to a Korea-like middle-income semi-industrial economy. Comparative numerical exercises show that this model with externalities captures the pattern of industrialization and TFP change in Korea and other countries following an ELG strategy much better than the standard neoclassical model does.

2. EXPORT-LED GROWTH: THE EVIDENCE

The superior performance of countries pursuing an ELG strategy is well documented in many comparative studies sponsored by the OECD, the

National Bureau of Economic Research and the World Bank.[1] From this literature, a number of suggestive 'stylized facts' have emerged.

First, countries undergoing ELG have industrialized by achieving high growth rates, increasing trade shares in gross domestic product (GDP) and dramatic structural change. As documented in Chenery *et al.* (1986b), countries pursuing ELG strategies had rapid structural change characterized by (i) rapid increases in the use of intermediate inputs ('deepening' of their input–output structure) and (ii) unbalanced growth led by increased demand for tradeable goods. Typically, the early phase of ELG industrialization is led by light manufacturing and is followed by development of the intermediate and capital goods sectors.[2]

Second, there is an acceleration in the rate of economic growth during the transformation associated with industrialization.[3] There is a positive correlation (at the economy-wide level) between aggregate growth and TFP growth. One common explanation for these observations is that there is continuing dynamic disequilibrium adjustment in the factor markets as the expanding industrial sectors pull resources from the agricultural and 'traditional' sectors.[4]

Third, supply-side sources of growth decompositions for countries that have followed an ELG strategy resemble more the pattern of developed countries than the pattern of other developing countries. For ELG countries, the contributions of capital accumulation and TFP growth to total output growth are higher than for other developing countries (and, indeed, than for developed countries).[5] By themselves, these TFP results do not help 'explain' differences between ISI and ELG patterns of development. Since the contribution to growth of TFP is calculated residually, the observed difference really amounts to a restatement of the problem.

Fourth, limited cross-country evidence using data for manufacturing sectors indicates a positive correlation between the role of export expansion and TFP growth at the sectoral level.[6] These results are consistent with the hypothesis that export expansion leads to higher TFP growth through exploiting economies of scale, technology transfer or increasing competitive incentives. There is also evidence that import substitution is correlated with low TFP growth rates at the sectoral level. These results are consistent with the hypothesis that import substitution (liberalization) leads to lower (higher) TFP growth by reducing (increasing) cost-reduction incentives.[7] However, cross-country variations in TFP growth rates are larger than within-country variations across sectors. This result suggests that the contribution to structural change of intersectoral variations in TFP growth rates does not suffice to explain the large differences in the structure of final demand between countries following ISI and ELG strategies.

These results have motivated a number of growth-accounting simulation exercises with neoclassical multisector models. One strand of work has sought to model the observed structural changes accompanying ELG.

Chenery and Syrquin (1986) and Kubo *et al.* (1986b) trace the impact of ELG and ISI strategies on the structure of production in open input–output models by imposing exogenously the changes in final demand and aggregate trade. Another strand of work with long-run computable general equilibrium models relates changes in aggregate growth and in trade structure to policy regimes characteristic of ISI and ELG strategies. For example, Chenery *et al.* (1986a) characterize an ELG strategy in a Korea-like economy by specifying neutral incentives (i.e., no anti-export bias) and an ISI strategy by pervasive import rationing resulting in premia of over 100 percent on all imported goods (largely intermediate and capital goods). Simulations representing a twenty-year period show a relatively small difference in growth rates between the two strategies. Even when exogenous differences in TFP growth rates between the two strategies are introduced, the model still does not adequately capture the differences in terminal year sectoral output and demand structure typical of ELG and ISI strategies.[8]

3. EXTERNALITIES AND GROWTH

The discussion above suggests that empirical work based on the neo-classical model only partially captures the stylized facts of ELG industrialization. Such models indicate that there are efficiency gains from introducing a policy regime of neutral incentives, but the gains are much too small to explain the observed differences in economic performance. The policy recommendation may be correct, but it cannot be justified using standard neoclassical models. The neoclassical framework must be expanded. One plausible way is to introduce externalities. Empirical case studies of countries pursuing ELG, and recent theoretical work, both support this approach.

Case studies indicate that ELG strategies have taken place with active government participation, well beyond simply preventing the development of an anti-export bias through dismantling policies to limit imports. On the export side, governments used large direct subsidies and, in addition, employed nonprice policies including the extensive use of export targeting and the establishment of 'trade-promoting organizations' (TPOs). For example, in Korea, KOTRA (the Korea Trade Promotion Corporation) was established as early as 1962 with government funds. During the early period of ELG industrialization in Korea, indicative export targets were set jointly by the government and various exporters' associations (with the government exerting leverage through its control of credit and other regulatory instruments).[9]

TPOs have played an important role in successful ELG strategies by providing trade information and inquiry services, trade promotion such as trade fairs, market development advice, and assistance to firms in specialized areas such as product design and packaging.[10] Keesing and Singer (1990) argue that TPOs (when efficiently designed and operated) promote exports of manufactured goods which, in turn, generate huge potential external benefits. These externalities cannot be internalized in earnings of an individual exporting firm (e.g., technology acquisition; learning and training; buyer's learning; economies of agglomeration; and general product quality improvement).[11] They are analogous to the role of infrastructure in big-push models (discussed briefly below).

On the import side, case studies indicate that countries pursuing ELG strategies have concentrated their imports more heavily in capital goods and selected intermediates compared with countries pursuing ISI strategies. Furthermore, ELG countries like Korea and Taiwan experienced very rapid increases in the import content of exports, a reflection not only of policies which have provided direct and indirect exporters with unrestricted access (and tariff exemptions) on imported inputs, but also of exporting itself, which gives exporters access to a tremendous range of technological improvements through the activities of the buyers of their exports.[12] In several papers, Westphal and his associates (Westphal, 1982; Westphal *et al.*, 1985) have argued that the infant industry exporting activity in Korea hastened the process of assimilating and mastering foreign technologies, thereby offsetting the static distortionary costs of the selective infant industry protection pursued by the Korean government. They argue that the promotion of infant industry exporting has enforced the mastering of foreign technology, since exporting of manufactures requires the ability to meet world market standards in specifications and quality, as well as distribution and marketing.[13]

Recent contributions to the growth theory literature also emphasize externalities.[14] Though couched in terms of steady-state dynamic models, these contributions have generated suggestive results for understanding ELG in developing countries (an inherently unbalanced process). Three approaches are especially interesting. First, some models introduce Marshallian externalities, in the form of either human capital accumulation (Lucas, 1988) or complementarity between disembodied knowledge and physical capital (Romer, 1986). These models, in effect, introduce increasing returns to scale at the economy-wide level, while maintaining constant returns to scale at the level of the firm. In addition to allowing for differences in growth rates over long periods of time, these models show that a decentralized equilibrium can exist despite the existence of a form of aggregate increasing returns in production (see Grossman and Helpman, 1991).

Second, some models include a mechanism whereby an externality generates an acceleration in the rate of growth. Such mechanisms arise in recent growth models with imperfect competition, either Schumpeterian (Helpman, 1988) or monopolistic (Romer, 1990; Young, 1991). In these models, disembodied knowledge is obtained by investment in research and development (R&D). This representation of how knowledge is created is really more appropriate for explaining the creation of new technology in developed countries than for explaining TFP growth in developing countries. However, the mechanism by which the rate of growth is a positive function of the number of products through investment in R&D is broadly compatible with some descriptions in the development literature on adopting and mastering foreign technology.

Third, some models incorporate pecuniary externalities that enter via demand spillovers between sectors. See, for example, models of a 'big push' such as Murphy *et al.* (1989a, b). In these models, a low level equilibrium growth path might arise in an uncoordinated market economy which generates an inefficiently low level of investment.[15] In such an environment, firms only capture in their profits a small fraction of the total contribution of their investment to aggregate income. Subsidies and grants to investment are essential. In the case of infrastructure, adequate investment may not be built without government assistance. Models with demand spillover effects are also consistent with the evidence from countries pursuing ELG strategies, where infant industry exporters acquired a wide range of foreign technologies. When mastered and assimilated by the firms engaged in exporting activities, these technologies spill over to other activities.

From these recent theoretical contributions, we take on the notions of pecuniary externalities, spillovers and the need for government participation either in the form of coordination of activities or in the form of subsidies to activities which take place at suboptimal levels. The importance of government participation will be apparent in the stylized model of an ELG–productivity link of Section 4. In the more complete representation of an ELG strategy in the model described in Section 5, there will be spillover benefits to non-industrial sectors from the improvement of capital equipment through the increase in the volume of imported capital goods.

From the case studies, we retain a stages approach to ELG industrialization. Export growth first takes place in light manufacturing and is followed by successful import substitution (and exports) in heavy industries. In our models, we emphasize the role of externalities as an engine of growth and industrialization during the first stage, when light manufacturing is the leading sector. We shall consider a single ten- to twenty-year transition period, rather than attempt to compare different long-run steady-state growth paths.

4. A MODEL WITH AN EXPORT EXTERNALITY

Table 1 presents a simple ELG model with an externality linked to exporting. To help the transition to the more elaborate model with factor

Table 1 An export externality model

$Q = F(M, D^D; \sigma)$	CES aggregation function	(1)
$\bar{X} = A\,G(E, D^S; \Omega)$	CET transformation function	(2)
$P^m = R\pi^m(1 + tm)$	import price	(3)
$P^e = R\pi^e(1 + te)$	export price	(4)
$P^t = P^d(1 + td)$	tax-ridden domestic price	(5)
$P^q = f_1(P^m, P^t; \sigma)$	consumer price	(6)
$P^x = g_1(P^e, P^d; \Omega)$	producer price	(7)
$M/D^D = f_2(P^m, P^t; \sigma)$	import demand equation	(8)
$E/D^S = g_2(P^e, P^d; \Omega)$	export supply equation	(9)
$A = \bar{A}\,(E/E_0)^{-\eta}$	export externality ($E > E_0$, $\eta > 0$, $A = \bar{A}$ if $E < E_0$)	(10)
$\pi^m M = \pi^e E$	balance of trade constraint	(11)
$D^D - D^S = 0$	domestic demand = supply	(12)

Variables

M, E	imports, exports
D^D, D^S	demand and supply of the domestic good
Q	composite consumer good
$\bar{X}$	fixed aggregate composite production
π^m, π^e	fixed world prices of imports and exports
R	conversion factor or 'nominal' exchange rate
P^m, P^e	domestic prices of imports and exports
P^d, P^t	domestic prices of domestic sales D, exclusive and inclusive of sales tax
P^q, P^x	domestic prices of composite consumer good Q and composite output X

Parameters

σ, Ω	elasticity of substitution (CES), elasticity of transformation (CET)
η, E_0	externality parameters

markets and intermediate inputs used in Sections 5 and 6, we introduce most of the functional forms to be used later. The model starts from de Melo and Robinson (1989).

There is a domestically produced good D which is an imperfect substitute in demand with an imported good M. There is a second domestically produced good E, which is sold on the export market and is not demanded domestically. The economy can produce combinations of D and E according to a production possibility frontier or 'transformation' function. In equations (1) and (2) the substitution and transformation possibilities are given by constant elasticity of substitution (CES) and constant elasticity of transformation (CET) functions respectively. Foreign trade takes place at fixed world prices, i.e., we make the small-country assumption (equations (3) and (4)). For now, aggregate production, $\bar{X}$, is fixed. The balance of trade constraint, equation (10), precludes any free lunch, and equations (6)–(9) specify profit maximization by producers and cost minimization by demanders. Equation (11) is the market-clearing condition.

The export externality is introduced in equation (10), which states that the amount of (composite) domestic production is an increasing function of exports beyond some base level volume of exports E_0. This is a true externality since the first-order condition, equation (9), does not take equation (10) into account. Producers do not see the benefits of exporting beyond the competitively determined level, and hence do not internalize the presence of equation (10).[16]

In equation (2), ignoring A, the transformation function is homogeneous of degree one in E and D. Just as in the recent growth models with externalities, where A represents disembodied technological knowledge that receives no compensation, here the function for A is also treated as purely external. In Arrow (1962) and Romer (1986), the choices concerning the rate of accumulation of capital make the evolution of productivity endogenous. In equation (10), there are assumed to be productivity-enhancing effects that are associated with exporting and so affect the A parameter.

Figure 1 illustrates both the competitive equilibrium in the stylized model of Table 1 and the optimum solution that takes into account the externality in equation (10). Quadrant I depicts the external balance of trade constraint, which is the 45° line since, by choice of units, we set $\pi^m = \pi^e = 1$ (and $R \equiv 1$ by choice of numeraire). Quadrant IV depicts the production possibility curve perceived by producers and the production possibility curve taking into account the externality. The corresponding consumption possibility frontiers are shown in quadrant II. Finally, quadrant III is the 45° line which specifies equilibrium in the market for domestic sales. The competitive solution is at points P and C, but the optimal solution is at P* and C*.[17] The optimal solution will obtain either as a result of government intervention, as discussed below, or as a result of producers' internalizing the externality, in which case equation (9) will be replaced by a first-order condition that includes η, yielding a full-information competitive model.

It should be obvious that, for a given initial structure, the welfare gain from an ELG strategy will be increasing in η. The gain will also depend on the values of σ and Ω, the (income-compensated) price elasticities of demand for imports and supply of exports respectively. As a typical case, consider an industrializing economy with 10 percent trade shares in GDP (assume $X = 100$ and $E = M = 10$). Sensitivity calculations for this

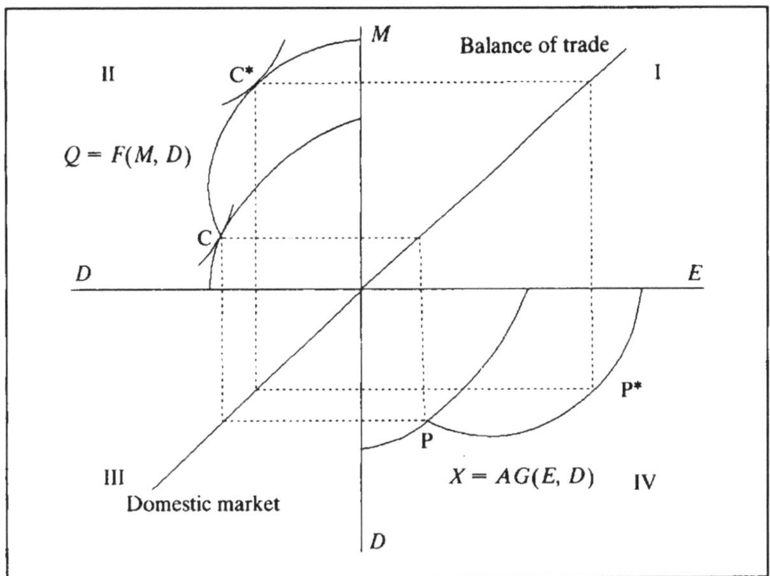

Figure 1 The export externality model.

hypothetical economy are shown in Table 2, which reports the full-information optimum solution values for absorption Q, which is the appropriate welfare indicator.[18] For given values of η, the welfare gain is increasing in σ and Ω. For example, for the first set of runs, with $\eta = 0.1$, the trade share in expenditure increases from 13.1 percent to 20.0 percent as the values of σ and Ω are raised from 0.75 to 3.0. For high values of both η and Ω, the transformation function becomes very flat. For values $\eta = 0.3$, $\sigma = 3.0$ and $\Omega = 3.0$, the model was infeasible.

What combination of parameter values best represents a typical country following an ELG strategy? If one takes the Korean experience between 1965 and 1975, the combination of parameters in run 12 ($\eta = 0.2$, $\sigma = 3.0$, $\eta = 1.5$) seems plausible. That combination gives a productivity–ELG link of 1.27 percentage points per year (12.7 percent increase in output divided by ten years) and an increase in export share in GDP from 10 percent to 25 percent under the assumption that the externality is fully exploited. Korea's performance was spectacular, and one would expect other more typical countries to achieve a similar transformation over, say, twenty rather than ten years.

Since, by definition, the externality is not perceived by the agents, it can only be exploited through policy intervention. The model in Table 1 includes three price-wedge instruments: (i) an export subsidy t_e; (ii) a tariff

Table 2 Sensitivity experiments

	Parameter values			Solution values		
Run	η	σ	Ω	$Q = Y$	$M = E$	$D^D = D^S$
1	0.1	0.75	0.75	101.6	13.3	88.8
2	0.1	1.50	0.75	101.9	13.9	88.4
3	0.1	0.75	1.50	102.2	14.7	88.5
4	0.1	1.50	1.50	102.8	16.1	87.6
5	0.1	3.00	1.50	103.3	17.2	86.7
6	0.1	1.50	3.00	103.7	18.4	86.8
7	0.1	3.00	3.00	104.6	20.9	85.1
8	0.2	0.75	0.75	106.6	16.9	91.5
9	0.2	1.50	0.75	107.5	17.4	91.0
10	0.2	0.75	1.50	109.2	20.7	92.2
11	0.2	1.50	1.50	111.1	22.9	91.2
12	0.2	3.00	1.50	112.7	24.8	90.0
13	0.2	1.50	3.00	114.5	28.7	91.2
14	0.2	3.00	3.00	117.4	33.2	88.6
15	0.3	0.75	0.75	116.4	21.7	98.4
16	0.3	1.50	0.75	118.2	22.9	97.8
17	0.3	0.75	1.50	123.2	29.4	102.1
18	0.3	1.50	1.50	127.1	32.1	100.9
19	0.3	3.00	1.50	130.2	35.3	99.2
20	0.3	1.50	3.00	135.8	44.6	103.4
21	0.3	3.00	3.00	NS	NS	NS

Notes: NS, no solution (infeasible).
Variables and parameters are defined in Table 1.

t_m; and (iii) an indirect tax on the domestic good, t_d. Any net taxes or subsidies are financed by nondistorting lump-sum transfers from or to the single household. The government does not demand goods. Given these instruments, we analyze three policy scenarios: an export subsidy alone; an export subsidy financed by an indirect tax, given a government revenue constraint; and export targeting.

We use the model to solve for optimal policy combinations. The problem is treated as a nonlinear program, maximizing absorption Q subject to the equations in Table 1 as constraints.[19] The tax rates are instrumental variables. In some experiments, it is possible to achieve the full-information optimum. In others, given additional constraints on government revenue or export targets, we consider the costs of not being able to attain the full-information solution.

The results of these scenarios, which all start from run 12 in Table 2, are reported in Table 3. Consider the tax and subsidy experiments. Using export subsidies alone would achieve the optimum and would require an export subsidy rate of 150 percent, at a fiscal cost representing 25 percent of GDP. GATT surveillance notwithstanding, this approach would raise the eyebrows of even the most outward-looking finance minister! In an economy with a well-established and efficient tax collection system, the full benefit of the externality could be achieved at no net cost to the treasury by combining a 25 percent production tax with a 98 percent export subsidy (experiment 4). Alternatively, by Lerner symmetry, the same production tax could be combined with a 50 percent subsidy to imports (experiment 5).[20]

It is unlikely that the full benefits of an externality are achievable by policy intervention, if only because of ignorance about the exact nature of the externality and thus about the optimal mix of policies.[21] Experiments imposing a government revenue constraint and export targeting give an idea of the cost of departing from the full-information optimum. The government revenue constraint experiments indicate that half of the benefits of the externality can be obtained with an export subsidy of 39 percent. Likewise, setting the volume of exports at 15 (about a third of the way between the competitive and full-information solutions) achieves over half of the externality benefits. The implication is that, if our representation of the externality is a reasonable approximation of how ELG works, the cost of policy errors is not large.[22]

5. A MODEL WITH IMPORT AND EXPORT EXTERNALITIES

The small model with an export externality illustrates the implications of capturing the potential role of export promotion in a development strategy. If such externalities are present, they are well worth exploiting. However, this model only captures some of the stylized facts characteristic of ELG discussed above. Also, while the stylized model is suggestive, it is highly aggregated and cannot capture the changes in sectoral structure that are typical of countries undergoing industrialization. In this section, we expand the model to incorporate a bit more sectoral structure and include an additional externality mechanism through which expanded trade is thought to affect economic performance.

In extending the neoclassical growth model to include externalities, the idea is to capture the major observed differences in the pattern of industrialization between ISI and ELG development strategies. A model of the transformation requires, at a minimum, four sectors: agriculture, light manufacturing, heavy manufacturing, and services. We start from arche-

Table 3 Policy experiments

		Variables and parameters											
Number	*Experiment*	$Q=Y$	$E=M$	D	P^x	P^e	P^m	P^d	ER	t_e	t_d	t_m	GR
1	Base run	100.0	10.0	90.0	1.00	1.00	1.00	1.00	1.00	0.0	0.0	0.0	0.0
2	Full info.	112.7	24.8	90.0	1.13	0.77	0.77	1.04	0.74	0.0	0.0	0.0	0.0
Tax and subsidy experiments													
3	t_e	112.7	24.8	90.0	1.41	1.91	0.77	1.04	0.74	1.50	0.0	0.0	−28.2
4	t_e and t_d	112.7	24.8	90.0	1.13	1.53	0.77	1.04	0.74	0.98	0.25	0.0	0.0
5	t_d and t_m	112.7	24.8	90.0	1.13	1.53	0.77	1.04	1.47	0.0	0.25	−0.5	0.0
Government revenue constraint experiments													
6	GR = −5	106.7	14.3	92.7	1.12	1.26	0.91	1.01	0.90	0.39	0.0	0.0	−5.0
7	GR = −10	109.8	17.3	93.0	1.20	1.44	0.86	1.02	0.84	0.67	0.0	0.0	−10.0
8	GR = −15	111.4	19.7	92.6	1.26	1.59	0.83	1.03	0.80	0.92	0.0	0.0	−15.0
9	GR = −20	112.3	21.9	91.8	1.32	1.72	0.80	1.03	0.78	1.14	0.0	0.0	−20.0
10	GR = −28.2	112.7	24.8	90.0	1.41	1.91	0.77	1.04	0.74	1.50	0.0	0.0	−28.2
Export target experiments													
11	$E=15$	107.6	15.0	92.9	1.08	0.90	0.90	1.01	0.88	0.0	0.0	0.0	0.0
12	$E=20$	111.5	20.0	92.5	1.12	0.82	0.82	1.03	0.80	0.0	0.0	0.0	0.0
13	$E=30$	111.4	30.0	85.0	1.11	0.72	0.72	1.06	0.68	0.0	0.0	0.0	0.0

Notes: For all these experiments $X=100$, $P^q=1$, $\sigma=3.0$, $\Omega=1.5$, $\eta=0.2$. The base run solution assumes that no actor sees externalities. The full-information solution is the optimum.

Variables and parameters are defined in Tables 1 and 2. ER is the real exchange rate, which equals R/P^d. The solution values for the nominal exchange rate R are the same as the solution values of P^m. GR is net government revenue from tax collection and subsidy disbursement.

type models of developing countries at different stages of development described in Chenery *et al.* (1986b).

We extend the model presented in Table 1 in a number of ways. Detailed equations are presented in the Appendix. The product differentiation assumptions with regard to both exports and imports are carried over to each of the four sectors.[23] We add inter-industry linkages, assuming a Leontief technology for demands for intermediate inputs. We include primary inputs, labor and capital, with sectoral Cobb–Douglas production functions for real value added.

On the demand side, we specify a single representative consumer with an extended Stone–Geary utility function that includes savings.[24] Final demand thus includes both consumer goods and capital goods, yielding the extended linear expenditure system (ELES). We chose as the numeraire price the cost function corresponding to the ELES utility function, so that maximizing supernumerary expenditure is equivalent to maximizing the indirect utility function.

As in the previous model, government collects indirect taxes and tariffs, pays subsidies and finances any difference through lump-sum transfers. We also retain the small-country assumption, with fixed international prices of sectoral exports and imports. The balance of trade is fixed exogenously, with the real exchange rate serving as the equilibrating variable.

Export externalities enter exactly as in the small model, but now appear in two sectors: light and heavy manufacturing. Exports of agriculture and services are assumed to generate no externalities. We also add an additional externality that works through imports. We assume that imported capital goods are more productive than domestic capital goods. Since the model is static, with a fixed aggregate capital stock, current imports cannot affect the current capital stock. However, we are doing comparative statics experiments designed to represent roughly a decade of rapid growth. We postulate a link between the import ratio in heavy manufacturing and the productivity of the capital stock in the comparative statics experiments. The functional form is analogous to that for the export externality:

$$B = (M/\bar{M})^{\eta} \qquad \eta > 0$$

$$K^{e} = B\bar{K}$$

where K^{e} is the economy-wide effective capital stock.

The effect of this formulation is to specify a link between the import ratio in heavy manufacturing and the size of the 'effective' capital stock. In the static model, this link is treated as an import externality that affects the aggregate capital stock. At the sectoral level, we assume either that producers do not see that raising the import ratio will increase the effective capital stock for their sector or that the productivity increase is not achieved unless it is widespread.

As in the small model, the existence of export and import externalities will lead to potential welfare gains from policy intervention. We include three price-wedge instruments: an export subsidy in both light and heavy manufacturing and an import subsidy in heavy manufacturing. In simulating alternative development strategies, we again solve the model as a nonlinear program, maximizing the utility of the representative consumer subject to all the model equations and solving for the optimum levels of the three subsidy instruments. The three policy instruments are not independent and, as in the small model, one could choose alternative instruments that would achieve the same optimum (e.g. domestic production taxes or subsidies).

In modelling both import and export externalities, we are postulating a link but are not specifying the mechanism by which the externality works. For example, the acquisition of technological mastery through imports of capital goods involves learning, requiring both time and resources. Likewise, on the export side, developing efficient institutional support for exporting involves investment. In the model, these links are costless and, in comparative statics experiments, timeless as well. The elasticities in the various externality equations should be interpreted as implicitly incorporating these costs.

Table 4 reports the structure of the model economy in the base year. The data are drawn from Chenery *et al.* (1986b) and represent an archetype semi-industrial country with per capita income of US $600 (in 1970 dollars). This economy is in the early to middle phase of the industrial transformation described by Chenery and Syrquin (1975). We seek to capture the transition to the next stage, which involves roughly doubling per capita income and lowering agriculture's share of GDP from 20 percent to about 15 percent.

During this transition, resources move out of agriculture, mostly into light manufacturing. Vernon (1989) describes technical change in the production of such goods as characterized by process rather than product innovation. In Vernon's view, the acquisition of technology in these sectors relies on machinery suppliers and in-house production engineers, rather than on in-house R&D. This view of technological change in light manufacturing is also consistent with Westphal's interpretation of Korea's experience with ELG. Thus, we do not try to capture the next stage of industrialization, during which growth shifts towards heavy industry with performance-sensitive products for which technical change requires substantial amounts of R&D expenditures.[25]

The elasticities of import demand and export supply specified for light and heavy manufacturing in Table 4 reflect this view. It is technically relatively easy to produce light manufactures for exporting, and relatively difficult for heavy manufacturing. It is also assumed to be difficult to produce a domestic substitute for imported heavy manufacturing goods.

Table 4 Structure of the economy in the base year

	Agriculture	Light manufacturing	Heavy manufacturing	Services	Total or average
Composition (%)					
Output	18.7	32.4	15.7	33.2	100.0
Value added	20.5	22.0	12.5	45.0	100.0
Employment	38.3	19.2	6.5	36.0	100.0
Capital stock	20.4	13.9	9.0	56.7	100.0
Exports	38.3	21.1	16.5	24.1	100.0
Imports	16.7	17.9	65.4	0.0	100.0
Ratios (%)					
Exports–output	22.8	7.2	11.7	8.1	11.1
Imports–output	12.1	7.5	56.4	0.0	13.5
Price elasticities					
Import demand[a]	4.0	1.1	0.8	4.0	
Export supply[b]	4.0	3.0	0.5	4.0	
Consumer demand[c]	−0.7	−0.8	−1.0	−1.0	
Income elasticity	0.8	0.8	1.3	1.3	
Productivity ratios (%)[d]					
Labor	61.5	124.7	122.2	123.8	100.0
Capital	84.1	143.7	193.9	80.1	100.0

Notes: [a]Compensated price elasticity (= σ).
[b]Compensated price elasticity (= Ω).
[c]Marshallian (uncompensated) own-price elasticity.
[d]Ratio to the economy-wide average.

Note that in Table 4, in line with the empirical evidence reviewed earlier, we assume that the marginal products of labor and capital are lower in agriculture than in industry. The model includes distortion parameters which specify a fixed ratio of sectoral marginal products for labor and capital relative to the economy-wide averages (a complete equation listing is given in the Appendix). Capturing the productivity gains from moving resources out of agriculture is achieved in the model by simply setting all these parameters to unity and resolving.[26]

6. ILLUSTRATIVE SIMULATIONS OF EXPORT-LED GROWTH INDUSTRIALIZATION

We now see whether the extension of the neoclassical model to include an export externality and an import externality captures the observed differences in growth and industrialization patterns between ISI and ELG strategies. As mentioned above, our simulations are intended to portray the transition to an industrial economy with a sizable 'light industry' sector.

The focus of the simulations is to see how far the trade externalities go toward endogenizing the contribution of TFP growth to overall growth and the pattern of structural change typical of ELG industrialization strategies. With the static model, the simulations consist of factor accumulation and exogenous technological change (in agriculture only) augmented by the presence of the externalities described in Section 5. The results are presented in Tables 5 and 6.

To isolate the contribution of the trade externalities, we report four experiments (see the bottom of Table 5). The first three experiments are cumulative. In the first experiment (E1) growth and structural change are entirely through factor accumulation and exogenous technological change

Table 5 Experiment results, aggregate variables

	Base solution	E1 Factor growth	E2 Factor reallocation	E3 Externality 1	E4 Externality 2
GDP change (%)	0.0	54.9	59.6	77.8	109.0
Growth contributions (%)					
Labor	0.0	30.5	28.1	21.5	15.3
Capital	0.0	68.5	63.2	48.5	34.8
Residual	0.0	1.0	8.7	30.0	49.9
Ratios (%)					
Exports–GDP	22.2	26.6	25.0	33.5	44.6
Imports–GDP	27.0	31.3	29.6	37.6	48.1
Foreign savings–GDP	4.8	4.2	4.6	3.5	2.7
Real exchange rate index	100.0	111.5	98.5	106.5	124.0
Agricultural terms of trade	100.0	82.6	103.9	106.8	109.7
Export subsidy (%)					
Light manufacturing	0.0	0.0	0.0	42.3	44.3
Heavy manufacturing	0.0	0.0	0.0	51.4	79.5
Import subsidy (%)					
Heavy manufacturing	0.0	0.0	0.0	24.6	49.7
Externality indices					
Effective production					
Light manufacturing	100.0	100.0	100.0	118.6	143.3
Heavy manufacturing	100.0	100.0	100.0	103.0	106.3
Effective capital stock	100.0	100.0	100.0	102.5	112.8

Note: Description of experiments: E1, factor accumulation + exogenous technological change in agriculture (see text and Appendix); E2, E1 + removal of factor productivity differentials; E3, E2 + low externality parameters (see text); E4, E2 + high externality parameters (see text).

Productivity and externalities 57

Table 6 Experiment results, sectoral variables

	Base solution	E1 Factor growth	E2 Factor reallocation	E3 Externality 1	E4 Externality 2
Agriculture					
Output index	100.0	233.1	195.2	161.6	138.5
Producer price index	100.0	85.2	102.3	114.1	127.9
Consumer price index	100.0	84.2	102.4	113.3	121.8
Exports–output (%)	22.8	29.2	21.8	10.6	5.4
Imports–output (%)	12.1	7.8	12.9	33.8	72.5
Light manufacturing					
Output index	100.0	145.1	161.1	215.6	267.8
Producer price index	100.0	109.7	103.8	107.7	113.7
Consumer price index	100.0	109.2	103.8	84.0	69.4
Exports–output (%)	7.2	4.1	6.7	27.6	44.0
Imports–output (%)	7.5	9.6	7.8	6.0	5.0
Heavy manufacturing					
Output index	100.0	172.0	208.1	226.0	230.8
Producer price index	100.0	97.8	81.9	82.8	85.1
Consumer price index	100.0	95.5	87.2	70.6	57.3
Exports–output (%)	11.7	11.3	13.0	16.1	17.6
Imports–output (%)	56.4	60.6	45.6	53.9	75.0
Services					
Output index	100.0	166.4	174.4	167.8	172.0
Producer price index	100.0	100.4	103.0	121.1	141.0
Consumer price index	100.0	101.1	103.1	122.6	143.1
Exports–output (%)	8.1	5.4	7.5	3.0	1.3
Imports–output (%)	0.0	0.0	0.0	0.0	0.0
Composition of real GDP (%)					
Agriculture	20.5	27.1	22.2	18.0	14.7
Light manufacturing	22.0	18.1	19.7	25.7	30.4
Heavy manufacturing	12.5	12.2	14.5	15.3	14.9
Services	45.0	42.6	43.6	41.0	40.0

in agriculture that combines deepening of inter-industry linkages and exogenous TFP growth (see the Appendix). The net effect is a residual contribution of TFP to total growth of less than 1 percent. Experiment E1 reflects the growth and structural change that would be generated by the neoclassical growth model. The second experiment (E2) recognizes that a productivity gain is realized by moving factors out of low-productivity agriculture. As can be seen from the top of Table 5, the contribution of the 'residual' to growth is now almost 9 percent. In terms of GDP growth, this factor relocation effect raises GDP by 5 percentage points.

The next two experiments introduce externalities in exporting of light and heavy manufactures and in importing of heavy manufactures. In E3, the values of all externality parameters are set at 0.1, and in E4 the export externality parameters are set at 0.15 and the import externality parameters at 0.20. The contributions of the two externalities to effective production and to the economy-wide effective capital stock are reported at the bottom of Table 5. The empirical result is a contribution of TFP growth to total growth of 30–50 percent, which is consistent with empirical evidence.

Experiment E1 represents an 'equilibrium' neoclassical description of an ELG strategy. Adding the 'disequilibrium' assumption of differential factor productivity growth during the transformation stabilizes the agricultural terms of trade index, a widely observed stylized fact of development over relatively long time periods. For an economy following a manufacturing ELG strategy, the factor reallocation effect also contributes towards stabilizing the value of the relative price of tradeables because tradeables (which are concentrated in manufacturing) benefit from cheaper capital and labor through the reallocation effect. Note, however, that the factor reallocation effect has little effect on the openness of the economy, as the aggregate ratios of exports and imports to GDP are very similar for E1 and E2. As a first approximation, E2 corroborates numerically the acceleration hypothesis during the transition, but does not contribute toward an explanation of structural change.

In E3, where externality effects are small, there is some change in the real exchange rate and terms of trade indices compared with E2, but nothing dramatic. Openness is increased by about a third, with exports and imports reaching 35 percent of GDP.[27] The factor accumulation rates in the experiments approximate those realized by Korea during 1975–85. Assuming the experiments represent a decade, the implied compound growth rate is 5.2 percent per annum under E3, which is much less than the 7.7 percent rate achieved by Korea during that period. The externality effects assumed in E4 result in an annual compound growth rate of 7.7 percent, matching historical performance. However, E4 overestimates structural change (in terms of openness) during that period, whereas E3 yields an increase in openness very close to that achieved by Korea during 1975–85.

Table 5 indicates the implications for structural change of incorporating 'disequilibrium' in factor markets and externalities into the basic neoclassical computable general equilibrium model. The factor reallocation effect (experiment E2) prevents the agricultural sector from increasing its share in GDP, but it misses entirely the change in the sectoral structure of foreign trade that takes place during a manufacturing ELG industrialization strategy. In experiment E2, import and export shares in gross output are too high for agriculture and too low for industry, particularly for heavy manufacturing. By contrast, with externalities, the computerized general equilibrium model captures much better the surge in light manufacturing exports (e.g., textiles and other consumer goods) and heavy manufacturing imports (e.g., capital goods), as well as the declining share of agricultural exports and rising share of agricultural imports. The patterns of structural change in output and foreign trade under E3 and E4 replicate fairly closely those observed during the early to middle phase of ELG in countries such as Korea and Taiwan, when growth was greatest in light manufacturing sectors.

One last stylized feature of ELG growth is nicely captured by the modified model with trade externalities. Williamson (1979), citing the Kim and Roemer (1979) study of Korea's industrialization, notes that, in contrast with most other developing countries, Korea's relative (to GDP) price index of investment goods declined by approximately 40 percent during the period 1962–75. Table 6 shows that with the subsidy to imports of heavy manufacturing necessary to induce the acquisition of heavy manufacturing imports, there is a dramatic decline in the domestic purchaser's price index of heavy manufacturing products. The producer price index of heavy manufacturing increases between E3 and E4 because of the more than doubling of the export subsidy to heavy manufacturing in E4 compared with E3. It is also interesting to note that the subsidy rates in experiments E3 and E4 are in line with the subsidies to infant industry exports described by Westphal (1982). The patterns of structural change in Table 6 are, of course, only suggestive, but they do capture the salient differences in structural change observed between ISI and ELG strategies.

In these experiments, the policy mix involves only subsidies to exporting manufactures and importing heavy manufactures. As with the small model, the total expense of the program is large. In the high elasticity externality experiments (E4), the cost of all subsidies equals 12 percent of gross sales and 27 percent of GDP. We did an additional experiment that started from E4 but added a uniform indirect tax rate t_d of 15 percent. The result is a similar pattern of subsidies but effectively no net tax on households. It is certainly feasible to design a mix of indirect taxes and subsidies that exploit the externalities with little impact on total net tax revenue. The implied sectoral tax and subsidy rates are also within observed ranges for semi-industrial countries.

7. CONCLUSION

In spite of their extreme simplicity, there are a couple of lessons to be learned from the stylized models incorporating export and import externalities. First, from a theoretical perspective, the approach appears to be fruitful. The models capture well the major stylized facts of growth and structural change in countries undergoing ELG. They also overcome a major shortcoming of the neoclassical model. In the neoclassical model, TFP growth appears by magic, with no link to changes in economic structure or policy choices. These trade-externality models provide a first step toward endogenizing major driving forces generating measured TFP growth in ELG countries. They also provide a better framework for analyzing the links between aggregate economic performance, structural change and policy choices.

Second, there is a lesson for policy analysts. In the presence of externalities, many of the simple policy rules arising from the neoclassical general equilibrium model are no longer valid. Policy rules that seek to minimize static efficiency losses may miss potential gains arising from policy links to externalities. As is common in economics, there appear to be some tradeoffs – in this case, between static efficiency costs and dynamic gains from exploiting externalities linked to export performance and import structure. The empirical results with the small export externality model and the second model adding an import externality support this view and suggest a change in policy perspective. If there are externalities to be exploited, policymakers should pursue them aggressively, and not worry overmuch about getting the instruments just right. The simulations indicate that when there are rectangles to be gained, an economy can easily afford to lose some triangles along the way.

The simple stylized models of ELG presented here are based on the empirical experience of countries that have pursued successful ELG strategies. Yet they are only skeletal models that emphasize one possible explanation of TFP growth: Marshallian externalities. In this environment, the empirical results support the view that policymakers should pursue an interventionist policy regime to coordinate private sector activities. Further work is needed to explore the channels through which the externalities operate and interact with the structural changes that accompany industrialization. The models developed here are only a first step in that direction.

APPENDIX

This appendix completes the description of the model presented in Section 5. The following notation is adopted throughout. If double subscripts are employed, the first subscript denotes the sector of origin, the second the sector of destination. Upper-case letters are reserved for endogenous variables, unless they have a bar, in which case they are exogenous variables or normalizing constants. Parameters and policy variables are denoted by Greek or lower-case Latin letters. Variables with a tilde over them represent nominal magnitudes. There are four sectors indexed over i or j: agriculture, light manufacturing, heavy manufacturing, and services (A, H, L and S respectively).

We use CES and CET functions to describe substitution possibilities in trade. To save on notation, note that CES and CET functions can be written symmetrically, using the same share parameter α and exponent ρ: $X = \mathrm{CES}(F_1, F_2; \alpha, \rho, \bar{A})$ where the CES substitution elasticity σ and

CET transformation elasticity Ω are given by $\sigma = 1/(1 - \rho)$, $-\infty < \rho < +1$, in the CES case and $\Omega = 1/(\rho - 1)$, $1 < \rho < +\infty$, in the CET case. In both cases, the function is written:

$$X = \bar{A} \left[\alpha\, F_1^{\rho} + (1 - \alpha)\, F_2^{\rho} \right]^{1/\rho}$$

Table A1 lists the equations describing the model underlying the simulations reported in Section 6. The model includes the export externality, the import externality and an assumption of differential factor productivities for capital and labor across sectors. The export externality is the same as that introduced for the simple model in Section 4 except that it now applies to exports of light and heavy manufacturing (see equation (A8)). The import externality (equation (A7)) increases aggregate effective capital and hence has economy-wide implications. Finally, the assumption of differential factor productivity across sectors is reflected by fixed distortion parameters in the first-order conditions for factor demands (see equations (A6) and (A7)).

Since there is only one consumer who maximizes utility given by the equations of the ELES, we have chosen as numeraire the cost function corresponding to the ELES so that, given our choice of numeraire, maximizing supernumerary expenditures (see equation (A1)) is equivalent to maximizing utility. Also note that exogenous foreign transfers $\bar{B}$, expressed in foreign currency units, are given to the representative household and that the government's activity is restricted to collecting and disbursing tax revenues.

The values for the externality parameters are discussed in the main text. The factor productivity differentials, or distortion parameters, are drawn from evidence reported in Chenery *et al.* (1986b), particularly chapters 3, 5 and 8. The assumed values for the base solution are

$$\lambda_1^K = 0.84 \qquad \lambda_2^K = 1.44 \qquad \lambda_3^K = 1.94 \qquad \lambda_4^K = 0.80$$

$$\lambda_1^L = 0.62 \qquad \lambda_2^L = 1.25 \qquad \lambda_3^L = 1.25 \qquad \lambda_4^L = 1.24$$

The assumed values for sectoral technology and the structure of the base solution sectoral outputs are given in Table A2, and the social accounting matrix for the base data is given in Table A3. The elasticities for the CET, CES and ELES functions describing export supply, import demand and consumer demand are described in Table 5 in the main text.

In all experiments, the following assumptions are made about factor accumulation and exogenous technological progress in agriculture. The labor force is augmented by 32 percent and the capital stock (net of depreciation) by 79 percent. These figures, representative of Korea during 1975–85, imply annual compound growth rates of 2.8 percent and 6 percent respectively. In agriculture, exogenous technological progress (on real value added) of 79 percent is combined with increasing intermediate-

62   **The Journal of International Trade & Economic Development**

Table A1 A multisector model with trade externalities

Welfare indicator

$$W = \dot{Y} - S - \sum_i \mathrm{PQ}_i \, \gamma_i \tag{A1}$$

Technology

$$X_i = \overline{\mathrm{AX}} K_i^{\alpha_i} L_i^{1-\alpha_i} \tag{A2}$$

$$V_i = \sum_j a_{ij} X_j \tag{A3}$$

$$Q_i = \mathrm{CES}(D_i, M_i; \beta_i, \sigma_i, \overline{\mathrm{AQ}}_i) \tag{A4}$$

$$X_i = \mathrm{CET}(D_i, E_i; \delta_i, \Omega_i, \mathrm{AT}_i) \tag{A5}$$

Factor markets

$$K_i^{\mathrm{D}} = \frac{\alpha_i \, \mathrm{PN}_i \, X_i}{\lambda_i^K \, W_K} \tag{A6}$$

$$L_i^{\mathrm{D}} = \frac{(1 - \alpha_i) \, \mathrm{PN}_i \, X}{\lambda_i^L \, W_L} \tag{A7}$$

Externalities

$$\mathrm{AT}_k = \overline{\mathrm{AT}}_k \left[\frac{E_k}{\bar{E}_k} \right]^{-\eta_k} \qquad k \in \mathrm{L, H \; and} \; E_k \geq \bar{E}_k \tag{A8}$$

$$\mathrm{AT}_k = \overline{\mathrm{AT}}_k \qquad k \in \mathrm{A, S \; or} \; E_k < \bar{E}_k$$

$$B = \left[\frac{M_\mathrm{H}}{\bar{M}_\mathrm{H}} \right]^{\psi} \qquad M_\mathrm{H} \geq \bar{M}_\mathrm{H}$$

$$B = 1 \qquad M_\mathrm{H} < \bar{M}_\mathrm{H} \tag{A9}$$

Resource constraints and effective capital stock

$$\sum_i L_i^{\mathrm{D}} = \bar{L} \tag{A10}$$

$$\sum_i K_i^{\mathrm{D}} = K^c \tag{A11}$$

$$K^e = B \, K \tag{A12}$$

Export supply and import demand

$$\frac{D_i}{E_i} = \left[\frac{\delta_i \, \mathrm{PD}_i}{(1 - \delta_i) \, \mathrm{PE}_i} \right]^{\Omega_i} \tag{A13}$$

$$\frac{D_i}{M_i} = \left[\frac{\beta_i \, \mathrm{PD}_i}{(1 - \beta_i) \, \mathrm{PM}_i} \right]^{-\sigma_i} \tag{A14}$$

Prices

$$PQ_i = (PM_i \, M_i + PD_i \, D_i)/Q_i \tag{A15}$$

$$PN_i = PX_i - \sum_j a_{ji} \, PQ_j \tag{A16}$$

$$PK = \sum_j PQ_j \, b_j \tag{A17}$$

$$PX_i = (PE_i \, E_i + PD_i \, D_i)/X_i \tag{A18}$$

$$PM_i = \overline{PWM}_i \, R \, (1 + tm_i) \tag{A19}$$

$$PE_i = \overline{PWE}_i \, R \, (1 + te_i) \tag{A20}$$

Demand

$$S = \beta_0 \, Y \tag{A21}$$

$$Z_i = b_i \, S/PK \tag{A22}$$

$$PQ_i \, C_i = PQ_i \, \gamma_i + \frac{\beta_i}{\Sigma_j \beta_j} \, (\tilde{Y} - S - \sum_j PQ_j \, \gamma_j) \tag{A23}$$

Balance of trade constraint

$$\sum_i (\overline{PWM}_i \, M_i - \overline{PWE}_i \, E_i) = B \tag{A24}$$

Income and government revenue

$$\tilde{Y} = W_L \, L + W_K \, K + \tilde{G} + B \, R \tag{A25}$$

$$\tilde{G} = \sum_i (tm_i \, M_i \, \overline{PWM}_i - te_i \, E_i \, \overline{PWE}_i) \, R \tag{A26}$$

Market equilibrium

$$Q_i = V_i + Z_i + C_i \tag{A27}$$

Numeraire

$$P = PK^{\beta_0} \prod_i (PQ_i)^{\beta_i} \tag{A28}$$

input requirements. The input–output coefficients for intermediate inputs into agriculture from the non-agricultural sectors are increased by 40 percent. The elements of the first column in Table A2 become 0.170, 0.100, 0.169 and 0.125. In addition, the entry from agriculture to light manufacturing is doubled. As can be seen from the contribution of the residual to growth in Table 5, this combination of technological progress and deepening intermediate-input structure yields a contribution of the residual to value-added growth in agriculture of 4.3 percent.

64   *The Journal of International Trade & Economic Development*

Table A2 Input–output coefficients and factor ratios

| | Input–output coefficients | | | | Ratios | | Output |
Sector	Agriculture	Light manufacturing	Heavy manufacturing	Services	K/XD	K/L	XD
Agriculture	0.170	0.111	0.080	0.048	1.44	1.61	224
Light manufacturing	0.071	0.250	0.191	0.108	0.65	2.20	388
Heavy manufacturing	0.121	0.180	0.239	0.050	0.76	4.21	188
Services	0.089	0.119	0.090	0.113	2.27	4.79	397

Table A3 Social accounting matrix

| | Expenditures | | | | | | |
Receipts	Commodity	Activity	Value added	Households	Capital account	Rest of world	Total
Commodity		597		509	120		1,226
Activity	1,064					133	1,197
Value added		600					600
Households			600				600
Capital account				120			120
Rest of world	162			−29			133
Total	1,226	1,197	600	600	120	133	

NOTES

The views are those of the authors. They should not be attributed to their respective affiliations.

1   For early comparative case studies see Little *et al.* (1970), Balassa *et al.* (1971, 1982), Bhagwati (1978) and Chenery *et al.* (1986b). Cross-country correlations between export growth and aggregate growth are presented in Michaely (1977), Balassa (1978), Heller and Porter (1978), Feder (1983) and Jung and Marshall (1985). For more recent cross-country evidence, see Harrison (1991) and Roubini and Sala-1-Martin (1991), and Levine and Renelt (forthcoming) on how to interpret results from these econometric models.

2   See Chenery *et al.* (1986b), chs 3, 6 and 7. Balassa (1979) describes these

phases in terms of 'stages' of comparative advantage. See also de Melo (1985), who compares Korea and Taiwan.

3   Evidence in support of the acceleration hypothesis during the industrialization of today's developed countries is given in Kuznets (1971). Evidence for today's developing countries is reviewed in Syrquin (1986).

4   The classic two-sector development model is Lewis (1954). Bruno (1968), Robinson (1971) and Feder (1986) present two-sector models in which they econometrically estimate the contribution of disequilibrium adjustment in the factor markets to growth. Syrquin (1986) presents some computations for archetype economies.

5   The evidence is detailed in Chenery (1986).

6   The evidence is from Nishimizu and Robinson (1984). The countries are Japan (1955–70), Korea (1965–73), Turkey (1953–73) and Yugoslavia (1962–72). The data cover sixteen manufacturing sectors.

7   An alternative, but not exclusive, hypothesis is that export expansion and import liberalization increase TFP growth by relaxing the foreign exchange constraint, facilitating imports of nonsubstitutable intermediate and capital goods.

8   See also Lewis *et al.* (1987) who compare different models of Korea's ELG period.

9   See Westphal (1978).

10   For a description of the activities of TPOs in four countries pursuing ELG policies, see Keesing (1988).

11   This evidence suggests that the benefit of the externality is achieved through government investment. In the models presented below, we do not incorporate this link explicitly, though it could be handled along the lines suggested by Barro (1990).

12   See de Melo (1985), who shows that Korea and Taiwan doubled the import content of exports within a decade.

13   This argument is different from learning by doing (Arrow, 1962), where labor productivity increases with the level of cumulative gross investment or output, although both arguments are largely consistent with the data. Westphal argues, however, that the successful assimilation of imported technology (the learning) is itself dependent on the policy environment.

14   For a survey of these recent contributions, see Easterly (1991). On the channels through which policies affect the rate of growth, see Easterly *et al.* (1991).

15   There is an early literature on similar 'low level traps' in economic development. See, for example, Nelson (1956).

16   This specification is similar to that in other trade theory models analyzing arguments for 'infant export industry' protection. See Bhagwati (1968) and the dynamic model by Mayer (1984).

17   An interesting question is whether the competitive solution is always stable. In our empirical applications it is stable, but it is easy to pick parameter values where it is not.

18   We also choose Q as the numeraire good, setting $P^q \equiv 1$.

19   The model is solved using the GAMS software. See Brooke *et al.* (1988).

20   Accounting for the numeraire, the product of the exchange rate and export subsidy in row 4 of Table 3 equals the exchange rate multiplied by the import tariff in row 5.

21   In a different context, authors such as Harberger (1988) have argued that uniform tariffs should be pursued even granted the theoretical argument that they are not optimal because of ignorance of the parameters needed to compute optimal tariffs.

22 Of course, this result depends crucially on the particular functional form chosen for the externality linkage.
23 There is a two-way trade in every sector except services, in which there are no imports.
24 The expenditure system is the extended linear expenditure system (ELES). See Lluch *et al.* (1977).
25 Korea has recently increased its share of R&D expenditures in GNP from 0.57 percent in 1980 to 3.0 percent in 1986. This current trend is more consistent with the recent theoretical literature on R&D externalities discussed earlier, and is indicative of Korea's maturation.
26 The Appendix describes the equations and data sources.
27 Because foreign saving is maintained to fixed value currency units in E3 and E4, its share in GDP declines with increasing externalities.

REFERENCES

Arrow, K. (1962) 'The economic implications of learning by doing'. *Review of Economic Studies* 29, 154–74.

Balassa, B. (1978) 'Exports and growth: further evidence'. *Journal of Development Economics* 5, 181–9.

—— (1979) 'A "Stages Approach" to Comparative Advantage'. In Adelman, I. (ed.) *Economic Growth and Resources*, vol. 4, *National and International Issues*. London: Macmillan, 121–56.

—— (1985) 'Exports, policy choices, and economic growth in developing countries after the 1973 oil shock'. *Journal of Development Economics* May–June, 23–36.

Balassa, B. and associates (1971) *The Structure of Protection in Developing Countries*. Baltimore, MD: Johns Hopkins University Press.

Balassa, B. and associates (1982) *Development Strategies in Semi-Industrial Countries.* tries. Baltimore, MD: Johns Hopkins University Press.

Barro, R. (1990) 'Government spending in a model of endogenous growth'. *Journal of Political Economy* 98, S103–25.

Bhagwati, J. (1968) 'The theory and practice of commercial policy: departures from unified exchange rates'. Special Papers in Economics 8, Princeton University.

—— (1978) *Foreign Trade Regimes and Economic Development: Anatomy and Consequences of Exchange Control Regimes.* Cambridge, MA: Ballinger.

—— (1988) 'Export-promoting trade strategy: issues and evidence'. *World Bank Research Observer* 27–58.

Brooke, T., Kendrick, D. and Meeraus, A. (1988) *GAMS: A User's Guide.* New York: Scientific Press.

Bruno, M. (1968) 'Estimation of factor contribution to growth under structural disequilibrium'. *International Economic Review* 9, 49–62.

Chenery, H. (1986) 'Growth and Transformation'. In Chenery, H., Robinson, S. and Syrquin, M. (eds) *Industrialization and Growth: A Comparative Study.* London: Oxford University Press, ch. 2.

Chenery, H. and Syrquin, M. (1986) 'Typical Patterns of Transformation'. In Chenery, H., Robinson, S. and Syrquin, M. (eds) *Industrialization and Growth: A Comparative Study.* London: Oxford University Press, ch. 3.

Chenery, H., Robinson, S. and Syrquin, M. (eds) (1986b) *Industrialization and Growth: A Comparative Study.* London: Oxford University Press.

Chenery, H., Lewis, J.D., de Melo, J. and Robinson, S. (1986a) 'Alternative Routes to Development'. In Chenery, H., Robinson, S. and Syrquin, M. (eds)

Industrialization and Growth: A Comparative Study. London: Oxford University Press, ch. 11.

Easterly, W. (1991) 'Economic stagnation, fixed factors, and policy thresholds'. Mimeo, World Bank, Washington, DC.

Easterly, W., King, R., Levine, R. and Rebelo, S. (1991) 'How do national policies affect long-run growth? A research agenda'. PRE Working Paper Series 794, World Bank, Washington, DC.

Feder, G. (1983) 'On exports and economic growth'. *Journal of Development Economics* 12, 59–73.

—— (1986) 'Growth in semi-industrial countries: a statistical analysis'. In Chenery, H., Robinson, S. and Syrquin, M. (eds) *Industrialization and Growth: A Comparative Study.* London: Oxford University Press, ch. 9.

Grossman, G. and Helpman, E. (1991) *Innovation and Growth: Technological Competition in the World Economy.* Cambridge, MA: MIT Press.

Harberger, A. (1988) 'On uniform tariffs'. Mimeo, World Bank, Washington, DC.

Harrison, A. (1991) 'Openness and growth: a time-series, cross-country analysis for developing countries'. PRE Working Paper Series 808, World Bank, Washington, DC.

Heller, P. and Porter, M. (1978) 'Exports and growth: an empirical reinvestigation', *Journal of Development Economics* 5, 191–4.

Helpman, E. (1988) 'Growth, technological progress, and trade'. *Austrian Economic Papers* 15 (1), 5–25.

Jung, W. and Marshall, P. (1985) 'Exports, growth and causality in developing countries'. *Journal of Development Economics* 1–12.

Keesing, D. (1988) 'The four successful exceptions: official export promotion and support for export marketing in Korea, Hong Kong, Singapore and Taiwan, China'. UNDP–World Bank Trade Expansion Program, Occasional Paper 2, World Bank, Washington, DC.

Keesing, D. and Singer, A. (1990) 'How support services can expand manufactured exports: new methods of assistance'. PRE Working Paper 544, World Bank, Washington, DC.

Kim, K.S. and Roemer, M. (1979) *Growth and Structural Transformation.* Cambridge, MA: Harvard University Press.

Krueger, A. (1985) 'The Experience and Lessons of Asia's Super Exporters'. In Corbo, V., Krueger, A. and Ossa, F. (eds) *Export-Oriented Development Strategies: the Success of Five Newly Industrializing Countries.* Boulder, CO: Westview Press.

Kubo, Y., Robinson, S. and Urata, S. (1986b) 'The impact of alternative development strategies: simulations with a dynamic input–output model'. *Journal of Policy Modeling* 8 (4), 503–29.

Kuznets, S. (1971) *Economic Growth of Nations: Total Output and Production Structure.* Cambridge, MA: Harvard University Press.

Levine, R. and Renelt, D. (forthcoming) 'A sensitivity analysis of cross-country growth regressions'. *American Economic Review.*

Lewis, J.D., de Melo, J. and Robinson, S. (1987) 'Simulating alternative development strategies: some suggestions from Korea's experience'. *International Economic Journal* 1 (3), 1–19.

Lewis, W. (1954) 'Economic development with unlimited supplies of labor'. *Manchester School of Economic and Social Studies* 139–91.

Little, I.M.D. (1982) *Economic Development: Theory, Policy, and International Relations.* New York: Basic Books.

Little, I.M.D., Scitovsky, T. and Scott, M. (1970) *Industry and Trade in Some Developing Countries: A Comparative Study.* London: Oxford University Press.

Lluch, C., Powell, A. and Williams, R. (1977) *Patterns in Household Demand and*

Saving. London: Oxford University Press.

Lucas, R.E., Jr. (1988) 'On the mechanics of economic development'. *Journal of Monetary Economics* 22, 3–42.

Mayer, W. (1984) 'The infant industry export argument'. *Canadian Journal of Economics* 17 (2), 249–69.

de Melo, J. (1985) 'Sources of Growth and Structural Change in the Republic of Korea and Taiwan: Some Comparisons'. In Corbo, V., Krueger, A. and Ossa, F. (eds) *Export-Oriented Development Strategies: the Success of Five Newly Industrializing Countries*. Boulder, CO: Westview Press.

de Melo, J. and Robinson, S. (1989) 'Product differentiation and the treatment of foreign trade in CGE models of small economies'. *Journal of International Economics* 27, 47–67.

Michaely, M. (1977) 'Exports and growth: an empirical examination'. *Journal of Development Economics* 4, 149–53.

Murphy, K.M., Shleifer, A. and Vishny, R. (1989a) 'Industrialization and the big push stage of industrial development'. *Journal of Political Economy* 97, 1003–27.

—— (1989b) 'Income distribution, market size, and industrialization'. *Quarterly Journal of Economics* August, 537–64.

Nelson, R.R. (1956) 'A theory of the low level equilibrium trap'. *American Economic Review* December, 864–908.

Nishimizu, M. and Robinson, S. (1984) 'Trade policies and productivity change in semi-industrialized countries'. *Journal of Development Economics* 16 (1–2), 177–206.

Robinson, S. (1971) 'Sources of growth in less developed countries: a cross-section study'. *Quarterly Journal of Economics* 85 (3), 391–408.

Romer, P. (1986) 'Increasing returns and long-run growth'. *Journal of Political Economy* 94, 1002–37.

—— (1990) Endogenous technological change'. *Journal of Political Economy* 98, S71–S102.

Roubini, N. and Sala-I-Martin, X. (1991) 'The relation between trade regime, financial development and economic growth'. *NBER Fourth Annual Inter-American Seminar on Economics*. Cambridge, MA: National Bureau of Economic Research.

Syrquin, M. (1986) 'Productivity Growth and Factor Reallocation'. In Chenery, H., Robinson, S. and Syrquin, M. (eds) *Industrialization and Growth: A Comparative Study*. London: Oxford University Press, ch. 8.

Vernon, R. (1989) 'Technological development: the historical experience'. EDI Seminar Paper 39, World Bank, Washington, DC.

Westphal, L. (1978) 'The Republic of Korea's experience with export-led industrial development'. *World Development* 6, 347–82.

—— (1982) 'Fostering Technological Mastery by Means of Selective Industry Promotion'. In Syrquin, M. and Teitel, S. (eds) *Trade, Stability, Technology and Equity in Latin America*. New York: Academic Press.

Westphal, L., Kim, L. and Dahlman, C. (1985) 'Reflections on Korea's Acquisition of Technological Capability'. In Rosenberg, N. and Frischtak, C. (eds) *International Technology Transfer*. New York: Praeger.

Williamson, J.G. (1979) 'Why do Koreans save so little?' *Journal of Development Economics* 6, 343–62.

Young, A. (1991) 'Learning by doing and the dynamic effects of international trade'. *Quarterly Journal of Economics* 106 (2), 369–406.

The Economic Journal, **91** *(December* 1981*),* 891–906
Printed in Great Britain

A GENERAL EQUILIBRIUM ANALYSIS OF FOREIGN EXCHANGE SHORTAGES IN A DEVELOPING ECONOMY*

Kemal Dervis, Jaime de Melo and Sherman Robinson

An acute shortage of foreign exchange has been a recurring problem for many developing economies. In the development planning literature, the problem is usually discussed within the framework of the 'two-gap' or 'multi-gap' models developed and elaborated during the sixties. These models assume fixed input–output coefficients and limited possibilities for export expansion. As a result, a foreign exchange shortage becomes an almost absolute constraint on growth in that even if domestic savings were available in sufficient amounts to allow an increase in investment, the absence of the required complementary foreign exchange makes such an increase impossible. The neoclassical answer to this 'structuralist' view has always been to stress the role of relative prices and, in particular, exchange rate adjustment as a means of overcoming any foreign exchange shortage.[1] Stated simply, this view treats the alleged foreign exchange gap as only reflecting an overvalued real exchange rate. If the exchange rate is allowed to clear the foreign exchange market, there can be no foreign exchange gap.

However, the experience of developing countries indicates that it is extremely difficult to achieve the necessary rise in the effective exchange rate to restore equilibrium in the foreign exchange market. As Krueger (1978) has documented for a group of developing countries, the typical pattern of adjustment policies often involves an unsuccessful devaluation followed by a return to various forms of foreign exchange rationing. The reasons why devaluations are often unsuccessful are myriad and much discussed in the literature (see Krueger (1978), Bruno (1979), Diaz-Alejandro *et al.* (1979)), but the main point which we wish to pursue in this paper is that countries often rely on other policies whose quantitative impacts need to be systematically explored. In understanding different adjustment mechanisms, all students of trade and exchange rate policy in developing countries agree that the elimination of persistent foreign exchange imbalances requires substantial adjustments in the real sphere of the economy. While macroeconomic phenomena may be important, there must also be a reallocation of resources towards sectors where there is scope for import substitution and/or where exports can be expanded. The relationship between different policy regimes and these necessary structural adjustments provides the major focus of our analysis.

---

* We would like to thank Adrian Wood for helpful comments and criticisms. The views expressed in this article are the authors' and do not necessarily reflect those of the World Bank.

[1] For a presentation of these contrasting views, see Findlay (1973, Chapter 10) and Diamond (1978).

[891]

This paper re-examines the foreign exchange gap issue and the debate between structuralists and neoclassicists by providing a quantitative assessment of the role of different assumptions about the values of key trade elasticities. Perhaps more importantly, the paper also seeks to complement the existing descriptive analysis of the consequences of alternative adjustment mechanisms with a quantitative analysis that indicates the relative importance of different behavioural assumptions and policy regimes. The empirical analysis is based on a computable general equilibrium (*CGE*) model which is Walrasian in spirit and captures price mechanisms, market interactions and structural interdependence in a non-linear multi-sector framework.[1] The next section describes the main features of the model, concentrating on the specification of foreign trade. Section II describes the alternative adjustment mechanisms to be considered and Sections III and IV present the empirical results. Finally, conclusions follow in Section V.

I. OUTLINE OF THE MODEL

The analysis is based on a nineteen-sector *CGE* model which endogenously determines relative commodity and factor prices so as to equate demands and supplies for commodities resulting from the independently pursued optimising behaviour of various actors in the economy: producers, consumers, and the government (the latter not assumed to be a formal 'optimiser'). The parameter values and initialisation of the model are based on Turkish data and the selection of adjustment mechanisms is inspired by the policies undertaken by Turkey and other developing countries during periods of foreign exchange shortages. The model should, however, be viewed as a stylised one which attempts to capture the main structural interactions between the internal and external sectors in a 'typical' semi-industrial economy.

The equations of the flexible exchange rate version of the model are summarised in Table 1. The adaptations to the model required to incorporate a fixed exchange rate and alternative adjustment mechanisms are described in the next section. The specification of foreign trade and its interaction with the rest of the economy are the most important building blocks of the model. First, consider imports. Our fundamental assumption is that domestically produced and foreign goods of the same sector category are imperfect substitutes.[2] This treatment is a compromise between the assumption of perfect substitutability found in trade theory and the assumption of perfect complementarity found in 'two-gap' models. More specifically, define for each commodity category a 'composite' commodity which is a CES aggregation of imports and domestic goods. Consumers and producers demand this composite commodity so that the demands for imports and domestic goods become derived demands just as the demands for factors are derived demands in the traditional production model. Assuming that demanders seek to minimise the cost of acquiring a given

---

[1] For a survey of *CGE* models, see Dervis *et al.* (1981). Chenery and Raduchel (1971) used a related small, non-linear model to analyse the foreign exchange gap issue, but did not explicitly model market mechanisms or focus on different policy regimes.

[2] See Armington (1969).

Table 1

Equations of the Flexible Exchange Rate Model

I. *Prices*

(1) $PM_i = \overline{PW}_i\,(1 + tm_i)\,ER$

(2) $PWE_i = PD_i/[(1 + te_i)\,ER]$

(3) $P_i = (PD_i + PM_i\,M_i/D_i)/f_i(M_i/D_i, 1)$

(4) $PN_i = PD_i - \Sigma_j P_j a_{ji} - td_i PD_i$

(5) $\Sigma \Omega_i P_i = \overline{P}$

ER	exchange rate,
tm_i	tariff rate,
$\overline{PW}_i$	world price of imports,
PM_i	domestic price of imports,
te_i	export subsidy rate,
PD_i	domestic price,
PWE_i	world price of exports,
P_i	composite good price,
td_i	indirect tax rate,
a_{ji}	input–output coefficients,
PN_i	net price or value added,
Ω_i	price index weights,
$\overline{P}$	exogenous level of aggregate price index,
M_i	imports,
D_i	domestic demand for domestic production.

II. *Production and Employment*

(6) $X_i^s = \bar{A}_i F_i\,(\overline{K}_i, L_i)$

(7) $L_i = \lambda_i\,(L_{1i}, \ldots, L_{mi})$

(8) $PN_i\,(\partial X_i^s / \partial L_{ki}) = W_k$

(9) $L_k^D = \Sigma_i L_{ki}$

(10) $L_k^D - \overline{L}_k^s = 0$

$\bar{A}_i$	productivity parameter in production,
$\overline{K}_i$	exogenous sectoral capital stock,
L_{ki}	labour of category k in sector i,
L_i	aggregate labour in sector i,
W_k	average wage of labour category k,
L_k^D	total demand for labour category,
$\overline{L}_k^s$	exogenous labour supply for category k.

III. *Foreign Trade*

(11) $E_i = \bar{E}_i\,(\Pi_i/PWE_i)^{\eta_i}$

(12) $M_i/D_i = g_i\,(PD_i/PM_i)$

(13) $\Sigma_i \overline{PW}_i M_i - \Sigma PWE_i E_i - \overline{F} = 0$

$\bar{E}_i, \eta_i$	parameters of export demand function,

Π_i	exogenous world price of other-country goods,
$\overline{F}$	exogenous net inflow of foreign exchange.

IV. *Income and Investment*

(14) $R_L = \Sigma\Sigma_{ik} W_k L_{ki}(1 - t_k)$

(15) $R_K = \Sigma_i(PN_i X_i - \Sigma_k W_k L_{ki})\,(1 - tk_i)$

(16) $R_G = \Sigma\Sigma_{ik} t_k W_k L_{ki} + \Sigma_i tk_i\,(PN_i X_i^s$
$\quad\quad - \Sigma_k W_k L_{ki}) + \Sigma tm_i\,\overline{PW}_i\,ER\,M_i$
$\quad\quad - \Sigma_i te_i\,PWE_i\,ER\,E_i + \Sigma_i td_i$
$\quad\quad X_i^s PD_i + \overline{F}ER$

(17) $TINV = \overline{S}_L R_L + \overline{S}_K R_K + \overline{S}_G R_G$

(18) $Y_i = \theta_i\,TINV$

(19) $Z_i = \Sigma_j b_{ij} Y_j$

t_k	tax rate on labour income, category k,
R_L	after-tax labour income,
rk_i	tax rate on non-wage income in sector i,
R_K	after-tax capital income,
R_G	government revenue net of export subsidies,
$\overline{S}_L, \overline{S}_K, \overline{S}_G$	exogenous savings rates,
$TINV$	total investment,
Y_i	investment by sector of destination,
θ_i	sectoral investment allocation shares,
b_{ij}	capital composition coefficents,
Z_i	investment by sector of origin.

V. *Product Markets*

(20) $C_i = C_{iL} + C_{iK} + C_{iG}$

(21) $C_{ij} = \bar{q}_{ij}\,(1 - \overline{S}_j)R_j/P_i\quad j = L,\ K,\ G$

(22) $V_i = \Sigma_j a_{ij} X_j^s$

(23) $D_i = d_i\,(Z_i + C_i + V_i)$

(24) $d_i = 1/f_i\,(M_i/D_i, 1)$

(25) $X_i^D = D_i + E_i$

(26) $X_i^D - X_i^s = 0$

C_{ij}	consumption, sector i, demander j,
C_i	consumption demand, sector i,
$\bar{q}_{ij}$	expenditure share parameters,
V_i	intermediate demand,
d_i	domestic demand ratio,
X_i^D	total demand for domestic production.

Notes:

Endogenous variables are denoted by capital letters. Lower case letters (except d), Greek letters, and letters with a bar are exogenous variables or parameters.

In equations (3) and (24), $f(-)$ denotes the CES trade aggregation function. In equation (12), $g(-)$ is derived from the associated first order conditions. $F(-)$ and $\lambda(-)$ in equations (6) and (7) are CES functions.

amount of the composite goods, the desired ratio of imports to domestic goods is derived from the first-order conditions and is a function of the ratio of prices (to the demander) of domestic and imported goods (equation (12) in Table 1). Solving the first-order conditions also yields the desired ratio of domestic to composite goods and, through the cost-function dual, the price of the composite good.[1]

Since imports are assumed to be in infinitely elastic foreign supply, world prices, $\overline{PW}_i$, are fixed and the country is 'small' on the import side. Import prices to the domestic user are given in equation (1) and equal the world price times the exchange rate times one plus the tariff rate.

This treatment of imports conveys a certain autonomy to the domestic price system not found in models where domestically produced and foreign goods are perfect substitutes. The specification also has the advantage of allowing two-way trade. A pure non-traded sector whose relative price is entirely determined in the domestic market is one for which there are no imports or exports. For other sectors, the relative price depends on commercial policy embodied in the exchange rate, tariffs and subsidies. The relative importance of each of these factors in determining domestic prices depends on the relative importance of imports and exports in total domestic supply as well as on the trade substitution elasticity in the CES aggregation function.

Turning to exports, we assume a downward-sloping foreign demand curve for exports whose form is given in equation (11). PWE_i is the foreign currency price of exports and is obtained by dividing the domestic price, PD_i, by the exchange rate multiplied by one plus the rate of export subsidy – equation (2). On the export side, the country is not assumed to be 'small'.[2]

Built around this specification of foreign trade is a general equilibrium system with price-responsive demand functions and sectoral neoclassical production functions linked around an input–output core into a model that simultaneously determines quantities and prices. The core equations of the system are the excess-demand equations for labour, commodities and foreign exchange (equations (10), (26) and (13)). Once solved, the model determines wages, product prices and an exchange rate (in the flexible exchange rate version) which yield zero excess demands and hence clear these three markets.[3]

Equations (6) to (10) describe the labour market. The production technology is two-level CES in labour and capital, with intermediate goods required by fixed input–output coefficients (equation (22)). The labour markets always

---

[1] However, given linear homogeneity, then $f(M, D) = D f(M/D, 1)$, and these latter two magnitudes can be expressed in terms of the trade aggregation function, $f_i (M_i, D_i)$, evaluated at $(M_i/D_i, 1)$. Equations (3) and (24) show the relationships.

[2] The magnitude of the export demand elasticity depends not only on the country's market share, but also on the degree of product differentiation characterising products from other countries. Thus, the higher the market share or the more differentiated the product in question, the lower the export demand elasticity. Other specifications of export markets are also feasible and would not change the essential nature of the adjustment mechanisms we seek to capture. One could, for example, specify export supply functions and allow an endogenous wedge between domestic and export prices.

[3] For a survey of different approaches to solving *CGE* models and a description of our approach, see Dervis *et al.* (1981).

clear, with no open unemployment.[1] Capital is assumed sectorally fixed. Investment – equations (17), (18) and (19) – is savings determined and its allocation by sector of destination is given by exogenously specified shares.

Equations (20) to (26) describe the product markets. The various demands (Z_i, V_i and C_i) are all for composite goods, with the demands for domestic goods being given by multiplying the composite good demand by the domestic demand ratio (d_i). Since the various supply and demand functions, and the d_i ratios themselves, are all price sensitive, the excess-demand equations can be seen as functions of domestic prices and the exchange rate. With the balance of payments, equation (13), there are as many excess-demand equations as there are prices, wages and the exchange rate. However, by Walras' Law, the excess-demand equations are not independent and we require some price normalisation rule to close the system. We have chosen to set an aggregate index of composite prices exogenously – equation (5) – which represents an overall index of prices to buyers in all markets, including imports and intermediate goods.

In the flexible exchange rate model, the real variables depend only on relative prices and hence the choice of price normalisation is only a matter of a convenient choice of numeraire. However, as discussed in the next section, there are alternative specifications of adjustment mechanisms in which the exchange rate is fixed and balance of payments equilibrium is achieved by means of import rationing. In this case, the choice of the aggregate price index matters since it defines the 'no-inflation' benchmark against which the exchange rate is fixed and will affect real variables in the solution. Our choice implies that the monetary authorities are fixing an overall price index that includes transactions in all product markets in the economy including imports, intermediate goods and final demand. The ·actual monetary mechanisms at work are not explicitly modelled in what is, after all, an essentially Walrasian model.[2]

II. ALTERNATIVE ADJUSTMENT MECHANISMS TO FOREIGN PAYMENTS IMBALANCES

To explore the role of alternative adjustment mechanisms, we assume a sudden shortfall in the 'normal' flow of foreign resources ($\bar{F}$ in equation (13)). Assuming that the country can no longer borrow and that foreign exchange reserves have run out, it faces a foreign exchange crisis and will somehow have to adjust

---

[1] Other specifications of the labour markets (e.g. rigid wages and open unemployment) are certainly feasible and have been used in other *CGE* models.

[2] A similar approach is used by Bruno (1976) and Jones and Corden (1976) who also assume that appropriate fiscal and monetary policies are pursued to maintain price stability and full employment. The assumption of full employment could be easily relaxed and investigated in this framework. Explicit consideration of monetary factors would be a considerably more difficult matter which would be better undertaken in a short-term macro model including asset behaviour and expectations. Note, however, that the assumption of price stability is not without empirical support. After reviewing the evidence on twenty-two devaluations in developing countries Krueger (1978, p. 146) concludes that 'the net results of devaluation, import liberalisation, and monetary and fiscal policy were such that, on balance, the percentage price increase in the several years following devaluation was no higher than before'.

to it. Three alternative adjustment mechanisms will be examined: (1) devaluation; (2) fixprice rationing; and (3) premium rationing.

Adjustment by Devaluation

Suppose that the country is initially in a position of internal and external equilibrium with the demands for all commodities and foreign exchange equal to their supplies. A shortfall in the inflow of foreign resources, $\bar{F}$, generates an excess demand for foreign exchange and a matching excess supply of domestic goods creating upward pressure on the exchange rate, ER.[1] Given the fixed overall price level, this exerts downward pressure on domestic prices as a whole. However, as will be shown in Section IV, domestic prices do not fall uniformly. At this stage, it is sufficient to note that the upward adjustment in the real exchange rate is achieved by the combination of a fall in the price of domestically produced goods and a rise in the domestic currency price of both exports and imports.

Adjustment by Fixprice Rationing

In spite of a movement towards greater exchange rate flexibility in the 1970s, trade regimes based on fixed exchange rates and exchange controls remain characteristic of many developing countries. In such regimes, the exchange rate is not, at least initially, allowed to adjust. Instead, imports are rationed and we must try to model the rationing mechanism. Because there exists a multitude of different rationing schemes, we distinguish only two extreme cases: fixprice rationing and premium rationing.

In the absence of rationing, the total value of desired imports is $\Sigma \overline{PW}_i M_i^*$ where M_i^* is obtained from equation (12).[2] With a fixed exchange rate there is nothing to guarantee that this sum does not exceed export earnings and net foreign resource inflows. Usually what is assumed in fixed exchange rate models is that changes in foreign exchange reserves or additional short-term borrowing make up any excess of desired expenditure over foreign exchange earnings. We assume that the country can no longer find additional funds and has run out of reserves, so the trade balance in dollars must remain fixed across experiments. Realised imports then amount to whatever is allowed by available foreign exchange revenues. Desired imports based on the customs clearance price (c.i.f. + tariffs) may, however, add up to a much larger magnitude than the sum of export earnings and foreign resource transfers. A rationing mechanism is then introduced to bring about an ex-post equality between receipts and expenditure of foreign exchange.

Let RM denote the ratio of total available foreign exchange $TFEX$, to total desired imports:

$$RM = TFEX/\Sigma \overline{PW}_i M_i^*.$$

A simple rationing rule is to allocate foreign exchange to the various sectors in proportion to desired imports M_i^*. Actual realised imports are then obtained by multiplying desired imports in each sector by the overall excess demand

---

[1] Note that it is an upward pressure because the exchange rate is expressed in £'s per dollar.

[2] Using an asterisk to denote a desired quantity.

parameter, RM. The particular quantity adjustment mechanism outlined above is clearly a stylised and simplified story.[1] We call it 'fixprice' rationing to underline the fact that the user price of foreign exchange remains fixed in spite of an overall shortage.[2] It is appropriate for countries where imports of producer goods are tied to user-specific quotas and licences, where resale is prohibited, and where consumer goods imports are insignificant. What is crucial here is the assumption that the users of imports do not have to pay more than the c.i.f. + tariff price, so quantity allocations are directly channelled to users without going through some kind of auction or market system. The exchange rate is truly fixed: except for (fixed) tariffs and export subsidies, both exporters and importers pay ER units of domestic currency for one dollar's worth of imports. This implies that the entire burden of adjustment falls on domestic prices.

Adjustment by Premium Rationing

Alternatively, it is possible that under rationing a legal or semi-legal parallel 'free' market develops for the scarce imports or, more directly, for the scarce foreign exchange. Let us define such a system as rationing by premium.

Assume again that the demand for imports exceeds the supply of foreign exchange necessary to buy those imports at a given fixed exchange rate. Now, contrary to the case of fixprice rationing, assume that the government tolerates the emergence of a parallel or 'free' market for foreign exchange allocations. In that case, those who demand foreign exchange will bid up its price until at the new price demand again equals supply. If PR is the premium that emerges in this parallel market and ER is the official exchange rate, the user cost of imports will now be:

$$PM_i = \underbrace{PW_i \; ER}_{\substack{\text{The price of} \\ \text{imports in} \\ \text{domestic} \\ \text{currency}}} + \underbrace{PW_i ER \;\; tm_i}_{\substack{\text{The value of the} \\ \text{tariff}}} + \underbrace{PW_i ER \;\; PR}_{\substack{\text{The value of the} \\ \text{premium due to} \\ \text{rationing}}}$$

Viewed in this way, the premium acts as a variable, but sectorally uniform, import surcharge. Under rationing with premium, producers adjust by cost minimising given domestic prices and premium-inclusive import prices. Neglecting distribution effects between the government and the private sector, such a mechanism works as if the exchange rate was flexible on the import side only.[3] Desired imports are again equal to actual imports because the price

---

[1] Note that being forced off their demand curve for imports, each demander should solve a new quantity-constrained maximisation problem. Strictly speaking, one should not maintain the two-stage formulation presented above where consumers are allowed to remain on their demand function for the composite good. This two-stage specification is easier to implement empirically and is justifiable in our particular model since sectors with large import ratios represent intermediate goods whose demand is by fixed coefficients and hence there is little scope for changing demand proportions in response to changes in relative composite prices.

[2] Note that domestic prices and wages are not fixed, in contrast with other recent rationing models. See Malinvaud (1977) and Muellbauer and Portes (1978).

[3] There are also major distributional differences between the three adjustment mechanisms. We do not explore these effects in this paper, and they can have no impact on the demand side because all consumers are given the same average expenditure shares.

mechanism has been allowed to adjust the demand for imports to the supply of foreign exchange.

The three adjustment mechanisms described above are somewhat extreme cases when compared to how adjustments actually take place.[1] However by confining ourselves to these three possibilities in the following empirical illustration, we are able to bring out more sharply the contrasts between them, particularly at the microeconomic level.

III. MACROECONOMIC EFFECTS OF ALTERNATIVE ADJUSTMENT MECHANISMS

This and the following section present a quantitative analysis of the three adjustment mechanisms described above.[2] We start from an equilibrium position where desired expenditures on imports are equal to the sum of export earnings and a $1·2 billion net foreign resource inflow. The 'crisis' takes the form of a $600 million shortfall in the exogenous foreign resource transfer, amounting to about 3% of GDP.

To analyse the impact of foreign exchange shortage and the effects of the three alternative adjustment mechanisms, we discuss six experiments, two for each of the three adjustment mechanisms:

E-1: Devaluation, low trade elasticities
E-2: Premium rationing, low trade elasticities
E-3: Fixprice rationing, low trade elasticities
E-4: Devaluation, high trade elasticities
E-5: Premium rationing, high trade elasticities
E-6: Fixprice rationing, high trade elasticities.

By assuming, in each case, high and low values for the crucial trade substitution and export demand elasticities, we can evaluate the importance of elasticity pessimism and elasticity optimism in discussions of adjustment policies. The low elasticity case is closer to the fixed coefficients view of the structuralist school. The high elasticity case, on the other hand, brings us closer to neoclassical trade theory models that tend to assume perfect substitutability between domestic goods and imports and very high export demand elasticities.[3]

Table 2 presents the macroeconomic results. Consider first the flexible exchange rate case. There is a 21·5% devaluation when we assume low trade elasticities and a much smaller 8·7% devaluation with high trade elasticities, which highlights the role of trade elasticities in determining the required

---

[1] For a full description of exchange control regimes, see Bhagwati (1978).

[2] The empirical model used here is based on Dervis and Robinson (1978). The data base and parameter estimation are described in that paper.

[3] See Table 3 below for a summary of parameter values. The values for all nineteen sectors used in the experiments are available from the authors upon request. The 'high' trade elasticities (reported in Columns 5 and 6 of Table 3), range from 6 for primary commodities to 0·75 for capital goods and 0·50 for services. The corresponding set of low elasticities is set equal to one third of the values for the high set. In turn, export elasticities range from 6 for manufactured goods in the 'high' set to 2 for primary goods and processed agricultural goods in the 'low' set.

degree of exchange rate adjustment. The reduced need for relative price adjustment when elasticities are high is, of course, also reflected in the smaller change in import and export prices.

Table 2

Macroeconomic Impact of Alternative Adjustment Mechanisms

(% Changes from Base Run)

	Devaluation		Premium Rationing		Fixprice Rationing	
	Low (E-1)	High (E-4)	Low (E-2)	High (E-5)	Low (E-3)	High (E-6)
Exchange rate	21·5	8·7	—	—	—	—
User price of imports*	21·5	8·7	71·6	32·0	—	—
Dollar price of exports†	−17·1	−6·6	−2·7	−1·2	−0·7	−0·4
Imports (volume and dollar value)	−9·3	−8·2	−19·6	−20·4	−21·5	−22·4
Exports (volume)	44·6	37·0	5·6	4·8	0·7	0·9
Exports (value)	21·5	27·1	2·7	3·8	0·2	1·0
Non-agricultural wage	−1·1	−0·5	−9·7	−5·0	−2·3	−1·2
GDP	−0·4	−0·3	−1·3	−1·0	−2·4	−1·3

* Weighted average using import share weights.
† Weighted average using export share weights.

Under either kind of rationing the official exchange rate remains fixed. However, under rationing with premium, the user price of imports rises by 71·6 and 32·0 % respectively with low and high elasticities. This rise is between three and four times greater than the rise in import prices that occurs with devaluation, reflecting the fact that the entire burden of adjustment has shifted to the import side. Thus imports become much more expensive to domestic users when there is rationing with premium than with devaluation, a fact that is not always appreciated. This result also emphasises that the 'black market' exchange rate (i.e. the official rate plus the premium) should not be taken to equal the underlying equilibrium exchange rate. Quite apart from considerations of risk that may stem from the extra-legal nature of the black (or parallel) market, the fact that exports do not usually benefit from the black market premium implies that the equilibrium exchange rate that would rule if adjustment were permitted on both the import and the export sides must be substantially below the parallel market rate that rules for imports when there is premium rationing.

In the case of fixprice rationing, the user cost of imports is kept constant by forcing users off their demand curves. Thus, from the point of view of the user price of imports, fixprice rationing and premium rationing represent two extreme cases, with devaluation in between. Fixprice rationing may, in fact, reflect a desire to avoid any rise in import prices. Public enterprises which may already be in a precarious financial situation often press for some form of fixprice rationing. Who exactly is forced off his demand curve and to what extent will vary widely from case to case. Our experiments reflect only one possible way to distribute the burden of adjustment.

The change in the terms of trade is determined entirely by the change in the average dollar price of exports, since the dollar price of imports is assumed to be exogenous. Variations in the average domestic price of exportables (not reported in Table 2) are small, so changes in the terms of trade are largely determined by changes in the exchange rate. Thus, the decline in the terms of trade is 6·6% for devaluation with high elasticities and 17·1% with low elasticities.

Corresponding to the changes in the user price of imports and the average dollar price of exports, there are changes in the volume of imports and exports which are shown in Table 2. Not surprisingly, the reduction in the volume of imports is greater when there is no expansion of exports, and it reaches 22·4% under fixprice rationing. It is especially interesting to note the wide range in the implied aggregate import and export demand elasticities (with respect to the average user price of imports and the average dollar price of exports) under each of the adjustment mechanisms. Our results indicate that one must be careful when speaking of such aggregate elasticities since their values are likely to vary widely depending on what is held fixed (and it is not always clear from statistical analyses which variables are held fixed).[1]

Finally, note that GDP declines in all three cases. The decline is always greater when elasticities are low (i.e. the economy has more difficulty in adapting to a shortfall of foreign exchange). In terms of minimising GDP changes, devaluation is the best and fixprice rationing is the worst adjustment policy. This result reflects the increasing violation of marginal efficiency conditions as one moves from devaluation to fixprice rationing. Premium rationing introduces a gap between the domestic resource cost of exports and import substitutes while fixprice rationing goes further by interfering with the equalisation of the marginal productivity of imports across sectors. But there are, of course, a host of other factors that influence policy choice, not least of which is the sectoral impact of alternative adjustment policies. We turn in the next section to a discussion of resource allocation and sectoral production effects.

IV. RESOURCE ALLOCATION EFFECTS OF ALTERNATIVE ADJUSTMENT MECHANISMS

To examine what is happening at the microeconomic level, it is necessary to consider carefully each sector's trade orientation, i.e. the relative importance of imports and exports at the sectoral level. Bearing in mind that in general sectors will have both exports and imports, it is easy to see that an adjustment via a devaluation (*DEV*) is neutral in the sense that it affects both exports and imports in each sector. On the other hand, adjustment via premia (*PREM*) and via fixprice rationing (*FIX*) are asymmetric since the foreign currency

---

[1] For a summary of cross-section evidence on aggregate elasticities with respect to trade incentives, see Balassa (1981, Chapter 3). It is noteworthy that the estimates of the import elasticities (0·4) and the export elasticities (1·3) stand roughly in the same ratio to each other as our analysis suggests.

price of exports is not affected directly as it is by a devaluation. This asymmetry of the burden of adjustment between exports and imports is fundamental to an understanding of how resource allocation is affected by each one of the experiments.

Consider the sources of demand for each sector's output given in equation (25): domestic demand, D_i, and export demand, E_i. A devaluation, which raises the value of ER leads both to an increase in foreign demand, E_i (due to the fall in export prices expressed in currency units) and to an increase in domestic demand, D_i (as the price of imports, PM_i, rises and diverts demand to domestic substitutes). An adjustment via premium will not affect exports directly since ER remains fixed.

While the effect of a change in the exchange rate on the demand for exports is direct, the effect on domestic demand is indirect since it operates through the demand for the composite good. Therefore, the price of the composite good, P_i, defined in equation (3), must also be considered. An increase in the exchange rate or the application of a premium will raise the price of the composite good since the foreign currency price of imports is fixed and the domestic price of imports necessarily rises. A rise in P_i, in turn, leads to a fall in demand.[1] However, the ultimate effects of the alternative adjustment mechanisms on resource allocation depend on how they are translated into changes in net prices and wages. The effect on wages is straightforward and depends on the relative factor intensities (in the direct and indirect sense). It is more difficult, however, to explain the change in net prices since they depend on both the domestic and composite prices. The analysis requires a categorisation of sectors according to their role in foreign trade.[2]

Table 3 gives the necessary information to explore how different sectors will react to the different adjustment mechanisms. Sectors which are 'exportables' have a high ratio of exports to domestic supply (i.e. consumer goods and, to a lesser extent, services). Sectors which are 'non-tradables' have a low export ratio, a low ratio of imports to domestic goods in domestic use, and a low trade-substitution elasticity (i.e. construction). Sectors which are 'import dependent' have a high ratio of imported to total intermediate inputs (i.e. intermediate goods, capital goods, and construction).

Sectors characterised by high shares of imports in total domestic use can be divided into import substitutes and import complements depending on the ease of substitution between domestic and foreign goods. This distinction reflects the traditional distinction between competitive and non-competitive

---

[1] Ignoring general-equilibrium and/or income effects, the extent of this fall in demand depends, of course, on the own-price elasticity of demand for the composite good. In the present application, demand equations for private and government final demands have constant expenditure shares (as does investment demand) which implies a unitary own-price elasticity of demand. Intermediate demand has a zero price elasticity of demand. Therefore, consumer goods and capital goods producing sectors will be more responsive to a change in composite prices than intermediate goods producing sectors.

[2] In the discussion below, we have aggregated the results from the experiments with the nineteen-sector model and present them at a six-sector level, including: agriculture, consumer goods, intermediate goods, capital goods, construction, and infrastructure and services. The share of each of these sectors in total gross output is given in Table 3, Column 1. As with the other figures in that table, these shares refer to those prevailing in the base run prior to the $600 million foreign resource shortfall.

Table 3

Structure of the Economy in the Base Run

	Sectoral shares in total output	Ratio of imports to domestic goods	Ratio of imported to total intermediate inputs	Ratio of exports to total output	Trade substitution elasticities (High)	Export demand elasticities (High)
	(1)	(2)	(3)	(4)	(5)	(6)
Agriculture	21·5%	1·6%	8·4%	1·6%	6·0	4·0
Consumer goods	17·2	1·5	3·8	10·9	2·0	4·0
Intermediate goods	14·4	26·5	19·5	3·8	1·5	6·0
Capital goods	5·5	56·7	29·6	0·8	0·75	6·0
Construction	6·1	—	15·3	—	—	—
Infrastructure and services	35·3	1·6	8·4	5·0	0·5	4·0

imports, but it allows for variations in the degree of substitutability rather than specifying a dichotomous classification between perfect substitutes and perfect complements. An import substitute sector is one for which the price will rise if the price of imports rises. As the trade substitution elasticity rises, these sectors behave as the traditional perfect substitutes for competitive imports. If, on the contrary, the trade substitution elasticity is low, the sector behaves as if sectoral imports are complements. In this case, imports are non-competitive in the sense that a tariff on imports does not protect the corresponding domestic sector.

Whether or not a sector is an import substitute depends also on the elasticity of demand for the composite good. It can be shown in a partial equilibrium framework that if the trade substitution elasticity is less than the composite good demand elasticity, a rise in the import price (e.g. by a tariff) will lead to a fall in the domestic price.[1] Such a sector is an import complement.

A sector which will be most strongly protected by a devaluation or premium on imports is one which is an import substitute and is not import dependent. Protection will always attract resources into such a sector. In the six-sector aggregation, the two sectors which have the highest import shares (intermediate and capital goods) are also the most import dependent. Intermediate goods have a higher trade-substitution elasticity and are less import dependent than capital goods, and so should be more protected by a devaluation or import premium. Construction, which is import dependent but non tradable, will be adversely affected by any policy that raises import prices.

In the case of fixprice rationing (*FIX*), the whole burden of adjustment falls on domestic prices since both the exchange rate and the user price of imports are held fixed. Thus, in the *FIX* experiment, actual imports are only 65% of

---

[1] See Dervis *et al.* (1981), Chapter 6, for a proof. Diaz-Alejandro (1965, Chapter 2), and more recently Corden in several places, have strongly argued for the need to extend the standard tradable-home good dichotomy in the manufacturing sector of semi-industrialised countries to include a distinction between sectors that do and do not compete with foreign products.

desired imports and so producers and consumers are forced into using domestic goods. A useful way to visualise the adjustment mechanism is to think of rationing as an outward shift of the demand curve for the domestic good. The shift is largest for sectors which have a high import ratio, and the elasticity of demand for the domestic good is greatest for sectors which have a high trade substitution elasticity. Thus, fixprice rationing results in an increase in the domestic price of sectors which have a high import ratio and, for a given ratio, the adjustment in domestic prices is greater the lower is the trade-substitution elasticity (i.e. the more non-competitive are imports).

Note also that fixprice rationing has a different impact on intermediate input costs than does devaluation or premium rationing. Import-dependent sectors gain from fixprice rationing insofar as they are able to buy scarce imported intermediate goods at the fixed price. The final effect depends on the net impact on composite intermediate input prices of cheaper imports but higher domestic prices for import substitutes.

Table 4 summarises the results on resource allocation of the alternative adjustment mechanisms.[1] The table gives percentage changes from their base values of net prices (Columns 1–3), gross output (Columns 4–6), imports (Columns 7–9), and exports (Columns 10–12). Consider first the effect of a devaluation (*DEV*) which, from Table 2, raises the user price of imports by 8·7% and lowers the average dollar price of exports by 6·6%. From the discussion above, the exportable and import substitute sectors should draw resources from the rest of the economy – which, in fact, is what happens. Consumer and intermediate goods are the only sectors which show an increase in net price and gain in output after the devaluation.[2] The net price of capital goods falls with the devaluation in spite of its high import share because of its low trade substitution elasticity (it is effectively an import complement) and its high degree of import dependence. Finally, note that the devaluation results in an across-the-board increase in exports.

In the premium rationing experiment (*PREM*), the burden of adjustment falls on imports and the user price of imports rises by 32% while the average dollar price of exports only falls by 1·2%. An immediate consequence is that the relative position of the exportable sectors will be most affected since there is no increase in demand for exports and no upward pressure on their price, as in the case of a devaluation. This effect is compounded by the substantial rise in intermediate-input costs for the import-dependent sectors. The final result is – with the exception of intermediate goods which are strong import substitutes – a general fall in net prices, with consumer goods suffering the largest decline, compared with the devaluation experiment. However, the increase in intermediate input costs is more than offset by a decline in the wage rate (shown in Table 2). Thus capital goods output does not fall despite a fall in its net price of 5·4%. Because their output price has fallen, sectors such as

---

[1] Only the high-elasticity results are reported in Table 4 since nothing fundamentally different is involved with low-elasticities.

[2] Infrastructure and services shows no fall in output even though its net price falls because there was also a fall in the wage rate.

Table 4

Sectoral Impact of Alternative Adjustment Mechanisms

(% Changes from Base Solution, High Elasticity Experiments)

Experiment	Net prices			Output			Imports			Exports		
	(DEV)	(PREM)	(FIX)	(DEV)	(PREM)	(FIX)	(DEV)	(PREM)	(FIX)	(DEV)	(PREM)	(FIX)
	(1)	(2)	(3)	(4)	(5)	(6)	(7)	(8)	(9)	(10)	(11)	(12)
Agriculture	−0·6	−1·9	−3·5	0·0	0·0	0·0	−40·3	−81·0	−45·4	40·4	4·6	11·3
Consumer goods	0·4	−5·0	−2·1	1·5	−0·2	−1·1	−18·2	−45·7	−38·9	36·0	6·3	5·7
Intermediate goods	2·8	1·9	12·2	0·4	1·0	3·8	−6·6	−18·1	−18·5	29·7	−28·4	−33·7
Capital goods	−2·0	−5·4	21·2	−0·8	0·3	10·1	−6·5	−15·3	−20·8	52·7	−15·7	−59·7
Construction	−1·8	−6·5	−3·4	−1·8	−1·8	−3·3	0·0	0·0	0·0	0·0	0·0	0·0
Infrastructure and services	−0·7	−5·6	−2·5	0·0	0·1	−0·8	−5·8	−16·6	−37·0	39·8	15·9	7·1

consumer goods and infrastructure and services increase their volume of exports.

Finally, consider the impact of fixprice rationing (*FIX*). The effects of changes in incentives to import which previously worked indirectly via changes in the use prices of imports now become direct, with the burden of adjustment on domestic prices becoming magnified. Intermediate and capital goods – which have the highest import ratios, low export ratios, and low trade substitution elasticities – are the only sectors whose prices rise.[1] A comparison of net price and output changes with those from the premium rationing experiment (*PREM*) shows how much larger and more biased are adjustments by fixprice rationing compared to what happens with a price rationing system. Note that the capital goods sector expands by 10% under fixprice rationing whereas it shows little expansion under premium rationing. This result is due to the combination of low substitutability in use between imported and domestic capital goods and the large share that imported intermediates, whose price remains fixed, have in total production costs.

V. CONCLUSION

This paper illustrates the difficulties besetting policy makers in semi-industrial countries facing a shortage of foreign exchange. The adjustments in relative prices, including the real exchange rate, and in incomes necessary to restore equilibrium may be so dramatic that they are considered very undesirable or politically infeasible. Moreover, none of the alternative adjustment mechanisms provides any easy way out of the dilemma. Both fixprice and premium rationing schemes lead to large changes in relative prices and, at the economy-wide level, they are more costly. Even with high foreign trade elasticities, adjusting to an exogenous fall in foreign exchange inflow by means of rationing is three to four times more costly in terms of lost GDP than adjusting by means of devaluation. Assuming low foreign trade elasticities, and hence less flexibility, makes the contrast even more dramatic.

At the microeconomic level, the results show that the choice of adjustment policy has a strong impact on economic structure. In general, export-oriented consumer goods industries benefit from devaluation, while domestic capital and intermediate goods industries benefit from fixprice rationing. Indeed, it is precisely these differences in structural impact that may determine the choice of adjustment mechanism since politically relevant groups in the society may be affected differently by the various policies. Analysis of such distributional issues is beyond the scope of this paper, but is clearly important.

Our analysis lends support to the structuralist view that it is not sufficient to look at problems of adjustment only at the macroeconomic level. By incorporating the exchange control regimes typical of many developing countries in a general equilibrium model rich enough to capture important structural rigidities and imperfect substitution, it has proved possible to quantify and

---

[1] Although domestic prices are not reported in Table 4, the magnitude of their increase for (*PREM*) and (*FIX*) can be assessed by examining the corresponding decline in exports in Columns 11 and 12.

hence understand better the implications of following different policy regimes. Such a model, by focusing on microeconomic market mechanisms in a multi-sector framework, usefully complements more aggregated analyses which focus on macroeconomic flow-of-funds mechanisms. That both types of analysis indicate that there are no easy choices for policy makers should come as no surprise, but it is important to understand that problems of macroeconomic adjustment are usually linked with problems of structural adjustment.

The World Bank

Date of receipt of final typescript: January 1981

REFERENCES

Armington, P. (1969). 'A theory of demand for products distinguished by place of production.' *IMF Staff Papers*, vol. 16, pp. 159–78.

Balassa, B. and Associates (1981). *Growth Strategies in Semi-Industrial Countries* (forthcoming).

Bhagwati, J. (1978). *Foreign Trade Regimes and Economic Development: Anatomy and Consequences of Exchange Control Regimes*, Cambridge, Mass: Ballinger.

Bruno, M. (1976). 'The two-sector open economy and the real exchange rate.' *American Economic Review*, vol. 66, pp. 566–77.

—— (1979). 'Stabilization and stagflation in a semi-industrialized economy.' In *International Economic Policy: Theory and Evidence* (ed. R. Dornbusch and J. Frenkel). Baltimore: Johns Hopkins Press.

Chenery, H. and Raduchel, W. (1971). 'Substitution in planning models.' In *Studies in Development Planning* (ed. H. Chenery). Cambridge, Mass: Harvard.

Dervis, K. and Robinson, S. (1978). 'The Foreign Exchange Gap, Growth and Industrial Strategy in Turkey: 1973–1983', World Bank Staff Working Paper, No. 306, World Bank, Washington, D.C.

——, de Melo, J. and Robinson, S. (1981). *General Equilibrium Models for Development Policy*. Cambridge University Press (forthcoming).

Diamond, M. (1978). 'Towards a change in the economic paradigm through the experience of developing countries.' *Journal of Development Economics*, vol. 5, pp. 19–53.

Diaz-Alejandro, C. (1965). *Exchange Rate Devaluation in a Semi-Industrialized Economy: The Experience of Argentina, 1955–1961*, MIT., Cambridge, Mass.

—— et al. (1979). 'Exchange rate policy in semi-industrialized countries: a symposium.' *Journal of Development Economics*, vol. 6, No. 4, pp. 459–548.

Findlay, R. (1973). *International Trade and Development Theory*. New York: Columbia University Press.

Jones, R. and Corden, W. (1976). 'Devaluation, non-flexible prices and the trade balance for a small country.' *Canadian Journal of Economics*, vol. 9, pp. 150–61.

Krueger, A. (1978). *Foreign Trade Regimes and Economic Development: Liberalization Attempts and Consequences*, Cambridge, Mass: Ballinger.

Malinvaud, E. (1977). *The Theory of Unemployment Reconsidered*. Oxford: Basil Blackwell.

Muellbauer, J. and Portes, R. (1978). 'Macroeconomic models with quantity rationing.' ECONOMIC JOURNAL, vol. 88, pp. 788–821 (December).

Productivity Growth, External Shocks, and Capital Inflows in Chile: A General Equilibrium Analysis

Timothy Condon, Vittorio Corbo, and Jaime de Melo,
The World Bank

This paper uses a computable general equilibrium model to analyze the growth path of the Chilean economy during 1977–81. During that period a comprehensive package of reforms liberalized international trade and removed restrictive labor legislation. As a result of the reforms, there were large changes in relative prices and in the structure of production and demand, and the economy enjoyed unprecedented growth with declining inflation. But large macroeconomic imbalances become evident toward the end of the period and in 1982 Chile experienced an abrupt and severe recession. Taking the real exchange rate as an exogenous policy variable, and using the observed levels of employment growth and foreign capital inflows, this paper compares model-generated growth paths with those of the economy. First, the benchmark simulation path is used to estimate the magnitude and pattern of growth and productivity change during the 1971–81 period. Next, counterfactual simulations are used to assess how Chile's economic performance would have differed if (a) external events had been different; and (b) foreign capital inflows had been different. The analysis suggests that the macroeconomic imbalances that led to the crisis in 1982 were exacerbated by the large capital inflows and real exchange rate appreciation that resulted from the use of the exchange rate as a stabilization device.

1. INTRODUCTION

Between 1974 and 1981 the Chilean economy recovered from an internal crisis, successfully confronted a large external shock, and undertook a major reform package that spanned commodity and factor markets. As part of the recovery, the public sector deficit, at 24 percent of GDP in 1973, was completely eliminated by 1977, the inflation rate reduced from more than 600 percent to 84 percent. But as an oil

Address correspondence to Jaime de Melo, The World Bank, 1818 H Street NW, Washington, DC.

An earlier version of this paper was presented at the Second Task Force Meeting on Applied General Equilibrium Analysis, Sopron, Hungary, June 18–20, 1984. This paper is part of the World Bank Research Project on liberalization with stabilization in the Southern Cone (RPO 672-85). We thank conference participants and Bruce Ross-Larson for helpful comments. The views are those of the authors and should not be interpreted as reflecting those of the World Bank.

Received October 1984; accepted January 1985.

Journal of Policy Modeling 7(3):379–405 (1985)
© Society for Policy Modeling, 1985

379

0161-8938/85/$3.30

380   T. Condon, V. Corbo, and J. deMelo

importer, Chile suffered from the successive oil price shocks. And the price of copper, Chile's main export, fell 50 percent in 1975 and 30 percent during 1979–82.

In addition, relative incentives shifted greatly as a result of the liberalization policies. Nominal tariffs, which had averaged around 100 percent, were brought down through successive reductions to a uniform 10 percent by early 1979. Domestic commodity prices and interest rates were deregulated, more than 500 public enterprises were returned to private hands, and legislation impeding labor mobility was abolished. A change in the conduct of stabilization policy resulted in the implementation in February 1978 of an active (preannounced) crawling peg exchange rate. A decreasing rate of crawl culminated with the fixing of the exchange rate in June 1979, when wages were fully indexed on past inflation. The rate of inflation dropped from 40 percent in 1978 to 20 percent in 1981, indicating an apparently successful stabilization program. Furthermore, GDP grew at an average annual rate of 7.5 percent during 1977–81. This growth was accompanied by a cumulative increase in external debt of $12.8 billion and a cumulative current account deficit of $9.6 billion.

Despite these successes, 1982 was one of the worst recession years in Chilean economic history. Several reasons have been advanced for this collapse. One set of explanations focuses on external factors: low copper prices, a strong dollar, and high international real interest rates. Another set focuses on faulty policies: opening the capital account too quickly, deregulating the domestic banking system with too little control, and basing wage indexation on past inflation in a period when inflation was slowing and the nominal exchange rate was fixed. Unemployment, moreover, had remained in the 12–14 percent range while the economy was booming. And even though gross fixed investment rose from 14 percent of GDP in 1977 to 19 percent in 1981, net national savings as a fraction of GDP never exceeded 5 percent. These figures raise the questions, what were the sources of Chile's economic growth during this period—and what were the causes of the collapse?

In this paper we use a simple multisector general equilibrium model to examine the sources of growth of the Chilean economy during 1977–81 and to isolate the relative contribution of various factors in explaining the collapse of the economy in 1982. Section 2 outlines Chile's growth and major shifts in relative prices and quantities—and notes the puzzles the paper addresses. Section 3 outlines the structure of the model used for counterfactual simulation analysis. Section 4 uses the model to approximate the likely magnitude of the sources of growth and productivity gains during 1977–81. The results show that the growth of

EXTERNAL SHOCKS IN CHILE   381

productivity and capacity utilization must have been strong during the period. Finally, Section 5 sets up some counterfactual experiments to examine the effects of a different external environment and different government policies. The experiments suggest that the large and unsustainable external imbalance, a major reason for the economy's collapse in 1982, was made worse by the wage and exchange rate policies adopted in 1979 in combination with reduced restrictions on capital inflows. A more "reasonable" profile of capital inflows—at an annual rate of 7 percent of GDP, amounting to a cumulative current account deficit of $7.3 billion over 1977–81—would have led to a 17 percent increase in the equilibrium real exchange rate by 1981 and 7.4 percent annual GDP growth over the period.

2. THE RECORD FOR 1977–82

To help focus the presentation, we review the growth and the main quantity and relative price shifts during 1977–82 to be simulated with the general equilibrium model (Tables 1–4). Though 1982 is not included in our simulations, we include it to show how the economy reacted to the macroeconomic imbalance that had developed in 1981. The sectoral pattern of growth was highly uneven (Tables 1 and 2). The fastest-growing sectors were construction, trade, and financial services. The construction and services sector boom can be attributed to absorption growth exceeding GDP growth. Moreover, much of the growth in trade reflects an increasing volume of imports coupled with a rise in trade margins. Another important element was the government revenue from foreign trade, which more than doubled during the import boom and which by 1981 contributed more to GDP than the mining sector.

The manufacturing sector performed well until 1980. This was true even though the dismantling of trade barriers would be expected to shift resources toward agriculture and mining, which had been discriminated against in the period of highly protected industrialization. The reduction in impediments to trade thus appears to have led to improved resource allocation, including higher productivity growth and greater technical efficiency. The importance of productivity gains is the subject of Section 4.

Exports were growing well above the growth of GDP until 1981, but imports were growing at close to 20 percent a year, resulting in an increasing absorption to income gap. Private consumption was growing slightly slower than GDP until 1981, and government consumption even fell 8 percent in 1979. In sum, this left room for a respectable growth of investment, which was up 23 percent in 1978 and 31 percent in 1980.

Table 1: Real GDP at Market Prices by Sector of Origin[a]

Sector	Scheme[b]	GDP by sector (millions of 1977 pesos)	Annual percentage change				
			1978	1979	1980	1981	1982
Primary	(1)	28.2	−3.5	5.9	4.2	5.0	−1.9
Mining	(2)	23.1	1.7	5.1	5.3	8.1	5.7
Manufacturing	(3)	62.5	9.3	7.9	6.2	2.6	−21.6
Electricity, gas, and water	(5)	6.4	7.8	5.8	5.5	2.6	−0.2
Construction	(4)	11.7	8.1	23.9	23.9	21.1	−29.0
Trade	(5)	44.8	20.0	11.0	12.4	6.7	−17.8
Transport and communications	(5)	15.3	8.4	9.0	11.1	1.1	−9.9
Nonfinancial services	(5)	72.4	.1.1	1.9	0.7	0.5	−5.3
Financial services	(5)	18.1	20.4	28.0	22.6	16.1	−9.0
Imputed cost of banking services	(5)	−9.1	−0.3	45.6	41.0	29.2	−13.6
Value added		273.7	10.4	7.2	6.4	4.4	−14.4
Import taxes		14.0	16.9	19.1	22.4	24.2	−42.8
Total GDP[c]		287.7	8.2	8.3	7.8	5.7	−14.3

[a]*Source: Indicadores Economicos y Sociales, 1960–82*, Banco Central de Chile, p. 23.
[b]Figures in parentheses denote the aggregation scheme for the model used below.
[c]GDP = value added + import taxes. Components may not sum to total due to rounding.

Table 2: (a) Real GDP by Expenditure[a]

	1977 (millions of 1977 pesos)	Annual percentage change				
		1978	1979	1980	1981	1982
Private consumption	209.5	7.5	6.5	6.8	14.3	−14.4
Government consumption	41.9	6.7	9.2	−8.0	0.2	−7.8
Total investment, *of which*:	41.5	23.3	29.1	31.5	5.6	−65.4
Domestic savings	30.7	17.9	27.6	21.2	−41.9	NA[b]
Inventory stocks	3.2	96.8	118.0	67.3	−19.7	−179.7
Imports of goods and services	59.3	17.5	22.7	18.7	14.8	−32.9
Exports of goods and services	64.5	11.9	14.1	14.7	−5.2	10.4
GDP[c]	287.7	8.2	8.3	7.8	5.7	−14.3

(b) Other Macroeconomic Indicators[a]

	1977	1978	1979	1980	1981	1982
		Annual percentage change				
Employment	2,838	2.7	3.4	3.1	3.2	3.3
Primary	527	0.6	0.6	0.6	0.6	NA
Nonprimary	2,311	4.0	3.6	3.8	3.8	NA
		Percentage				
Unemployment rate for Greater Santiago	13.2	14.0	13.6	11.8	11.1	22.1
Public sector surplus/GDP	0.0	1.8	4.7	5.5	0.8	−3.4

[a]*Sources: Indicadores Economicos y Sociales 1960–82. Cuentas Nacionales de Chile, 1960–82.*
[b]NA: Data not available.
[c]Components may not sum to total due to rounding.

384   T. Condon, V. Corbo, and J. deMelo

Table 3: Balance of Payments[a]

	1977	1978	1979	1980	1981	1982
	Millions of current U.S. dollars					
Merchandise trade						
Exports (fob)	2,185	2,460	3,835	4,705	3,960	3,798
Imports (cif)	−2,417	−3,242	−4,708	−6,146	−7,218	−4,023
Net nonfinancial services	−029	114	279	287	076	−207
Net financial services and transfers	−240	−419	−595	−817	−1,328	−1,950
Current account	−551	−1,088	−1,189	−1,971	−4,814	−2,382
Capital inflows + errors and omissions (net of reserves)	664	1,800	2,236	3,215	4,884	1,217
Change in reserves	113	712	1,047	1,244	70	−1,165
	Percentages					
Capital inflows in relation to GDP[b]	4.5	12.6	10.8	11.5	14.4	5.2
Current account in relation to GDP[b]	4.1	7.1	5.7	7.1	14.6	9.9

[a]*Source: Indicadores Economicos y Sociales, 1960–82*, p. 237.
[b]Expressed in pesos at the average exchange rate for the year.

EXTERNAL SHOCKS IN CHILE   385

But this acceleration in investment had some disquieting signs. First, it started from a low base in 1977—14 percent of GDP. Second, an increasing part of the investment effort went into inventory accumulation. Third, the share of construction in fixed investment increased. Fourth, the growth rate of investment fell back to 5 percent in 1981, when consumption grew nearly three times faster than GDP. Fifth, domestic savings were extremely low during the period. Furthermore, unemployment rates were high despite the rapidly growing economy (Table 2b). These figures are puzzling in view of the rising real wages (Table 4) and the much lower rates of unemployment during the 1960s.

The financing of the import boom shows up in the balance of payments figures (Table 3). The current account deficit rose from $551 million in 1977 to a staggering $4.8 billion in 1981, when it was 14.6 percent of GDP. The deficits were financed by increased foreign borrowing, as can be seen from the relative unimportance of the government budget deficit during the period (Table 2b). The capital inflows materialized for two reasons. On the supply side, there was the gradual liberalization of the economy to capital flows—starting in September 1977 when commercial banks were allowed for the first time to borrow externally. On the demand side, there was a portfolio shift toward dollar-denominated loans in response to the increase in the difference between the peso-denominated and the dollar-denominated real interest rate.

After the establishment of the active crawling peg system in February 1978, and even more after the fixing of the exchange rate in June 1979, capital inflows accelerated. The resulting decrease in the interest rate and the rapid growth of the economy could also have increased perceived permanent wealth and thus expanded expenditures financed by the capital inflow. It is also noteworthy that the capital inflows more than covered the current account deficit, so that the Central Bank was accumulating international reserves.[1]

June 1979 was a major turning point for other reasons as well. It marks the time when restrictions on medium- and long-term capital flows were removed. It also is the time when the value of the peso was

---

[1]It is likely that capital inflows influenced the general revaluation of assets (the stock market price index rose sevenfold between January 1977 and December 1980). These inflows, by relaxing the capital market disequilibrium, probably resulted in a perceived increase in permanent wealth. If this effect was quantitatively important, as Harberger (1982) has suggested, it would help explain the poor domestic savings performance observed in Table 2.

Table 4: Relative Prices and Wage Indices (1977 = 100)

	Row	1978	1979	1980	1981	1982
GDP deflator[a]	(1)	156	229	296	335	373
Official CPI[a]	(2)	140	187	252	302	332
Corrected CPI[b]	(3)	150	205	276	331	364
$\frac{\text{Import}}{\text{Nontradable}}$ price index[c]	(4)	104	105	95	79	87
$\frac{\text{Export}}{\text{Nontradable}}$ price index[c]	(5)	90	104	102	74	73
Price of tradables/wages in manufacturing[c]	(6)	102	97	79	58	66
Copper price index[a]	(7)	104	152	167	133	113
Nominal exchange rate[a]	(8)	147	173	181	181	236
Official wages and salaries index[a,d]	(9)	160	236	346	451	494
Wages and salaries index for nonagriculture[e]	(10)	158	227	322	383	NA
Real exchange rate[c]	(11)	96	103	97	76	82

[a]*Source: Indicadores Economicos y Sociales, 1960–82.*

[b]Corrected by the Cortazar–Marshall index for 1978 and 1979.

[c]*Source*: Corbo (1984), Table 4. The real exchange rate is constructed as the relative price of tradables to nontradables. Export price index excludes copper. Both tradable indexes are constructed as Divisia indexes. The import price index is the trade-weighted WPI index of Chile's main trading partners. The export price index is the quantity-weighted index of Chile's export prices.

[d]This index does not include social security taxes. The increasing gap between indices in rows (9) and (10) is partly due to the decline in social security tax.

[e]Wage bill figures include social security taxes. Source: *Cuentas Nacionales de Chile, 1960–82* and employment figures from *Indicadores Economicos y Sociales, 1960–82*.

fixed at 39 to the dollar and when wage indexation would begin to have as a floor the previous 12 months' rate of inflation.

The panorama of major developments is completed by the changes in relative prices and wages (Table 4). Major changes took place between tradables and nontradables (i.e., the strong real exchange rate appreciation), among tradables, and in the wage index in relation to the CPI. Coupled with the changing structure of output and expenditures, these relative price shifts suggest that modeling the Chilean economy of the late 1970s should emphasize the role of relative prices. Starting in 1979 when the nominal value of the exchange rate was fixed while non-agricultural wages were fully indexed on past inflation, the influx of

EXTERNAL SHOCKS IN CHILE   387

capital put pressure on nontradables and the real exchange rate started its sharp appreciation. Between 1979 and 1981 the real exchange rate appreciated by 26 percent. What would have happened to the real exchange rate had capital inflows been maintained at more "reasonable" levels? The model outlined below provides a tool to answer this question.

3. A MULTISECTOR GENERAL EQUILIBRIUM MODEL OF CHILE

Because the public sector deficit was negligible over the period, the sustained current account deficits must be entirely accounted for by changes in investment and private savings. Recent discussions (Harberger 1982; Corbo 1984; Dornbusch 1984) have emphasized several channels for such adjustments. These channels rely on expectations that are not explicitly modeled in the analysis. First, dissaving may take place because of the combination of the following: a transitory real appreciation, an increase in wealth along with the removal of borrowing constraints, and an increase in purchases of consumer durables when their real price is low. Second, a transitory real appreciation will also lead to stockpiling of investment and inventory goods in anticipation of capital gains. The two effects can be adequately captured only with forward-looking agents facing an intertemporal budget constraint (e.g., Sachs 1981) and will be the subject of a future paper. Although the model captures the dissaving effect in an *ad hoc* manner, given our assumptions about savings and investment, it should be primarily viewed as investigating other factors, namely, relative price changes.

The computable general equilibrium (CGE) model of trade, production, and employment used in this paper is of the type described in Dervis et al. (1982, Chaps. 5 and 7). The complete set of equations describing the model is in the Appendix. We emphasize here only the main assumptions about functional forms that guide the determination of relative prices and savings and investment. The model has five sectors (Table 1) and is calibrated to 1977, the base year.[2] Output in each sector is a CES function of capital and labor and a Leontief function between value added and intermediates. CES functions also describe the aggregation of domestically and foreign-produced intermediates of a given sectoral classification, but no substitution takes place across intermediates. Capital equipment, once in place, is fixed, but gross investment responds to intersectoral differences in profit rates.

---

[2]See Mansur and Whalley (1982), and the discussion by Lau on calibration in general equilibrium models.

Journal of Development Economics 32 (1990) 113–131. North-Holland

EXCHANGE RATE-BASED DISINFLATION, WAGE RIGIDITY, AND CAPITAL INFLOWS*

Tradeoffs for Chile 1977–81

Timothy CONDON, Vittorio CORBO and Jaime DE MELO

The World Bank, Washington, DC 20433, USA

Received March 1986, final version received July 1988

This paper studies two effects that accompanied the real exchange rate appreciation in Chile during 1979–81. First, econometric and simulation evidence is given that an alternative policy restricting capital inflows to a lower level would have led to a disproportionately larger fall in absorption than in income, and the decline in absorption would have fallen disproportionately more on consumption than on investment. Second, econometric and simulation evidence is given of the extent to which a more flexible wage indexation rule would have offset the adverse impact on the protected sector employment of lower capital inflows.

1. Introduction

The use of exchange rate-based disinflation gained much support in the late 1970s and early 1980s, especially among semi-industrial countries wishing to avoid the usual contractionary effects of orthodox stabilization policies. The theoretical literature on this topic is vast, ranging from intuitive reasoning [Dornbusch (1982, 1985)] to more formal analysis [Helpman and Razin (1987)]. This paper adds to the less extensive body of empirical work examining one aspect of exchange rate-based disinflation; namely, how it affects the composition of expenditure switching and expenditure reduction adjustment in the presence of partial wage indexation in some segments of the labor markets. The analysis is carried out for Chile where exchange rate-based disinflation policy was actively pursued for four years.

In February 1978, Chile adopted the policy of pre-announcement of the exchange rate to reduce inflation. At the same time, restrictions on medium- and long-term capital flows were relaxed. The authorities devalued, at a decreasing pace, until June 1979 when the value of the peso was fixed. Also

*This paper is an extensive revision of Condon, Corbo and de Melo (1986). The views are those of the authors, not those of the World Bank. We thank Jorge Miranda-Meave for much appreciated assistance and Maria D. Ameal for logistic support. We thank Patrick Conway, Shantayanan Devarajan, Arnold Harberger, James Tybout, two referees and the editor for comments but remain solely responsible for any shortcomings that remain.

at that time legislation was introduced stating that wage indexation for workers subject to collective bargaining (essentially all workers outside of agriculture and other services) would begin to have as a *floor* the previous twelve months' rate of inflation (backward wage indexation, based on a *maximum* of 100 percent of the previous year's inflation, had been in place since November 1974). Capital inflows accelerated after the establishment of the active crawling peg system in February 1978 and even more after the fixing of the exchange rate in June 1979. The current account deficit rose steadily to reach a staggering 15% of GDP in 1981.[1]

The paper re-examines two of the remaining controversies about Chile's policies during this period. The first relates to the extent the loss of competitiveness that resulted from Chile's exchange rate policy would have been tempered had Chile followed a more restrictive external borrowing policy by not liberalizing the capital account of the balance of payments. The second relates to the high unemployment levels that persisted during Chile's economic boom. Productivity increases that accompanied the tariff dismantling are partly responsible for the high unemployment, but the issue of how sensitive employment was to wages remains. The first issue is analyzed in the context of a model where the domestic savings rate is linked to the level of external borrowing. The second issue is treated in the context of a Phillips curve and a portfolio model which links the money supply to capital inflows. These augmented linkages more realistically portray the response of employment to more 'reasonable' levels of capital inflows. The empirical analysis is carried out with a five-sector simulation model that emphasizes the implications of adjustments in domestic savings behavior to lower capital inflows and the implications of partial wage rigidity on employment and macroeconomic equilibrium.[2]

From a more general perspective, the paper shows how certain macroeconomic phenomena can be approximately incorporated into an otherwise microeconomic general equilibrium analysis. The approximation is somewhat ad hoc but it fits the Chilean stylized facts relatively well and may offer

[1]During 1977–81 capital inflows more than financed the current account deficits, so that the Central Bank was accumulating international reserves. The inflows materialized for two reasons. First, on the supply side, there was the gradual liberalization of the economy to capital flows – starting in September 1977 when commercial banks were allowed for the first time to borrow externally. Second, on the demand side, there was a portfolio shift toward dollar-denominated loans in response to the increase in the difference between the peso-denominated and the dollar-denominated real interest rate that resulted from fixing the exchange rate [Corbo (1986)]. It is likely that capital inflows influenced the general revaluation of assets (the stock market price index rose sevenfold between January 1977 and December 1980). These inflows, by relaxing the capital market disequilibrium, probably resulted in a perceived increase in permanent wealth, which in turn led to a reduction in domestic savings.

[2]The level of disaggregation (five sectors), and assumptions about foreign trade elasticities, are the same as those used in our earlier analysis of reform-induced productivity gains [Condon, Corbo and de Melo (1985)]. External closure, labor market specifications (and supporting evidence) depart from our previous analysis.

suggestions for other applications. Section 2 introduces a one-sector model that includes the major features of the more detailed model from which are derived the simulations reported in section 3. The simulations from the five-sector model show that the loss in GDP growth would have been small, even for large cuts in foreign capital inflows. Macro–micro linkages via the determination of the price level and the labor-market specification are explored, again in a one-sector model, in section 4. The simulation results from the resulting expanded five-sector model show a favorable employment–inflation tradeoff to lower capital inflows in 1980 and 1981. Conclusions follow in section 5.

2. Capital inflows, the real exchange rate and investment: A one-sector analysis

Consider an economy which has to adjust to a reduction in capital inflows. The standard Salter–Swan analysis indicates that if there is full wage and non-tradable price flexibility, a real exchange rate depreciation will be necessary provided that non-tradables and tradables are gross substitutes in consumption (the usual case). If, on the other hand, there is some degree of price inflexibility, then, as shown by Jones and Corden (1976) for the case of fixed nominal wages, there is an indeterminacy because the new equilibrium will lie inside the (full-employment all markets cleared) production possibility curve.

In the standard analysis, no distinction is made between the various components of absorption. This precludes taking into consideration contributions to the analysis of the current account which have emphasized the usefulness of modelling adjustments in savings and investment behavior [e.g. Sachs (1981), and Svensson and Razin (1983)]. Implications for the current account of real exchange rates temporarily in disequilibrium have also focused on savings and investment behavior [Dornbusch (1985)].

We introduce now a one-sector simplified version of the more complex multisector model used in section 3. The key features of the model are: (1) a fixed real wage to reflect wage indexation; and (2) private savings depend negatively on capital inflows. The model is useful to show the implications of the postulated private savings behavior on investment (and hence on medium-term growth) when there is a reduction in capital flows. To save on notation, time subscripts are omitted. The model consists of eq. (1)–(12) below.

$$XD = f(L; \bar{K}), \qquad \text{production function,} \tag{1}$$

$$\bar{W} = \partial f / \partial L, \qquad \text{labor demand,} \tag{2}$$

$$E/D = g(e \cdot PE/PD), \text{export supply,} \tag{3}$$

$$M/D = h(e \cdot \overline{PM}/PD), \qquad \text{import demand,} \qquad (4)$$

$$\overline{F} = \overline{PM} \cdot M - \overline{PE} \cdot E, \qquad \text{external balance,} \qquad (5)$$

$$XD = k(D, E), \qquad \text{composite output,} \qquad (6)$$

$$X = l(D, M), \qquad \text{composite expenditure,} \qquad (7)$$

$$PS \cdot XD = PD \cdot D + e\overline{PE} \cdot E, \qquad \text{income,} \qquad (8)$$

$$P \cdot X = PD \cdot D + e\overline{PM} \cdot M, \qquad \text{absorption,} \qquad (9)$$

$$P \cdot C = PS \cdot XD - S, \qquad \text{consumption,} \qquad (10)$$

$$P \cdot I = S + e\overline{F}, \qquad \text{investment,} \qquad (11)$$

$$S = S(PS \cdot XD, e\overline{F}), \qquad \text{savings function,} \qquad (12)$$

where XD = output; L = employment; $\overline{W}$ = fixed real product wage (i.e. $\overline{W} = W \cdot P\overline{S}$); K = (putty clay) capital; D, E = output for domestic and export markets respectively; M = imports; e = the price of foreign exchange in domestic currency units; $\overline{F}$ = exogenous transfer of purchasing power (i.e. net capital inflows) measured in foreign currency units; $\overline{PM}, \overline{PE} = 1$ exogenous world prices of imports and exports (reflecting the small country assumption); k and l are respectively the CET and CES aggregator functions for composite output and composite expenditure; PS, P = prices of the composites; C, I = consumption and investment. The first distinctive feature of the model is the assumption of product differentiation for exports [via the constant elasticity of transformation – i.e. CET – function in eq. (6)] and imports [via the CES aggregation function in eq. (7)]. This assumption is supported by detailed microeconometric evidence [Morande (1985)] and is largely responsible for why the multisector model tracks the large structural shifts observed in Chile during 1977–81 relatively well [see Condon, Corbo and de Melo (1985)]. The second distinctive feature is the assumption, embodied in eq. (12), that domestic savings is negatively related to foreign

T. Condon et al, Exchange rate-based disinflation 117

capital inflows (i.e. $s_2 < 0$). Economic evidence supporting this formulation is provided below. The model is homogeneous of degree zero in prices so that only relative prices are determined, and *PD* serves as numéraire. Using this formulation, changes in e approximate changes in the real exchange rate.

Fixing the real product wage dichotomizes the system: eqs. (1) and (2) determine employment and output. For a given output level, XD, eqs. (3)–(6) co-determine equilibrium imports, exports, domestic use of output and the real exchange rate. Equilibrium is depicted in fig. 1a as the intersection of the external balance equation (FF) and the allocation schedule for domestic sales, $D(e; XD)$. The FF curve slopes upward because, at a given real exchange rate, a diversion of sales from the export market to the domestic market creates excess demand for foreign exchange, which is eliminated by a real exchange rate depreciation. The slope of $D(e; XD)$ reflects the fact that the allocation of output to the domestic market is negatively related to the real exchange rate. A reduction in the capital flows shifts FF rightward and a decrease in the real wage shifts $D(e; XD)$ rightward.

Fig. 1b shows the implications of the assumption about domestic savings behavior for investment, taking output as fixed. If domestic savings is independent of capital inflows, real investment is positively related to a change in e by virtue of the revaluation of the net foreign transfer. [The revaluation effect was first noted by Hirschman (1948).] This effect is mitigated by the assumption that domestic savings is negatively related to the size of the transfer $(s_2 < 0)$. Note that from eq. (11) a decrease in the foreign transfer, $\bar{F}$, shifts the investment line downward, and the shift is greater when there is no offsetting change in domestic savings (i.e. $s_2 = 0$).

We can now depict the effect of a reduction in foreign transfers. As shown in the top quadrant, the FF schedule shifts rightward resulting in a real exchange rate depreciation. The medium-term implications are found by tracing the new real exchange rate, e_1, to the lower figure and seeing where it intersects the new investment line, $I'(S_2 < 0)$. This new lower investment level, I_1, is, however, greater than it would be in the absence of the assumption that the domestic savings rate rises to offset reductions in foreign savings. (In fig. 1b, I_1' is the investment level that would result in the case where $s_2 = 0$).

There are two other channels through which a reduction in foreign capital inflows affects macroeconomic equilibrium. First, the multisector model captures the effect of a change in the relative price between tradables and non-tradables on the cost of a unit of composite capital equipment installed in each sector, and hence on the volume of real investment. This allows us to capture the construction boom that occurred [Corbo (1986)]. Second, as explained below, the real consumption wage rather than the real product wage is fixed, which complicates the outcome because output is no longer fixed because the real product wage is not fixed. It remains that the main determinants of how the economy will adjust to lower foreign transfers are

1a

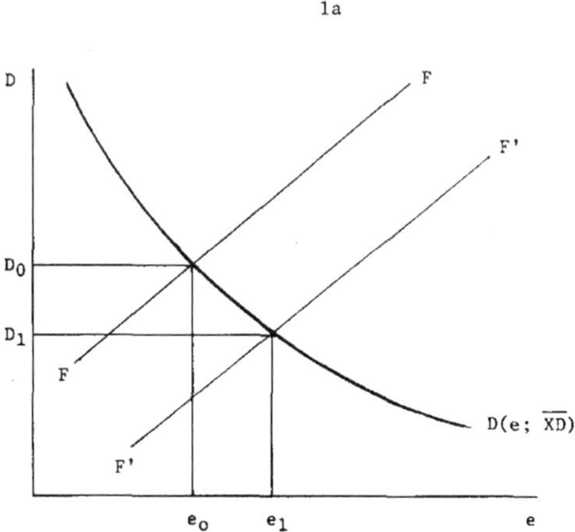

1b

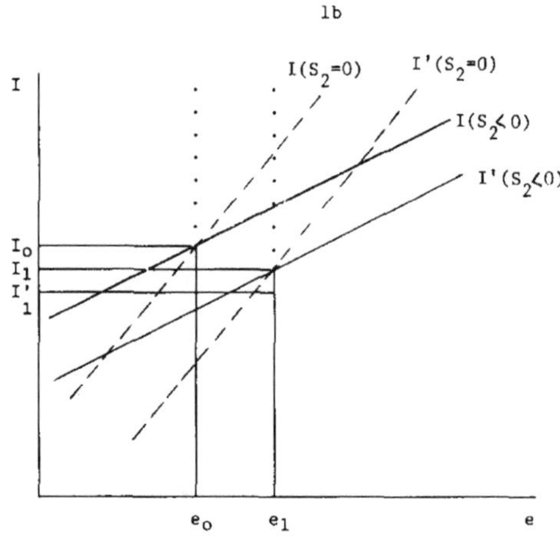

Fig. 1. Investment and real exchange rate adjustment to capital inflows.

the extent of short-run price rigidity and the domestic savings response to variations in the net foreign transfer. Hence we shall focus on the empirical characterization of these two channels.

3. Capital inflows and the real exchange rate: A multisector analysis

During the boom years of 1977–81, high unemployment rates (above 10%) coexisted with rising real wages. The consensus [see Edwards (1986), Riveros

T. Condon et al, Exchange rate-based disinflation   119

(1986)] is that the high unemployment levels of the late seventies are not explained by changes in labor participation rates, but rather by the extreme real wage rigidity that resulted from automatic wage indexation. The stylized representation of the labor market which most closely fits the facts is the segmented labor market hypothesis [see e.g. Stiglitz (1974)]. Edwards (1986) gives evidence that labor market adjustment during the period is consistent with the hypothesis that unemployment is involuntary with respect to the protected segment of the market covered by wage indexation, but voluntary with respect to the remaining (free) segment. In the model the free segment is approximated by agriculture and social, personal and domestic services, with the rest of the economy in the protected segment. Wages in the primary sector and services sectors clear the market. Wages in the protected sector are fixed in terms of the cost of living index.[3] For the protected sector, the average wage in period t, WA_t, is given by

$$WA_t/WA_{t-1} = 1 + \gamma[(\bar{P}_t/\bar{P}_{t-1})^{-1}], \tag{13}$$

where $\gamma = 1$, and $\bar{P}_t$ is the CPI index defined below.

Gross investment is set equal to total national savings:

$$TINV = S_p + S_G + CA \cdot ER \tag{14}$$

where (S_G) is government saving, CA is the current account deficit and ER is the price of foreign exchange. Real gross private saving, $S_p/\bar{P}$, is a function of real disposable income, Y, and foreign capital inflows denominated in pesos, $\bar{F}_2 \cdot ER$. After correcting for heteroskedasticity, the estimated equation over the period 1960–81 gives the following results:

$$S_p/\bar{P} = 1.7 + 0.16\,Y - 0.39(\bar{F}_2 \cdot ER)/\bar{P}, \tag{15}$$
$$\quad\;\; (0.15)(4.55)\quad(3.50)$$

where t-statistics are reported in parentheses. This equation is a proxy for several adjustment channels not directly captured in the model.[4] One is that capital inflows lowered the real interest rate, thus raising expenditure.

---

[3]Commerce, transportation, utilities, government and other services comprise the aggregate services sector. Output in the services sector is a Cobb–Douglas aggregation of fixed-wage labor and flex-wage labor, with shares derived from the data in Edwards (1986, appendix).

[4]The parameter estimates are in line with those reported in Weisskopf (1972). We emphasize that our equation is an attempt to capture various intertemporal effects that the static nature of the model would otherwise ignore [see also Grinols and Bhagwati (1976)]. The formulation in eq. (14) is close in spirit to the Laursen–Metzler (1950) effect. The small country assumption in our model implies that changes in purchasing power via terms-of-trade changes must come exogenously, whereas in the Laursen–Metzler analysis, a devaluation implies a terms-of-trade change. This is in line with Dornbusch (1985) who gives forceful arguments why capital inflows are (often correctly) perceived by private agents as transfers rather than loans.

Table 1

Parameters and structure of the Chilean economy in 1977.

	Primary	Copper	Manufacturing	Construction	Services
Sectoral shares in total output (percent)	11.1	5.9	37.2	4.3	41.5
Ratio of imports to domestic goods (percent)	27.2	3.8	37.6	0.0	3.9
Value-added ratio	0.54	0.55	0.30	0.49	0.64
Ratio of imported intermediates to total intermediate inputs (percent)	14.6	17.4	17.5	24.0	14.9
Depreciation rates	3.5	3.5	3.5	3.0	3.5
Ratio of exports total output (percent)	10.5	83.6	7.0	0.0	4.6
Capital–labor ratio	0.4	1.2	0.2	0.7	0.4
Capital–labor elasticity of substitution	0.9	0.9	1.2	1.5	1.5
Trade substitution elasticity[a]	3.0	3.0	3.0	0.5	0.5
Export transformation elasticity[b]	3.0	2.0	3.0	2.0	2.0

[a]The trade substitution elasticity is the compensated price elasticity of demand for imports.
[b]The export transformation elasticity is the compensated price elasticity of supply of exports.

Second, insofar as the real exchange rate appreciation caused by the capital inflow was viewed as temporary, consumers would have substituted present for future expenditure in durables, which in Chile are imported or import-competing.

Although the sustained current account deficit corresponded to changes in private savings and investment, the model includes a government sector. Government savings is derived by subtracting exogenous real government spending on goods and services from total government revenue. Foreign savings is equal to the current account deficit. The model has five sectors, and is calibrated to 1977, the base year. The key elasticities are the elasticities of substitution in the production functions, the trade substitution elasticities, and the export transformation elasticities (see table 1). All elasticities are best guesses but sensitivity analyses from earlier work suggest they are reasonable values. Equilibrium is defined as a set of relative prices for goods and factors such that excess demand in all markets is zero.[5]

In the multisector model the real exchange rate, e, is defined as

[5]The five sectors are: Primary, Mining, Manufacturing, Construction, Services. The solution strategy and algorithms used are described in Dervis, de Melo and Robinson (1982, appendix 3). The complete set of model equations is available upon request.

Table 2

Capital inflows and the real exchange rate in the base run.

	1977	1978	1979	1980	1981	Cumulative 1977–81
Exogenous total capital inflow[a]	530	1,150	1,590	3,140	5,320	11,370
Endogenous real exchange rate index[b]	100	97	96	90	82	–

[a]Millions of dollars.
[b]1977 = 100.

$$e = \left(\sum_i W_i^m \overline{PM_i} + \sum_i W_i^e \overline{PE_i} \right) ER \bigg/ \sum_i W_i^x PD_i, \qquad (16)$$

where the i subscript refers to sectors, superscripts m, e, x denote imports, exports and domestic production respectively, the W's are variable quantity weights (summing to unity), and all variable mnemonics are as defined in section 2. Finally, the numeraire, which is set to the observed CPI index, is given by

$$\bar{P} = \sum_i \Omega_i P_i, \qquad (17)$$

where the Ω_i are fixed quantity weights. The model endogenously determines the equilibrium real exchange rate consistent with different levels of capital inflows. The model-predicted relation between capital inflows and the real exchange rate is shown in table 2. The real exchange rate appreciation predicted by the model is close to other estimates [see e.g. Corbo (1985)]. Note the acceleration that occurred in 1980 – the first full year when the rate of crawl of the nominal exchange rate was zero and total capital inflows began rising dramatically.

To simulate the response of the economy to lower levels of capital inflows, the total capital inflow in table 2 for 1980 and 1981 is reduced by 10%, 25% and 50% (experiments E–1, E–2, and E–3, respectively). At the initial exchange rate there is excess demand for traded goods. The extent of relative price adjustment depends on the importance of capital inflows in total absorption and on the relative import intensity of consumption and investment expenditures. In 1980, capital inflows represented about 10% of absorption in Chile.

Adjustment occurs mainly through expenditure reduction. Expenditure is reduced by: (1) the fall in capital inflows, and (2) an increase in unemployment because of real wage rigidity. Real wage rigidity thus implies that external balance comes at the expense of an increase in unemployment. It

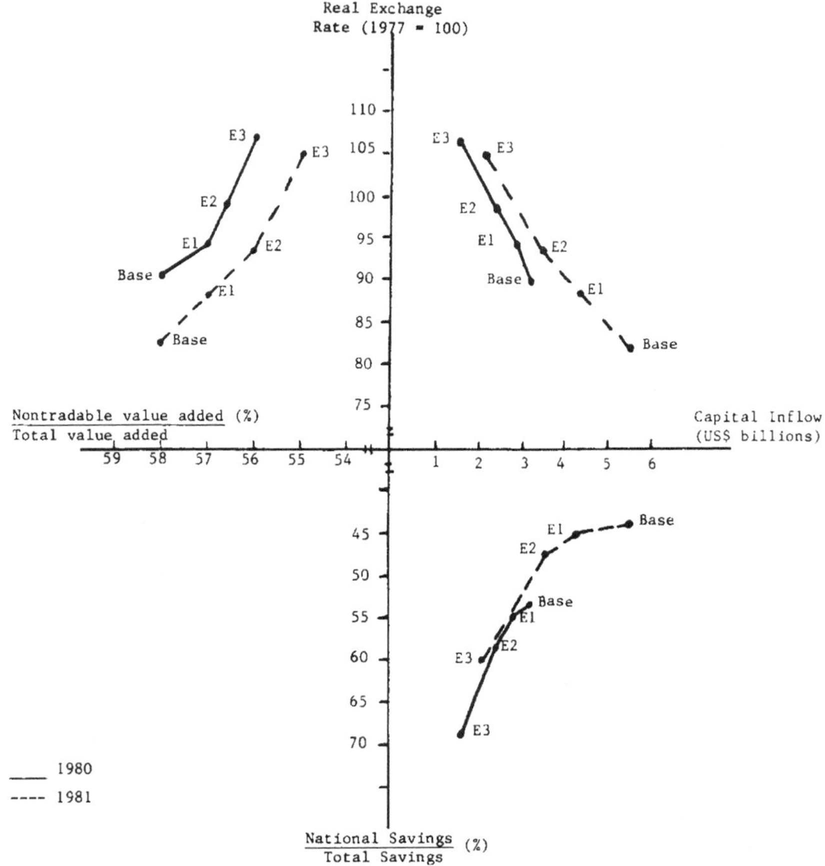

Fig. 2. Model predicted tradeoffs from lower capital inflows.

also implies that compositional shifts in demand are minimal (see fig. 2, quadrant 2). The shift from consumption toward investment demand in 1980, however, raises the 1981 GDP level beyond what it would have been in the absence of the link between domestic savings and capital inflows.

Table 3 reports the consequence for GDP, absorption and non-primary employment of the different capital inflow levels, and fig. 2 traces the tradeoffs for the real exchange rate (and hence the distribution of production between tradables and non-tradables), and the composition of savings at different capital inflow levels. The fall in absorption is much larger than the fall in income. One reason for this is the shift from consumption toward

Table 3

GDP, absorption, and non-primary employment levels with lower capital inflows in 1980 and 1981 (percentage deviation from base run).

	1980				1981			
	Capital inflows[a]	GDP	Absorption	Non-primary employment	Capital inflows[a]	GDP	Absorption	Non-primary employment
E–1	1.1	–	−2.3	−0.4	1.5	−0.5	−3.3	−0.9
E–2	2.8	−0.6	−5.8	−1.1	3.8	−1.2	−8.5	−2.0
E–3	5.4	−1.5	−11.9	−2.3	7.6	−2.9	−17.5	−4.3

[a]Decline in capital inflows expressed as a proportion of base run GDP.

investment demand, which raises employment because investment goods are labor intensive relative to the consumption bundle. Still, as noted below, the employment consequences of the reduction in capital inflows with a fixed real wage are negative overall. Table 3 also shows that the cost of adjustment to lower capital inflows rises more than proportionately with the decline in capital inflows.[6] This is because producers who use imported intermediates as inputs find it increasingly difficult to substitute domestic intermediates and have to pay a higher price for imported intermediates. As a result, the economy-wide value added to gross output ratio falls.

4. Capital inflows, disinflation and employment

The disinflation policy based on the fixing of the exchange rate was partly thwarted by the inflationary pressures created by the capital inflows since full sterilization of these inflows could not be achieved by the monetary authorities. It is also likely that wages were affected by the expenditure boom, adding a cost–push element to inflationary forces. We now turn to an examination of the linkages between capital inflows, inflation, wages, and employment by adding macroeconomic elements to the microeconomic model. It is obvious that the macroeconomic issues raised here are best studied on their own, but a multisector model is eventually needed if one wishes to study employment implications.

As in section 2 we present the main features with a one-sector macro model which abstracts from the determination of internal–external balance already covered in section 2. The equations of the macro model are given by (18)–(21).

$$M^S = g(\bar{F}), \qquad g' > 0, \tag{18}$$

$$M^D = kPy, \tag{19}$$

$$y = f(w/\tilde{p}), \qquad f' < 0, \tag{20}$$

$$w = h(\tilde{y}_{-1}, \tilde{p}), \qquad h_{\tilde{y}} > 0, h_{\tilde{p}} > 0. \tag{21}$$

Following econometric evidence in Corbo (1986), we assume that the money supply (18) is partly under the control of monetary authorities, i.e., that there is less than perfect capital mobility.[7] Money demand is given by

---

[6]A variant of experiment E–3 in which the coefficient of $(\bar{F}_2 \cdot ER)/P$ in eq. 15 is set to zero results in a 3.4 percent drop in non-primary employment in 1980 compared with a drop of 2.3 percent in E–3.

[7]Quarterly estimates (over the period 1975–1982) of a portfolio model similar to Kouri and Porter (1974) gave strong empirical support for the model, with the offset coefficient on domestic internal credit estimated at -0.32.

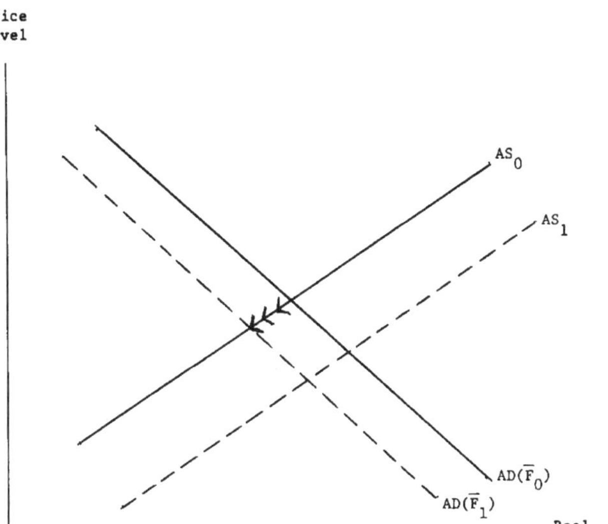

Fig. 3. Effects of a reduction in capital inflows on output and the price level.
Note: $\bar{F}_1 < \bar{F}_0$ (capital inflows).

the Cambridge equation (19). As before, real GDP is a decreasing function of the real wage in the sector under wage legislation (20). Finally wage contracts are given by a Phillips curve, where $\tilde{y}_{-1}$ is the deviation of GDP from trend last period and $\tilde{p}$ is expected inflation formed last period.[8] Neglecting lags, or equivalently considering the effect of a change in $\bar{F}$ last period, we drop the tildes in (21) and derive the aggregate demand and supply schedules by equating (19) and (20) and by substituting (21) into (20). The resulting equilibrium is shown in fig. 3. The aggregate demand schedule is downward sloping, and it can be shown that the aggregate supply is upward sloping unless the effects of changes in output have a strong effect on wages.[9] From the demand side, a reduction in capital inflows reduces GDP as in the simulations presented above. In addition, on the supply side, lower inflation translates into lower nominal wages through (21). For the estimated Phillips curve coefficients reported below in (22), the real wage falls, which implies a downward shift of the aggregate supply curve in fig. 3.

Before turning to simulation experiments, we report the econometric

[8]During the period of analysis, wage contracts in Chile were typically negotiated once a year. Evidence supporting a Phillips curve approach to wage determination is given in Corbo (1985) and below.

[9]This is most unlikely, especially in view of the fact that only approximately two thirds of the labor market was under wage indexation. The condition for AS to be upward sloping in fig. 3 is $(1 - hy) > 0$.

evidence supporting the Phillips curve determination of manufacturing wages proposed in (21). After performing model specification tests[10] to choose between perfect foresight, full backward wage indexation and alternatives, we settled on the following estimates (corrected for first-order autocorrelation) derived from quarterly data over the period 1976(1)–1982(4):

$$W\hat{A}_t = -0.007 + 0.23(y_{t-1} - y^*_{t-1}) + 1.22(_{t-1}\hat{P}_t),$$
$$\quad\;\; (-0.99) \quad (3.17) \qquad\qquad (24.78)$$

$$\bar{R}^2 = 0.92, \quad DW = 2.01,$$
$$\tag{22}$$

where $\hat{}$ denotes a percentage change between t and $t-1$, y_t is GDP, y^*_t is trend GDP, and

$$_{t-1}\hat{P}_t = 0.5\,\hat{P}_{t-1} + 0.5\,\hat{P}_t. \tag{23}$$

This formulation encompasses the formulation in (13) as a special case.[11]

To carry out the simulations, we use the estimated offset coefficient from Corbo (1986, p. 122). His estimate, using quarterly data from 1975 to 1982 derived from a three-asset portfolio model similar to Kouri and Porter (1974), indicates that a 10 peso increase in domestic credit is offset by a 6.8 peso loss in reserves. This implies a 3.2 peso increase in the money supply. Eq. (19) then determines the new price level associated with the lower level of capital inflows. Because the estimated value of the offset coefficient would have likely changed in a regime with greater capital controls like the one implicit in our experiments, we only report simulations for 10% and 25% cuts in capital inflows.

To isolate the effect of a lower level of capital inflows on wages and on protected sector employment, the base run simulation was recalibrated with protected sector wages determined by eq. (22) rather than by eq. (13) and with the price level determined by eqs. (18)–(21). The calibration results in a new base simulation where the equilibrium real wage increase is the same as the one incorporated exogenously in the base run reported in section 3. Then we performed again the same simulations consisting of 10% and 25% cuts in capital inflows during 1980–81. The results of the new simulations are reported in table 4 in the form of ratios to the equilibrium levels of the same variables in the earlier set of simulation experiments (e.g. the value of 97 in

---

[10]The selection of weights in determining price expectations formation in (23) was based on the model selection procedure suggested by Davidson and MacKinnon (1981). We were able to reject both perfect foresight and full backward wage indexation when tested against the 'half and half' alternative adopted in (23) as a special case.

[11]In (13) the coefficient on deviation from trend output is assumed to be zero, the coefficient on expected inflation one and the coefficients on $\hat{P}_{t-1}$ and $\hat{P}_t$ in (23) one and zero, respectively.

Table 4

Real wages and real GDP with Phillips curve wage determination.[a]

	1980		1981	
	Real wage[b]	GDP	Real wage[b]	GDP
EXP1	97	101	93	102
EXP2	92	102	82	105

[a]Ratio to corresponding values in table 3 and fig. 2.
[b]Protected sector.

the upper left-hand corner of table 4 means that the real wage is now 3 percent lower in 1980 than it was in the corresponding previous simulation).

The results indicate that the alternative to full backward wage indexation represented by eq. (22) would have resulted in lower real wages in the protected sector. Thus, for example, for a 25% decline in capital inflows, real wages in 1981 are 18% below the level reached in the earlier experiment. As a result, GDP is 5% higher. The reason for the lower real wages lies in the replacement of full backward wage indexation by a process linking wage growth to current inflation and to deviations from trend growth. As a result, there is an element of expenditure switching in the economy's response to deflation that was not previously accounted for. This evidence supports earlier conjectures [Corbo (1986), Edwards and Edwards (1987)] which blame the policy of full backward wage indexation for exacerbating the output loss resulting from the sharp fall in capital inflows that eventually occurred in Chile in 1982.

5. Conclusions

A real exchange rate appreciation usually accompanies exchange rate-based stabilization programs. One mechanism that leads to real exchange rate appreciation is capital inflows that may follow capital account and financial market liberalizations. The real exchange rate appreciation is further exacerbated if there is some price rigidity, as, for instance, when there is a wage indexation, and if money supply control is partial. All these features were present in the Chilean experiment with exchange rate-based disinflation between 1978 and 1981.

This paper has studied two effects that accompanied the real exchange rate appreciation in Chile during 1979–81. First, we give econometric and simulation evidence that an alternative policy restricting capital inflows to a lower level would have led to a proportionately larger fall in absorption than in income, and the decline in absorption would have fallen disproportion ately more on consumption than on investment. Second, we give econometric and simulation evidence of the extent to which a more flexible wage indexation rule would have offset the adverse impact on protected sector employment of lower capital inflows.

Appendix

A. Model equations

This appendix sets out the model equations in block form. A bar on a variable indicates that the variable is exogenous. In general, i and j subscripts refer to sectors (5), and k subscripts refer to labor categories (2). Equations appear in table A.1 and corresponding variables are defined in table A.2.

The simulations reported in section 3 involve eqs. (A.1)–(A.26), with the coefficients reported in eq. (15) in the text substituted into eq. (A.19). In addition, the real wage for protected sector labor is not determined by (A.11) but is fixed as in eq. (13) in the text.

The simulations reported in section 4 require the following additional changes: eq. (13) of the text is replaced by eq. (22) of the text; and the overall price level is endogenously determined (along with the money supply) according to text eqs. (18)–(19).

B. Data

The primary data source is the 1977 input–output table, *Matriz de Insumo–Producto de la Economía Chilena: 1977*, ODEPLAN. The model contains a five-sector aggregation of the twelve-sector data in the publication. Data on employment, wage bills and balance of payments statistics came from *Indicadores Economicos y Sociales: 1960–82* and *Cuentas Nacionales de Chile: 1960–82*, both published by the Banco Central de Chile. The capital stock data and capital-composition matrix were compiled by researchers at the Universidad Catolica based on 1977 data. World price indexes for Chile's exports and imports were computed as Divisia indexes. The import price index is the trade-weighted wholesale price index of Chile's main trading partners. The export price index is the quantity weighted index of Chile's export prices. Values for both indexes are taken from Corbo (1985).

T. Condon et al, Exchange rate-based disinflation   129

Table A.1

Model equations.

---

1. Prices

$$PM_i = \overline{PW}_i(1 + tm_i)(1 + tmv_i)(1 + trp_i)ER \tag{A.1}$$

$$PE_i = \overline{PWE}_i(1 + te_i)ER \tag{A.2}$$

$$PS_i = (D_i/X_i)[PD_i + PE_i(E_i/X_i)] \tag{A.3}$$

$$P_i = (D_i/X_i)[PD_i + PM_i(M_i/D_i)] \tag{A.4}$$

$$PN_i = PS_i - \sum_j P_j a_{ji} - td_i PD_i \tag{A.5}$$

$$\sum_i \Lambda_i P_i = \bar{P} \tag{A.6}$$

2. Production and employment

$$X_i^S = g_i(L; \bar{K}_i) \tag{A.7}$$

$$L_i = \lambda_i(L_{i1}, \ldots, L_{ik}) \tag{A.8}$$

$$L_k^D = \sum_i L_{ik} \tag{A.9}$$

$$PN_i((\partial x_i/\partial L_i)(\partial L_i/\partial L_{ik})) = W_k \tag{A.10}$$

$$L_k^D = L_k^S \tag{A.11}$$

3. Foreign trade

$$X_i^S = h_i(E_i, D_i) \tag{A.12}$$

$$Q_i = f_i(M_i, D_i) \tag{A.13}$$

$$\sum_i \overline{PW}_i M_i - \sum_i \overline{PWE}_i E_i - F_1 = F + \bar{F}_2 \tag{A.14}$$

4. Savings and investment

$$R_L = \sum_k \sum_i W_k L_{ki}(1 - tl_k) \tag{A.15}$$

$$R_K = \sum_i (PN_i X_i - \sum_k W_k L_{ki} - \delta_i K_{-1})(1 - tk_i) + \bar{F}_1 ER \tag{A.16}$$

$$R_G = \sum_k \sum_i W_k L_{ki} tl_k + \sum_i tk_i (PN_i X_i - \sum_k W_k L_{ki}) \tag{A.17}$$
$$+ \sum_i tm_i \overline{PW}_i ER\, M_i + \sum_i tmv_i \overline{PW}_i ER\, M_i(1 + tm_i)$$
$$- \sum_i te_i \overline{PWE}_i ER\, E_i + \sum_i td_i X_i PD_i$$

$$TINV = S_p + \left(R_G - \sum_i P_i G_i\right) + \left(\sum_i \overline{PW}_i ER\, M_i - \sum_i \overline{PWE}_i ER_1 E_i - ER\bar{F}_1\right) \tag{A.18}$$

$$S_p = \alpha_0 \bar{P} + \alpha_1(R_L + R_K) - \alpha_2 \bar{F}_2 ER + \sum_i \delta_i K_{-1} \tag{A.19}$$

$$Y_i = \Theta_i TINV / \sum_j b_{ji} P_j \tag{A.20}$$

$$Z_i = \sum_j b_{ij} Y_j \tag{A.21}$$

5. Demand and market equilibrium

$$C_i = \bar{g}_i(R_L + R_K - S_p)/P_i + \bar{g}_{zi}\bar{G} \tag{A.22}$$

$$V_i = \sum_j a_{ij} X_j^S \tag{A.23}$$

$$D_i = d_i(Z_i + C_i + V_i) \tag{A.24}$$

$$d_i = 1/f_i(M_i/D_i, 1) \tag{A.25}$$

$$D_i - [1/h_i(E_i/D_i, 1)] X_i^S = 0 \tag{A.26}$$

Table A.2

Definition of variables.

C_i	= Consumption demand, sector i		g_i	= CES production function
g_i	= Fixed private expenditure shares		$\bar{K}_i$	= Sectoral capital stock (fixed within a period)
g_{zi}	= Fixed government expenditure shares		L_i	= Aggregate labor in sector i
V_i	= Intermediate input demands		L_{ki}	= Labor of type k in sector i
d_i	= Domestic demand ratio		L_k^D	= Demand for category k labor
$\underline{PM_i}$	= Domestic price of imports		L_k^S	= Supply of category k labor
PW_i	= Exogenous world prices of imports		W_k	= Nominal wage of labor category k
ER	= Exchange rate		R_L	= After-tax labor income
tm_i	= Tariff rate		tl_k	= Tax rate on labor income of category k
tmv_i	= Import value added tax rate		tk_i	= Tax rate on non-wage income of sector i
trp_i	= Trade margin rate		R_K	= After-tax capital income
$\underline{PE_i}$	= Domestic price of exports		R_G	= Government revenue
PWE_i	= Exogenous world export price		G_i	= Sectoral real government consumption
te_i	= Export subsidy rate			(note that $\sum_i G_i = \bar{G}$ is fixed exogenously.)
PS_i	= Average sales price		$TINV$	= Total investment (equal to domestic plus
PD_i	= Domestic good price			foreign saving)
P_i	= Composite good price		Y_i	= Investment by sector of destination
PN_i	= Value added or net sales price		Θ_i	= Sectoral investment allocation shares
td_i	= Indirect tax rate		b_{ij}	= Capital composition coefficients
a_{ij}	= Input–output coefficient		Z_i	= Investment by sector of origin
Δ_i	= Price index weights equal to base year shares of		δ_i	= Capital stock depreciation rate
	composite good output		Q_i	= Composite good supply
$\bar{P}$	= The price index, equal to the GDP deflator		$\bar{F}_1$	= Net non-factor service receipts payments
D_i	= Output for domestic use		$\bar{F}_2$	= Net foreign capital inflows
E_i	= Exports		F	= Endogenous reserve loss (equals zero if the
M_i	= Imports			exchange rate is endogenous)
X_i^S	= Gross domestic output of sector i		λ	= Labor aggregation function

References

Banco Central de Chile, Cuentas Nacionales de Chile, 1960–1982 (Direccion de Politica Financiera, Banco Central de Chile, Santiago).
Banco Central de Chile, Indicadores Economicos y Sociales, 1960–1982 (Direccion de Politica Financiera, Banco Central de Chile, Santiago).
Condon, T., V. Corbo and J. de Melo, 1985, Productivity growth, external shocks, and capital inflows during 1977–81: A general equilibrium analysis, Journal of Policy Modelling 7, 379–405.
Condon, T., V. Corbo and J. de Melo, 1986, Capital inflows, the current account and the real exchange rate: Tradeoffs for Chile 1977–81, DRD discussion paper no. 108 (The World Bank, Washington, DC).
Corbo, V., 1985, International prices, wages and inflation in an open economy: A Chilean model, Review of Economics and Statistics 57, 564–573.
Corbo, V., 1986, The use of the exchange rate for stabilization purposes: The case of Chile, in: M. Connolly and C. Gonzalez-Vega, eds., Economic reform and stabilization in Latin America (Praeger, New York).
Davidson, R. and J.G. MacKinnon, 1981, Several tests for model specification in the presence of alternative hypotheses, Econometrica 49, 781–793.
Dervis, K., J. de Melo and S. Robinson, 1982, General equilibrium models for development policy (Cambridge University Press, Cambridge)..
Dornbusch, R., 1982, Stabilization policies in developing countries: What have we learned?, World Development 10, 701–708.
Dornbusch, R., 1985, External debt, budget deficits and disequilibrium exchange rates, in: G. Smith and J. Cuddington, eds., International debt and the developing countries (The World Bank, Washington, DC).
Edwards, A., 1986, The Chilean labor market 1970–83: An overview, DRD discussion paper no. 152 (The World Bank, Washington, DC).
Edwards, S. and A. Edwards, 1987, Monetarism and liberalism in Chile (Ballinger, Cambridge, MA).
Fischer, S., 1986, Indexing, inflation and economic policy (MIT Press, Cambridge, MA).
Grinols, E. and J. Bhagwati, 1976, Foreign capital, savings, and dependence, The Review of Economics and Statistics 58, no. 4, 416–424.
Helpman, E. and A. Razin, 1987, Exchange rate management, intertemporal tradeoffs, American Economic Review, March, 107–123.
Hirschman, A., 1948, Devaluation and the trade balance: A note, Review of Economics and Statistics 31, 50–53.
Jones, R. and W. Corden, 1976, Devaluation, non-flexible prices and the trade balance for a small country, Canadian Journal of Economics 9, no. 1, 150–161.
Kouri, P. and M. Porter, 1974, Inflationary capital flows and portfolio equilibrium, Journal of Political Economy 82, 443–467.
Laursen, S. and L. Meltzer, 1950, Flexible exchange rates and the theory of employment, Review of Economics and Statistics 2, 281–299.
Morande, F., 1985, Domestic price of importable goods in Chile and the law of one price: 1975–82, Journal of Development Economics 21, no. 1, 131–148.
Riveros, L., 1986, The Chilean labor market: From the structural reforms of the 1970s to the crisis of the 1980s, DRD discussion paper no. 173 (The World Bank, Washington, DC).
Sachs, J.D., 1981, The current account and macroeconomic adjustment in the 1970s, Brookings Papers on Economic Activity, 201–268.
Stiglitz, J., 1982, Wage determination and unemployment in LDCs, Quarterly Journal of Economics 88, 194–227.
Svensson, L. and A. Razin, 1983, The terms-of-trade, spending and the current account: The Harberger–Laursen–Metzler effect, Journal of Political Economy 91, 97–125.
Weisskopf, T., 1972, The impact of foreign capital inflows on domestic savings in underdeveloped countries, Journal of International Economics 2, no. 1, 25–38.

Adjustment and income distribution
A micro–macro model for counterfactual analysis*

François Bourguignon

Delta, Paris 75014, France
EHESS, Paris 75006, France

William H. Branson

Princeton University, Princeton, NJ 08544, USA
CEPR and NBER

Jaime de Melo

The World Bank, Washington, DC 20433, USA
University of Geneva, Geneva, Switzerland and CEPR

Received March 1989, final version received December 1990

This paper presents a structural macro simulation model to quantify the effects of alternative stabilization packages on the distribution of income and wealth. The model combines the explicit microeconomic optimizing behavior characteristic of computable general equilibrium models with asset portfolio behavior of macroeconomic models in Tobin's tradition. In this model there are four main mechanisms by which policy changes affect the distribution of income and wealth. First, changes in factor rewards affect directly household income distribution. Second, household real incomes are affected by changes in their respective cost of living indexes. Third, household real incomes are affected by changes in real returns on financial assets since household incomes include income from financial holdings. Fourth, household wealth distribution is affected by capital gains and losses. Illustrative simulations with the model are carried out for a representative economy subject to the interest rate and terms-of-trade shocks of the early 1980s. The simulations suggest a large adverse impact on the distribution of income of a sharp contractionary package.

*This paper builds on work financed by the OECD Development Centre in the context of a project, 'Adjustment Programmes and Equitable Growth'. Support from the OECD Development Center and the World Bank under RPO (675-18) is gratefully acknowledged. The views are those of the authors, not those of their respective affiliations, nor those of the supporting agencies. We thank Akiko Suwa for many helpful suggestions and very helpful research assistance, and Maria D. Ameal and Rebecca Sugui for their unfailing logistic support. We also thank two referees, seminar participants at Berkeley, EHESS and at the Federal Reserve Board of Governors for helpful comments.

18   *F. Bourguignon et al., Adjustment and income distribution*

1. Introduction

Declining terms-of-trade, rising real interest rates on external debt and a virtual halt of commercial bank lending were the major contributors to the crisis environment under which were executed many adjustment programs supported by the World Bank and IMF. A characteristic of these programs has been the joint participation of the institutions and hence the simultaneous emphasis on stabilization and structural adjustment. Stabilization policies placed emphasis on demand management, while structural adjustment programs placed emphasis on supply-side effects. The two concepts, however, are not easily defined and separated: for example, exchange rate policies are a fundamental element of both Fund-supported stabilization packages and of Bank-supported structural adjustment packages.

Recently, distributional implications of these adjustment packages have received increasing scrutiny. In particular, they have been criticized for their lack of focus on the welfare of the poor. These adjustment packages have been criticized for causing excessive reduction in aggregate demand, thus resulting in an unwarranted contraction of output, employment, and living standards of the poor. These adjustment programs have also been criticized for their lack of emphasis on mitigating the adverse distributional implications of external shocks on the poor.

The most thorough critique is in Cornia, Jolly and Stewart (1987) where a strong argument is also made for an activist role for adjustment programs. In their outline proposal for 'Adjustment with a Human Face', Cornia et al. suggest a combination of expansionary macro policies and sectoral (and micro) policies that are targeted towards the poor and designed to increase equity and efficiency. In support of their targetting approach, they cite evidence showing that increases in nutrition, education and health raise productivity and that small farms where the landless poor are located have higher productivity than large farms. They further offer suggestive time paths of adjustment and incomes of the poor under their proposed targetted package [Chapter 6 in Cornia et al. (1987)].

While very informative and thoroughly researched, this approach offers no framework which ties the macro and micro policies they suggest.[1] Neither is there a coherent analytical framework underlying the studies undertaken by the IMF and World Bank in response to this rising concern. For example, the sensible methodology proposed by Heller et al. (1988, ch. 3) is to: classify the poor across economically meaningful socioeconomic groups; describe how the policies included in a typical adjustment package are likely to affect these groups: then to speculate on how the poor fared during adjustment,

---

[1]See World Bank (1986), IMF (1986) and, more recently, Heller et al. (1988). Kanbur (1987) is an exception. He develops practical measures to measure poverty at the household level using expenditure survey data.

usually without attempting to impute whether any change in their status was due to the effects of the adjustment program or to the (unsustainable?) preprogram situation [Heller et al. (1988, p. 8)].

The purpose of this paper is to go a step beyond these earlier efforts by using counterfactual simulation analysis to derive orders of magnitude about the likely distributive implications of alternative adjustment strategies for the poor. Our analysis relies on the socio-economic classifications proposed in the studies cited above. The paper also relies on previous estimates of the magnitude of adjustment that was required during the period when the adjustment programs supported by the Bank and the Fund were in effect. These previous efforts allow us to build sensible base scenarios and counterfactuals as well as a representative classification of the poor by meaningful socio-economic groups.

The distinctive characteristic of our simulation model is that it links the short-run impact of macroeconomic policies that affect the distribution of income through inflation, the interest rate and other price changes, with the more-often emphasized medium-run impacts of adjustment policies (i.e. incentive reforms) that affect the distribution of income through relative commodity and factor price changes. We are therefore able to address many of the criticisms that have been raised against the recent adjustment packages (e.g. their lack of emphasis on supply response and their excessive use of demand management policies).

The remainder of the paper is organized as follows: Section 2 outlines the model which is described in skeletal form in the appendix. (A complete description of the model is available on request from the authors.) Section 3 sets out the features of an application of the model to a representative semi-industrial economy. The selection of alternative adjustment packages is presented in section 4 and simulation results in section 5. Conclusions follow in section 6.

2. Model outline

The model used for our simulation analysis is designed to capture the short and medium to long-run effects of stabilization and structural adjustment policies on the distribution of income. Analytically, one can distinguish three interacting channels through which these adjustment packages may have adversely affected income distribution. The first, and more easily quantifiable channel, has to do with the medium to long-run effects of cuts in government expenditures and changes in production incentives brought about by changes in relative prices following changes in tariffs, other taxes, and the exchange rate. For a given mix of expenditure reduction, the extent of relative price rigidities (e.g. fixed real wages or mark-up pricing), the extent of factor mobility (e.g. supply elasticities), and differences in consumption expenditure patterns across socioeconomic groups will determine the medium to long-run distributional impacts of the resulting structural adjustment. [De Melo and Robinson (1982) give a numerical exercise quantifying these various effects.]

Second, a stabilization program will have short-run effects through changes in the levels of aggregate demand and in asset prices. To the extent that the latter impact on investment, they will feed into the medium-run effects. For example, most programs include some degree of fiscal and monetary tightening. If the system has any nominal rigidity, as for instance when there is nominal wage or price stickiness, these rigidities will lead in the short run to a reduction in employment and capacity use, and to an increase in the real interest rate. These effects will, in turn, reduce investment spending and medium-term growth.

Third, portfolio shifts in response to changes in asset prices generate capital gains and losses that affect the distribution of wealth, and therefore income and consumption. As an example, foreign exchange controls may be ineffective in preventing capital flight by households when expectations mount that a stabilization program will soon be abandoned. First noted by Diaz-Alejandro (1979), stabilization programs in an environment with relatively high capital mobility have often resulted in portfolio shifts from domestic to foreign assets, with a capital gain for owners of foreign-currency-denominated assets after the subsequent devaluation.

So far these short-run channels, by which stabilization programs affect the distribution of income and wealth, have not been quantified. Though our emphasis is not on short-run dynamics and expectations,[2] the simulation model developed here quantifies the interaction of these three channels through which the distribution of income and wealth is affected by adjustment packages. The first channel is captured by the multi-sector computable general equilibrium (CGE) models where distributional shifts mostly occur through changes in relative prices. The second two channels are conveniently captured by the standard $IS-LM$ macro framework for an open economy [e.g. Tobin (1969), Branson (1989)], where asset prices are endogenously determined. The model described here incorporates features from these two traditions and we refer to the model as a 'maquette' because it is intended to be applicable to a wide range of countries and situations depending on parameter specification.

In the remainder of this section, we start with an overview of how policies and changes in the external environment affect the distribution of income and wealth in a 'period' equilibrium. Next, we discuss our treatment of the financial and government sectors, and close with a description of linkages between the financial and the goods and factor markets.

---

[2]All markets are assumed to clear in the representative period and there are no lags. Therefore, the model does not address the short-run dynamics of adjustment as in e.g. Khan and Zahler (1983).

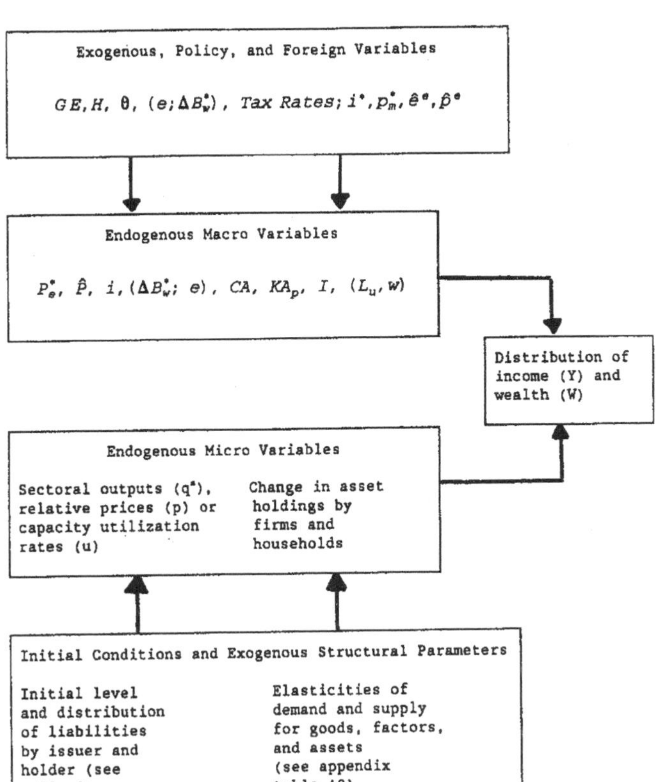

Notation: See text, table 1, and appendix. All variables refer to variables in table A.1.

Fig. 1. Macro–micro linkages and income distribution.

2.1. Period equilibrium

The linkages through which adjutment policies affect the distribution of income and wealth are summarized in fig. 1 which shows the determination of a 'period' equilibrium. (See the appendix for a one-sector version of the maquette.) The distribution of income, *Y*, and wealth, *W*, at the household (socioeconomic group) level is affected by the endogenously determined values for macroeconomic and microeconomic variables. In turn, the jointly determined values of macroeconomic and microeconomic variables depend on the exogenously given values of policy variables and exogenous structural variables (elasticities, expectations, and initial conditions). Typically, the values of exogenous structural variables are invariant across simulations while the values of policy variables depend on the selected policy choices in the adjustment package.

The exogenous policy variables (notation follows in table A.1 in the appendix) in the maquette are: the level and composition of nominal government expenditures (GE); the money supply (H) or, more generally, the degree of monetization of foreign capital flows (θ); the nominal exchange rate (e) or government borrowing abroad (ΔB_w^*); and various tax rates. This menu of policy variables allows the maquette to capture the major policy instruments applied in a typical adjustment package. Additional exogenous variables include: the foreign interest rate (i^*); import prices (P_m^*) expressed in foreign currency; and expectations about inflation $(\hat{p}^e)$ and about devaluation $(\hat{e}^e)$.

The endogenous macroeconomic variables determined in the maquette are: the foreign currency price of exports (P_e^*); inflation $(\hat{P})$; the domestic nominal interest rate (i); the government foreign borrowing or the nominal exchange rate; the current account (CA) and the private capital account (KA_p) if there are no foreign exchange controls; investment (I); unemployment (L_u) or the nominal/real wage (w). The endogenous microeconomic variables are: sectoral outputs and the use of domestic and foreign-produced intermediates; relative prices (p), or sectoral capacity utilization rates (u) if exogenously specified mark-up rates (m) are in effect; and asset holdings.

How model closures and behavioral assumptions determine the period equilibrium shown in fig. 1 is described next.[3]

2.2. The financial sector

We distinguish five financial units: government, households, firms, the consolidated banking system, and the foreign sector. We assume that governments do not lend and that households do not borrow. Because of thin or non-existent equity markets in most developing countries, the equity market is modelled in a rudimentary manner and the endogenously determined proportion of household savings allocated to equity is made directly available to firms. The distinction between firms and households allows us to separate productive and distributional implications of adjustment packages. However, to avoid modeling the details of the process of creating inside

---

[3]Equilibrium solution values in any given 'period' only depend on current and past values of endogenous and exogenous variables. Labor force growth is exogenous and capital accumulation is endogenous (see appendix).

Table 1

Monetary sector balance sheet.[a]

	Assets	Liabilities
	Rest of the world	
	$eL_w^* + eB_w^*$	$eF_h^* + eR^*$
	Government	
		$B_b + B_h + eB_w^*$
	Monetary survey	
	$eR^* + B_b + L_b$	$H_h + H_f + \text{Net Worth}$
	Private sector	
Firms	H_f	$eL_w^* + L_b + p_a E$
Households	$H_h + B_h + eF_h^* + p_a E$	

[a]Changes in Central Bank Net Worth are assumed to absorb changes in the home-currency value of foreign exchange reserves given by $R^* \Delta e$. Thus the latter do not affect the money supply.

money, following IMF practice we integrate the commercial banks and the Central Bank into an aggregate monetary survey.

The balance sheets of the five financial entities are summarized in table 1. The rest of the world (ROW) may lend to domestic firms (L_w^*) or to the government (B_w^*), domestic households may hold assets abroad (F_h^*), and the Central Bank holds reserves (R^*). The government borrows from banks (B_b), households (B_h), and the ROW. The integrated banking system holds reserves, lends to the government and to firms (L_B); its liabilities are money held by households (H_h) and firms (H_f). In the private sector, firms hold money balances and borrow from banks and the ROW, while households' wealth is divided between money, equity ($p_a E$), government debt, and foreign assets.

The households' asset demands are modelled in the specific form of the money–bonds–capital model of Tobin (1969). Household wealth is allocated first to money via a transaction-based interest-elastic money demand. The remainder is allocated between equity and total (domestic plus foreign) bonds as a function of the ratio of the real return on capital to the average bond yield. The final allocation between domestic and foreign bonds depends on their relative returns. The households' accumulation of equity capital is supplied directly to firms, at a price which is the cost of new investment goods. The firms finance their new investment (fixed and working capital) by equity issue (household equity capital), retained earnings, and borrowing from banks or from abroad with the borrowing division depending on the relative cost of capital.

The dynamics of the financial sector are driven over time by asset accumulation. The government deficit moves the debt stock. The current account balance less government borrowing abroad drives the sum of reserve accumulation and net foreign lending by the private sector. Firms' investment moves the capital stock, and saving drives household wealth.

2.3. The government sector

Critics of Bank–Fund supported programs point out that excessive reductions in government expenditures fall disproportionately on capital expenditures, and within current expenditures, disproportionately on health and education expenditures. In an analysis with a macroeconomic focus, one cannot capture meaningfully a direct link between type of government expenditure, productivity, and income distribution. Hence we assume that a peso's worth of government investment expenditure has the same return as a peso's worth of private investment expenditure.

Following the notation in the appendix, government revenue (GR) comes from tax collection on domestic $(t_i pq_s)$ and imported $(e\bar{p}_m^* t_m M)$ goods. Government expenditure (GE) has several components: government workers $(\bar{L}_G)$, paid an exogenous wage $(\bar{W}_G)$; expenditures on commodities $(P_c \bar{G})$ and investment $(p_c \bar{I}_g)$; and interest payment on the domestic and foreign debt. Investment and current expenditures on commodities are exogenous. The government deficit (GD) is financed by a mix of borrowing from the private sector, (ΔB_h), foreign borrowing, $(e\Delta B_w^*)$, and financing from the Central Bank (ΔB_b). The government's budget constraint $(GD \equiv GR - GE)$ is therefore given by

$$\Delta B_h + e\Delta B_w^* + \Delta B_b \qquad\qquad (GD)$$

$$= t_i pq_s + e\bar{p}_m^* t_m M \qquad\qquad (GR) \qquad (2.1)$$

$$-(p_c \bar{G} + \bar{W}_G \bar{L}_G + p_c \bar{I}_g + i_{-1} B_h + i_{-1}^* B_w^* e_{-1}) \quad (GE)$$

where a subscript (-1) indicates a one period lag of the variable and p_c indicates the price of expenditures in terms of a composite aggregate of domestic and imported goods.

2.4. Goods and factor markets

Assumptions about goods and factor markets are familiar from the literature on CGE models. Capital once installed is fixed within the period, and intersectoral capital mobility is achieved through time by capital stock depreciation. Technology for gross output assumes a separable production function for value-added and intermediates, with a CES for value-added and a Leontief between intermediates and value-added and within intermediates. For each sectoral demand, some substitution is allowed between the use of domestically produced goods in that sector and competitive imports to that sector. However, a fraction of intermediate imports is non-competitive. In the simulations reported below, imports are available in perfectly elastic supply but foreign export demand may be less than infinitely elastic, in which case the terms of trade are endogenous. Thus a devaluation or a change in protection gives some scope for import substitution, but export expansion may involve some deterioration in the terms of trade.

In the simulations, two closures are adopted with respect to the foreign sector. In one closure, the exchange rate is fixed, in which case government borrowing abroad (expressed in foreign currency) is endogenous and given by

$$-\Delta B_w^* = CA + KA_p, \tag{2.2}$$

where CA is the interest-inclusive current account expressed in foreign currency and $KA_p = \Delta L_w^* - \Delta F_h^*$ is the private sector's capital account. In the other, government borrowing abroad is exogenous and the exchange rate adjusts so that

$$CA + KA_p = -\Delta \bar{B}_w^*. \tag{2.3}$$

We assume that a proportion, θ, of private capital movements is monetized, so that the money supply depends on the capital account, i.e.,

$$\Delta H = \Delta L_b + e\theta KA_p + \Delta B_b \tag{2.4}$$

where a positive value of KA_p indicates a net private capital inflow.

This completes the descriptive overview of the maquette. Specific assumptions about market behavior will vary according to country institutional characteristics. The remainder of the paper describes a numerical application.

3. A numerical application: Aggregations and initial conditions

We now turn to a numerical application. In this section we describe briefly the level of disaggregation across product and factor markets and across socioeconomic (or household) groups. We also indicate the assumptions we make about the distribution of financial assets and the mapping of physical and human wealth by socioeconomic class. The sectoral disaggregation and wealth ownership mapping is described in table 2.

The economy is disaggregated into six sectors. There are two primary sectors: an export-oriented sector and an agricultural sector that may

Table 2

Private sector distribution of assets and liabilities.

Sectors		Factors of production	Physical and human wealth distribution by socioeconomic class						Firms		
			Capitalists	Big farmers	Small farmers	Landless agricultural workers	Modern workers (incl. gvt.)	Informal workers	Liabilities/ Assets	Working capital/ Sales	Foreign debt/ Total debt
Primary export	(1)	Specific factor	20	80					5	15	0
		Agr. labour		5	24	71					
Agriculture	(2)	Specific factor	10	55	35				5	15	0
		Agr. labor		5	24	71					
Consumer goods	(3)	Modern labor	6				94		30	15	20
Intermediate and capital goods	(4)	Modern labor	6				94		30	15	20
Non-traded formal	(5)		6				94		30	15	20
Informal non-agriculture	(6)	Informal labor						100	0	15	0
All sectors	(7)	Capital[a]	35.4	10.7	0.5	1	16.4	6			

			Financial wealth distribution by socioeconomic class						Economy-wide ratio values	
Foreign assets/ Financial wealth	(8)		30	20					Debt/Exports	150
Domestic bonds/ Allocation	(9)		70	30					Money supply/ Sales	40
Money/Income	(10)		10	10	10	10	10	10	Domestic bonds/ Govt. debt	25
Savings/Income	(11)		64	32	3	13	3	8		

[a]Does not add up to 100 because of retained profits by firms.

compete with imports. Three formal urban sectors (consumer goods, intermediate and capital goods, and nontraded formal) employ 'modern labor' and may adopt mark-up pricing. Finally, is the informal non-agricultural sector, which is also assumed to be nontraded.

Turn now to the description of wealth ownership. As suggested by Kanbur (1987), Heller et al. (1988), the poor are among the following socioeconomic groups: (1) landless rural laborers who receive their income from the labor they supply to the primary export and agricultural sectors; (2) agricultural smallholders (or small farmers) who receive their income from the land they own and from their supply of labor; (3) the urban informal sector here represented by informal workers who receive their income from their services in the informal non-agricultural sector where they are paid their average value product (no other factor is employed in that sector). In addition to these groups, the urban formal sector is represented here by the 'modern labor' socioeconomic group, a group which includes government workers as well as labor employed in the three manufacturing sectors and in the formal nontraded sector (see table 2). The description of socioeconomic groups is completed by capitalists who receive their non-financial income from several sources: land and natural resources in the primary export sector (e.g. mining activity, labor supply to the modern industrial sectors), and income from the capital they own in all sectors. The mapping of physical and human wealth (originating from factor incomes) across socioeconomic groups is meant to be representative of the fact that households, when classified in such large socioeconomic groups, receive their income from several sources.[4] It should be noted that the assumption that socioeconomic groups receive income from several sources mitigates the distributional effects of policy simulated below.

Initial distributions of financial assets and liabilities (see bottom part of table 2) are also meant to be representative of an economy with a relatively low debt/equity ratio with private sector debt mostly concentrated in domestically-issued debt. Only capitalists hold a fraction of their financial wealth abroad. Also capitalists and big farmers are the only socioeconomic groups holding domestic bonds. For the remaining socioeconomic groups, money is the only financial asset. Initial economy-wide financial ratios indicate an economy with a moderate initial stock of public foreign debt (150% of exports) and a small volume of internally held debt. Because firms' liabilities to the banking system are relatively low (about 10% of the value of the economy's capital stock), financial wealth is only about 10% of the value of physical wealth (land and capital).

In sum, the economy portrayed here is intended to be representative of a

---

[4] The ownership of capital does not add up to 100 because firms are assumed to have a retained earnings rate of 30 percent ($\alpha = 0.3$). On the determination of capital shares and household savings rate through calibration, see the appendix.

middle-income semi-industrial economy. The production and final demand structure is a slight modification of what Chenery and Syrquin call the 'standard' middle-income archetype derived from their cross-country model [see Chenery et al. (1987, table 3.5)]. However, because of our assumptions about capital mobility (see section 4 below), one can think of our application as more representative of adjustment in a Larin American than in an East Asian economy.

The selected elasticity specification is summarized in table A.2 in the appendix. As is typical of such simulation exercises, the elasticities reflect a combination of averages of borrowed econometric estimates (e.g. for household consumption, technology, foreign trade) and guesstimates (e.g. portfolio response elasticities). Income and price elasticities of demand are lower for the poorer socioeconomic groups, price elasticities of demand are lower for imported intermediates, and portfolio elasticities are high reflecting high capital mobility.

4. Description of external shock and adjustment packages

The adjustment programs supported by the IMF and World Bank that were subject to the criticisms noted in the introduction took place in an unfavourable external environment. An indication of how unfavourable the environment was for middle-income countries, is given by the magnitude of external shocks. These have been estimated to amount to a loss of 4 percentage points of average GDP during 1982–1986 compared with 1978–1981. For the same group of countries, average GDP growth during 1982–1986 was 2 percent per year down from 4.8 percent during 1978–1981 and the ratio of investment to GDP fell sharply [see Faini et al. (1991, table 2)]. It is well documented that this sharp deterioration in performance was greatly due to the limited access to foreign borrowing which would have helped cushion the effects of declining terms of trade and rising real interest rates on foreign debt.

Table 3 describes the simulations. A base run (BR) simulation is contrasted with four simulations describing how an economy might be expected to react to an external shock of the type experienced during the early eighties with rising interest on foreign debt, declining terms of trade, and limited foreign borrowing. All simulations are over a seven-year period.

In BR, the economy grows at 5.9 percent per year with the investment share in GDP rising slightly from 20 to 21 percent of GDP. Expectations about inflation and devaluation are 'correct' with both actual inflation and actual nominal devaluation at 15 percent per year so that the real exchange rate is constant. Public sector real wages grow at 3 percent annually and government recurrent and investment expenditures grow at 7 percent annually in real terms. Wage and price flexibility insure full employment and full

Table 3

Description of simulations.[a]

Base run (BR)
- $\hat{H}=18\%$; $\hat{e}=15\%$; ($\hat{p}^c=\hat{e}^e=15\%$); $t=1,\dots,7$.
- Flexible wages and prices.
- No foreign exchange controls.
- $\hat{w}_G=3\%$; $\hat{I}_g=\hat{G}=7\%$ (all growth rates in real terms).

Shock with rigidity (SR)[b]

Same as BR with:
- $i^*=7\%$; $t=1$ and $i^*=12\%$ $t=2,\dots,7$; $\hat{p}_m^*=10\%$; $t=2$.
- Exchange controls (see text).
- Accommodating monetary policy: $\hat{H}=23\%$; $t=2,\dots,7$.
- Modern sector wages indexed 100% on cost of living index.
- Profit margins fixed in modern sector.

Shock with non-accommodating monetary policy (SN)

Same as SR with:
- $\hat{H}=18\%$; $t==1,\dots,7$.

Shock with fiscal tightening (SF)

Same as SR with:
- Growth in nominal public expenditures (wages, investment and consumption): 10% for $t=2,\dots,4$; 15% for $t=5$; 17% for $t=6$; 23% for $t=7$.

Shock with credit squeeze (SC)

Same as SR with:
- Money base increases at half the rate of SR.
- Modern sector wages indexed at 50% of cost-of-living index.

Shock with human face package (SH)

Same as SR with:
- Public works (see text).
- Food subsidies (5%) and protection ($t_m=t_m+0.15\ t_m$ for all sectors).

---

[a]All symbols refer to variables defined in the text or in the appendix.
[b]The unanticipated shock occurs in year 2.

capacity utilization. The domestic real interest rate is approximately constant at 10 percent per year. In this scenario, the economy faces no external borrowing constraint. The fiscal deficit remains constant at around 5 percent of GDP and the current account is approximately in balance. Since there is no sterilization, approximate current account balance implies that the actual growth of the money supply is about equal to the exogenously set growth rate of 18 percent ($\hat{H}=18$ percent). The public sector's external debt declines from 40 to 30 percent of GDP. In terms of GDP, household assets held abroad remain constant at 12 percent while firms increase their leverage from 12 to 16 percent of GDP and decrease their domestic levrage from 46 to 43 percent of GDP. In sum, BR describes an economy in an almost stationary growth path.

The shock is applied in period 2. It consists of increasing the foreign currency price of imports by 10 percent in period 2, and the foreign interest rate (i^*) from 7 to 12 percent throughout the entire simulation (starting also in period 2). Exchange controls are introduced in period 2 as a reflection of the deteriorating external environment. Except for households, all agents face an external borrowing constraint. Henceforth, firms can no longer borrow abroad, while the government is allowed to borrow (exogenously) approximately the combined amount borrowed by firms and households in BR. By design, combined borrowing is as much as in BR. Hence, the shock is a relatively mild one, and is intended to take into account debt reschedulings and other de facto postponements on debt repayments. Households, however, can continue to hold assets abroad. This assumption reflects the capital flight amply documented during the crisis in the eighties. With the borrowing constraint, the nominal exchange rate is now endogenously determined so as to clear the exogenously set external borrowing constraints [i.e. so as to satisfy eq. (2.3)]. This description of the external environment and of the closure for the external account is maintained for all simulations except BR.

There is no typical country adjustment to such an external shock, but it is safe to assume that some wage and price rigidity characterized the adjustment experience of developing countries, especially for middle-income Latin American economies. Simulation SR in table 3 describes how we fix wages and prices along with the external shock. In SR monetary policy is accommodating and fiscal policy is unchanged form BR, so that adjustment by massive exchange rate devaluation is the only adjustment in this policy package. We view SR as representative of an economy unable to carry out the necessary adjustment policies.

In the following three simulations, we examine successively the effects of: a non-accommodating monetary policy (SN); a fiscal squeeze (SF); a credit squeeze (SC); and a human face adjustment scenario (SH). All experiments are variants on SR. In SN, the monetary authorities try to maintain the same money supply path as in BR by expanding the monetary base at the same rate as in BR. However, because we assume no sterilization of capital flows ($\theta = 1$), the money supply becomes endogenous so that part of the voluntary monetary reduction is offset by capital movements. In the adjustment package with fiscal tightening SF, government expenditures are cut during periods 2 to 5 before resuming growth rates they had in BR. With the credit squeeze package SC, monetary base is expanded at half the rate of SR and wages for modern workers are only indexed to half of the increase in the cost of living index. Finally, in the human face package SH, public works (increase in public employment with a reduction in the average public sector wage that maintains the wage bill constant) is combined with food subsidies financed by an increase in tariffs so as to prevent a fiscal deterioration. All policies in this package are applied in year 2 and maintained throughout.

Fig. 2 summarizes the effect over the seven periods of a simulation of the

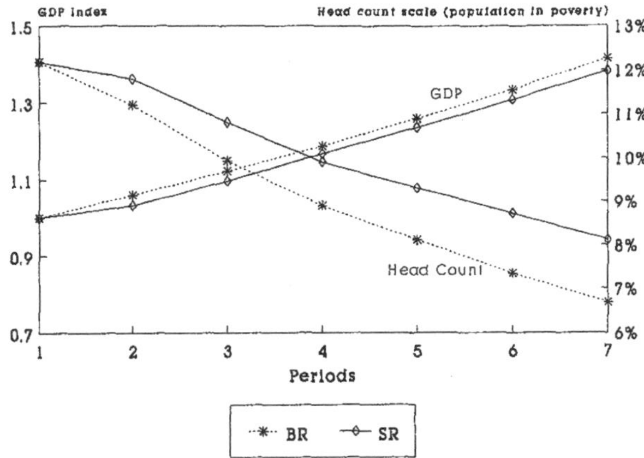

Fig. 2. GDP and head counts paths: A comparison of BR and SR. (*Note:* For definitions of simulations and abbreviations, see table 3.)

external shock on an index of GDP and on a measure of poverty, the head count ratio (i.e. the fraction of the population below an exogenously specified income level). The loss in output is concentrated in year 2 with a corresponding worsening of the head count ratio as a larger fraction of the population is in poverty. There are reasons why the loss in growth is relatively small. First, the accommodating monetary policy results in a real interest rate that is, on average, about the same as in BR. Second, unemployment (1.9 percent) only occurs in period 2, when the shock is applied. And third, less than full capacity utilization also only occurs in period 2. Thus, because of the accommodating monetary policy, the effects of wage and price rigidities are hardly felt, and the economy is able to adjust relatively painlessly, even though the external shock results in a depreciation of the real exchange rate of 15 percent.

5. A comparison of alternative adjustment packages

We now describe briefly the macroeconomic and distributional consequences of the alternative adjustment packages described above. All comparisons are with respect to SR. The aggregate effects on the growth and head count paths are shown in figs. 3a and 3b with other macroeconomic and distributional indicator values displayed in table 4 for periods 2, 4 and 7.

Fig. 3 indicates that the growth rates of SR, SF and SH are about the

32   *F. Bourguignon et al., Adjustment and income distribution*

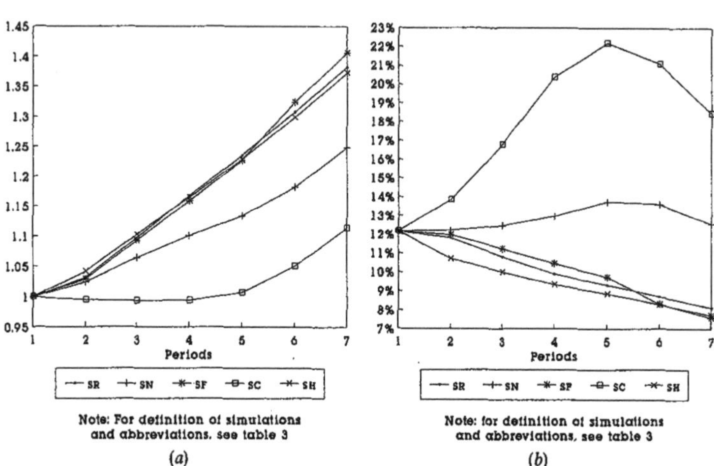

Fig. 3a. GDP index (period $1=1$). 3b. Head count (percentage). (*Note:* For definition of simulations and abbreviations, see table 3).

same and that there is very little difference in the head count path for the three simulations. However, the growth rate is lower for the SN and SC packages because of the lower capacity utilization rates under the restrictive monetary policies of these packages. As indicated in table 4, the real interest rate is much higher under these two packages. Firms have to pay higher interest payments on their domestic loans which cuts in their profit margins. Because of the assumption of mark-up pricing, firms in the modern sector (sectors 3–5) increase their mark-up to maintain profits, and adjustment occurs through reduced capacity utilization. Hence the lower GDP growth in these two packages. With lower growth, the head count worsens especially in the credit squeeze package SC, adjustment package where the head count increases by as much as 10 percentage points. Such an adjustment package where average GDP growth falls to 1.5 percent per year can be considered representative of some of the more extreme adjustment experiences in Latin America in the 1980s.

In the less drastic non-accommodating monetary policy package, SN, the supply-side contractionary effect is less pronounced: capacity utilization in the modern sector, shown in table 4, does not fall below 73 percent and consequently growth does not fall as much. So the head count indicator remains constant throughout the adjustment period. Here GDP growth is just sufficient to keep up with population growth.

The fiscal adjustment package, SF, is relatively successful in bringing down the fiscal deficit without worsening growth or income distribution. The

Table 4

Macroeconomic and distributional outcomes of alternative adjustment packages.[a]

Simulation	SR			SN			SF			SC			SH		
Period	2	4	7	2	4	7	2	4	7	2	4	7	2	4	7
INV/GDP[b]	15.5	17.8	19.3	15.2	16.2	18.6	16.1	20.0	22.6	14.1	13.9	18.1	14.4	16.7	19.0
GD/GDP[c]	−5.6	−4.8	−5.3	−5.8	−6.2	−7.0	−4.3	−1.7	−1.6	−6.6	−9.3	−9.8	−7.0	−5.6	−5.4
Capacity utilization[d]	0.99	0.99	1.00	0.96	0.82	0.73	0.98	0.95	0.99	0.83	0.59	0.52	1.00	1.00	1.00
Real interest rate	9.5	9.0	8.1	11.6	12.3	8.9	10.1	8.3	6.3	15.8	19.1	8.6	10.0	9.1	8.3
Inflation	15.7	14.5	14.9	14.0	11.3	10.6	14.3	12.7	14.7	11.1	3.6	9.7	16.3	15.0	14.9
Theil	65.6	68.3	70.0	66.0	72.6	73.8	69.8	70.4	70.0	70.1	80.3	76.7	64.7	67.7	70.0
Poverty gap	3.4	2.8	2.3	3.5	3.7	3.6	3.2	3.0	2.2	4.0	5.8	5.3	3.1	2.7	2.2

[a]SR: shock with rigidity; SN: shock with non-accommodating monetary policy; SF: shock with fiscal tightening; SC: shock with credit squeeze; SH: shock with human face package.
[b]Real Investment/Real GDP.
[c]Fiscal Deficit/Nominal GDP.
[d]Utilization rates for the formal urban sectors.

reduction in public expenditures in real terms during period 2, 3 and 4 leads to a sharp fall in the fiscal deficit and to a crowding-in effect as private investment recovers. Public finances also recover because of the lesser burden on servicing the domestic debt.

Finally, the human face development package, SH, mitigates sharply the adverse distributional effect of the shock in year 2 (lower values for the Theil and poverty gap indicators). However, this relief, crucial as it may be for the long-term sustainability of any adjustment package, is short-lived. By the end of the seven-period simulation, poverty and distributional indicators have values similar to those under SR.

6. Concluding remarks

This paper has presented a micro–macro simulation model to quantify the likely distributional shifts that would occur under different packages. The distinguishing feature of the model is that it links the micro elements by which structural adjustment policies affect income distribution through relative price shifts with the macro elements of the stabilization components of adjustment packages that affect income distribution through the level of economic activity. An advantage of the model is that it is able to handle a large number of different parameterizations and closures. To underscore this flexibility, we refer to the model as a 'maquette'. Because of our focus on income distribution in the application, the model is fairly disaggregated across sectors, markets, and socioeconomic groups. As a result of the added complexity due to disaggregation, expectations, which also affect income and wealth distribution, are treated exogenously.

Illustrative simulations with the model were carried out for a representative middle-income economy subject to interest rate and terms-of-trade shocks. Alternative adjustment packages were designed to illustrate the likely adverse distributional consequences of these shocks. Of the packages considered, adjustment by real exchange rate depreciation was found to dominate adjustment packages with contractionist monetary policy, and would probably dominate packages with fiscal contraction if one took into account the likely distributive cost of foregone current public expenditures. The predicted distributional shifts are likely to endanger the sustainability of any adjustment package even though the simulations suggest that the distribution of income becomes more equal when normal policies are resumed upon completion of the required adjustment to the shocks. Furthermore, alternative packages appear to have small effects on distributional indicators. However, these small changes were mostly attributed to the relatively mild external shock imposed in the simulations.

F. Bourguignon et al., Adjustment and income distribution   35

Appendix: Model outline

This appendix describes the model outlined in section 2 which extends an earlier version [Bourguignon, Branson and de Melo (1988)] to include an equity market. Functional forms describing technology and household consumption are summarized in the text and are as in our earlier paper. Table A.1 describes decisions by firms, households and government, market equilibria under different model closures and dynamics. To simplify notation, the presentation is for a one-sector model, but the reader should think of accompanying subscripts for goods markets, labor markets, and household consumption and financial decisions. Lagged values are indicated by a subscript (-1) and exogenous expectations about inflation, devaluation, and the foreign interest rate by $\hat{p}^e$, $\hat{e}^e$ and $i^{*e} \equiv (1+i^*)(1+\hat{e}^e) - 1$. A superscript asterisk denotes a variable denominated in foreign currency units. A bar on a variable indicates that it is exogenous.

Start with firms and households. The representative firm makes decision about output supply and investment demand. Output supply derives from profit maximization with full capacity utilization $(u=1)$ under a Walrasian regime (see below) and variable capacity utilization $(u<1)$ under a Keynesian closure with mark-up pricing. Technology F is given by a constant-returns-to-scale production function (A.1) with short-run diminishing returns to labor, the only variable factor (along with intermediate demand not specified here). Once installed, capital (k) can only be varied through factor accumulation (see A.30) or through depreciation at the rate δ. Labor demand (A.2) is derived from profit maximization and investment demand (A.3) is a modified version of Tobin's q theory of investment to account for adjustment costs. Firms require working capital (A.5), and investment financing (A.6) comes from retained earnings $(\alpha\pi)$, household savings in equity (S_k) with the balance from bonds (ΔL). Note that the borrowing allocation between domestic and foreign bonds (A.8) depends on relative bonds prices with a constant elasticity of substitution (ε_0).

Household income (A.9) includes income from domestic and foreign bonds as well as distributed profits and wages. A wealth effect is included in the aggregate consumption/savings decision (A.11), and wealth allocation is a three-stage budgeting decision (implying zero cross-price effects). Money demand comes first (A.14) and depends negatively on the rate of interest and expected inflation. Next the decision to save in equity (i.e. to invest in physical capital) (A.15) depends on the relative return on physical and aggregate financial assets. The third stage decision involves the portfolio allocation between domestic and foreign bonds (A.16–A.17) which has the same functional form as the corresponding decision for firms.

The government's expenditure decisions (A.22) are exogenously determined

36   *F. Bourguignon et al., Adjustment and income distribution*

Table A.1

---

1. Firms

(A.1) $q^s = uF(k, p, w)$ Supply (u is capacity utilization)

(A.2) $L^d = \lambda(w/p)q^s$ Labor demand

(A.3) $I = (g+\delta)k + I(ru/(\delta + i_I - \hat{p}^e))$ Investment demand
with $i_I \equiv \bar{i}(1-g_0) + i^{*e}g_0$
where $r \equiv (p\,\partial f/\partial k)/p_k$ Gross marginal revenue product of capital (p_k is price of capital goods)

(A.4) $\pi = pq^s - wL^d - ei^*_{-1}L^*_{w,-1} - i_{-1}L_{b,-1}$ Profits (π)

(A.5) $H_f = H\left[\dfrac{g_0(1+i) + (1-g_0)(1+i^{*e})}{1+\hat{p}^e}\right]^{\gamma} pq^s$ Working capital (H_f)

(A.6) $\Delta L = p_k I + \Delta H_f - \alpha\pi - S_k - \rho(L_{b,-1} + eL^*_{w,-1})$ Investment financing (L) (ρ is repayment rate; α is retained profits share)

(A.7) $L = L_{b,-1} + eL^*_{w,-1} + \Delta L$ Firm's debt (bonds)

(A.8) $eL^*_w = (1-g_0)B; \; g_0 \equiv \phi_0\left(\dfrac{1-i}{1+i^{*e}}\right)^{\varepsilon_0}$ Borrowing allocation between domestic (L_b) and foreign bonds ($\bar{i}$ is shadow rate of interest)

2. Households

(A.9) $Y = wL^d + \bar{w}_G\bar{L}_G + (1-\alpha)\pi + iB + ei^*F_h$ Income constraint

(A.10) $W = H_h + B_h + eF^*_h + p_a E$ Wealth constraint (W)
$WG \equiv (H_{h,-1} + B_{h,-1}/i + eF^*_{h,-1}/i^* + p_a E_{-1}) - W_{-1}$ Definition of wealth gain (WG)

(A.11) $C = [(1-s)Y + \gamma(WG)]/p_c$ Consumption (p_c is price of composite good)

(A.12) $S = sY - \gamma(WG)$ Savings

(A.13) $W = W_{-1} + S$ New wealth

(A.14) $\ln(H_h/\bar{p}) = a\ln(Y/\bar{p}) - z_i i - z_p \hat{p}^e$ Money demand ($\bar{p}$ is the cost of living)

(A.15) $p_a E = g_1(W_{-1} + S - H_h)$ Demand for equity (E)

$g_1 = \psi_1\left[\dfrac{1+r-\delta+\hat{p}^e}{g_2(1+i) + (1-g_2)(1+i^{*e})}\right]^{\varepsilon_1}$

(A.16) $B_h = g_2(1-g_1)(W_{-1} + S - H_h)$ Demand for domestic bonds

$g^*_2 = \psi_2\left[\dfrac{(1+i)}{(1+i^{*e})}\right]^{\varepsilon_2}$

(A.17) $eF^*_h = (1-g_2)(1-g_1)(W_{-1} + S - H_h)$ Demand for foreign bonds

(A.18) $p_a = [k_{-1}(p_k(1-\delta) - p_{k,-1}) + \alpha\pi + \Delta H_f + E_{-1}p_{a,-1}$ Price of equity (p_a)

(A.19) $S_k = p_a(E - E_{-1})$ Net increases in equity and direct financing of investment

(A.20) $p_c = dp(1+t_i) + (1-d)e\bar{p}^*_m(1+t_m)$ Price of composite good (d is share of domestic good in total expenditure)

Table A.1 (continued)

3. Government and balance of payments

(A.21)	$GR = t_i pq^s + e\bar{p}_m^* t_m M$	Tax revenue (t_i is indirect tax and t_m is tariff)
(A.22)	$GE = p_c \bar{G} + \bar{W}_G L_G + p_c \bar{I}_g + i_{-1} B_h + i_{-1}^* B_w^* e_{-1}$ $GD \equiv GR - GE$	Spending Government deficit
(A.23)	$GD = \Delta B_h + e\Delta B_w^* + \Delta B_b$	Deficit financing
(A.24)	$CA = p_e^* X - \bar{p}_m^* M - i_{-1}^* [B_{w,-1}^* + L_{w,-1}^* - F_{h,-1}^*]$	Current account
(A.25)	$KA_p = \Delta L_w^* - \Delta F_h^*$	Capital account (private)

4. Market equilibria

	$q^s = q^d$	Walrasian regime
(A.26)	or	or Goods market
	$p = (1+m)\lambda W$	Keynesian regime
	$\hat{W} = \psi_0 + \psi_1 \bar{p} + \psi_s(L_u^{-1} - L_{u,-1}^{-1})$	Phillips curve
	$L_u = 1 - (\bar{L}_G + L^d)/\bar{L}^s$	Unemployment rate
(A.27)	or	or Labor market
	$\bar{L}^s = L^d + \bar{L}_G$	Flex wage ($\Psi \to \infty$)
	$\Delta H_f + \Delta H_h = \Delta H + \theta eKA_p,\ i \leqq i_{max}$	Market clearing
(A.28)	or	or Money market
	$\Delta L_b(\bar{i}) = \Delta H + \theta eKA_p - B_b,\ \bar{i} > i_{max}$	Credit rationing
	$CA + eKA_p = -\Delta \bar{B}_w^*$	Flexible exchange rate
(A.29)	or	or Foreign exchange market
	$-\Delta B_w^* = CA + KA_p$	(Fixed exchange rate)

5. Dynamics

(A.30)	$\Delta k = I + k(1 - \delta)$	Capital accumulation
(A.31)	$\Delta L^s/L^s = n$	Labor force growth (n)

while the government's revenue (A.21) depends on activity and tax levels. As explained in the text, deficit financing (A.23) comes from the sale of bonds, foreign borrowing or borrowing from the Central Bank.

Market equilibria are determined by the selection of market closures. In the goods market, the choices are between a Walrasian closure with price adjustment and a Keynesian closure with mark-up pricing, in which case capacity utilization is endogenous (A.26). Typically a mixture of the two closures is adopted with a Walrasian closure for agriculture and a Keynesian closure for manufacturing. The same mixture usually applies to the labor markets with the agricultural labor market characterized by a flexible wage and the modern labor market by wage indexation (A.27). In the money

Table A.2

Elasticity specification.[a]

Households	
Consumption	*Portfolio*
Household expenditure elasticity (0.4, 1.4)	Money:
Frisch parameter (-1.25, 2.00)	z_i (semi-interest elasticity) $= 0.02$
Household savings rate (0.02, 0.15)	a (income elasticity) $= 0.6$
Proportion of wealth change consumed (0.10)	Bond allocation ($\varepsilon_2 = 3.0$)
Capitalist and farmers' population growth (0.01)	Physical/financial ($\varepsilon_1 = 1.0$)
Firms	
Technology	*Portfolio*
Capital-labor substitution elasticity in value-added (0.7, 1.1)	Working capital ($\gamma = 0.5$)
Labor share (0.48, 1)	Bonds ($\varepsilon_4 = 6.0$)
Depreciation rate ($\delta = 0.04$)	
	Investment
Labor force growth (0.03)	Investment demand elasticity with respect to profits (0.05, 0.12)
Technical progress (0.015, 0.025)	
Foreign Trade	
Price elasticity of foreign export demand (1.0, 3.0)	Price elasticity of import demand (0.6, 1.5)

[a]Intervals for elasticities refer to ranges across sectors and socioeconomic classes. All parameter values remain unchanged across simulations.

market, note that when there is credit rationing (A.28) firms borrow at the shadow interest rate ($\bar{\imath}$) while households receive interest at the fixed rate (i). Finally the foreign exchange market is closed either by a flexible exchange rate with exogenous foreign government borrowing or vice-versa (A.29).

The dynamics are decomposable in time and consist of capital accumulation and exogenous labor force growth. There is also migration across labor categories in response to wage differentials and the updating of exogenous variables (e.g. technological progress) not described here.

Elasticities of demand and supply, elasticities of substitution among assets and other parameters are summarized in table A.2. To save on space, only the range of elasticities across sectors is reported in table A.2.

The calibration is common to CGE applications: initial prices and quantities are combined with parameters (e.g. tax rates, etc.) and elasticities to obtain share parameters and exogenous constraints that validate the read-in prices and quantities. However, the presence of assets complicates calibration in two respects. First, since income flows depend on income earned (or interest paid for firms) from assets, the model is calibrated to the wealth ownership matrix in the text iteratively to ensure that desired portfolio holdings comply with the read-in wealth matrix. This explains the calibrated values for capital ownership and household savings rates in table 2. Second, savings rates by socioeconomic groups are adjusted so that, for the given wealth matrix, physical capital accumulation by each socioeconomic group would leave wealth distribution unchanged in the absence of changes in factor incomes and relative prices. This explains the derivation of the calibrated values for capital ownership and household savings rates in table 2.

References

Bourguignon, F., W. Branson and J. de Melo, 1989, Macroeconomic adjustment and income distribution: A macro–micro simulation model, Technical papers, no. 1 (OECD Development Centre, OECD, Paris) April.

Branson, W.H., 1989, Macroeconomic theory and policy (Harper and Row, New York).

Chenery, H., S. Robinson and M. Syrquin, eds., 1987, Industrialization and growth: A comparative study (Oxford University Press, Oxford).

Cornia, Giovanni Andrea, Richard Jolly and Frances Stewart, 1987, Adjustment with a human face: Protecting the vulnerable and promoting growth (Oxford University Press, Oxford).

Diaz-Alejandro, C., 1979, Southern cone stabilization plans, in: W. Cline and S. Weintraub, eds., Stabilization policies in developing countries (Brookings, Washington, DC).

Faini, R., J. de Melo, A. Senhadji-Semlali and J. Stanton, 1991, Growth-oriented adjustment programs: A statistical analysis, World Development.

Heller, P., A. Bovenberg, T. Catsambas, K. Chu and P. Shome, 1988, The implications of fund-supported adjustment programs for poverty: Experiences in selected countries, Occasional paper no. 58 (IMF, Washington, DC).

International Monetary Fund, 1986, Fund-supported programs, fiscal policy, and income distribution: A study by the fiscal affairs department of the International Monetary Fund, IMF Occasional paper no. 46 (International Monetary Fund, Washington, DC) Sept.

Kanbur, R., 1987, Measurement and alleviation of poverty: With an application to the effects of macroeconomic adjustment, Staff Papers 34, no. 1 (International Monetary Fund, Washington, DC) March.

Khan, M. and R. Zahler, 1983, The macroeconomic effects of changes in barriers to trade and capital flows: A simulation analysis, Staff Papers, pp. 223–283 (International Monetary Fund, Washington, DC).

Melo, J. de and S. Robinson, 1982, Trade adjustment policies and income distribution in three archetype developing economies, Journal of Development Economics, pp. 67–92.

Tobin, James, 1969, A general equilibrium approach to monetary theory, Journal of Money, Credit and Banking, 15–29.

World Bank, 1986, Targeted programs for the poor during structural adjustment: A summary of the symposium on poverty and adjustment (World Bank, Washington, DC).

Computable General Equilibrium Models for Trade Policy Analysis in Developing Countries: A Survey

Jaime de Melo, *Trade Policy Division, Country Economics Department, The World Bank*

This paper surveys the contributions of computable general equilibrium (CGE) simulation models designed to quantify the implications of alternative trade policy scenarios in developing countries. The paper starts with a review of the basic structure of CGE models, using a one-sector model with product differentiation on the import and export side. The basic properties of CGE models are established and a series of applications to trade policy, internal–external balance and growth, and intertemporal issues are discussed.

INTRODUCTION

The use of computable general equilibrium (CGE) models for policy analysis has become widespread for both developed and developing economies. For developed economies, with a few notable exceptions, applications have focused on microeconomics with the analysis concentrating on estimating the welfare impact of alternative tax structures or energy policies.[1] In developing countries, CGE models have been used for a wider range of issues, from medium- to long-term macroeconomic policy analysis to the more traditional microeconomic issues analyzed in developed countries as well.[2] Several reasons account for this wider range of applications, particularly the fact that notwithstand-

---

[1]Applications to international trade and taxation issues are surveyed in Shoven and Whalley (1984). For models with a focus on energy policies, see Hudson and Jorgenson (1978). An exception is Dixon et al. (1982), who use a CGE model for Australia to analyze a wide range of macroeconomic and microeconomic issues.

[2]Robinson (1988) surveys CGE applications for developing countries with an emphasis on macroclosure and applications rather than on international trade. The two surveys are therefore complementary.

Address correspondence to Jaime de Melo, The World Bank, 1818 H. Street, N.W., Washington, D.C. 20433.

I thank Sherman Robinson for comments and Jackson Magargee and Julie Stanton for much appreciated support. The views are those of the author, not those of the World Bank.

Journal of Policy Modeling 10(4):469–503 (1988)

© Society for Policy Modeling, 1988

469

0161-8938/88/$3.50

ing the use of econometric models in the framework of LINK, developing countries are usually not well suited to economy-wide policy analysis relying on econometric techniques. This is so for three reasons. First, reliable time-series data for sufficiently long periods are usually not readily available; second, when available, the data are often not appropriate for standard econometric analysis without considerable further preparation to remove inconsistencies; and third, significant changes in policy regimes often take place, calling for different structural models, thereby reducing the time span available for hypothesis testing with a selected model.

CGE models have been used frequently for medium- to long-term policy analysis in developing countries. The policy applications have ranged from long-run issues such as the the impact of alternative development strategies on growth and resource allocation or on policy concerning exhaustible resources, to medium-run issues such as rural–urban migration, labor markets and employment, the functional and size distribution of income, and tax reform. Because foreign exchange has great scarcity value in most developing countries, the issue of foreign trade policy has occupied center place in the majority of applications. Even in the applications that do not have a foreign trade focus, the way the foreign trade sector is modeled has a decisive influence on the outcome of policy simulations. For example, in a model focusing on income distribution, changes in the equilibrium value of the agricultural terms of trade in response to a change in policy will depend on assumptions about the behavior of exports and imports. The issue of foreign trade policy and the interaction between the domestic economy and the foreign trade sector is also particularly well suited for general equilibrium rather than partial equilibrium policy analysis because of the sensitivity of domestic resource allocation to developments in the external sector. The extent to which the scarcity value of foreign exchange is affected by a change in policy cannot be easily estimated in partial equilibrium analysis because of the difficulty of estimating excess demand functions for tradables and nontradables without specifying the appropriate economy-wide budget constraint.

This survey reviews the contributions made to the modeling of foreign trade and provides examples from numerical applications. Deliberately, the focus is on policy issues and how to model them, rather than on an exhaustive review of contributions in each policy area.[3]

---

[3]Devarajan, Lewis, and Robinson (1986) and Decaluwe and Martens (1986) provide bibliographic surveys.

Section 2 presents the simplest model for dealing with external–internal balance. This one-sector model is then extended to a multisectoral version in section 3. The discussion of policy applications starts in section 4, which examines the impact of tariffs and quantitative restrictions on welfare and resource allocation, as well as the design of tariff policy when the government has a revenue constraint. Model extensions for dealing with a growing economy are surveyed in section 5, with applications to problems of external–internal balance in the medium run. Finally, applications that deal with policy choice when the economy faces an intertemporal budget constraint are raised in section 6.

2. A ONE-SECTOR MODEL

It is widely accepted that for medium-run issues, the Salter–Swan dependent economy model is the most appropriate specification for representing the external sector in a developing economy. In that specification, foreign prices are given and hence the external terms of trade are exogenous and domestically produced tradable goods are perfect substitutes for foreign-produced goods. In applied work, however, with the exception of a few homogeneous primary commodities, the implication of this specification— namely, that changes in foreign prices or trade policy are entirely passed through to competing domestic traded goods—is unrealistic for most traded goods. Indeed, the empirical evidence at the most disaggregated levels (see, for example, Isard 1977; Aspe and Giavazzi 1982) shows that the pass-through of exchange rate changes on domestic prices is small.[4] In addition, trade statistics indicate significant cross-hauling even at a very disaggregated commodity level, also suggesting the inappropriateness of the perfect substitution assumption of the Salter–Swan framework.

The alternative, now found in most CGE models, is to assume that foreign goods and domestic import-competing goods are imperfect substitutes in use. This specification, which is used on the import side, should also be incorporated on the export side for similar reasons. Then domestically produced goods for export sale

---

[4]A recent example of a pass-through, although for a developed economy, is that of the dollar appreciation during 1981–85. Dornbusch (1987) observes that a 20 percent appreciation in the dollar resulted in only a five percent increase in the index for manufactured imports. He goes on to show that this relative price behavior among traded goods is consistent with a number of competing hypotheses about firm behavior and product characteristics, including the one presented here. Krugman (1986c) develops other pricing models that are consistent with this observation.

are imperfect substitutes for domestically produced goods for sale on the domestic market. This assumption, while appropriate for economy-wide models that are fairly aggregated, is not without drawbacks. As Dixon (1977) has convincingly argued, empirical estimates of the costs of protection that are not sufficiently disaggregated to accommodate both economies of scale at the product level and the appropriate degree of complementarity/substitutability in use are likely to seriously understate the costs of protection. This criticism thus applies to the models that use the product differentiation assumption presented here when the models are used to give welfare estimates of the cost of protection.

A one-sector full employment model with symmetric product differentiation is presented in Table 1 and analyzed in Figure 1.[5] Because of Walras' law, the economy-wide budget constraint is omitted. Because of homogeneity of demand and supply functions, only relative prices are determined. Let $e = 1$ be the numeraire. Then the model determines the following 10 endogenous variables: X, E, D^d, D^s, M, p^m, p^e, p^d, Q, p^x. In numerical applications, the functions $G(\ )$ and $F(\ )$ are usually given by constant elasticity of transformation (CET) and constant elasticity of substitution (CES) functions.[6]

The equilibrium in this stylized economy is represented in Figure 1. The external constraint for $\bar{B} = 0$ is given in quadrant 1, and the full-employment transformation frontier represented by the CET is shown in quadrant 4. By choice of units, let $\bar{\pi}^e = \bar{\pi}^m = 1$. Then the economy's consumption possibility frontier, which is given by CC in quadrant 2, is symmetric with the production possibility frontier in quadrant 4. Finally, II represents the indifference map. It is easy to see that equilibrium in the economy is characterized by the following familiar condition:

$$\frac{\delta Q/\delta D}{\delta Q/\delta M} = \frac{\bar{\pi}^e}{\bar{\pi}^m} = \frac{\delta G/\delta D}{\delta G/\delta E} = \frac{p^d}{p^m} = \frac{p^d}{p^e}, \tag{1}$$

which states that the marginal rate of transformation in production is equal to the marginal rate of substitution in consumption at equilibrium. Furthermore, when there are no trade or consumption taxes, these

---

[5]The presentation here follows de Melo and Robinson (1986).

[6]The CET and CES formulations in this context were first introduced by Powell and Gruen (1967) and Armington (1969), respectively.

TRADE ANALYSIS IN DEVELOPING COUNTRIES   473

Table 1: A One-Sector Small-Country Model With Differentiated Trade

(1) $Q = F(M,D^d)$	Import aggregation function
(2) $X = G(E,D^s)$	Export transformation function
(3) $p^m = e\,\bar{\pi}^m$	Import price
(4) $p^e = e\bar{\pi}^e$	Export price
(5) $p^q = f_1(p^m,p^d)$	Consumer price
(6) $p^x = g_1(p^e,p^d)$	Producer price
(7) $\dfrac{M}{D^d} = f_2(p^m,p^d)$	Import demand equation
(8) $\dfrac{E}{D^s} = g_2(p^e,p^d)$	Export supply equation
(9) $\bar{\pi}^m M - \bar{\pi}^e E = \bar{B}$	Balance of trade constraint
(10) $D^d - D^s = 0$	Domestic demand–supply equilibrium

where:

M,E	= Imports, exports
D^d,D^s	= Demand and supply of the domestic good
Q	= Composite consumer good
X	= Composite production
$\bar{\pi}^m$	= World price of imports
$\bar{\pi}^e$	= World price of exports
e	= Numeraire
p^m	= Domestic price of imports, M
p^e	= Domestic price of exports, E
p^d	= Domestic price of domestic sales, D
p^q	= Domestic price of composite consumer good, Q
p^x	= Domestic price of composite output, X
$\bar{B}$	= Exogenous balance of trade, or net foreign capital inflow (or outflow for negative $\bar{B}$)

---

marginal rates are equal to the foreign rate of transformation and Pareto efficiency occurs.

The equilibrium in Figure 1 is given by A and B. This apparatus is useful for examining the effects of terms of trade shifts and changes in the (exogenous) level of foreign transfers $\bar{B}$ and ad valorem trade taxes (tariffs and subsidies are not incorporated in the equation summary of Table 1). Several characteristics of this model are worth noting. First, the sign of the slope of the domestic offer curve—obtained by perturbing the terms of trade—is determined by the value of the elasticity of substitution in use, σ, between imports and domestically produced goods. As shown by de Melo and Robinson (1989), the domestic offer curve is upward (backward) sloping when σ is greater (less) than one. This is an important point in numerical applications

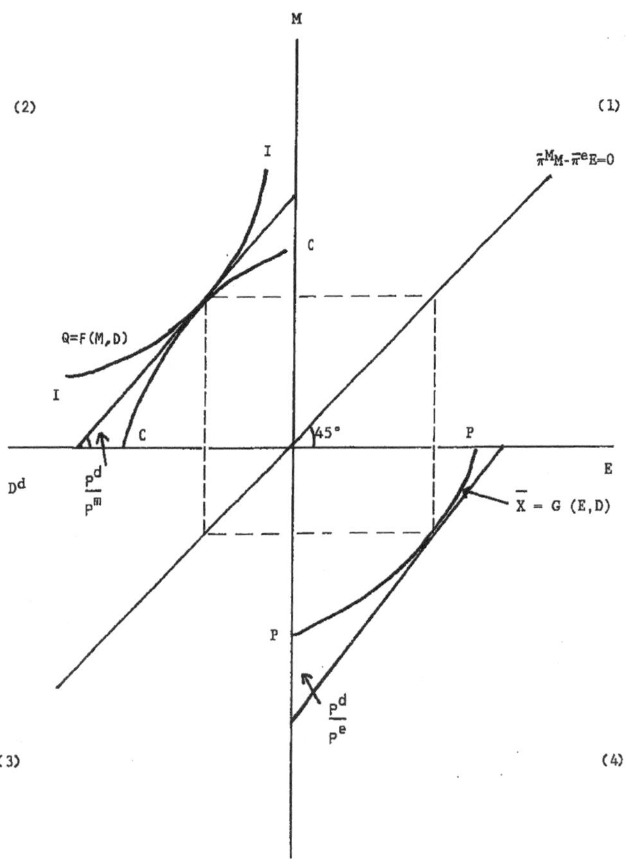

Figure 1. A one-sector full employment model.

since it will determine whether a policy change will cause a real exchange rate appreciation or depreciation.

Second, the model determines an equilibrium real exchange rate, e^r, which is the relative price of the foreign-produced and the domestically produced goods. Note that for the selected numeraire, $e = 1$, the real exchange rate is defined as $e^r = 1/p^d$. However, the computed value of e^r will differ according to the choice of weights in defining the price index for the domestically produced good. Thus, results from multisectoral simulations computing the percentage change in the equilibrium real exchange rate from a policy scenario can be used to determine how sensitive the values of e^r are to the selection of weights in defining the price indices that enter into the definition of the real exchange rate.[7]

3. THE DOMESTIC PRICE SYSTEM IN MULTI-SECTOR MODELS

The stylized model above is too simple in structure for policy analysis, although it contains the elements necessary to expand the dependent-economy model. The first extension that adds structure to the model is the inclusion of sectors and intermediate goods. The implications of this extension for the effects of trade policy changes on resource allocation are discussed next. The analysis is partial equilibrium.[8]

To start out, consider the problem of specialization in production in response to trade policy change when the perfect substitution assumption ($p^m = p^d = p^e$) is joined to the small country assumption. Suppose the economy has n sectors, of which i, $j = 1, \ldots, m$ are traded and the remainder $k = m+1, \ldots, n$ are nontraded. Following most CGE applications, technology is described by a separable function between value added and intermediates. A Leontief production function describes the fixed input/output coefficients for value added and the aggregate of intermediates, as well as the substitution possibilities within intermediates.

To illustrate the specialization problem, assume that nontraded intermediates do not enter into traded goods production. As before, by choice of units, $\overline{\pi}^m = \overline{\pi}^e = 1$. Suppose there are $l = 1, \ldots, s$ intersectorally mobile factors of production with unit input coefficients k_l under cost minimization. Then the zero- profit condition of perfect competition for traded sectors implies that unit value added prices will just cover unit costs when production takes place. If t_i denotes the ad valorem tariff/subsidy rate, the zero-profit condition is:

$$PN_i \leq \sum_s k_s w_s \qquad\qquad \begin{aligned} i,j &= 1, \ldots, m \\ s &= 1, \ldots, s \end{aligned} \qquad\qquad (2)$$

where $PN_i = 1 + t_i - \sum_j a_{ji} t_i$. It is immediately evident that the system of equations described in equation 2 is underdetermined for a change in tariff/subsidy rates if $m > s$, that is, if there are more traded

---

[7]Edwards and Ng (1985) discuss alternative definitions of the real exchange rate and of the indices used in computing it.

[8]The analysis below draws on de Melo and Robinson (1985).

sectors than primary factors of production. This is of course the case in most empirical applications. Allowing for nontraded intermediate inputs to enter into traded goods production will help somewhat, but not much, unless they weigh heavily and cross-price effects are strong enough within the nontraded sectors that relative prices change considerably when tariff/subsidy rates are altered. An obvious solution is to add primary factors; however, this approach is not entirely satisfactory because one quickly runs out of information for disaggregating labor categories. The alternative is to assume decreasing returns to scale (e.g., land as a naturally fixed factor or entrepreneurial talent that is sector specific).[9]

Another alternative is to return to the product differentiation assumption presented in section 2, which has the added advantages of allowing for cross-hauling and of leading to a characterization of sectors by their degree of tradability, as will be shown shortly. Define

$$E^m \equiv \frac{dp^d}{dp^m}\frac{p^m}{p^d} \text{ and } E^e \equiv \frac{dp^d}{dp^e}\frac{p^e}{p^d},$$

the elasticities of the domestic price response to a change in the domestic currency price of imports and exports, respectively (sector subscripts are omitted to save on notation). It is clear that under the assumption of perfect substitution, $E^e = E^m = 1$, an increase of say 10 percent in the domestic currency price of imports or exports (due to a change in their world price, a change in the exchange rate, or a change in the trade tax) will lead to a 10 percent increase in the price of the domestically traded sector. However, for the model introduced in section 2, it can be shown that

$$E^m = \frac{(\sigma - \epsilon^q)\,\theta^m}{(1 - \theta)\,\epsilon^s + \epsilon^q + \theta^e\Omega + (\sigma^e - \epsilon^m)\,\theta} \tag{3}$$

$$E^e = \frac{(\Omega - \epsilon^s)\,\theta^e}{(1 - \theta^e)\,\epsilon^s + \epsilon^q + \theta^e\Omega + (\sigma - \epsilon^q)\,\theta^m}, \tag{4}$$

where $\theta^e = p^e{\cdot}E/P^x{\cdot}X$, $\theta^m = P^m{\cdot}M/P^qQ$, $\epsilon^q \equiv \dfrac{dQ}{dP^q}\dfrac{P^q}{Q} < 0$, ϵ^s is the elasticity of supply of X, and σ and Ω are the elasticities of substitution and transformation for the CES and CET trade aggregation functions

---

[9]This was done by Taylor and Black (1974) in one of the first trade policy simulations with a CGE model.

introduced in section 2.[10] Clearly, dropping the assumption of perfect substitution between imports and domestic goods solves the specialization problem noted above. Furthermore, this formulation is well suited for addressing empirically the arguments raised in the development literature between "structuralists" who maintain that developing countries are characterized by low elasticities, and "neoclassicists" who maintain that elasticities are high.[11] When σ, Ω $\rightarrow \infty$, the domestic price system loses its independence, and we are back to the traditional trade theoretic model.

Once intermediates are included, the formulation acquires quite a degree of realism for studying the impact of trade policy changes on resource allocation. A four-part classification of sectors according to their degree of tradability follows naturally: (1) nontradables are sectors with low export (θ^e) and import (θ^m) shares; (2) exportables are sectors with high export and low import shares; (3) importables must be distinguished according to two subgroups, depending upon whether they are substitutes ($\sigma > \epsilon^q$) or complements ($\sigma < \epsilon^q$); and (4) import-dependent sectors are the sectors, like construction, that may be nontradable on the final demand side but that have a high ratio of imported intermediate inputs to total intermediate inputs.

This formulation has a number of desirable attributes due to the relatively small number of parameters and elasticities required for its implementation. Furthermore, equations like (3) and (4), once augmented for oligopolistic pricing possibilities, can be used for interpretation of microeconometric estimates of the link between exchange rate movements and producer prices.[12] When applied to simulations of the effects of changes in trade taxes on resource allocation, however, this formulation's reliance on constant elasticities may overestimate the degree of autonomy of the domestic price system, especially when simulations involve large changes in relative incentives.

---

[10]These expressions are derived in de Melo and Robinson (1985), who compute values of E^e and E^m for different parameter configurations in equations (3) and (4). They also show that this formulation can easily be extended to accommodate a less than infinitely elastic foreign demand for exports, with or without product differentiation on the export side, thereby extending the analysis for homogeneous primary commodities.

[11]Chenery (1975) reviews the structuralist debate.

[12]Feinberg (1986a,b) uses the model presented here and augments it by a term that captures the presence of oligopolistic interactions on the price-cost margin. He uses a Cournot model to estimate econometrically the pass-through of changes in the real value of the dollar to relative producer prices at the microeconomic level.

4. APPLICATIONS TO TRADE POLICY

The model structure outlined in sections 2 and 3 reflects the essential characteristics of the trade policy reform simulations carried out in practice. Three examples of model-based simulations are presented in the following subsections.

4.1. The Welfare Costs of Quantitative Restrictions and Rent-Seeking Activities[13]

The foreign trade regimes in many developing countries are rife with quantitative restrictions. For example, import programs in Turkey in the late 1970s were issued semiannually, with imported commodities classified under three main lists: a liberalization list, consisting essentially of raw materials and spare parts not in competition with domestic production, for which importation was free; a restricted list, consisting of intermediate and final goods most of which were manufactured in Turkey, for which an import license was required; and a quota list, with commodity-specific quotas further allocated between industrialists and importers.

Students of Turkey's foreign trade regime have noted that industrialists have responded to these extensive quantitative restrictions with rent-seeking activity.[14] Grais, de Melo, and Urata (1986) draw on the concept of "virtual" prices introduced by Neary and Roberts (1980) to estimate the welfare costs of rationing in Turkey, using an eight-sector CGE model calibrated to 1978 Turkish data. The use of virtual prices (prices that would induce an unrationed household or firm to behave in the same manner as when faced with a vector of ration constraints) allows reoptimization over unrationed quantities, thereby allowing for spillover into other markets when adjustment to the quota is by quantity rather than price.

In the simulations, consumers are rationed in their purchases of imports of final goods, and producers are rationed in their purchases of imports of intermediates.[15] Furthermore, producers are assumed to

---

[13]This application was formulated in the transactions value (TV) approach to modeling (see Drud, Grais, and Pyatt 1986, and Pyatt 1987).

[14]Krueger's (1974) is the original work in this area. Bhagwati and Srinivasan (1980) and Dervis, de Melo, and Robinson (1982) add to the discussion. Lewis and Urata (1984), Ahmed et al. (1985), Robinson and Tyson (1985), Clarete and Whalley (1986), and Ahmed and Grais (1987) also provide estimates of the costs of quantitative restrictions and rent-seeking activities.

[15]The specification of foreign trade in this application is close to the one in Table 1, although final demand is broken down into investment and public and private consumption.

engage in rent-seeking activity. The approach to implementing rent-seeking behavior is to assume that the production function for rent seeking is the same as that for what the authors refer to as "traditional" output. Producers, however, must purchase both the traditional and the rent-seeking commodities. Furthermore, the authors assume that the entire value of the rents, R, is spent on the production of the rent-seeking activity. At equilibrium the following will hold (sector subscripts have been dropped to simplify the notation):

$$X_t^d(p^d) + X_r^d(p^d) = X^s(p^d, p^v; \bar{k}) \tag{5}$$

$$X_r^d \cdot p^d = M(p^v - p^m) = R, \tag{6}$$

where p^d, p^v, and p^m are, respectively, the domestic, virtual, and import prices; M is the volume of rationed intermediate imports; X_t^d, X_r^d are the demand for traditional and rent-seeking output; and X^s is short-run output supply, given capital stock. Thus the effect of rent seeking is to reduce the supply of the traditional output and to raise the price to the final user. In the spirit of the literature on directly unproductive activities, rent seeking creates income since more output is produced, but at the same time the output generated by rent seeking, X_r^d, does not enter the utility function since it does not appear as an element of final demand.

The loss to the economy from rationing and rent seeking is summarized in Figure 2, which conveniently aggregates the economy into one sector. Because producers purchase imported intermediates, any rationing of these intermediates will raise the marginal costs of production. This is shown in Figure 2 by the leftward shift of XX_0s to XX_1s beyond X_0, the point at which rationing becomes effective. As a result of rationing, there is a deadweight loss, ADE. The effect of rent seeking is to push the supply curve up even further to $X_2^s = X_1^s - X_R^d$ because of the diversion of output toward rent seeking. The result is to raise the price (in terms of the numeraire) to PD_2. The area *HBCI* is equal to the value of the rents, and the horizontal distance between X_1^s and X_2^s shows the output of rent-seeking activity. The extra deadweight loss from rent seeking is given by *ABD*. At the new equilibrium, *FG* and *BF* are the additional costs due to rationing and rent seeking, respectively.

The welfare benefits resulting from the removal of quantitative restrictions are reported in Table 2. Measured in terms of GDP, the welfare costs of quantitative restrictions in Turkey in 1978 were estimated at over five percent of GDP. Most of the costs come from quotas on intermediates since consumer imports had a small share in

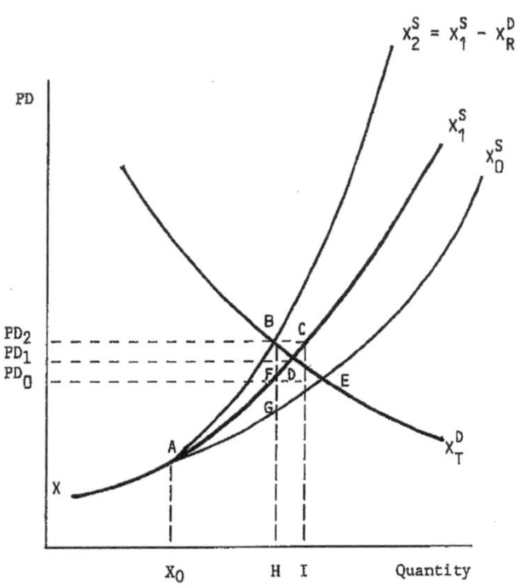

Figure 2. Welfare cost of rationing and rent seeking.

overall imports. Of course, the magnitude of the results is driven by the assumed rent-seeking behavior and by the estimated value of the premium rates incorporated in the calibrated solution for the base simulation. The results are thus only indicative, but they help to focus on the costs in terms of foregone consumption and, more important, foregone growth due to reduced real investment caused by quantitative restrictions and rent-seeking behavior.

Table 2: Welfare Benefits Resulting From the Removal of Quotas in Turkey (Ratio to Base Simulation Value)

	Removal of Quotas on Intermediate Imports Removed	Removal of Quotas on Intermediate and Consumer Imports
Real GDP	1.052	1.054
Real Household Consumption	1.038	1.042
Real Investment	1.112	1.110

Source: Grais, de Melo, and Urata (1986, Table 7).

4.2. Interactions Between Quantitative Restriction-Based Foreign Trade Regimes and Industrial Organization

Rent-seeking activity under foreign trade regimes based on quantitative restrictions is only one aspect of the potential welfare costs that extend beyond the standard welfare costs of protection. Another and potentially more costly aspect of such trade regimes derives from the noncompetitive behavior made possible by the market structure in many developing countries. In the following application, a quantitative restriction-based trade regime does not give rise to rent seeking.

Students of industrial organization in developing countries have often noted that concentration is high in the manufacturing sector and that these high concentration ratios probably understate the extent of market power enjoyed by leading oligopolists.[16] This is so because entry is restricted by industrial policies that regulate investment through complex licensing procedures and because credit incentives are exhausted among incumbent firms. Likewise, weak capital markets imply that investment funds are internally generated, which also restricts entry. Most important, the widespread use of quantitative restrictions eliminates foreign competition. Furthermore, exit from the market is also difficult because of the lack of bankruptcy legislation. As a result, markets in these countries are often characterized by both market power and an ossified industrial structure. When restrictiveness on investment licensing is not too great, too many firms operate. This has become known as the *excessive entry problem*, reflecting the observation that too many firms have typically coexisted behind protective walls despite official licensing policies.[17]

Condon and de Melo (1986), starting from the analysis by Harris (1985) and Cox and Harris (1985) for Canada, illustrate the costs of quantitative restriction-based protection in a semi-industrial economy. They use several variants of a model in which economies of scale and oligopolistic behavior interact when rationing of consumer and intermediate imports takes place. Although expressed in dual rather than primal form, the model is similar to the model presented in Table 1

---

[16]The evidence on market structure and performance in developing countries is surveyed in Kirkpatrick, Lee, and Nixson (1984). Krugman (1986a,b) reviews the issues raised here along the same lines. Stewart (1984) takes an opposing view, claiming that the literature on trade and industrial organization provides new arguments for protection.

[17]The excessive-entry problem was first noted by Eastman and Stykolt (1960) for Canada. A well-known example of excessive entry is that of the automobile industry in developing countries.

in its specification of the foreign trade sector since it assumes symmetric product differentiation on the import and export sides.

Before examining the welfare costs of rationing, it is instructive to indicate how the standard costs of protection are modified by the presence of economies of scale and by the departure of pricing from average cost implied by noncompetitive behavior. Let the consumer side be represented by a single consumer with expenditure function E $(P_1, \ldots P_n, W)$, where W is a welfare index. Let sectoral production take place in identical firms $(X_i = n_i x_i)$, with unit cost functions $c_i(w, X_i)$, where w is the vector of factor prices, x_i is firm output, and $\theta_i = c_i[\delta(c_i x_i)/\delta\, x_i]$ is the ratio of average to marginal cost (i.e., the inverse of the scale elasticity). Then, as shown by Rodrick (1987), the wlefare effect of a change in trade policy can be decomposed into the following expression:

$$E_w dW = \sum_i (P_i - \pi_i^*)dC_i - \sum_i (c_i - \pi_i^*)dX_i + n_i c_i \left[1 - \frac{1}{\theta_i}\right] dX_i, \qquad (7)$$
$$\quad\;\;(1)\qquad\qquad\quad(2)\qquad\qquad(3)$$

where P_i is the domestic price and π_i^* is the corresponding world price.

Equation (7) decomposes the welfare change into three terms. The first term is the familiar consumption effect, which states that consumption should be expanded wherever marginal value exceeds marginal cost. The second term departs from the traditional costs of production and states that output should contract whenever unit domestic price exceeds world price because of the effects of imperfect competition. The degree of monopoly is represented by the extent to which $P_i > c_i$. Whenever $P_i > c_i$, the correct policy goal should be to expand output to remove monopoly power. In the end, the second term states that output should contract if $c_i > \pi_i^*$. Thus, for a given degree of oligopoly, the production costs of protection are less than under perfect competition. Finally the third term states that, for a fixed number of firms, production should be expanded whenever there are unexploited economies of scale.

Table 3 reports the welfare cost calculations obtained from a stylized three-sector model (primary, manufacturing, and nontraded activities) in which only the manufacturing sector is characterized by economies of scale and noncompetitive behavior. The welfare costs of rationing are obtained by starting from a free trade situation and then rationing consumer and intermediate imports, first by 20 percent and then by 50 percent (that is, reducing the volume of imports by 20 percent and 50 percent). Rationing is modeled as in the previous example, but there is no rent seeking.

Table 3: A Comparison of the Welfare Costs of Rationing Under Alternative Market Structures

	Rationing rate (M_0/M_1)	Variant 1:[a] CRTS	Variant 2: IRTS	Variant 3: IRTS; Firm Entry, No Collusive Behavior	Variant 4: No Entry, IRTS; Collusive Behavior
Welfare Costs:[b]					
(% of base national	0.8	1.7	6.1	6.5	6.5
income)	0.5	13.0	16.0	16.7	17.1
Profits (P/AC-1)	0.8	0	0	0	6.6
	0.5	0	0	0	25.7
Number of firms	0.8	1	1	107	1
(ratio to base)	0.5	1	1	124	1

Source: Condon and de Melo (1986, Table 5).

Notes: The calibration of the parameters determining the extent of economies of scale in manufacturing are from Cox and Harris (1984). Profits and firm entry are calibrated so as to replicate the change in price–cost margin and number of firms in the Chilean manufacturing sector after trade liberalization (see de Melo and Urata 1986). In the base simulation, foreign trade is 40 percent of GDP with 5% in consumer goods.

CRTS = Constant returns to scale.

IRTS = Increasing returns to scale.

[a]Variants are discussed in the text.

[b]Computed as the Hicksian compensation variation from the Linear Expenditure System (LES) indirect utility function representing consumer expenditure choice.

Variant 1 gives the cost of rationing with constant returns to scale. Variant 2 gives the cost of rationing when there are economies of scale in manufacturing. Variant 3 captures the excessive-entry phenomenon observed in the manufacturing sector of developing countries by incorporating the assumption that the number of firms in a sector is an increasing function of the rents in manufacturing arising from rationing. Variant 4 captures the fact that rationing provides opportunities for manufacturing firms to depart from average cost pricing in the domestic market. Rents accruing from rationing are used as the proxy for entry barriers (since imports are restricted), and the departure of unit domestic price, p^d, from unit average cost is an increasing function of the per unit rents conferred by rationing.[18] Table 3 shows that the

---

[18]Calibratrion procedures are described in Table 3.

welfare costs of excessive entry or collusive pricing can be well over 10 percent of national income. These calculations are only suggestive because more disaggregation would be desirable to better distinguish sectors that are subject to economies of scale and noncompetitive behavior. Nonetheless, the calculations are suggestive of the potential costs of quantitative restrictions when interaction is specified between the trade regime and the industrial organization structure.

4.3 Optimal Trade Policy in the Presence of a Government Revenue Constraint

With limited administrative capacity to raise taxes, developing countries often have a government revenue constraint. Some sectors in the economy (e.g., agriculture) or some categories of demand (e.g., consumer goods) cannot be taxed, and rampant tax evasion for certain kinds of taxes, such as income taxes, forces the government to rely on trade and producer taxes as its main source of revenue. The policy issue then is how to raise a given amount of revenue at minimum distortionary cost, given the presence of nonremovable distortionary taxes and the further constraint that trade taxes are needed to raise revenue.[19]

Dahl, Devarajan, and van Wijnbergen (1986) and Mitra (1986) derive conditions for optimal tariff structures for raising government revenue at minimum distortionary cost under the conditions specified above. They derive a number of rules analogous to those derived in the optimal taxation literature. For example, they show that in the absence of cross-price effects, the optimal tariff rate is inversely proportional to the import demand elasticity. Furthermore, when there is cross-elasticity of import demand with respect to the export price, account must be taken of the fact that a tariff acts as an export tax, so that imports that are the closest substitutes for export goods should be taxed the least. These theoretical results imply that the recommendation for uniform nominal (and hence effective) tariffs advocated in the literature on trade liberalization should be revised to take into account the inherent weaknesses of developing country fiscal systems.

Dahl, Devarajan, and van Wijnbergen (1986) incorporate these features in a CGE model similar to the one outlined in Table 1 except that their eight-sector model for Cameroon also includes uniform less-

---

[19]As shown by Dixit (1985), in the absence of nondistortionary taxes, consumer taxes should be used to raise revenue.

Table 4: Actual and Optimal Revenue-Constrained Tariff Rates

	Indirect Production Tax Rate	Actual Tariff Rates	Optimal Revenue-Constrained Rates	
			Ind. Taxes > 0	Ind. Tax = 0
Food Crops	0.02	0.22	−0.06	0.09
Cash Crops	0.19	0.23	−0.28	0.13
Forestry	0.06	0.28	9.31[a]	0.12
Food Processing	0.04	0.35	0.27	0.11
Consumer Goods	0.10	0.38	0.28	0.11
Intermediate Goods	0.03	0.18	0.22	0.15
Services	0.00	0.00	0.04	0.19
Uniform Rate			0.16	0.15

Source: Dahl, Devarajan, van Wijnbergen (1986, Table 2).

Note: The simulations assume zero export taxes.

[a]The 931 percent tariff on forestry is due to the fact that imports in this sector are minuscule.

than-infinitely-elastic demand for sectoral exports ($\zeta = -20$). Table 4 presents the results from a model run using optimal tariffs to raise the same level of government revenues as was collected in Cameroon during 1979. Although similar in structure to the prevailing tariff structure (in column 1), the optimal tariff structures (in columns 2 and 3) are far from uniform. Note in particular the results in column 2 for the case in which the prevailing set of indirect taxes is kept at its existing level: the optimal tariff for food and cash crops is negative. Because virtually all output of the cash crop sector is exported, the production tax acts like an export tax. The negative optimal tariff dampens the effect of this tax, which is excessive given the high elasticity of demand for exports.

Of course, as with the other empirical exercises, greater disaggregation would help in the design of trade reform packages, but the essential message of this analysis would remain, namely that uniform protection is not optimal in the presence of fiscal (or other) constraints.

5. APPLICATIONS TO INTERNAL-EXTERNAL BALANCE AND GROWTH

I now turn to issues of internal–external balance in a growing economy. Table 5 augments the skeleton model presented in Table 1 to deal with a growing economy. Neither the process of growth nor the

Table 5: A One-Sector Small-Country Growth Model

(1)	$Q = F(M,D^d)$	Import Aggregation Function
(2)	$X = G(E,D^s)$	Export Transformtion Function
(3)[a]	$X = A(t)\,H\,(L_t;\ \bar{K}_t)$	Production Function
(4)[a]	$\underline{W} = P^x\,\delta H/\delta L_t$	Labor Demand
(5)[a]	$K_t = K_{t-1} + I_{t-1}$	Capital Accumulation
(6)[a]	$L_t = L_{t-1}(1+g_L)$	Labor Accumulation
(7)	$p^m = e\bar{\pi}^m$	Import Price
(8)	$p^c = e\bar{\pi}^c$	Export Price
(9)	$p^q = f_1(p^m,p^d)$	Consumer Price
(10)	$p^x = g_1(p^c,p^d$	Producer Price
(11)[a]	$p^I = k_1(p^m,p^d)$	Investment Price
(12)	$\dfrac{M}{D^d} = f_2(p^m,p^d)$	Import Demand
(13)[a]	$\dfrac{I^d}{I^m} = k_2(p^m,p^d)$	Investment Demand
(14)	$\dfrac{E}{D^s} = g_2\,(p^c,p^d)$	Export Supply
(15)	$\bar{\pi}^m I^m + \bar{\pi}^m M - \bar{\pi}^c E = \bar{B}$	Balance of Trade constraint
(16)[a]	$Y = p^x X + e\bar{B}$	Income
(17)[b]	$p^q Q = p^d D^d + P^m M + P^I I$	Absorption
(18)[a]	$p^q C = P^x X^d - S(\underline{Y})$	Consumtion
(19)[a]	$P^I I = S(Y) + e\bar{B}$	Investment

[a]Equation was not included in Table 1.

[b]This absorption equation replaces equation 10 in Table 1.

A time subscript is included only for the factor accumulation and factor demand equations to save on notation. $A(t)$ is the exogenous rate of disembodied technical progress, and g_L is the exogenous rate of growth of the labor force. Also to save on notation, it is assumed that domestic and foreign investment goods have the same prices as their final demand counterparts.

interaction between growth and policy is addressed in the model, except in a very limited sense, as discussed further on.

The distinguishing feature of the augmented model is the presence of a more complete production side, which includes factor allocation and factor accumulation equations. Here the capital stock is assumed to be immobile across sectors, whereas labor migrates to equate the value of marginal products across sectors. This specification is common in many applications where limited within-period factor mobility is handled in this manner. For example, rural and urban labor are often distinguished, with limited rural–urban migration in response to wage differences. The model also assumes that all of the resource gap $e\bar{B}$ is invested and that investment includes a domestic and an imported

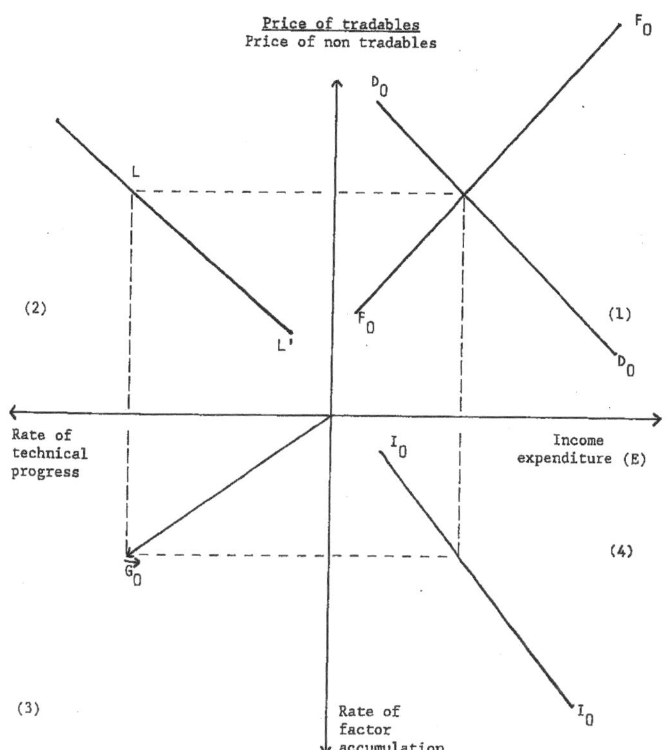

Figure 3. Internal-external balance and growth.

component; therefore, any change in the equilibrium value of relative prices will have an impact on the amount of real investment forthcoming from a given savings effort.

To see more clearly how external–internal balance and factor accumulation interact to determine growth in this augmented model, consider the simple case with no differences in factor intensities across sectors but with greater technical progress in tradables than in nontradables (perhaps because of learning by doing). The contribution of technical progress to growth can be related to the structure of production, as shown by line LL' in Figure 3, quadrant 2. Internal–external balance for a given level of exogenous capital inflow ($\bar{B}_0$) is given by F_0F_0 in quadrant 1. The internal balance is downward sloping because, starting from an equilibrium position, expenditure exceeds income and the relative price of home-produced goods must rise to eliminate excess demand. By the same line of reasoning, the external balance schedule is upward sloping because the excess demand for tradables caused by an excess of expenditure over income requires an increase in the relative price of tradables (i.e., a depreciation of the real exchange rate) to eliminate the excess demand.[20] The model is closed in quadrant 4 by the assumption that a constant fraction of income is invested. The rate of growth is measured by the vector $\overrightarrow{OG_0}$ in quadrant 3. The model closure assumes that investment is determined by savings. As Dewatripont and Michel (1987) show, other closures are possible. One such example is the application reported in section 5.2.

The apparatus can be used to examine the effects on growth resulting from a change in the terms of trade, in the exogenous level of foreign transfers (a shift in the F_0F_0 schedule), or in the relative price of investment goods (a shift in the investment schedule I_0I_0). The simulations reported below involve applications that amount to either exogenous or policy-induced shifts in the schedules of quadrants 1 and 4. A typical exercise with a model of the type described in Table 5 starts with a validation of the model from historical data; the modeler chooses a plausible set of parameters and elasticities that produce a base run scenario close to the observed aggregate and sectoral growth rates. No formal econometric procedures are used to test the validity of the chosen model structure.[21] After satisfactory validation, counterfactual simulations are undertaken to examine the likely evolution of equilibrium values of relative prices and medium-term adjustments under different policy scenarios.

5.1 Causes of Turkey's Foreign Exchange Crisis in 1977

The modern theory of exchange rate determination recognizes that the equilibrium exchange rate is determined by a combination of monetary and real factors, going beyond differences in inflation rates of the economy and the rest of the world as advocated by the strictest version of purchasing power parity (PPP). To show this, we assume following Dornbusch (1976), that there is goods arbitrage, so that for tradables

---

[20]The slopes of the internal and external balance schedules reflect the assumption of gross substitutability between tradables and nontradables in demand. See, for example, Dornbusch (1980, chapter 6) for a fuller derivation.

[21]CGE models have been described so far as though relative prices were always assumed to adjust to clear markets. In practice, all models rely on a mix of price and quantity clearing assumptions in product and factor markets.

$$P_T = e\, P_T^*, \tag{8}$$

where subscript T refers to a tradable sector. Let P denote the price level and θ, θ^* the equilibrium relative price of traded goods, so that

$$P_T = \theta P; \quad P_T^* = \theta^* P^*, \tag{9}$$

where the asterisk denotes a variable for the rest of the world. In introducing the monetary sector, assume monetary equilibrium where L and L^* denote domestic and foreign demand for real balances

$$M/P = L(\ ); \quad M^*/P^* = L^*(\ ). \tag{10}$$

By combining equations (8)–(10) and taking log differentials, it can be shown that the determinants of the equilibrium exchange rate combine real and monetary aspects according to the following:

$$\hat{e} = (\hat{M} - \hat{M}^*) + (\hat{L} - \hat{L}^*) + (\hat{\theta} - \hat{\theta}^*), \tag{11}$$

where the first term captures the effect of different rates of monetary growth and the second and third terms capture the effects of real money demand and changes in relative price structure, respectively. In the exercise to be described, the monetary sector is treated rudimentarily, as it is assumed that the monetary authorities effectively control the domestic price level, which is set exogenously in the model. The analysis concentrates on decomposing the role of the various real factors that contribute to the equilibrium value of the real exchange rate.[22]

Following a successful devaluation in 1970, accompanied by a set of macro policies to correct imbalances, Turkey achieved a \$0.5 billion current account surplus in 1973. By 1978, however, Turkey had a deficit of \$3 billion, or nine percent of GDP. With its foreign reserves exhausted, Turkey only postponed the crisis by massive foreign borrowing. As is often the case in such circumstances, Turkey did not devalue sufficiently during the post-1973 period to correct for the differential in inflation so the real exchange rate was back to its pre-1970 value by 1976 (the differential in inflation between Turkey and OECD countries was eight to 10 percentage points while devaluations averaged five percent).

What were the causes of this foreign exchange crisis? More specif-

---

[22]More precisely, values for $\hat{P}$ and $\hat{P}_T^*$ are taken exogenously where $\hat{P}$ is Turkey's inflation rate and $\hat{P}_T^*$ is the OECD's rate of inflation. The exercise thus assumes equilibrium in the money market, with the government having full control over the money supply. In terms of the results in Table 6, the effects of differential inflation are captured by the first two terms on the right side of equation 11.

490   J. de Melo

Table 6: Factors Contributing to the Change in the Equilibrium Real Exchange Rate in Turkey in 1977 (%)

Differential Inflation	37
Oil Price Rise	21
Higher OECD Export Prices	11
Lower Remittances	18
Other Factors (residual)	13
	100

Source: Dervis and Robinson (1982, Table 5)

ically, what were the contributions of the inflation differential, the rise in oil prices of 1973, the massive foreign borrowing in 1976 and 1977, the rise in the index of OECD-country export prices, and the unexpected fall in worker remittances (which had been financing half of imports by 1973)? Dervis and Robinson (1982) used a 15-sector CGE model similar to the one described in Table 3 to assess the relative impact of each of these effects.[23]

After validating their model over the period 1973–77, Dervis and Robinson performed a set of cumulative experiments (adding one new factor after another). They sought to determine what the equilibrium real exchange rate would have been had inflation in Turkey equaled OECD inflation, had external borrowing been equal to GDP growth, had there been no rise in oil prices or OECD-country export prices beyond the rise in world prices in Turkey's export markets, and had workers' remittances grown at the same rate as GDP.

The results of the contribution of each element of this counter-factual history are reported in Table 6. The exercise shows that differential inflation was only a small part of the story. Of course the model structure was imposed rather than tested, and there was certainly interaction among some of the variables that were treated exogenously or feedback from endogenous to exogenous variables. But it remains that in a world in which economies are exposed to multiple exogenous shocks, partial equilibrium analysis or simplistic calculations are likely to be misleading.

---

[23]The numerical results are from Dervis and Robinson (1982), who summarize the full structure of the model and recent Turkish economic history.

5.2. Absorption Under Disequilibrium Exchange Rates: Chile, 1979–1981

A second application dealing with internal–external balance illustrates the difficulty in modeling agents' expectations and incorporates a practical—albeit not entirely satisfactory—way of overcoming the difficulty. The model follows the recent contributions to the analysis of the current account that emphasize the role of expectations and the usefulness of modeling the adjustments in savings and investment behavior (see, for example, Sachs 1981; Svensson and Razin 1983). Studies of the implications for the current account of a temporary disequilibrium in exchange rates have also focused on savings and investment behavior (see, for example, Dornbusch 1985). In great part, these contributions have been inspired by country experiences, some involving unsustainable current account deficits fostered by protracted periods of low real exchange rates resulting from "excessive" capital inflows. These contributions drawn from intertemporal models show that expenditure smoothing takes place to offset temporary changes in purchasing power.

A vivid example of this smoothing effect is the consumption increase that followed the 25 percent appreciation of the real exchange rate in Chile between 1979 and 1981. The problem was exacerbated by the pegging of the peso to the dollar in mid-1979 while the minimum wage was fully indexed to past inflation and domestic inflation exceeded world inflation. Capital inflows averaged five percent of GDP between 1977 and 1979 and jumped to an average of nine percent during 1979–81, with the current account deficit reaching 15 percent of GDP in 1981. With no public sector deficit, this increase in capital inflows (induced by the fixed exchange rate coupled with unregulated domestic interest rates) resulted in an expenditure boom. During 1977–79 private consumption grew at a rate that was one percent less than the growth in GDP, but during 1979–81 it grew at an average annual rate of 11 percent, while GDP was growing at the rate of seven percent. The crisis emerged when the capital inflows necessary to finance the deficit ceased.

Condon, Corbo, and de Melo (1986) use a simulation model similar to the one presented in Table 3 to ask what might have happened had Chile not followed the fixed exchange rate policy that led to the surge in capital inflows described above. The mechanism leading to capital inflows is not modeled explicitly; rather, the exercise consists of asking what would have been the absorption and real exchange rate trajectories had capital inflows been lower during 1979–81. Their model departs from the one described in Table 3 to allow for a rising real consumption wage that reflects the wage indexation mechanism then prevailing in

Chile. In addition, private savings behavior is modified to incorporate expenditure smoothing by considering savings as a positive function of real income and a negative function of (exogenously determined) real capital inflows, $e\bar{B}$, with coefficients drawn from econometric estimation with Chilean data.[24]

This model closure applied to a five-sector model for Chile during 1977–81 fits well with the adjustment patterns in production, relative price, and expenditure that occurred in Chile during that period. The authors then use the model to ask how the Chilean economy would have adjusted to lower capital inflows during 1979–81, taking as given the wage indexation mechanism prevailing in Chile. The model is used to trace the combination of real exchange rate depreciation and increases in unemployment caused by real wage rigidity. By taking into account different factor intensities across sectors, the model also captures the effect on GDP of compositional shifts in demand induced by expenditure switching and by expenditure reductions.

Figure 4 shows the predicted tradeoffs from lower capital inflows during 1979–81 with reductions in capital inflows of 10 percent, 25 percent, and 50 percent (E–1, E–2, E–3) during both 1980 and 1981. Elasticities of the real exchange rate with respect to the equilibrium expenditure levels range between -0.6 and -0.8 for 1980, and -0.5 and -0.7 for 1981. In addition, the model shows that much of the adjustment to lower capital inflows could have been achieved by expenditure switching, in spite of the institutionally determined real wage rigidity, because of the positive effect on employment of compositional shifts in demand. Again, these counterfactual simulations are only indicative, but as in the preceding exercises, the addition of structure (in the labor market and in the composition of demand) to an otherwise standard dependent-economy model, provides an enhanced tool for policy analysis.

5.3. Simulating Alternative Development Strategies[25]

The last application is a long-run exercise using CGE simulation analysis to distill the growth implications of alternative foreign trade

---

[24]The counterfactual is well visualized in terms of Figure 3 since, during 1977–81, total factor productivity growth patterns induced by the trade reforms corresponded to those shown in Figure 3. Reducing capital inflows (with a fixed real wage) results in an upward shift of the F_0F_0 schedule, an inward shift of the D_0D_0 schedule, and a leftward kink in the I_0I_0 schedule for expenditure levels below the initial equilibrium.

[25]The specifics of the model are reported in Chenery et al. (1986).

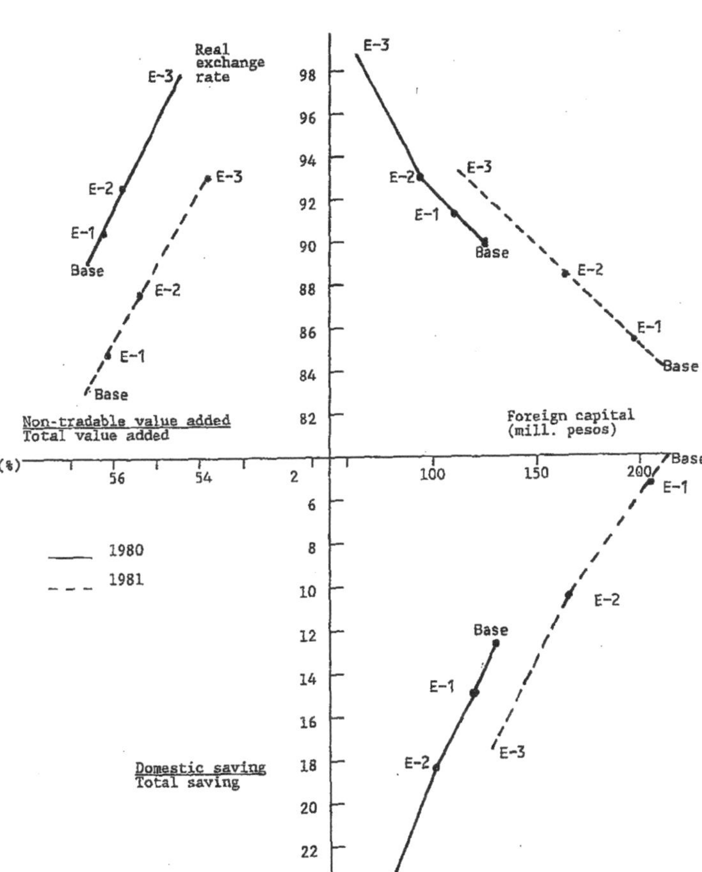

Figure 4. Model predicted tradeoffs from lower capital inflows.

strategies. The results of the exercise, consisting of 20-year simulation
runs, are sensitive to the linkages built into the (mostly) exogenous
determinants of growth. Again, the model structure corresponds quite
closely to that described in Table 3 and Figure 3. Three new features,
however, deserve attention. First, exogenous trends have to be imposed
on the parameters describing the response of imports and exports to
relative price shifts (See table 7); otherwise, the model is not capable
of reproducing the development patterns that result from the selection

of alternative trade strategies (described below).[26] This is a serious shortcoming of the functional forms advocated in section 2, at least for long-run applications, and suggests that the foreign trade specifications adopted in applied general equilibrium analysis need improvement. Second, as indicated in Table 7, the inward-looking (IS) strategy is modeled by assuming that macroeconomic adjustment comes entirely on the import side via rationing of imports when there is excess demand for imports, rather than by a real exchange rate devaluation, which would also relieve the foreign exchange constraint by stimulating exports. The implication of this adjustment mechanism is that a premium on imports develops in the IS strategy, resulting in the strong bias against exporting in the trade regime shown in Table 7. The third new feature is the significant effect on the relative price of capital goods. This effect, equivalent to an upward shift of the $I_0 I_0$ schedule in Figure 3, results in less real investment from a given savings rate. Thus, policy choices affect growth via the bias in the trade regime and the cost of capital goods.

Table 7 reports the results of simulations designed to provide rough bounds on the extent to which the choice of development strategy is likely to affect growth. Although not reported here, the model was also used to examine the marginal productivity of foreign aid under different trade strategies. Based upon extensive sensitivity analysis to key parameters in the model, the exercise suggests that up to one percent of average annual growth (over a 20-year period) can be explained by the mechanisms incorporated in the model to describe alternative trade strategies.

6. APPLICATIONS TO INTERTEMPORAL ISSUES[27]

Although the role of forward-looking decisions was alluded to in the application to Chile for absorption under a disequilibrium real exchange rate (see section 5.2), all the models considered so far have been intertemporally decomposable. That is, the solution values for endogenous variables in period t depended only on the solution values of endogenous variables in previous periods. For the problems examined, this assumption was adequate, although the example for Chile

---

[26]This led the authors to update exogenously the trade share parameters in the import demand and export supply equations. Analytical expressions are provided by de Melo and Robinson (1985) that show such a procedure is necessary to diminish the degree of independence of the domestic price system from foreign prices.

[27]See Devarajan (1987), who covers intertemporal issues in greater depth.

TRADE ANALYSIS IN DEVELOPING COUNTRIES   495

Table 7: Representative Trade Strategies and Macroeconomic Indicators

Components	Import Substitution (IS)	Balanced (B)	Exort Promotion (EP)
Trade Policy/Trends			
Sectoral trends (i.e., exogenous variation in trade shares)	Low/falling	Constant	Rising
Macroeconomic policy instruments	Tariffs/import rationing[a]	Real echange rate adjustment[b]	Real exchange rate adjustment[b]
Productivity growth	Low/intermediate	Intermediate	High
Macroeconomic Indicators[c]			
Incremental capital-output ratio, terminal, year	3.26	3.02	2.95
Export growth rate	7.9	10.3	14.1
Import growth rate	4.5	6.4	9.3
GDP growth rate	5.7	6.2	6.5
Bias of the trade regime in terminal year[d,e]	200	100	95
Relative price of capital goods in terminal year[d]	120	105	95

Source: Chenery et al. (1986, Chapter 4).

[a]Import rationing implies that ex ante excess demand for foreign exchange is eliminated by endogenously determining the premium on foreign exchange.

[b]No rationing of imorts.

[c]Level of cumulative capital inflow is $1,900 million in 1964 dollars.

[d]Index = 100 in initial year.

[e]The bias of the trade regime is defined as $B = EER_M/EER_x$, where EER is the effective exchange rate (inclusive of tariffs, subsidies, and premiums on foreign exchange), and subscripts refer to imports and exports respectively.

points out that such an assumption is not tenable when the economy is in strong macroeconomic disequilibrium. The assumption of intertemporally decomposable growth paths is also inadequate for inherently forward-looking policy issues such as the optimal extraction rate for an exhaustible resource, or decisions about external borrowing strategy. In such circumstances a forward-looking intertemporal model is the appropriate framework.

This section briefly reviews the equilibrium properties of the two-sector tradable/nontradable dependent-economy model in a two-period framework, and then illustrates results from an application to optimal borrowing strategies for Thailand derived from a five-sector, seven-period model. The intertemporal aspects of the two-period model carry over to the multiperiod model.

Following Glick and Kharas (1986), consider a small open economy that can borrow any amount, D, in the first period at a fixed world interest rate, r. The country's welfare maximization problem consists of choosing consumption and investment levels for traded and non-traded goods that maximize discounted utility:

$$W = \sum_{t=1}^{2} C_t^{1-b}/[(1-b)(1+\delta)^{t-1}], \tag{12}$$

where $C_t \equiv C_{Tt}^a C_{Nt}^{1-a}$; $b>0$, $0<a<1$.

Subject to the intertemporal budget constraint

$$C_{T1} + p_1 C_{N1} + I + (C_{T2} + p_2 C_{N2})/(1+r) \tag{13}$$
$$- Q_{T1} - p_1 Q_{N1} - (Q_{T2} + p_2 Q_{T2})/(1+r) = 0,$$

where $P_t \equiv \dfrac{P_{Nt}}{P_{Tt}}$ is the relative price of nontraded goods or the inverse of the real exchange rate. Subscripts T and N distinguish tradables from nontradables, and Q refers to output. Note that investment, I, is all in tradables. In this formulation, δ is the pure rate of time preference, and the utility function is assumed to be intertemporally separable, with a constant intertemporal elasticity of substitution $1/b$, as in the simulation exercise below. As $b \rightarrow \infty$, greater smoothing of consumption is desired. Let $\rho_2 \equiv \delta Q_{T2}/\delta k_2 + p_2 \, \delta Q_{N2}/\delta k_2$ represent the return to capital in period 2. Then the first-order conditions to the maximization problem are:

$$(1 + \delta)(C_2/C_1)^b = (1 + r)(p_2/p_1)^{1-a} = \rho_2(p_2/p_1)^{1-a}. \tag{14}$$

This familiar condition from intertemporal models states that the real social discount rate in equilibrium is set equal to the real cost of foreign borrowing and the real rate of return on capital, all rates and costs being expressed in terms of the aggregate consumption bundle. The real cost of foreign borrowing and the real return to capital depend on two factors: (1) the cost (return) in terms of traded goods, and (2) changes in the aggregate consumer price index over time. Thus changes in relative prices over time are an important determinant of intertemporal substitution.

With no investment, given supply functions, borrowing (lending) will occur for $\delta > r$ ($\delta < r$) because there is a fall (rise) in consumption of tradables and nontradables in the second period. With positive investment—the case relevant to the CGE applications—Glick and Kharas show that borrowing not only affects production and consumption through relative prices, but also through factor intensities in each sector. Only for the case of $b=0$ (that is, when consumption is perfectly substitutable across time periods) are relative price movements independent of investment. Otherwise, the relative factor intensity in production will influence the outcome. Thus, while it is possible to isolate the factors that determine whether borrowing or lending will take place, it is difficult to derive analytical results, even in the simple case in which all investment goods are produced in the tradable sector. Also, the outcome is quite sensitive to the value assumed by the intertemporal elasticity of substitution, a parameter for which it is difficult to give an intuitively satisfying value.[28]

6.1. Optimal Foreign Borrowing Strategies: A Case Study of Thailand, 1985–1992

As the recent debt repayment difficulties of developing countries have shown, it is critical that external borrowing be conducted within a consistent macroeconomic policy environment, lest capital flight occur when credibility wanes. The debt crisis of the early 1980s also showed creditors the fragility of sovereign borrowing and debtors the realities of credit rationing. For example, the empirical evidence shows that lenders' willingness to lend is positively related to the borrower's fiscal position (Kharas and Shishido 1984). This suggests that borrowers will find it appropriate to achieve high fiscal savings in order to reduce the probability of being cut off from credit.

Kharas and Shishido (1986) use a model similar to the one described above to examine optimal borrowing strategies for Thailand over the period 1985–92. In addition to the intertemporal equilibrium conditions described in equation 14, their multisectoral model captures some aspects of uncertainty insofar as the expected terminal year fiscal surplus is a parameter that depends on the weight attached by the borrower to the possibility of losing creditworthiness. To ensure smooth in-

---

[28]Glick and Kharas (1986) also study the properties of the model when the economy no longer faces a perfectly elastic supply of foreign funds. They do so by incorporating an endogenous lending constraint whereby lenders limit the credit extended below the worth of the "collateral" given by the penalties of default proxied by a given loss of tradable goods production. In particular they show that the presence of a lending constraint provides a case for subsidizing tradable goods production.

vestment and borrowing paths, the model postulates an absorptive capacity constraint on investments in each period so that there is a diminishing marginal efficiency of investment within any period. Likewise, the more the country borrows relative to outstanding loans in each period, the more costly the loans become, reflecting the assumption that the borrower must shift to new lenders and more expensive financial instruments. Finally, as in the applications discussed in section 5, technology is putty-clay with new investment being directed to sectors with the highest profit rates and capital being removable from a sector only through depreciation.[29] The model is solved numerically by resorting to the turnpike theorem (Burmeister and Dobell 1970), so that a balanced growth state is reached by the end of the simulation, with all real values growing at the same rate in the post-terminal period.[30] This implies that the model evaluates the penalty for the outstanding debt and the premium for the existing capital stocks in the terminal year by calculating the impact of these on future consumption.[31]

After calibrating the model on historical data for the period 1975–85, Kharas and Shishido use it to determine optimal borrowing and investment strategies after a policy change when the economy is subjected to external or internal shocks. As in the other simulation exercises, the model determines the equilibrium real exchange rate and other relative prices and quantities; but in these dynamic simulations, the model also determines the borrowing and investment paths that maximize welfare subject to the constraints discussed above.

As an example, consider the implications of a tariff reform that would reduce the average tariff on manufactured imports from 16 percent to 10 percent. The dashed and solid line simulation paths in

---

[29]This implies that profit rates are not equalized within period, although there is a tendency toward equalization within period. Note that these adjustment costs on investment and borrowing and partial capital mobility are necessary in dynamic multi-period models to avoid extreme behavior (e.g., all investment or borrowing in one period).

[30]The transversality condition requiring that the net present value of post-terminal debt service payments be equal to the debt outstanding is incorporated in the model by insuring that the balanced-growth increase in the stock of debt is less than the interest rate. The additional constraint (mentioned above) requiring that a predetermined fiscal surplus be maintained in the post-terminal year, ensures that funds will always be available along the transition path during the simulation period.

[31]The specification of the foreign trade sector is akin to that discussed earlier, although exports from the primary sector are modeled exogenously and manufactures exports have a less than infinitely elastic demand. Imports have either a zero elasticity of substitution (i.e., are noncompetitive) or a positive elasticity, as in Tables 1 and 2.

TRADE ANALYSIS IN DEVELOPING COUNTRIES   499

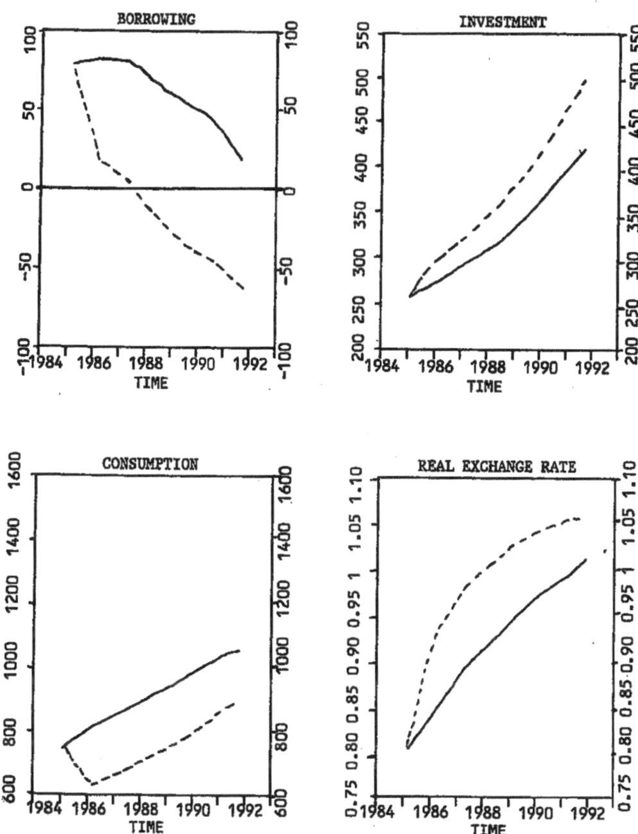

Figure 5. Impacts of a lower tariff rate in Thailand: experiment and base-run simulations (real figures in 1975 billion bahts). Solid lines, base run; dashed lines, simulation. Source: Kharas and Shishido (1986, Figure 22).

Figure 5 show the simulated values under the experiment and the base simulation.[32] In the absence of a lending constraint, lower tariffs would generate positive effects on growth because of reduced distortions. With a lending constraint, however, the situation is quite different.

---

[32]Similar paths arise from an increase in the world interest rate or lower world demand for Thai exports. The relative position of the base and simulation paths is reversed for simulations that raise the rate of technical progress or the domestic supply of natural gas.

500   J. de Melo

The loss in public revenue (24 percent) increases the risk of debt repudiation, so lenders reduce credit lines and borrowing is only 18 percent of what would be available without the policy change. As shown in Figure 5, consumption must fall and the real exchange rate depreciate so as to achieve the required reduction in the current account deficit forced by the borrowing constraint. Investment, however, rises because of the improved returns in the economy associated with the real exchange rate depreciation.

The results presented here are of course even more tentative than those drawn from the simulations reported in section 5 because they rely on parameters whose values are even harder to obtain, such as the intensity of the lending constraint or the intertemporal elasticity of substitution. Nevertheless, the simulations point out the need to take macroeconomic considerations into account while undertaking microeconomic reforms, and the advisability of not postponing adjustment in the face of an adverse change in external or internal conditions.

7. CONCLUSIONS

This paper has surveyed recent contributions in foreign trade-focused applied general equilibrium analysis for developing countries. The structure and properties of the models commonly employed have been analyzed and numerical exercises have been reviewed to show how simulation analyses can provide a useful tool for policy analysis. The strengths and weaknesses of the models were clear from their theoretical properties and implementation methods. It is evident that there is room for much improvement, especially in the area of parameter estimation and in the development of more formal methods of testing model validity. Nonetheless, it is hoped that the variety of applications illustrated in this paper show the range of foreign trade policy issues in developing countries for which CGE models can be used.

REFERENCES

Ahmed, S., and Grais, W., (1987) Reforming Egypt's Pricing System. Industrial Bank of Kuwait Papers Series No. 25. Kuwait.

Ahmed, S., Bhattacharya, A., Grais, W., and Pleskovic, B., (1985) Macroeconomic Effects of Efficiency Pricing in the Public Sector in Egypt. World Bank Staff Working Paper No. 726. Washington, D.C.: World Bank.

Armington, P. (1969) A Theory of Demand for Products Distinguished by Place of Production, *IMF Staff Papers* 16:159–78.

Aspe, P., and Giavazzi, F. (1982) The Short-Run Behavior of Prices and Output in the Exportables Sector: The Case of German Machinery, *Journal of International Economics* 12:83–93.

Bhagwati, J. (1965) On the Equivalence of Tariffs and Quotas. In *Trade, Growth and the Balance of Payments* (R. Baldwin, Ed.). Amsterdam: North Holland.

Bhagwati, J., and Srinivasan, T. N. (1980) Revenue-Seeking: A Generalization of the Theory of Tariffs, *Journal of Political Economy* 88:1069–1087.

Burmeister, E., and Dobell, M. (1970) *Mathematical Theories of Economic Growth*. New York: MacMillan.

Chenery, H. (1975) The Structuralist Approach to Development Policy, *American Economic Review* (May) 65:310–316.

Chenery, H., Lewis, J., Melo, J. de, and Robinson, S. (1986) Alternative Routes to Development. In *Industralization and Growth: A Comparative Analysis* (H. Chenery, S. Robinson, M. Syrquin, eds.). London: Oxford University Press.

Clarete, R., and Whalley, J., (1986) Equilibrium in the Presence of Foreign Exchange Premia. The University of Western Ontario. Processed.

Condon, T., Corbo, V., and Melo, J. de, (1986) Capital Inflows, the Current Account, and the Real Exchange Rate: Tradeoffs for Chile: 1979–81. Washington, D.C.: World Bank. Processed.

Condon, T., and Melo, J. de (1986) Industrial Organization Implications of QR Trade Regimes: Evidence and Welfare Costs. Washington, D.C.: World Bank.

Cox, D., and Harris, R. (1985) Trade Liberalization and Industrial Organization: Some Estimates for Canada, *Journal of Political Economy* 93 (1):115–45.

Dahl, H., Devarajan, S., and van Wijnbergen, S. (1986) Revenue Neutral Tariff Reform: Theory and an Application to Cameroon. Washington, D.C.: World Bank. Processed.

Decaluwe, B., and Martens, A. (1986) CGE Modelling and Developing Economies: A Concise Empirical Survey of 56 Applications to 24 Countries. C.R.D.E. Study No. 1686. Montreal: University of Montreal.

Dervis, K., and Robinson, S. (1982) A General Equilibrium Analysis of the Causes of a Foreign Exchange Crisis: The Case of Turkey, *Welwirtschaftliches Archiv* 118:259–279.

Dervis, K., Melo J. de, and Robinson, S. (1982) *General Equilibrium Models for Development Policy*. Cambridge: Cambridge University Press.

Devarajan, S., Lewis J., and Robinson, S. (1986) A Bibliography of Computable General Equilibrium (CGE) Models for Developing Countries. HIID Discussion Paper No. 224. Cambridge, Massachusetts: Harvard University.

Devarajan, S. (1988) Natural Resources and Taxation in Computable General Equilibrium Models of Developing Countries, *Journal of Policy Modeling* 10:505–528.

Dewatripont, M., and Michel, G. (1987) On Closure Rules, Homogeneity and Dynamics in Applied General Equilibrium Models, *Journal of Development Economics* 26(1):65–76.

Dixit, A. (1985) Tax Policies in Open Economies. In *Handbook of Public Economics* (A. Auerbach and M. Feldstein, eds.). Amsterdam: North Holland.

Dixon, P. B. (1977) Economies of Scale, Commodity Disaggregation and the Costs of Protection, *Australian Economic Papers* 17(30):63–80.

Dixon, P. B., Parmenter, B., Ryland, G., and Sutton, J. (1982) *Orani: A General Equilibrium Model of the Australian Economy, Vol. 2*. Canberra: Government Publishing Service.

Dornbusch, R. (1976) The Theory of Flexible Exchange Rate Regimes and Macroeconomic Policy, *Scandinavian Journal of Economics*, 78(2):255–275.

Dornbusch, R. (1980) *Open Economy Macroeconomics*. New York: Basic Books.

Dornbusch, R. (1985) External Debt, Budget Deficits, and Disequilibrium Exchange Rates. In *International Debt and the Developing Countries* (G. Smith and J. Cuddington, eds.). Washington, D.C.: World Bank.

Dornbusch, R. (1987) Exchange Rates and Prices, *American Economic Review* 77(1):93–106.

Drud, A., Grais, W., and Pyatt, G. (1986) Macroeconomic Modelling Based on Social Accounting Principles, *Journal of Policy Modeling* 8(1):25–36.

Eastman, H., and Stykolt, S. (1960) A Model for the Study of Protected Oligopolies, *Economic Journal* 70:336–347.

Edwards, S., and Ng, F. (1985) Trends in Real Exchange Rate Behavior in Selected Developing Countries. CPD Discussion Paper No. 1985–16. Washington, D.C.: World Bank.

Feinberg, R. A. (1986a) The Effects of Foreign Exchange Movements on U.S. Domestic Prices, Pennsylvania State University, Mimeo.

Feinberg, R. A. (1986b) The Interaction of Market Power and Exchange Rate Effects on German Domestic Prices, *Journal of Industrial Economics* 35:61–70.

Glick, R., and Kharas, H. (1986) Optimal Foreign Borrowing and Investment with an Endogenous Lending Constraint. Washington, D.C.: World Bank. Processed.

Grais, W., Melo, J. de, and Urata, S. (1986) A General Equilibrium Estimation of the Effects of Reductions in Tariffs and Quantitative Restrictions in Turkey in 1978. In *General Equilibrium Trade Policy Modelling* (T. N. Srinivasan, J. Whalley, eds.). Cambridge, Massachusetts: M.I.T. Press.

Harris, R. (1985) Applied General Equilibrium Analyses of Small Open Economies with Scale Economies and Imperfect Competition, *American Economic Review* 74(5):1017–1032.

Hudson, E., and Jorgenson, D. (1978) Energy Prices and the U.S. Economy, 1972–76, *Natural Resources Journal* 18(4):877–897.

Isard, P. (1977) How Far Can We Push the Law of One Price? *American Economic Review* 67:942–948.

Kharas, H., and Shishido, H. (1984) Credit Rationing in International Capital Markets: An Empirical Analysis. CPD Discussion Paper No. 1984–24. Washington, D.C.: World Bank.

Kharas, H., and Shishido, H. (1986). Foreign Borrowing Strategies for an Uncertain Future: A Cast Study of Thailand. Washington, D.C.: World Bank. Processed.

Kirkpatrick, C., Lee, N., and Nixon, F. (1984) *Industrial Structure and Policy in Less Developed Countries*. London: George Allen & Unwin.

Krueger, A. (1974) The Political Economy of the Rent-Seeking Society, *American Economic Review* 64(3):291–303.

Krugman, P. (1986a) Industrial Organization and International Trade, NBER Working Paper No. 1957, Cambridge, Mass.

Krugman, P. (1986b) New Trade Policies for Small Economies. Cambridge Mass.: MIT. Mimeo.

Krugman, P. (1986c) Pricing to Market When the Exchange Rate Changes. Cambridge, Mass.: MIT. Mimeo.

Lewis, Jeffrey, and Urata, S. (1984) Anatomy of a Balance of Payments Crisis: Application of a Computable General Equilibrium Model to Turkey, 1978–80, *Economic Modelling* 1(3):281–303.

Melo, J. de, and Urata, S. (1986) The Influence of Increased Foreign Competition on Industrial Concentration and Profitability, *International Journal of Industrial Organization* 4: 287–304.

Melo, J. de, and Robinson, S. (1985) Product Differentiation and Trade Dependence of the Domestic Price System in Computable General Equilibrium Trade Models. In *International Trade and Exchange Rates in the Late Eighties* (T. Peeters, et al., eds.) Amsterdam: North Holland.

Melo, J. de, and Robinson, S. (1989) *Product Differentiation and The Treatment of Foreign Trade in Computable General Equilibrium Models of Small Economies. Journal of International Economics* (forthcoming).

Mitra, P. (1986) Revenue Raising Tariffs: Theory and an Application to India. Washington, D.C.: World Bank. Processed.

Neary, P., and Roberts, K. (1980) The Theory of Household Behavior Under Rationing, *European Economic Review* 13:25–42.

TRADE ANALYSIS IN DEVELOPING COUNTRIES 503

Powell, A., and Gruen, F. (1967) The Constant Elasticity of Transformation Production Frontier and Linear Supply System. *International Economic Review* 8:315–328.

Pyatt, G. (1988) A SAM Approach to Modeling, *Journal of Policy Modeling* 10:327–352.

Robinson, S. (in press) Multisector Models of Developing Countries: A Survey. In *Handbook of Development Economics* (H. Chenery and T. N. Srinivasan, eds.). Amsterdam: North-Holland.

Robinson, S., and Tyson, L. (1985) Foreign Trade, Resource Allocation, and Structural Adjustment in Yugoslavia: 1976–80, *Journal of Comparative Economics* 9:46–70.

Rodrik, D. (1987) Imperfect Competition, Scale Economies, and Trade Policy in Developing Countries. Processed, Cambridge, Massachusetts: Harvard University.

Sachs, J. D. (1981) The Current Account and Macroeconomic Adjustment in the 1970s, *Brookings Papers on Economic Activity* 1:201–268.

Shoven, J., and Whalley, J. (1984) Applied General Equilibrium Models of Taxation and International Trade, *Journal of Economic Literature* 22:1007–1051.

Stewart, F. (1984) Recent Theories of International Trade: Some Implications for the South. In *Monopolistic Competition and International Trade* (H. Kiezkowski, ed.) Oxford: Clarendon Press.

Svensson, L., and Razin, A. (1983) The Terms-of-Trade, Spending and the Current Account: The Harberger–Laursen–Metzler Effect, *Journal of Political Economy* 91(1):97–125.

Taylor, L., and Black, S. (1974) Practical General Equilibrium Estimation of Resource Pulls under Trade Liberalization, *Journal of International Economics* 4(1):37–58.

Part II:

Archetype Economies

11 *Alternative Routes to Development*

HOLLIS CHENERY

JEFFREY LEWIS

JAIME DE MELO

SHERMAN ROBINSON

UP TO NOW, our analysis has focused on real activity in the economy and its implications for aggregate growth, factor accumulation, resource allocation, productivity growth, and changes in the structure of production and of demand. The role of market mechanisms and of relative prices in determining resource allocation and structural change has been left in the background. Yet in mixed economies, the policy instruments that are designed to promote development work through markets and prices. In this chapter, therefore, we explicitly consider how market mechanisms and relative prices affect industrialization under different development strategies.

Similarly, the models we have used up to now to provide the framework for the analysis have focused on real variables and neglected the role of prices. In this chapter, we turn to the Walrasian model, in which market-clearing prices achieve equilibrium in a set of interdependent commodity and factor markets. Specifically, we use a computable general equilibrium (CGE) model that simulates the operation of a market economy and into which price incentive policies such as taxes, subsidies, and tariffs are explicitly incorporated. With this framework, we can sort out some of the main causal mechanisms that operate through changes in relative prices and that determine the effects of different policy choices.

Our approach is to use a CGE model of a single country as a simulation laboratory for doing controlled experiments designed to explore different development strategies. Chapter 3 used a model of several representative or archetypal economies that was based entirely on comparative data. In this chapter, we start instead with data for a particular country, Korea, in 1963. At that time, Korea had just completed a period of growth based primarily on import substitution and was poised for a major shift in development strategy. In many ways, its economic structure at that time was typical of those of other semi-industrial countries setting out on a path of rapid industrialization. Where Korea differs from the average, we have adjusted the data to obtain a more typical economy. We are interested in

311

creating a stylized version of Korea for the purpose of comparative analysis, not in analyzing the strategic choices available to Korea in 1963.[1]

The first section defines three development strategies that differ mainly in their trade policies and that span the range of strategies actually followed in semi-industrial countries. We also consider how differences in the external environment—such as the nature of export markets and access to foreign capital—can affect the success of a given strategy choice. The second section describes the theoretical structure of the dynamic CGE model, and the third section analyzes the macroeconomic features of some model experiments designed to isolate the chief mechanisms at work. In the fourth section, we provide a more detailed analysis of the experimental results at the sectoral level, focusing on the role of changes in commodity and factor prices and in the exchange rate.

Three Development Strategies

We have seen in earlier chapters that even in those economies in which manufactured exports burgeoned following the shift to an outward-oriented development strategy, rapid industrialization led to increasing demands for imports of intermediate and capital goods. Only late in the process did the industrial sector become a net contributor of foreign exchange. In an industrializing economy, the balance of payments pressure arising from increases in import demand can be met in three ways: by import substitution, by export expansion, or by increased foreign borrowing. Either the demand for imports must be limited or the supply of foreign exchange must be increased. As shown in chapter 6, different trade strategies can be classified according to the relative importance they give to each of these components.

We define three options that cover a spectrum wide enough to encompass the experience of most semi-industrial countries. These three options provide the starting point for the experiments with the CGE model. In all cases, we assume an economy that has achieved a significant industrial base and that is not rich in natural resources—and so cannot generate ample supplies of foreign exchange through primary exports.

The first option is the strategy of export expansion, which is illustrated in an extreme form by the experience of Korea after 1963. Starting from a situation in which production for the domestic market had been strongly favored, Korea implemented a strategy that called for, first, reduced protection to imports; second, real devaluation to provide incentives to shift resources toward the tradable sectors; and third, elimination of incentives with a bias against exporting. Among the economies that have pursued such a strategy for a shorter or longer time, the most successful—in addition to Korea—include Malaysia, Singapore, and Taiwan.

---

1. For an analysis of the Korean case, see Kim and Roemer (1979). Chapters 4, 6, and 7 provide comparative data that include Korea.

Common features of their experience are export expansion well in excess of GNP growth, substantial reduction of the bias in incentives against exports, and sufficient foreign capital inflow to permit a sustained period of trade liberalization.

The second option is the strategy of import substitution, the elements of which are also taken from the experience of countries that have followed it with some success—Mexico and Turkey in our sample. Its three essential characteristics are a limitation on imports through both tariff protection and foreign exchange rationing; maintenance of an overvalued real exchange rate, which exacerbates the bias in incentives against exporting; and a relatively low foreign capital inflow, the result primarily of creditworthiness constraints arising from the low level of exports.

These two options represent extreme cases. In terms of policy choice, they are mutually exclusive. The protectionist policies supporting the import substitution strategy necessarily generate a bias against sales abroad and in favor of the domestic market; this applies to nontradables as well as tradables. Slower export growth also leads to less foreign borrowing, and this leads to still more limitations on imports.

Between the two extremes of export expansion and import substitution, a third option, a balanced strategy, combines elements of both. This alternative calls for more equal adjustments in the three components and a phasing of capital inflows. Import demand is limited through exchange rate policy rather than through tariff protection and foreign exchange rationing. The net effect is less bias against exporting and hence more exports than in the import substitution strategy. Since removing the bias against exports generally takes time, the strategy leads to more foreign borrowing in the early periods to finance more imports and so requires less devaluation of the real exchange rate. The components of the strategy include a reduction in import growth as a result of devaluation, but less than in the second option; an increase in exports, but less than in the first option; and higher foreign capital inflows in the early period. For countries with access to foreign capital, this strategy is less demanding than either the first option, which calls for a rapid shift of resources toward exports, or the second option, which calls for severe constraints on imports. In the sample, Israel is the best example of a country pursuing such a strategy.[2]

A Dynamic Computable General Equilibrium Model

The computable general equilibrium model presented in this section provides a framework for making systematic comparisons among the

2. Although the choice among these three options is primarily a domestic policy matter, external factors may impinge on a country's ability to pursue a given strategy successfully. For example, export performance is responsive to economic conditions and policies in the developed countries, and access to foreign borrowing is also affected by world economic conditions.

three strategies. Given our emphasis on alternative trade strategies, the model focuses on the markets for tradable commodities and on the incentives facing domestic producers and demanders of imports. Moreover, since our concern is with the effect of alternative development strategies on growth and structural change in the long run, the model is simulated for a twenty-year period (in five four-year intervals).[3] The long-run CGE model incorporates the market mechanisms through which domestic policy choices affect incentives, and it endogenizes the supply and demand reactions of domestic economic actors to such policies. Because the model is for a single economy, external conditions are reflected in exogenous variables.

In the development literature, CGE models trace their lineage back to the multisector input-output models widely applied to problems of planning in developing countries in the 1960s.[4] While firmly based on the foundation of Walrasian general equilibrium theory, CGE models can also be seen as a logical culmination of a trend in the literature on planning models to add more and more substitutability and nonlinearity to the basic input-output model.[5] The models tend to be highly nonlinear—to have neoclassical production and expenditure functions—and to incorporate a variety of substitution possibilities in production, demand, and trade.

CGE models applied to developed countries have generally stayed relatively close to the Walrasian paradigm.[6] In applications to developing countries, however, most researchers have introduced certain structuralist features into CGE models to capture the stylized facts characterizing these countries. Our model is very much in this tradition; it starts from a family of models developed by Dervis, de Melo, and Robinson to explore questions of foreign trade policy in semi-industrial countries characterized by many structural rigidities.[7] The model is presented in three stages. First, we outline the model structure, distinguishing between the static part, during which an equilibrium is achieved, and the dynamic part, which updates exogenous variables and parameters. A description of markets, agents in

---

3. The model is not designed to explore the short-run problems of making a transition to a new development strategy. Such issues of "structural adjustment"—in the terminology of the World Bank—are better addressed with an annual model designed to track the adjustment process in more detail.

4. The model of the Norwegian economy developed by Johansen (1960) was the first empirical implementation of a general equilibrium model in a developed country.

5. There are also theoretical similarities between CGE models that simulate a multisector market equilibrium and planning models, either linear or nonlinear, that specify an explicit objective function within the framework of a programming model. See Ginsburgh and Robinson (1984) for a discussion of the relationship.

6. For a survey of CGE models focusing on issues of tax policy and international trade in developed countries, see Shoven and Whalley (1984).

7. See Dervis, de Melo, and Robinson (1982) for a detailed discussion of the structure and theoretical properties of CGE models in general and of models applied to problems of foreign trade in particular. See also Robinson (1986).

the markets, and functional forms governing agents' behavior follows. Second, we outline the adjustment mechanisms that operate under each of the three development strategies defined above. Third, we describe the dynamic processes that drive the model forward in time.

Structure of the Model

The dynamic model consists of two parts. First, there is a static CGE model which solves for a one-year equilibrium. In this model, a set of markets for factors, commodities, and foreign exchange is assumed to clear subject to a variety of structural rigidities and to choices of exogenous variables, including policy parameters. Given these constraints, the static equilibrium represents an optimum for producers and consumers. Second, intertemporal linkage equations update exogenous variables and parameters that are dependent on policy choices and specify cumulative dynamic processes such as factor accumulation and productivity growth. The intertemporal equations provide all exogenous variables needed for the next period (four years later) by the CGE model, which is then solved for a new equilibrium. The model is thus solved forward in a dynamically recursive fashion, with each static solution depending only on current and past variables. The model does not incorporate any behavioral role for future expectations, and in its present form it cannot be used to explore issues of dynamic optimality except through sensitivity analysis.

Table 11-1 schematically organizes the main features of the model around blocks of equations and equilibrium conditions. The first two columns describe the overall structure of the within-period CGE model, while the third column summarizes the cumulative processes incorporated into the dynamic part. The equilibrium conditions in the CGE model include a supply-demand balance in three different types of market: labor, commodities, and foreign exchange. A fourth macroeconomic equilibrium condition is a balance between investment and savings—the macro "closure" of the model. A detailed description of the mathematical equations of the CGE model, supplementing the briefer discussion here, will be found in appendix A to this chapter.

The CGE model simulates the working of a market economy. In each period, it solves for wages, prices, and an exchange rate (or import premium rate) that clear the markets for labor, commodities, and foreign exchange. The model is Walrasian in that only relative prices matter. The numeraire against which all relative prices are measured is defined as an index of domestic prices.[8] The model also satisfies Walras's law so that, by construction, there cannot be a situation of aggregate excess demand or supply. Thus the model cannot address macro issues such as the role of

---

8. This choice is especially important in interpreting the role of the exchange rate, which will be discussed in more detail below.

Table 11-1. *Schematic Outline of the Static and Dynamic* CGE *Models*

| Economic relations | Static model | | Dynamic model: cumulative processes |
	Principal relations	Structural features	
Factor markets			
Labor	Labor demand equations	Segmented rural-urban labor markets	Labor force growth
Capital	Marginal product equations	Fixed sectoral capital stocks	Capital stock growth
Product markets			
Production	Production functions	—	Productivity growth
Demand	Expenditure functions	—	Composition changes
Foreign trade			
Exports	Export supply functions	Segmented domestic and export markets	World market trends
Imports	Trade aggregation functions	Imperfect substitutability	Induced import substitution
Trade balance	Exchange rate or premium rate	Foreign exchange rationing, exogenous inflow	Sequence of capital inflows
Macroeconomic balance			
Savings-investment	Domestic savings rates	—	Trends in savings rates
External capital	Endogenous foreign capital inflows	Fixed exchange rate	—

— Not applicable.

inflation or Keynesian unemployment. Given its long-run focus, it is appropriate to ignore such cyclical effects.[9]

Except for the structuralist features listed in table 11-1, the model is very neoclassical in spirit. Sectoral production is given by mixed two-level constant elasticity of substitution (CES) and linear functions. Intermediate inputs are required according to fixed input-output coefficients, aggregate labor and capital are combined to create value added according to a CES function, aggregate labor is a CES aggregation of labor of different types,

9. There are CGE models that have been designed to explore issues of inflation and unemployment, with some strain to the Walrasian paradigm. See J. D. Lewis (1986) for such a model and for a discussion of the modeling issues raised.

and the aggregate capital used in each sector is a linear aggregation of capital goods from different sectors. Sectors are assumed to maximize profits, and labor demand functions come from the first order conditions equating the wage with the marginal revenue product of labor of each category.

The labor market is segmented, with four distinct categories of labor: agricultural, unskilled, skilled (in the industrial sector), and service-oriented. Migration from the agricultural sector is specified exogenously over time; there is no mobility within periods. There is full employment of aggregate labor in each period, with the sectoral allocation of labor by different categories determined endogenously.[10] Sectoral capital stocks are fixed within periods; they change over time given aggregate growth of the capital stock and the sectoral allocation of investment. Investment in the industrial sectors is allocated endogenously to make sectoral rental rates approximately equal by the terminal year (although the rates differ across sectors in the intervening years).

Expenditure functions for demanders arise from Cobb-Douglas utility functions, which yield constant expenditure shares and unitary income elasticities of demand within periods. To capture the impact of Engel's law, exogenous trends are imposed on the expenditure shares dynamically. Thus, income elasticities all equal one within periods but differ from one over time. The model determines the flow of funds to all economic agents, including wage earners, recipients of capital income, and government (whose income consists of tax revenue).

The supply of exports by sector is a function of the ratio of the price in domestic currency of exports (determined by the world price, the exchange rate, and any subsidies) to the price of output sold in the domestic market. This treatment partially segments the export and domestic markets. Prices in the two markets are linked but need not be identical. Imports and domestic products are assumed to be imperfect substitutes—an assumption widely used in CGE models of trade. Imports and domestic goods are combined according to a CES trade aggregation function, with consumers demanding the resulting composite good.[11] The trade substitution elasticity determines the extent to which import shares adjust in response to changes in relative prices. For both exports and imports, the world price in dollars is assumed to be constant—the small country assumption.

Adjustment Mechanisms under Alternative Strategies

There are three mechanisms by which the CGE model can achieve equilibrium in the balance of trade under different assumptions about the

---

10. The model thus has no surplus labor or underemployment. It would be feasible to specify a model with surplus labor (and a fixed real wage). See de Melo and Robinson (1982), who explore the effect of trade policy on income distribution in such a model.

11. See Dervis, de Melo, and Robinson (1982) and de Melo and Robinson (1985) for a discussion of the implications of this treatment. Armington (1969) used this specification in

(Note continues on the following page.)

availability of foreign borrowing. These alternative mechanisms are used in different experiments depending on the issues being addressed. Two of them assume a fixed foreign capital inflow, reflected in an exogenous value for the balance of trade, so that adjustment depends primarily on relative price effects.

For the first mechanism, endogenous variation in the real exchange rate provides the equilibrating mechanism. The real exchange rate is defined as the relative price of tradables and nontradables. Since we use an index of domestic prices as numeraire, variations in the nominal exchange rate in the model directly affect the ratio of the price—in domestic currency—of imports and exports to the price of domestic sales and so represent a change in the real exchange rate. For example, a devaluation raises the domestic price of imports and exports relative to domestic sales and so encourages exports and import substitution. The model determines the equilibrium real exchange rate by manipulating the nominal rate relative to the fixed numeraire index of domestic prices.

For the second mechanism, import rationing provides the equilibrating mechanism. We assume that the rationing is efficient in that the marginal value of a dollar is the same across sectors: this is equivalent to assuming that import licenses can be sold in an open market.[12] In effect, a uniform import premium is imposed on top of any official tariffs; the premium rate is determined endogenously to equate import demand with the available aggregate supply, given exports and the exogenous foreign capital inflow. The result is the same as a devaluation applied only to imports, and the scheme yields a bias in incentives against exporting since it operates like a tariff.

For the third mechanism, we assume that the exchange rate is fixed and the balance of trade is endogenous, so that foreign capital inflow adjusts. Given the numeraire, this specification effectively fixes the real exchange rate. With a fixed relative price, the model achieves equilibrium through a quantity adjustment mechanism—in this case, through changes in foreign capital inflow. Because of the dual role of foreign capital inflow in permitting both increased investment and imports (as in two-gap models), external capital plays an important macroeconomic role as well.

The balance between savings and investment in the model is achieved by setting total investment equal to the sum of domestic and foreign savings.[13]

---

estimating import demand functions: the trade aggregation function is sometimes called an Armington function.

12. This treatment is a proxy for the wide range of second-best quantitative and licensing restrictions that are often imposed in developing, as well as developed, economies. For a discussion of modeling alternative rationing schemes, see Dervis, de Melo, and Robinson (1982).

13. This specification is termed neoclassical closure. Much of the debate on the appropriate macro closure revolves around issues of adjustments in the short to medium run in models that allow unemployment by, for example, assuming a fixed wage. Given our long-run focus and full-employment assumption, the neoclassical closure is an obvious choice. See Rattso (1982), Lysy (1983), and Robinson (1986) for surveys of the issues involved.

Domestic savings is modeled as a rising function of real GDP, so that a higher growth rate is associated with an increase in the domestic savings effort. The specification of foreign savings reflects empirical evidence that the propensity to save out of foreign capital inflows is less than one. In the CGE model, 40 percent of the inflow goes directly into savings. The remainder is funneled to capitalists, who in turn save a fraction; the remainder is consumed or taxed. The net effect is that the overall marginal savings rate from external resources is about 0.6, a value similar to that estimated by Chenery and Syrquin (1975).

Cumulative Dynamic Processes

The dynamic equations capture cumulative processes that drive the CGE model forward in time. These processes reflect three different types of forces: exogenous trends, policy choices, and past history incorporating solutions of the model for previous periods. The variables and parameters that are updated dynamically in the model can be classified into three categories:

- Updated by exogenous trends
    Aggregate labor force growth
    Sectoral total factor productivity growth
    Input-output coefficients
    Government consumption shares
    Private consumption shares
- Updated by policy choices
    Tariff rates
    Foreign capital inflows
    Exchange rate
- Updated by economic behavior
    Sectoral investment allocation
    Sectoral capital stocks
    Labor force allocation by category
    Sectoral export shares
    Sectoral import ratios

Variables updated by exogenous trends follow the same dynamic path in all experiments. The aggregate labor force is assumed to grow 3 percent annually. Total factor productivity growth rates are drawn from the results discussed in chapter 10. The other parameters—input-output coefficients and expenditure shares—are interpolated in each period between exogenously specified initial and terminal values.

Variables updated by policy choices are the chief policy instruments of the three trade strategies. While the CGE model includes a large number of policy instruments, the variations in these three define the three trade strategies. We vary different combinations of these instruments and solve others endogenously to meet certain targets.

Variables updated by economic behavior have values that are generated as part of the history of the model. The sectoral allocation of investment is assumed to adjust over time to equate rental rates in the industrial sectors by the terminal year.[14] Sectoral capital stocks in any year depend on investment allocation and the depreciation rate. Whereas aggregate growth of the labor force is exogenous, the composition by category is determined by a combination of two factors: exogenously specified migration of agricultural labor to one of the three categories of urban labor and migration among categories in response to changing real wage differentials. Over time, real wage differentials will induce an offsetting migration response.

Within a period, export supply shares and import demand shares respond to changes in relative prices. In some experiments, we also add a trend component to these shares. For exports, the assumption is that changes in world demand or increased market penetration lead to increased exports without any change in relative prices in the domestic market. With only supply behavior included in the model, such a specification is necessary to capture actual export behavior under the export expansion trade strategy.[15]

The dynamic specification of import demand also varies according to the trade strategy pursued. Under an import substitution strategy or a balanced strategy, it is assumed that the long-run trade substitution elasticity is higher than the short-run elasticity.[16] The effect is to allow for "successful" import substitution: the efficient ratio of imports to domestic supply for a given set of relative prices will gradually fall. Demanders can replace imports with domestic production more easily between periods than within periods and so avoid experiencing diminishing returns to further import substitution.

Macroeconomics of Alternative Strategies

In this section we describe the simulations of the three strategies in general terms and discuss their policy differences. All simulations begin from a common starting point in the base year, after which policy choices and the paths of exogenous variables differ. The purpose is to measure the effect of each strategy under different conditions, to illustrate the effects of various policy packages, and to examine the strains that emerge from the interactions among groups of policies.

---

14. In the base year, by construction, the economy is assumed to start from an initial solution with equal rental rates across the industrial sectors.

15. We chose not to include both supply and demand functions for exports because we did not wish to endogenize the effects of international terms of trade. Models with such behavior are described in Dervis, de Melo, and Robinson (1982).

16. There is a long-run envelope curve for each level of composite good (analogous to isoquants in production functions) with the short-run curves applicable to each period tangent to the long-run curve at a point.

Table 11-2. *Representative Trade Strategies*

Components	Import substitution (IS)	Balanced (B)	Export promotion (EP)
Trade policy			
Sectoral trends	Import reduction	Import reduction	Export penetration/ import liberalization
Main policy instruments	Tariffs/import rationing	Real exchange rate	Real exchange rate
Trade bias	Inward	Neutral	Outward
Trade shares	Low/falling	Constant	Rising
Borrowing policy	Limited by low exports	Maintain neutrality	Sustain trade liberalization
Indirect effects			
Productivity growth	Low/intermediate	Intermediate	High
Capital goods	High cost	World prices	World prices
Examples (1960s)[a]	*Turkey*	*Israel*	*Korea*
	Mexico	Thailand	*Taiwan*
	Philippines	Tunisia	Singapore
	Colombia	Greece	Malaysia
	Argentina		
	Brazil		

a. Examples are taken from chapter 4. Economies in italics are those analyzed in chapters 6 and 7.

The main features of each strategy are compared in table 11-2, and the influence of these factors on growth is summarized in table 11-3.[17] Each strategy is characterized by typical exogenous elements, the policy rules for maintaining external balance, and other policy choices.

A successful export promotion (EP) strategy is reflected in an average export growth of 14 percent annually.[18] Given the pattern and cumulative level of capital inflow, the real exchange rate varies to achieve external balance. Over a twenty-year period, this strategy results in substantial trade liberalization, shown by the rise in the share of imports in GDP from 14 to 24 percent. The capital inflow required to finance import requirements declines steadily from an initial level of 8 percent of GDP to less than 1 percent in the terminal year. GDP growth averages 6.5 percent, of which 1.7 percent is the result of assumed growth of total factor productivity.[19]

17. The numbers cited in table 11-3 and in the description of strategies are for a moderate level of foreign capital inflow for each strategy. The implications of different cumulative inflows are discussed more fully below.

18. Of this 14 percent, about 2.5 percent is attributable to market penetration and other effects not reflected in relative prices.

19. While this GDP growth is representative of the outward-oriented economies identified in table 4-4, it is less than the growth rate of 8 to 9 percent observed in Korea and Taiwan during the 1960s.

322   DEVELOPMENT STRATEGY

Table 11-3. *Macroeconomic Indicators of Alternative Trade Strategies*

Indicator	Import substitution (IS-2)	Balanced (B-2)	Export promotion (EP-2)
Average ratio of capital inflow to GDP	4.5	4.4	4.1
Ratio of imports to GDP, terminal period	10.7	18.1	24.0
Incremental capital-output ratio, terminal period	3.26	3.02	2.95
Export growth rate	7.9	10.3	14.1
Import growth rate	4.5	6.4	9.3
GDP growth rate	5.7	6.2	6.5

Note: In the abbreviations IS-2, B-2, and EP-2, the number "2" refers to one of four levels of capital inflow, defined in table 11-4 as 1,900 million 1964 dollars. All figures are percentages except for the incremental capital-output ratio.

The import substitution (IS) (inward-oriented) strategy maintains external balance by rationing foreign exchange through an import premium that provides incentives for import substitution. By increasing the cost of imported inputs, this strategy also makes exports less profitable. To maintain this policy over the twenty-year period, the import premium rises rapidly. This steadily increases the incentive bias in favor of import substitution over export promotion. The implications of this bias for relative prices are discussed more fully in the next section.

The macroeconomic effect of the IS strategy is a considerable closing of the economy. Imports fall from 14 percent of GDP to under 11 percent. The incremental capital-output ratio is 10 percent higher in the terminal year than it is in the EP strategy, and average GDP growth declines by nearly a percentage point.

The balanced (B) strategy contains elements of both the EP and IS strategies. The balanced strategy eliminates the inefficiency and price distortions associated with protection in the IS strategy without calling for the rapid growth of exports of the EP strategy. This is accomplished by combining successful import substitution with devaluation of the real exchange rate, which encourages exports and avoids the anti-export bias inherent in the IS strategy. Elimination of this bias increases export growth to 10 percent, which permits substantially more rapid growth in imports.[20] GDP growth over the period is 6.2 percent, only slightly less than growth with the EP strategy.

In summary, the balanced strategy combines efficient import substitution with moderate export expansion. In some of the countries pursuing

20. The balanced strategy simulations do not include the export growth through market penetration that is part of the export promotion simulations.

this strategy, access to more external borrowing and the resulting increase in investment can offset the gains from further specialization that occur in the export-led strategy. The choice between the two strategies then depends on the preferences of a country and the feasibility of implementing the necessary trade and borrowing policies.

In considering the three alternative strategies, it is important to emphasize that the sectoral rates of total factor productivity growth used in each strategy have been held constant. This assumption conflicts with the conclusions of chapters 2, 8, and 9, in which it was argued that the import restrictions, price distortions, and loss of specialization inherent in the aggressive pursuit of an import substitution strategy result in significantly lower rates of total factor productivity growth. We have assumed similar productivity growth to facilitate comparisons across strategies; however, we explore in other experiments how economic performance is affected by assuming lower factor productivity growth rates in the IS strategy.

Elements of Policy

To clarify the effects of the main elements of external policy—the trade bias, degree of openness, and capital inflow—it is useful to vary them separately while holding other aspects constant. This procedure is illustrated in table 11-4, which gives solutions for each strategy with the cumulative capital inflow held constant at four different levels. This set of simulations is used to identify the effects of individual policy changes when all else remains unchanged.

TRADE BIAS. The effect on growth of eliminating the trade bias (holding capital inflow constant) is shown in table 11-4 by comparing the balanced strategy (B) with the inward-oriented strategy (IS) in column 1. The import premium as an endogenous equilibrating variable is replaced by a flexible exchange rate, so that external balance is achieved both by increasing exports and by reducing imports in proportion to their respective elasticities. The exchange rate devaluation needed is only 35 percent instead of the 170 percent premium needed in IS. More than half the adjustment in the B strategy takes place through expanding exports.

This shift to a neutral trade policy raises GDP growth from 5.2 to 5.9 percent. In addition to the small static allocative gains from more efficient trade, the decline in the relative cost of investment goods leads to a significant rise in the real rate of investment and contributes to GDP growth.[21]

The marginal benefits of eliminating the trade bias decline as the capital inflow rises because the more plentiful supply of foreign exchange reduces the need for import substitution. Whereas the elimination of trade bias at

---

21. This phenomenon will be analyzed in more detail in the section below on prices, incentives, and structural change.

Table 11-4. *Trade Strategies, Capital Inflows, and Growth*

	Level of cumulative capital inflow (millions of 1964 dollars)			
Strategy	900 (1)	1,900 (2)	3,000 (3)	4,500 (4)
Import substitution (IS)				
GDP growth rate (percent)	5.2	5.7	6.2	—
Elasticity of imports to GDP	0.65	0.79	0.97	—
Ratio of imports to GDP, terminal period (percent)	9.4	10.7	13.4	—
Ratio of total debt to GDP, terminal period (percent)	0.31	0.54	0.78	—
Ratio of average capital inflow to average GDP (percent)	2.9	4.5	6.3	—
Balanced (B)				
GDP growth rate (percent)	5.9	6.2	—	6.6
Elasticity of imports to GDP	1.07	1.05	—	1.17
Ratio of imports to GDP, terminal period (percent)	17.6	18.1	—	17.7
Ratio of total debt to GDP, terminal period (percent)	0.27	0.50	—	1.10
Ratio of average capital inflow to average GDP (percent)	2.7	4.4	—	8.4
Export promotion (EP)				
GDP growth rate (percent)	6.3	6.5	—	6.9
Elasticity of imports to GDP	1.49	1.43	—	1.50
Ratio of imports to GDP, terminal period (percent)	23.9	24.0	—	24.0
Ratio of total debt to GDP, terminal period (percent)	0.26	0.47	—	1.02
Ratio of average capital inflow to average GDP (percent)	2.6	4.1	—	8.4

— Figures are not available because simulations with that cumulative capital inflow were not undertaken.

Note: Levels of capital inflow are identified by column numbers.

low levels of capital inflow (IS-1 versus B-1, where "1" refers to column 1 in table 11-4) increases GDP growth by 0.7 percentage points, doing so at moderate levels of inflow (IS-2 versus B-2) increases GDP growth by only 0.5 percentage points. With capital inflows as high as in B-4, the premium falls to zero, eliminating the bias between the IS and B strategies.

OPENNESS. An increase in exports and imports beyond the level specified by the balanced strategy leads to greater specialization and lower

ALTERNATIVE ROUTES TO DEVELOPMENT   *325*

resource costs for tradable goods as a whole. This result is the essence of trade liberalization (see chapter 6). The increase in export growth from 10 percent in B-2 to 14 percent in EP-2 leads to cumulative levels of both imports and exports that are 50 percent higher over twenty years.

The aggregate effect of this greater specialization is to increase the growth rate by 0.4 percentage points, which is about half the effect of eliminating the trade bias at low levels of capital inflow. Although the increase in openness (as measured by the ratio of imports to GDP) from B-1 to EP-1 is similar to the increase from IS-1 to B-1, the reduction in the resource cost for tradable goods is considerably less.

CAPITAL INFLOW. External resources perform two distinct functions in a development strategy: they add to the level of investment and they supply additional imports. In modeling the first function, we have assumed that 60 to 70 percent of the capital inflow represents a net addition to investment, in line with econometric estimates of this effect.[22]

On the trade side, capital inflows are not a perfect substitute for exports since they do not have the cumulative benefits of market penetration and eventually need to be repaid. In addition, slower export growth limits the amount of external borrowing that can be sustained over the long run.[23] Borrowing does alleviate the need to undertake types of import substitution or export subsidization that may prove inefficient once export performance improves. It also allows a lower real exchange rate in the early period of import substitution.

The examples in table 11-4 suggest that an increase in capital inflow may add half a percentage point to the long-run growth rate within the feasible limit of the debt-export ratio. This increased growth from higher borrowing capability adds to the direct benefits of shifting from an inward-oriented to an outward-oriented strategy.

Dynamic Growth Paths

We now turn from a consideration of the cumulative effects of alternative strategies to an examination of the dynamic aspects of growth. How do trade bias, openness, and capital inflows interact to determine the pattern of growth under each strategy? Table 11-5 and figures 11-1, 11-2, and 11-3 show the dynamic effect of changes in these policy components.

The effects of trade policy on the openness of the economy (as measured by the ratio of imports to GDP) and on the growth of GDP are shown in

22. The proportion varies somewhat depending on the level of real GDP since the domestic savings effort is a rising function of national income.

23. In the model simulations, we approximate the borrowing constraint by restricting cumulative foreign borrowing to four times the level of exports. Among major borrowers, this was approximately the ratio of Argentina, Mexico, and the Phillipines in 1983. It was exceeded by Brazil (5.3) and Turkey (4.5). In contrast, the outward-oriented countries (for example, Korea, Malaysia, Thailand, and Yugoslavia) had ratios ranging from 0.9 to 2.0.

Table 11-5. *Dynamics of Alternative Strategies*

Period or variable	Base Time 0[a]	Import substitution (IS-2)		Balanced (B-2)		Export promotion (EP-2)	
		Time 2	Time 5	Time 2	Time 5	Time 2	Time 5
Variable—internal aspects							
Percent of GDP							
Domestic savings	8.6	13.8	24.3	13.5	24.7	13.5	26.3
Foreign savings	5.1	3.5	1.9	4.2	2.3	4.4	0.6
Investment	13.7	17.3	26.2	17.7	26.9	17.9	26.9
Real investment	13.7	17.2	23.6	17.5	26.4	18.0	27.1
Growth rate[b]							
Primary output		3.5	2.9	3.3	2.9	3.5	3.2
Manufacturing output		7.4	9.1	8.9	11.6	9.1	11.5
GDP		5.6	6.4	5.7	7.3	6.0	7.9
Incremental capital-GDP ratio		2.83	3.26	2.78	3.02	2.65	2.95
Variable—external aspects							
Percent of GDP							
Import share	14.1	11.6	10.7	15.1	18.1	17.3	24.0
Export share	5.7	6.3	8.1	8.7	15.1	10.5	23.3
Trade balance	8.4	5.4	2.6	6.5	3.0	6.8	0.8
Growth rate[b]							
Imports		3.5	6.8	5.0	9.8	8.8	10.7
Exports		7.3	9.5	9.6	11.3	14.2	14.4
Exchange rate	1.00	1.00	1.00	1.19	1.22	1.00	1.00
Premium rate (percent)	0	35	118	0	0	0	0

Note: The cumulative trade balance in all runs is the same.

a. Each twenty-year simulation is composed of five four-year "times." Time 0 is the base year; time 2 is eight years later; time 5 is the last year in the twenty-year simulation.

b. Growth rates for time 2 are for the first eight years; growth rates for time 5 are for the last four years.

figure 11-1. In the import substitution strategy (IS-2), the initial import ratio of 14 percent falls to 11 percent by the fourth four-year period.[24] This decline in openness is accompanied by lower GDP growth. The balanced strategy (B-2) is characterized by a steady rise in the import ratio, which reaches 18 percent by the end of the twenty-year span; in the export promotion strategy (EP-2), the import ratio reaches 24 percent.

Figure 11-2 shows the changing import ratio, and the relative importance of exports and of capital inflows in financing imports, for the three trade strategies. The moderate capital inflow of EP-2 is sufficient to maintain a constant real exchange rate over the twenty years.[25] External capital

24. Recall that each twenty-year simulation with the model is composed of five four-year periods. Declines of this magnitude have been observed in Argentina, Brazil, Turkey, and some other countries following implementation of an inward-oriented policy. Such declines eventually end either because of the increasing cost of import substitution or because of a change in policy to offset the anti-export bias in selected sectors.

25. This result was achieved by construction to provide a base for comparisons. The model was run with a fixed exchange rate and endogenous capital inflow.

Figure 11-1. *Import Requirements under Alternative Strategies*   327

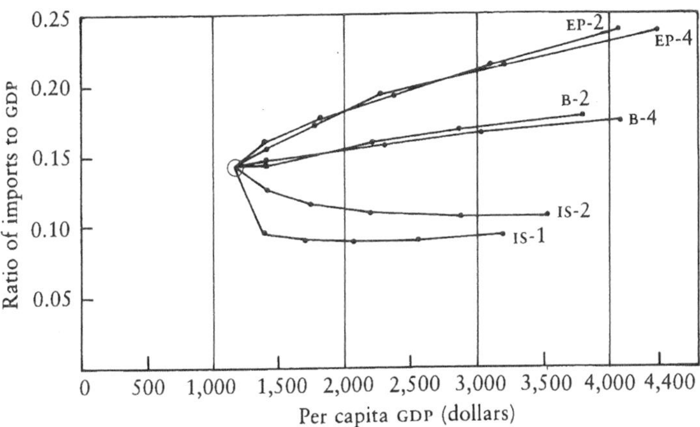

Figure 11-2. *Financing of Imports under Alternative Strategies*

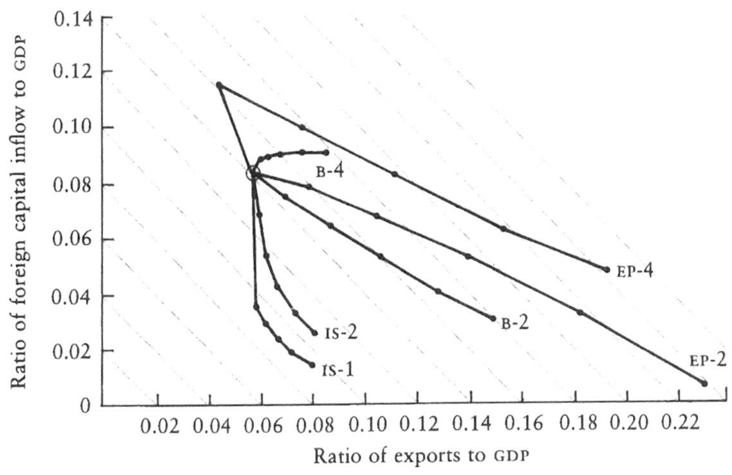

Note: See table 11-4 for key to simulations in figure. Dashed lines indicate ratios of investment to GDP.

Figure 11-3. *Financing of Investment under Alternative Strategies*

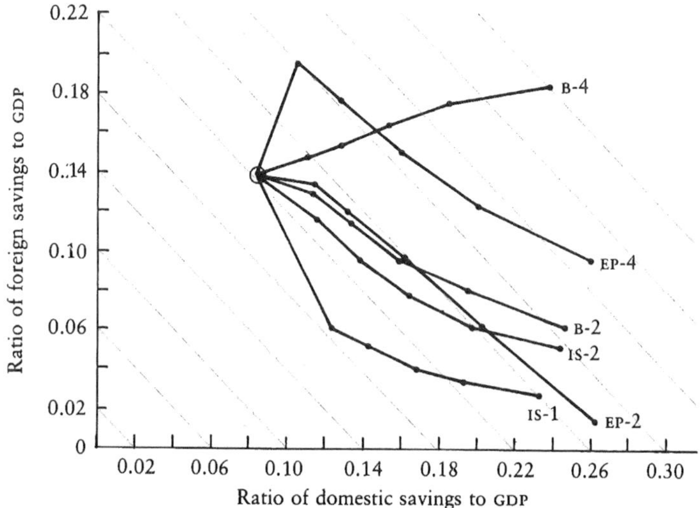

Note: See table 11-4 for key to simulations in figure. Dashed lines indicate ratios of investment to GDP.

is more concentrated in the earlier periods, during which it sustains higher imports and more rapid growth.[26] With the high capital inflow of EP-4, the importance of exports in GDP actually declines in the second period, as the large capital inflow results in a revaluation of the exchange rate and a corresponding decline in export growth.[27]

The moderate inflow of B-2 is also distributed in a manner which maintains a fairly constant real exchange rate from the second period onward.[28] It is characteristic of this strategy to reduce dependence on external capital more slowly. Although the opening up of the economy takes place more slowly than in EP-2, the corresponding loss in aggregate growth is relatively small. With the initial increase in external dependence associated with the higher inflow of EP-4, dependence is actually lower in B-4 than in EP-4 in the second period. The export growth of EP-4 rapidly

26. Analysis of the optimal distribution of capital inflows (Chenery and MacEwan 1966) shows that this pattern persists under a wide variety of assumptions.
27. This initial decline in the contribution of exports under an export promotion strategy is in keeping with the empirical conclusions of chapter 7.
28. Although the CGE model does not determine optimal aid patterns, experiments with alternative paths for capital inflow showed very little improvement over the pattern in B-2.

overtakes the balanced path, however, so that from the third period onward, the balanced path is more dependent on external inflows. After twenty years, dependence on external resources in B-4 remains unchanged.

Table 11-5 compares the economy's performance during time 2, after the major dislocations associated with policy changes have occurred, to that during time 5, which reflects the cumulative effects of twenty years of growth and structural change. From this table, which supplements figures 11-2 and 11-3, we can distinguish the common features of all strategies as well as the main differences among them:

- Acceleration of aggregate growth takes place in all strategies. GDP growth rates increase nearly 30 percent in the two neutral strategies (EP-2 and B-2). The increase is less with import substitution.
- Accelerated growth has two main sources: a rise in the domestic savings rate for a given income level and increasing openness of the economy. Whereas the first effect is similar in all strategies, the second occurs only in the two neutral strategies.
- Several factors act to offset accelerated growth. Higher domestic savings are partially offset by declining foreign savings (figure 11-3) and by rising incremental capital-output ratios. Greater openness is partly offset by rising import costs, particularly under the import substitution strategy.
- The combined effects of these factors is to widen the range of growth rates, since the slower growth that characterizes the inward-oriented strategy is more affected by the adverse factors than the other strategies. For the runs reported in table 11-4, GDP growth rates toward the end of the period range from less than 6 percent to more than 8 percent, three times the range observed at the beginning.

A summary of the effects on terminal GDP and terminal capital stocks of varying both the choice of strategy and the level of capital inflow is given in figure 11-4. The greater efficiency of the outward-oriented strategies is shown by the higher output-capital ratios of the EP and B curves compared with the IS curve. The relative slopes of these curves reveal the marginal productivity of external capital in each case. Since the inward-oriented strategy becomes increasingly inefficient at low import levels, the marginal productivity of external resources is correspondingly higher, as indicated by the steeper slope of the IS curve starting from the low inflow of IS-1.

Productivity Growth and Trade Strategies

Evidence from earlier chapters points to a strong positive association between the outward orientation of an economy and the growth rates of total factor productivity in the economy. In the characterizations of alternative strategies undertaken thus far, however, no distinction has been made in the sectoral rates of productivity growth according to the strategy pursued. If inward-oriented, import substitution strategies do

Figure 11-4. *Productivity of Capital under Alternative Strategies*

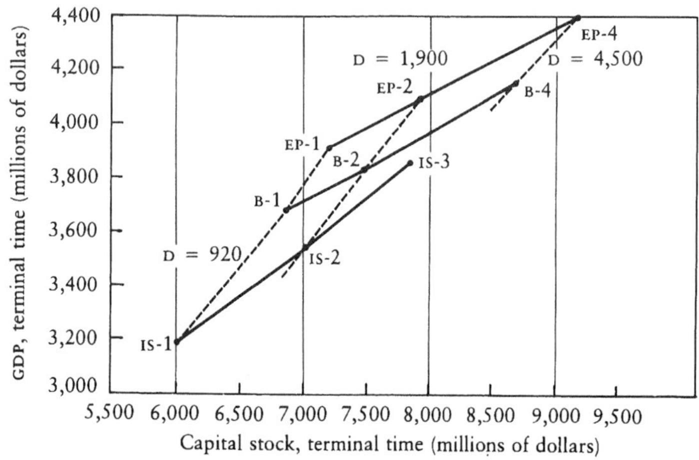

Note: See table 11-4 for key to simulations in figure. The points on the dashed lines indicate terminal-time GDP and capital stocks under different strategies for a given level of cumulative capital inflow (D). Lines further from the origin indicate higher capital inflow. The slopes of the solid lines indicate the marginal productivity of capital under each strategy.

imply lower rates of productivity growth, then the differences in growth performance by strategy will be larger than those described above.

To provide some indication of how economic performance is affected by the lower productivity growth associated with inward-oriented strategies, table 11-6 compares IS-1 with a scenario (IS-1L) in which sectoral rates of productivity growth are reduced by half. All other policies are the same, so that differences in performance are attributable to the lower productivity growth.

The reduction in TFP growth slows GDP growth by about 1 percent.[29] Nominal investment, which rises with GDP growth, remains lower as well. Incremental capital-output ratios are substantially higher in IS-1L, with even larger differentials observed in earlier periods. The slower growth does reduce import requirements, so that the premium rate required to achieve external balance is actually lower than in IS-1 (134 percent compared with 170 percent), although it remains quite high. The openness of the economy is largely unchanged, although export and import growth is slower since GDP growth has dropped. GDP growth accelerates less, in-

---

29. The TFP growth is assumed to apply only to value added. Changes in intermediate input coefficients are specified separately and are not altered in this experiment.

Table 11-6. *The Effect of Lower Productivity Growth*

Variable	Normal productivity (IS-1)	Low productivity (IS-1L)
Percentage of GDP, terminal year		
Domestic savings	23.2	19.5
Foreign savings	1.0	1.3
Investment	24.2	20.8
Real investment	20.9	18.0
Imports	9.4	9.7
Exports	7.9	7.8
Growth rate		
Primary output	3.0	2.0
Manufacturing output	8.8	7.5
GDP	5.2	4.0
Imports	7.3	6.0
Exports	3.4	2.4
Other values		
Incremental capital- GDP ratio	3.14	3.38
Premium rate (percent)	170	134

Note: For a description of these experiments, see the text. Further discussion of these results can be found in appendix B.

creasing from 3.5 percent in the first four-year period to 4.5 percent in the final four-year period. By incorporating the adverse impact of inward-oriented strategies on productivity growth, IS-1L is more representative of the experience of countries pursuing such strategies over a long time.

Although not reported here, additional experiments were conducted to analyze the sensitivity of the results to such main elasticity assumptions as trade substitution elasticities and capital-labor substitution elasticities.[30] The principal finding is that the IS strategy is more adversely affected than the others by reductions in the substitution elasticities: when both trade substitution and capital-labor elasticities are reduced by 50 percent, the GDP growth acceleration disappears completely. In the two neutral strategies (EP and B), acceleration is reduced but not eliminated. As substitution possibilities are reduced, the economy behaves more like the traditional two-gap model.

Prices, Incentives, and Structural Change

The macroeconomic policy choices discussed in the previous section work primarily through their influence on relative prices. Since sectoral

30. These sensitivity experiments are discussed in detail in appendix B to this chapter.

factor allocation responds to price incentives, we can trace the mechanisms through which policy changes affect structural change and hence the growth of the economy. After a discussion of the structural features of the economy and the sectoral sources of growth, we focus on the relative price movements underlying the alternative trade strategies. In particular, we examine the exchange rate regime and the bias it creates toward producing for export markets or for domestic import substitution, and the relative price of capital goods and its influence on real capital accumulation.

Structural Change and Development Strategy

Each strategy leads to a different economic structure in the terminal period, primarily because of the differing pattern of international trade. In particular, the degree of tradability of a sector—defined here in terms of the share of imports and exports in domestic supply—together with the responsiveness of output supply determine the distribution of adjustment across sectors. For example, more tradable sectors will benefit from a depreciation of the real exchange rate since both import substitution and export expansion will be stimulated.

The columns of table 11-7 contain measures of sectoral trade dependence and supply responsiveness. Sectors with low value added ratios are more adversely affected than others by a rise in the price of intermediate goods.[31] The ratio of imported intermediates to total intermediates measures the dependence of each producing sector on imported goods—the higher the ratio, the greater the impact of an increase in the prices of imported intermediate goods. Since capital stocks are fixed within a given period, the capital-labor ratio is a proxy for the supply elasticity of the sector. The trade substitution elasticity measures the substitutability of domestic for imported goods, which together with the composition of final demand will determine demand elasticities.[32]

To summarize the pattern of structural change implicit in the three strategies, we decompose the growth of output using the sources-of-growth methodology developed in chapter 5. Sectoral output growth is decomposed into four components: domestic demand expansion, export expansion, import substitution, and changes in input-output coefficients.[33]

Table 11-8 contains the sectoral growth decompositions for the full twenty-year period. (The three service sectors have been aggregated.) The

31. This is especially true in a model such as this one that assumes fixed input-output coefficients, since no price-responsive substitution between intermediates and value added is possible. Note, however, that there is substitution between imports and domestic goods within each cell of the input-output matrix.

32. The composition of final demand is important because different components of final demand have different elasticities of demand. Intermediate demand has a zero price elasticity, while consumption has an elasticity of one.

33. Since the changes in input-output coefficients are exogenous and identical in all strategies, the contribution of this component varies little, with aggregate differences explained by variations in the composition of output.

Table 11-7. *Sectoral Trade Dependence and Elasticities*

Sector	Gross output structure	Value added ratio	Imported inter-mediate ratio	Export supply ratio	Import supply ratio	Capital-labor ratio	Trade elastic-ity
Primary	32.6	73.7	10.8	2.4	10.9	0.22	1.10
Food processing	9.4	10.8	8.2	3.7	6.4	0.21	1.30
Consumer goods	16.0	33.6	6.3	3.0	3.4	0.63	1.10
Intermediate goods	7.9	33.6	12.7	4.7	38.7	0.68	0.60
Machinery	3.0	42.4	20.3	2.6	64.5	0.49	0.50
Construction	5.6	33.3	16.2	2.0	0.0	0.12	0.33
Social overhead	4.7	51.3	15.4	7.5	1.1	2.19	0.33
Services	20.8	69.6	5.5	3.9	1.1	1.02	0.33
Total	100.0	53.2	10.0	3.3	9.9	0.51	—

— Not applicable.
Note: Imported intermediate ratio = ratio of imported intermediates to total intermediates
Export supply ratio = ratio of exports to domestic output
Import supply ratio = ratio of imports to domestic supply
(domestic supply = domestic output − exports)
Trade elasticity = elasticity between imports and domestic goods
Source: World Bank data.

economywide results reveal the importance of trade strategy to the pattern of growth in the economy. With an export-led strategy, export expansion accounts for 27 percent of the overall expansion in output, while import substitution is negligible. In the more neutral balanced strategy, the contribution of export expansion falls to 13 percent, only half that of the export-led strategy but still substantially larger than the 6 percent contribution of import substitution. Finally, in the import substitution strategy, the import substitution contribution reaches 12 percent, surpassing the export contribution of 8 percent.

The sources of growth presented in table 11-8 are comparable with the empirical results presented in chapter 6 (see, for example, table 6-4). The typical strategies analyzed here avoid the extreme episodes observed for limited periods in certain economies; this reflects the focus on long-run structural change. The negligible contribution of import substitution to growth under the export promotion strategy differs from the experience of some outward-oriented economies and arises from the assumption of a degree of trade liberalization as part of the strategy.

Effects of the Trade Incentive Bias

One direct impact of alternative development policies is reflected in the incentives to domestic producers to sell products in domestic rather than foreign markets. The policies that influence these incentives include sectoral policy instruments such as tariffs and subsidies as well as macroeconomic variables such as the real exchange rate.

The upper graph of figure 11-5 shows the incentive to substitute for imports, represented by the ratio of import to domestic prices.[34] The lower graph portrays the bias of the trade regime, which corresponds to the ratio of import prices to export prices—in domestic currency—and summarizes the aggregate incentives for import substitution and for export. A higher bias value signals relatively greater incentives to produce import substitutes rather than exports.[35]

The differences in strategy are apparent in the figure. With the EP strategy, the rapid growth in export earnings achieved through market penetration and increased market shares is sufficient to finance import needs without substantial import substitution. Price incentives further encourage increased exports as average tariffs are lowered from 17 to 11 percent by the end of the period. The successful penetration of export markets and the availability of adequate capital inflows obviates the need for increased export incentives that would require real devaluations of the exchange rate.[36]

With the B strategy, an exclusive reliance on export expansion is replaced by more neutral policies that increase exports as well as gradually reduce import dependence through successful import substitution. With lower export growth and the same inflow as with EP-2, external balance is achieved through devaluations of the real exchange rate. Since devaluation affects export and import prices uniformly, the bias of the trade regime remains unchanged. The real devaluation necessary is about 20–25 percent, and it occurs in the early portion of the twenty-year period.[37]

The IS strategy assumes the same successful import substitution as in the B strategy. The real exchange rate is held constant, however, so that adjustment to the foreign exchange constraint occurs entirely through import reduction brought about by a rising import premium. Since this premium affects import prices but not export prices, the bias of the trade regime more than doubles as increasingly costly and inefficient import

---

34. Although the results shown are only for a moderate level of capital inflow, the pattern is largely unchanged for other levels of inflow as well.

35. A measure of the bias is given by B, defined as:

$$B = \frac{M_i}{E_i} \frac{\mathrm{PWM}_i}{\mathrm{PWE}_i} \frac{(1 + \mathrm{TM}_i + \mathrm{PR})\,\mathrm{ER}}{(1 + \mathrm{TE}_i)} \frac{}{\mathrm{ER}},$$

where M and E are base-year weights, PWE and PWM are world prices, TE and TM are subsidies and tariffs, PR is the import premium, and ER is the exchange rate. In the current case, however, with no export subsidies and no change in world prices, the bias is determined as $B = (1 + \mathrm{ATM} + \mathrm{PR})$, where ATM is the appropriate average tariff rate.

36. This pattern is in fact characteristic of the East Asian superexporters. Westphal (1978) shows, for example, that the real exchange rate in Korea remained constant throughout a period of substantial penetration of foreign markets.

37. This policy is representative of the crawling peg policies pursued by some Latin American and other countries starting in the mid-1960s; the real exchange rate was held constant, with periodic discrete devaluations to increase export competitiveness and curtail imports.

Table 11-8. *Sources of Output Growth
for Twenty-Year Simulation Period*

Strategy and sector	Output growth	Share of output change	Percentage contribution			
			Domestic demand	Exports	Import substitu-tion	Change in input-output coefficients
EP-2						
Agriculture	3.2	9.0	103.4	31.2	−4.6	−30.2
Food processing	7.3	9.1	79.4	23.4	−0.7	−2.1
Consumer goods	9.4	24.9	64.4	38.1	0.2	−2.6
Intermediate goods	12.4	23.0	51.0	30.9	1.7	16.4
Machinery	12.6	8.9	70.1	16.4	−1.5	14.9
Services	6.6	25.1	89.5	14.9	0.1	−4.5
Total	7.5	100.0	73.0	26.7	−0.2	0.4
B-2						
Agriculture	3.2	9.4	101.3	16.6	13.2	−31.1
Food processing	6.8	8.6	89.2	10.0	3.4	−2.6
Consumer goods	8.1	20.0	85.5	13.9	3.8	−3.2
Intermediate goods	12.6	25.5	56.2	17.0	9.4	17.5
Machinery	12.9	10.1	70.4	6.4	6.4	16.8
Services	6.5	26.4	90.4	11.6	2.3	−4.3
Total	7.2	100.0	79.6	13.2	5.9	1.2
IS-2						
Agriculture	3.2	10.2	95.3	8.8	26.8	−30.8
Food processing	6.6	8.7	89.8	5.4	7.5	−2.7
Consumer goods	7.9	20.1	86.7	9.1	7.1	−3.0
Intermediate goods	12.3	25.9	52.6	11.4	17.0	19.1
Machinery	12.2	9.5	65.4	3.5	12.2	18.9
Services	6.2	25.6	92.4	7.6	4.3	−4.3
Total	6.9	100.0	78.4	8.4	11.5	1.7

Note: The first column gives sectoral output growth rates. The second column expresses sectoral growth as a share of total change in output. The remaining four columns show the percentage contribution of each demand component to sectoral output change and sum to 100.0 for each sector.

substitution opportunities are pursued. Thus, although the large foreign borrowing in the base year (8 percent of GDP) has been substantially reduced, evidence of continued external imbalance is apparent in the import premium of nearly 200 percent in the terminal period.[38]

The Cost of Capital and Growth

One important implication of the choice of a development strategy—an implication stemming from sectoral interdependence—concerns the rela-

---

38. In practice, of course, such continued disequilibrium would almost inevitably result in major policy changes as the economy was increasingly crippled by a shortage of foreign exchange. The results described here illustrate the strains inherent in such circumstances but have nothing to say about how the situation would be resolved.

Figure 11-5. *The Level of Incentives*

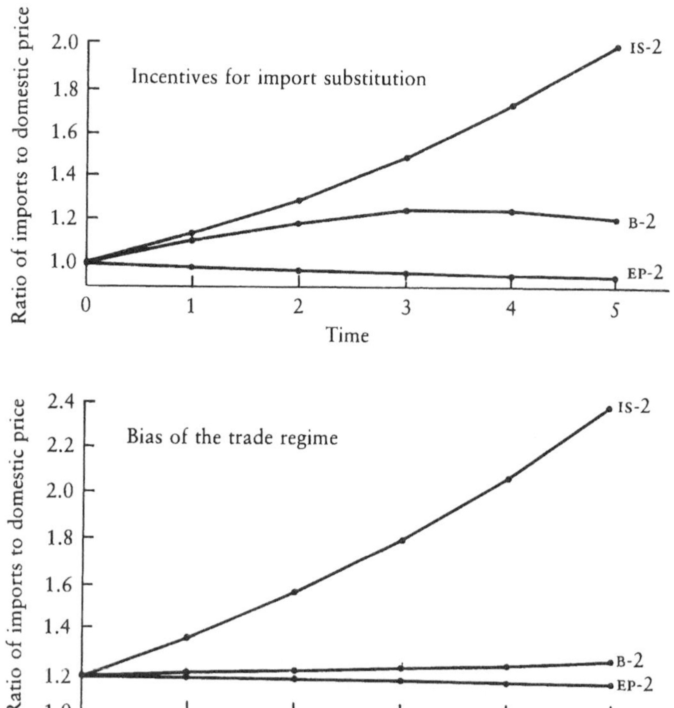

Note: See table 11-4 for key to simulations in figure. See table 11-5 for explanation of times.

tive price of capital goods and its effect on capital accumulation and growth. Capital accumulation in the economy occurs as investors in each sector purchase capital goods. As noted in chapter 8, a unit of capital goods is composed primarily of machinery and construction inputs in a proportion that remains more or less stable over the course of development.[39]

The relative price of capital goods will determine the real investment resulting from a given investment expenditure. This capital goods price is,

---

39. In the data used in this chapter, the average composition is: machinery, 36 percent; construction, 56 percent; other sectors, 8 percent.

in turn, strongly influenced by trade policy, since a large portion (40 percent in the base year) of the machinery purchased domestically is imported. Thus any policy that raises the domestic price of imported machinery will raise the price of capital goods, since substitution possibilities are limited.

Figure 11-6 illustrates this effect for the three trade strategies. In the upper graph, the average price of a unit of capital goods is plotted for the moderate inflow simulation of each strategy. For the export promotion strategy, the relative price of capital goods declines over most of the period. This fall in capital costs has been noted for Korea, where the relative price of capital goods declined by over 40 percent between 1962–65 and 1972–75.[40]

The average price of capital goods in the final period is 20 percent higher with the IS strategy than with the EP strategy. Furthermore, the price is rising most rapidly in the final period, reflecting the increasing scarcity of foreign exchange manifested in a rising import premium. The implication for real investment and growth is shown in the lower graph of figure 11-6. The divergence in the unit cost of capital goods translates into a ratio of real investment to GDP that is 2 percentage points higher with the EP strategy than with the IS strategy.[41] This real investment differential yields an aggregate capital stock that is 13 percent higher in the EP strategy than in the IS strategy.

In the IS strategy, the 16 percent rise in the average price of capital goods masks substantial sectoral variation. In the final period, increases in the prices of sectoral capital goods range from 1 percent in the construction and services sectors to 25–30 percent in the manufacturing sectors. These sectoral differences are caused by compositional differences in capital goods. The high premium rate of the IS strategy raises the price of machinery to domestic purchasers because of the high share of imports in total supply. Capital goods prices for the manufacturing sectors increase since machinery is the largest component of the capital stock in these sectors. In the service sector, in contrast, the share of machinery is smaller and that of construction (a nontraded good) larger, so that the impact of higher import prices is less severe.

Conclusions

The CGE model has proved useful for tracing the causal mechanisms through which trade policies affect economic performance in a market economy. In exploring the effects of the three development strategies

40. See Williamson (1979, p. 350). This effect is analyzed in Corden (1971) and de Melo and Dervis (1977).

41. The difference in investment rates also reflects the impact of savings propensities rising with GDP growth, but this effect is quite small compared with the relative price effect. Ratios of nominal investment to GDP differ by only 0.7 percentage points across the three strategies in the final period.

338   Figure 11-6. *The Cost of Capital Goods and Real Investment*

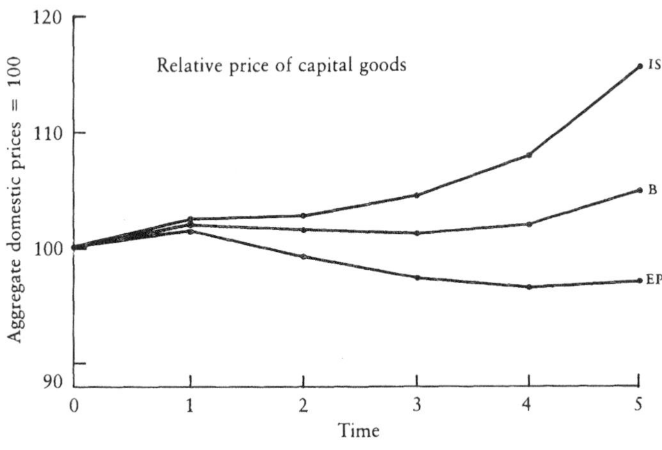

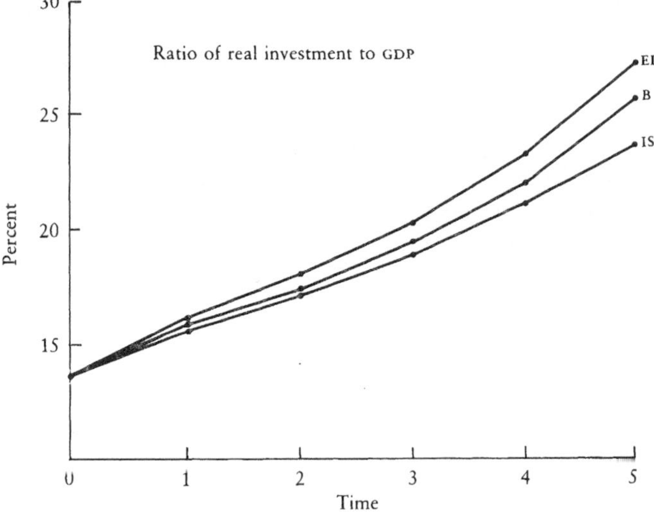

Note: See table 11-4 for key to simulations in figure. See table 11-5 for explanation of times.

(export promotion, import substitution, and balanced), we have been able to follow the links from incentive policies through changes in prices to changes in resource allocation, output, and trade. Our experiments with the CGE model also indicate some of the limitations of an exclusive focus on price incentives and market mechanisms in policy analysis. These are not the whole story, especially in developing countries where structural rigidities and more limited substitution possibilities constrain the effective operation of some markets and the responsiveness of the system as a whole.

In our experiments with the model based on the Korean experience, we found only moderate variation in aggregate growth rates under different development strategies—certainly less variation than we have observed among the semi-industrial countries whose experience was analyzed in chapter 4. The main reason for this is that our model was designed to describe an economy that starts with a significant industrial base (although it need not be a large share of GDP) and reasonably effective factor markets. For example, the model assumes that the choice of development strategy does not affect aggregate employment in the long run. This assumption is reasonable for an economy such as Korea's, which reached the end of its surplus labor phase in the late 1960s. In a dualistic economy characterized by massive underemployment, one would seek to model the employment creation effects arising from different development strategies. This would increase the contrasts between strategies.

Our results indicate the importance of interactions between foreign capital inflows and domestic investment. Holding either one fixed, we found significant diminishing returns in terms of growth from increases in the other. Note that the causal mechanisms are complex and involve changes in the structure of production arising from shifts in demand, variations in sectoral factor proportion, and the composition of sectoral investment. Thus even though the model embodies a variety of substitution possibilities in production, demand, and trade, it nonetheless exhibits the behavior characteristic of a two-gap model. Although there are no binding constraints of the type that a programming model would exhibit, there are increasing costs (and corresponding declines in growth) when an economy is forced to adjust to large imbalances in trade and in its domestic structure.

In many ways, the model economy embodies our current state of knowledge about the interactions among the various components of a development strategy. We focus on market incentives and leave out exogenous factors whose links with policy are only imperfectly understood. Especially important among these are: the relation between total factor productivity growth and policy choices; the determinants of successful import substitution, whereby domestic producers acquire the technological capability to produce close substitutes for foreign goods (exports as well as import substitutes); and the determinants of export supply behavior beyond simple price differential incentives, including issues of quality and market penetration. In each of these areas, we were forced to specify exogenous trends, the effect of which could therefore only be explored by parametric variation. These elements are empirically very important. Endogenous effects working through incentives and market channels only explain a part of the differences in performance.

Policies designed to "get the prices right" may be necessary to achieve rapid growth and structural change, but at this stage of our knowledge we cannot conclude that they suffice. Our results in this chapter support the analysis in chapter 4 and part III suggesting that a combination of factors influences performance. The success of an export promotion development strategy cannot be entirely attributed to the direct effects of the trade strategy.

Appendix A. Equations of the CGE Model

The Flexible Exchange Rate Version

This appendix gives a more formal mathematical description of the static CGE model used in chapter 11.

Capital letters without a bar denote endogenous variables. Lower-case letters, Greek letters, and letters with a bar are exogenous variables or parameters. The subscripts i and j refer to sectors and the subscript k refers to labor categories. There are n sectors and m labor categories. Nonlinear functions are not written out explicitly. Instead, the symbol for a function $f(\cdot)$ is used, and the form of the particular function is explained with each such equation.

PRICES

$$(11\text{-}1) \qquad PM_i = \overline{PW_i}(1 + tm_i)ER$$

$$(11\text{-}2) \qquad PE_i = \overline{PWE_i}(1 + te_i)ER$$

$$(11\text{-}3) \qquad P_i = f(PD_i, PM_i)$$

$$(11\text{-}4) \qquad PS_i = S_i^e PE_i + (1 - S_i^e)PD_i$$

$$(11\text{-}5) \qquad PN_i = PS_i(1 - td_i) - \Sigma_j a_{ji} P_j$$

$$(11\text{-}6) \qquad \Sigma \delta\delta_i PD_i = \bar{P}$$

Endogenous variables:

ER = exchange rate
PM_i = domestic price of imports
PE_i = domestic price of exports
P_i = price of a composite good
PS_i = average price of domestic and export sales
PN_i = net or value added price

PD_i = domestic price of domestic sales
a_{ji} = input-output coefficients
S_i^e = export share in sectoral sales

Exogenous variables and functions:

$\overline{PW}_i$ = world price of imports
$\overline{PWE}_i$ = world price of exports
tm_i = tariff rate
te_i = export subsidy rate
td_i = indirect tax rate
Ω_i = aggregate price index weights
$\bar{P}$ = exogenous level of price index
$f(x)$ = equation 11-3, cost function dual of the CES trade aggregation function (CES is the constant elasticity of substitution).

PRODUCTION AND EMPLOYMENT

(11-7) $$X_i^S = f(\bar{K}_i, L_i, VD_i)$$

(11-8) $$L_i = f(L_{li}, \ldots, L_{mi})$$

(11-9) $$VD_i = \Sigma_j\, a_{ji}\, X_i^s$$

(11-10) $$WL_k = (1 - tv_i)\, PN_i(\partial X_i/\partial L_i)(\partial L_i/\partial L_{ki})/\gamma_{ki}$$

(11-11) $$WK_i = (1 - tv_i)\, PN_i(\partial X_i/\partial K_i)$$

(11-12) $$L_k^D = \Sigma_i L_{ki}$$

(11-13) $$L_k^D - \bar{L}_k^S = 0$$

Endogenous variables:

X_i^S = sectoral production
L_i = aggregate labor input
VD_i = aggregate intermediate input by sector of destination
L_{ki} = labor of category k in sector i
WL_k = average wage of labor category k
WK_i = market profitability rate
L_k^D = demand for labor of category k

Exogenous variables and functions:

$\bar{K}_i$ = exogenous sectoral capital stock
tv_i = value added tax
γ_{ki} = ratio of sectoral wage rate to average wage rate for labor category k
$\bar{L}_k^S$ = exogenous labor supply of category k
$f(x)$ = equation 11-7, two-level Cobb-Douglas or CES production function
$f(x)$ = equation 11-8, Cobb-Douglas or CES labor aggregation function

FOREIGN TRADE

$$(11\text{-}14) \qquad S_i^e = f(PE_i/PD_i)$$

$$(11\text{-}15) \qquad E_i = S_i^e \cdot X_i^S$$

$$(11\text{-}16) \qquad M_i/D_i = f(PD_i/PM_i)$$

$$(11\text{-}17) \qquad \Sigma \overline{PW}_i M_i - \Sigma \overline{PWE}_i E_i - \bar{F} = 0$$

Endogenous variables:

E_i = exports
M_i = imports
D_i = domestic demand for domestic production

Exogenous variables and functions:

$\bar{F}$ = exogenous net inflow of foreign exchange
$f(x)$ = equation 11-16 derived from first-order conditions associated
         with the trade aggregation function

INCOME AND FLOW OF FUNDS

Endogenous variables calculated:

$$(11\text{-}18) \qquad GY = \text{total government revenue}$$

$$(11\text{-}19) \qquad HY = \text{total income of households}$$

$$(11\text{-}20) \qquad TZ = \text{total investment}$$

$$(11\text{-}21) \qquad GC = \text{total government consumption}$$

$$(11\text{-}22) \qquad HC = \text{total consumption by households}$$

Total investment, TZ, is equal to the sum of domestic and foreign savings. A fixed fraction of the foreign capital inflow is assumed to enter directly into savings, while the rest is distributed to institutions, with part of it being saved and part of it ending up as household consumption. Domestic savings is made up of government and private savings, with the private savings rate assumed to be an increasing function of GDP.

PRODUCT MARKETS

$$(11\text{-}23) \qquad ZD_i = \overline{SZ}_i TZ/\Sigma_j b_{ji}\, P_j$$

$$(11\text{-}24) \qquad Z_i = \Sigma_j b_{ij} ZD_j$$

$$(11\text{-}25) \qquad G_i = \frac{\overline{SG}_i GC}{P_i}$$

$$(11\text{-}26) \qquad C_i = \frac{\overline{SP}_i HC}{P_i}$$

$$(11\text{-}27) \qquad\qquad V_i = \Sigma_j a_{ij} X_j^S$$

$$(11\text{-}28) \qquad\qquad D_i = S_i^d (Z_i + G_i + C_i + V_i)$$

$$(11\text{-}29) \qquad\qquad S_i^d = f(PD_i/PM_i)$$

$$(11\text{-}30) \qquad\qquad X_i^D = D_i + E_i$$

$$(11\text{-}31) \qquad\qquad X_i^D - X_i^S = 0$$

Endogenous variables:

ZD_i = investment by sector of destination
Z_i = investment by sector of origin
G_i = government demand by sector
C_i = private demand by households
V_i = intermediate demand by sector of origin
S_i^d = domestic demand ratio
X_i^D = total demand for domestic production

Exogenous variables and functions:

$\overline{SZ_i}$ = total sectoral investment allocation shares ($\Sigma_i \overline{SZ_i} = 1$)
b_{ji} = capital composition coefficients ($\Sigma_j b_{ji} = 1$)
$\overline{SG_i}$ = government expenditure shares ($\Sigma_i \overline{SG_i} = 1$)
$\overline{SP_i}$ = private expenditure shares ($\Sigma_i \overline{SP_i} = 1$)
$f(x)$ = equation 11-29, derived from first-order conditions associated with the trade aggregation function

The Import Premium Version

The equations above describe the flexible exchange rate version of the static CGE model. In certain simulations in chapter 11, the exchange rate is fixed, and an endogenous premium on imports is the equilibrating variable in the foreign exchange market. Since this premium generates an income flow, certain equations must be modified. The import and export price equations become:

$$(11\text{-}1a) \qquad\qquad PM_i = \overline{PW_i}(1 + tm_i + PR)\,\overline{ER}$$

$$(11\text{-}2a) \qquad\qquad PE_i = \overline{PWE_i}(1 + te_i)\,\overline{ER}$$

where

PR = uniform import premium rate
$\overline{ER}$ = exogenously fixed exchange rate

All other variables are defined as before. Total income of households (equation 11-19) now includes premium income, which equals $ER \cdot PR \cdot \Sigma pw_i M_i$.

Appendix B. The Critical Parameters of the CGE Model

This appendix explores systematically the macroeconomic effects of alternative assumptions about three sets of parameters: the rate of productivity growth; the substitutability of domestic production for imports; and the substitutability of labor for capital.

Productivity Growth

In chapter 11, we assumed relatively high rates of total factor productivity (TFP) growth, averaging 1.7 percent across all sectors. The rates were unaffected by the choice of a development strategy, a specification which is contrary to the evidence of chapters 9 and 10 but enables us to isolate the effects of other factors. We shall now assume that this rate of productivity growth is associated with trade liberalization and examine the effects of lower TFP growth on the other two strategies.

Lower productivity growth initially implies a smaller increase in output and in income from a given increase in capital and labor. In subsequent periods, lower income leads to less savings and investment, which augments the initial effects. The total adjustment to lower productivity growth through the general equilibrium model is shown in the terminal-year figures in table 11-9 for both the import substitution and the balanced strategies. There is a cumulative reduction of about 17 percent in the rates of saving and real investment under both strategies. The growth rate of GDP declines by about 1.2 percentage points, which is comparable with the effects of either a change in strategy or the maximum variation in capital inflow, as discussed previously.

There is much more reason to associate lower productivity growth with the excessive import substitution and distorted prices characteristic of the inward-oriented strategy than with the balanced strategy, in which the trade bias has been eliminated. Chapters 9 and 10 point to an association of lower productivity growth with the policy environment of inward-oriented countries rather than with particular types of sectors. Within our sample, the export-promoting economies (Korea and Taiwan) have clearly benefited from high productivity growth, while the import substitution economies (Mexico and Turkey) were shown in chapters 2 and 9 to be average performers. The difference between the two pairs is of the same order of magnitude as that assumed here. There are clearly other factors than trade policy, however, that explain productivity growth (see chapter 8).

Substitution in Production and Trade

The basic difference between the CGE model and the input-output model of earlier chapters is the omission from the latter of almost all forms of substitution: between capital and aggregate labor in each sector, between domestic production and imports in satisfying domestic demand, and

Table 11-9. *Lower Productivity Growth and Trade Strategy*

| | Trade strategy | | | |
| | Import substitution | | balanced | |
Variable	IS-1	IS-1L	B-1	B-1L
Percentage of GDP, terminal year				
Domestic savings	23.2	19.5	24.3	20.1
Foreign savings	1.0	1.3	1.2	1.4
Investment	24.2	20.8	25.5	21.5
Real investment	20.9	18.0	25.2	21.1
Imports	9.4	9.7	17.6	16.8
Exports	7.9	7.8	16.0	14.8
Growth rate				
Primary output	3.0	2.0	3.0	2.0
Manufacturing output	8.8	7.5	9.4	8.0
GDP	5.2	4.0	5.9	4.6
Imports	7.3	6.0	6.3	4.9
Exports	3.4	2.4	11.9	9.1
Other values				
Incremental capital-GDP ratio	3.14	3.38	2.83	3.38
Premium rate (percent)	170	134	0	0
Exchange rate	1.00	1.00	1.15	1.12

Note: IS-1L and B-1L have TFP growth rates reduced by 50 percent in all sectors compared with the growth rates used in IS-1 and B-1. The trade strategies are identified in table 11-4.

between exports and supplying domestic markets.[42] Since we have assumed relatively high elasticities for each of these relations, the performance of the economy is quite neoclassical in its ability to adjust to changes in the constraints on labor, capital, and foreign exchange that have been considered.

We now investigate how assuming lower elasticities of substitution in critical areas affects the aggregate performance of the economy. For example, the effects of limited capital-labor substitution have been analyzed in general terms in the surplus labor model, in which capital becomes the principal determinant of growth as the productivity of labor falls. The limited substitutability of domestic production for certain types of imports plays a similar role in two-gap models of development. Both these phenomena are produced in the present model when the relevant elasticities of substitution are sufficiently reduced. Furthermore, since trade provides an

42. The formulation of these relations has been discussed in appendix A. Substitution among commodities in domestic demand is omitted in the present specification, in which Cobb-Douglas expenditure shares are used.

indirect way of substituting capital for labor, the effects of lowering both elasticities together tend to be cumulative.[43]

Here we are concerned with the differential effects of lower elasticities on the three external strategies. Our experiment consists of lowering the elasticities of capital-labor substitution and imports-domestic production (or trade) substitution first by 50 percent and then by 75 percent in each sector. For capital-labor substitution, reductions of this magnitude cover the range of estimates of this parameter in empirical studies. Since trade substitution—which means replacing imports of commodities such as machinery and capital-intensive intermediate goods by domestic production—involves a complex combination of factors, such as quality differentials and economies of scale, there are few statistical estimates available.

The results of selected simulations for different strategies, levels of capital inflow, and combinations of elasticities are given in table 11-10. They illustrate the following conclusions for each strategy:

- The import substitution strategy is quite sensitive to the reduction in trade elasticities but is much less affected by capital-labor substitution. Reducing trade elasticities by 50 percent forces the premium rate to more than double (from 118 to 276) and produces a moderate reduction in the growth rate of GDP (from 5.7 to 5.4 percent). If the supply of foreign exchange is further reduced by cutting the capital inflow, the effect on growth is quite marked, and the required premium (385 percent) becomes implausibly high. In effect, this is the CGE equivalent of a two-gap model in which foreign exchange becomes the main factor limiting growth. Since discrimination against exports is inherent in this strategy, the elasticity of demand for exports is irrelevant to the outcome. In these experiments, changing the capital-labor elasticity has relatively little effect.

- The balanced strategy is much less sensitive to lower trade elasticities than is the import substitution strategy. When both elasticities are lowered by 50 percent, the economy adjusts by expanding exports to offset the more limited opportunities for import substitution. This is accomplished by a moderate increase in the devaluation required (from 20 to 30 percent). It is only under the extreme assumptions of a 75 percent reduction in both elasticities combined with lower capital inflow that growth drops substantially (from 6.1 to 5.6 percent).[44]

The reason for the greater sensitivity of the import substitution strategy to lower elasticities of substitution between capital and labor is easy to

---

43. The interaction among elasticities of substitution in production, domestic demand, and trade is analyzed in Chenery and Raduchel (1979).

44. These conclusions derive from a more extensive process of sensitivity analysis, which is not reported in the table. The results for export promotion were less sensitive and are omitted from the discussion here.

Table 11-10. *Effects of Lower Substitution Elasticities*

| Trade strategy experiment | Elasticities | | Exchange rate | | Premium rate (percent) | | GDP growth (percent) |
	Capital-labor	Trade	Time 2	Time 5	Time 2	Time 5	
Import substitution							
IS-2	1.00	1.00	1.0	1.0	35	118	5.7
IS-2A	1.00	0.50	1.0	1.0	70	276	5.4
IS-2B	0.50	0.50	1.0	1.0	68	256	5.3
IS-1	1.00	1.00	1.0	1.0	84	170	5.2
IS-1A	0.50	0.50	1.0	1.0	182	385	4.5
Balanced							
B-2	1.00	1.00	1.19	1.20	0	0	6.2
B-2A	0.50	0.50	1.30	1.17	0	0	6.0
B-2B	0.25	1.00	1.19	1.16	0	0	5.8
B-2C	0.25	0.25	1.39	1.13	0	0	5.7

Note: The elasticity numbers shown are the multiplicative factors applied to the original sectoral elasticities in each run. The trade strategy experiments are identified in table 11-4; the times in table 11-5.

understand: a lower elasticity value only matters when the economy departs from a "balanced" growth path, that is, from the set of relative prices in the base year around which the model is calibrated. Since the import substitution strategy is the strategy for which relative product and factor prices change the most, it is the strategy for which the effect of low elasticity of substitution is the greatest. This holds for both the trade substitution and capital-labor substitution elasticities.

It has been shown that more pessimistic assumptions about trade elasticities increase the differences between the import substitution strategy and the two neutral strategies. These differences could in turn be reduced by cutting the export elasticity in the neutral strategies.

Journal of Development Economics 10 (1982) 67–92. North-Holland Publishing Company

TRADE ADJUSTMENT POLICIES AND INCOME DISTRIBUTION IN THREE ARCHETYPE DEVELOPING ECONOMIES*

Jaime de MELO and Sherman ROBINSON

The World Bank, Washington, DC 20433, USA

Received November 1980, final version received April 1981

This paper explores quantitatively the macroeconomic and distributional impacts on non-oil producing, semi-industrial developing countries of external shocks originating in the world economy — in particular, rising costs of imports and shrinking export markets. The empirical analysis is done with a computable general equilibrium (CGE) model. The effects of the same external shock are modelled for three different archetype economies: a primary exporter, a manufacturing exporter, and a closed economy. Three different policy-adjustment regimes are considered: devaluation, premium rationing of imports (import licenses), and premium rationing in an environment with a fixed real wage for unskilled labor. By making simple assumptions about the way socioeconomic groups operate to influence decision-making, the paper also examines how the struggle between the gainers and losers is likely to affect the policy regime to be chosen.

1. Introduction

Shocks emanating from the international economy in the decade of the seventies have had a major impact on both developing and developed countries. The resulting structural adjustments have required, and will continue to require, changes in market conditions which necessitate changes in resource allocation and in product and factor prices to restore equilibrium. In turn, these changes in relative prices alter the distribution of income among socioeconomic groups. In the structuralist environment characterizing many developing countries, there is little doubt that the attempts of different socioeconomic groups to protect their relative position in society greatly affect the choice of government policies. Thus, in evaluating the feasibility of different adjustment policies, one must consider their impact on income distribution.

A good deal of insight about the distributional impact of alternative adjustment policies can be obtained from the standard trade model with limited factor mobility when appropriately modified to incorporate both traded and

*An extended version of this paper is available in the World Bank Staff Working Paper series (no. 442). De Melo wishes to acknowledge financial support from the Agency for International Development and from the World Bank. Our work has greatly benefited from other work undertaken jointly with Kemal Dervis, and we should also like to thank Hollis Chenery, Martha de Melo, Joan Nelson, Larry Westphal, and a referee for comments on an earlier draft. Neither they, AID, nor the World Bank are responsible for any views and interpretations expressed in this paper, which are solely those of the authors.

home goods. See, for example, Jones (1971), Mussa (1974), and Corden and Neary (1980). However, even when this model is reduced to its bare essentials by ignoring the existence of intermediate inputs and assuming all demanders have identical tastes, the effect of a change in the relative prices of traded goods on the real income of the mobile factor is ambiguous. Attempts to incorporate realistic extensions rapidly lead to intractable algebra, and it becomes impossible to maintain any unambiguous qualitative results. One must consider the relative magnitudes of various offsetting effects and so one is forced to rely on empirical analysis. In this situation, empirical simulation models can be used to provide insights into the relative importance of different mechanisms at work.

In this paper, we start from an empirical simulation model whose theoretical structure is quite close to what has become known as the Australian model.[1] The model structure is given by a computable general equilibrium (CGE) model which extends the simple trade model to include intermediate inputs and greater disaggregation across sectors, factors of production and consumers. The model incorporates imperfect substitutability between imported and domestically produced goods, limited factor mobility and the possibility of fixed real wages for certain labor categories.[2] The model includes eight sectors, four labor categories and seven socioeconomic groups. This disaggregation represents the simplest we could devise which nonetheless captures essential structural features of semi-industrial countries.

Rather than basing the study on the historical, political and economic circumstances in a particular country, we have instead created three representative or archetype economies whose empirical structures reflect a range of semi-industrial countries. Our goal is to investigate how a common external shock and trade policy response might have different effects in different environments. We thus subject our three archetype economies to an identical external shock and to identical choices of policy response and then compare the different results.

In constructing the three representative economies, we draw heavily on a variety of cross-section work describing the trade, production and demand structures in semi-industrial countries.[3] To keep the analysis and interpretation of results manageable, we emphasize distinguishing characteristics of our archetype economies and make them quite similar in other, non-essential aspects. The insights from the simulation analysis thus arise from the impact of differences in factor endowments, composition of output, and structure and volume of trade in an otherwise identical model.[4]

---

[1]See Salter (1959). There are some differences, especially in the incorporation of foreign capital inflows and savings.

[2]See, for example, Brecher (1974) for a simple model with fixed real wages.

[3]See Chenery and Syrquin (1975), Lluch et al. (1977), and Kubo and Robinson (1979).

[4]A complete description of how the data sets were constructed and of the equations of the model is given in de Melo and Robinson (1980b). A related model applied to Colombia is discussed in de Melo and Robinson (1980a). A simplified summary of the model equations is given in the appendix.

The next section describes briefly the external shocks and adjustment mechanisms examined in the paper. Section 3 summarizes the characteristics of the archetype economies and describes the experiments. Section 4 analyzes the impact of alternative adjustment mechanisms on the distribution of income in each economy and contrasts the effects of each policy response across the three representative economies. Section 5 discusses how the political struggle among socioeconomic groups is likely to influence policy selection. Conclusions follow in section 6.

2. External shocks and macroeconomic adjustment

The common external shock simulated below takes the form of an increase in the world price of imports and a decrease in the demand for exports (see section 4 below). We also assume that the country cannot borrow abroad to finance the gap between desired expenditures and income and so must adjust fully to the shock.[5] The first and by no means least painful adjustment requires that aggregate expenditure be cut to reflect the fall in the terms of trade. Second, a rise in the effective exchange rate for imports will be necessary to remove the excess demand for foreign exchange. Through changes in relative product prices and wages resulting in an increase in the relative price of sectors in which there is scope for import substitution, there will be a movement of resources into these sectors away from the more exportable sectors and away from the pure non-traded sectors. In addition, the relative price shifts necessary to attain macroeconomic equilibrium will also affect the cost of investment goods and hence future productive capacity.

How adjustment takes place is influenced by a variety of factors. In the first place, it depends on the structure of production and trade and on the volume of trade. Secondly, it depends on how the various socioeconomic groups perceive that they are affected by the adjustment and the extent to which they manage to protect themselves by influencing the selection of adjustment policy. For example, if labor is sufficiently well-organized so that real wages are sticky, then adjustment will rely more heavily on expenditure reduction rather than on expenditure switching.[6] The simulation analysis with the CGE model provides a quantitative assessment of the role of expenditure-reducing and expenditure-switching effects in achieving external and internal balance. As in the Australian model referred to above, it does not capture inflationary mechanisms.[7] The

---

[5]For an analysis of borrowing to cushion the adjustment costs to an external shock, see Martin and Selowsky (1981).

[6]For a model with fixed real wages and markup pricing in the home goods sector where adjustment is entirely by expenditure switching see Findlay (1973, ch. 10).

[7]This is not to say that the distribution of income, broadly defined, is only affected by the structural changes described above. For example, one can postulate disequilibrium adjustment with an inflationary spiral that will, of course, affect income distribution. See Rodriguez (1978). However, the recent external shocks suffered by developing countries are structural rather than monetary and, in spite of their monetary consequences, they call for structural adjustments in the economy. It is the distributional consequences of these structural adjustments that we focus on in this analysis.

emphasis on income and relative price adjustments makes the structural differences built into the three archetype economies all the more important since they largely determine the comparative results.

3. The three archetype economies

The three economies are all assumed to be 'semi-industrial' countries with an income per capita around \$500 (1970 US\$). Such countries are in a transitional phase with their economic structure closer to that of the industrialized countries than to the very poor low income countries in which the overwhelming bulk of economic activity is in the primary sector. While they have quite different structures of trade, production and employment, we have also assumed them to be similar in a number of important respects. First, they are identical in size with the same total physical output and size of the labor force. Second, they share virtually the same technology. This assumption is common in cross-country comparisons where universal access to a common technology is often assumed. The input–output coefficients differ very little across the three countries, the capital structure (B) matrices are identical and capital/output ratios are the same. We do assume different labor endowments by skill categories which implies that labor/output and hence capital/labor ratios differ.[8]

It is a difficult matter requiring compromise to come up with a satisfactory definition of socioeconomic groups which is useful both for economic and political analysis and is also closely related to the variables generated endogenously by a CGE model. The socioeconomic classification described below represents one such compromise. Table 1 summarizes the socioeconomic classification of individuals, the sectors from which their income is derived and whether that income is from wages or profit income. Finally, it provides the assumed within-group logvariance of the distribution of income within each socioeconomic group.[9]   By 'farmers' we mean agricultural workers and small landowners or 'minifundistas' who own a plot of land that provides enough income to support a family. What distinguishes them from marginal labor, besides their slightly higher income, is that they are tied to the land and earn, in

---

[8]In addition to the same sectoral classification, uniformity across the archetypes was also imposed in the selection of parameters describing consumer and producer response to relative price changes. Trade elasticities, elasticities of substitution in production, and income and price elasticities of demand for consumption by socioeconomic groups are the same. Each socioeconomic group makes expenditure decisions according to the Linear Expenditure System (LES). The parameters of the LES vary across socioeconomic groups, but are the same for a given type of group across countries. To simplify further, production functions are assumed to be Cobb–Douglas in capital and labor, with fixed input–output coefficients for intermediate inputs. Finally, the logvariances describing the distinction of income within socioeconomic groups are the same for a given socioeconomic group in all three archetype economies.

[9]The distribution of income within each socioeconomic group is given by a lognormal distribution with an exogenously specified logvariance. The overall distribution is derived by numerically aggregating the within-group distributions. The technique is described in Adelman and Robinson (1978).

Table 1

Socioeconomic classification of individuals.

Type	Sectors of activity	Income source	Within-group logvariance
Farmers	1	Wages + profits[a]	0.50
Marginal laborers	1–8	Wages	0.20
Industrial laborers	2–7	Wages	0.40
Service sector laborers	8	Wages	0.25
Agricultural capitalists	1	Profits[a]	0.60
Industrial capitalists	2–7	Profits	0.60
Service sector capitalists	8	Profits	0.50

[a]25 percent of agricultural profits go to farmers, the rest to agricultural capitalists.

addition to their wage income, a share of agricultural profits. Because there is considerable variation in the size and quality of land owned by smaller farmers, we have assumed this group has a fairly high within-group logvariance. By contrast, marginal labor — the only group which is mobile across all sectors — is fairly homogenous. With an income a shade above half of the economy-wide mean income, they are the largest and poorest group in society and their income is fairly equally distributed. Industrial laborers, or organized labor, are employed in the manufacturing sector. The smallest wage-earning group in society, they are fairly disparate in composition and include white collar workers, clerical workers, technicians and engineers. Their income is about 1.5 times that of marginal labor. Service sector laborers include government workers and, finally, we have the three capitalist groups who get their income from profits. Their number is fixed exogenously with the income of the industrial capitalists about ten times the economy-wide mean income and about 30 percent above that of agricultural capitalists. Service sector capitalists include a large group of self-employed (such as retail traders, etc.) and have an income about five times the mean income.

These groups whose incomes are determined by the model represent the minimum necessary to capture the diversity of socioeconomic groups found in semi-industrial countries. Clearly there is considerable range of variation in mean income and, at this level of aggregation, a considerable degree of heterogeneity within socioeconomic groups. The countries are characterized by a fairly high degree of inequality, with Gini coefficients of approximately 0.50 (or overall logvariance of 0.60). About 45 percent of the overall logvariance is due to between-group variation and corresponds to that part of total inequality which is endogenous to the model.

We now come to the distinguishing characteristics built into the production side of the three archetype economies. The distinctions introduced into the otherwise similar structures fall under three categories. First, the economies are distinguished by their volume of trade. Two of the economies are open in the sense that the volume of exports as a proportion of GDP is large (15 percent).

Second, they are distinguished by their structures of production and trade. Of the two open economies, one is a primary exporter and the other is a manufacturing exporter. Accordingly, the structure of production is biased toward the primary sector in the first and towards manufacturing in the second. The third distinguishing characteristic, which provides the basis for the structural differences described above, is a variation in factor endowments, tariffs and subsidies that are assumed to account for the differences in production and trade structures between the three economies.

There are thus three archetype economies: primary exporter (PE), manufacturing exporter (ME) and closed economy (CL).[10] They differ in: sectoral structure of production, employment and capital; volume of trade; sectoral composition of exports and imports; skill composition of the labor force; and past trade policies reflected in different sets of tariffs and subsidies. These differences are summarized in tables 2 to 4.

Table 2 compares the structure of production and trade in the Base Run (prior to any shock) across the three archetypes. All of the variation in structure comes from the relative sizes of the industrial and primary sectors, and from variations within the manufacturing sector itself. The PE economy, with a larger primary sector (and hence a smaller manufacturing sector), has a distinctively different gross output structure. The differences between the CL and ME structures are less pronounced, although the ME economy has a much larger consumer goods sector which provides its main source of foreign exchange while the CL economy has larger primary and food sectors to assure self-sufficiency.

The overall export and import ratios (see also table 3) indicate the sharp difference in volume of trade between the closed and open economies. Note that with world prices exogenous (and equal to unity), the foreign capital inflow is the same for all three economies and is maintained at its Base Run level throughout the experiments. The variation in exports and imports is most obvious at the 3-sector level of aggregation. The PE and ME economies have opposite structures and the CL economy resembles the PE economy on the importing side, while on the export side it has a balanced structure with half of its exports originating from the primary sector. Within the manufacturing sector, note that the CL economy is almost as dependent on imports of intermediates and capital goods as the other economies.[11]

Table 3 provides information on the sectoral trade orientation of the three

---

[10]Note that the import vector describing the CL economy corresponds more closely to that found in countries like Mexico and Turkey than to the import structure of Brazil or India.

[11]Accompanying, and responsible for, this foreign trade structure are the following trade incentives: tariffs of 25 percent, 35 percent, 20 percent for consumer goods, intermediates and capital goods for ME and PE; 15 percent across the board export subsidies for PE and 75 percent export subsidies for manufacturing in ME; no export subsidies for CL and the following tariffs: consumer goods (75 percent), intermediates (75 percent) and capital goods (20 percent). All three economies have the following trade substitution elasticities: primary (3.0), food (1.5), consumer goods (1.25), intermediates (0.75), capital goods (0.25).

Table 2

Three archetype economies: Structure of production and trade in the base run (percent).

Sectors		Gross production			Imports			Exports		
		CL	PE	ME	CL	PE	ME	CL	PE	MF
Primary	(1)	20.7	27.2	19.6	6.6	8.7	17.3	48.2	80.9	9.9
Food	(2)	13.4	11.5	12.0	4.0	13.4	14.2	12.8	4.5	6.2
Consumer	(3)	11.7	9.2	14.4	5.0	12.9	7.4	22.5	9.3	52.9
Intermediate	(4)	11.6	9.1	11.1	51.2	34.4	36.8	13.9	4.5	23.2
Capital goods	(5)	5.4	3.9	4.9	33.2	30.6	24.3	2.6	0.8	7.8
Construction	(6)	5.8	7.0	6.9	—	—	—	—	—	—
Social overhead	(7)	8.9	10.2	9.7	—	—	—	—	—	—
Services	(8)	22.5	21.9	21.4	—	—	—	—	—	—
Primary	(1)	20.7	27.2	19.6	6.6	8.7	17.3	48.2	80.9	9.9
Industry	(2–7)	56.8	50.9	59.0	93.4	91.3	82.7	51.8	19.1	90.1
Services	(8)	22.5	21.9	21.4	—	—	—	—	—	—
Total		*100.0*	*100.0*	*100.0*	*100.0*	*100.0*	*100.0*	*100.0*	*100.0*	*100.0*
Ratio to GDP		175.3	150.3	159.5	11.2	18.7	19.0	7.4	15.2	15.5

Table 3

Three archetype economies: Sectoral trade ratios in the base run (percent).

Sector	Imports/ domestic supply[a]			Imported inputs/total[a] intermediate inputs			Exports/ domestic production		
	CL	PE	ME	CL	PE	ME	CL	PE	ME
Primary	2.3	5.7	11.0	9.7	13.7	14.7	9.8	30.3	4.9
Food	2.0	15.1	14.8	6.1	9.9	12.2	4.0	4.0	5.0
Consumer	3.0	19.2	9.5	12.0	19.2	15.7	8.1	10.2	35.7
Intermediates	29.8	49.3	49.2	17.1	25.1	23.5	5.0	5.1	20.2
Capital goods	39.8	98.8	69.2	28.0	38.5	32.2	2.0	2.0	15.4
Construction	—	—	—	24.8	30.9	27.3	—	—	—
Social overhead	—	—	—	25.1	31.6	27.4	—	—	—
Services	—	—	—	17.0	20.5	17.8	—	—	—
Average	6.7	13.8	13.2	15.8	20.7	19.5	4.2	10.2	9.7

[a]Domestic supply = domestic production − exports.

Table 4

Three archetype economies: Composition of the labor force (percent).

Archetype	CL	PE	ME
Farmers	30	40	25
Marginal laborers	30	27	33
Organized labor	10	9	15
Service sector labor	30	24	27
Total	100	.100	100

archetype economies. It is crucial for understanding how the common external shock gets transmitted across sectors and across archetypes. The most tradable sectors in the sense that their domestic prices are closely tied to the exogenous world prices are the sectors which have high ratios of imports to domestic supply and/or high ratios of exports to domestic production. Note also that although there are three pure non-traded sectors in the economy, these are among the most import dependent sectors due to the high import content of total intermediate inputs.

The final distinction between the three archetypes relates to labor endowments which are given in table 4. All three economies have a total labor force of 10 million. As one would expect on the basis of the factor endowment theory of international trade, the pattern of trade is closely related to each archetype's factor endowments. Thus the PE economy has the largest supply of farmers while the ME economy has the greatest supply of marginal labor and especially of organized labor which are intensively used in the manufacturing sector. As is the case with most other indicators, the CL economy, which has the most balanced trade and production structure, has an employment pattern between those of the two open economies.

4. The macroeconomic impact of an external shock and its effect on the distribution of income

The external shock we impose on each of the archetype economies has two components. On the import side, the exogenous world prices of imports are raised by 25 percent across the board. On the export side, physical exports are lowered by 25 percent in all sectors and are essentially fixed to their new values.[12] World prices of exports, however, remain fixed. This experiment is intended to capture the essence of the events that occurred in the second half of the seventies. First, the increase in the purchase price of developing countries imports spurred by the rise in energy prices and compounded by the inflationary situation that developed in

[12]In the model, it is convenient to cut exports by lowering all the sectoral export supply ratios (see table 3). This, however, does permit a slight export supply response through changes in the sectoral composition and level of output. In the experiments, this effect is very small.

the industrialized countries; second, the world recession that led to restrictionist policies in industrialized countries which in turn resulted in both a sharp decline in their demand for developing countries' exports along with the imposition of quantitative restrictions. We have deliberately chosen to ignore the induced terms-of-trade losses that occurred to the extent that developing countries face downward sloping demand curves for their exports. Rather, we have emphasized the effects associated with export quantity restrictions coupled with an exogenous change in the foreign terms of trade.[13]

To study the interactions between adjustment policies and the distribution of income, we compare the following three adjustment policies: devaluation, premium rationing and premium rationing with a fixed real wage for marginal labor. There are important political as well as economic differences between the three adjustment mechanisms. A policy of devaluation, because of its fairly even spread across sectors, could be viewed as a political compromise reflecting some minimal degree of consensus among socioeconomic groups. A policy of granting import licenses giving rise to premia reflects a situation where political power is concentrated in the hands of the capitalists and would accentuate income concentration. Finally, a policy of premia on imports coupled with fixed real wages for marginal labor reflects a situation where no socioeconomic group is firmly in control of policymaking. Businessmen manage to appropriate the premia associated with a system of import control by licensing but, on the other hand, workers are sufficiently well organized to prevent a fall in real wages.

The macroeconomic effects of alternative adjustments to the external shock are reported in table 5 which contrasts the magnitudes of changes in the major components of GDP at constant prices across the three countries for each of the alternative adjustment mechanisms. Consider first the case of devaluation. At constant prices, the fall in real GDP ranges between 8.7 percent for CL to 2.3 percent for PE.[14] The ME economy is harder hit than the PE economy because the latter has a production structure biased toward the primary sector which, next to food, is the least import dependent sector in the economy.

As expected, under devaluation, private consumption falls the least in the PE economy since agricultural and food exports are now supplied to the domestic market, dampening the cut in aggregate consumption expenditure. With a 7.5 percent decline, the fall in private consumption expenditures is highest in the ME economy which has to bear the brunt of higher prices for food imports.

[13]In selecting the external shock, we have tried to facilitate the comparison across archetypes in a number of ways. First, combining equal across-the-board rises in import prices with equal across-the-board reductions in export ratios yields an undifferentiated external shock for all three economies so that the impact effect depends only on the total volume of trade in the economy. Second, by fixing the world price of exports, the decline in the foreign terms of trade is the same for all three economies so that the resulting income loss depends on the initial volume of trade and not on its composition.

[14]At first sight, this result seems counterintuitive since the economy which trades the least is the most severely affected. This is because the CL economy has the highest ratio of intermediate input requirements and, moreover, its imports are concentrated in the intermediate sector which has a low trade substitution elasticity. This is also the reason why devaluation is highest in the CL economy.

Table 5
The macroeconomic impact of the external shock.

	Experiment: Devaluation			Premium rationing			Premium rationing with fixed real wage		
	CL	PE	ME	CL	PE	ME	CL	PE	ME
Change from base run (%)[a]									
GDP	−3.7	−2.3	−3.2	−3.3	−2.0	−3.2	−4.9	−2.9	−6.5
Private consumption	−7.7	−4.2	−7.5	−4.4	−4.0	−6.6	−5.7	−5.0	−10.4
Government consumption	11.6	9.3	8.8	5.3	10.7	7.4	5.3	10.7	7.4
Investment	−12.8	−16.7	−7.1	−18.3	−16.7	−9.5	−19.3	−17.4	−12.7
Exports	−23.8	−22.8	−27.8	−23.8	−23.8	−28.9	−26.2	−23.8	−33.0
Imports	−32.9	−35.5	−37.8	−32.8	−35.5	−39.5	−34.4	−36.3	−41.2
Exchange rate	62.0	37.4	33.9	0.0	0.0	0.0	0.0	0.0	0.0
Selected ratios (%)									
Unemployment rate	—	—	—	—	—	—	3.6	1.6	7.1
Premium rate	—	—	—	86.7	51.0	42.7	84.1	50.4	41.6
Total premia/GDP	—	—	—	9.2	8.3	6.6	9.0	8.2	6.5
Price indices[b]									
Investment goods price deflator	118	119	106	118	120	104	118	120	105
Net price agricultural terms of trade	95	100	141	87	78	137	83	76	127
Composite price agricultural terms of trade	74	71	117	74	64	111	72	63	106

[a]All variables are real, except the exchange rate.
[b]Ratios to base run, percent.

Government consumption rises by approximately 10 percent across all three economies, largely because government domestic currency revenues from tariffs increase both because they are levied on higher foreign prices and because the currency has devalued.

While, under devaluation, the differences in adjustments between countries are not great for exports and imports, they are quite significant for investment. In the model, fixed savings rates are assumed for the government and for each socioeconomic group which implies that the model is 'savings driven'. Foreign capital inflows are assumed to be part of savings. To understand why real investment falls by more than 16 percent in PE but only by 7 percent in ME we need more information about the composition of investment and the sources of savings. First, note that one expects to find variations in relative prices and hence differences in the prices of capital goods. As can be seen from looking at the investment goods price deflator at the bottom of table 5, the same nominal investment would, after the shock, yield different real investment.[15]

There is also a second effect due to the change in the composition of savings in current domestic prices. The trade deficit, measured in world prices, is identical and remains fixed across the three economies and also is assumed to be part of savings. But this saving takes place in domestic prices and hence varies with devaluation. The foreign component of domestic savings — 22 percent in the base run — rises dramatically across all three economies with devaluation. And of course it rises most in CL where devaluation is greatest. Thus real investment falls less in CL than in PE, even though both economies experience essentially the same rise in capital goods prices.[16]

Whether and to what extent foreign capital inflows are channelled into investment is an issue which has often been debated in the literature. After having been much discussed in the context of two-gap models, the issue has resurfaced in the debate on the role of alternative closure rules on the distribution of income. Likewise, how investment is determined may have a significant impact on the distribution of income. For example, had real investment been fixed, with increases in the prices of capital goods from 6 to 19 percent, there would have been significant forced savings which might have worsened the distribution of income, depending on the nature of the forced-saving mechanism assumed.[17]

Since exports are essentially fixed, the main difference between adjustment by devaluation and adjustment by premium rationing is the income transfer to capitalists. Thus, many of the differences in the pattern of adjustment between the three economies remains when adjustment takes place by premium rationing.

---

[15]The investment goods price deflator varies widely across the three economies, changing least for the ME economy because of the increased availability of capital goods on the domestic market.

[16]This effect, often referred to as the Hirschman (1949) effect, has been noted and investigated in the context of developing countries by Cooper (1971). The foreign savings component of total savings rises by 59 percent in CL, by 41 percent in PE and 36 percent in ME.

[17]See Taylor (1980).

Premium payments as a percent of GDP range from 6.6 percent for ME to 9.2 percent for CL. The potential rents accruing to the private sector from a system of licenses can therefore be enormous and it is no surprise that it is important what method of adjustment is used. Although more sensitivity analysis would be needed before one could establish a correspondence between devaluation and associated premia, these results are consistent with the often-made observation that huge rents are commonplace in economies which choose to maintain external balance with a system of import controls.[18]

Finally, we come to adjustment by premia combined with fixed real wages. The fall in GDP due to the contractionary impact of the external shock is exacerbated by induced unemployment ranging from 1.6 percent for PE to 7.1 percent for ME. As a result, GDP falls substantially more, except in the primary exporter.[19]

In addition to variations in real investment, the different policy adjustments have important variations in incidence among socioeconomic groups. Which groups bear the brunt of adjustment across the three economies and is it the same groups that lose the most under both devaluation and premium rationing? Can any group benefit in absolute terms and experience a rise in real income?

Before examining the magnitudes of distributional shifts, it is useful to review the various mechanisms whereby the external shock affects the distribution of earned income. First, on the supply side the change in relative net prices affects the distribution of value added between sectors and, within sectors, the distribution of value added between wages and rents. These shifts determine, after taxes, the distribution of earned nominal income among the socioeconomic groups. Second, the distribution of income is affected by differential changes in the cost of living across groups. The relevant prices are those of composite goods (which include imports). The evolution of the net price agricultural terms of trade (see table 5) varies across experiments and adjustment mechanisms; so does the composite price agricultural terms of trade which follows a similar course as the net price terms of trade and is important in determining real income. Not surprisingly, the agricultural terms of trade increases the most in the ME economy which must replace agricultural products previously imported.[20] Third, the distribution of income is affected by transfers which here arise from the distribution of import licenses and hence premia.

---

[18]Note that the premium rate is higher than the devaluation rate even though the composition and volume of imports and exports are similar. This is entirely because of the price normalization rule which maintains a weighted sum of composite prices constant. Thus the domestic currency price of exports does not rise in the case of premia rationing whereas it does in the case of devaluation. It follows that to maintain the same price level, the domestic prices of imports do not rise as much.

[19]If we had instead made the short-run assumption that nominal rather than real wages remain fixed, the impact of adjustment on the distribution of income would have been quite different. Indeed, with real wages falling, the demand for labor would have increased. Such an assumption is not justified in a medium-turn model and, in any case, would require an analysis of inflationary mechanisms which is beyond the scope of the present analysis.

[20]There is also a large spread in the shifts in cost of living indices between socioeconomic groups. On average, the spread is over 10 percentage points.

Table 6 provides the group mean real incomes in the base run along with the percent changes from the values in the base run. It thus indicates which groups gain or lose in absolute terms. In turn, table 7 provides information on the relative distribution of incomes by giving changes in group shares in total income. It is noteworthy that some groups gain in absolute terms after the external shock in spite of the sizable fall in the economy-wide mean income (see last row). Some striking patterns emerge: for the manufacturing exporter, regardless of the adjustment mechanism, farmers and agricultural capitalists always gain in absolute terms relative to the Base Run. In the other two economies, no group gains significantly when adjustment is by devaluation. However, when there is adjustment by premium rationing, industrial capitalists gain absolutely along with service sector capitalists and, to a lesser extent, service sector labor. What emerges from these figures is that starting from a reasonable spread in mean incomes among groups in the base run, the distribution of premia, amounting to close to 10 percent of GDP, raises the mean income of some recipient groups by up to 25 percent. No wonder that the choice of policy instruments is such a politically sensitive topic.

Consider, for example, service sector capitalists. They are the largest and least well-off of the capitalist groups. With adjustment by devaluation, even their relative position in society is likely to deteriorate as a result of the increase in the relative price of traded goods. However, when they receive the premia associated with the licenses they are granted for importing consumer goods, their mean income rises by almost 10 percent in the PE economy and by 7 percent in the CL economy. But in the ME economy, where import substitution in the primary sector is assumed achievable in the medium run, the farmers and agricultural capitalists appropriate these rents through higher domestic agricultural prices. In that economy, service sector capitalists gain little from a system of import licenses since imports of consumer goods become effectively replaced by domestic substitutes.

Finally, one can take a more aggregate view of the distribution of income along broad functional lines and lump all capitalists together in one group. Table 7 indicates that, taken as a group, capitalists always improve their relative position when they get premia, but in the case of devaluation they only improve their position in the SM economy. It would thus appear that devaluation is not a politically easy adjustment policy to implement.

The relative position of marginal labor, the largest labor group in each of the economies, declines in virtually all instances. As is typical in developing countries, we assume that the employed support the unemployed by direct income transfers.[21] Struggling to maintain real wages leads the marginal labor group as a whole (including the unemployed) to mitigate their relative income loss (4.4–2.2

---

[21]In this model, this is done through transfers so that the unemployed receive half the mean income of the employed.

Table 6

Group mean real incomes.

| | Values: Base run | | | Change from base run (percent) | | | | | | | | |
| | | | | Devaluation | | | Premium rationing | | | Premium rationing with fixed wages[a] | | |
	CL	PE	ME	CL	PE	ME	CL	PE	ME	CL	PE	ME
Farmers	2.5	2.9	2.9	−6.9	0.7	12.3	−13.5	−16.0	8.1	−16.7	−17.7	1.8
Marginal labor	2.3	3.2	2.6	−8.2	−1.9	−16.4	−9.9	−4.4	−20.6	−4.3	−1.0	−13.0
Org. labor	4.1	5.3	4.4	−7.2	−2.1	−17.0	−11.6	−3.6	−26.2	−10.4	−3.2	−26.9
Serv. labor	3.2	3.7	3.2	−2.2	−7.0	−21.6	0.6	4.1	−15.9	−1.6	2.2	−20.0
Ag. capital	31.7	40.5	37.1	−13.3	−7.9	26.8	−15.6	−21.2	22.8	−19.7	−23.1	13.9
Ind. capital	46.1	55.0	50.1	−11.8	−6.7	−13.3	23.7	24.4	−2.1	23.3	24.3	−3.8
Serv. capital	23.1	28.3	25.9	−5.8	−13.0	−14.7	7.1	9.8	−1.0	3.9	7.0	−6.0
Mean income	4.1	5.1	4.7	−7.5	−4.7	−7.4	−3.4	−4.1	−6.4	−5.3	−5.3	−10.0

[a]Unemployed marginal labor has mean incomes of 1.2, 1.6 and 1.3 for CL, PE and ME economies. Their mean income is assumed to be 0.5 that of employed marginal labor.

Table 7

Group shares in total income.

| | Shares: base run | | | Change from base run[a] | | | | | | | | | | | |
| | | | | Devaluation | | | Premium rationing | | | Premium rationing with fixed real wage | | |
	CL	PE	ME	CL	PE	ME	CL	PE	ME	CL	PE	ME
Farmers	17.0	21.8	14.4	0.1	1.3	3.1	−1.8	−2.6	2.2	−2.1	−2.8	1.9
Marginal labor	16.1	15.9	17.5	−0.2	0.4	−1.7	−1.1	−0.1	−2.6	−1.9	−0.5	−4.4
Unemployed	—	—	—	—	—	—	—	—	—	1.1	0.6	2.2
Org. labor	9.4	8.9	13.2	0.0	0.2	−1.0	−0.8	0.0	−2.8	−0.5	0.2	−2.5
Serv. labor	21.8	16.5	17.5	1.3	−0.4	−2.7	0.9	1.4	−1.8	0.8	1.3	−1.9
Ag. capital	13.7	17.8	11.7	−0.9	−0.6	4.3	−1.7	−3.2	3.7	−2.1	−3.4	3.1
Ind. cap.	12.1	11.5	17.7	−0.5	−0.2	−1.1	3.4	3.4	0.8	3.7	3.6	1.2
Serv. cap.	9.9	7.6	8.0	0.2	−0.7	−0.6	1.1	1.1	0.5	1.0	1.0	0.4
All	35.7	36.9	37.4	−1.2	−1.5	2.6	2.8	1.3	5.0	2.6	1.2	4.7
Total	*100.0*	*100.0*	*100.0*	*0.0*	*0.0*	*0.0*	*0.0*	*0.0*	*0.0*	*0.0*	*0.0*	*0.0*
Gini	0.51	0.52	0.52	−0.01	−0.01	0.02	0.02	0.01	0.03	0.02	0.01	0.03
Theil index	0.59	0.62	0.63	−0.02	−0.03	0.07	0.07	0.04	0.12	0.07	0.04	0.11

[a]In percentage points.

=2.2 percent loss) compared to premium rationing (2.6 percent loss). With or without fixed real wages, the alternatives facing the poorest are gloomy indeed.[22]

5. Class conflict and policy choice

The picture that emerges from comparing the impact of alternative adjustment mechanisms on the distribution of income in different economic environments is complex. There are certainly significant changes in the relative distribution among socioeconomic groups, with some groups gaining in absolute terms in spite of an overall decline in real income due to the external shock. Differences in economic environment alone suffice to make different groups gain or lose, even with the same adjustment policy. Different adjustment policies also have quite different effects on the distribution. The fact that the choice of policies has a significant impact on the distribution of income leads one to wonder how the struggle between the gainers and losers decides the final choice of policy. Assuming that one can analyze how policies are selected on the basis of conflicting group interests, is it likely that the same policy will be selected in different economic environments?

To explore these questions, we make a number of drastic simplifying assumptions. First, assume that each group realizes how its income would be affected under each policy regime. Second, assume that socioeconomic groups are distinct and care only about their own interests. We thus assume that we have partitioned the society into the important or politically relevant power groups, each pursuing its own interests with perfect knowledge. Third, assume that the intensity with which any group cares about a given policy change is measured by the relative difference in its income between the two situations. Define $Y_i(P)$ as the mean income of group i under policy regime P. In our experiments, P can be the following: B (Base Run), D (devaluation), P (premium rationing), and $P, \bar{W}$ (premium rationing with fixed real wage). For example, the intensity with which group i is for $(+)$ or against $(-)$ devaluation compared to premium rationing as a function of its relative change in income is defined by

$$R_i(D; P) = (Y_i(D) - Y_i(P))/Y_i(B). \tag{1}$$

Next consider the problem of determining the weight of each socioeconomic group in influencing policy choice. There is certainly little agreement about how to derive such weights, so we have specified three different schemes which are consistent with different views about the sources of power or influence and which

[22]In these experiments, aggregate measures of income inequality such as the Gini coefficient hide more than they reveal. Even when the share of marginal labor falls over 4 percentage points relative to capitalists, the Gini coefficient never changes by more than 3 percentage points. More revealing from a distributional standpoint is an analysis of the composition of poverty. The results show that a large fraction of society can be adversely affected, even when aggregate measures of the relative distribution show little variation. See de Melo and Robinson (1980b).

should provide a reasonable range of values. It should be stressed that the analysis is not concerned with more fundamental and difficult issues relating to the theory of how the political process works. Rather, given a political system, we are trying to capture in a stylized manner some of the elements which are likely to determine the course of policy selection by those who are already in power. The mechanisms by which political power is exercised or altered are not considered.

The first scheme assumes that relative influence is given by shares in total population — 'one person, one vote'. The second scheme assumes that influence is measured by relative shares in total income — 'one rupee, one vote'. Finally, the third scheme assumes that the political system is dominated by the economic elite and hence that the influence of different groups is measured by their share in the elite. In this third case, we assume that the elite is defined as the top 5 percent of the overall personal income distribution and that influence in decision-making is measured by the socioeconomic composition of this group.

The first scheme is rather naive but appealing to utilitarian welfare economists, if not to cynical political scientists. The second scheme is a kind of 'effective demand' theory of the distribution of influence with groups able to buy influence in proportion to their shares in total income. Large groups are still important, even if they have a relatively low mean income. The third scheme is really a simple oligarchy that might characterize a naive Marxist view of how a capitalist society works. This last measure, though somewhat extreme, is intended to provide a first approximation of how policy decisions are made in countries where power is concentrated in the hands of the capitalists class.[23]

With the 'political power' shares and the information on changes in the mean incomes of the socioeconomic groups, we can undertake an analysis of the selection of different policy regimes. Eq. (1) defined $R_i(P_1; P_2)$ which measures the relative gains or loss for group i between policy regimes P_1 and P_2. Expressions for the average gain of the gainers and the average loss of the losers, weighting by influence shares, are given by

$$G(P_1; P_2) = \sum_i W_i R_i(P_1; P_2) \bigg/ \sum_i W_i \quad \text{for all } R_i > 0,$$

$$(2)$$

$$L(P_1; P_2) = -\sum_i W_i R_i(P_1; P_2) \bigg/ \sum_i W_i \quad \text{for all } R_i < 0,$$

where P_1, P_2 are policy regimes, W_i is the relative influence of group i, and R_i is the relative gain of group i from eq. (1).

[23]The population shares are given in table 4 except for the capitalist groups whose shares are very small (from 1.1 to 2.2 percent). Income shares are in table 6. For elite shares, the capitalists are the most important (from 20.1 to 39.5 percent). The choice of the top 5 percent is completely arbitrary. In general, the smaller the elite, the more relative power is ascribed to capitalists. See de Melo and Robinson (1980b) for a more detailed discussion.

The average gain and loss functions reflect the intensity with which different groups support or reject one policy compared to another. The political feasibility of one policy compared to another depends, in addition, on the relative influence of the gainers compared to the losers. Given that we used relative influence weights in defining the average gains and losses, G and L, the political feasibility of a particular policy choice depends on whether the weighted difference between G and L is positive or negative. We can thus define an index of political feasibility, F, which is equal to this weighted difference. It is also just equal to the weighted average of the relative gains, R_i, over all groups, gainers and losers:

$$F(P_1; P_2) = \sum_i W_i R_i(P_1; P_2). \tag{3}$$

Note that since we have three different weighting schemes, there are three different feasibility indices for pairwise comparison of policy regimes.

Table 8 presents the average gains and losses of the gainers and losers, G and L, as well as the index of feasibility, F, for all pairwise comparisons of the three different policy regimes. In each pairwise comparison of policies, the first column gives the relative influence of the gainers. We have already discussed which groups gain and lose and it is important to remember here that the group composition of the gainers and losers does vary across archetype economies and policy regimes. However, within each archetype and pairwise comparison, the differences in G, L and F are due only to the different weighting schemes used.

Consider, for example, the comparison of devaluation with premium rationing. As the weighting scheme goes from population shares to elite shares — democracy to oligarchy — the relative power of the gainers declines substantially. In the comparison of premium rationing with and without a fixed real wage (the last four columns), the effect is reversed, with the weight of the gainers increasing with the more oligarchic weights. In the first comparison, the gainers tend to be the small farmers and laborers whose population share is high but whose representation in the top 5 percent is small. In the last comparison, the gainers are everybody but marginal and organized labor, so their weight is high under all three schemes, but especially so for elite shares.

The average gains and losses, G and L, measure the intensity with which the gainers and losers care about the outcome. For the first two policy comparisons, with a few exceptions (six out of eighteen, given the different weighting schemes and archetypes), the feasibility index indicates that those who care the most will determine the policy choice. In the third pairwise comparison, between premium rationing with and without a fixed real wage, the opposite is the case in all three archetypes for the first two weighting schemes. Even though the losers lose more than the gainers gain, their weight is so low that the feasibility index is always positive.

Table 8

Policy comparisons.[a]

Archetype economy	Weighting scheme	Devaluation vs. premium rationing				Devaluation vs. premia with fixed wage				Premia vs. premia with fixed wage			
		Political weight of gainers	Average gain G	Average loss L	Feasibility index F	Political weight of gainers	Average gain G	Average loss L	Feasibility index F	Political weight of gainers	Average gain G	Average loss L	Feasibility index F
CL	Population shares	68.5	4.1	4.6	1.4	39.9	8.1	2.9	1.4	61.9	2.9	4.5	0.1
CL	Income shares	56.1	3.8	14.2	−4.1	40.0	7.1	10.0	−3.0	74.6	2.7	4.0	1.0
CL	Elite shares	46.8	15.6	14.0	−0.2	46.6	6.3	18.8	−7.2	90.9	2.8	1.3	2.5
PE	Population shares	74.7	10.0	12.6	4.2	49.0	15.2	5.8	4.6	65.7	1.8	2.7	0.3
PE	Income shares	64.4	10.2	20.0	−0.6	48.6	14.1	13.1	0.1	73.2	1.6	2.4	0.6
PE	Elite shares	55.9	11.8	26.0	−5.1	55.6	13.3	24.3	−3.4	90.6	1.7	0.5	1.5
ME	Population shares	71.1	5.2	6.3	1.9	39.6	10.4	2.9	2.3	68.5	4.2	7.6	0.5
ME	Income shares	56.8	5.3	9.4	−1.1	39.3	11.0	5.4	−1.0	82.5	4.2	7.6	2.2
ME	Elite shares	43.4	5.3	12.1	−4.5	43.2	11.8	8.9	0.0	99.8	4.6	7.6	4.6

[a]See text for definition of G, L and F.

Table 9

Policy rankings.[a]

Archetype economy	Weighting scheme	Policy ranking
CL	Population shares	$(D)>(P)>(P,\bar{W})$
CL	Income shares	$(P)>(P,\bar{W})>(D)$
CL	Elite shares	$(P)>(P,\bar{W})>(D)$
PE	Population shares	$(D)>(P)>(P,\bar{W})$
PE	Income shares	$(P)>(D)>(P,\bar{W})$
PE	Elite shares	$(P)>(P,\bar{W})>(D)$
ME	Population shares	$(D)>(P)>(P,\bar{W})$
ME	Income shares	$(P)>(P,\bar{W})>(D)$
ME	Elite shares	$(P)>(P,\bar{W})=(D)$

[a](D): devaluation, (P): premium rationing, $(P,\bar{W})$: premium rationing with fixed real wage, $>$: preferred to, and $=$: indifferent to.

Table 9 summarizes the ranking of different policies based on the pairwise comparisons in table 8. It is interesting to note that the various pairwise comparisons never violate transitivity. That is, if policy P_1 is preferred to P_2 and P_2 is preferred to P_3, it is always true that the pairwise comparison shows that P_1 is preferred to P_3, as would be predicted by assuming transitivity.

Devaluation, which skews the distribution of income the least, always prevails in a more democratic political system. Noting that historically more democratic political processes tend to emerge in the more developed countries, one might speculate that the Kuznets U hypothesis (that the distribution of income first becomes worse and then improves as the process of development unfolds) is at least partly related to changing policy choices as political power shifts over time.

There is remarkable agreement in policy rankings, given the choice of weights, across the three archetype economies. This is true in spite of the fact that the particular groups which gain or lose, and the magnitudes of their gains and losses, vary widely. Although our particular choices of policy regimes to compare were purposely made to enhance their differences, it is tempting to conclude that there are generalizations about the feasibility of implementing different policies that are valid for a wide variety of economic environments. The universal dominance of devaluation under a democratic weighting scheme and of premium rationing under the other schemes is certainly consistent with casual observation of a wide variety of countries, although our three simple weighting schemes do not capture adequately the wide variety of political systems represented in the world.

6. Conclusions

By constructing three archetype economies that cover a broad range of initial conditions — resource endowments, past trade policies, and economic structure — this paper has examined the quantitative importance of different initial conditions in adjusting to an identical external shock. While all three economies suffered, for the particular external shock we simulate (a decline in export markets and an adverse movement in the international terms of trade), the closed, rather than the open, economy is the most severely affected. This result is due to the relative importance of imported intermediate inputs in the closed economy. These inputs are crucial and cannot be easily replaced by domestically produced intermediates, so the economy has to bear the full brunt of their rising costs.

The composition of imports determines to a large extent whether the burden of adjustment falls on consumption or investment. For the manufacturing exporter (a food importer), the consumption loss tends to be high. On the other hand, for the closed economy and for the primary exporter (which both import capital goods), the decline in GDP falls most heavily on investment. The rate of real investment, which is around 20 percent of GDP prior to the shock, falls to 17 percent in the closed and primary exporting economies.

How the distribution of income among socioeconomic groups is affected by the external shocks depends both on initial conditions and on the choice of adjustment policy. In general, the distributional shifts are most pronounced for the manufacturing exporter where farmers and agricultural capitalists gain regardless of the selected policy while all categories of labor lose. In the other economies the response is more varied with industrial capitalists losing under devaluation but gaining under a policy of premium rationing of imports. Finally, when real wages are fixed, the contractionary effect of the external shock is more pronounced for the manufacturing exporter, which experiences a 10 percent fall in mean income along with an unemployment rate of 7.1 percent.

The picture that emerges from comparing the impact of alternative adjustment mechanisms on the distribution of income in different economic environments is complex. In particular, the distribution of premia, amounting to close to 10 percent of GDP, raises the mean income of some recipient groups by up to 25 percent, in spite of a sizable decline in overall mean income. With so much at stake, it is no surprise that the choice of policy instrument is such a politically sensitive topic.

The fact that the choice of policies has a significant impact on the distribution of income leads to a set of political questions that go beyond the usual economic analysis of policy choice. By making quite strong assumptions about the way socioeconomic groups operate in the political process, one can determine the policy most likely to be chosen. The analysis proceeds with three different measures of relative influence of socioeconomic groups, reflecting decision making under political regimes ranging from democratic to oligarchic. The simple assumptions we have made certainly do not do justice to the relevant theories of political and economic conflict, yet they roughly capture how vested interests are likely to influence policy making. The model-based results indicate that the likely outcome is a selection of adjustment policies resulting in a deterioration of the distribution of income.

Appendix: The equations of the model

Table A.1 provides a summary of the equations of the flexible exchange rate version of the model. Note that imports and domestically produced goods are assumed to be imperfect substitutes in use and all demands are for a composite good defined for each sector. Since all demanders are assumed to minimize costs, the price of this composite good in eq. (3) is given by the cost function dual to the CES trade aggregation function. Exports in each sector are determined by fixed shares of sectoral supply — eq. (10).

In table A.1, the income and flow-of-funds equations are not explicitly written out. The average incomes of all socioeconomic groups — different types of wage earners, farmers and recipients of non-wage income — are determined endogenously by mapping from factor incomes. The distribution of income within each group is given by a two-parameter lognormal distribution function. The logvariance is specified exogenously and the logmean is a function of the logvariance and the endogenous group mean income. All aggregate distributional statistics are derived numerically by summing the within-group distributions. Note that cost-of-living indices are computed for each group separately so that real incomes for socioeconomic groups are defined using appropriate separate deflators.

Aggregate savings and investment is determined by applying fixed savings rates to the income of the various institutions in the economy: enterprises, households and government. Foreign capital inflow is also assumed to be saved. The allocation of total investment to sectors is given by exogenous shares — eq. (18) — and the demand for investment goods by sector of destination is calculated by assuming a fixed composition of aggregate capital which differs across sectors — eq. (19).

In the flexible exchange rate version of the model, the exchange rate (ER) is determined endogenously to clear the market for foreign exchange, satisfying eq. (12). In the premium rationing version, the exchange rate is fixed and a uniform premium is added to sectoral tariffs in eq. (1), thus affecting the domestic price of imports (PM). The premium rate is solved endogenously to satisfy eq. (12). Except for the use of adjustment by premium rationing with fixed real wages, the labor market is specified so that all wages are solved endogenously to clear the labor markets. In the version with a fixed wage, the real wage for unskilled labor is set exogenously and the excess demand function for the corresponding labor category in eq. (9) is dropped. For further discussion of this type of model, see Dervis, de Melo and Robinson (1982).

Table A.1
Equation of the flexible exchange rent model.[a]

(I) Prices

(1) $PM_i = \overline{PW_i}(1 + tm_i)ER$
(2) $PE_i = \overline{PWE_i}(1 + te_i)ER$
(3) $P_i = f(PD_i, PM_i)$
(4) $PN_i = PD_i - \sum_j F_i a_{ji} - td_i PD_i$
(5) $\sum \Omega_i P_i = \bar{P}$

ER : exchange rate,
tm_i : tariff rate,
$\overline{PW_i}$: world price of imports,
$\overline{PM_i}$: domestic price of imports,
te_i : export subsidy rate,
$\overline{PWE_i}$: world price of exports,
P_i : composite good price,
td_i : indirect tax rate,
a_{ji} : input–output coefficients,
PN_i : net price or value added,
Ω_i : price index weights,
$\bar{P}$: exogenous level of price index.

(II) Production and employment

(6) $X_i^S = f(\bar{K}_i, L_{1i}, \ldots, L_{mi})$
(7) $PN_i(\partial X_i^S / \partial L_{ki}) = W_k$
(8) $L_k^D = \sum_i L_{ki}$
(9) $L_k^D - \bar{L}_k^S = 0$

X_i^S : sectoral production,
$\bar{K}_i$: exogenous sectoral capital stock,
L_{ki} : labor of category k in sector i,
W_k : wage of labor category k,
L_k^D : total demand for labor category k,
$\bar{L}_k^S$: exogenous labor supply for category k.

(III) Foreign Trade

(10) $E_i = \varepsilon_i X_i^S$
(11) $M_i/D_i = f(PD_i/PM_i)$
(12) $\sum \overline{PW_i} M_i - \sum \overline{PWE_i} E_i - \bar{F} = 0$

E_i : exports,
ε_i : export shares,
M_i : imports,
D_i : domestic demand for production,
$\bar{F}$: exogenous net inflow of foreign exchange.

(IV) Income and flow of funds

Variables calculated:

(13) GY : total government revenue,
(14) Y_g : income of socioeconomic groups,
(15) TZ : total investment,
(16) GC : total government consumption,
(17) C_g : total consumption by socioeconomic groups.

(V) Product markets

(18) $ZD_i = \theta_i TZ$
(19) $Z_i = \sum_j b_{ij} ZD_j$
(20) $GC_i = \sigma_i GC/P_i$
(21) $C_{ig} = f(C_g, P_1, \ldots, P_n)$
(22) $V_i = \sum_j a_{ij} X_j^S$
(23) $D_i = d_i(Z_i + GC_i + \sum_g C_{ig} + V_i)$
(24) $d = f(PD_i/PM_i)$
(25) $X_i^D = D_i + E_i$
(26) $X_i^D - X_i^S = 0$

(V) Product markets, cont.

ZD_i : investment by sector of destination,
θ_i : sectoral investment allocation shares,
b_{ij} : capital composition coefficients,
Z_i : investment by sector of origin,
GC_i : government demand by sectors,
σ_i : expenditure share parameters,
C_{ig} : private demand by groups and sectors,
V_i : intermediate demand,
d_i : domestic demand ratio,
X_i^D : total demand for domestic production.

---

[a]Endogenous variables are denoted by capital letters. Lower case letters (except d), Greek letters, and letters with a bar are exogenous variables or parameters. There are n sectors and m labor categories. The letter f denotes a function. In eq. (6) it is a Cobb–Douglas production function. In eq. (3) it is the cost function dual of the CES trade aggregation function. In eqs. (11) and (24) it is derived from the first-order conditions associated with the trade aggregation functions. In eq. (21) it is the linear expenditure system.

References

Adelman, I. and S. Robinson, 1978, Income distribution policy in developing countries: A case study of Korea (Stanford University Press, Stanford, CA).

Brecher, R., 1974, Minimum wage rates and the price theory of international trade, Quarterly Journal of Economics 88, 98–116.

Chenery, H. and M. Syrquin, 1975, Patterns of development: 1950–1970 (Oxford University Press, London).

Cooper, R.N., 1971, Currency devaluation in developing countries, Princeton Essays in International Finance, no. 86 (Princeton, NJ).

Corden, W.M. and P. Neary, 1980, Booming sector and de-industrialization in a small open economy, Mimeo.

Dervis, K., J. de Melo and S. Robinson, 1982, General equilibeium models for development policy (Cambridge University Press, Cambridge).

Findlay, R., 1973, International trade and development theory (Columbia University Press, New York).

Hirschman, A., 1949, Devaluation and trade balance: A note, Review of Economics and Statistics 31, 50–53.

Jones, R., 1971, A three factor model in theory, trade and history, in: J. Bhagwati et al., eds., Trade, balance of payments and growth: Essays in honor of C.P. Kindleberger (North-Holland, Amsterdam).

Kubo, Y. and S. Robinson, 1979, Sources of growth and structural change: A comparative analysis of eight countries, Mimeo (World Bank, Washington, DC).

Lluch, C., A. Powell and R. Williams, 1977, Patterns of household demand and saving (Oxford University Press, London).

Martin, R. and R. Selowsky, 1981, Energy prices, substitution, and optimal borrowing in the short run: An analysis of adjustment in oil importing developing countries, Mimeo. (World Bank, Washington, DC).

Melo, J. de and S. Robinson, 1980a, The impact of trade policies on income distributions in a planning model for Colombia, Journal of Policy Modeling 2, no. 1, 81–100.

Melo, J. de and S. Robinson, 1980b, Trade adjustment policies and income distribution in three archetype developing economies, World Bank Staff Working Paper no. 442 (Washington, DC).

Mussa, M., 1974, Tariffs and the distribution of income: The importance of factor specificity, substitutability and intensity in the short and long-run, Journal of Political Economy 82, no. 6 1191–1203.

Rodriguez, C., 1978, A stylized model of the devaluation–inflation spiral, Staff Papers, 76–89.

Salter, W., 1959, International and external balance: The role of price and expenditure effects, Economic Record 35, 226–238.

Taylor, L., 1980, Macro models for developing countries (McGraw-Hill, New York).

Distributional Effects of Adjustment Policies: Simulations for Archetype Economies in Africa and Latin America

François Bourguignon, Jaime de Melo, and Akiko Suwa

For developing countries the 1980s was a decade of external shocks whose adverse effects were compounded by domestic macroeconomic imbalances and structural ineffi-ciencies. The performance of developing countries during this decade, however, was not uniform. The effects of terms of trade and interest rate shocks are simulated for two model economies, one representing an average Latin American economy and the other representing an average African economy. In addition to the effects of the shocks, the effects of different adjustment policies are examined. As expected, identical shocks and adjustment packages yield different outcomes for growth, poverty, and income distri-bution in the two economies. The differences in results can be traced to specific features of the models, and, to the extent that the archetypes created are representative of real economies, have implications for adjustment policy prescriptions.

It has long been recognized that so long as basic social services are provided to the poor, economic growth remains the primary means of reducing poverty and improving the quality of life. When growth slows markedly, however, as it did during the 1980s, the focus shifts toward the role of public policy in reducing poverty. Confronted with the macroeconomic crises of the 1980s, policies to alleviate poverty become more difficult to design because of the need to both stabilize the economy and promote restructuring so as to ensure long-term growth. The interaction of initial macroeconomic conditions and economic structure with stabilization and structural adjustment policies (or lack thereof) explains the divergent growth and distribution performance across countries during the past decade.

To recount briefly, the 1980s will be remembered as a decade of external shocks for developing countries. Weak demand from developed countries, de-clining terms of trade (prices for many primary commodities fell to their lowest

François Bourguignon is in the Departement et Laboratoire d'Economie Théorique et Appliquée (DELTA) and the Ecole des Hautes Etudes et Sciences Sociales. Jaime de Melo is with the Trade Policy Division of the World Bank and Centre for Economic Policy Research. Akiko Suwa is also in the Département et Laboratoire d'Economie Théorique et Appliquée (DELTA). The authors thank Rebecca Sugui for her unfailing logistical support and the three referees for their comments on an earlier draft.

levels since World War II), a diminishing supply of external finance, and an increase in the level and volatility of interest rates combined to produce an unusually unfavorable external environment. For many countries the need to adjust was also compounded by macroeconomic imbalances resulting from overly expansionary fiscal policies made possible by external borrowing before the crisis.

For all countries, a reduction in absorption was required to adjust to the terms of trade and interest rate shocks. But in countries where initial conditions were relatively favorable because of manageable macroeconomic imbalances and relatively little need to restructure, adjustment was accompanied by an acceleration of growth and an alleviation (or containment) of poverty. This was largely the case for East and South Asian countries, whose average real gross domestic product (GDP) per capita grew 1.5 to 2.0 percentage points faster per year during 1980–89 than during 1973–80.

In Sub-Saharan Africa and in Latin America and the Caribbean, initial macroeconomic imbalances were large or the need for structural adjustment was greater because of many years under heavily distorted incentive systems. Implementing the right policies was also often harder because of structural rigidities caused by weak institutions (Sub-Saharan Africa) or by distributional conflicts (Latin America and the Caribbean). The outcome was an average annual per capita GDP growth of −2.2 percent in Sub-Saharan Africa and −0.6 percent in Latin America and the Caribbean during the 1980s. For Sub-Saharan Africa per capita GDP growth during 1973–80 had been barely positive, but for Latin America and the Caribbean average per capita GDP growth had been 2.6 percent. It is, therefore, no surprise that the past decade has been called a lost decade for the poor in these regions. The *World Development Report 1990* (World Bank 1990) estimates that in 1985, 30 percent of the population in Africa and 12 percent in Latin America was in extreme poverty.

The strikingly different performance between the East and South Asian countries, on the one hand, and the African and Latin American and Caribbean countries, on the other, raises several issues. Was the difference mostly attributable to market characteristics (flexible versus nonflexible economies), levels of development (middle-to-high income versus low income), institutional development (economies financially developed and integrated into the world financial markets versus financially underdeveloped economies)? It would be useful to investigate how important these various differences are in practice. In particular how will growth and income distribution respond to similar (or identical) policies in these different economic environments? Is it likely that poverty and income distribution indicators will react in the same way in the African and Latin American economies?

This article is concerned with the interaction of "typical" stabilization and structural adjustment policies on income distribution in what we shall refer to as "typical" Latin American and African economies. This label is, of course, only suggestive, and one could just as well think of our archetypes as representative of low-income and middle-income economies or of flexible and rigid economies.

Because of stylized differences between the two archetype economies, the same packages or shocks can be expected to have different distributional effects in spite of the same classifications of sectors and socioeconomic groups.

To anticipate what is described in greater detail in the body of the article, we build two archetypical economies to which we apply the same external shock that will result in different effects because of different structures and initial conditions. The first typical adjustment package is arrived at by roughly calibrating the model to produce changes in average values of key macroeconomic variables like growth, external debt, and investment rates that were observed between 1979–81 and 1986–89. The result of this rough calibration exercise is labeled the *standard* (or average) adjustment package. It includes countries that implemented stabilization and adjustment policies advocated by the World Bank and International Monetary Fund (IMF) as well as countries that did not or that did so only intermittently. To keep things simple and to identify more clearly the effects of structural differences across archetypes, we identify the standard adjustment package with exchange rate adjustments. We first analyze in some detail the macroeconomic and distributional effects of this standard adjustment pattern with the alternative scenario of a no-shock growth path.

We then compare this standard adjustment package with three other typical packages. The rationing adjustment package can be characterized by the failure to reduce imbalances and alter economic structures by changing policy incentives. In our framework this amounts to resisting real exchange rate depreciation. The structural reform package corresponds to adjustment packages supported by the World Bank and the IMF. In that typical package, rationalization of trade and fiscal incentives is intended to help reduce the fiscal imbalance and restructure the economy. Finally, the redistribution package combines the reforms of the previous package with redistributive measures along the lines advocated in recent studies on poverty alleviation. One can think of this package as approximating the strategy advocated in the *World Development Report 1990*.

The remainder of the article is organized as follows. In the following section, we describe in some detail the main features of the simulation model, including the differences in model closures between the two archetype economies with respect to the functioning of labor, goods, and foreign exchange markets. Calibration to initial macroeconomic conditions in the early 1980s is then described, along with an analysis of the effects of the shock under the standard adjustment scenario. We compare adjustment under the standard package with adjustment under the three other typical packages described above, and then draw our conclusions.

I. MODEL OUTLINE

The model is designed to capture the short- and medium- to long-run effects of stabilization and structural adjustment policies on the distribution of income. It is fully described in Bourguignon, Branson, and de Melo (forthcoming) and is available upon request. We refer to the model as a "maquette" because of the variety of closures afforded by the "micro-macro" linkages built into it. Micro-linkages come from the interactions across the six sectors included in the model. These long-run linkages are well known from the literature on computable general equilibrium (CGE) models and are not discussed here. Macro-linkages come from the standard IS-LM macro framework for an open economy (see Tobin 1969). These linkages are not discussed either, although they will become apparent from the description of the differences in our modeling of the labor, goods, and financial markets in the two archetype economies.

The construction of the archetypes draws on the work of Chenery and his colleagues (Chenery and Syrquin 1975 and Chenery, Robinson, and Syrquin 1987) and is detailed in the appendix. Archetypical economies have the same disaggregation across labor markets, goods markets, and socioeconomic groups, but, to reflect differences in their levels of development and economic structures, the relative importance of sectors, labor markets, and socioeconomic groups differ. For example, the agricultural labor market is more important in the African archetype economy than in the Latin American one. Initial conditions such as the size of the external debt and the rate of interest on the external debt also differ. Further, demand and supply elasticities are usually lower in the African than in the Latin American archetype, and, most important, the functioning of labor, goods, and financial markets differs between the two archetype economies.

In both archetype economies we distinguish five financial units: government, households, firms, the consolidated banking system, and the foreign sector. By assumption, governments do not lend, households do not borrow, and, because of thin (or nonexistent) equity markets in most developing countries, the equity market is modeled rudimentarily so that the endogenously determined proportion of household savings allocated to equity is made directly available to firms.

The different modeling assumptions are summarized in table 1. In the African archetype there is no market for government debt, the government holds all foreign debt, and household financial wealth is made up entirely of domestic financial assets (money and equity). By contrast, in the more developed financial markets of the Latin American archetype, part of the government debt is held in domestic bonds, households hold foreign assets, and firms have part of their debt in foreign currency.

Because it is difficult to sterilize capital flows in Latin American economies with relatively integrated financial markets, it is assumed that monetary authorities can only partially control the money supply in the Latin American archetype. The change in base money, H, is given by:

$$\Delta H = \Delta L_b - e\theta KA_p + \Delta B_b$$

where L_b is the liability of the banking system, e is the exchange rate (units of domestic currency per unit of foreign currency), KA_p is the private capital account, B_b is government issued domestic debt, and θ ($0 < \theta < 1$) measures the

Table 1. *Assumptions of the Model*

African archetype	Latin American archetype
Financial sector	
• Money supply exogenous ($\theta = 0$)[a]	• Money supply partly endogenous ($\theta = 0.3$)[a]
• No bond market; government holds only foreign debt (B_w^*)	• Bond market; government holds domestic debt (B_b) and foreign debt (B_w^*)
• Households hold cash (H_h) and equities in firms ($p_a E$)	• Households hold cash and foreign bonds (F_h^*) in their portfolio as well as equities in firms ($p_a E$)
• Firms use working capital (H_f) and liabilities of the banking system (L_b)	• Firms use working capital (H_f), liabilities of the banking system (L_b), and foreign-denominated debt (L_w^*)
Foreign exchange market	
• Limit on government borrowing (B_w^*); firms and households have no access to the foreign capital market	• Limit on government borrowing (B_w^*) and on firm borrowing (L_w^*), but no limit on foreign assets held by households (foreign and domestic assets are imperfect substitutes)
Labor market	
• Flexible wages for agricultural labor; downward nominal rigidity for modern sector labor	• Flexible wages for agricultural labor: full indexation on cost of living (full real wage rigidity) for modern sector labor
Goods market	
• Flexible prices for all sectors	• Mark-up pricing in modern sector; flexible prices in other sectors

a. θ is the monetized proportion of private capital movements.

degree of sterilization of foreign capital flows. Also, because of the evidence that inflation leads to flight from money, households' real demand for money, H_h, is

$$(1) \qquad H_h = H_h(\, y, i, \dot{p}^e)$$
$$ + \; - \; -$$

where signs under the variables indicate the signs of the corresponding partial derivatives, y is real income, i is the nominal interest rate, and $\dot{p}^e$ is the exogenously given expected inflation rate.

In the foreign exchange market with a normal external environment, that is, without shock, there is no constraint on foreign borrowing. The exchange rate is then predetermined, and endogenous government borrowing ΔB_w^* is given by:

$$(2) \qquad -\Delta B_w^* = CA(\, i, e) + KA_p(i, e)$$
$$ - \; + \qquad\quad + \; -$$

where CA is the interest inclusive current account and, for the Latin America archetype, $KA_p = \Delta L_w^*(i, e) - \Delta F_h^*(\, i, e)$, where L_w^* is firm borrowing from
$$ + \; - \qquad\quad - \; +$$
abroad, and F_h^* is households' holdings of foreign bonds. For a given domestic price, the current account responds positively to the exchange rate and negatively to the interest rate because of investment demand. For given expectations private firms (households) shift toward domestic debt (foreign assets) when the

exchange rate devalues (revalues) and when the interest rate rises (falls). In the African archetype the capital account is exogenous by assumption. In all simulations, except the no-shock scenario, it is assumed that each archetype faces an exogenously determined foreign exchange constraint and the government borrows an exogenously set amount ΔB_w^*. Money is the only financial asset held in the African archetype, so that when the amount of foreign borrowing is fixed, the fiscal deficit is financed from seignorage on the cash holdings of firms and households. In the Latin American archetype big farmers and capitalists hold a fraction of their financial portfolio in foreign assets and domestic bonds. The fiscal deficit is therefore also partly financed from domestic borrowing. Also, in the Latin American economy not only does the government face a foreign borrowing constraint, but firms can no longer borrow abroad, that is, $\Delta L_w^* = 0$. Households, however, continue to hold foreign bonds in their portfolios even when there is foreign exchange rationing. In addition we assume that foreign exchange controls are ineffective in the Latin American archetype, so that we are able to capture the widely documented phenomenon of capital flight. Thus, although foreign borrowing is constrained in both economies, households can shift their portfolios toward foreign-denominated assets in the Latin American archetype in response to changes in the domestic economic environment.

In both archetypes the economy is divided into six sectors—primary export, agriculture, nontraded informal (private services and cottage shop activities), consumer goods, intermediate and capital goods, and nontraded formal (construction and utilities)—and six socioeconomic groups—two capitalist groups (large farmers and modern-sector capitalists), small farmers, and three worker groups. The primary export sector is the standard export sector (a mineral or cash crop sector), whereas agriculture includes activities that compete with imported agricultural products. In both archetypes after-tax profits are largely distributed to the capitalist socioeconomic groups, whereas worker income comes primarily or exclusively from the sale of labor services. The appendix describes in more detail the output and final demand structures, taxes, the mapping of factor incomes into socioeconomic groups, and the holding of financial assets.

In the labor markets agricultural workers are assumed to be paid a competitive wage, and informal workers earn their average product. In the African archetype modern sector wages are downwardly rigid in nominal terms, but there is usually enough inflation to clear the modern labor market. In the Latin American archetype wages for modern sector workers are fully indexed to the cost of living. This reflects the combination of union power and workers' resistance to a cut in living standards. With real wage rigidity any disequilibrium in the modern labor market resulting in an excess supply of labor results in unemployment.

In the goods markets we assume that prices adjust to clear markets in the African archetype. In the Latin American archetype we assume that capitalists in the modern sector will resist cuts in their profit rates. This implies a mark-up pricing rule of the type:

$$(3) \qquad p^v = w_{-1}(1 + m)(1 + \alpha\, \hat{p}^e)$$

where p^v is the value added price, w_{-1} is last period's labor cost per unit of output, m is the mark-up rate, and $\alpha < 1$ depends on how much resistance there is to a cut in profits. In the modern sector, the rate of capacity utilization U is adjusted to clear the market in case of excess supply. Hence supply is given by $q^s = UF(\bar{K}, L)$, where $\bar{K}$ is the fixed capital stock, L stands for labor, and $F(\ )$ is the sectoral production function. Thus in the Latin American archetype the combination of wage indexation with a mark-up pricing rule leads to an extremely rigid modern sector.

The government sector is modeled identically in both archetypes. The government collects taxes on domestic and imported goods and pays interest on internal and external debt. Noninterest government expenditures are divided into three components: wages, consumption expenditures, and investment expenditures. Government workers, whose employment level is exogenous, receive an exogenous wage. To simplify the interpretation of results, we assume that the marginal productivity of government investment is the same as for private investment. We also assume that all components of noninterest expenditures grow at 3 percent per period in all simulations. Thus we abstract from any productivity effects that would arise from changes in patterns of government expenditures. However, for a given monetary and exchange rate policy, any change in the fiscal deficit has an effect on private investment demand by clearing the money market.

The immediate effect of the external shock considered here is to require a reduction in absorption relative to income. There is no room to increase supply since the economies are initially assumed to be at a full-employment equilibrium. With more rigidity in goods and labor markets in the Latin American archetype, the shock moves the economy inside its production possibility frontier, and the reduction in absorption is greater than in the more flexible African archetype. Of course resources are not actually fully and efficiently employed in the no-shock scenario, and structural adjustment policies were intended to move economies closer to their production frontier. We do not model directly this supply-augmenting effect, which structural adjustment policies were presumed to have, because of the lack of reliable information on the extent of resource idleness caused by inappropriate incentives. Rather we implicitly assume that in the no-shock scenario economies would have had sufficient access to external funding to have normal capacity use. In particular we do not take into account the possibility of immiserizing capital inflows caused by distortions (see Brecher and Diaz-Alejandro 1977).

In the longer run there is also an effect of adjustment on growth resulting from changes in the composition of absorption. Household savings of capitalists are

346   THE WORLD BANK ECONOMIC REVIEW, VOL. 5, NO. 2

negatively affected by the incorporation of a wealth effect in the consumption function, and, for a given amount of savings, the allocation of savings to physical capital depends on the relative price of equities (that is, of physical capital) compared with other financial assets.

The other component of absorption is private investment. How it reacts to changes in the endogenously determined macroeconomic variables will largely determine the relative success of stabilization and structural adjustment policies. Investment demand by the private sector I_p is given by:

$$(4) \qquad I_p = I_p\left(\frac{U(p^v \partial F/\partial K)/p_k}{(i_r - \dot{p}^e)}\right).$$

Investment demand is a positive function of capacity utilization and that sector's marginal revenue product of capital $p^v \partial F/\partial K$ and a negative function of the cost of capital p_k and the opportunity cost of borrowing $i_r - \dot{p}^e$, where i_r is a weighted sum of domestic and foreign interest rates adjusted for exchange rate changes. In turn the price of capital goods and the opportunity cost of borrowing is affected by the value of the real exchange rate.

How adjustment affects income distribution among socioeconomic groups is influenced by three factors. First is the standard effect coming from the mapping of factor incomes into socioeconomic groups. Incomes of factors employed relatively intensively in expanding sectors will rise. Likewise rents will rise in sectors that expand, with the real income of immobile factors changing more than those of mobile factors. Second, poor socioeconomic groups, which have consumption patterns that are not price responsive—because they are concentrated in necessities with low price (and income) elasticities of demand—will be more severely affected by changes in relative prices and real income. Third, poor socioeconomic groups, which have little equity and hold financial assets mostly in the form of noninterest-bearing money, will lose more from shocks that raise the inflation rate and lead to a real exchange rate depreciation. However, rich socioeconomic groups, which have more diversified portfolios and hold interest-bearing assets or assets denominated in foreign currency, are better protected against inflation and capital losses.

II. Adjustment to an External Shock in the Two Archetype Economies

We now turn to an analysis of how interest rate and terms-of-trade shocks affect macroeconomic and distributional indicators in the two archetype economies. The terms-of-trade shock is a 20 percent increase in the foreign currency price of imports (p_m^*) in period 2 only. The interest rate shock is a permanent doubling of the interest rate (i^*) on foreign debt beginning in period 2 (simulations run for seven periods). Because the typical African economy holds publicly guaranteed debt disbursed under donor assistance, it has a relatively high grant element compared with the stock of external debt held by the typical Latin American country, where the proportion of commercial debt with a variable interest rate is high. Hence the interest rate on foreign debt in the African archetype is doubled from 4 to 8 percent per year, whereas for the Latin American archetype the interest rate is doubled from 8 to 16 percent.

Assuming that the parametrization of the external shock is sensible, the plausibility of the archetypes and of the differing assumptions about market behavior, parameters, and initial conditions can be judged by comparing model outcomes with realized values of macroeconomic variables averaged over African and Latin American economies during 1979–86. We assume that if the external environment in the 1980s had been benign, average performance achieved during 1978–81 would have continued throughout the 1980s. We compare these average realized values for 1978–81 with period 1 values obtained with the simulation model, which indicate macroeconomic outcomes for most flow indicators over the entire simulation in the absence of an external shock. The realized average values of variables during 1986–89 are taken to represent the combination of the unfavorable environment resulting from the external shock and the standard adjustment to that shock. They are compared with model results from period 7 after the economies have settled down from the effects of the shock and of the standard adjustment package.

The realized values of macroeconomic indicators and the values generated by the model under the standard adjustment package are compared in tables 2 and 3. Looking at the realized values, four stylized outcomes stand out. First, growth slowed much more in Latin America than in Africa. But the larger population growth rate in Africa (3.2 percent per year versus 2.2 percent for Latin America) resulted in declining average per capita income in Africa. Second, the investment share in GDP fell drastically in both regions. Although some portion of the fall in investment rates was certainly compensated for by increases in the marginal efficiency of investment, it is implausible that efficiency gains compensated for the loss in investment volume. Third, the current account deficit worsened slightly for both regions because of the surge in interest payments on the external debt in spite of the sharp real exchange rate devaluation. Fourth, inflation skyrocketed in Latin America, whereas it remained stable in Africa in great part because of the influence of countries in the franc zone.

The model results broadly replicate these stylized outcomes, although there are some discrepancies. For the Latin American archetype the treatment of rigidities in the model magnifies the fall in growth rates when compared with the average realized values. Regarding inflation, in the Latin American archetype the exogenous treatment of expectations about inflation and devaluation in the simulations makes any outcome possible. In view of the very uneven inflation patterns both within and across countries, we have assumed "strong" inflationary expectations only during the period when the shock occurs. As a result an inflation bout occurs in period 2, and the economy settles back to a "normal" inflation pattern thereafter. Hence we are not modeling the dynamics of hyperinflation. With respect to the real exchange rate index, the two indicators are not strictly comparable, since the index calculated from the model corresponds

Table 2. *GDP Growth and Inflation: Africa and Latin America, 1978–81 and 1986–89*
(annual average in percent)

	Africa				Latin America			
	Actual value		*Value generated by the model*		*Actual value*		*Value generated by the model*	
Indicator	*1978–81*	*1986–89*	*Without shock*	*With shock*	*1978–81*	*1986–89*	*Without shock*	*With shock*
GDP growth per year	2.9	2.8	3.0	2.6	3.7	2.4	4.4	1.1
Inflation rate per year (CPI)	20.9	22.1	16.4	18.3	21.1	271.3	30.5	37.5

Note: Actual values are unweighted averages for the periods indicated. The values generated by the model are compounded seven-year average annual growth rates for the no-shock and shock simulations.
Source: World Bank data and authors' calculations.

Table 3. *Macroeconomic Indicators: Africa and Latin America, 1978–81 and 1986–89*
(percent unless otherwise indicated)

	Africa				Latin America			
	Actual value		*Value generated by the model*		*Actual value*		*Value generated by the model*	
Indicator	*1978–81*	*1986–89*	*Period 1*	*Period 7*	*1978–81*	*1986–89*	*Period 1*	*Period 7*
Investment/GDP	22.70	18.10	21.60	15.50	22.30	17.30	22.60	14.80
Current account/GDP	−4.80	−5.90	−4.60	−5.40	−4.60	−5.20	−3.30	−7.40
External debt/exports	0.89	3.59	1.07	1.89	1.16	3.35	0.99	2.89
Interest payments/exports	3.40	11.10	3.70	15.10	9.90	24.30	9.50	42.50
Real exchange rate (1930=1)	1.02	1.46	1.00	1.09	1.01	1.14	1.00	1.08

Note: Actual values are unweighted averages for the periods indicated.
Source: World Bank data and authors' calculations.

to the relative price of tradables, whereas the calculated value for regional averages corresponds to an index of external competitiveness rather than to an index of resource allocation within the economy. Because the model was designed for counterfactual analysis and not forecasting, one should not require exact replication of realized values. The comparisons indicate, however, that the main changes observed during the 1980s are captured by the standard adjustment package built into the model.

We now evaluate the effects of the external shock on income distribution under the standard adjustment package. In the favorable external environment base simulation, expectations are realized. The money supply, inflation, and expected devaluation (and actual devaluation) all grow at 30 percent per period for the Latin American base simulation and 15 percent for the African base simulation (except for the money supply in Africa, which grows at 20 percent per period). Under this scenario there is no foreign borrowing constraint, real exchange rates and real interest rates are nearly constant, and there is full employment of labor and full capacity use. As shown in table 4, the debt-to-export ratio doubles by the end of the seven-period simulation, with the fiscal deficit worsening in Africa mainly because of the rising external debt service. The value of exports grows less rapidly in Africa than in Latin America because of a bias toward primary products with low price and income elasticities of demand. This difference reflects the difficulties that African countries have had in expanding export earnings.

Because of higher population growth, the normal external environment for the African archetype is just sufficient to maintain poverty indicators constant throughout the simulation, although the distribution of income becomes significantly more equal according to the Theil index of inequality. However, the combination of higher GDP growth and lower population growth enables the Latin American archetype to achieve a reduction in poverty and a marginally more equal income distribution.

In the simulations with the unfavorable external environment, in which the interest rate on external debt is doubled for periods 2 to 7 and the foreign currency price of imports is hiked by 20 percent in period 2, the standard adjustment package is derived as follows. In the African archetype a limit on external borrowing is imposed with no changes in expectations or monetary policy. In the Latin American archetype the limit on public borrowing is complemented by a freeze on the portfolio choice of firms that see their foreign-denominated debt frozen to its period 2 value. No constraints are imposed on portfolio choices by households. Because of the rigidities built into this archetype, expectations of inflation and the rate of devaluation are raised to 35 percent in period 2 and 40 percent in period 3, with a corresponding increase in the money supply. For subsequent periods expectations and monetary growth resume preshock values. To simplify this adjustment package we have assumed no contractionary change in fiscal (or monetary) policy as a result of the shock. In other words we assume that the limit on foreign borrowing is met by varia-

Table 4. *Macroeconomic and Distributional Indicators for the Two Archetypes with and without Shock*
(percent unless otherwise indicated)

| | African archetype | | | | Latin American archetype | | | |
| | Without shock | | With shock | | Without shock | | With shock | |
Indicator	Period 2	Period 7	Period 2	Period 7	Period 2	Period 7	Period 2	Period 7
GDP (period 1 = 100)	103.0	120.0	103.0	117.0	104.0	129.0	101.0	107.0
Export value (in foreign currency units)	21.6	23.6	23.8	28.9	17.1	21.5	19.7	21.2
Investment/GDP (real)	21.5	20.5	18.9	15.5	21.4	23.6	13.8	14.8
Inflation rate (CPI)	16.8	16.9	20.7	18.1	35.4	30.0	108.3	30.0
Devaluation rate	15.0	15.0	27.0	17.6	30.0	30.2	108.0	31.4
Interest rate	20.1	21.2	20.3	23.4	35.9	34.1	49.0	42.1
Overall deficit/GDP	4.0	6.2	5.2	9.0	6.2	6.7	8.2	17.4
Primary deficit/GDP[a]	3.1	4.6	3.2	5.2	3.9	3.0	4.4	5.8
Debt/exports[b]	113.0	239.0	103.0	189.0	124.0	224.0	107.0	289.0
Debt service/exports[b]	4.5	9.3	8.3	15.1	11.3	21.0	17.2	46.2
Domestic debt/GDP	n.a.	n.a.	n.a.	n.a.	3.4	4.0	5.8	7.0
Domestic debt service/government revenue	n.a.	n.a.	n.a.	n.a.	7.1	9.0	4.7	18.0
Household foreign assets/exports	n.a.	n.a.	n.a.	n.a.	34.4	42.0	48.2	57.2
Theil index[c]	66.4	58.6	61.5	50.8	37.1	35.0	33.4	43.2
Poverty gap[d]	2.68	2.71	2.77	2.71	0.84	0.63	0.91	1.49
Poverty rate	30.4	31.1	29.9	29.5	11.8	10.5	12.1	19.5

n.a. Not available.
a. Does not include interest payments on public debt.
b. Public and private external debt.
c. A decrease in the value of the index indicates less income inequality.
d. The poverty gap indicates the percentage of income that must be redistributed to bring all those below the poverty line up to the poverty line.
Source: Authors' calculations.

tions in the exchange rate alone. This clearly overstates the laxity of fiscal policies pursued in a standard adjustment package, but it makes it easier to interpret the effects of differences in economic structure, initial conditions, and market mechanisms on adjustment policies.

The impact of the shock and the standard adjustment on macroeconomic variables in periods 2 and 7 is given in table 4. Private investment declines sharply in both economies (public investment grows exogenously), because of the combined effects of a higher price for imported capital goods (resulting from the devaluation of the real exchange rate) and a higher real interest rate (resulting from larger government borrowing from the Central Bank to finance interest payments). This effect is particularly strong for the Latin American archetype and is certainly in accord with the sharp rise in real interest rates that occurred during the past decade in many Latin American economies.

A second clear pattern is the deterioration in fiscal indicators, which is particularly pronounced for the Latin American archetype. Although the deterioration is rather extreme because we have purposely not built in contractionary fiscal policies in the standard adjustment package, it is interesting that the exploding fiscal deficit in the Latin American archetype is almost entirely due to interest payments on the internal and external debt.

This sharp fiscal deterioration in the Latin American archetype results from the price rigidities impairing resource use. Unemployment goes up sharply because of real wage rigidity in period 2, and capacity falls with a lag because of the resistance of capitalists to a fall in the profit rate in the modern sector. As a result, in contrast with the African archetype, in which the real exchange rate devaluation achieves expenditure switching with a concomitant increase in export earnings, in the Latin American standard adjustment pattern, export earnings remain at the same level as in the base simulation. Stagnant export earnings and a severe output contraction imply less government tax revenue. The deterioration in government revenue along with rising interest payments results in a large crowding out of private sector investment and a tripling of the real interest rate (compared with the no-shock simulation) by period 7.

For the African archetype the assumption of wage and price flexibility minimizes the adverse growth effects of the shock, and poverty and income distribution actually improve. As discussed below, the improvement in the poverty and distributional indicators comes from the expenditure switching policies, which raise the real income of the poor and improve their relative position. However, poverty and distributional indicators in the Latin American archetype are significantly worse because of three factors. First, wage and price rigidity slows growth and raises the fraction of the population in poverty. Second, the richer socioeconomic groups, which own capital, resist the cuts in living standards. Third, big farmers and capitalists are able to avoid capital losses by shifting their portfolios toward foreign-denominated assets.

The evolution of the distribution of income across socioeconomic groups is shown in figures 1 and 2. In the African archetype the real exchange rate

352   THE WORLD BANK ECONOMIC REVIEW, VOL. 5, NO. 2

Figure 1. *Distributional Effects of External Shock in the African Archetype*
(real income per capita index)

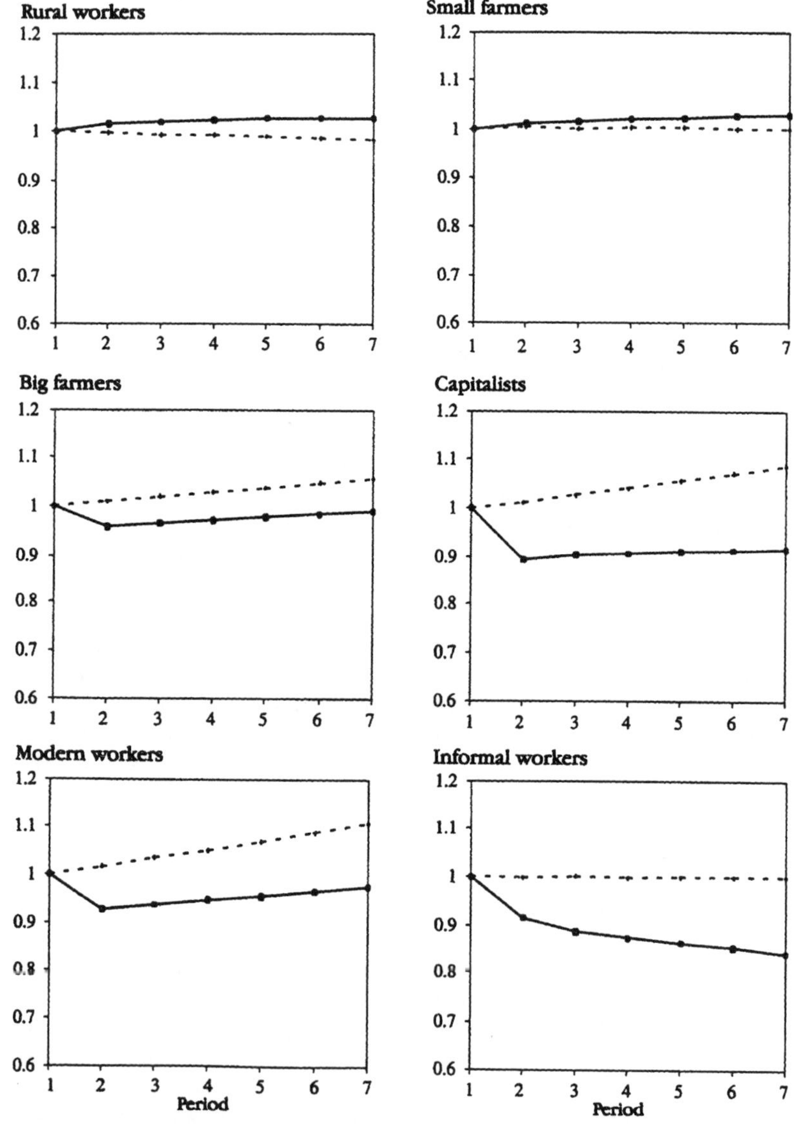

Note: ▫——— With shock, +- - - without shock.
Source: Authors' calculations.

Figure 2. *Distributional Effects of External Shock in the Latin American Archetype*
(real income per capita index)

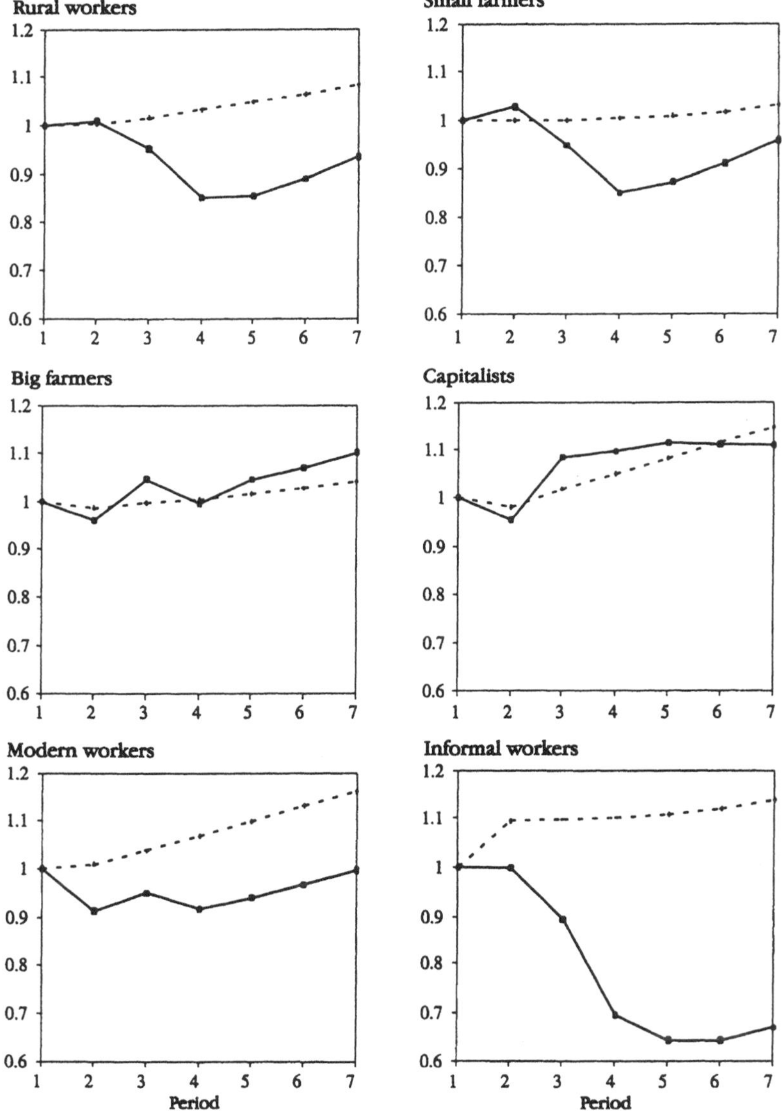

Note: o——— With shock, +- - - - without shock.
Source: Authors' calculations.

devaluation raises the real income of rural workers beyond levels reached in the no-shock environment, and small farmers, who earn part of their income from wages in the export sector, lose very little from the shock. The burden of adjustment falls most heavily on workers in the nontraded informal sector, who lose not only because of the fall in the relative price of nontradables but also because of the decline in the real income of capitalists, who have a high income elasticity of demand for informal sector services. Modern sector workers lose somewhat less than capitalists because their average wage includes the exogenously set real wage of civil servants. Mobility across modern sectors also mitigates the effects of the shock. The distribution of income becomes less unequal in the African archetype as a result of the shock because devaluation protects the poorest socioeconomic groups, rural workers, and small farmers.

A strikingly different pattern emerges under the standard adjustment pattern in the Latin American archetype. Despite the sharp recession under adjustment, capitalists and big farmers manage to maintain and even improve their absolute real income. All wage earners suffer, and real income falls in the informal sector. Modern sector workers lose on average in spite of real wage resistance in great part because of increased unemployment, which results in decreased per capita income in the sector. Finally, the fate of small farmers and rural workers is similar, with both losing because of recession. Clearly, under this adjustment scenario in which the poor have to share income with the unemployed and cannot protect their money holdings from the inflation tax, the shock widens income disparities among socioeconomic groups.

III. DISTRIBUTIONAL EFFECTS OF ALTERNATIVE ADJUSTMENT PACKAGES

We have seen that differences in assumptions about market adjustment and about household opportunities to protect themselves from shocks can account for radically different distributional effects of identical external shocks and adjustment policies. We now evaluate the distributional effects of the three adjustment packages described in the introduction. As before all policy changes occur in period 2.

In the rationing adjustment package, adjustment occurs through import rationing, with the Central Bank sticking to an exchange rate policy that maintains a constant real exchange rate pegged to CPI domestic inflation. This adjustment scenario reflects a policy of postponing adjustment, which we assume can last for the seven years in the simulation. The proceeds of the rents accruing from the premium on imports are distributed pro-rata (as dividends) to each sector. (Rents from the premiums on noncompetitive imports are distributed to the formal nontraded (commercial) sector.) Otherwise all other assumptions are identical to those describing the standard adjustment package. Again, to clearly trace the effects of the differences built into each archetype, we abstract from the use of the standard fiscal, monetary, and exchange rate instruments.

In the structural reform package, starting from the standard adjustment package, we apply the trade and tax reforms advocated by the IMF and the World Bank. (Tax and tariff structures across sectors in each archetype are given in appendix tables A-1 and A-2.) Export taxes are abolished for both archetypes. Uniform tariff rates are set at 15 percent for Africa and 20 percent for Latin America. Sales taxes are also equalized at 7 percent for Latin America and 3 percent for Africa, and profit and income taxes on modern sector capitalists are set at 10 percent in both archetypes. To reflect difficulties in tax administration, all tax reforms apply only to the modern sector; the nontraded informal and the two agricultural sectors are not taxed. The equalization of tax rates is designed to yield broadly the same revenue levels in period 2 as in the standard adjustment package. These tax rates may not be at the exact level actually found in the regions, but the composition of tax receipts across the categories of trade taxes, direct taxes, and indirect taxes broadly conforms to average patterns for low- and middle-income countries.

Finally, in the redistribution package the structural adjustment package is augmented by food subsidies and a public works program. Because our simulation model is not sufficiently disaggregated, especially with respect to the social sectors, this strategy, which is intended to simulate the elements of the strategy advocated in the *World Development Report 1990*, cannot reflect all the targeting and redistributive policies that would be included in a complete strategy of poverty alleviation. A food subsidy of 7 percent for the African archetype and of 5 percent for the Latin American archetype is applied to sales of agricultural products from period 2 on. The public works program is implemented so as to result in the same exogenous government nominal wage bill as in previous experiments while achieving full employment at the same time. In the African archetype average public sector wages are frozen in real terms with an increase in public employment, thereby drawing labor out of the formal sector. In the Latin American archetype average public sector real wages fall, reflecting the hiring of unskilled workers in the public works program. In this archetype government sector increases in employment come out of the pool of unemployed.

The macroeconomic and aggregate distributional effects of each one of these packages are contrasted with the standard adjustment package in table 5 and figure 3. For both archetypes the rationing adjustment package results in severe import rationing by the end of the simulation period, with premium rates on imports exceeding 100 percent. Under this scenario both poverty indicators also worsen, which is not surprising since the rents accruing from rationing redistribute real income from the poor and middle to the richer socioeconomic groups. Figure 3 indicates that the population in poverty increased from 30 to 40 percent in Africa and from 12 to 36 percent in Latin America. These estimates are very high and may exaggerate the actual adverse impact on poverty of adjustment in an economy in which rent-seeking and nonmarket mechanisms

Table 5. *Macroeconomic and Distributional Indicators for the Two Archetypes under Different Adjustment Packages*
(percent unless otherwise indicated)

Archetype and indicator	Standard adjustment		Rationing adjustment		Structural reform		Redistribution	
	Period 2	Period 7	Period 2	Period 7	Period 2	Period 7	Period 2	Period 7
African archetype								
GDP (period 1 = 100)	103.0	117.0	102.0	121.0	103.0	117.0	103.0	117.0
Investment/GDP (real)	18.9	15.5	20.5	25.5	19.3	15.3	17.2	13.1
Inflation (CPI)	20.7	18.1	22.3	16.7	19.6	18.3	19.3	19.4
Devaluation rate	27.0	17.5	22.0	17.3	22.0	18.0	21.0	18.2
Premium rate[a]			27.5	102.3				
Interest rate	20.3	23.4	18.4	15.0	19.8	23.0	21.5	26.6
Government revenue/GDP	15.3	15.0	15.5	16.5	15.0	15.2	12.5	12.8
Overall deficit/GDP	5.2	9.0	6.8	12.6	5.5	8.5	8.0	11.1
Theil index[b]	61.5	50.8	61.1	47.9	57.6	46.6	55.8	45.4
Poverty gap[c]	2.8	2.7	3.5	4.8	2.3	2.3	1.9	2.1
Poverty rate	29.9	29.5	33.9	39.2	26.0	26.0	22.9	24.3
Latin American archetype								
GDP (period 1 = 100)	101.0	107.0	100.0	100.0	101.0	108.0	104.0	108.0
Investment/GDP (real)	13.8	14.8	13.9	16.1	14.4	14.6	13.4	14.2
Inflation (CPI)	108.3	30.1	102.8	27.8	102.6	30.7	108.9	30.6
Devaluation rate	108.0	31.4	100.0	26.3	103.0	31.9	109.0	32.1
Premium rate[a]			10.0	115.4				
Interest rate	49.0	42.1	48.4	37.4	47.9	42.7	49.3	43.3
Government revenue/GDP	11.5	12.6	13.7	12.9	10.9	12.8	10.2	11.5
Overall deficit/GDP	8.2	17.5	8.7	23.9	8.7	17.8	9.3	18.4
Theil index[b]	32.7	43.0	32.6	45.6	31.8	41.0	32.4	42.3
Poverty gap[c]	0.9	1.5	1.0	3.8	0.7	1.2	0.6	1.2
Poverty rate	12.1	19.5	12.5	28.2	10.3	16.9	9.7	17.3

n.a. Not available.

Note: Under the standard adjustment package the exchange rate is devalued, with the rationing adjustment package there is import rationing, with the structural reform package there is tax equalization, and under the redistribution package there are tax equalization, food subsidies, and public works.

a. Premium rate on imports under rationing.

b. A decrease in the value of the index indicates less income inequality.

c. The poverty gap indicates the percentage of income that must be redistributed to bring all those below the poverty line up to the poverty line.

Source: Authors' calculations.

Figure 3. *Growth and Poverty under Alternative Adjustment Packages*

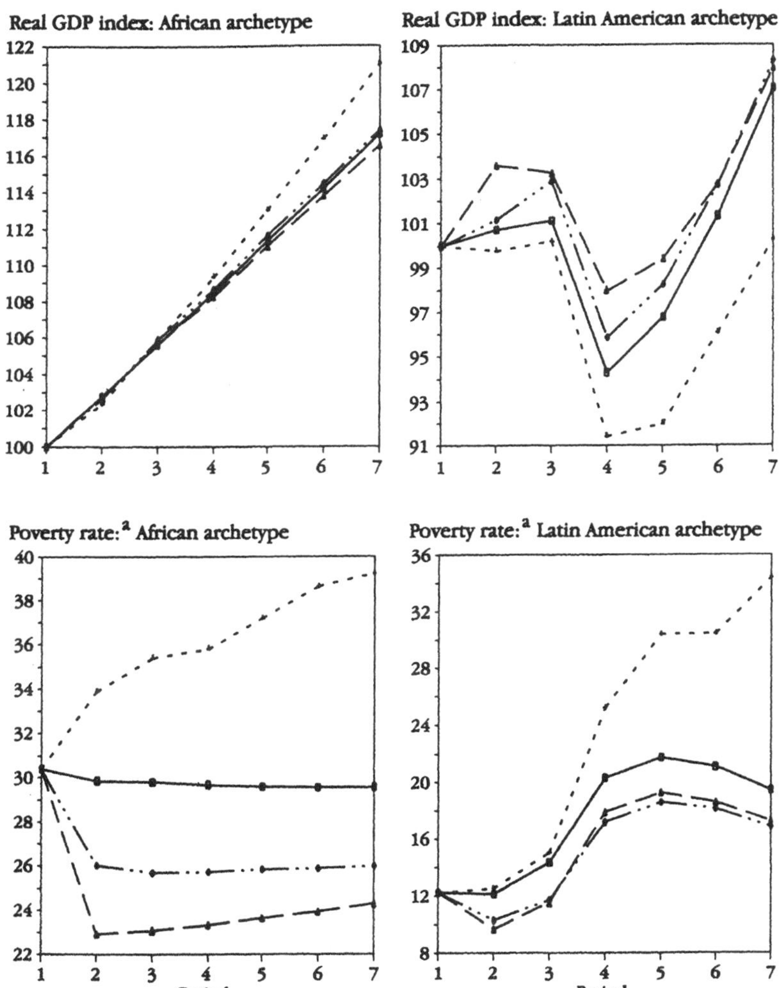

Note: ○—— Standard adjustment, +- - - rationing adjustment, ◆—— structural reform,
▸—— redistribution.
a. Head count index.
Source: Authors' calculations.

358 THE WORLD BANK ECONOMIC REVIEW, VOL. 5, NO. 2

are commonplace. The higher growth in Africa with the rationing adjustment package is induced by a strong Kaldorian effect. Income is redistributed from households to firms and capitalists through the quasi-rents on imports. Given that capitalists have a higher propensity to save, the rate of interest drops and investment expenditures increase. Of course this expenditure-switching phenomenon occurs because wage and price flexibility ensures that the economy is at full employment. Over time the increased share of investment in GDP also leads to substantially faster growth.

The overall effect on income distribution is mixed. The drop in household consumption contributes to a fall in agricultural prices and thus in the real income of all rural groups, including poor rural workers and smallholders. Big farmers in the primary export sector also lose a substantial proportion of their income, however, because the real exchange rate does not fall as in the standard adjustment scenario. Since the Theil measure of inequality is very sensitive to changes at the top of the distribution, the overall result is a slight drop in inequality. Some other measures of inequality would indicate the opposite.

Although the preceding effects also operate in the Latin American archetype, resistance to real wage cuts and price rigidity in modern sectors prevents the preceding Kaldorian expenditure-switching phenomenon. Because of price rigidities, import rationing cuts real expenditures and reduces economic activity. The rate of unemployment thus is much higher than in the standard adjustment package, with a consequent deterioration in poverty indicators. The outcome is that real GDP stands at the same level as in the base year at the end of the seven-year simulation. At the same time, in spite of a lower real cost of servicing the external (and internal) debt, the overall fiscal situation is worse under this scenario because of forgone trade tax revenues caused by the refusal to devalue the real exchange rate. In sum the rationing adjustment scenario has strongly adverse effects on poverty.

Compared with the rationing adjustment scenario, the two reform packages (structural reform and redistribution) yield relatively smaller effects of the shock precisely because the reforms are once-and-for-all measures introduced in period 2. Overall, with either reform package, the macroeconomic indicators are very close to the values achieved under the standard adjustment package, although there is a slightly larger fiscal deficit in the redistribution package at the end of the simulation. As can be seen in figure 3, the change in the poverty rate occurs in period 2, as soon as the reforms are implemented. Significantly, the redistributive effect achieved in the African archetype in period 2 is largely maintained throughout the entire simulation. Clearly, if it is possible to carry out trade and tax reforms that improve allocative efficiency by equalizing incentives across sectors and to implement revenue-neutral redistributive measures, then it is possible to reduce poverty.

At a more general level structural reforms will be largely unsuccessful when there are rigidities, as in the Latin American archetype, that prevent adjustment in relative prices. Under those circumstances reforms will not induce firms to work closer to full capacity. From the simulations with the African archetype, in which (effective) indirect taxes are relatively low and production structures are relatively rigid because of largely noncompetitive imports, reforms have a negligible effect in the small modern sector. Hence efficiency gains are small. Of course abolishing export taxes benefits the agricultural sector, reduces poverty, and equalizes income, but the expansionary effect on output is negligible because of diminishing returns in agriculture.

IV. Conclusion

The question raised in the introduction to this article was whether differences in economic and market structure and levels of institutional development were important in the analysis of adjustment policies on poverty and income distribution. We asked whether these differences could result in identical adjustment policies applied in response to a common external shock having radically different, and even opposite, effects on poverty and income distribution. Although such an outcome is not in itself surprising, differences in magnitudes and in the channels that account for these results were often found to be interesting and at times surprising. These results suggest a payoff to the careful modeling of relevant differences across countries in an economywide setting when analyzing the effects of adjustment policies on poverty and income distribution.

Several important differences emerged in the comparisons of different adjustment packages across the two archetype economies. As an illustration, we recall three results. The first is the result that, in the standard adjustment package, inequality increased significantly for the Latin American archetype but decreased significantly for the African archetype. We traced these differences to two factors: the ability of the rich to protect their financial assets through capital flight in the Latin American archetype and the flexibility in the African archetype, which helps the poor as the real incomes of the rural areas are raised through higher export earnings induced by the real exchange rate depreciation. The second result, often stressed by structuralists, is that adjustment can lead to a sharp redistribution of income from groups with low marginal propensities to save toward groups with high marginal propensities to save. In the context of supply- (rather than demand-) constrained economies, such Kaldorian redistributive effects will tend to raise investment and growth, which helps reduce poverty. The third result is that redistributive policies through trade and tax reforms that improve allocative efficiency by equalizing incentives across sectors can reduce inequality significantly, provided that governments are able to implement these revenue-neutral redistributive measures.

There were also other interesting differences. These included the relatively small effects of reforms on growth and income distribution in both archetypes, even though the reasons for this were found to be different for each one. Perhaps most significantly, we showed that our macro-micro model replicated broadly the stylized changes in the value of the macroeconomic indicators during the

1980s (lower growth, a fall in the investment share in GDP, a current account deterioration because of higher interest payments on the external debt, and a surge in inflation in Latin America). In this context wage and price rigidities built into the Latin American archetype caused the distribution of income to worsen significantly as a result of the external shock. However, wage and price flexibility built into the African archetype insulated the distribution of income from the external shock.

APPENDIX

This appendix details briefly the assumptions made in the construction of each archetype economy. The production and final demand structure for the two archetype economies and the tax structure across sectors and socioeconomic groups is given in tables A-1 and A-2. The structure is a slight modification of what Chenery and Syrquin call the "standard" cross-country model (see Chenery, Robinson, and Syrquin 1987, chapter 3). We constructed the African (Latin American) archetype from their low-income (middle-income) cross-country model. In addition to differences in structural composition, the two economies have differences in interindustry linkages, as reflected in the lower value added to gross output ratio in the Latin American archetype. Interindustry linkages for the two archetypes are adapted from table 5.2 of Chenery, Robinson, and Syrquin (1987).

Tables A-3 to A-5 describe the initial distribution of physical and financial assets across socioeconomic groups, and the assumptions about initial publicly held foreign debt and the share of total debt held in domestic bonds. Assumptions about financial ratios for firms and the economy as a whole are given in table A-5. The African archetype initially has a lower share of external debt. The same log variance of income is used for corresponding socioeconomic groups across economies, and dispersion in within-group income is assumed to be higher for capitalists than for workers.

Table A-1. *Production and Demand Structure of the African Archetype*
(percentage of total value added)

Sector	Output	Value added	Consumption		Investment		Exports	Imports	Intermediate demand
			Private	Public	Private	Public			
Primary exports	16.7	13.0	0.0	0.0	0.0	0.0	16.7	0.0	0.0
Agriculture	30.0	24.8	18.8	0.7	0.0	0.0	0.0	3.9	14.5
Light industry	28.6	10.7	7.8	0.7	0.0	0.0	0.7	6.7	26.1
Heavy industry	8.4	3.6	1.3	0.7	5.6	1.9	0.2	13.7	12.4
Services	47.3	27.9	21.0	1.2	11.3	3.9	2.2	4.6	12.4
Government	9.0	9.0	0.0	9.0	0.0	0.0	0.0	0.0	0.0
Informal	13.0	11.0	10.83	0.0	0.0	0.0	0.0	0.0	2.2
Total	153.0	100.0	59.7	12.3	16.9	5.8	19.8	28.8	67.4

Sector	Tax structure (percent)			
	Indirect tax	Corporate tax	Tariff	Export tax
Primary exports	14	0	0	8
Agriculture	0	0	10.6	0
Light industry	4	0	24.8	0
Heavy industry	5	0	16.8	0
Services	9	0	0	0
Noncompetitive imports			16.0	
Percentage of total tax revenue	49	0	25	10
Income tax on capital: 10 percent (16 percent of total tax revenue)				

Source: Adapted from Chenery, Robinson, and Syrquin (1987), tables 3.4 and 5.2.

Table A-2. *Production and Demand Structure of the Latin American Archetype*
(percentage of total value added)

Sector	Output	Value added	Consumption		Investment		Exports	Imports	Intermediate demand
			Private	Public	Private	Public			
Primary exports	6.1	4.3	0.0	0.0	0.0	0.0	4.6	0.0	1.5
Agriculture	11.4	8.0	7.7	0.0	0.0	0.0	0.0	3.0	6.7
Light industry	46.1	17.0	21.0	0.0	0.0	0.0	4.6	4.0	24.5
Heavy industry	31.4	15.7	3.6	0.0	7.8	1.1	2.9	13.2	29.2
Services	55.4	32.8	22.0	0.0	12.8	1.9	5.1	4.3	17.9
Government	6.0	6.0	0.0	6.0	0.0	0.0	0.0	0.0	0.0
Informal	20.0	16.2	15.0	0.0	0.0	0.0	0.0	0.0	5.0
Total	170.4	100.0	69.4	0.0	20.6	3.0	17.2	24.5	84.8

Sector	Tax structure (percent)			
	Indirect tax	Corporate tax	Tariff	Export tax
Primary exports	2	0	0	5
Agriculture	0	0	8	0
Light industry	1	8	45	0
Heavy industry	2	8	40	0
Services	4	8	0	0
Noncompetitive imports			41	
Percentage of total tax revenue	31	5	48	2
Income tax on capital: 10 percent (14 percent of tax revenue)				

Source: Adapted from Chenery, Robinson, and Syrquin (1987), tables 3.5 and 5.2.

Table A-3. *Private Sector Distribution of Assets and Liabilities in the African Archetype*
(percent unless otherwise indicated)

Factor of production	Production sector	Socioeconomic group						
		Capitalists	Big farmers	Small farmers	Landless agricultural workers	Modern workers	Informal workers	Total
Distribution across socioeconomic groups								
Land	Primary export	20	80					100
	Agriculture		55	45				100
Labor	Primary export		1.8	7.8	11.8			21.4
(labor units)	Agriculture		4.2	18.2	27.4			49.8
	Consumer goods		0.8			3.2		4.0
	Intermediate and capital goods					0.4		0.5
	Nontraded formal		1.2			4.6		5.8
	Informal						14.0	14.0
	Total		8.1	26.0	39.2	8.2	14.0	95.5
Capital	All sectors	62.0	27.4	1.4	6.3	0.7	2.2	100.0
Financial assets ratios								
Money/income		10	10	10	10	10	10	
Savings/income		42	26	2	1	6	3	

Source: Authors' calculations.

Table A-4. *Private Sector Distribution of Assets and Liabilities in the Latin American Archetype*
(percent unless otherwise indicated)

		Socioeconomic group						
Factor of production	*Production sector*	*Capitalists*	*Big farmers*	*Small farmers*	*Landless agricultural workers*	*Modern workers*	*Informal workers*	*Total*
Distribution across socioeconomic groups								
Land	Primary export	20	80					100
	Agriculture	10	55	35				100
Labor	Primary export		0.3	1.8	5.6			7.7
(labor units)	Agriculture		0.8	4.2	12.3			17.3
	Consumer goods	0.8				11.6		12.4
	Intermediate and capital goods	0.4				6.7		7.1
	Nontraded formal	0.8				11.4		12.2
	Informal						27.0	27.0
	Total	2.0	1.1	6.0	17.9	29.7	27.0	83.7
Capital[a]	All sectors	33.6	4.7	0.2	0.5	16.3	4.7	60.0
Financial assets ratios								
Foreign assets/financial wealth		30	20					
Domestic bonds/nonmonetary assets		70	30					
Money/income		10	10	10	10	10	10	
Savings/income		41	21	2	2	8	5	

a. This does not add up to 100 percent because of the assumption of 40 percent retained earnings.
Source: Authors' calculations.

Table A-5. *Financial Assumptions*
(percent)

| | Firm financial ratio | | | | | |
| | African archetype | | | Latin American archetype | | |
Sector	Liabilities/ assets	Working capital/sales	Foreign debt/ total debt	Liabilities/ assets	Working capital/sales	Foreign debt/ total debt
Primary export	5	10	0	5	15	0
Agriculture	5	10	0	5	15	10
Consumer goods	30	10	0	25	15	10
Intermediate and capital goods	30	10	0	25	15	10
Nontraded formal	30	10	0	25	15	0
Informal nonagriculture	0	10	0	0	0	0

| | Economywide ratio | |
	African archetype	Latin American archetype
Debt/exports	164	100
Money supply/sales	15	40
Domestic bonds/government debt	0	25

Source: Authors' calculations.

366 THE WORLD BANK ECONOMIC REVIEW, VOL. 5, NO. 2

REFERENCES

Bourguignon, François, W. Branson, and Jaime de Melo. Forthcoming. "Adjustment and Income Distribution: A Micro-Macro Model for Simulation Analysis." *Journal of Development Economics*.

Brecher, Richard, and Carlos Diaz-Alejandro. 1977. "Tariffs, Foreign Capital, and Immiserizing Growth." *Journal of International Economics*: 317–22.

Chenery, Hollis, and Moshe Syrquin. 1975. *Patterns of Development: 1950–70*. New York: Oxford University Press.

Chenery, Hollis, Sherman Robinson, and Moshe Syrquin, eds. 1987. *Industrialization and Growth: A Comparative Study*. New York: Oxford University Press.

Tobin, James. 1969. "A General Equilibrium Approach to Monetary Theory." *Journal of Money, Credit, and Banking* (February): 15–29.

World Bank. 1990. *World Development Report 1990: Poverty*. New York: Oxford University Press.

Journal of Development Economics 4 (1977) 149–172. © North-Holland Publishing Company

MODELLING THE EFFECTS OF PROTECTION IN A DYNAMIC FRAMEWORK

Jaime A.P. DE MELO*

Georgetown University, Washington, DC 20007, U.S.A.

Kemal DERVIS

Princeton University, Woodrow Wilson School, Princeton, NJ 08540, U.S.A.

Received September 1976, revised version received January 1977

The effects of alternative trade strategies on development performance are analyzed using a small, dynamic, computable general equilibrium model. The static allocation costs of protection are quantitatively weighed against the dynamic benefits resulting from heterogenous capital goods and imperfect foresight. An attempt at quantifying the effects of protection on employment and savings behavior is made by using submodels specifying distortions in labor-markets and alternative savings functions.

1. Introduction

The debate over the appropriate trade strategy for developing countries has been and continues to be a lively one. Belief in the need for a development strategy based on protection of the manufacturing sector is powerful in most LDCs. The argument for protection in this context is essentially based on dynamic considerations. It is conceded that trade distortions have static welfare costs but it is then argued that the dynamic benefits associated with a protectionist growth strategy are well worth the static costs. Since the times of Hamilton and List these dynamic considerations essentially relate to some variant of the 'infant industry' argument. The precise form taken by the argument varies, but it is always based on a divergence between static and dynamic considerations and an emphasis on dynamic effects. Trade theorists have on the other hand emphasized the static distortions caused by departures from unified exchange rates and have tended to advocate a movement to freer trade. Although recent investigations of the gains from trade in a growth theoretic context have somewhat qualified the static results, most policy prescriptions derived from trade theory favour free trade.

*We are grateful to the Editor and an anonymous referee for helpful comments. We would also like to thank Sherman Robinson, Peter Kenen, Anne Krueger and Mieko Nishimuzu for fruitful discussions.

But an adequate quantitative analysis of the relationships between trade policy and development performance, weighing the static costs against the potential dynamic gains from alternative trade strategies, remains to be developed. It is with this in mind that we present a dynamic general equilibrium model that can be used for a quantitative investigation of some of these issues.

The model is part of the general family of computable non-linear Walrasian models that incorporate direct substitution in both production and demand.[1] Behavioral equations derived from profit and utility maximization by firms and consumers combine with market clearing equations and technological relations to determine the growth path of the economy. It is the first of these models that addresses itself to the issue of trade policy in a dynamic context. Section 2 presents the equations of the model. Section 3, relating our model to the trade and welfare literature, discusses the major mechanisms that will determine the performance of alternative trade strategies. Sections 4, 5, and 6 present and evaluate the results.

2. A general equilibrium model of trade and growth

We spell out some of the salient features of the model before presenting the set of equations describing it. Behavior is assumed to be competitive and commodity markets must clear in each period. Capital is heterogeneous and once installed cannot be moved across sectors. Since we do not assume perfect foresight or perfect capital markets, profit rates in general will vary between sectors. Several alternative specifications in the labor market are combined with endogenous and exogenous savings behavior.

In the spirit of the barter theory of international trade, the economy faces fixed terms of trade and monetary effects are excluded from the model. However, in line with recent developments in the field, we emphasize the dichotomy between: (1) tradable goods whose prices are fixed with quantities traded clearing their markets, and (2) home goods whose prices adjust to clear their markets.

The structure of the model is general and can accommodate any number of sectors.[2] However, some of its most important properties can be captured with a three sector specification. This also allows better understanding of the rather complex causal chains running through the model and facilitates the interpretations of results. In our experiments based on Turkish data we shall distinguish between agriculture, manufacturing and a nontradable sector, and run the model over forty years. In the presentation of the model $n = q_1 + q_2$ refers to the number of sectors in the economy, q_1 of which are traded, and t is the time subscript.

---

[1]For models of this type see Johansen's (1960) pioneering study of the Norwegian economy, Taylor and Black (1974), Dervis (1975), de Melo (1975), Adelman and Robinson (1976). For a model specifying noncompetitive pricing behavior, see Staehlin (1976).

[2]The solution algorithm can handle a very large number of sectors and has been tested for a 12-sector version of the model.

J.A.P. de Melo and K. Dervis, The effects of protection   151

Greek letters, lowercase roman letters and roman letters with bars are pre-determined variables or parameters. All endogenous variables are denoted by uppercase roman letters.

Below we present the main components of the model along with the complete set of equations describing the foreign trade sector, the producing and consuming sectors, the labor markets and the dynamic linkage equations.

The price equations for tradable sectors are

$$P_{it} = \bar{\pi}_{it}\,(1+\bar{\imath}_i)\,E_t, \qquad i = 1, \ldots, q_1,$$
$$t = 1, \ldots, T. \tag{1}$$

Eq. (1) states that the domestic price of tradable sector i, P_{it}, equals the world price, $\bar{\pi}_{it}$, multiplied by one plus the ad valorem tariff rate, $\bar{\imath}_i$, times the exchange rate, E_t. If commodity i is exported, $\bar{\imath}_i$ is the rate of export subsidy. The relative price of tradables are entirely determined by the exogenously specified world prices via the tariff structure, itself determined by government trade policy. In contrast to the nontradable sectors where domestic prices adjust to equate domestic supply and demand, in the tradable sectors quantities traded clear the domestic markets.

This dichotomy between tradables and nontradables is an extreme one. Domestic and foreign tradable goods are perfect substitutes so that the country will either export or import a commodity, but not both.[3] We have chosen to retain this extreme specification and the small country assumption because they are commonly used in trade theory and in the literature on the welfare costs of protection to which this paper is addressed.

The balance-of-payments equations are

$$\sum_{i=1}^{q_1} \pi_{it}\,T_{it} + \bar{\pi}_0\,M_{0t} = \bar{D}_t, \qquad t = 1, \ldots, T, \tag{2}$$

where

$$M_{0t} = \sum_{i=1}^{n} s_{i0}\,Y_{it}.$$

Since we choose to predetermine the trade gap $\bar{D}_t$ (with balance-of-trade when $\bar{D}_t = 0$), the exchange rate adjusts until the balance-of-payments equation is satisfied; T_{it} denotes the quantities traded and we adopt the convention that $T_{it} > 0$ for imports and $T_{it} < 0$ for exports. Noncompetitive imports enter the

---

[3]In reality, even for a very fine commodity classification, product differentiation is sufficient to allow persistent price differentials as well as two-way trade. For a discussion of these problems, see Armington (1969), Deardorff, Stern and Baum (1976), and Robinson and de Melo (1976).

model and are denoted by M_{0t}. They are assumed to be related to investment by sector of destination, Y_{it}, through noncompetitive import coefficients, s_{i0}.

In a fixed exchange rate variant, not considered here, E_t would be fixed and (2) would become a side equation.

The price normalization equations are

$$\sum_{i=1}^{n} P_{it} \bar{X}_{i0} = \sum_{i=1}^{n} \bar{P}_{i0} \bar{X}_{i0}, \qquad t = 1, \ldots, T. \tag{3}$$

Only relative prices are determined by the model and one has to choose a normalization rule. The normalization equations above set a base year weighted price index equal to its initial value for all years throughout the plan period. An appropriate price stabilizing monetary policy is thus implicitly assumed. The base period is denoted by time subscript 0.

It should be noted that eqs. (1) and (3), and the assumption of constant world prices, imply that the exchange-rate adjustment between time periods is given by the change in the relative value of nontraded goods. By manipulating eqs. (1) and (3) it can be shown that

$$\frac{E_t}{E_0} = 1 + \frac{\displaystyle\sum_{i=q_1+1}^{q_2} P_{i0} \bar{X}_{i0} - \sum_{i=q_1+1}^{q_2} P_{it} \bar{X}_{i0}}{\displaystyle\sum_{i=1}^{q_1} P_{i0} \bar{X}_{i0}}.$$

Eqs. (1)–(3) complete the description of the foreign trade sector.

The production functions are

$$X_{it} = \bar{A}_{i0} (1+\bar{g}_i)^t K_{i,t-1}^{\alpha_i} L_{it}^{\beta_i}, \qquad i = 1, \ldots, n, \tag{4}$$
$$t = 1, \ldots, T.$$

Output of sector i, X_{it}, is a Cobb–Douglas function of capital installed at the end of the past period, $K_{i,t-1}$, and currently employed labor, L_{it}. The shift parameters, $\bar{A}_i$, grow at exogenously specific rates, g_i. These technical progress rates play a crucial role in determining dynamic comparative advantage and the price of nontradables.

The material balance equations are

$$C_{it} = X_{it} + T_{it} - \sum_{j=1}^{n} a_{ij} X_{jt} - \sum_{j=1}^{n} s_{ij} Y_{jt}, \qquad i = 1, \ldots, n. \tag{5}$$

Domestic private consumption, C_{it}, is equal to domestic production, X_{it}, plus imports (minus exports), T_{it}, minus intermediate demand, minus investment demand; Y_{jt} stands for investment by sector of destination; a_{ij} and s_i are the elements of the input–output and capital composition matrices.

The consumer demand functions are

$$C_{it} = \bar{q}_{it}\left(\sum_{i=1}^{n} P_{it}\,C_{it}\right)\bigg/ P_{it}, \qquad i = 1, \ldots, n,$$
$$t = 1, \ldots, T,$$

where

$$\sum_{i=1}^{n} P_{it}\,C_{it} = C_t = \text{income consumed.}$$

These demand functions are derived from a Cobb–Douglas utility function

$$(U = \prod_i C_i^{\bar{q}_i}).^4$$

Multiplying each equation in (5) by P_{it}, summing over i and substituting (2) into this sum, it can be checked that with a zero balance of trade the following identity holds:

$$\sum_{i=1}^{n} P_{it}\,C_{it} = \text{Gross National Income} - \text{Investment,}$$

where Gross National Income itself is given by the expression: $GNI =$ total value of output − value of intermediate inputs + or − the trade tax or subsidy.

The net price equations are

$$V_{it} = P_{it} - \sum_{j=1}^{n} a_{ji}\,P_{jt}, \qquad i = 1, \ldots, n,$$
$$t = 1, \ldots, T.$$

The net price V_{it} equals the domestic price minus the costs of intermediate inputs. Note that the cost of tariffs are included in the P_{jt}, and that changes in the prices of nontradables affect the cost of producing tradables.

The specification of labor markets.   We shall experiment with three alternative specifications of the labor market: a full-employment model, a fixed-wage

---

[4]The parametric restrictions imposed on the utility function rule out inferior and complementary goods and the resulting Engel curves are linear. For this truncated version of the linear expenditure system, the own price elasticity of demand is unity and there are no cross-price effects.

model and a migration model. The full-employment model has the following equations:

$$W_t = \frac{\beta_i V_{it} X_{it}}{L_{it}}, \qquad i = 1, \ldots, n,$$

$$t = 1, \ldots, T, \tag{8a}$$

and

$$\sum_{i=1}^{n} L_{it} = L_0 (1+g_n)^t, \qquad t = 1, \ldots, T. \tag{8b}$$

Here an exogenously growing labor supply, $L_0 (1+g_n)^t$, must be fully employed and the endogenous full employment wage is equalized across all sectors.

The fixed-wage model has the following equations:

$$\gamma_i \overline{W}_t = \frac{\beta_i V_{it} X_{it}}{L_{it}}, \qquad i = 1, \ldots, n,$$

$$t = 1, \ldots, T, \tag{8'b}$$

where

$$\gamma = 1, \quad i = 2, \ldots, n \quad \text{and} \quad \gamma_1 = \bar{\gamma},$$

and

$$\overline{W}_t = \overline{W}_0 (1+g_w)^t \frac{\displaystyle\sum_{i=1}^{n} P_{it} C_{i0}}{\displaystyle\sum_{i=1}^{n} P_{i0} C_{i0}}.$$

Here the real wage, defined in terms of a Laspeyres consumer price index, is specified to grow exogenously at equal rates, g_w, in agriculture and in the urban sectors, preserving a fixed rural urban wage differential, $\bar{\gamma}$. The supply of labor to all sectors is perfectly elastic at the going wage.

The migration model has an expanded set of equations.

$$\overline{W}_t = \frac{\beta_i V_{it} X_{it}}{L_{it}}, \qquad i = 2, \ldots, n,$$

$$t = 1, \ldots, T, \tag{8''a}$$

$$W_1 = \frac{\beta_1 V_{it} X_{1t}}{L_t^A}, \qquad t = 1, \ldots, T. \tag{8''b}$$

J.A.P. de Melo and K. Dervis, The effects of protection   ·155

$$L_t^A = L_0^A (1+g_n)^t - MIG_t, \qquad t = 1, \ldots, T, \qquad (8''\text{c})$$

$$L_t^U = L_0^U (1+g_n)^t + MIG_t, \qquad t = 1, \ldots, T, \qquad (8''\text{d})$$

$$MIG_t = \mu \left(\frac{W_t^e}{W_1} - 1 \right) L_{t-1}^A, \qquad t = 1, \ldots, T, \qquad (8''\text{e})$$

$$W_t^e = \overline{W}_t \left(\sum_{i=2}^{n} L_{it}/L_t^u \right), \qquad t = 1, \ldots, T, \qquad (8''\text{f})$$

This is the most popular model in the development literature; L_t^A and L_t^U denote the supply of labor in agriculture and in the urban sectors;[5] in agriculture the wage is allowed to clear the labor market but the urban wage is exogenously fixed as in the fixed-wage model and an endogenous rural urban migration mechanism regulates the supply of urban labor. Migration MIG_t is a function of the expected urban wage W_t^e which is equal to the urban wage multiplied by the urban employment rate. It is clear that this model becomes inconsistent when $\sum_{i=2}^{n} L_{i:} > L_t^u$, i.e. when urban unemployment disappears. At that stage we switch to a full employment specification and an endogenous determination of the urban wage. Migration will continue as long as the expected urban wage, now simply equal to the urban wage, exceeds the wage in agriculture.

The capital-price equations are

$$U_{it} = \sum_{j=1}^{n} s_{ji} P_{jt} + s_{0i} \pi_0 (1+t_0) E_t, \qquad j = 1, \ldots, n, \qquad (9)$$

$$t = 1, \ldots, T.$$

The price of capital, U_{it}, in each sector is the weighted sum of the prices of its components including the price of noncompetitive imports, $\pi_0 (1+t_0) E_t$.

The profit-rate equations are

$$R_{it} = \frac{V_{it} X_{it} - W_t L_{it}}{U_{it-1} K_{it-1}} - \frac{U_{it} - (1-\bar{d}_i) U_{i,t-1}}{U_{i,t-1}}, \qquad i = 1, \ldots, n, \qquad (10)$$

$$t = 1, \ldots, T.$$

The sectoral profit-rates, R_{it}, equal the rental rates plus the depreciation adjusted rate of capital gains; $\bar{d}_i$ are the exogenously fixed depreciation rates. Profit rates will not in general be equal across sectors.[6]

---

[5] See Harris and Todaro (1969), Ahmed (1974) and Fields (1975).
[6] See Dervis (1975) for a discussion of profit rates in multi sector growth models in an intertemporal equilibrium model that equalizes profit rates across sectors for all periods.

156   **J.A.P. de Melo and K. Dervis, The effects of protection**   .

Eqs. (4) – (10) complete the description of the producing and consuming sectors in the economy. We now turn to the intertemporal linkages which govern the dynamic structure of the model.

The investment allocation equations are:

$$Y_{it} = H_{it} \sum_{i=1}^{n} Y_{it} = H_{it}\, INV_{t}, \qquad i = 1, \ldots, n, \qquad (11)$$

$$t = 1, \ldots, T,$$

$$U_{it}\, Y_{it} = H_{it} \sum_{i=1}^{n} U_{it}\, Y_{it} = H_{it}\, INV_{t}, \qquad i = 1, \ldots, n, \qquad (11')$$

$$t = 1, \ldots, T.$$

H_{it} is the share of total investment, INV_{t}, that goes to sector i in period t. The sum of H_{it} must equal one. We have two alternatives: H_{it} may be the share in terms of base year prices (11) or it may be the share in terms of current prices (11').[7] It remains to determine these shares.

The investment shares equations are

$$H_{it} = SK_{i,t-1} + \delta\, SK_{i,t-1} \left(\frac{R_{i,t-1} - AR_{t-1}}{AR_{t-1}} \right), \qquad i = 1, \ldots, n, \quad (12)$$

$$t = 1, \ldots, T.$$

The investment theory adopted here specifies that the allocation of investment by sector of destination depends on sectoral profit shares and sectoral profit rates; SK_{i} is the share of total profits originating in sector i; AR_{t-1} is the average profit rate experienced in the previous period; δ is an investment mobility parameter.[8]

The share of investment going to sector i is determined by the share of sector i in total profits of the previous period and the percentage deviation of sector i's profit rate from the average profit rate. When $\delta = 0$ there is no intersectoral mobility of investment funds and the share of each sector in capital formation is identical to its share in profits. This would be the case if all investment were to be financed by retained profit earnings. When δ is positive, investment funds will respond to profit rate differentials: high profit rate sectors will attract profits from other sectors. Thus δ is an index of the intersectoral mobility of investment funds Note however that it is *not* an index of foresight exhibited in capital markets.

---

[7] Unless otherwise stated we shall use (11').

[8] It may easily be checked that given $\sum_{i=1}^{n} SK_{i} \equiv 1$ we have $\sum_{i=1}^{n} H_{i} \equiv 1$.

J.A.P. de Melo and K. Dervis, *The effects of protection*   ·157

The economy-wide capital accumulation equations are:

$$INV_t = \sum_{i=1}^{n} Y_{it} = \overline{GRK} \sum_{i=1}^{n} K_{it-1} + \sum_{i=1}^{n} \bar{d}_i K_{it-1}, \qquad t = 1, \ldots, T, \tag{13}$$

$$INV_t = \sum_{i=1}^{n} U_{it} Y_{it} = \bar{S} \times GNI, \qquad t = 1, \ldots, T, \tag{13'}$$

$$INV_t = \sum_{i=1}^{n} U_{it} Y_{it} = \overline{SP} \times \text{profits}, \qquad t = 1, \ldots, T. \tag{13''}$$

We have three alternative specifications. In (13) we exogenously specify the growth rate of capital, $\overline{GRK}$, in base year prices. We shall refer to (13) as the 'exogenous investment' or 'open-loop savings' specification. It has been used almost exclusively in most previous computable general equilibrium models mainly because of its computational convenience.

The mechanism through which the economy realizes any predetermined $\overline{GRK}$ remains unspecified. An explicit and more elaborate closing of the government and income accounts would be required to specify alternative mechanisms through which any given level of real investment could be achieved. We implicitly rely here on the existence of appropriate Robinsonian 'animal spirits'!

In (13') and (13'') we postulate neoclassical and classical savings functions with a constant fraction of national income saved in the first case and a constant fraction of capitalist income saved in the second. Investment now becomes endogenous.

Finally, the capital updating equations are

$$K_{it} = K_{i,t-1} (1 - \bar{d}_i) + Y_{it}, \qquad i = 1, \ldots, n, \tag{14}$$

$$t = 1, \ldots, T.$$

These are simply accounting relations updating the depreciated sectoral capital stocks in each period.

The dynamic linkage equations close the growth model. Eqs. (11) to (14) are sufficient to determine for any time period t the variables INV_t, H_{it}, Y_{it} and K_{it}, given the exogenous parameters and the values of the remaining variables. Taking for example the full employment specification of the labor market, with sectoral capital stocks given from the previous time period and sectoral investment allocation determined through the linkage equations, eqs. (1)–(10) determine in each period the following endogenous variables:

P_{it}	n		domestic prices
E_t	1		the exchange rate
T_{it}	q_1		imports (exports)
X_{it}	n		output levels
L_{it}	n		sectoral employments
C_{it}	n	$\times T$	sectoral consumption
U_{it}	n		capital stock prices
V_{it}	n		net prices
R_{it}	n		sectoral profit rates
W_t	1		the wage rate

There are $(7n + q_1 + 2) \times T$ equations to determine these variables. The model can thus be run forward from initial capital stock prices, U_{i0}, and sectoral capital stocks, K_{i0}. It may easily be checked that for the fixed-wage and Harris–Todaro versions the changes in the number of variables equals the change in the number of equations and the model remains determinate.[9]

3. Static costs, dynamic benefits and imperfect markets

Before turning to the quantitative results, it is worth dwelling on the major causal chains implicit in our specification. It is not easy in a general equilibrium model to trace all the determining mechanisms, but we can isolate those that are likely to be most important for a dynamic analysis of trade policy.

We have two tradable sectors, agriculture and manufacturing, and one sector of nontradables.[10] We shall refer to protection as a policy that imposes a 50% tariff on the manufacturing sector and compare the 'protected' growth path to a 'free trade' path of unified exchange rates. Whenever manufacturing becomes the export sector, the 50% differential between the domestic price and the world price must be reinterpreted as an export subsidy. World prices remain constant throughout the analysis. The demand parameters also remain fixed. Changes in tastes thus play no role in determining the dynamics of the growth path.

There is exogenous, neutral, disembodied technical change in all three sectors. But manufacturing, our 'infant' sector is characterized by more rapid technical progress. For our basic runs we used $g_1 = 0.5\%$ in agriculture, $g_2 = 3.0\%$ in manufacturing, and $g_3 = 1.0\%$ in nontradables.

In the exogenous investment specification, capital stock, valued in base-year prices, is assumed to grow at an annual rate of 9%. In the full-employment

---

[9]It is of course not enough, in principle, to count equations and variables to establish the existence, let alone uniqueness of a solution. However, in rather well behaved general-equilibrium models of this kind the equality of equations and unknowns can be taken as both necessary and sufficient for the existence of a solution.

[10]The parameters for the three sectors given in the appendix were obtained by aggregating the 37-sector data base that underlies the third Turkish Five-Year Plan.

model, the work force grows at 3% per annum while in the fixed-wage model it is the real wage that grows at a 3% rate. In all variants there will be differential factor accumulation characteristic of the development process: the economy-wide capital–labour ratio will increase.

Agriculture is the labor intensive sector, with manufacturing and nontradables relatively more capital intensive. Initially there is a comparative advantage in agriculture but differential rates of factor accumulation and technical progress combine to shift comparative advantage towards manufacturing.

If profit rates were instantaneously equalized across all sectors due to homogeneous and shiftable capital or due to an assumption of perfect futures markets, and if there were no learning externalities that could not be internalized, the fact that comparative advantage was shifting over time would not cause the free trade path to be inefficient. In the absence of distortions, free trade remains optimal even if comparative advantage is shifting.

But in a world of heterogenous nonshiftable capital, changes in the structure of comparative advantage due to the pattern of technical progress and factor accumulation can lead to an infant industry type argument when foresight and capital markets are imperfect or when private discount-rates deviate from social discount-rates. Note that for there to be dynamic benefits associated with protection one does not need to assume the existence of 'learning' externalities that cannot be internalized. Our model does not contain such externalities. But it does specify imperfect foresight and heterogenous imperfectly mobile capital. This is sufficient for an allocation of investment based on the present structure of comparative advantage to be intertemporally inefficient. This does not of course constitute a first-best argument for protection. It does, however, suggest that protection can have a beneficial dynamic effect when compared to a policy of nonintervention. This should be quantitatively weighted against the more familiar static welfare costs of protection, future benefits being discounted at some appropriate social rate.[11]

Quite apart from the infant industry argument, it is well known that protection may be superior to 'laisser faire' in the presence of domestic distortions although, again, tariffs will never, in a small country model, constitute a first-best policy. The specification of labor markets takes on crucial importance in this context.[12]

A full-employment model with no distortions and free labor mobility between rural and urban sectors constitutes our basic specification. It is not a very realistic

---

[11]If, in addition, the 'infant' sector generates learning externalities that could not be internalized even in a perfect market setting, the argument is further reinforced. For a full discussion of infant industry protection, see Johnson (1971) and Corden (1974, ch. 9).

[12]Excellent surveys of the theory of distortions and first-best remedies in a static context are provided by Bhagwati (1971) and Magee (1973). The welfare effects of imperfect foresight, discussed in multi-sector growth theory, have generally not been discussed in the trade and development literatures. For an exception see however, the interesting analysis in Findlay (1973, ch. 8).

160   ***J.A.P. de Melo and K. Dervis, The effects of protection***

one in the context of developing countries. We therefore have experimented extensively with two alternative specifications: a model postulating perfectly elastic labor supplies at fixed and exogenously growing real wages, and a Harris–Todaro type model with an endogenous migration mechanism as the third case. Depending on the situation in labor markets, tariffs should be expected to have different effects on the level of welfare. In the full employment model without distortions, tariffs will always have negative static allocation effects. But in both the fixed-wage and the Harris–Todaro models, total employment becomes a variable affected by trade policy. It has been shown by Brecher (1974) in the context of the standard 2-by-2 static model of trade theory that in a minimum wage economy tariffs may decrease or increase total employment depending on whether free trade leads to the export or the import of the labor-intensive commodity.[13] The same basic result should be expected from our three-sector model and the direction of the total-employment effect of protection should depend on the direction of trade in the absence of intervention.

In the Harris–Todaro model, however, the increase in the relative price of agriculture generated by a movement to free trade will no longer have a positive employment effect because labor is no longer fully mobile. A fall in the relative price of manufactures will lead to higher urban unemployment that is not fully compensated by an increase in rural employment.

These are the major mechanisms that theory and an analysis of our specification suggests will determine our results in the case of the exogenous investment specification. Section 4 turns to an evaluation of these quantitative results. Section 5 will deal with the alternative neoclassical and classical endogenous investment or closed-loop saving specifications.

4. The quantitative results

A general-equilibrium model of the type specified leads to a great deal of microeconomic and macroeconomic results but we shall here concentrate on the welfare effects of alternative trade strategies. The welfare indicator used throughout is the Cobb–Douglas utility function, with sectoral consumption as arguments, from which the demand system can be derived.[14] Unless otherwise stated, the investment mobility parameter was set at $\delta = 0.10$ for all experiments we shall report on, implying moderate intersectoral mobility of investment funds.

Table 1 presents the level of utility reached in several years for the basic full employment, exogenous investment version of our model. At a 5% discount rate the protected path is slightly superior to the free trade path in terms of the sum of discounted utility reached at the end of the 40-year plan period. At a

---

[13]Provided that there is incomplete specialization. See also Lefeber (1971).

[14]Note that percentages are unaffected by multiplicative changes in welfare units. The natural origin of the utility function is given by zero consumption levels.

J.A.P. de Melo and K. Dervis, The effects of protection   161

6% discount rate, free trade would become superior. Fig. 1 summarizes the results graphically.

Table 1

Welfare under free trade and protection: The full-employment model.

	Annual utility levels for years:					Total utility discounted at 5%
	2	10	20	30	40	
Free trade	30.6	52.0	104.0	255.7	662.3	1910
Protection	29.5	48.0	109.5	273.4	674.4	1955
Percentage difference (2−1)/1	−3.6	−7.7	+5.3	+6.9	+1.8	+2.3[a]

[a]Protection slightly superior.

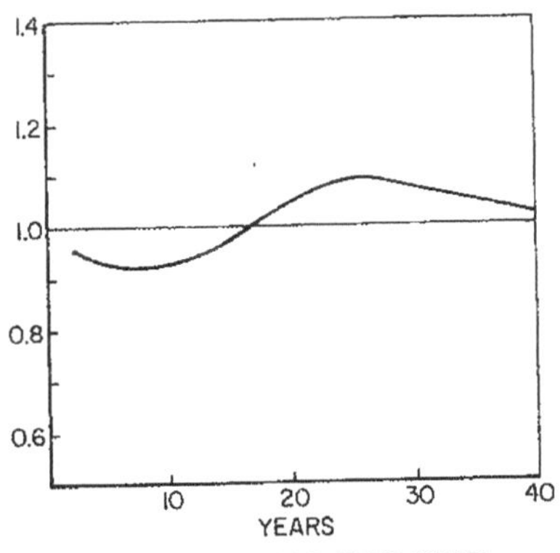

Fig. 1. The ratio of the level of utility under protection to the level of utility under free trade.

As shown in table 1 and fig. 1, at first the static allocation effects predominate, and in year 10 the welfare loss due to protection reaches almost 8%. But the dynamic effects favorable to protection are at work throughout and the protected path 'overtakes' the free trade path in year 17. It is not until year 28, however, that the discounted sum of utility is greater under protection than under free trade. Towards the end of the plan period the relative weight of agriculture in domestic production becomes insignificant for both growth paths. The dynamic investment allocation effect therefore loses its significance which explains the shape of the graph in fig. 1.

Table 2 describes the differences in investment allocation generated by the two alternative trade strategies. The difference in investment allocation reaches its peak in year 10 with manufacturing getting 61.7% under protection as opposed to only 31.5% under free trade. After the first 30 years the allocation of investment begins to look similar in both cases. Since the static effect is still at work in each period and the dynamic effect has lost much of its force, the superiority of the protected path starts to decline again.

Table 2

Profit rates and investment allocation shares: The full-employment model (percentages).[a]

	Years									
	2		10		20		30		40	
	R_i	H_i	R_i	H_i	R_i	H_i	R_i	H_i	R_i	H_i
Free trade										
Agri.	48.1	33.1	39.4	29.7	26.3	16.1	13.1	2.6	7.2	0.2
Mfgr.	16.0	23.7	33.4	31.5	43.4	48.7	45.7	58.7	44.4	56.1
N.T.	36.8	41.2	36.2	38.8	37.6	34.2	46.3	38.7	47.9	43.7
Protection										
Agri.	32.4	15.4	22.1	6.5	9.6	0.5	6.3	0.0	0.0	0.0
Mfgr.	43.2	46.7	52.2	61.7	50.3	64.0	49.7	60.6	50.2	57.4
N.T.	43.4	37.9	44.6	31.8	53.0	35.5	53.2	39.4	52.3	42.6

R_i = profit rates,
H_i = investment shares.
N.T. = non-tradables.

The results presented confirm and quantify the trade-off between static costs and dynamic benefits of protection and show that in our model a protectionist strategy pays-off at discount rates below 5%. There are however many qualifications.

As expected, the result is largely due to the substantial differences in technical progress rates. To verify this we have experimented with different rates. In the case of a 'neutral' run with $g_i = 1.5\%$ in all sectors the discounted sum of the utilities is no longer higher but 3.7% lower under protection and free trade remains superior even with a zero discount rate. Note however that even in this case differential factor accumulation preserves a much weakened but still positive dynamic allocation effect that leads the protected path to 'overtake' the free trade path in year 31.[15]

---

[15]It is this particular effect, linked to the Rybcznski theorem, that has been qualitatively analyzed by Findlay (1973, ch. 8).

J.A.P. de Melo and K. Dervis, *The effects of protection*   163

Increasing the investment mobility parameter δ strengthens the dynamic allocation effect favorable to protection by leading to more pronounced investment misallocation under free trade at the beginning of the plan period, but it also weakens its impact on welfare because the eventual correction of the misallocation is also more rapid. Moderate variations in assumed investment mobility do not affect the overall ranking of policies although they do affect the growth path.

What stands out in the results from the full-employment model is the relative smallness of the overall differences in the discounted sum of utilities. This is due to the fact that the static and dynamic effects tend to cancel out. Given that the spread postulated between the technical progress rates can be considered as a rather extreme upper-bound, table 1 should not be interpreted as justifying a policy of continued protection.

Indeed an intermediate policy of 'gradual' trade liberalization may dominate both paths so far presented. A growth path generated by a policy that lets the tariff decline geometrically starting in year 10 yields a discounted sum of utilities that is slightly greater than in the case of continued protection.

Fig. 2 summarizes the comparisons of growth paths in the fixed-wage and the Harris–Todaro type migration models. Here total employment effects complicate the picture and the percentage differences can no longer be considered as small.

For the fixed-wage case it is now the free trade path that very clearly dominates in terms of discounted utility. It remains true however that the protected path eventually overtakes and in the terminal period it generates a welfare level that is almost 35% greater than under free trade. Fig. 2a depicts the behavior of the two welfare paths.

The major explanation behind these results is the very strong total employment effect. This underlines the importance of trade policy for employment problems. Table 3 summarizes the alternative employment paths. It should be stressed that a rigidly fixed rate of real wage growth that is independent of the other variables in the system is not a realistic specification for a period as long as 40 years. In particular, the extension of the assumption of an infinitely elastic supply of labor at a fixed wage to the agricultural sector is not really justified. The assumption is often made for the urban sector but massive instantaneous reverse migration back to agriculture implied in the free-trade version of the fixed wage model is clearly unrealistic. An increase in the relative price of agriculture generated by a movement to free trade would not be able to generate the dramatic increase in agricultural employment if labor mobility between the urban and rural sectors was imperfect. The total employment effect would therefore lose much of its force. Urban employment would actually fall, leading to a worsened overall employment situation, at least initially. This is reflected in fig. 2, which summarizes the performance of our alternative trade strategies for the third variant of the model specifying an endogenous Harris–Todaro

164   **J.A.P. de Melo and K. Dervis, *The effects of protection***

type migration mechanism. In what is probably the most realistic specification of the labor markets, protection now clearly dominates. Indeed, except between years 7 and 14, the protected path is now consistently above the free trade alternative. The total employment effect is initially detrimental to free trade

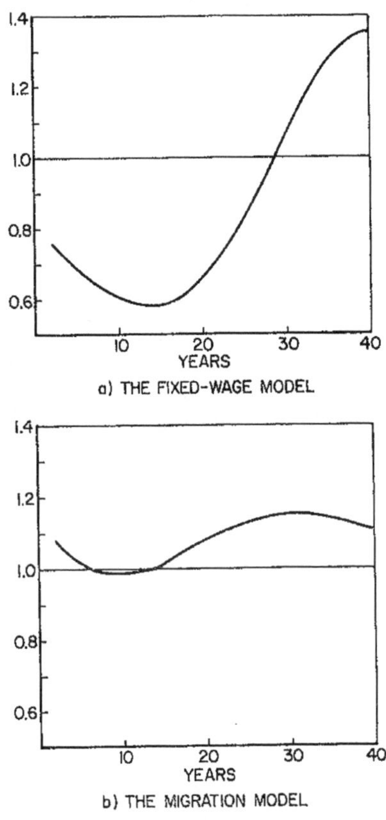

Fig. 2. The ratio of the level of utility under protection to the level of utility under free trade.

actually reducing economy wide employment. Table 4 describes the details of the results.

The conclusions derived from a Harris–Todaro type specification are thus exactly the opposite of those obtained in the fixed-wage case because the employment effect tends to work in opposite directions. This shows that it is extremely important when assessing the impact of alternative trade strategies on employment to analyze the actual degree of intersectoral labor mobility.

J.A.P. de Melo and K. Dervis, The effects of protection   165

Table 3

Economy-wide employment under free trade and protection: The fixed-wage model (thousand workers).

	Years				
	2	10	20	30	40
Free trade	14700	26700	41100	50798	54000
Protection	9071	12131	17930	32024	65796
Percentage difference (2−1)/1	−38	−55	−56	−37	+22

Table 4

Economy-wide employment, migration and urban unemployment under free trade and protection: The migration model (thousand workers).

	Years				
	2	10	20	30	40
Free trade					
Economy-wide employment	8300	12100	17500	26300	31700
Rural–urban migration	108	163	219	417	562
Urban unemp. rate	48%	22%	–	–	–
Protection					
Economy-wide employment	9200	12100	17500	23400	31700
Rural–urban migration	108	205	375	289	150
Urban unemp. rate	25%	14%	–	–	–

We have until now assumed that the economy-wide capital stock valued at base year prices grows exogenously. One could alternatively specify savings functions of the classical or neoclassical type. It is to a brief discussion of the issues relating to the interaction between trade policy and saving behavior that we turn in the next section. To conclude the report on the 'exogenous investment' specification of the model, table 5 summarizes the basic characteristics of the growth paths generated by the three variants discussed in this section.

166   *J.A.P. de Melo and K. Dervis, The effects of protection*

Table 5
Summary characteristics of the growth paths for the exogenous investment case.

	The full employment model		The fixed wage model		The migration model	
	Free trade	Protection	Free trade	Protection	Free trade	Protection
Average annual GNI growth	8.5%	8.7%	8.8%	9.5%	8.3%	8.8%
Average annual growth in base-year valued total consumption	8.4%	8.5%	8.6%	9.5%	8.3%	8.6%
Exports of manufactures starts in year	10	2	31	4	14	4
Average annual growth in the real wage	4.7%	5.4%	3.0%[a]	3.0%[a]	3.9% (2.7%)[b]	4.4% (1.9%)[b]
Total sum of discounted utilities in year 40	1910	1955	2413	2.87	1772	1932
Rankings in terms of utility	protection slightly superior		free trade superior		protection superior	

[a]The wage grows exogenously in all sectors.
[b]The urban wage grows exogenously.

5. Specifying explicit savings behavior

On the growth paths we have discussed so far, a certain fraction of national income was implicitly saved each year and spent on the acquisition of new capital goods. By using the 'exogenous investment' version [eq. (13)] of our model, we implied that the 'real' rate of capital accumulation is somehow determined independently of trade policy.

In this section we shall instead attempt to capture the interaction between trade policy and aggregate capital formation by specifying neoclassical and classical savings functions [eqs. (13') and (13'')] familiar from descriptive growth theory. As has recently been emphasized in the theoretical literature,[16] the relative price and income changes generated by changes in trade policy may have important effects on savings behavior, real growth, and therefore development performance. Note that our model with its nontraded sector that includes construction and its treatment of capital as a composite commodity will always retain some domestic production of capital goods in contrast to the 2-by-2 models where generally investment goods are either only exported or only imported.

[16]See, for example, Corden (1971), Johnson (1971) and Deardorff (1973).

The impact of trade policy on savings behavior can essentially be decomposed into income, substitution and distribution effects.

If real income increases, due to changes in trade policy, there will be greater saving and therefore greater real capital accumulation. This is the essence of the income effect and it strengthens the argument for free trade. As noted above, in the early phase of our plan period the static allocation effects favorable to free trade are dominant. If this leads to greater capital accumulation free trade will now itself have a positive dynamic effect that must be set against the dynamic investment allocation effect favorable to protection. The situation may however, reverse itself if, because of strong dynamic allocation effects, income under protection were ever to overtake income under free trade. At that point the income effect would start reinforcing the positive effect of protection.

Turning to the substitution effect, its direction depends on which kind of trade policy leads to a fall in the relative price of investment goods. Tariffs on imported capital goods will clearly increase their relative prices. On the other hand, the higher exchange rate implied in a free trade strategy will increase the cost of capital goods that can be imported without a tariff. In our model the noncompetitive import component of capital goods is more expensive under free trade, while the machinery component domestically produced or competi-tively imported is cheapened by freer trade. Moreover, the price of nontradable capital (construction) is substantially lower under free trade so that, netting out, free trade leads to a significant reduction in the relative price of capital goods. Table 6 describes the behavior of capital prices.

Table 6

The impact of trade policy on the relative prices of capital goods (U_i) with full employment and neoclassical savings.

| | Years | | | | |
	2	10	20	30	40
Free trade					
Agri.	0.780	0.719	0.718	0.792	0.860
Mfgr.	0.848	0.840	0.839	0.850	0.859
N.T.	0.787	0.724	0.723	0.799	0.870
Protection					
Agri.	0.806	0.801	0.895	0.969	1.016
Mfgr.	0.921	0.921	0.929	0.935	0.939
N.T.	0.805	0.800	0.898	0.970	1.024

With the income and substitution effects working together in the same direction whenever initially free trade increases national income, the results obtained when specifying a neoclassical saving function should be expected to be more favorable to free trade than those reported on in section 4.

If however, we specify a classical savings function so that savings depends only on total profits, a distribution effect will work in conjunction with the income and substitution effects discussed above. A trade policy that increases the relative prices of the goods that use capital more intensively will tend to increase real accumulation. In our model, manufacturing and nontradables being capital intensive, the distribution effect will be favorable to protection.

Fig. 3 summarizes the results obtained for the full employment version of our model when a neoclassical or a classical savings function is specified. These results should be compared to those given in table 1 and fig. 1. While protection was slightly better than free trade for the exogenous investment specification, free trade is now clearly preferable for the neoclassical and even the classical savings function. Note that the dynamic allocation effect is still at work but in the case of the neoclassical savings function it is never powerful enough to wholly offset the combined static allocation, income and substitution effects. When a classical savings function is specified, the protected path overtakes the free trade path for a few years. But as the relative weight of agriculture becomes insignificant towards the end of the plan-period, the dynamic allocation and distribution effects lose their strengths and the free trade path again overtakes the protected path (see fig. 3). In terms of total discounted utility, free trade remains superior.

The nature of the results remains basically unchanged for the fixed wage and migration variants of our model. Specifying a neoclassical savings function substantially strengthens the case for free trade particularly in the fixed-wage model. In the migration model, where free trade lowers urban employment without being able to rapidly increase agricultural employment, the income effect is favorable to protection but it is only with a classical savings function when it is combined with a distribution effect, that it is able to offset the substitution effect and actually strengthen the case for protection. Protection remains superior in the migration model: by 4% with the neoclassical savings function (less than the 8.9% obtained with the exogenous investment specification) but by 10% with the classical savings function.

6. Conclusion

The small 'stylized' general-equilibrium model presented was able to capture and quantify many of the relationships that should be considered and quantified when designing trade policy in a developing country. In principle it could easily be extended into a fully disaggregated multisector model and it is such disaggregation based on extensive and reliable data that would transform it into an actual planning model. The kind of data needed to properly estimate the structure of the model are difficult to obtain but not beyond reach. It should also be noted that in a disaggregated model a much more careful analysis of technological change incorporating the concept of international product cycles could yield qualitatively new results.

If an overall conclusion can be drawn from our model, it is that when labor is mobile only very strong dynamic effects can make protection a superior

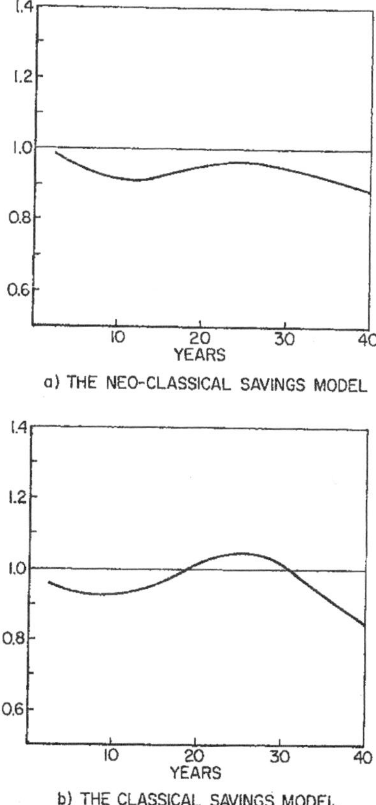

Fig. 3. The ratio of the level of utility under protection to the level of utility under free trade under the full employment specification.

strategy. Whenever labor supply is very elastic to labor intensive export sectors, free trade will be preferred. If, moreover, economy wide employment is a variable, a very strong total employment effect reinforces the case for free trade, provided again that labor is intersectorally mobile. On the other hand, when labor is relatively immobile most of the static and dynamic mechanisms that lead to improved welfare under free trade can no longer fully work and protection may dominate free trade.

Our experiments also indicate that the kind of savings behavior specified is important and that the substitution, income and distribution effects that trade policy generates in this context are as important as the more traditional allocation effects.

Finally, it should be stressed that comparing two extreme trade strategies does not lead to knowledge of an optimal strategy. Future research may have to concentrate on finding optimal paths for tariff rates. If the model could be extended into an optimizing direction that would allow the computation of optimal tariffs and subsidies, the solution may well prove to be an in between strategy of gradual and carefully phased trade liberalization.

Appendix

This appendix presents the parameters that have remained constant during the computations and that have not been explicitly given in the text. They have been derived by aggregation and rounding from the 37-sector data base of the Third Turkish Five-Year Plan. Sectors 1, 2 and 3 are agriculture, manufacturing and nontradables.

The input–output matrix: a_{ij}.

	1	2	3
1	0.220	0.180	0.030
2	0.040	0.260	0.170
3	0.100	0.200	0.150

The capital composition matrix: s_{ij}.

	1	2	3
1	0.000	0.000	0.000
2	0.200	0.500	0.150
3	0.700	0.300	0.700

The noncompetitive import coefficients: s_{0j}.

1	2	3
0.100	0.200	0.150

The base-year shift parameters in the
production functions: $\bar{A}_{i0}$.

1	2	3
0.920	1.500	1.350

The Cobb–Douglas elasticities.

1	2	3	
0.300	0.650	0.700	Capital α_i
0.700	0.350	0.300	Labor β_i

The base-year capital stocks (billion
1967 TL.).

1	2	3
36.0	70.0	62.0

The consumption shares: q_i.

1	2	3
0.28	0.40	0.32

The base-year urban labor supply (million workers) = 4.0.
The base-year total labor force (million workers) = 10.0.
The base-year urban wage (1967 TL. per year per worker) = 6600.
The savings parameters $\bar{S} = 0.25$, $\overline{SP} = 0.45$.

References

Adelman, I. and S. Robinson, 1976, Income distribution policy in developing countries: A case study of Korea (Stanford University Press, Stanford, CA).

Ahmed, F., 1974, Migration and employment in a multi-sector model – An application to Bangladesh, unpublished Ph.D. Dissertation (Princeton University, Princeton, NJ).

Armington, P., 1969, A theory of demand for products distinguished by place of production, Staff Papers 16, 159–178.

Bhagwati, J., 1971, The generalized theory of distortions and welfare, in: J. Bhagwati et al., eds., Trade, balance-of-payments and growth: Papers in international economics in Honor of C.P. Kindleberger (North-Holland, Amsterdam).

Brecher, R., 1974, Minimum wage rates and the pure theory of international trade, Quarterly Journal of Economics 88, 98–116.

Corden, W.M., 1971, The effects of trade on the rate of growth, in: J. Bhagwati et al., eds., Trade, balance-of-payments and growth (North-Holland, Amsterdam).

Corden, W.M., 1974, Trade policy and economic welfare (Oxford University Press, Oxford).

Deardorff, A.V., 1973, The gains from trade in and out of steady state growth, Oxford Economic Papers 25 July, 173–191.

Deardorff, A.V., R. Stern and C. Baum, 1976, A stimulation model of world trade and production, paper presented to the International Finance Seminar, Princeton University, November.

De Melo, J.A.P., 1975, A multi-sector, price endogenous trade model applied to Colombia, unpublished Ph.D. Dissertation (Johns Hopkins University, Baltimore).

Dervis, K., 1975, Substitution, employment and intertemporal equilibrium in a non-linear multi-sector planning model for Turkey, European Economic Review 6, January, 77–96.

Fields, G., 1975, Rural–urban migration, urban unemployment and underemployment, and job search activities in LDCs, Journal of Development Economics 2, no. 2, 165–187.

Findlay, R.E., 1973, International trade and development theory, (Columbia University Press, New York).

Harris, J. and M. Todaro, 1970, Migration, unemployment and development: A two-sector analysis, American Economic Review 60, 126–142.

Johansen, L., 1960, A multi-sector study of economic growth (North-Holland, Amsterdam).

Johnson, H.G., 1971, Aspects of the theory of tariffs (Allen and Unwin, London).

Johnson, H.G., 1971, The theory of trade and growth: A diagrammatic analysis, in: J. Bhagwati et al., eds., Trade, balance-of-payments and growth (North-Holland, Amsterdam).

Lefeber, L., 1971, Trade and minimum wage rates, in: J. Bhagwati et al., eds., Trade, balance-of-payments and growth (North-Holland, Amsterdam).

Magee, S., 1973, Factor market distortions, production and trade: A survey, Oxford Economic Papers 25, 1–43.

Robinson, S. and J.A.P. de Melo, 1976, A planning model featuring trade, intra-sector product differentiation and income distribution, Research Program in Development Studies, Princeton University, November.

Staelin, C.P., 1976, A general equilibrium model of tariffs in a non-competitive economy, Journal of International Economics 6, no. 1, 39–63.

Taylor, L. and S. Black, 1974, Practical general equilibrium estimation of resource pulls under trade liberalization, Journal of International Economics 4, no. 1, 37–58.

Lobbying, Counterlobbying, and the Structure of Tariff Protection in Poor and Rich Countries

Olivier Cadot, Jaime de Melo, and Marcelo Olarreaga

A political economy model of protection is used to determine endogenously the intersectoral patterns of protection. Three propositions are derived that are consistent with the stylized patterns of tariff protection in rich and poor countries: Nominal protection rates escalate with the degree of processing, protection is higher on average in poor countries, and rich countries protect agriculture relatively more than they protect manufacturing, whereas poor countries do the reverse. Numerical simulations for archetypal rich and poor economies confirm that the endogenously determined structure of protection is broadly consistent with observed patterns of protection.

Tariff protection in rich and poor countries displays several stylized patterns. Three stand out as particularly robust. First, nominal rates of protection escalate with the degree of processing, which contributes to the widely observed escalation of effective rates of protection with the degree of processing. Second, protection is higher on average in poor countries. Third, rich countries protect agriculture more than they do manufactures, whereas poor countries do the reverse.

Until recently, analysts explained these patterns of protection largely by calling on the theory of second best. They pointed out, for example, that in rich countries farming provides a groomed landscape that benefits the whole population.[1] In poor countries high trade taxes (including taxation of agriculture) are justified by the revenue constraint that because of weak fiscal administration cannot be met by less distortionary instruments. In turn, protection of manufacturing has been justified on infant-industry grounds. In each case, second-best considerations provided efficiency-based arguments justifying protection.

Olivier Cadot is professor of Economics at École de Hautes Études Commerciales, Univerité de Lausanne; his e-mail address is olivier.cadot@hec.unil.ch. Jaime de Melo is professor of Economics, Department of Political Economy, University of Geneva; his e-mail address is demelo@ecopo.unige.ch. Marcelo Olarreaga is senior economist in the Development Economics Research Group at the World Bank; his e-mail address is molarreaga@worldbank.org. This article is part of a research project on the political economy of trade protection supported by the World Bank's Research Support Budget. The authors thank Francis Ng for the data in table 1; Sanoussi Bilal, François Bourguigonn, Maurice Schiff, Alan Winters, participants at seminars at the University of Geneva and the World Bank; and three referees for comments on an earlier draft.

1. Noneconomic objectives, such as a certain degree of self-sufficiency or an income distribution objective are also often invoked as explanations for the observed pattern of protection. See Corden (1974) for an early treatment.

THE WORLD BANK ECONOMIC REVIEW, VOL. 18, NO. 3,

doi:10.1093/wber/lhh042　　　　　　　　　　　　　　　　　　　　18:345–366

While recognizing the validity of these considerations, this article argues that an equally if not more important reason for the observed pattern of protection is rooted in the political economy considerations identified in the new political economy literature.[2] This body of literature views governments not as passive executors of a trade policy to maximize social welfare but as agents interacting with organized interest groups to maximize an objective function in which social welfare is just one argument. This article shows that such an approach can generate endogenously—and perhaps more readily so than the traditional second-best literature—a predicted cross-sectoral pattern of protection that broadly fits the three stylized patterns.

I. Literature Background

Empirically, Anderson (1995) was the first to quantitatively investigate the tariff-protection pattern of agriculture relative to industry in rich and poor countries. Using a Ricardo-Viner model similar to the one developed here, data for archetypal rich and poor economies, and parameter values similar to those used here in, he shows that support to farmers in rich countries raises their incomes substantially while reducing manufacturing incomes only marginally. Conversely, agricultural taxation in poor countries reduces farmers' incomes marginally while benefiting capitalists and workers substantially. These simulations, he concludes, explain the observed pattern of protection of agriculture relative to manufacturing in rich and poor countries. Although highly suggestive, the simulations fall short of endogenizing the level and sectorial pattern of protection.

More recently, in a model nesting the economic (terms of trade) and political (redistribution toward powerful favored groups) arguments, Freund and Djankov (2000) find support for the political economy argument of protection. In a cross-section they find that proxies for political power (past share of income in the hands of the 20 percent richest groups and an index for corruption) and for favoritism (the share of public expenditures on nonpublic goods defined as expenditures other than health, education, and the social safety net) are positively related to the degree of protection. The results are robust to omitted-variable bias (distance and endowments) and to reverse causation (openness to trade, by enhancing competition, could reduce rent-seeking activity and have a negative effect on corruption; see Ades and Di Tella 1999).

Freund and Djankov's finding that favoritism has been an obstacle to trade liberalization is supportive of the approach taken here, and their finding that protection is not correlated with relative country size (the proxy for market

2. Recent empirical work (see Djankov and others 2002) also suggests that distortionary taxation of market entry tends to be associated with indicators of poor governance, themselves largely associated with low income levels. This evidence points toward explanations for observed patterns of taxation that are broadly consistent with the new political economy literature. We are grateful to a referee for attracting our attention to this point.

power) is not surprising because tariff-setting policy is usually not associated with a country's desire to improve its terms of trade. Their approach is also consistent with the common small-country modeling approach taken here and in most of the endogenous protection literature.

This article derives Anderson's results by extending the influence-driven approach to the endogenous determination of tariffs proposed by Grossman and Helpman (1994), itself an extension of the political support approach proposed by Hillman (1982). The Grossman-Helpman approach has the advantage of relating the predicted structure of protection to potentially measurable technology and preference parameters. However, in its original formulation, it predicts that for organized sectors (those with active political lobbying) equilibrium tariff protection increases with domestic output and hence decreases with import penetration. As Rodrik (1995) points out, this prediction is not entirely realistic because it suggests, for instance, that agriculture rather than manufacturing should be protected in poor countries and is at odds with the bulk of existing empirical evidence. As argued later in this article, this apparently counterintuitive implication is not the result of a particular artifact of the Grossman-Helpman model but rather a direct consequence of Hotelling's lemma that is bound to appear in any model of influence activity.[3] If the new political economy's descriptive power is to be taken seriously, therefore, reconciling the model's logic with the empirical evidence is essential.

Several solutions have been proposed to the puzzle, both empirically and theoretically. Empirically, Koujiannou-Goldberg and Maggi (1999) show that when organized and unorganized sectors are treated separately, the estimated relationship between equilibrium trade protection and import penetration is broadly in line with the Grossman-Helpman model's prediction (decreasing for organized sectors and increasing for unorganized ones). Gawande and Bandyopadhyay (2000) have similar results. Maggi and Rodriguez-Clare (1999) show theoretically that when public funds have a distortion cost and trade protection can take the form of either tariffs or quantitative restrictions, trade protection may increase with import protection under plausible conditions in the Grossman-Helpman model.

Although these studies have helped reconcile theory with the observed patterns of protection, the empirical results of Koujiannou-Goldberg and Maggi (1999) and Gawande and Bandyopadhyay (2000) are not without ambiguity,[4] and Maggi and Rodriguez-Clare's (1999) extension comes at the price of substantial complication. They are thus unlikely to be the last word on an issue that is sufficiently important to deserve further exploration.

This article takes a different approach. It keeps the political game untouched but puts flesh on the underlying economy. It introduces factor-market rivalry

---

3. Hotelling's lemma states that at the profit-maximizing output level the derivative of profits with respect to prices is equal to output.

4. For instance, Koujiannou-Goldberg and Maggi (1999) find stronger results for unorganized sectors than for organized ones, which is problematic for a model that focuses on the effects of lobbying.

and input-output linkages, giving rise to counterlobbying (by organized sectors other than the direct beneficiary of trade protection) and altering the equilibrium pattern of protection in a way that can reduce the gap between prediction and evidence. Indeed, it turns out that this extended model, when applied to archetypal data, yields an endogenous structure of protection that is consistent with the three stylized patterns: Nominal protection escalates with the degree of processing (because of weaker counterlobbying for processed goods), protection is higher on average for poor countries (because of sparse interindustry linkages), and rich countries protect agriculture more than they do manufactures, whereas poor countries do the reverse (because of differences in interindustry linkages and rivalry in factor markets).

In sum, this article extends the Grossman-Helpman model and the simulations by Anderson, providing a simple political economy–based account of observed protection patterns. In doing so, it provides a basis for examining the forces behind trade protection in developing and industrial countries, which is a necessary first step to any successful (and therefore lasting) trade reform.

II. PATTERNS OF TARIFF PROTECTION IN DEVELOPED AND DEVELOPING ECONOMIES

This section provides prima facie evidence for the three stylized facts. Average tariffs by degree of processing for agricultural and industrial products for 37 developing economies and 7 industrial countries (the European Union is counted as one country), the largest available sample, provide evidence for the first two stylized facts (table 1).[5] For agricultural products the average rate of

TABLE 1. Tariff Escalation in Developing and Industrial Countries, 1997–99 (Unweighted Averages in %)

Stage of production	Developing	Industrial
Agricultural products		
First stage processing	19.0	5.2
Semiprocessed	26.3	5.4
Fully processed	29.6	5.8
Ratio of countries without escalation to sample size	4/37	1/7
Industrial products		
First stage processing	9.5	0.5
Semiprocessed	13.1	4.0
Fully processed	15.2	4.6
Ratio of countries without escalation to sample size	1/37	0/7

Source: WTO 2000 Integrated Data Base CD-ROM and WTO *Trade Policy Reviews*, various issues.

5. The data are from the World Trade Organization (WTO) Integrated Data Base version 4 and the WTO *Trade Policy Reviews*.

protection rises by degree of processing for both the developing country group and the industrial country group. Fully processed agricultural goods have a 55 percent higher tariff on average than goods in their first stage of processing in developing areas and a 12 percent higher tariff in industrial countries.[6] Protection also rises on average with the degree of processing for industrial products. However, fully processed industrial products receive about 55 percent more protection than first-stage processing products in developing economies and 450 percent more in industrial countries.

Because classifying products by degree of processing is subject to error, a more robust estimate of the effect that processing has on tariff structure might compare first-stage and fully processed products. For agriculture products only five countries do not conform to the prediction that tariffs are higher for fully processed goods: China, Republic of Korea, South Africa, Thailand, and Norway). For industrial products, only, Romania does not conform. By this classification the predicted pattern holds in 93 percent of the cases.[7]

On the second stylized fact, that protection is higher in developing economies, a quick look at table 1 suggests that this is the case for both agriculture and industry across all levels of processing.

The third stylized fact is that industrial countries tend to protect agriculture more than manufacturing, whereas the opposite is true for developing areas. The ploting of a curve linking the average relationship (by decile) between protection of manufacturing relative to agriculture and gross domestic product (GDP) per capita of a sample of 81 countries shows a negative relation (figure 1).[8] The relative protection variable is t_M/t_A, where t_M and t_A are unweighted average tariffs for manufactures and agriculture for a sample of 81 countries (the largest available sample with data on tariffs and GDP per capita, Y_P). The gain in number of countries covered by using only tariffs rather than all forms of protection, comes at a cost, however. Because these estimates do not include the effects of other price measures (such as export taxes) and nonprice measures (such as nontariff barriers), figure 1 cannot be said to be representative of

6. Note however, that all developed countries use specific tariffs intensively in agriculture and that the WTO's Integrated Data Base does not provide ad valorem equivalents of these tariffs. Including specific tariffs could show a more dramatic picture.

7. One could also object that the pattern of protection in manufactures is the result of bargaining through successive rounds of tariff negotiations rather than determined noncooperatively at the national level, as predicted by the political economy approach developed here. However, because the current observed pattern is largely the result of successive linear across-the-board reductions, it is likely that the current pattern reflects, as a first approximation, patterns established before the multilateral tariff cuts. Ray (1990) discusses how these patterns were established along political economy grounds similar to those explored in this article.

8. The data on agriculture and manufacturing tariffs are compiled from various sources, including WTO, UNCTAD, and the World Bank and are available online at www.worldbank.org/research/trade. The GDP per capita data are from World Bank (2000). Note that the sample is larger than that in table 1 because the disaggregated tariff data necessary to compute average tariffs by levels of processing are not available for some countries.

350   THE WORLD BANK ECONOMIC REVIEW, VOL. 18, NO. 3

FIGURE 1. Relative Protection of Manufacturing and Income per Capita, 1995–2000

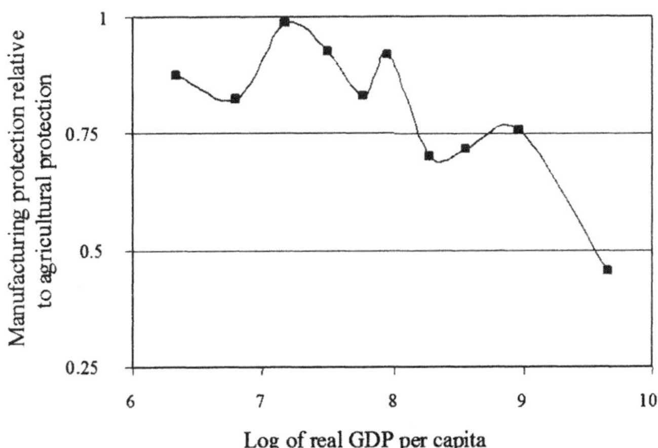

Source: WTO 2000 CD-ROM *International Trade Statistics* and WTO *Trade Policy Reviews,* various issues for tariff data; World Bank 2000 for GDP per capita.

the relative incentives to agriculture and manufactures as income per capita varies.

The negative relation between protection of manufacturing relative to agriculture and the log of income per capita is confirmed by the results of the following regression, for which $F(1,79) = 9.27$, with the t-statistic in parentheses.

$$(1) \qquad t_M/t_A = \underset{(5.77)}{1.68} - \underset{(3.04)}{0.11} \ Y_P$$

The relation, which is significant despite a few outlier observations (including Australia and Turkey), indicates that the relative tariff of agriculture over manufactures increases by 1.1 percent for each 10 percent increase in GDP per capita.

It is likely that the positive relation between the relative protection of agriculture and the level of GDP per capita would have been even more striking had data been available on producer subsidy equivalents for all countries and had more indicative data been available on protection for agriculture in developing countries, along the lines of the Krueger and others (1989) estimates.

III. DETERMINANTS OF THE STRUCTURE OF PROTECTION

The model presented next is an extension of the basic Grossman-Helpman model, with which it shares several elements. First, the political game is the same. Namely, lobbies "bid for protection" through monetary contributions conditioned on the level of tariffs, and the government maximizes a weighted average of social welfare and contributions. Alternatively, the government can be seen as acting as the common agent of the lobbies. The government's objective function is a linear (but not necessarily convex) combination of welfare and monetary contributions from the lobbies.

Second, the underlying economy is similar in most regards. The lobbies represent the interests of specific-capital owners in a Ricardo-Viner model, and individuals have identical quasilinear preferences. The differentiating elements introduced here are that specific-capital ownership is assumed to be sufficiently concentrated that lobbies care only about protecting their industry (they do not internalize the effect of protection on consumer prices), all sectors are assumed to be politically organized (actively lobbying), and all sectors combine specific capital with mobile labor. This symmetry in factor use across sectors relaxes a key assumption in the Grossman-Helpman model—that the existence of a sector operating with labor only under constant returns to scale fixes the wage rate. The interest of relaxing this assumption is that a flexible wage rate introduces intersectoral rivalry in the labor market, with one sector's protection raising the cost of labor for other sectors.

Finally, all goods may enter as input into the production of all other goods, so that one sector's protection raises the costs of other sectors. This creates a second channel of intersectoral rivalry, through input-output linkages.

These new elements create the possibility of counterlobbying: In this model one sector's lobbying for protection meets political opposition from other sectors. The equilibrium pattern of protection results from the net effect of these opposing forces. These extensions generate a pattern of protection that no longer needs to share the unfortunate features of the basic Grossman-Helpman model.

Lobbying in a Specific-Factor Model

Consider a small open economy with $n+1$ tradable sectors, in which good 0 serves as numéraire and export good. All n other goods are import competing. Individuals have different endowments but identical tastes, represented by a utility function:

$$(2) \qquad\qquad U = c_0 + u(\mathbf{c}),$$

where c_0 is consumption of the numéraire good, and $\mathbf{c}$ is the vector of consumption of the n non-numéraire goods, $u' > 0$ and $u'' < 0$.

All goods produced in the economy are potential inputs in other sectors, and all industries are perfectly competitive. Each sector's technology is Leontief between intermediate consumptions and value added. Thus, value added is nested in the Leontief production function and is created using a specific factor (κ_j) and a mobile factor (ℓ_j) under a general constant returns to scale technology (f^j). Letting a_{ij} be the requirement of good i necessary to produce one unit of good j, and letting x_{ij} be sector j's demand for good i as an intermediate input,

352   THE WORLD BANK ECONOMIC REVIEW, VOL. 18, NO. 3

$$(3) \qquad y_j = \min \left\{ f^j(\kappa_j, \ell_j); \; x_{0j}/a_{0j}; \; \ldots \; ; x_{nj}/a_{nj} \right\}.$$

The world prices of all goods are fixed and assumed to be unity. The domestic price of good i is thus $p_i = 1 + t_i$, where t_i is the specific tariff (or subsidy if it is negative) applied to it. Let $\mathbf{p} = (p_1, \ldots, p_n)$ be the vector of domestic prices and w the wage rate, and let $\tilde{p}_j = p_j - \sum_{i=0}^{n} a_{ij} p_i$ be the net price of good j. Given the technology postulated, industry j's restricted profit function can be written as $\pi_j[\kappa_j; \mathbf{p}; w(\mathbf{p})] = \tilde{p}_j y_j - w\ell_j$. Lobbies representing import-competing sectors (all are assumed to be organized) bid simultaneously for protection with "truthful" contribution schedules $C_j(\mathbf{p}) = \max\{0; \pi_j - b_j\}$ for some nonnegative constant b_j.[9] The form of the contributions reflects the assumption that lobbies are very small in the population. Thus, from their point of view, the effects of protection on consumer surplus and tariff revenue are not commensurate with the direct effect of protection on producer surplus, and they take only that direct effect into account in their lobbying activity.

Faced with such contributions, the government chooses best-response tariffs (domestic prices) maximizing

$$(4) \qquad V(\mathbf{p}) = \sum_{j=1}^{n} C_j(\mathbf{p}) + a W(\mathbf{p})$$

where $W(\mathbf{p})$ is social welfare and a is a constant representing the weight the government attaches to social welfare.[10] Domestic prices satisfy the first-order condition:

$$(5) \qquad \partial V(\mathbf{p})/\partial p_i = \sum_{j=1}^{n} (\partial \pi_j/\partial p_i) + a(\partial W/\partial p_i) = \mathcal{P}_i + a\mathcal{E}_i = 0,$$

which picks up the net effect of protection in sector i on economywide rents and measures the incentive for the government to depart from the optimal second-best tariff in sector i. The first term in the equation is the "net political-power component," because it measures the ability of lobby i to make its voice heard above that of opposing lobbies; this term is denoted by $\mathcal{P}_i$. Using Hotelling's lemma, $\partial \pi_j/\partial p_i = (1_{j=i} - a_{ij}) y_j - \ell_j \partial w/\partial p_i$, where $1_{j=i}$ is an indicator function equal to one when $j = i$ and zero otherwise. Thus, under the assumption that all sectors are politically organized, the effect of a change in p_i on aggregate political contributions (on producer surplus in all sectors) is:

<hr>

9. The vector of constants b_j determines how the rents from trade protection are shared between the government and lobbies; see Grossman and Helpman (1994).

10. Grossman and Helpman (1996) show that this objective function emerges in a political system in which lobbies use campaign contributions to influence the outcome of the election, while two parties compete for seats in Parliament. However, whether such an objective function is representative of the objective function in low-income countries is more debatable. For a skeptic's view, see Findlay (1991).

(6) $$P_i \equiv \sum_j (\partial \pi_j / \partial p_i) = y_i - \sum_j a_{ij} y_j - \ell (\partial w / \partial p_i)$$

where $\ell = \sum_j \ell_j$ is the economy's total labor force.

The first term in P_i reflects the direct effect of trade protection on the profits of sector i—the rent accruing to owners of sector-specific capital in sector i. This term is at the origin of the import-penetration controversy. To see this, observe that the larger an industry's domestic output, the larger is (through Hotelling's lemma) the impact of a given tariff increase on its profits. Through the truthfulness assumption, this implies a higher lobbying intensity, which raises the power of the incentive given to the government. Accordingly, in equilibrium the government grants larger protection. But for a given level of demand a larger domestic output reduces the import-penetration ratio, hence the negative association between import-penetration ratios and equilibrium protection. As mentioned, this result is not a modeling artifact but goes to the heart of the influence-activity logic: Whenever lobbying is done by an industry's residual claimants, through Hotelling's lemma a larger domestic output will raise the return to lobbying.

In the Grossman-Helpman model, the story stops here. The only way out of this unfortunate prediction is to note, as Koujiannou-Goldberg and Maggi (1999) do, that the positive relationship between output size and equilibrium protection holds only for organized industries. For unorganized ones the relationship is reversed, at least provided that special interests take consumer effects into account.

Though not contesting this observation, the model here focuses on another effect that also solves the puzzle but generates distinct predictions as by-products. All sectors are assumed to be organized, an assumption that is easily relaxed but at the cost of additional notation. The novelty here comes in the next two terms in equation 6, which reflect the two components of rivalry between lobbies; the stronger the rival lobbies, the lower the level of rent extraction by lobby i. The first term $(\sum_j a_{ij} y_j)$ represents the impact of protection in i on downstream sectors through input-output linkages. An increase in the tariff on good i reduces the net price $\tilde{p}_j$ of all downstream sectors (all sectors j such that $a_{ij} > 0$), giving rise to counterlobbying. The last term in equation 6 represents crowding out through the wage rate: As the tariff on good i rises, sector i expands, bidding up the wage rate, penalizing other sectors, and giving rise to counterlobbying. In general, the political power component, P_i, need not be positive, as general-equilibrium spillovers through input-output and labor-market linkages may more than offset any gains from protection accruing to sector i.

The second term $(\partial W / \partial p_i)$ in equation 5 picks up the effect of protection on social welfare and summarizes second-best considerations. It is labeled the "efficiency component" and is denoted by $\mathcal{E}_i$. (The derivations of P_i, $\mathcal{E}_i$ are given in appendix 1.)

Although protection in one sector generates negative downstream spillovers through input-output linkages, it does not generate positive spillovers in

354   THE WORLD BANK ECONOMIC REVIEW, VOL. 18, NO. 3

upstream (tradable) sectors, because tradables prices (equal to $1 + t_i$ for all i) are unaffected by variations in domestic demand. By contrast, if there were an upstream nontradables sector—a situation not considered formally here or in the simulations for space considerations—its profits would be boosted by protection downstream, because the nontradable's price would be sensitive to variations in domestic demand. Ad hoc coalitions of interests could then form between tradables and nontradables sectors.

Explaining the Three Stylized Facts

Proposition 1 shows that when interindustry linkages are taken into account, the net political power of an industry increases with the amount of that industry's sales to final consumers rather than with its overall output. The first two corollaries help explain the first two stylized facts (tariff escalation and higher levels of protection in poor countries). Proposition 2 shows that sectors that employ a large share of the labor force face stronger counter-lobbying due to factor market rivalry. Corollary 3 helps explain the third stylized fact (higher levels of agricultural than manufacturing protection in rich countries and the reverse in poor countries).

Proposition 1. *The net political power of sector* i *increases with the level of sector* i*'s sales to final users. Moreover, when its free-trade level of output falls short of other sectors' intermediate requirements of good* i *by a sufficiently large amount, sector* i *may get negative protection in equilibrium.*

Proof. The first statement follows directly from the observation that P_i is an increasing function of $y_i - \sum_j a_{ij} y_j$, which is that part of final domestic consumption covered by domestic output. For the second statement, fix all prices except p_i at their equilibrium level and p_i at its free-trade level ($p_i = 1$). If $y_i < \sum_j a_{ij} y_j$, $P_i < 0$, provided that the second-best term ε_i is nonpositive or, if positive, not sufficiently large as to offset the political power term P_i, $\partial V / \partial p_i = P_i + a \varepsilon_i < 0$. Under the second-order condition, $\partial V / \partial p_i$ is a decreasing function of p_i; therefore, the equilibrium value of p_i must be lower than 1, which implies negative protection for good i.

Thus, it is the fraction of sector i's output that is sold to final consumers (or exported in the case of an export industry bidding for subsidies) that determines how much protection sector i gets in equilibrium. This is because unlike domestic downstream industries, neither final consumers nor foreign users are organized. Proposition 1 yields a second result as a by-product.

Corollary 1. *The net political power of final-goods industries is greater, ceteris paribus, than that of intermediate-goods industries.*

In a political equilibrium final-goods industries, which in most cases correspond to the fully processed goods industries mentioned earlier, are likely to obtain more protection than intermediate-goods industries unless output levels vary systematically and inversely with the degree of processing and this systematic variation is large enough to undo the negative effect of the term $\sum_j a_{ij} y_j$. Barring this, the overall structure of protection will display tariff escalation.[11] This result accords with the data in table 1 (see also Ray 1990) and helps explain the first stylized fact. It is also in accordance with the more detailed accounts in industry case studies of protection. For example, Moore (1996) notes in his study of protection in the U.S. steel industry that organized steel users joined forces to prevent an extension of the 1984 voluntary restraint agreement on steel imports. Destler and Odell (1987) offer similar arguments on the importance of counterlobbying.

If one is willing to accept that more developed economies have more sophisticated and interlinked production techniques (a lower share of value added to output), then the second stylized fact is also a corollary of proposition 1:

Corollary 2. *Tariffs are higher, ceteris paribus, in countries with sparse interindustry linkages (developing countries).*

To see this, note that $\partial \mathcal{P}_i / \partial a_{ij} < 0$. Thus poor countries tend to have higher levels of protection, because there are few incentives for other sectors to counterlobby increases in protection on intermediate inputs when interindustry linkages are sparse.

Proposition 2. *Incentives for owners of sector-specific capital in sector i to lobby for protection decrease with that sector's share of labor in value added.*

Proof. Abstract from interindustry linkages so that $\mathcal{P}_i$ in equation A6 in appendix 1 becomes $\mathcal{P}_i = y_i[1 - \tilde{\varepsilon}_i^w \tilde{\alpha}_i / \lambda_i]$, where $\tilde{\varepsilon}_i^w$ is the elasticity of the wage with respect to the price of good i, λ_i is the share of employment in sector i in the total labor force ($\lambda_i = \ell_i / \ell$), and $\tilde{\alpha}_i = w\ell_i / \tilde{p}_i y_i$ is the share of labor in value added. Given that labor is in fixed supply, $\tilde{\varepsilon}_i^w = (\eta_i \ell_i / \sum_j \eta_j \ell_j)$ where η_i is the real wage elasticity of labor demand in sector i. Furthermore, assuming that η_i is identical across sectors, $\tilde{\varepsilon}_i^w = \lambda_i$. Then, $\mathcal{P}_i = y_i[1 - \tilde{\alpha}_i]$. Finally, $\partial \mathcal{P}_i / \partial \tilde{\alpha}_i < 0$.

Thus the labor rivalry term is increasing in the share of labor in sector i's value added. In a setting with flexible wages incentives to lobby for protection by owners of sector-specific capital are likely to be small in industries where a large share of value added can be attributed to labor.

Finally, if one is willing to accept that the share of labor in value added in agriculture relative to manufacturing is higher in developing economies—as suggested by the calibration of Anderson (1995) and Chenery and Syrquin's (1986) data in the simulations below (table B-2)—then the explanation for the third stylized fact is that:

Corollary 3. *The ratio of agricultural to manufacturing tariffs will be lower, ceteris paribus, in countries where the share of labor in value added is higher in agriculture than in manufacturing (low-income developing countries).*

---

11. Note that the Leontief technology implies that downstream users of a protected intermediate good are trapped, as they cannot escape the intermediate good's increased domestic price by substituting away from it. With a different technology, input substitution would be an alternative to lobbying against the intermediate good's protection; with a lesser incentive to counterlobby, the tariff-escalation result would be weakened.

356   THE WORLD BANK ECONOMIC REVIEW, VOL. 18, NO. 3

According to the data calibration in the next section, in developing areas the share of labor in value added is two times greater in agriculture than in manufacturing. In industrial countries, by contrast, the share of labor in value added is 30 percent larger in manufacturing than in agriculture. According to corollary 3, this could help explain the third stylized fact.

IV. SIMULATIONS: ENDOGENOUS PROTECTION IN ARCHETYPAL RICH AND POOR ECONOMIES

The propositions are ceteris paribus results pertaining only to the political power term in the endogenous-tariff formula, with second-best terms held constant. Relaxing this assumption in simulations can help show how consistent the model's predictions are with the stylized facts presented earlier. Partial equilibrium simulations are conducted for archetypal rich and poor economies with data for three-sector economies with two tradables sectors, agriculture and industry, and one nontradeables sector.[12] The simulations are based on a disaggregation of the economy that includes interindustry flows, a key element of lobby rivalry highlighted by the model. Data sources and parameters representing demand and supply elasticities are described in appendix B and come mainly from Anderson (1995) and Chenery and Syrquin (1986).

On the basis of the data on the two archetypal economies, Anderson calculated the effects on the income of farmers and industrialists of a 10 percent rise in the relative price of industrial products as a result of a tax on agricultural exports. This relative price change reduced farmers' incomes by less than 4 percent while boosting industrialists' real incomes by 40 percent. Results were similar for an increase in the relative price of industrial products that had a small negative effect on farm incomes. By contrast, for the rich economy, a 10 percent increase in agricultural relative prices would boost real farm incomes by 23 percent while lowering industrial incomes by only 3 percent. His simulations suggest that farmers in poor countries who successfully seek price supports or oppose industrial protection would get only one-sixth to one-ninth the benefits of farmers in rich countries who successfully engage in the same activities. Likewise, industrial capitalists in poor countries would have more than 10 times the incentive to seek policies to protect manufacturing and reduce agricultural prices than would industrialists in rich countries.

Anderson conjectures that this adjustment pattern helps explain the difficulties encountered in concluding the Uruguay Round of negotiations, because farm lobbies in industrial countries opposed reductions in farm support. But this observation falls short of fully explaining the observed pattern of protection

---

12. The words "rich" and "poor" other are used only to indicate the differences in economic structure observed between countries, as in Chenery and Syrquin (1986), for example. This is the choice of names in Anderson (1995), kept here for continuity.

in rich and poor economies. The simulations reported in this article show that Anderson's conjecture emerges endogenously in this model of tariff determination. Moreover, the ability of the Grossman-Helpman model to generate this particular pattern of protection comes specifically from the extensions introduced here.

The simulations are based on a numerical evaluation of equations 5, A-6, and A-5, which are indexed over two tradables sectors (agriculture and manufacturing), though the economy also includes a third, nontradables sector (for consistency with Anderson [1995] and with the Chenery and Syrquin [1986] data). The wage appears as a variable in these equations. This requires adding an equation for determining labor demand for each sector as well as a labor-market constraint ($\sum_i \ell_i = \ell$) determining the equilibrium wage rate.

Thus, the three-sector model used here has seven equations: two determine the tariffs, three determine cost-minimizing labor demand (ℓ_i), and one determines the market-clearing wage rate (w). (Appendix B describes the equations used in these partial-equilibrium simulations.) Because the income–expenditure link is not specified in this system of equations, the model is closed by fixing the price of the nontradables sector.[13] The solution to this model yields tariffs for tradables sectors, labor allocations that clear the labor market, and the value of the wage in terms of the price of the nontradables sector.

This model is best viewed as an approximate local calculation of an equilibrium tariff structure for the selected elasticities of demand and supply (described in table A-2) and an exogenously given preference (given by the parameter a) for the welfare of the representative consumer.[14] For low enough values of the weight attached to welfare (a), the first-order condition of the optimization problem might yield a minimum of the function V, rather than a maximum. In other words, tariffs may be high enough to give rise to negative value-added prices. Such cases are not considered here.

For variations in the weight attached to welfare (a), the model predicts the endogenous tariff rates for the two archetypal economies (table 2). As expected, for both economies the greater the weight politicians attach to welfare, the lower the rate of protection. For sufficiently large weights, tariffs tend to zero. Next, note that the average level of protection is lower in the rich economy. The ratio of value added to output is lower for the rich economy (55 percent) than

---

13. Eliminating the tradables–nontradables link by omitting the income–expenditure link is justifiable for this illustrative exercise. Simulations here are meant to check only whether the model can reasonably support the stylized facts. Conditions under which this partial equilibrium approach is valid in a general equilibrium model identical to this one are given in Dornbusch (1974).

14. Evaluation of the formula in the text is based on elasticities that are valid only for small changes around the equilibrium. Moreover, some of those elasticities are endogenously determined; for instance, price elasticities of the wage rate depend, at a cost-minimizing equilibrium, on the elasticity of substitution and on the elasticity of labor demand, whose calculation depends on domestic prices, which in turn include a guess about the tariff value. Systematic experimentation with several starting values always yielded the same solution.

358　THE WORLD BANK ECONOMIC REVIEW, VOL. 18, NO. 3

TABLE 2. Endogenous Tariff Structure in Rich and Poor Countries (%)

	Rich			Poor		
	$a = 1.5^a$	$a = 2$	$a = 10$	$a = 1.5^b$	$a = 2$	$a = 10$
Average agricultural tariff	52.5	27.7	3.3	30.1	23.3	5.9
Average manufacturing tariff	16.8	11.5	1.9	69.7	47.7	9.2
Aggregate tariff	20.9	13.3	2.0	35.6	26.7	6.4

Note: a is the weight politicans attach to the welfare of the representative consumer.
[a]If $a < 1.25$, the solution is not unique.
[b]If $a < 1.25$, the optimization problem yields a minimum.
Source: See appendix B.

for the poor economy (74 percent), so that stronger counterlobbying by downstream users in the rich economy reduces the average rate of protection. But the most striking result is the pattern of protection. In accordance with the stylized facts, the pattern of incentives systematically favors manufacturing in the poor economy and agriculture in the rich economy. In the simulations reported in table 2, agriculture is a net exporting sector in the poor economy and industry is in the rich economy. Thus it is not necessarily true that the endogenous tariff and subsidy structure results in large sectors receiving higher protection because of their larger political weight.

There is no doubt that other factors—limited means of taxation in poor countries and lack of political power by all but a tiny minority of farmers to organize themselves into lobbying activities—are important in explaining the relative pattern of incentives between agriculture and industry in poor and rich economies. Nonetheless, by taking account of intermediate goods and assuming a greater variation in the pattern of elasticities across sectors in poor countries, this model generates a pattern of protection that conforms to the one observed: higher protection and greater variance of tariff rates in poor than in rich economies. But because manufacturing activities are aggregated into a single activity, it is difficult to verify whether the endogenously determined tariff structure captures the escalation in protection by degree of processing. Overall, however, these archetypal representations appear to capture adequately the main differences in the pattern of protection between rich and poor economies. They are broadly consistent with the stylized facts on the pattern of protection in rich and poor countries.

Sensitivity calculations for the rich country archetype help establish the robustness of results to underlying assumptions about parameter values (table 3). For reference, the results from applying the Grossman-Helpman formula are also reported. Not surprisingly, because the Grossman-Helpman model has no intermediate goods, their formula yields a higher level of protection.

Column 1 of table 3 reproduces the result of table 2 for $a = 2$; the other columns report the results of one-by-one variations from this baseline case. Columns 2 and 3 cut the input-output delivery coefficients for manufacturing

TABLE 3. Sensitivity Analysis for the Rich Economy

	Base[a]	$a_M/2$	$a_A/2$	$\varepsilon_M^w = 0$	$\varepsilon_A^w = 0$	$\varepsilon_{MM}^c/2$	$\varepsilon_{AA}^c/2$	$\sigma^A = 0.8 \; \sigma^M = 1.2$	G-H[b]
	(1)	(2)	(3)	(4)	(5)	(6)	(7)	(8)	(9)
T^A	27.7	39.8	86.2	24.2	56.3	22.2	31.6	38.3	42.4
T^M	11.5	32.5	11.4	25.3	10.8	12.1	11.3	7.2	30.6
$\overline{T}$	13.3	33.3	20.0	25.2	16.0	13.3	13.7	10.6	31.9

[a]Base results are for the rich economy from table 2 for $a = 2$.

[b]Calculated from Grossman and Helpman (1994), Proposition 2, and note 10 under the assumption of no consumer participation in interest groups.

Source: See appendix B.

and agriculture in half. In both cases smaller intermediate sales reduce counterlobbying from other sectors, yielding higher protection for the sector. When the manufacturing sector's input-output delivery coefficients are cut, protection of agriculture also rises. This is because the reduction in the agricultural sector's requirement for manufactured goods raises its equilibrium profits (in spite of the higher price of manufactured goods), leading to stronger agricultural lobbying.

Columns 4 and 5 isolate the general equilibrium effects of the wage rate adjustment by setting the price elasticity of the wage rate to zero. This may be viewed as the most relevant closure empirically, because it could be argued that general equilibrium effects are not central to lobbyists' decisions. Although not reported, the pattern of protection in which agriculture is protected relative to manufacturing holds when both elasticities are simultaneously set to zero. This closure amounts to determining the tariff of a small sector in the sense that changes in that sector's demand for labor have no influence on the equilibrium wage rate. As explained in section II, there is less counterlobbying, and in this highly aggregated model with only three sectors this effect is quantitatively important, resulting in a near doubling of the sector's endogenous tariff.[15]

Columns 6–8 consider second-best effects by varying demand and supply elasticities. A reduction in the own-price elasticity of demand in one sector reduces its elasticity of import demand, in turn reducing the welfare cost of protection in that sector.[16] The same effect is at work in the simulation reported in column 8: A departure from unitary elasticities of substitution in production

---

15. Though in a different context, this experiment is reminiscent of the thought experiment performed by Mayer (1984) in a direct democracy setting. In a Ricardo-Viner economy he showed that sectors with weaker wage complementarities (by which he meant weaker effects of one sector's tariff on the equilibrium wage rate) are more likely to get support and obtain protection.

16. Ramsey effects also explain why cutting the price elasticity of demand in manufacturing reduces the variance of tariffs, whereas cutting the same elasticity in agriculture raises their variance. In the case of the reduction in the elasticity of demand for manufacturing, the differential in the pattern of elasticities is reduced, whereas in the case of agriculture the opposite occurs. Thus a reduction in the elasticity of demand for manufacturing leads to a more uniform pattern of protection, but the opposite occurs with a reduction in the elasticity of demand for agriculture.

also raises the differential in elasticities of supply. By second-best considerations, this results in a greater dispersion of the tariff structure.

V. Concluding Remarks

This article introduced two extensions to the Grossman-Helpman framework: vertical (input-output) linkages and interindustry rivalry on labor markets. These extensions, though involving minimal additional complication, are potentially useful in several ways.

First, they help overcome a basic contradiction between the logic of influence-activity models and empirical evidence (and intuition). According to the model's logic, a higher level of domestic output raises the return to lobbying. In a common-agency context this leads lobbies to face governments with steeper incentive schedules, leading to more generous trade protection in equilibrium. Intuition and empirical evidence, however, suggest that lobbying intensity and the government's protectionist response should increase with the perceived threat of import competition (with rising import-penetration ratios). The gist of the approach here is to show that equilibrium protection is the result not just of lobbying pressures from direct beneficiaries of protection but also of counter-lobbying by negatively affected downstream industries. This argument is distinct from the Grossman-Helpman notion that producer lobbies internalize consumption effects, which requires them to be large enough in the population. This extension of the Grossman-Helpman approach suggests that, empirically, the relationship between domestic output and equilibrium protection may be blurred by potentially larger effects having to do with counterlobbying.

Second, these extensions suggest a pattern of trade protection that displays tariff escalation by degree of processing, an empirical regularity that cannot be accounted for by the basic version of the Grossman-Helpman model, which superimposes a sophisticated political game on an overly stripped-down economy.

Finally, the extended Grossman-Helpman model can generate endogenously a pattern of protection suggested by Anderson (1995), whereby poor countries protect industry relative to agriculture while rich ones do the reverse. Thus the message is that the apparent difficulty of reconciling the logic of the Grossman-Helpman model with stylized facts comes not so much from the political game at the center of their analysis as from the straitjacket of an overly simplistic underlying economy. Once the straitjacket is relaxed, the model proves capable of generating a wealth of plausible implications.

The analysis is perforce essentially positive rather than normative, a characterization that applies to the entire political economy literature. Indeed, the central tenet of this literature is that irrespective of what economists think governments ought to do, economists first need to understand what governments actually do and why they do it, which requires a realistic view of the objectives and constraints of elected political representatives. Normative prescriptions are thus thrown back one step, into recommendations for institutional arrangements capable of mitigating policy capture by special interests.

However, useful if somewhat impressionistic policy considerations can emerge as by-products of this positive analysis. For instance, the emphasis on counterlobbying suggests that in conformity with the general logic of common-agency models, good policies do not necessarily come from politicians maximizing "welfare-friendly" objective functions or operating under tight rules, but possibly from the balance of conflicting special-interest pressures. Conversely, bad policies can result from imbalances in lobbying pressures and from institutional arrangements that weaken pressure from one side aggravate distortions. For instance, duty-drawback schemes can be expected to weaken antiprotectionist pressure from downstream users of import-competing goods, which may well lead to higher tariffs on intermediate products. This idea is pursued theoretically and shown to hold empirically in Cadot and others (2003).

APPENDIX A. DERIVATION OF THE EFFICIENCY AND POLITICAL EFFECTS

At any point the economy is characterized by its income-expenditure identity, namely

$$(A\text{-}1) \qquad E(1, \mathbf{p}, W) \equiv R(1, \mathbf{p}, \mathbf{k}, \ell) + T(\mathbf{p})$$

where 1 is the price of the numéraire, $E(.)$ is the economy's expenditure function, $R(.)$ is its revenue function, $\mathbf{k}$ is the vector of $n + 1$ specific factors, and $T(.)$ is tariff revenue. The homogeneity properties of equation A-1 implies that only relative prices can be determined. Differentiating this identity with respect to p_i and letting E_i stand for the partial derivatives of the expenditure and R_i for revenue functions with respect to p_i gives

$$(A\text{-}2) \qquad E_i + E_W(\partial W / \partial p_i) = R_i + (\partial T / \partial p_i).$$

Let m_i stand for sector i's import-demand function, c_i and y_i being respectively the domestic consumption and production of good i, and a_{ij} the input-output coefficients. Rearranging equation A-2 and using Shephard's and Hotelling's lemmas, together with the fact that the marginal utility of income is 1 under equation 2, we have

$$(A\text{-}3) \qquad \partial W / \partial p_i = -m_i + (\partial T / \partial p_i).$$

Choose units so that all international prices are equal to one, and let $t_i = p_i - 1$ be the tariff rate. Tariff revenue can be written as $T(p) = \sum_j t_j m_j(p)$, so that

$$\partial T / \partial p_i = m_i + \sum_j t_j (\partial m_j / \partial p_i).$$

Substituting this into equation A3 gives

$$\partial W/\partial p_i = \sum_j t_j \left(\partial m_j/\partial p_i\right) = \sum_j t_j \left([\partial c_j/\partial p_i] + \sum_k a_{jk} [\partial y_k/\partial p_i] - [\partial y_j/\partial p_i] \right).$$

which confirms that supply of good j is a function of the "net price" of good j, $\tilde{p}_j = p_j - \sum_j a_{kj}p_k$, and of the wage rate. Thus,

$$\partial y_k/\partial p_i = (\partial y_k/\partial \tilde{p}_k)\,(\partial \tilde{p}_k/\partial p_i) + (\partial y_k/\partial w)\,(\partial w/\partial p_i).$$

Collecting terms,

$$\partial W/\partial p_i = \sum_j t_j(c_j/p_i)\varepsilon_{ij}^c$$

$$+ \sum_j t_j \left[\sum_k a_{jk}[\partial y_k/\partial \tilde{p}_k]\,[\partial \tilde{p}_k/\partial p_i] - [\partial y_j/\partial \tilde{p}_j]\,[\partial \tilde{p}_j/\partial p_i] \right.$$

$$\left. + \left(\sum_k a_{jk}\,[\partial y_k/\partial w] - [\partial y_j/\partial w] \right) - (\partial w/\partial p_i) \right].$$

Let $\tilde{\varepsilon}_i^s = \partial \log y_i/\partial \log \tilde{p}_i\;(> 0)$ be the elasticity of supply to the net price of good i, $\mu_i = -\partial \log y_i/\partial \log w\;(> 0)$ the wage elasticity of supply in sector i, and $\varepsilon_{ij}^c = \partial \log c_j/\partial \log p_i$ the cross-price elasticity of final demand in sector i. Using the fact that

$$\partial \tilde{p}_k/\partial p_i = \begin{cases} 1 - a_{ii} & \text{for } k = i \\ -a_{ik} & \text{otherwise,} \end{cases}$$

yields

$$\sum_k a_{jk}(\partial y_k/\partial \tilde{p}_k)\,(\partial \tilde{p}_k/\partial p_i) = a_{ji}(1 - a_{ii})\,(\varepsilon_i^s y_i/\tilde{p}^i) + \sum_{k \neq i} -a_{jk}a_{ik}(\varepsilon_k^s y_k/\tilde{p}^k)$$

$$= a_{ji}(\varepsilon_i^s y_i/\tilde{p}^i) - \sum_{k=0}^{n} a_{jk}a_{ik}(\varepsilon_k^s y_k/\tilde{p}^k).$$

Similar calculations give

$$\sum_j t_j(\partial y_j/\partial \tilde{p}_j)\,(\partial \tilde{p}_j/\partial p_i) = \varepsilon_i^s t_i y_i/\tilde{p}^i - \sum_{j=0}^{n} -a_{ij}(\varepsilon_j^s y_j/\tilde{p}^i),$$

$$\sum_j t_j \left(\sum_k a_{jk}[\partial y_k/\partial w] \right) = -\sum_j \sum_k t_j a_{jk}(\mu_k y_k/w)$$

and

$$\sum_j t_j(\partial y_j/\partial w) = -\sum_j (\mu_j t_j y_j/w).$$

Finally, let $\tilde{\varepsilon}_i^w = \partial log\, w/\partial log\, \tilde{p}_i\ (> 0)$ be the elasticity of the wage rate to a change in the net price of good i. The expression for the wage-rate adjustment term is given by:

$$\partial w/\partial p_i = \sum_k (\partial w/\partial \tilde{p}_k)\,(\partial \tilde{p}_k/\partial p_i) = \sum_k (\partial w/\partial \tilde{p}_k)\,(1_{k=i} - a_{ik})$$

(A-4)
$$= \tilde{\varepsilon}_i^w w/\tilde{p}_i - \sum_k a_{ik}\tilde{\varepsilon}_k^w w/\tilde{p}_k.$$

Combining these gives:

$$\varepsilon_i = \sum_j (t_j c_j/p_i)\varepsilon_{ij}^c + \sum_j t_j\left(a_{ji}[\varepsilon_i^s y_i/\tilde{p}^i]\sum_{k=0}^n a_{jk}a_{ik}[\varepsilon_k^s y_k/\tilde{p}^k]\right)$$

$$-\left([\varepsilon_i^s t_i y_i/\tilde{p}^i] + \sum_{j=0}^n a_{ij}[\varepsilon_j^s y_j/\tilde{p}^j]\right)$$

$$-\left[\left(\sum_j [\mu_j t_j y_i/w]\right) - \left(\sum_j \sum_k t_j a_{jk}\,[\mu_k y_k/w]\right)\right]\left(\tilde{\varepsilon}_i^w w/\tilde{p}i - \sum_k a_{ik}\tilde{\varepsilon}_k^w w/\tilde{p}_k\right).$$

(A-5)

If $P_i > 0$, the existence of an interior solution with positive protection requires that $E_i < 0$. As in the Grossman-Helpman model, the first term and the following two in parentheses are Ramsey terms minimizing the deadweight loss due to the tariff on good i. They are decreasing in the own-price elasticity of supply (ε_i^s) and in (the absolute value of) the own-price elasticity of demand ($|\varepsilon_{ii}^c|$); that is, $E_i \to -\infty$ (driving down the equilibrium tariff toward zero) when either $\varepsilon_{ii}^c \to -\infty$ or $\varepsilon_i^s \to \infty$. The expression in square brackets is a sum of second-best terms reflecting the presence of positive tariffs on other goods; it is multiplied by a wage-adjustment factor in parentheses. Clearly, if there is no tariff other than i ($t_j = 0$ for all $j \neq i$) there is no second-best argument for a positive t_i on efficiency grounds. But even with positive tariffs on other goods, the second-best argument for a tariff in i vanishes when all general equilibrium linkages picked up by cross-price elasticities of demand, input-output coefficients, and wage-rate adjustment are simultaneously zero, as in Grossman-Helpman.

Using the notation introduced in this appendix, equation 6 can also be rewritten in terms of elasticities and shares. Using equation A4, let $\tilde{\alpha}_i = w\ell_i/\tilde{p}_i y_i$ be the share of labor in sector i's value added, and let $\lambda_i = \ell_i/\ell$ be the share of sector i in total employment,

$$(A\text{-}6) \qquad P_i = y_i - \sum_j a_{ij} y_j - \left((\tilde{\alpha}_i/\lambda_i)\varepsilon_i^w - \sum_k a_{ik}(\tilde{\alpha}_k/\lambda_k)\tilde{\varepsilon}_k^w \right) y_i.$$

APPENDIX B. EQUATIONS AND CALIBRATION OF THE SIMULATION MODEL

The first two equations in the simulation model are the government's first-order condition, given by equations A-6 and A-5, which are indexed over tradables sectors (agriculture and manufacturing). Labor demand is indexed over all activities, and assuming that the nested value-added function is of the CES type, labor demand in sector i (i = agriculture, manufacturing, or nontraded) is given by

$$\ell_i = (\tilde{\alpha}_i \tilde{p}_i/w)^{\sigma i} yi.$$

Finally, the following equation determines the equilibrium wage:

$$\ell = \sum_i \ell_i.$$

Several elasticities in table B-2 are calculated internally from the data. This is the case for μ_i, the wage elasticity of supply used in equation A-5, and η_i, the elasticity of labor demand used in the calibration of $\tilde{\varepsilon}_i^w$ ($\tilde{\varepsilon}_i^w = \eta_i \ell_i / \sum_j \eta_j \ell_j$), the elasticity of the wage rate to a change in the net price of i used in equations A4 and A5.

Data Sources

Tables B-1 and B-2 give the data used in the simulations. Parameters describing technology and demand and production structures (like ratios of sectoral consumptions and productions) are taken from Anderson (1995, table 1). So are price elasticities of demand and the assumption of a Cobb-Douglas technology (except for sensitivity analysis). Anderson, however, does not provide information on input-output relationships. For the rich economy these were taken from de Melo and Tarr (1992). For the poor economy the coefficients are aggregated

TABLE B-1. Input-Output Coefficients for Rich and Poor Archetypes

	Agriculture		Manufacturing		Nontradables	
	Rich	Poor	Rich	Poor	Rich	Poor
Agriculture	0.38	0.22	0.04	0.09	0.028	0.03
Manufacturing	0.26	0.04	0.42	0.10	0.26	0.05
Nontradables	0.07	0.05	0.08	0.10	0.11	0.05

Source: See appendix B.

TABLE B-2. Output Composition and Elasticities for Rich and Poor Archetypes

	Agriculture		Manufacturing		Nontradables	
	Rich	Poor	Rich	Poor	Rich	Poor
C	7	35	12	10	31	20
Y	6	61	46	10	68	29
$\tilde{\alpha}_i^a$	0.35	0.70	0.50	0.35	0.60	0.60
σ_i	1	1	1	1	1	1
μ_i^b	0.54	2.33	1	0.54	1.5	0.43
η_i^c	1.54	3.33	2	1.54	2.5	1.43
λ_i^d	0.031	0.761	0.379	0.065	0.590	0.175
$\tilde{\varepsilon}_i^e$	0.02	0.774	0.258	0.06	0.722	0.166
$\varepsilon^{i,i}$	−0.12	−0.25	−0.52	−0.69	−0.21	−0.49

[a] $\tilde{\alpha}_i = w\ell_i/\tilde{p}_i y_i$.
[b] $\mu_i = \varepsilon_i^s(\sigma_i\tilde{\alpha}_i)/(1 - \tilde{\alpha}_i)$.
[c] $\eta_i = \sigma_i/(1 - \tilde{\alpha}_i)$.
[d] For $w = 1$.
[e] For $w = 1$ and from expression $\tilde{\varepsilon}_i^w = (\eta_i\ell_i/\sum_j \eta_j\ell_j)$.
Source: See appendix B.

from information used in Chenery and Syrquin (1986, chap. 4) for a typical economy with a \$500 GDP per capita (in 1970 dollars). The main difference in interindustry structure between the rich and poor economies in table B-1 is the higher value-added ratio in the poor economy due partly to the higher value-added ratio in agriculture (see Chenery and Syrquin, figures 3.3 and 3.4). Table B-2 gives the remaining elasticities and shares.

REFERENCES

Ades, A., and R. Di Tella. 1999. "Rents, Competition and Corruption." *American Economic Review* 89(4):982–93.

Anderson, K. 1995. "Lobbying Incentives and the Pattern of Protection in Rich and Poor Countries." *Economic Development and Cultural Change* 43(2):401–23.

Cadot, O., J. de Melo, and M. Olarreaga. 2003. "The Protectionist Bias of Duty Drawbacks." *Journal of International Economics* 59(1):161–82.

Chenery, H., and M. Syrquin. 1986. "Typical Patterns of Transformation." In H. Chenery, S. Robinson, and M. Syrquin, eds., *Industrialization and Growth*. New York: Oxford University Press.

Corden, W. M. 1974. *Trade Policy and Economic Welfare*. Oxford: Clarendon Press.

Destler, I. M., and J. S. Odell. 1987. "Anti-Protection: Changing Forces in US Trade." Policy Analysis 21. Institute for International Economics, Washington, D.C.

Djankov, S., R. La Porta, F. Lopez-de-Silanes, and A. Shleifer. 2002. "The Regulation of Entry." *Quarterly Journal of Economics* 117(1):1–37.

Dornsbusch, R. 1974. "Tariffs and Nontraded Goods." *Journal of International Economics* 4(2):177–85.

Findlay, R. 1991. "The New Political Economy: Its Explanatory Power for LDCs." In G.M. Meier, ed., *Political Economy and Policy Making in Developing Countries*. San Francisco, Calif.: ICS Press.

366   THE WORLD BANK ECONOMIC REVIEW, VOL. 18, NO. 3

Freund, C., and S. Djankov. 2000. "The Politics of Trade Liberalization." World Bank, Washington, D.C.

Gawande, K., and U. Bandyopadhyay. 2000. "Is Protection for Sale? Evidence on the Grossman-Helpman Theory of Endogenous Protection." *Review of Economics and Statistics* 87(1):139–52.

Grossman, G., and E. Helpman. 1994. "Protection for Sale." *American Economic Review* 84(4):833–50.

———. 1996. "Electoral Competition and Special Interest Politics." *Review of Economic Studies* 63(2):265–86.

Hillman, A. L. 1982. "Declining Industries and Political-Support Protectionist Motives." *American Economic Review* 72(5):1180–87.

Koujianou-Goldberg, P., and G. Maggi. 1999. "Protection for Sale: An Empirical Investigation." *American Economic Review* 89(5):1135–55.

Krueger, A. O., M. Schiff, and A. Valdes. 1989. "Agricultural Incentives in Developing Countries: Measuring the Effect of Sectoral and Economy-wide Policies." *World Bank Economic Review* 2(3):255–73.

Maggi, G., and A. Rodriguez-Clare. 1999. "Import Penetration and the Politics of Trade Protection." *Journal of International Economics* 51(2):287–304.

Mayer, W. 1984. "Endogenous Tariff Formation." *American Economic Review* 74(5):970–85.

Melo, J. de, and D. Tarr. 1992. *A General Equilibrium Analysis of U.S. Foreign Trade Policy.* Cambridge, Mass.: MIT Press.

Moore, M. 1996. "Steel Protection in the 1980's: The Waning Influence of Big Steel?" In A. O. Krueger, ed., *The Political Economy of American Trade Policy.* Chicago: Chicago University Press.

Ray, E. J. 1990. "Empirical Research on the Political Economy of Trade." In C. A. Carter, ed., *Imperfect Competition and Political Economy.* Boulder, Colo.: Westview Press.

———. 1991. "Protection of Manufactures in the United States." In D. Greenaway, ed., *Global Protectionism: Is the U.S. Playing on a Level Field?* New York: St. Martin's Press.

Rodrik, D. 1995. "The Political Economy of Trade Policy." In G. Grossman and K. Rogoff, eds., *Handbook of International Economics,* vol. 3. New York: North Holland.

World Bank. 2000. *World Development Indicators 2000.* Washington, D.C.

WTO (World Trade Organization). Various issues. *Trade Policy Reviews.* Geneva.

8   Globalization and migratory pressures from developing countries: a simulation analysis

RICCARDO FAINI, JEAN-MARIE GRETHER
AND JAIME DE MELO

1   Introduction

Opposition to immigration in the North has been on the rise, notably in the EU and in the USA. This rising opposition can be traced to the regime shift in their labour markets which have moved from tight labour markets up to the early 1970s to rising unemployment (in the EU) and increasing wage inequalities (in the USA) since then. On the other hand, migratory pressures have not subsided. For many developing countries, stagnant growth in the wake of the debt crisis and explosive demographics have led to a marked deterioration in labour market conditions. The thawing of East–West relations has also contributed to greater migration pressure. Paradoxically, Western European governments, who used to criticise socialist regimes in Eastern Europe for imposing draconian restrictions on people mobility, reacted to the 1989 events by swiftly implementing new and more effective migration control measures.

As pointed out by Schiff (1996), the change in attitude in the North towards immigration from the South is well exemplified by the change in attitudes in the International Labour Organisation (ILO). Not surprisingly, during the period of tight labour markets in the North, the ILO recommended attracting suitable labour from the South (ILO, 1949). But by the mid-1980s, the ILO was recommending that the receiving countries should

> endeavour to cooperate more fully in the development of such countries by appropriate intensified capital movements, the expansion of trade, the transfer of technical knowledge.   (ILO, 1984)

More recently, the ILO (1992) has recommended that developed countries provide foreign assistance to developing countries to reduce migratory pressures.

This policy shift on migration can be criticised on both ethical and economic grounds (see, for example, Bhagwati, 1992). Yet, migration policy is

190

"

Globalization and migratory pressures from developing countries   191

not made in a vacuum, but reflects the values and the attitudes of voters and pressure groups reflected in what Schiff (1996) calls 'social capital'. The fact is that the attitude toward migration has changed markedly in industrialised countries. According to an EC survey, 64 per cent of respondents in Italy believe that migrants are 'too many'. In France, Germany and the UK the percentage of those who believe migration to be excessive is over 50 per cent. Since 1989, Europe's newspapers have been filled with stories of racial intolerance. Under these conditions, Europe's policy-makers have little choice but to try to stem the flow of new immigrants while at the same time promoting the social and economic assimilation of old ones. This pressure is likely to subsist in spite of the ageing of European population. The issue then arises of how industrial countries can discourage massive and largely undesired population flows. That is the issue investigated in this chapter.

The policy options appear to be limited. Migration controls can work in the very short run but are often ineffective in the medium to long run, as typified by the recurring use both in Europe and in the USA of migration regularisation programmes, invariably coupled with the promise that future controls will be tightened up. Foreign aid as well as trade policies have often been advocated as more effective tools to cope with rising migrations. Foreign aid can boost growth in sending countries, thereby reducing the incentive to emigrate to the North. Similarly, trade liberalisation can foster factor-price convergence and limit the incentive for factor mobility. The diffusion of North–South regional trade integration agreements during the 1990s has often been attributed to the desire to stem migration pressure, as epitomised by President Salinas' quote that 'Mexico wants to export goods, not people'. The EU's drive toward signing Association Agreements with its close trading partners in the East and in the South has been similarly motivated.

Two channels of action have been identified in the policy debate. The first are what one could call 'direct measures'. These take the form of increased aid to raise income in the South. Increased costs to migration through, say, more effective border controls represent an alternative direct measure. The second channel includes 'policy reform measures' whose effects on migratory pressures are less direct. Paramount here are the trade reforms of the Uruguay Round and beyond, leading to a reduction in barriers to trade in goods (especially in agriculture and light manufactures such as textiles and apparel) and in services (a reduction in barriers to Foreign Direct Investment (FDI) and eventually to trade in services).

The impact on migratory pressure of any measure will depend mostly on the determinants of migration in sending countries in response to changes in incentives to migrate. To take an example, one would expect that migrants from Sub-Saharan African (SSA) countries would be mostly low-skill labour whereas Southern Mediterranean migrants in Northern countries

192 **Riccardo Faini** *et al.*

would be more predominantly medium- and high-skill labour. Migrants from SSA countries would also tend to be viewed as more permanent in receiving countries whereas migrants from Mediterranean countries would be more susceptible to responding positively to an improvement in economic conditions in their home countries, and thus would exhibit 'return' migration behaviour.[1] If one considers SSA countries as typical of Low-Income (LI) economies and Southern Mediterranean countries as typical of Middle-Income (MI) economies, one would expect different patterns of migratory pressures in each group. This chapter uses simulation analysis to investigate if direct and indirect measures are likely to elicit different migratory pressures in different countries. Two questions are asked: (1) Would direct and indirect attempts to reduce migratory pressures yield qualitatively different migratory responses for an archetypical developing country, be it a LI or a MI economy? (2) Would identical measures have different effects in LI and MI economies?

Simulations are carried out in a single-country framework with modelling efforts directed at the sending country. To this effect we build a Ricardo–Viner (RV) economy with traded and non-traded sectors.[2] The economy is disaggregated on the labour and household sides with households offering labour services at home and abroad. Calibration is carried out for two 'archetype' LI and MI economies. The archetypes differ systematically in the structure of production, consumption, trade and factor supply across sectors while elasticities and the mapping of factor income to households is purposely kept the same. This allows us to investigate quite systematically the likely effect of differences in economic structure on migratory pressures.

One might object that modelling should be carried out in a two-country North–South world. Such an approach would be desirable for an analysis of systemic changes in which repercussion effects are likely to be important. A North–South trade model would also be desirable to study factor-price-convergence effects and for a more thorough analysis of the complementarity–substitutability issue between trade and migration. A more elaborate model than the one offered here would also be desirable to investigate some of the issues which the theoretical literature has identified such as migration in response to relative deprivation, risk and uncertainty and sunk costs in migration. We ignore or only partially address these issues. Nonetheless, our focus on a single-country model enables us to give a better road-map of the channels through which Southern countries' migratory pressures exert themselves. Finally, since the receiving country is not modelled, increased migratory pressure in this single-country framework translates directly into an increased supply of workers abroad (in effect, we assume an infinitely elastic demand for labour from the sending country over the relevant range).

Globalization and migratory pressures from developing countries   193

The remainder of the chapter is organised as follows. Section 2 develops the modelling of migration in this RV framework. It also outlines the main features of the simulation model which is given in the appendix (p. 212). Section 3 describes the calibration to the two archetype economies and the simulations proposed to decompose the likely effects of globalisation on South–North migratory pressures. Section 4 reports on the simulation results comparing the effects on migratory pressures across archetypes for a base model cloture. Section 5 examines the sensitivity of results to changes in model cloture (elasticities and assumptions about the mapping of factor income to households). It also proposes likely orders of magnitude for what one might call the most relevant model for each 'archetype'. Since much of the data is constructed or invented, it is probably best to interpret the results in relative terms – i.e. differences in results across archetypes or between measures. Section 6 draws some conclusions.

2   A Ricardo–Viner model of migration

The traditional reason for migration is earnings differential: the prospect of a higher net (of moving and other fixed costs) expected wage in the receiving country is the main reason for migration. In the traditional literature derived from Harris and Todaro (1970), risk-neutrality on the part of homogeneous migrants implies that expected earning differentials are the sole determinants of migration. It has been recognised, however, that migration costs are also a determinant of migration. These include non-monetary costs (idiosyncratic tastes for location as in Djajic and Milbourne, 1988, or Faini and Venturini, 1994) and monetary costs (Lopez and Schiff, 1995). If agents are risk-averse, matters are somewhat more complicated. First, risk considerations may have an ambiguous impact even from the point of view of an individual agent. On the one hand greater uncertainty about perspectives in the destination region should deter migration. Conversely, higher income risk at home may encourage agents to move. However, if migration is at least partially irreversible, as would happen if it were subject to sunk costs, then potential migrants might prefer to wait for uncertainty to dissipate before making their location decision (Burda, 1993). At the household level, on the other hand, greater uncertainty may boost migration provided that incomes in different location are not perfectly correlated. Under these circumstances, the household can indeed reduce its total risk exposure by having some of its members migrate to a different location (Stark, 1991). The theoretical literature has also investigated additional factors, such as relative deprivation and asymmetric information, that might affect the migration decision.

While there is some evidence to support these suggestions (see Schiff,

1996, for a survey of the evidence and Daveri and Faini, 1996, for recent evidence from Southern Italy), by and large the evidence is scant. Also we have little knowledge of the relative importance of these (and other) factors in determining the supply of migrants. For this reason, we develop a simple model that accommodates the traditional motive based on earnings differentials and we assume that, in their location decision, households face concave costs to relocation. This implies that households will diversify, i.e. they will not locate entirely in one country.

2.1   *Modelling migration*

Consider a heterogeneous household (households are indexed over $h \in H$) that maximises a utility function that includes leisure and the consumption of goods as arguments. In view of the numerical application that follows, for simplicity, we assume strong separability in the choice of labour supply and consumption of goods. This gives us a two-stage decision process. In a first stage the household decides on the amount of labour to supply, and in a second stage on the allocation of labour between the home and foreign labour markets. In the first stage, the supply of labour by household, LS_h, is determined from the maximisation of the following LES utility function:

$$U^h(.) = \prod_{i=0}^{n} (C_{i,h} - \delta_{i,h})^{\beta i,h},\tag{1}$$

where $\Sigma_{i=0}^{n}\beta_{i,h} = 1$ and C_0 is leisure. Maximisation of (1) subject to the household's budget constraint ((25) in table 8A.1) determines the household's supply of labour services ((12) in table 8A.1) and the consumption of goods ((17) in table 8A.1). Given that we choose an LES, this means that leisure and goods are substitutes as are all goods. The allocation of labour services LS_h between the domestic (L_h) and foreign (L_h^*) labour market takes place in the second stage. It depends on the relative wage in each destination with increasing costs to relocate from one labour market to the other. This gives a concave locus describing how the households' labour services can be relocated. A convenient form is the familiar Constant Elasticity of Transformation (CET) function given by:

$$\begin{aligned}LS^h &= \overline{B}_h[(1 - v_h)^{-\Omega_h}(L_h)^{1+\Omega_h} + (vh)^{-\Omega^h}(L_h^*)^{1+\Omega_h}]^{1/(1+\Omega_h)}\\ &= \Psi_h(L_h, L_h^*, \Omega_h)\\ &= \Psi_h(.),\end{aligned}\tag{2}$$

where $\overline{B}_h$ and v_h are positive parameters ($0 \iota v_h \iota 1$) and Ω_h is the elasticity of transformation.

The CET function, $\psi_h(.)$, is concave implying increasing costs to labour

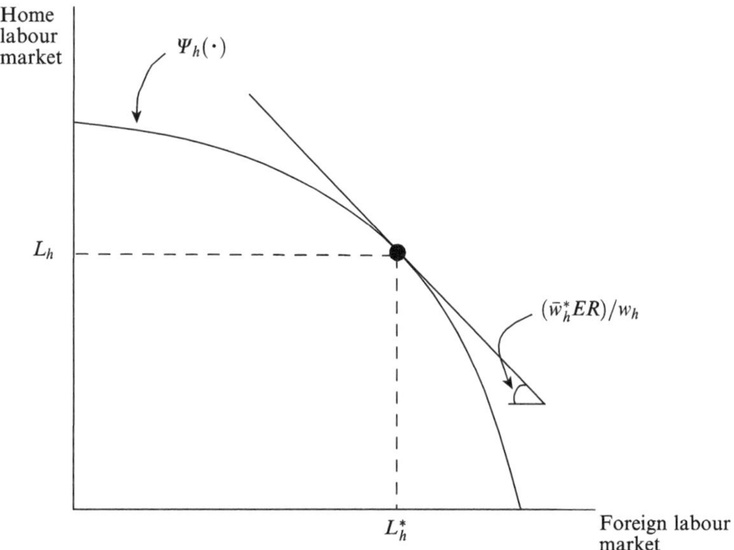

Figure 8.1   Labour-allocation decision

relocation. It has the advantage of tractability: it is easy to calibrate numerically as it requires only one parameter Ωh for implementation. In the second stage, household h maximises labour income, $\tilde{W}_h LS_h$, where $\tilde{W}_h$ is the revenue-maximising wage under the condition of increasing relocation costs ((11) in table 8.A1 gives the expression for $\tilde{W}_h$). Maximisation of wage income is subject to the constraint that labour relocation between the home and foreign labour markets takes place under increasing costs, i.e.

$$\max \mathbf{L}(L_h, L_h^*, \lambda_h) = w_h L_h + ER \bar{w}_h^* L_h^* - \lambda_h \Psi_h(.), \tag{3}$$

where λ_h is a Lagrange multiplier, ER is the conversion factor of foreign currency units into domestic currency units, and w_h is the domestic wage. In this maximisation, the foreign wage, $\bar{w}_h^*$ is exogenous, reflecting an infinitely elastic foreign demand for labour over the relevant range. The result of the maximisation of (3) is the allocation of labour services, L_h and L_h^* ((13) and (14) in table 8A.1).

Figure 8.1 depicts the allocation of labour services for a given aggregate household labour supply, LS_h. Wage-income-maximisation leads to the solution (L_h, L_h^*). Since by the choice of numéraire, a price index of non-traded goods is kept fixed (see (28) in table 8A.1), ER is in effect the value of the real exchange rate – i.e. the relative price of tradables. Hence, we assume in (3) that the household makes its labour-allocation decision on the basis of the purchasing power of foreign wages in terms of home (non-traded) goods.

196   **Riccardo Faini *et al.***

Labour will then be reallocated either in response to a change in the domestic wage, or to a change in the value of the real exchange rate, *ER*.

In the above formulations, we are modelling a medium-term labour-allocation decision rather than an irreversible migration decision. As argued above, this 'guest-worker' view of migration is perhaps more prevalent among MI than LI developing countries. There is recent evidence in the case of Mexican migration to the USA that Mexico–US migration patterns are responsive to changes in the Mexican-US bilateral exchange rate (see Markusen and Zahniser, 1997, table 1). As an alternative, we assume that migration is more permanent at least in the sense that the household does not consider the domestic currency purchasing power of foreign wages. This amounts to fixing *ER* to its initial value in (3). We shall call this version the 'permanent-migration' view. It is offered here both as an alternative relevant to the migration decision in LI economies and as a way of isolating the real exchange rate component of migratory pressures.[3] It is considered in section 5.

Whether these views of the labour allocation are realistic or not is a moot point: all that can be said is that they are 'consistent' with observations on household diversification.[4] As will be confirmed in the simulations below, this formulation implies that there is a resource cost to a relocation of labour across the border because of the concavity of the CET function.[5]

2.2   *The simulation model*

In the specification of the RV simulation model, atomistic firms with constant-returns-to-scale (CRS) production functions maximise profits and atomistic households maximise utility. Each agent has a constraint, and the economy has an external constraint. Firms have a Cobb–Douglas technology for value-added and Leontief technology for intermediates and between intermediates and value-added. As in the traditional RV model, the economy is a price-taker in the markets for traded goods. There are however, non-traded activities as well, for which there is an endogenous market-clearing price. To accommodate the fact that much of imports in developing countries are non-competitive with local production (the structure of imports reveals that intermediates and capital goods account for the bulk of imports), we assume that each sector also uses non-competitive imports. Firms pay their mobile factors, the different categories of labour, their value marginal product.

As some sectors are non-traded, the real exchange rate adjusts to maintain external and internal balance. In turn, adjustments in the real exchange rate affect both the allocation of labour as depicted in figure 8.1 as well as the domestic-currency value of remittances. For traded goods, domestic and foreign-produced goods are perfect substitutes which would tend to lead to extreme specialisation among traded activities in response to relative price

Globalization and migratory pressures from developing countries   197

changes. It is the presence of sector-specific factors that gives enough concavity to the production possibilities frontier to prevent extreme specialisation.

The mapping from factor to household income is described below in section 3 (see table 8.2, p. 200), and in the appendix, which gives the full specification of the model. Suffice it to note here that, to simplify, each household only supplies one type of labour, and we exclude the possibility that households would invest capital income abroad. The income from capital (the specific factor in each sector) is distributed across households (see table 8.2). This mapping of factor income to households implies that there is some diversification in each household's source of income, a diversification which attenuates household income fluctuations.

It is clear that this model is very close to the standard RV model with non-traded goods, except that it is augmented to include migration and that there are several mobile factors of production and several households. To approximate the standard model as closely as possible, the government's only role is to tax trade (tariffs and export taxes are the only distortions in the model). Government revenue is redistributed lump-sum to each household in proportion to that household's income. Remittance income adjusted for the (exogenous) trade deficit in foreign-currency units is distributed to households, also according to each household's share in total income. Thus changes in trade policy do not have a direct effect on income distribution via government transfers.

In this set-up, policy changes such as a trade liberalisation that alters relative prices affects both the aggregate supply of labour on the part of each household according to the resulting changes in household wage income and total income and the allocation of labour between the domestic and foreign labour market depending on changes in relative wages in the home and foreign labour market. An appreciation of the real exchange rate, for example, will make the home labour market more attractive if there is no compensating change in the domestic wage. On the other hand, the home market wage rate for each labour category will change following traditional Heckscher–Ohlin (HO) factor- intensity differentials across sectors. When protection is reduced, for example, if export sectors are relatively intensive in the use of medium-skill labour, the wage rate for medium-skill labour will rise relative to other wages.

3   Decomposing the effects of globalization on the supply of migrants for two archetype economies

We now examine numerically how changes in the economic environment via either changes in policy or in the external environment are likely to affect the supply of migrants from the South to the North. This section

198   **Riccardo Faini *et al.***

describes the two archetype economies to which the RV model is calibrated and the set of simulations to decompose the direct and indirect channels through which policy changes and changes in the external environment are likely to affect South–North migratory pressures.

3.1   The archetype economies

The RV model is calibrated to data for two archetypical developing economies. The data are adapted from Bourguignon *et al.* (1992). As explained in the appendix, these data are representative (in the sense of Chenery and Syrquin, 1986) of a low-income (LI) developing economy (say, a SSA economy) and a middle-income (MI) developing economy (say, a Latin American or North African economy). The details on the data are provided in the appendix. To control for the dimension along which the MI and LI economies differ, we assume that the two archetypes are of equal size, have the same sectoral disaggregation, the same factor-use mapping by sectors and the same household composition. This limited difference between archetypes makes it much easier to interpret simulation results.

The two archetypes differ in structure in the following stylised way. The principal structural characteristics of the LI and the MI economies are given in tables 8.1a and 8.1b (also see tables 8A.3 and 8A.4 in the appendix). Tables 8.1a and 8.1b show the difference in production structure, trade, trade barriers and labour allocation across sectors and abroad. The two economies engage in the same activities: subsistence agriculture for the LI economy which is a non-traded activity by definition and import-competing agriculture in the MI economy. In the LI economy, the output of the export agriculture sector (which could also represent a mining activity) is entirely exported as there is no domestic final and no intermediate consumption (cocoa or copper). It is taxed and is the only export activity in the calibrated scenario for the LI economy. This representation of the LI economy corresponds to the traditional stylised description of small LI economies that export only a few commodities (i.e. 'monoculture' economies).[6]

Two manufacturing activities (light and heavy manufacturing) are distinguished, the latter essentially a non-competing import-substituting activity, the former representing the typical HO labour-intensive exports. Note the structure of trade taxes in each archetype: imports and exports are taxed, with taxation higher in the LI archetype. Otherwise, the archetypes also differ in their inter-industry linkages, these being weaker in the LI economy which also has a larger share of non-competitive imports in total imports (see tables 8A.3a and 8A.3b in the appendix). This calibration results in the LI archetype having a much larger share of activity in

Globalization and migratory pressures from developing countries   199

Table 8.1. *Structure of production, demand and factor allocation*

a low-income *(L1)* archetype

	Out. struc (1)	Net exp. out. (2)	Tariff exp. tax (3)	Low skill (4)	Medium skill (5)	High skill (6)
Sub. ag.	0.20	0.0	0.0	0.65	0.0	0.0
Exp. ag.	0.10	1.0	−0.2	0.0	0.25	0.0
Light mfg.	0.22	−0.2	0.5	0.0	0.17	0.31
Heavy mfg.	0.04	−1.5	0.4	0.0	0.0	0.07
Services	0.31	0.0	0.0	0.0	0.31	0.57
Informal	0.13	0.0	0.0	0.26	0.17	0.0
Lab abroad[a]			(0.2)[c]	0.09	0.09	0.05
Lab abroad[b]				0.63	0.32	0.05

b middle-income (*M1*) archetype

	Out. struc (1)	Net exp. out. (2)	Tariff exp. tax (3)	Low skill (4)	Medium skill (5)	High skill (6)
Sub. ag.	0.09	−0.3	0.2	0.46	0.0	0.0
Exp. ag.	0.05	0.4	−0.1	0.0	0.06	0.0
Light mfg.	0.24	0.2	0.0	0.0	0.19	0.18
Heavy mfg.	0.14	−0.3	0.4	0.0	0.0	0.33
Services	0.33	0.0	0.0	0.0	0.46	0.45
Informal	0.15	0.0	0.0	0.45	0.21	0.0
Lab abroad[a]			(0.1)[c]	0.09	0.09	0.05
Lab abroad[b]				0.35	0.47	0.18

Notes:
[a] Share of migrants in skill category.
[b] Share of skill category in total migrants.
[c] Tariff on non-competitive imports.

agriculture. However, to control for the sources of differences in economic structure, the same Cobb–Douglas technology for value-added is imposed for each archetype (see table 8A.4 in the appendix). Both the Service and the Informal sectors are non-traded activities in both economies. Thus, a substantial share of GDP is non-traded in both calibrated archetypes. These differences in production structure are reflected in the allocation of the three labour categories – (low-skill = LSL), (medium-skill = MSL), (high-skill = HSL) – across sectors. (The percentage distribution across

200   **Riccardo Faini** *et al.*

Table 8.2. *Factor–household mapping: L1 and L2 archetypes*

	Low-skilled LS HH	Medium-skilled MS HH	High-skilled HS HH	Capitalist household CAP HH
Mobile factor:				
LSL	1	0.0	0.0	0.0
MSL	0.0	1	0.0	0.0
HSL	0.0	0.0	0.75	0.25
Specific factor:				
Sub. ag.	0.5	0.0	0.0	0.5
Exp. ag.	0.0	0.5	0.0	0.5
Light mfg.	0.0	0.25	0.25	0.5
Heavy mfg.	0.0	0.0	0.25	0.75
Services	0.0	0.25	0.25	0.5
Informal	0.5	0.5	0.0	0.0

sectors is given in columns (3)–(6) in tables 8.1a and 8.1b.) Note in row 7 of the table, the percentage of each category of labour abroad. These figures are assumed to be the same for each archetype, even though the composition of migrants abroad from the LI and MI archetype is different (see row 8).

Finally, table 8.2 gives the mapping from factor to household income. It is the same for both archetypes. The top part of the table gives the mapping of the mobile factor to each one of the four households (LS HH, MS HH, HS HH, CAP HH) and the bottom part of the table gives the mapping of the fixed factor to these households. Except for the HSL labour category which is supplied by both the HS HH (75 per cent) and the CAP HH (25 per cent), each labour category is supplied by only one household. LSL is the least diversified labour category as it is employed in only two sectors, both of which are non-tradable in the LI archetype. The other labour categories are employed in three or four sectors, with a split between tradable and non-tradable activities, so that the effects of changes in the relative price of tradables on household income is dampened by this assumed diversification in sectoral employment.

3.2   *Decomposing the effects of globalisation*

To study the determinants of migratory pressures in this single-country framework three sets of policy experiments are carried out to find out the

Globalization and migratory pressures from developing countries   201

Table 8.3. *Policy experiments*

Direct intervention

E-1   Increased transfer of resources [*ITR*] to the South (a relaxation of the
external constraint by 10 per cent)

E-2   Increase of migration costs ($E-1$ + decrease in the wage in the North by 10
per cent)

Trade liberalisation in the South

E-3   Trade liberalisation in the South [*TLS*] (removal of tariffs on imports and
taxes on traditional exports)

E-4   Increase in FDI in the south [*FDI*] (*E*-3 + 10 per cent increase in capital
stock in agricultural export and light manufacturing with profit repatriation
to the North)

Trade liberalisation in the North

E-5   Agricultural trade liberalisation in the North [*ATLN*] (a 10 per cent
increase in the world price of agricultural exports)

E-6   Manufacturing trade liberalisation in the North [*MTLN*] (a 10 per cent
increase in the world price of light manufactures)

E-7   Across-the-board trade liberalisation in the North [*TLN*] (*E*-5 + *E*-6)

Increased globalisation

E-8   Global trade liberalisation in North and South [*GTL*] (combination of *E*-7
and *E*-4)

best way to achieve the 'Export goods, not people' objective. These are
described in table 8.3. Within each set, experiments are usually cumulative.
In the first experiments (*E*-1 and *E*-2), the attempt is direct: increase in
foreign aid to the South or raise migration costs by lowering the (exogenous) effective wage in the North. In the second set (*E*-3 and *E*-4), trade
liberalisation in the South is examined with the potential by-product of an
increase in Northern FDI in the actual (and potential) exporting sectors.
The third set (*E*-5–*E*-7) attempts to capture the effects of a reduction in the
protection of agricultural and manufactured products exported by the
North. Finally we consider the potential effects of increased globalisation
of economic activity by combining increased openness to trade in the
North and the South (*E*-8). In this single-country model, it is difficult to
capture the effects of a trade liberalisation in the North. It is done here by
an exogenously imposed improvement in the terms of trade for the South
(except in *E*-6 for the LI archetype which is a net importer of light manufactures – see tables 8.1a and 8.1b). Arguably, this may not be an accurate
description of the likely effects of trade liberalisation in the North, as it is
not clear that it would improve the terms of trade for the South, thereby

202   **Riccardo Faini** *et al.*

presumably stemming migratory pressures. We are aware of this, but wished to capture the hoped-for increase in the demand for exports of manufactures from the South that increased integration of world markets would presumably bring about. In any event, it is these simulations that are carried out for the two archetype economies mentioned above.

4   Simulation results

In this RV model, the simulations described above affect the supply of migrants to the North through several channels. At the macro level, changes in purchasing power (via transfers or changes in the terms of trade) affect the aggregate supply of labour as the relative price of leisure changes. At the household level, income changes result from changes in the purchasing power (in terms of home goods) of remittances and from changes in remunerations via adjustments in relative wages across labour categories and in sectoral rents. Finally there is also a redistribution of purchasing power via changes in the cost of living as a given change in relative prices has a differential impact across households (here mostly via Engel effects in consumption as LS HH have both a lower income and a lower price elasticity of demand for agricultural products). In addition to changes in purchasing power, there are also changes in relative rewards for fixed and mobile factors which affect household income and hence both the supply and the location of labour activities. We report first the aggregate effects, then the compositional effects at the household and sectoral levels.

4.1   *Aggregate migratory pressures*

Tables 8.4a and 8.4b give the aggregate results in terms of total labour supply, its allocation at home and abroad, along with the changes in the equilibrium value of the real exchange rate and real GDP. A first glance at the results in tables 8.4a and 8.4b reveal both that economic structure matters and that the objective of decreased migration is not always met for the LI archetype. In fact, because trade liberalisation in the LI economy is accompanied by a strong real depreciation, it becomes more profitable to seek employment abroad. While FDI attenuates this effect, and trade liberalisation in the North as well, one still gets an increase in migratory pressure with globalisation. It would appear that LI economies are more prone to exhibit trade–migration complementarity than MI economies. Indeed, for the MI economy, under all scenarios, there is a reduction in aggregate labour supply abroad even though some labour categories increase their allocation abroad (see table 8.5b, p. 206).

   The contrast between the two archetypes has several causes, but the prominent one is the different effect of trade liberalisation in the South

Globalization and migratory pressures from developing countries   203

Table 8.4. *Macro results: labour supply and home–foreign-labour allocation*

a *L1* archetype[a]

		TLab.[b]	TFLab.[c]	TDLab.[d]	RER[e]	RGDP[f]
E-1	*ITR*	− 0.1	− 1.5	0.2	− 1.4	0.1
E-2	*IMC*	− 0.3	− 9.3	1.6	− 0.2	0.8
E-3	*TLS*	0.1	8.0	− 1.5	18.7	− 3.1
E-4	*FDI*	0.0	2.6	− 0.5	13.4	− 1.3
E-5	*ATLN*	− 0.4	− 7.5	1.1	− 6.0	0.5
E-6	*MTLN*	0.1	− 3.8	0.9	− 4.2	0.3
E-7	*TLN*	− 0.3	− 10.6	1.9	− 9.5	0.9
E-8	*GTL*	− 0.2	− 7.5	1.4	2.8	− 0.3

b *M1* archetype

		TLab.[b]	TFLab.[c]	TDLab.[d]	RER[e]	RGDP[f]
E-1	*ITR*	− 0.1	− 0.8	0.0	− 0.9	0.0
E-2	*IMC*	− 0.4	− 11.4	1.8	− 0.8	0.9
E-3	*TLS*	− 0.2	− 2.0	0.1	− 0.2	− 1.9
E-4	*FDI*	− 0.4	− 5.6	0.6	− 3.7	− 0.7
E-5	*ATLN*	− 0.2	− 3.9	0.6	− 3.3	0.1
E-6	*MTLN*	− 0.3	− 7.5	1.1	− 7.7	0.3
E-7	*TLN*	− 0.5	− 10.4	1.5	− 10.1	0.6
E-8	*GTL*	− 0.9	− 14.6	1.9	− 13.5	− 1.1

Notes:
[a] Percentage changes from initial values.
[b] Aggregate labour supply.
[c] Foreign labour allocation.
[d] Domestic labour allocation.
[e] Real exchange rate index.
[f] Real GDP.
See table 8.3 for definition of policy experiments.

(*TLS*) on the equilibrium value of the real exchange rate. Whereas for the LI economy *TLS* is accompanied by a strong real exchange rate depreciation (18.5 per cent), for the MI economy, *TLS* brings about a slight real exchange appreciation. This is because of greater supply response to the change in relative prices in the MI economy than in the LI economy which exhibits what is called 'structuralism'. Indeed, the elimination of the export tax on agricultural exports generates a stronger export-supply response in the MI economy as agriculture exports (or mining) are also consumed domestically whereas in the LI economy agriculture exports are not. Hence a removal of the export tax induces a strong export- supply response in the MI economy which must be matched by an increase in imports to meet the exogenous current-account constraint. Hence the real exchange rate appreciation to induce the resource shift out of import-competing activities (see also the results in table 8.6, p. 207).[7]

On the other hand, there are similarities in the pattern of results. This is so because we have only allowed for selected differences between the two archetypes. Consider for instance trade liberalisation in the North (*TLN*). For both archetypes, there is approximately the same 10 per cent reduction in labour supply abroad. This is because this simulation results in the same improvement in the terms of trade for both economies which induces the same amount of real exchange appreciation. For both economies, a decline in real GDP occurs for the simulations that involve large labour relocations. As explained in section 2, this is due to the concavity of the labour alloca-tion frontier and reflects adjustment costs.

The same pattern of results obtains when one compares *ITR* with *IMC* and *TLS* with *FDI* which are also cumulative experiments. Compare for example increased resource transfer (*ITR*) with *IMC* (increased migration costs) in which the increase in foreign transfer is also accompanied by increased migration costs. Reducing the wage received abroad (perhaps by tighter immigration controls) naturally increases the amount of return migration. This larger return migration induces a larger decline in the home wage which lowers the aggregate supply of labour.

Finally note the general equilibrium effects at work in the global trade liberalisation (*GTL*) experiment. Though *GTL* = *FDI* + *TLN* in design, the reduction in migratory pressure is less than would have been predicted in a partial equilibrium calculation that would have aggregated the results from *FDI* and *TLN* separately.

4.2   *Household and sectoral effects*

The aggregate results have identified the role of differential changes in the real exchange rate in the LI and MI economies, and its implications for the pattern of migratory pressures. These aggregate changes, however, mask composition effects at the household level. Also they are the result of different patterns of resource reallocation across sectors. Tables 8.5a and 8.5b give, for each household, the change in real income, the foreign rela-tive wage expressed in domestic-currency units, the change in labour supply abroad and the change in the distribution of income. Table 8.6 compares the resource shifts in the two archetypes for the *TLS* and *GTL* simulations.

Table 8.5. *Household incomes and labour-allocation decisions*

a L1 *archetype*[a]

		Gini coef.[b]	LSK INC[c]	LSK RW[d]	LSK FLS[e]	MSK INC	MSK RW	MSK FLS	HSK INC	HSK RW	HSK FLS	CAP INC	CAP RW	CAP FLS
E-1	ITR	−0.1	1.4	−1.5	−1.6	1.0	−0.8	−1.1	1.3	−1.2	−1.9	1.3	−1.2	−1.9
E-2	IMC	2.9	−1.0	4.1	−6.6	2.4	−0.1	−13.4	4.4	−2.2	−17.2	3.9	−2.2	−17.1
E-3	TLS	−5.3	0.1	9.7	10.0	10.6	−5.9	−7.8	−22.3	50.0	79.9	−3.7	50.0	75.4
E-4	FDI	−5.7	2.5	5.1	3.2	12.4	−10.1	−13.4	−19.8	42.4	67.2	−2.7	42.3	63.4
E-5	ATLN	0.4	2.6	−5.5	−6.0	4.9	−7.9	−10.7	1.8	−4.0	−5.9	4.3	−4.0	−6.2
E-6	MTLN	2.7	−3.3	−2.1	−1.9	−1.4	−4.6	−5.9	3.1	−9.1	−13.1	0.6	−9.1	−12.8
E-7	TLN	2.8	−0.7	−7.3	−7.7	3.2	−11.6	−15.3	4.6	−12.1	−17.3	4.5	−12.1	−17.3
E-8	GTL	−2.9	1.7	−2.0	−1.9	15.6	−19.8	−26.0	−15.5	24.3	38.1	1.9	24.3	35.1

b M1 *archetype*[a]

		Gini coef.[f]	LSK INC[c]	LSK RW[d]	LSK FLS[e]	MSK INC	MSK RW	MSK FLS	HSK INC	HSK RW	HSK FLS	CAP INC	CAP RW	CAP FLS
E-1	ITR	0.0	0.8	−0.3	−0.4	1.2	−0.8	−1.1	1.0	−0.5	−0.8	0.9	−0.5	−0.8
E-2	IMC	2.9	0.3	2.0	−9.2	1.4	0.6	−11.8	2.7	−0.5	−14.6	3.5	−0.5	−14.7
E-3	TLS	−6.5	−5.2	11.2	12.3	12.9	−15.8	−20.0	−4.5	11.9	17.1	−3.6	11.9	16.9
E-4	FDI	−6.9	−4.3	10.0	10.9	15.2	−19.3	−24.4	−2.7	8.0	11.3	−3.2	8.0	11.3
E-5	ATLN	−0.5	−0.0	−0.5	−0.6	3.5	−5.9	−7.4	0.0	−0.8	−1.2	1.2	−0.8	−1.4
E-6	MTLN	3.0	−2.3	−0.4	−0.3	3.9	−9.6	−12.1	3.5	−7.1	−10.1	2.4	−7.1	−9.9
E-7	TLN	2.4	−2.4	−0.8	−0.7	6.8	−13.7	−17.4	3.3	−7.6	−10.8	3.2	−7.6	−10.8
E-8	GTL	−3.0	−7.8	8.9	10.1	20.3	−29.4	−37.1	0.9	−3.0	−4.3	0.8	−3.0	−4.4

Notes:
[a] Percentage changes from initial values.
[b] Initial value G = 0.41.
[c] Real income.
[d] $\bar{w}_h^* \, ER/w_h$.

Globalization and migratory pressures from developing countries 207

Table 8.6. *Micro results: net price and sectoral output shifts[a]*

Experiment archetype	TLS LI Net price	TLS LI Sec. out.	TLS MI Net price	TLS MI Sec. out.	GTL LI Net price	GTL LI Sec. out.	GTL MI Net price	GTL MI Sec. out.
Sub. ag.	4.3	−3.6	−21.8	−12.9	3.7	−1.1	−36.6	−20.2
Exp. ag.	70.6	35.3	76.9	49.3	63.7	40.6	77.3	59.3
Light mfg.	−32.7	−32.7	20.1	16.8	−33.6	−29.1	19.0	25.3
Heavy mfg.	−35.7	−18.7	−42.5	−35.6	−53.6	−43.8	−53.5	−47.9
Services	−1.2	−1.1	3.6	0.8	5.7	2.7	8.5	3.9
Informal	13.9	−2.5	3.6	0.4	15.1	−0.7	1.0	2.5

Notes:
[a] Percentage change from initial values.
See table 8.3 for definition of policy experiments.

Start with the effects on households. As noted above, the largest differences between the two archetypes are for the *TLS* and *GTL* simulations. Comparing the effects of trade liberalisation, there a striking difference in the effects across households even though *TLS* reduces income inequality by approximately the same amount for both archetypes. In the LI economy the purchasing power of the low-skill household (LS HH) does not fall whereas it declines by 5 per cent for the MI economy. This is because the real depreciation lowers the cost of living following the fall in the price of non-traded subsistence agriculture. However, in the absence of HO effects, one would have also expected that the relative wage (*RW*) for the LS HH would have fallen more in the LI economy (because of the depreciation). But *TLS* increases the demand for low-skill labour (LSL) in the LI economy, thereby attenuating the decline induced by the real exchange rate depreciation. In fact, the fall in the relative wage is approximately the same for both economies. The HS HH is the great loser of *TLS* in the LI economy as the fall in the domestic wage exacerbates the effect of the real depreciation. Not surprisingly, *TLS* (and to a lesser *GTL*) brings an exodus of HS and CAP HH. However, because both households are only a small fraction of migrants abroad, the net effect on migratory pressure is small.

Except for the *TLS* and *FDI* results for the LI economy, we have seen that all other measures generate a net decrease in migratory pressure. Inspection of tables 8.5a and 8.5b indicates that return migration occurs for all HH groups. There are however some differences in the pattern of changes across HH. For example, even though the CAP and HS HH face the same relative wage, their incomes deviate because of their different pattern of specific-factor

208   **Riccardo Faini** *et al.*

ownership. Again *TLS* in the LI economy barely affects the income of CAP HH while decreasing the income of HS HH by 20 per cent. Also in the agricultural trade liberalisation in the North (*ATLN*), return migration is more pronounced for the LI economy. This is because the terms of trade improvement is not dampened in the LI economy as there households do not consume this good.

Other patterns could be drawn from a closer inspection of the results in tables 8.5a and 8.5b. Two will be mentioned here. First, insofar as migratory pressure could respond positively to increases in relative deprivation (see Stark, 1991), then *TLS* in the South, especially if accompanied by *FDI* in exporting activities, could lead to a decrease in migratory pressure as the distribution of income becomes less unequal. Second, migratory pressure affects the skill composition of the labour force. Here *TLS* in the LI economy has a particularly strong adverse effect on the skill composition of the labour force because of the Stolper–Samuelson (SS) effects leading to an exodous of *HSL*. Insofar as there are positive externalities associated with a higher skill content of the labour force in LI economies, trade liberalisation in the South could have adverse effects on future growth.

Table 8.6 compares the resource-pull effects of *TLS* and *GTL* across the two archetypes. Inspection of the results confirms the contraction in non-traded sectors in the LI economy (subsistence agriculture and informal sectors). A comparison of net price and output shifts does not give a clear pattern. This is mostly because, although both economies have the same Cobb–Douglas technology for value-added, the MI economy is more intensive in the use of intermediates and is better endowed in MS and HS labour.

5   Sensitivity analysis

It is obvious that the simulation results described above are likely to be sensitive to the choice of elasticities and, more importantly, to the modelling assumptions. In this section, we report briefly on the sensitivity of the results to changes in elasticities and in assumptions about migration. This is far from systematic sensitivity analysis as only a few parameter values are varied and only one change in model cloture is contemplated.[8] The results of these simulations are reported in table 8.7 using the following notation: *ES*-1(LI) indicates the results of sensitivity analysis on *E*-1 for the LI economy. Multiple variations are indicated by letters (a for fixed labour supply, b for financial constraints, etc.). In all the results in table 8.7, the initial calibrated solution is the same as in tables 8.4a and 8.4b so the results in table 8.7 are directly comparable with those in tables 8.4a and 8.4b.

Globalization and migratory pressures from developing countries   209

Table 8.7. *Sensitivity analysis: labour supply and home–foreign-labour allocation[a]*

		TLab. sup.	TFLab. sup.	TDLab. sup.	Real ER	RGDP
ES-1a(M1)[b]	*ITR*	−0.0	−0.6	0.1	−0.9	0.1
ES-8a(LI)	*GTL*	−0.2	−7.5	1.4	2.6	−0.3
ES-3b(LI)	*TLS*	0.0	1.1	−0.2	22.9	−2.4
ES-3c(LI)	*TLS*	0.1	8.1	−1.6	19.3	−3.1
ES-5d(MI)	*ATLN*	−0.2	−5.9	0.8	−3.3	0.3
ES-3e(LI)	*TLS*	−0.1	−7.0	1.4	21.7	−1.6
ES-8e(LI)	*GTL*	−0.3	−9.8	1.8	3.2	−0.1

Notes:
[a] Percentage change from initial values.
[b] Archetype in parenthesis.
See table 8.3 for definition of policy experiments.

a   Fixed labour supply

We consider first the sensitivity of the results to changes in the household elasticity of labour supply by assuming a zero income elasticity of labour supply for each HH. This change is done for the *ITR* and *GTL* simulations. In the aggregate for the *ITR* simulation for the MI economy, there is no change in labour supply. This is because the fall in the returns to working abroad are compensated by an increase in the domestic wage, leaving the aggregate HH wage $\tilde{W}$ unchanged.

b   Financial constraints to migration

The theoretical literature has pointed out that outmigration may be constrained by financial costs, especially for low-income potential migrants (see, for example, Schiff, 1995; Lopez and Schiff, 1995). There is also evidence that financing constraints and migration costs can be significant in the migration decision.[9] To test the sensitivity of our results to a potential financial constraint, we suppose that low-skill households face a financing constraint. We assume that only the LS HH faces a migration constraint – i.e. $\Omega_h = 0$ for this HH group. This means that this household cannot emigrate (or return home) in response to a change in relative earnings. Introducing a financial constraint on the migration of LS HH in the *TLS* for the LI economy has drastic effects as the aggregate migration pressure falls from 8 per cent to 1 per cent. This is because migratory pressure is from the LS HH.

210   **Riccardo Faini** *et al.*

c   Concentrated factor ownership

Though the mapping matrix of factor to household income is guesswork, it represents a view of the world in which households have some asset diversification as they receive both income from activities in several sectors and from several factors. While this is certainly closer to reality than the textbook case in which there is no asset-ownership diversification, it is interesting to see how sensitive results are to this assumption. To this end, we modified the factor ownership shares in table 8.2, assuming that the CAP HH receives all its income from the ownership of specific factors. Hence, it does not supply labour services, and therefore cannot migrate. In the aggregate, increased concentration of factor ownership does not affect migratory pressure. This is so because the CAP HH represents an insignificant share of migrants. However, this modification leads to a weaker improvement in income distribution (Gini decrease by 3.4 per cent versus 5.3 per cent).

d   Reduction in migration costs

A reduction in migration costs should increase both relocation of labour to relative wage changes and lead to less loss in GDP. In *ES*-5d(MI) (*ATLN*), for all households the value of Ω_h is increased from 1.5 to 2.5. As expected, there is a magnification effect on return migration. Also GDP increases more than in the corresponding scenario with higher migration costs.

e   Permanent migration

Finally we consider the effects of a household labour-allocation decision that does not take into account variations in the purchasing power of foreign wages in terms of domestic goods. As argued in section 2, this corresponds more closely to a permanent view of migration and is probably more applicable to LI economies. Hence we consider only the effects of this option for the LI economy for two scenarios: *TLS* and *GTL*. Now the HO wage effects of trade liberalisation dominate the results and instead of an 8 per cent increase in emigration, there is a 7 per cent decrease in foreign labour supply due the increase in the unskilled wage caused by the expansion of unskilled labour-intensive export industries. The same effects are at work in the *GTL* experiment with a magnification effect of return migration compared with the results in table 8.4a.

In the simulations and sensitivity analysis, the approach has been taxonomic, with variations in only one parameter at a time. If one were to choose the model most appropriate for a LI and MI economy, one could argue that a 'return migration' model is more relevant for a MI economy

Globalization and migratory pressures from developing countries   211

while a 'permanent migration' model with a financial constraint for unskilled labour migration is the more relevant model for a LI economy. Since the permanent migration closure results in return migration in the *TLS* and *GTL* experiments, the financial constraint cloture would not be binding. Thus the results from rows 6 and 7 of table 8.7 would probably be the more representative expected results for a LI economy. One would therefore conclude that direct or indirect channels to stem migration, at least as modelled in this chapter, would likely achieve their objective of reducing migratory pressure.

6   Conclusions

Whether direct and indirect measures aimed at reducing South–North migratory pressures are effective cannot be determined on *a priori* grounds, although for direct measures (e.g. foreign aid and tighter controls on migration), in the absence of financial costs to migration, the net impact is most likely a reduction in migratory pressure. It is for the indirect measures that both theoretical and empirical results are ambiguous. For example, at the theoretical level, the effect of a more liberal trade regime is ambiguous, since if trade and factor movements are substitutes (complements), then trade liberalisation will (will not) discourage migration.

This chapter shows that empirically, even in the context of a simple RV model, the effects of trade liberalisation are quite complex and could lead to ambiguous effects on migratory pressures. If the responsiveness of exports to the new set of incentives is strong enough, trade liberalisation will be accompanied by a real appreciation which could lead to return migration, at least if migration is not permanent, a prediction that has been corrobated by data on Mexican–US migration. However, if exports are slow to respond to the new trade regime, trade liberalisation will be accompanied by a strong real exchange rate depreciation. This depreciation will increase migratory pressure. It would thus appear that trade liberalisation in LI economies is more likely to lead to an increase in migratory pressure than in MI economies.

However, differences in structure and constraints between LI and MI economies should also be taken into account. Migration cost constraints for low-skill workers in LI economies will alleviate migratory pressure. Also, for LI economies, it is likely that the pattern of migratory pressure resulting from indirect measures such as trade liberalisation will adversely affect the skill composition of the labour force, as it is the medium and high-skill workers that will lose in relative terms and will find migration more attractive.

At a more general level, there are many analogies between the 'trade and jobs' controversy and the debate on how to cope with growing migration

212   **Riccardo Faini** *et al.*

pressure. Growing trade and investment links with developing countries are often faulted for the fall in unskilled wages in the USA and the growth in unemployment in Europe. There is indeed some evidence that trade with labour-abundant countries has been somewhat inimical to unskilled workers in industrial countries, albeit its effects are limited. Similarly, additional migration is typically resisted on the ground that it would lead to a marked deterioration in the labour market conditions of the unskilled. However, by creating jobs for the household groups most probably wishing to emigrate, FDI is likely to reduce South–North migratory pressure. The simulations in this chapter have identified only some of the channels through which policies and environmental changes might affect migratory pressures from the sending country. At the very least, a more complete analysis should also attempt to take into account adjustments during the transition. It is easy to imagine that changes in the human capital stock resulting from out- (or return) migration would have effects on investment and hence on transitional growth.

More than the numerical results and the differences across MI and LI archetypes and differences in institutional settings, what is to be retained from this chapter is that trade and migration policies cannot be assessed separately. A liberal trade regime is probably likely to lead, under most circumstances, to less migration. Conversely, a shift toward protectionism will add to migration pressure. Those opposing trade liberalisation with developing countries should reflect on the fact that protection breeds further migration, both by discouraging labour-intensive exports in sending countries and by boosting the demand for foreign labour in receiving countries. Moreover, in the light of the current debate, those favouring a cut in foreign aid to developing countries on the basis of its inefficiency should think about its consequences on migratory pressure. Hence industrial countries face a dilemma. They cannot reduce aid and become more protectionist with developing countries and still hope to reduce migratory pressures: they must make a choice.

APPENDIX

The appendix specifies the full set of equations of the model sketched in the main text and describes how we assembled the data for each archetype economy.

1   **The simulation model**

The model is a standard general equilibrium RV model. The economy is divided into $i = 1, \ldots, N$ sectors. These include traded and non-traded

Globalization and migratory pressures from developing countries   213

sectors with corresponding subscripts t and nt. There are $v = 1, ..., V$ categories of labour and $h = 1, ..., H$ categories of households. Sectors are indexed over i,j, factors of production over v and households over h. Prices denoted in foreign currency units have an asterisk – e.g. P_t^* is the foreign-currency price of tradables. An asterisk is also used to denote labour allocated abroad – e.g. L_h^* (L_v^*) is the amount of labour by household h (of category v) allocated abroad. Finally a bar over a variable indicates an exogenous variable.

The equations describing the simulation model used in the text are contained in table 8A.1. Table 8A.2 lists the endogenous variables and the exogenous variables and parameters. The first block of equations in table 8A.1 indicates a multi-factor Cobb–Douglas technology for value-added and a Leontief technology for intermediates and between intermediates and value-added ((4), (5)). Factor demands are determined by the first-order conditions for profit-maximisation (6) with (7) determining rents for the fixed factors. Note the presence of non-competitive imports in the definition of net prices (5).

The second block gives the factor-to-household mapping. In the notation used in (8) and (9) λ^L is a (V,H) matrix indicating the mapping of labour by category to labour ownership by household. In this application this is a matrix of ones and zeroes as each household only supplies one category of labour, though it may receive income from more than one factor and some labour categories are supplied by more than one household. Equation (10) gives the mapping of capital from sectors to households.

The third block describes the allocation of household labour between domestic and foreign destinations according to the description in the main text. Equation (11) is the cost function associated with (2). Maximisation of (3) gives the division of labour between home and foreign markets given by (13) and (14). The wage rate for each category of labour is determined by (16).

The following block determines net trade from the material balances for the traded sectors (19) while the material balance equations for non-traded sectors determines prices for the non-traded sectors (20). All final demand is for household consumption as in the standard trade-theoretic models. The small-country assumption is embodied in eq. (21) and (22). The exogeneity of the current account (24) insures that there are no free lunches while the choice of normalisation (28) insures that the value of ER is the equilibrium value of the real exchange rate (the price of tradables in terms of non-tradables). Finally the determination of household income (25) indicates that government and remittance redistributions do not affect the distribution of income between households.

In the simulations with FDI, the stock of capital in the agricultural export and light manufacturing sectors is exogenously increased with the

214 Riccardo Faini *et al.*

Table 8A.1. *Model equations*

<hr>

Technology and factor demand

$$X_i = \bar{A}_i \bar{K}_i^{\alpha_i} \prod_v (L_{i,v}^d)^{\gamma_{i,v}} \tag{4}$$

$$\sum_v \gamma_{i,v} + \alpha_i = 1$$

$$PN_i = P_i - \sum_i \bar{a}_{i,j} P_j - \bar{b}_{0,i} P_0 \tag{5}$$

$$L_{i,v}^d = (\gamma_{i,v} PN_i X_i)/w_v \tag{6}$$

$$Ri = \alpha_i (PN_i X_i)/\bar{K}_i \tag{7}$$

Factor-household income mapping

$$w_h = \sum_v w_v \lambda_{v,h}^L \tag{8}$$

$$\bar{w}_h^* = \sum_v \bar{w}_v^* \lambda_{v,h}^{*L} \tag{9}$$

$$\bar{K}_i = \sum_h HK_{i,h} \tag{10}$$

Household home–foreign-labour allocation

$$\tilde{W}_h = 1/\bar{B}_h [(1 - \nu_h)^{-\Omega_h}(w_h)^{1+\Omega_h} + (\nu_h)^{-\Omega_h}(\bar{w}_h^* ER)^{1+\Omega_h}]^{(1/(1+\Omega_h))} \tag{11}$$

$$LS_h = MH_h - (\beta_{0,h}/\tilde{W}_h)((Y_h - \phi_h)/(1 - \beta_{0,h})) \tag{12}$$

$$L_h = (1/\beta_h)^{(1+\Omega_h)}((1 - \nu_h)\tilde{W}_h/w_h)^{-\Omega_h} LS_h \tag{13}$$

$$L_h^* = (1/\beta_h)^{(1+\Omega_h)}(\nu_h \tilde{W}_h/\bar{w}_h^* ER)^{-\Omega_h} LS_h \tag{14}$$

Wage determination

$$L_v^s = \sum_h LS_h \lambda_{v,h}^L \tag{15}$$

$$L_v^s = \sum_i L_{i,v}^d \tag{16}$$

Demand and material balances

$$C_{i,h} = \delta_{i,h} + (\beta_{i,h}/P_i)(Y_h - \phi_h)/(1 - \beta_{o,h})$$

$$\phi_h = \sum_{i=1}^n P_{i,h} \delta_{i,h} \tag{17}$$

Globalization and migratory pressures from developing countries   215

Table 8A.1. (*cont.*)

$$\sum_i \beta_h + \beta_{0,h} = 1$$

$$ID_i = \sum_j \bar{a}_{i,j} X_j \tag{18}$$

$$X_t = \sum_h C_{t,h} + ID_t + NE_t \tag{19}$$

$$X_{nt} = \sum_h C_{nt,h} + ID_{nt} \tag{20}$$

Trade and external balance constraint

$$P_t = \bar{P}_t^* ER(1 + \bar{T}_t) \tag{21}$$

$$P_0 = \bar{P}_0^* ER(1 + \bar{T}_0) \tag{22}$$

$$TRB = \sum_t \bar{P}_t^* NE_t - \sum_i \bar{b}_0 \bar{P}_0^* X_i \tag{23}$$

$$CA = TRB + \sum_h L_h^* \bar{w}_h^* ER \tag{24}$$

Government revenue and income–expenditure constraint

$$Y_h = LS_h \tilde{W}_h + \sum_i R_i HK_{i,h} + s_h [GR - CA.ER] \tag{25}$$

$$GR = -\sum_t \bar{T}_t \bar{P}_t^* NE_t ER + \sum_i \bar{T}_0 \bar{b}_0 \bar{P}_0^* X_i \tag{26}$$

$$s_h = (LS_h \tilde{W}_h + \sum_i R_i HK_{i,h} / \left(\sum_h \left[LS_h \tilde{W}_h + \sum_i R_i \bar{H}\bar{K}_{i,h} \right] \right) \tag{27}$$

Price normalisation

$$\overline{PNORM} = \sum_{nt} (P_{nt} X_{nt}^0) / \left(\sum_{nt} P_{nt}^0 X_{nt}^0 \right) \tag{28}$$

216   Riccardo Faini *et al.*

Table 8A.2. *Variables and parameters*

Endogenous variables

$P_n t$	Non-traded price	nt
NE_t	Net trade	t
Y_h	Household income	H
ER	Real exchange rate	1
X_i	Sectoral gross output	N
PN_i	Net price	N
$L_{i,v}^d$	Labour demand for category v	N.V
w_v	Wage for labour category v	V
w_h	Wage for labour category h	H
R_j	Rental for fixed factor in sector i	N
$\tilde{W}_h$	Aggregate wage income for household h	H
LS_h	Labour supply for household h	H
L_h	Home-labour supply for household h	H
L_h^*	Foreign-labour supply for household h	H
$C_{i,h}$	Consumption by household h	N.H
s_h	Income share for household h	h
ID_i	Intermediate demand for sector i	N
NE_t	Net exports for sector t	t
CA	Current account	1
Y_h	Income for household h	H
GR	Government revenue	1

Exogenous variables and parameters

$\bar{P}_t^*$	World price for competitive imports	t
$\bar{P}_0^*$	World price for non-competitive imports	1
$\bar{TRB}$	Trade balance	1
$\bar{K}_i$	Specific factor	N
$\bar{MH}_h$	Maximum number of hourts available to h	H
$\bar{w}_h^*$	Household wage abroad	H
Ω_h	Elasticity of transformation	h
ϕ_h	Non discretionary expenditure for household h	h
$\delta_{i,h}$	Exogenous consumption of i	N.H
$\beta_{i,h}$	Marginal budget share of i	N.H
$\gamma_{i,v}$	Output elasticity for factor v	N.V
α_i	Factor-specific share in value-added	N

Globalization and migratory pressures from developing countries   217

Table 8A.3. *Output and final demand structure*

a *LI* archetype

	Output	Hous. cons.	Net exp.	Intm. sal.	Value-added	Non-comp. imports
Sub. ag	30.0	17.9	0.0	12.1	18.3	6.0
Exp. ag	15.7	0.0	15.7	0.0	11.0	1.9
Light mfg.	33.0	24.9	−6.6	14.7	15.1	2.3
Heavy mfg.	6.4	5.4	−9.6	10.6	1.8	1.9
Services	47.3	36.4	0.0	10.9	27.2	1.9
Informal	20.0	18.0	0.0	2.0	14.7	0.0

b *MI* archetype

	Output	Hous. cons.	Net exp.	Intm. sal.	Value-added	Non-comp. imports
Sub. ag	15.5	7.8	−4.7	12.3	7.7	0.8
Exp. ag	9.0	2.7	3.6	2.7	2.3	0.3
Light mfg.	40.7	11.1	8.1	21.5	13.8	2.0
Heavy mfg.	24.0	11.9	−7.2	19.3	12.4	2.4
Services	55.4	37.4	0.0	18.0	33.8	0.6
Informal	26.0	20.6	0.0	5.4	15.3	0.0

share of profits corresponding to the foreign-owned capital being repatriated abroad. In the simulations with a zero elasticity of labour supply to the foreign market $\Omega_{LSK}=0$, L^*_{LSK} is fixed, and (14) is dropped for this household.

2   The data

The data for the structure of production, for input–output coefficients and for the structure of trade are largely inspired from Bourguignon *et al.* (1992). In turn, these data were assembled from Chenery and Syrquin (1987), who construct what they call 'archetypical' primary and manufacturing exporters (they also consider a third archetype, the 'large' economy with a population over 20 million which is less open to trade). Roughly speaking, the two archetypes correspond to what Chenery and Syrquin call 'low-income' and 'middle -income' economies. Both economies are calibrated to be of the same size, but the LI archetype has a much larger share of resources in agriculture, a less dense input–output structure, and a larger

218   **Riccardo Faini** *et al.*

Table 8A.4. *Factor shares in value-added*

	Low skill	Medium skill	High skill	Capital stock
Sub. ag	0.5	0.0	0.0	0.5
Exp. ag	0.0	0.5	0.0	0.5
Light mfg.	0.0	0.25	0.25	0.5
Heavy mfg.	0.0	0.0	0.5	0.5
Services	0.0	0.25	0.25	0.5
Informal	0.25	0.25	0.0	0.5

share of non-competitive imports in total imports (see table 8A.3). The same sectoral technology was imposed for both archetypes. Output elasticities (and factor shares in value-added for the Cobb–Douglas technology specified here) are given in table 8A.4. Except for the sensitivity analysis, the same values for $\Omega h = 1.5$, the elasticity of transformation for labour allocation between home and foreign markets, was set for all households for both archetypes.

Household consumption patterns were calibrated in the usual way starting from income elasticities of demand for each household along with estimates of the Frisch parameter, F_h ($F_h = - Y_h/(Y_h - \phi_h)$ ranging from -3.0 for the LS HH to -1.5 for the CAP HH.

NOTES

We thank Sanoussi Bilal, Marcelo Olarreaga, André Sapir, Alessandra Venturini and Klaus F. Zimmermann for helpful comments on a draft and the FNRS for support under grant no. 12-42011.94.
1 For evidence of return migration in Southern European countries (Southern Italy, Spain and Turkey over the period 1962–88, see Faini and Venturini (1995).
2 For an empirical justification of the RV model, see Kohli (1993), who showed that it performs better than the HO framework in explaining the US experience.
3 Although this is a static model, the 'temporary-migration' view could also be interpreted as the inclusion of perfect foresight expectations about the exchange rate in the migration decision.
4 It is hard to predict to what extent households would diversify across countries in the absence of barriers to migration. It is likely, though, that heterogeneity within the household would be important enough to insure some diversification, even though one observes agglomerations of ethnic groups (e.g. Chinatowns and Little Italys) which suggests convex relocation costs.
5 It could be shown that risk-aversion by risk-neutral households receiving stochastic incomes from different sources would lead to concave iso-risk loci. These could be viewed as consistent with this approach as households would spread their labour services across destinations to reduce risk.

Globalization and migratory pressures from developing countries 219

6 A large LI economy like Bangladesh would have a more diversified economic structure that would call for a different archetype representation. The choice of agriculture as import-competing in the MI economy is, of course, arbitrary. It turns out, however, to be convenient in the simulations capturing the effects of trade liberalisation as it gives the same number of sectors with net imports for both archetypes.
7 Neary (1988), discusses the conditions under which a transfer and a change in the terms of trade will lead to an appreciation of the real exchange rate and Edwards and van Wijnbergen (1987) give conditions under which trade liberalisation in a RV model will lead to a depreciation of the real exchange rate. Neither study includes migration, but the reasoning is broadly applicable to the discussion here.
8 A systematic analysis of alternative cloture rules would have included the role of economies of scale in the possibility of generating a complementarity relationship between trade and migration. See Venables (1997) for a summary of the results in the trade-theoretic literature on the substitutability–complementarity relationship between trade and migration.
9 See, for example, Adams (1996); Freeman (1993); Funkhouse (1992).

REFERENCES

Adams, R. (1996). 'Remittances, Inequality and Asset Accumulation: The Case of Rural Pakistan', in D. O'Connor and L. Farsakh (eds.), *Development Strategy, Employment and Migration: Country Experiences* (Paris: OECD Development Centre), 149–70

Bhagwati, J. (1992). 'Free Traders and Free Immigrationists: Strangers or Friends?', *Working Paper*, **20** (New York: Russell Sage Foundation)

Bourguignon, F., J. de Melo and A. Suwa (1992). 'Distributional Effects of Adjustment Policies: Simulations for Archetype Economies in Africa and Latin America', *World Bank Economic Review*, **5**, 339–66

Burda, M. (1993). 'The Determinants of East–West German Migration', *European Economic Review*, **37**, 452–61

Chenery, H. and M. Syrquin (1987). 'Typical Patterns of Transformation', in H. Chenery, S. Robinson and M. Syrquin (eds.), *Industrialization and Growth* (Oxford: Oxford University Press)

Daveri, F. and R. Faini (1996). 'Where Do Migrants Go? Risk-Aversion, Mobility Costs and the Locational Choice of Migrants', University of Brescia, mimeo

Djajic, S. and R. Milbourne (1988). 'A General Equilibrium Model of Guest-Worker Migration', *Journal of International Economics*, **25**, 335–51

Edwards, S. and S. van Wijnbergen (1987). 'Tariffs, the Real Exchange Rate and the Terms of Trade: On Two Popular Propositions in International Economics', *Oxford Economic Papers*, **39**, 458–64

Faini, R. and J.M. Grether (1994), ' L'ouverture au commerce, peut–elle réduire la migration Nord–Sud?', University of Neuchâtel, mimeo

Faini, R. and J. de Melo (1995). 'Trade Policy, Employment and Migration: Some Simulation Results from Morocco', CEPR, *Discussion Paper*, **1198**

(1994). 'Migration and Growth: The Experience of Southern Europe', CEPR, *Discussion Paper*, **964**

220   **Riccardo Faini *et al.***

Faini, R. and A.Venturini (1995), 'Trade, Aid and Migration: Some Basic Policy Issues', *European Economic Review*, **37**, 435–42

Freeman, R. (1993). 'Immigration from Poor to Wealthy Countries: Experiences from the US', *European Economic Review*, **37**, 443–51

Funkhouse, E. (1992). 'Mass Migration, Remittances and Economic Adjustment: The Case of El Salvador', in G. Borjas and R. Freeman (eds.), *Immigration and the Work Force: Economic Consequences for the United States and the Source Areas* (Chicago: University of Chicago Press for the NBER)

Harris, J. and M. Todaro (1970), 'Migration, Unemployment, and Development: A Two–Sector Analysis', *American Economic Review*, **60**, 126–42

ILO (1949). *Migration for Employment Recommendation* (Geneva: ILO)

   (1984). *Employment Policy Recommendation* (supplementary provision) (Geneva: ILO)

   (1992). 'ODA as a Means to Reduce Economic and Social Emigration Pressure', paper for joint ILO–UNHCR Meeting in International Aid as a Means to reduce the Need for Emigration: Informal Summary Record, Geneva

Kohli, U. (1993). 'US Technology and the Specific–factors Model', *Journal of International Economics*, **34**, 115–36

Lopez, R. and M. Schiff (1995). 'Migration and the Skill Composition of the Labour Force: The Impact of Trade Liberalisation in LDCs', *PRWP*, **1493** (Washington, DC: World Bank)

Markusen, J. (1983). 'Factor Trade and Commodity Trade as Complements', *Journal of International Economics*, **13**, 341–56

Markusen, J. and S. Zahniser (1997). 'Liberalisation and Incentives for Labour Migration: Theory with Applications to NAFTA', Boulder, University of Colorado, mimeo

Massey, D.S. (1989). 'Theories of International Migration: A Survey', *Population and Development Review*, **19**, 431–66

Melo, J. de and Tarr, D. (1992). *A General Equilibrium Analysis of US Foreign Trade Policy* (Cambridge, MA: MIT Press)

Neary, P. (1988). 'Determinants of the Equilibrium Real Exchange Rate', *American Economic Review*, **78**, 211–15

Schiff, M. (1995). 'Trade Policy and International Migration in the Short and the Long Run', *Revue d'économie du Development*, **4**, 3–25

   (1996). 'South–North Migration and Trade: A Survey', *PRWP*, **1696** (Washington, DC: World Bank)

Stark, O. (1991). *The Migration of People* (Oxford: Basil Blackwell)

Venables, A. (1997). 'Trade Liberalisation and Factor Mobility:An Overview', LSE, mimeo; see also chapter 2 in this volume

Wong, K.-Y. (1995). *International Trade in Goods and Factor Mobility* (Cambridge, MA: MIT Press)

Part III:
Costs of Protection from Trade Policy Regimes in Developing Countries

DISTORTIONS IN THE FACTOR MARKET: SOME GENERAL EQUILIBRIUM ESTIMATES

Jaime A. P. de Melo*

I. Introduction

RECENT studies in the field of trade policy have investigated the welfare effects of distortions in the factor market. In general these studies deal exclusively with the theoretical aspects of distortions. On the empirical side, two recent studies by Dougherty and Selowsky (1972) on Colombia, and Fløystad (1975) on Norway have attempted to measure explicitly the production costs of imperfections in the factor market in the form of wage differentials across sectors. Their methodology consists of specifying sectoral production functions for primary factors for a number of sectors and solving the supply side of the system under different assumptions keeping product and factor prices fixed. The fixed-price assumption implies either that the economy is small and completely open (without non-traded goods) or that sectoral output changes are sufficiently small so as to leave relative product prices unchanged. The authors' estimates of the cost of factor market distortions are obtained by comparing actual observed sectoral outputs with those obtained under the optimal solution when the selected factors of production get equal returns across sectors.

The purpose of this paper is (1) to extend this partial equilibrium methodology by presenting a computable Walrasian general equilibrium model of resource allocation where both product and factor prices adjust to changes in factor market distortions, and (2) to present some illustrative results for Colombia. The remainder of the paper is organized as follows: section II describes the methodology and presents the application to Colombia; section III reports the empirical results; and finally section IV summarizes the results in the study.

II. Methodology

In contrast with programming models where maximization takes place via an objective function, Walrasian models rely on implicit optimization carried out separately by consumers and producers who maximize utility and profits subject to budget and production constraints. A distinctive feature of this approach is that the various agents in the economy may interact through a variety of specifications of market behavior that are particularly well-suited for the incorporation of price distortions in commodity and factor markets.[1] Essentially the solution problem is that of finding a fixed point for a set of simultaneous nonlinear demand and supply equations.

Some salient characteristics of the model presented in the appendix are briefly outlined here, and the reader is referred to de Melo (1975) for a full presentation of the model and a discussion of solution techniques and data sources. On the supply side producers maximize profits subject to a Leontief technology for intermediate inputs and non-competitive imports. Multi-factor Cobb-Douglas production functions are specified for value-added.[2] All primary factors (land, capital, skilled and unskilled labor) are in inelastic supply and are fully employed; factor returns are endogenously determined. On the demand side the representative consumer maximizes a Stone-Geary utility function which generates the linear expenditure system. Finally, in line with recent developments in the pure theory of trade, a distinction is made between tradable goods whose prices are determined in world

Received for publication January 5, 1976. Revision accepted for publication April 1, 1977.

*I am indebted to Bela Balassa, Michael Crosswell, Constantine Michalopoulos and two referees for helpful comments. This research was carried out while I was with the Agency for International Development. I take full responsibility for any remaining errors.

[398]

---

[1] For a discussion of Walrasian models see Adelman and Robinson (1977). The first multi-sector Walrasian model was formulated by Johansen (1960). For a dynamic model, see Dervis (1975).

[2] For a more detailed presentation of the model, see de Melo (1976). That paper also includes an alternative specification of technology with two-level CES production functions for value-added. Table 4 in that paper indicates the effects on resource allocation of systematic variations in the elasticity of substitution between capital and labor.

DISTORTIONS IN THE FACTOR MARKET   399

Table 1.—Actual Wages and Employment of Capital and Labor by Sector, 1969

Sector	Gross Output: Thousands of Pesos	Value-added (%)	Return on Capital (%)	Unskilled Wage: Pesos Per Man Year	Skilled Wage: Pesos Per Man Year	Capital Stocks: Thousands of Pesos	Unskilled Labor: Thousand Man Years	Skilled Labor: Thousand Man Years
Coffee (+)	548.6	97.2	8.0	370	1,080	1,206.1	470.0	32.1
Agriculture (+)	2,963.6	84.2	7.6	410	1,210	7,477.8	1,979.1	132.7
Food, Beverage, Tobacco (+)	1,403.4	32.1	24.9	1,850	3,730	1,092.7	42.5	14.5
Textiles and Apparel (+)	817.8	46.4	16.1	1,660	3,460	1,078.1	73.9	13.1
Paper, Wood, Leather (−)	310.2	41.2	15.9	1,850	4,160	380.8	18.6	4.7
Rubber and Chemicals (−)	662.5	63.1	30.1	2,660	6,070	823.2	20.8	12.1
Metals and Products (−)	443.4	37.0	14.7	1,820	3,460	552.3	25.1	5.9
Nonmetallic Products (+)	196.8	50.2	9.4	1,660	3,230	422.2	21.6	4.1
Mining and Petroleum (+)	482.4	63.2	12.8	800	4,440	1,349.9	76.3	2.4
Machinery (−)	218.0	59.9	22.7	2,560	4,780	252.5	14.1	5.0
Diverse Industries (−)	241.2	57.4	22.3	1,980	3,010	282.7	22.2	5.7
Light Domestic Industries	507.6	54.9	45.6	3,920	7,100	400.4	13.6	5.9
Construction	1,113.0	67.5	8.4	1,470	15,750	2,014.9	318.5	7.2
Transport and Communication	1,166.6	71.4	13.1	1,320	15,020	3,261.6	217.6	8.0
Services and Artisans	3,749.4	91.4	18.0	570	3,360	7,313.1	1,884.5	306.1
Column	(1)	(2)	(3)	(4)	(5)	(6)	(7)	(8)

markets with quantities traded clearing domestic markets, and home goods whose prices adjust to clear their markets. The exchange rate is endogenously determined so as to maintain equilibrium in the balance of trade.

Following the theory of wage differentials, distortions in the factor market are introduced by recognizing that rates of return to each factor are *not* equalized across sectors. Note that a differential which is autonomous (e.g., differences in age, skill, and experience among workers) is not a source of welfare distortion. In practice it is difficult to distinguish between a differential and a distortion. A crude attempt has been made here by assuming that the differential wage per factor between rural and urban areas is not a source of distortion so that it is maintained at its existing ratio in the base period. It is argued that in segmented dualistic economies such as Colombia, it is justifiable to assume that the dual wage structure between rural and urban areas would persist after a removal of distortions in the urban sector. Wage differentials in the industrial sector are viewed as distortionary, and to the extent that they are not the welfare results reported below will overstate the gains in efficiency from

equalizing wage rates.[3] The empirical experiments reported below therefore consist of removing the differentials observed in the labor market by equalizing the wage rates to skilled and unskilled labor in the urban sectors while maintaining a constant rural-urban wage differential.

The experiments are based on Colombian data for 1969. Of the fifteen sectors included in the model and described in table 1, sectors one to eleven are classified as tradable and the remainder are classified as non-tradable. The agricultural sector is disaggregated into coffee and other agriculture to take into account the fact that Colombia has a quota for coffee exports determined by the International Coffee Agreement. For that sector the export tax is endogenously determined so as to ensure that coffee producers supply the quantity fixed by their quota share in world supply. Goods that are imported but not processed domestically

[3] A more accurate distinction between distortionary and non-distortionary differentials would call for a greater degree of disaggregation between different skill classes of labor. Unfortunately available data did not allow for a greater level of skill differentiation at the level of sectoral disaggregation in the study.

are lumped into a non-competitive import sector.[4]

Table 1 describes the return to labor and capital in Colombia in 1969 along with the sectoral breakdown of the economy. The sign entered next to sector names indicates whether that sector is a net exporter (+) or a net importer (−). Multiplying column 2 by column 1 would yield sectoral value added in thousands of current 1969 pesos. The rate of return to capital shown in column 3 differs greatly across sectors ranging from 7.6% in agriculture to 45.6% in light domestic industries. This set of figures is the most unreliable among the data presented in the table since it is derived from the shaky estimates of capital stocks in column 6 and the factor shares in the sectoral production functions. For this reason, different rates of return to capital are not interpreted as distortionary although an unknown portion of the variances in these rates of return to capital are due to distortions in the capital market. Columns 4 and 5 show the average wage per worker per year for unskilled and skilled labor. As expected, the nominal wages for workers are well below average for agriculture and coffee sectors where there must be a fair amount of payment in kind not captured in these figures, which however, do attempt to correct for imputed income to non-paid workers. For the services and artisan sectors, which also indicate wages below the economy average, this may be expected since there is no unionization or foreign ownership, which would raise the wage rates.

III. The Empirical Results

Distortions have two major effects: the first one is on economic structure while the second one is on welfare. In turn the structural effects may be further subdivided into several categories including output effects, which will be the focus of attention in the following

experiments.[5] As indicated by Magee (1973) in his survey, a considerable amount of theoretical work has been concerned with the possibility of perverse results following the removal of a differential. A perverse result would occur when, as a result of the reduction in the differential t ($t > 1$) paid to labor in industry x (so as to equalize wage rates between industries x and y), either welfare decreased or the output of x decreased. An abnormal output response will occur only if there is a non-correspondence between the rankings of the physical and value factor intensities (Magee, 1973, p. 21). Such a possibility is ruled out for Cobb-Douglas production functions (Herberg and Kemp, 1971). Regarding welfare effects, Bhagwati (1971) has shown that the reduction of a differential with other distortions in the system may not increase welfare. Since the model includes distortions in the product market in the forms of tariffs, subsidies, and a quota, abnormal welfare results may obtain. Experiments consisting of removing differentials singly by equating the sector's wage to the economy-wide average wage confirmed this possibility. However this perverse result occurred only once. Removing the differential paid to unskilled labor in the construction sector reduced welfare slightly. This non-traded sector is large and has strong linkages with other sectors on the supply side so that the necessary price adjustment to eliminate excess demand in that sector affects value-added, and therefore comparative advantage. In the presence of other distortions in the form of tariffs and subsidies on traded goods, welfare declined by 0.1%.

Although the model outlined in section II is suitable for a wide range of experiments, only one experiment will be reported here, namely, removing distortions in the labor market. Two assumptions will be made with respect to capital mobility: (1) sectoral capital stocks remain fixed, and (2) all factors of production with the exception of land are mobile across sectors. When capital stocks are fixed to reflect short-run adjustments, sectoral rates of return are calculated residually from the equations

---

[4] Note that with more product prices fixed through trade than variable factor prices, the model will tend to specialize (Samuelson, 1953). Virtually all multi-sector trade models face this issue and the specialization problem is usually handled by setting arbitrary bounds on quantities traded or by assuming decreasing returns to scale (e.g., fixing capital stocks). Here returns to scale are arbitrarily set equal to 0.9 for all sectors and no bounds are placed on quantities traded. For further discussion and justification, see de Melo (1976).

[5] Other effects include the shrinkage of the production possibilities curve, non-tangency, convexity, factor market effects and trade effects. See Magee (1973) for a discussion of these other structural effects.

DISTORTIONS IN THE FACTOR MARKET   401

TABLE 2.—EFFECTS OF REMOVING URBAN LABOR MARKET DISTORTIONS
(all figures represent % changes)[a]

	Welfare	GDP[b]	Unskilled Wage	Skilled Wage	Rate of Return to Capital	Exchange Rate[c]	Coffee Tax Rate[d] (%)
Capital stocks fixed	1.3	2.7	34.6	44.8	0.4	−5.5	38.6
Capital stocks mobile	1.3	10.7	37.0	52.8	3.6	−6.0	39.9

Note: Wage rates are per worker.
[a]The figures in the last column are in per cent, not percentage change.
[b]GDP valued using current prices as weights.
[c]Revaluation (−).
[d]The coffee ad-valorem tax rate is 44% prior to removal of distortions.

determining sectoral demands for capital. When capital is mobile, it is assumed that the structure of differential rates of return across sectors reflects differences in risk or that they are temporary and are due to adjustment costs. In common with the other studies, no attempt is made at removing distortions in the sectoral shares of capital income. Removal of distortions in the urban sector is accomplished by setting all the differentials equal to unity ($d_{\lambda i} = 1$, $i = 3 \ldots 15$ in equation 3 in the appendix), recalculating the differentials for the agricultural sectors so as to maintain a constant rural-urban wage differential (RU_λ in equation 4), and solving the model under the new market structure.

A. Welfare Effects

Table 2 summarizes the results of this experiment and provides comprehensive estimates of the effects on welfare of removing differentials in the labor market. These estimates differ from those offered so far in two important respects. First they are estimated in a general equilibrium framework so that a change in production cost will affect quantities supplied; this in turn leads to a price adjustment to clear those markets. Second, they are undertaken in a framework which is in close agreement with the theoretical literature on domestic distortions since factor market distortions affect not only production but also trade and therefore comparative advantage. With quantities traded endogenously determined, the model takes into account this important effect of factor market distortions and, as a by-product, the exchange rate adjustment required to maintain balance of trade emerges from the solution of the model.

Because exogenous demand, which includes investment (which equals savings ex post), remains fixed, the comparative static experiments can be viewed as examining the effects of distortions in the factor market under an exogenously predetermined level of investment in base year prices with the welfare effects measured by the Stone-Geary utility indicator. Column 1 indicates that the welfare gains are the same under both sets of experiments. This result is interesting since one would expect on a priori grounds that the gains from removing distortions would be greater when capital is mobile. To understand this result it is necessary to trace the effects of removing differentials on net tax revenues from foreign trade. As mentioned above, there is a set of ad valorem tariffs, subsidies and taxes on traded goods. Although these trade distortions remain fixed, net tax revenues are affected insofar as quantities traded are affected by the removal of differentials in the labor market. When capital stocks are fixed, the extent of specialization is limited and the net revenue from trade taxes shows a small variation. However, when capital stocks are mobile a substantial number of sectors that were previously net exporters become net importers (e.g., agriculture) and vice versa (e.g., machinery and diverse industries). As a consequence of these trade reversals, net revenues from trade taxes decrease substantially. Thus, although GDP shows a substantial rise, disposable income remains unchanged because of the increase in taxes on factor incomes necessary to offset the decline in tax and tariff receipts and the increase in subsidies disbursed on exports.[6]

---

[6]When there is a trade reversal, tariffs become subsidies (and vice versa). As a result revenues become disbursements (and vice versa). Although there is no reason to believe that a government would grant to producers

This interesting result indicates the importance of the presence of other distortions in the system which are best captured in a general equilibrium setting.

Valued at base prices, the increase in GDP is 5.7% when capital is fixed and 13.3% when capital is mobile. It is interesting to note that this gain is well above the estimates of Dougherty and Selowsky (1972, p. 382) who note that "...the insensitivity of the level of output to the allocation of labor implies that the static first order conditions are of little relevance." Although their experiments refer to an earlier year, and although it is likely that their estimates are lower partly because they have a greater number of factors of production resulting in employment changes tending to offset one another, it is likely that the difference in magnitudes between the two sets of estimates is due to the differences in methodologies, and to the fact that these estimates allow for a migration of factors outside agriculture while theirs do not.[7]

Turning to labor markets, table 2 indicates that both skilled and unskilled labor would benefit from the removal of differentials as average wage rates per worker would rise substantially. However, most of these gains would accrue to rural labor because the assumption that the rural-urban wage differential per worker (see equation 4 in appendix) remains constant limits the movement of labor out of agriculture. Thus, with the migration of labor into the urban sector as labor is substituted for capital following the removal of distortions in the urban sector (see table 3), the average urban wage per worker changes very little, increasing by 1.4 percentage points for unskilled labor when capital is mobile. It is notable that fixing the rural-urban wage differential for workers reduces welfare gains by dampening factor migration. Therefore, if in

fact the rural-urban differential per worker is not distortionary, a removal of distortions in the urban sector would benefit labor in general, though the gains would mostly accrue to the remaining labor in agriculture in the form of higher wages for the remaining workers. Because differentials are not removed in the capital market, the average rate of return per unit of capital shows little variation.

Finally one can see that the removal of differentials would entail a small appreciation of the peso. The exchange rate adjustment determined by the normalization rule is given by the percentage change in the value of non-traded goods and the change in the coffee tax rate shown in the last column of table 2.[8] As can be seen from table 3, relative prices of non-traded goods do not all change in the same direction so that it is difficult to predict a priori the magnitude of the exchange rate adjustment. Lowering the tax rate on coffee raises the domestic price of coffee resulting in an appreciation of the peso. This effect is further strengthened by a small increase in the value of non-traded goods due to the large rise in the price of services.

B. Output Effects

Table 3 describes the new allocations of factors after a removal of differentials in both labor markets, along with the corresponding changes in output and value-added. The most notable feature of the table is that relative prices are affected by the removal of differentials. Consider post-distortion sectoral values-added as a percentage of initial values-added in column 1. For traded sectors prices are only affected by the exchange rate adjustment, which in this case is an appreciation of 5.7%. However due to the presence of non-traded goods, whose prices are endogenously determined, and to the linkages between traded and non-traded sectors, adjustments in net prices among traded sectors will differ. For non-traded goods, an increase in the price of inputs raises value-added as in the case for services and artisans, a sector whose wages are below average (see table 1).

---

subsidies at the same rate as they collect tariffs on imports, no attempt was made to alter the structure of distortions in product markets because it was felt that one could no longer isolate the effects of distortions in the factor market when other distortions in the system were also altered.

[7] Dougherty and Selowsky justify the fixed-price assumption on the grounds that all goods are traded and that the country has no monopoly in trade. While such an assumption may be defensible, a more satisfactory methodology would explicitly incorporate trade into the analysis by specifying demand relations and a balance of payments constraint.

[8] The coffee tax rate is endogenously determined so as to insure that coffee producers supply a fixed quantity of coffee for export after meeting domestic intermediate and final demand.

TABLE 3.—EQUILIBRIUM NET PRICES, EMPLOYMENT AND OUTPUT
(all figures are percentages of initial values)

Capital	Value-added		Unskilled Labor		Skilled Labor		Physical Output		Rate of Return on Capital	
	Fixed	Mobile	Fixed	Mobile	Fixed	Mobile	Fixed	Mobile	Fixed	Mobile
Coffee	103.5	100.9	106.2	95.7	98.7	87.9	101.9	90.4	106.3	96.0
Agriculture	93.2	92.8	89.4	74.3	82.2	65.4	95.2	67.9	88.2	81.0
Food, Beverage, Tobacco	89.7	87.5	215.2	138.1	87.3	53.7	112.4	63.2	100.8	74.4
Textiles and Apparel	89.9	88.6	221.5	262.7	92.4	105.1	128.2	133.4	87.0	156.8
Paper, Wood, Leather	90.3	87.9	253.0	305.3	114.3	132.3	131.1	139.6	118.9	165.2
Rubber and Chemicals	91.0	90.2	363.0	571.3	166.2	250.8	129.7	181.4	117.9	210.4
Metals and Products	91.1	88.9	243.4	284.6	92.6	104.0	127.0	132.2	115.6	154.4
Nonmetallic Products	89.0	88.0	225.8	276.6	88.1	103.5	132.2	140.9	85.9	166.8
Mining and Petroleum	95.9	94.1	85.5	53.9	95.5	57.7	96.8	57.0	92.2	63.1
Machinery	91.8	90.7	459.2	162.6	171.7	582.9	168.8	535.8	154.6	625.2
Diverse Industries	90.4	89.4	283.7	655.3	86.6	133.3	136.9	194.2	124.2	227.2
Light Diverse Industries	45.9	72.9	229.7	305.3	94.3	123.5	116.3	85.1	53.3	115.1
Construction	56.4	61.3	130.2	132.3	270.6	253.8	137.1	87.5	77.4	133.1
Transport & Communication	59.9	75.1	107.1	125.3	232.9	252.1	115.7	90.2	69.5	171.1
Services and Artisans	133.8	128.6	88.3	85.4	98.0	95.3	93.8	116.8	125.6	99.6

With capital stocks fixed, equating wages to their respective marginal revenue products would result in substantial output gains in the industrial sector. These gains would be mainly at the expense of agriculture, and services and artisans, which show a decline in output of 4.8% and 6.2%, respectively. The changes in the rate of return to capital are an indication of the resource pull on capital. Those sectors whose rates of return increase most would draw capital in from those sectors whose rates of return decline most. Relaxing the fixed capital stock assumption results in greater specialization among traded sectors as returns to scale move closer towards unity. In the case of non-traded goods, the price adjustment is dampened by increased factor mobility (e.g., the net price of services increases by 28.6% instead of 33.8%). This price adjustment is dampened because increased factor mobility reduces excess demand, which in turn reduces the price adjustment necessary to eliminate that excess demand.

Maintaining a constant rural-urban wage differential per factor for all factors precludes factor migration in response to a change in the wage structure between rural and urban areas following the removal of differentials. Yet both experiments indicate a migration of factors towards the urban sector. The explanation for this result is to be found in the substitution of labor for capital in the urban sector following the removal of distortions and in the adjustment of the relative prices of non-traded goods, which in turn affect the net prices of all sectors

in the economy. This change in relative prices alters the patterns of consumption and comparative advantage, provoking a migration of factors out of agriculture.[9]

Another interesting general equilibrium adjustment is captured by the model. When capital stocks are fixed coffee output expands by 1.9%; when capital stocks are mobile coffee output declines by 9.6%. Yet, in both instances quantities exported are the same and there is no private final demand for coffee. The difference in output adjustments is due to the deliveries from the coffee sector to the food industries, which expand when capital stocks are fixed but contract when they are not.

This last point illustrates some of the important adjustment mechanisms captured by a general equilibrium analysis which insures consistency between aggregate supply and aggregate demand. The results in table 3 show that there are substantial interactions between the agricultural and urban sectors. While this model does not provide a detailed treatment of the linkages between agricultural and nonagricultural sectors, as a resource allocation model portraying a dualistic economy, it attempts to incorporate some of the likely interactions between the rural and urban sectors. In addition, the results in that table

[9] In the spirit of the pure theory of international trade, domestically produced and foreign produced goods are perfect substitutes. For developing countries in particular, this assumption should be relaxed for industrial sectors to reflect limited substitution possibilities in the face of changes in relative prices.

indicate that the assumption of fixed prices found in other empirical estimates of distortions in factor markets is likely to seriously underestimate the reallocation of factors brought about by a removal of factor market distortions.

IV. Conclusion

This paper has presented a Walrasian computable general equilibrium model with an application to analyze the effects of factor market distortions on welfare and economic structure. The model has been built to incorporate the differential wage structures specified in the theoretical analyses of factor market distortions. The results in this paper indicate the possibility of perverse welfare results in the presence of other distortions in commodity markets. They also indicate that the efficiency gains from removing distortions in the labor market are likely to be significant, at least for developing countries like Colombia. Previous estimates of the effects of these distortions using a simpler methodology concluded that the gains from removing such distortions were likely to be of a second order of magnitude. It appears that the low magnitude of the efficiency gains were due to their partial equilibrium methodologies neglecting the effects of distortions on demand and therefore on welfare and resulting in fixed product and factor prices.

APPENDIX

The following notation is adopted throughout: Greek letters and lower case Roman letters refer to exogenous parameters whose values are given to the model; upper case Roman letters with a bar are used for exogenous variables. There are $n = q_1 + q_2$ goods produced in the economy; q_1 of these goods are traded; the remainder, q_2, are classified as non-traded. Non-competitive imports are lumped into a sector, 0. Superscripts are used to distinguish between the initial situation (zero) and any other situation (one).

Factor demand equations are derived from profit maximizing behavior on the part of producers. The sectoral wage $W_{\lambda i}$ for factor λ is related to the average economy-wide wage $\hat{w}_\lambda$ by the differential $d_{\lambda i}$. The exchange rate adjustment $E' = (E^1 - E^0)/E^0$ is determined by the normalization rule, which determines a price level such that base year GNP valued at current prices remains constant. Note that, although not explicitly described in the equation system, ad valorem tariffs, subsidies and taxes separate domestic prices from world prices so that the marginal equivalences for a Pareto optimum are also broken on the demand side since the marginal rate of substitution in consumption does not equal the marginal foreign rate of transformation. Thus domestic prices of traded goods equal world prices times one plus the ad valorem tariff, subsidy or tax times the exchange rate E (i.e., $P_k = \pi_k(1 + t_k)E$; $k = 1 \ldots q_1$).

On the demand side, the consumption equations are derived from maximizing utility given by $U = \Pi_i(C_i - \delta)^n$ subject to the budget constraint given by disposable income for consumption, Y. By substitution through the flow balance equations, it can be shown that under a zero balance of trade, disposable factor income for consumption is equal to gross domestic product minus exogenous investment minus net revenues from trade taxes, tariffs and subsidies. Therefore direct taxes on factor incomes cover the difference between government expenditures and revenues on foreign trade.

Including the equations linking domestic to world prices, there are $(4n + 2ns + 2s + q_1 + 1)$ equations to determine the following same number of endogenous variables: X_i, C_i, P_i, P_i^*, $R_{\lambda i}$, $W_{\lambda i}$, RU_λ, R_λ, T_i, and E.

Model Summary

	Number of Equations

Production Functions

1. $X_i = A_i \prod_\lambda R_{\lambda i}^{\alpha_{\lambda i}}$; $\quad i = 1 \ldots n$ $\quad \lambda = 1 \ldots s$ $\qquad n$

where $V_i = \sum_\lambda \alpha_{\lambda i}$

Factor Demand Equations

2. $\alpha_{\lambda i} P_i^* X_i = W_{\lambda i} R_{\lambda i}$; $\quad i = 1 \ldots n$ $\quad \lambda = 1 \ldots s$ $\qquad n.s$

Factor Differential Equations

3. $W_{\lambda i} = d_{\lambda i} \hat{W}_\lambda$; $\quad i = 1 \ldots n$ $\quad \lambda = 1 \ldots s$ $\qquad n.s$

Rural-Urban Wage Differential

4. $RU_\lambda^1 = RU_\lambda^0$ $\qquad s$

where $RU_\lambda = \dfrac{\sum_h w_{\lambda h} R_{\lambda h} \sum_j R_{\lambda j}}{\sum_j W_{\lambda j} R_{\lambda j} \sum_h R_{\lambda h}}$; $\quad h = 1, 2$ $\quad j = h + 1 \ldots n$

Net Price Equations

5. $P_i^* = P_i - \sum_j a_{ji} P_j - a_{0i} P_0$; $\quad i = 1 \ldots n$ $\qquad n$

Price Normalization Equation

6. $\sum_i P_i^{*1} X_i^0 = \sum_i P_i^{*0} X_i^0$; $\quad i = 1 \ldots n$ $\qquad 1$

Consumption Equations

7. $C_i P_i = P_i \delta_i + \gamma_i (Y - \sum_j P_j \delta_j)$; $\quad i,j = 1 \ldots n$ $\qquad n - 1$

where $Y = \sum_i C_i P_i$

Resource Constraints

8. $\sum_i R_{\lambda i} = \bar{R}_\lambda$; $\quad i = 1 \ldots n$ $\qquad s$

Flow Balance Equations

9. $X_i - T_i - \sum_i a_{ji} X_i - a_{0i} X_i = C_i + \bar{Z}_i$;

$\qquad T_i = 0$ for $i > q_1$; $\quad i = 1 \ldots n$ $\qquad n$

10. $\sum_k \pi_k T_k - \pi_0 \sum_i a_{0i} X_i = \Delta$; $\quad k = 1 \ldots q_1$ $\qquad 1$

DISTORTIONS IN THE FACTOR MARKET

List of Variables and Parameters

$X_i, C_i, \bar{Z}_i$—Gross output, private consumption and exogenous demand (government demand + investment demand + depreciation) in sector i.

$R_{\lambda i}$—Use of primary factor λ. Estimates of sectoral capital stocks are from Berry (1974).

$\hat{W}_\lambda$—Average wage of primary factor λ.

P_i, P_i^*—Domestic and net price (inclusive of tariffs and subsidies) of sector i.

T_k—Quantity traded (competitively) of sector k (>0 for exports). T_1 fixed by quota export coffee tax.

$\alpha_{\lambda i}$—The exponent for factor λ in sector i. The exponent for capital, α_{ki}, is derived residually, i.e., $\alpha_{ki} = V_i - \sum_{\lambda \neq k} \alpha_{\lambda i}$.

V_i—Returns to scale in sector i; $V_i = .9$, $i = 1, \ldots, n$.

a_{ij}, a_{0i}—Physical input-output coefficient and noncompetitive import of sector i.

$\bar{A}_i$—Normalizing constant (shift parameter) defining units of measurement for sector i; calculated from equation 1 using base year values.

Δ—Trade gap measured at world prices (equal to zero).

γ_i, δ_i—Marginal expenditure share and subsistence minimum for sector i. These were obtained from Howe (1974).

$d_{\lambda i}$—Differential wage scale parameter for primary factor R_λ. These parameters are the weights defining the average wage $\bar{W}$ in the base period so that $\sum_i d_{\lambda i}(R_{\lambda i}/\bar{R}_\lambda) = 1$.

Y—Total private expenditures.

π_k—World price of commodities produced by sector k; $k = 1 \ldots q_1$.

RU_λ—Ratio of the wage of factor λ in agriculture to the wage of factor λ in the urban sector.

REFERENCES

Adelman, I., and S. Robinson, *Income Distribution Policy in Developing Countries: A Case Study of Korea*, Stanford University, 1977.

Berry, R., "A Descriptive History of Colombian Industrial Development in the Twentieth Century" (mimeo) World Bank, Washington, D.C., 1974.

Bhagwati, J., "The Generalized Theory of Distortions and Welfare," in J. Bhagwati, R. Jones, R. Mundell, and J. Vanek (eds.) *Trade, Balance of Payments and Growth, Papers in International Economics in Honor of C. Kindleberger* (Amsterdam: North-Holland Publishing Company, 1971).

de Melo, J. A. P., "A Multi-Sector, Price Endogenous Trade Model Applied to Colombia," unpublished Ph.D. thesis, Johns Hopkins University, 1975.

———, "The Effects of Distortions in the Factor Market: Some General Equilibrium Estimates," Discussion Paper no. 34, Agency for International Development, Department of State, Washington, D.C., 1976.

Dervis, K., "Substitution, Employment and Intertemporal Equilibrium in a Non-Linear Multi-Sector Planning Model for Turkey," *European Economic Review* 6 (Jan. 1975), 77–96.

Dougherty, C., and M. Selowsky, "Measuring the Effects of the Misallocation of Labour," this REVIEW 55 (Aug. 1972), 386–390.

Fløystad, G., "Distortions in the Factor Market: An Empirical Investigation," this REVIEW 57 (May, 1975), 200–213.

Herberg, H., and M. Kemp, "Factor Market Distortions, the Shape of the Locus of Competitive Outputs, and the Relation between Product Prices and Equilibrium Output," in J. Bhagwati, R. Jones, R. Mundell and J. Vanek (eds.), *Trade, Balance of Payments and Growth, Papers in International Economics in Honor of C. Kindleberger* (Amsterdam: North-Holland Publishing Company, 1971).

Howe, H., "Estimation of the Linear and Quadratic Expenditure Systems: A Cross-Section Case of Colombia," unpublished Ph.D. thesis, University of Pennsylvania, 1974.

Johansen, L., *A Multi-Sectoral Study of Economic Growth* (Amsterdam: North-Holland Publishing Company, 1960).

Magee, S., "Factor Market Distortions, Production and Trade: A Survey," *Oxford Economic Papers* 25 (Mar. 1973), 1–43.

Samuelson, P., "Prices of Factors and Goods in General Equilibrium," *The Review of Economic Studies* 21 (54) (1953–54), 1–20.

TRADE POLICY AND RESOURCE ALLOCATION IN THE PRESENCE OF PRODUCT DIFFERENTIATION

Jaime de Melo and Sherman Robinson*

I. Introduction

TRADITIONALLY, the empirical analysis of the effects of trade policy on resource allocation has relied both on a partial equilibrium framework using effective rates of protection (Balassa (1971, 1981)) and on a multi-sector, general equilibrium framework (Evans (1972), Taylor and Black (1974), de Melo (1978)). Both approaches have usually been based on fairly aggregated data and have relied on the standard assumption often made in trade theory that domestically produced and imported goods are perfect substitutes in use. Recently, however, there has been a shift in empirical work that reflects a growing dissatisfaction with the assumption of perfect substitutability. For example, Baldwin, Murray and Richardson (1977) in their estimates of the effects of multilateral tariff negotiations on resource allocation and welfare explicitly introduce imperfect substitutability into their partial equilibrium analysis. Some recent empirical general equilibrium models, both multi-sector and multi-country, also introduce product differentiation between domestic and foreign goods.[1]

The motivation for this new approach is twofold. First, there has been an increasing amount of empirical evidence suggesting that, even for the most narrowly defined domestic and foreign goods for which prices can be matched (4 and 5 digit SITC categories), the "law of one price" is systematically violated (Isard, 1977). Second, substantial two-way trade is observed in trade

Received for publication August 13, 1979. Revision accepted for publication July 30, 1980.

* Georgetown University and the World Bank, respectively.

This paper has benefited greatly from and draws upon collaborative work undertaken with Kemal Dervis. We also wish to thank two anonymous referees for helpful comments. The views expressed in this paper are those of the authors and not necessarily those of the institutions with which they are associated.

[1] See, for instance, the single country models of Dixon, Parmenter, Ryland and Sutton (1977), Dervis, de Melo and Robinson (1981), and the multi-country models of Deardorff and Stern (1979), Petri (1976) and Whalley (1978).

statistics at similar levels of aggregation (Grubel and Lloyd, 1975). While other reasons for these observations are possible, the assumption that domestic and foreign goods are imperfect substitutes in use provides both a theoretically satisfying explanation and a specification that is implementable in empirical models. However, in spite of its recent popularity, there has been no systematic investigation of the implications of this new specification for the analysis of the impact of trade policy on relative prices and resource pulls. This paper aims to provide such an investigation.

The paper has two objectives: first, to discuss the theoretical properties and implications of one practical specification of product differentiation and, second, to explore quantitatively the impact of trade policy on relative prices and resource pulls with an empirical general equilibrium model which incorporates product differentiation. In section II we discuss the implications of product differentiation for the autonomy of the domestic price system. The analysis uses a partial equilibrium framework and leads to a classification of sectors according to the extent to which the domestic price is influenced by trade policy. Section III extends the analysis to include intermediate products and discusses the implications of product differentiation for the computation of effective rates of protection. In section IV, we use a computable general equilibrium model to explore the empirical impact of trade policy on relative prices and resource pulls and to compare the effects of changes in tariffs and subsidies in single sectors to changes across many sectors simultaneously.

II. Product Differentiation and Domestic Prices: A Partial Equilibrium Analysis

When domestically produced goods and foreign produced goods are perfect substitutes in use and when the country is small, an increase in the import price results in the same increase in the domestic price. Thus, with the exception of non-traded goods whose prices are determined by

[169]

internal conditions, the domestic price system is entirely determined by trade policy. However, if the domestic and foreign goods are imperfect substitutes then, for any sector i, the price of the domestic good, PD_i, is no longer identical with the domestic currency price of the import substitute, PM_i. For simplicity, assume that the degree of substitutability is the same for all internal uses: consumption demand, investment demand and intermediate demand. Let D_i denote the demand for internal use, and E_i export demand (which is a function of the dollar price of exports, PWE_i). Then, under partial equilibrium assumptions, the equilibrium condition in the market for the domestically produced good in sector i is

$$X_i^d = X_i^s \qquad (1)$$

where

$$X_i^d = D_i(PD_i, PM_i) + E_i(PWE_i) \qquad (2)$$

and

$$X_i^s = X_i(PD_i). \qquad (3)$$

A natural question is to investigate the extent to which trade policy affects the price of the domestic good. We shall thus discuss more specifically the treatment of imports and exports, using the functional forms adopted later in the quantitative analysis.

The Demand for Imports and the Demand for Exports

A convenient way of introducing product differentiation is to follow Armington (1969a) and to define for each commodity category an aggregate or composite commodity Q_i, which is a constant elasticity of substitution (CES) function of imports M_i, and domestic goods for internal use, D_i:

$$Q_i = \{\delta_i M_i^{-\rho_i} + (1 - \delta_i) D_i^{-\rho_i}\}^{-1/\rho_i} \qquad (4)$$

where δ_i and ρ_i are parameters and $\sigma_i = (1 + \rho_i)^{-1}$ is the "trade substitution elasticity" between foreign and domestic goods. Consumers and producers demand this composite commodity so that the demand for imports and domestic goods becomes a derived demand. If the country's import share in total world supply is small, imports are in infinitely elastic supply and world prices, $\overline{PW}_i$, are fixed exogenously. Import prices to domestic users are given by

$$PM_i = \overline{PW}_i (1 + tm_i)ER. \qquad (5)$$

Turning to exports, their supply is equal to the difference between total production and demand for domestic use. In turn, the demand for exports depends both on the country's market share and on the degree of product differentiation characterizing products from different countries. Thus the less substitutable the product in question, the lower the export demand elasticity, η_i. The foreign demand for exports is given by

$$E_i = \bar{E}_i(PWE_i)^{-\eta_i} \qquad (6)$$

where the dollar price of export, PWE_i, is obtained by dividing the domestic price by the exchange rate times one plus the rate of export subsidy:

$$PWE_i = PD_i/ER(1 + te_i). \qquad (7)$$

A Classification of Sectors by Their Degree of Tradability

Given the treatment of exports and imports, we can investigate how a change in tariffs and subsidies affects the equilibrium price of the domestic good. Start with partial equilibrium and assume the exchange rate is fixed. Then, assuming demanders minimize the cost of acquiring the composite good, we have the following equations (dropping subscripts):

$$D = (1 - \delta)^\sigma (P/PD)^\sigma Q \qquad (8)$$
$$M = \delta^\sigma (P/PM)^\sigma Q \qquad (9)$$
$$P = \{\delta^\sigma PM^{(1-\sigma)} + (1 - \delta)^\sigma PD^{(1-\sigma)}\}^{1/1-\sigma} \qquad (10)$$

where (8)–(9) are the first order conditions and (10) is the cost function derived from the CES aggregation function (4). Totally differentiate the equilibrium condition (1) to get

$$\hat{X}^s X^s = \hat{D}D + \hat{E}E \qquad (11)$$

where a " $\hat{\ }$ " denotes a percentage change.

To obtain expressions in terms of elasticities and shares, define the following:

$$\hat{X}^s = \epsilon^s \widehat{PD}; \ \hat{Q} = -\epsilon^d \hat{P}; \ \hat{E} = -\eta \widehat{PWE};$$
$$\theta_m = \frac{PM \cdot M}{PQ} = \delta^\sigma (P/PM)^{(\sigma-1)}.$$

Although the import share θ_m will vary when relative prices change (if $\sigma \neq 1$), it can be assumed constant for small changes around equilibrium. Total differentiation of (8)–(10) and substitution into (11) yields, after some manipulation, an expression for the percentage change in the domestic price for a small change in the rate of export subsidy, *te*:

$$\hat{PD} = \frac{\eta}{(\epsilon^s + \eta)/D + \{\epsilon^s + \epsilon^d (1 - \theta_m)\}/E} \, \lambda_e \hat{te}.$$

(12)

The corresponding expression for the case of a small change in the tariff rate, *tm*, is[2]

$$\hat{PD} = \frac{(\sigma - \epsilon^d)\theta_m}{(\epsilon^s + \eta) \, E/D + \epsilon^s + \epsilon^d + (\sigma - \epsilon^d)\theta_m} \, \lambda_m \hat{tm}$$

(13)

where

$$\lambda_m = \frac{tm}{1 + tm}, \quad \lambda_e = \frac{te}{1 + te}. \tag{14}$$

What can we conclude from these expressions? First, the demand for the domestic good is clearly a derived demand and the elasticity of supply appears in both expressions. Thus, other things equal, the higher the elasticity of supply, the smaller the adjustment in the domestic price necessary to restore equilibrium in the market. The same can be said of the role of the price elasticity of demand for the composite good, ϵ^d.

Second, the role of the elasticity of demand for exports is important in determining the extent to which a change in trade policy affects the domestic price. In the case of an export subsidy, the dominating effect of its value is quite obvious since the higher its value, the larger will be the corresponding domestic price change. Note, however, that export demand is also important when there is a change in the tariff rate, especially when the share of domestically produced goods being exported is large. The higher the elasticity of demand for exports, the smaller will be the domestic price change resulting from a change in tariff policy. A tariff will lead to a fall in exports as domestic output is channeled away from foreign markets towards domestic use and the easier this substitution process the smaller will be the price increase.

Third, expression (13) provides a necessary condition for a rise in import price to lead to a fall in the domestic price; namely, that the trade substitution elasticity be less than the elasticity of demand for the composite good.

2 For derivation of (12) and (13) and a discussion of limiting cases, see de Melo and Robinson (1978).

The specification of imperfect substitution allows for a richer and more realistic description of the role of different sectors in foreign trade. One is no longer faced with the extreme dichotomy in which sectors are either traded with their prices entirely determined outside the model, or non-traded with their prices entirely determined endogenously. Sectors are characterized by a continuum of "tradability" and even if all sectors are traded, the domestic price system can have a significant degree of autonomy from world prices.

In analyzing resource pulls, it is useful to distinguish four types of sectors: non-tradables, exportables, import substitutes and import complements. A sector produces "non-tradables" if both the share of exports in total production and the share of imports in domestic use is small (e.g. construction and services). A sector producing "exportables" is one in which the ratio of exports to domestic production is high. Sectors characterized by high shares of imports in total domestic use can be divided into "import substitutes" and "import complements" depending on the ease of substitution between domestic and foreign goods relative to the sectoral own demand elasticities for the composite good. Import substitutes are sectors for which the trade substitution elasticity exceeds the own composite good demand elasticity so that an increase in the tariff leads to an increase in the domestic price. As σ gets very large, these sectors behave as the traditional perfect substitutes for competitive imports. If, on the contrary, the elasticity of substitution in use between domestic and foreign goods is lower than the own demand elasticity, the relevant sectors behave as if sectoral imports are non-competitive in the sense that a tariff on imports does not protect the corresponding domestic industry. The distinction between import substitutes and import complements reflects the traditional distinction between competitive and non-competitive imports, but it allows for a continuum rather than the extreme treatment of imports as either perfect substitutes or perfect complements for domestic goods.

III. Intermediate Products and Effective Protection

A natural way to extend the analysis of section II is to allow for intermediate products. Assume that intermediate products are demanded in fixed proportions and so define value-added or the "net price" in sector i as

$$PN_i = PD_i - \Sigma_j a_{ji} P_j \tag{15}$$

where the a_{ji} are intermediate input coefficients expressed in units of composite goods per unit of domestic production.

Effective rates of protection (ERPs) express the protection to value-added accorded by a change in trade taxes and are defined as

$$ERP_i = PN_i^1/PN_i^0 - 1 \tag{16}$$

where PN_i^1 and PN_i^0 are the value-added or net prices in that sector before and after the change in trade policy. To simplify the notation, assume that units are defined so that initial prices are equal to unity. Then $PN_i = 1 - \Sigma_j a_{ji}$ and the effective rate of protection is given by

$$ERP_i = \frac{\widehat{PD}_i - \Sigma_j a_{ji} \hat{P}_j}{1 - \Sigma_j a_{ji}} \tag{17}$$

where a "$\,\hat{}\,$" indicates a percent change. It is desirable to relate the ERP directly to the change in trade policy, which can be done by totally differentiating equation (10) and substituting into (17). The expression for the ERP becomes

$$ERP_i = \frac{\widehat{PD}_i - \Sigma_j a_{ji}[\theta_{jm}\lambda_{jm} tm_j + (1 - \theta_{jm})\widehat{PD}_j]}{1 - \Sigma_j a_{ji}}. \tag{18}$$

In the presence of product differentiation an across-the-board change in tariffs will not lead to a proportional change in value-added across sectors unless changes in both tariff rates and domestic prices are identical across sectors ($\widehat{tm}_j = \widehat{PD}_j$ for all j). But we know that, with a few notable exceptions, the changes in domestic prices resulting from single changes in tariffs are not very large (especially when they are weighted by the share of domestic goods). Therefore, we may neglect the second terms in brackets in equation (18).[3] It then becomes clear that the

sectors which have a lower ERP when there is an equal across-the-board change in tariffs are those sectors for which the share of imported intermediate inputs ($\Sigma_j a_{ji}\theta_{jm}$) is high. Independently of its trade orientation, a sector is classified as "import-dependent" if it has a high ratio of imported to total intermediate inputs. As in the traditional measure of effective protection, the presence of tariffs on imported intermediate inputs lowers the ERP accorded to a sector.

IV.   A General Equilibrium Analysis of Resource Pulls

Although the model presented above can be implemented in its partial equilibrium form, it is natural to explore the impact of trade policy on resource allocation and relative prices by specifying a multi-sector general equilibrium. The latter has two distinct advantages. First it allows for an endogenous determination of variables such as the exchange rate which are held constant in a partial equilibrium framework. Second, whereas calculus techniques restrict the investigation to small changes around equilibrium, the direct solution of a general equilibrium model allows one to explore the impact of large changes in trade policy. Following is a brief summary description of the model used for the numerical application.[4]

The model is Walrasian in spirit and determines relative product prices, wages and the exchange rate so as to clear the markets for products, different types of labor, and foreign exchange. On the supply side producers minimize costs. Labor moves across urban sectors until the value of its marginal product is everywhere the same. The agricultural labor force is fixed. Capital stocks, once installed, are assumed to be fixed during the period considered. Sectoral technology is described by a CES production function for capital and labor. Intermediate technology takes place according to a Leontief production function with fixed coefficients (expressed in terms of composite goods).

---

[3] Note that if domestic and foreign goods were perfect substitutes, equal tariffs would lead to equal ERPs since, given that $tm_i = tm_j$ for all i and all j, it would always be true that

$$ERP_i = \frac{tm_i - \Sigma_j a_{ji} tm_j}{1 - \Sigma_j a_{ji}} = \frac{tm_i - tm_j(\Sigma_j a_{ji})}{1 - \Sigma_j a_{ji}} = tm_i.$$

In this expression it is assumed that all goods are traded and that the small country assumption holds for both imports and exports.

[4] For a detailed description of the structure of a computable general equilibrium model, see Dervis, de Melo, and Robinson (1981). An appendix with the complete set of equations is available upon request.

On the demand side, sectoral consumption demands are given by constant expenditure proportions. This implies that the own-price elasticity of demand for sectoral composite output is unity. This specification has the advantage of simplifying the interpretation of results since the elasticity of response of private final demand to a change in sectoral composite price, itself due to a change in trade policy, is the same across all sectors. Aggregate investment demand is held fixed in real terms which implies a zero own-price elasticity of demand for both the intermediate and the investment components of final demand. Savings are determined residually so as to maintain real investment. This formulation allows a focus on relative prices and resource allocation by leaving out the distributional impact of trade policy and the interactions between trade policy and growth via changes in the level of real investment.[5]

The model outlined above is the basis for the two sets of experiments reported in this section.

[5] Although not mentioned, there is a government sector whose presence is neutralized by a system of transfers to and from the private sector so as to prevent any policy-induced redistribution of income between the private sector and the government sector.

The first set of experiments consists of examining successively the impact on resource allocation of single 50% tariffs and subsidies on a sector by sector basis. They correspond closely to what one might expect from partial equilibrium estimates along the lines described in section II. The second set of experiments consists of across-the-board changes in tariffs and subsidies. The impact of general equilibrium effects is gauged by comparing a ranking of changes in sectoral outputs under both sets of experiments. The analysis is conducted at a 19 sector level of aggregation and the data are based on the 1973 Turkish input-output table.

The structure of the economy in the reference solution, which is a solution of the model without any trade interference, is provided in table 1. Columns 1 and 2 describe the structure of production across sectors. The next three columns provide information about each sector's trade-orientation as discussed in section II. Column 3 indicates that only five sectors export over 10% of their production, with food, textiles and petroleum products being the most export-oriented sectors in the economy. These ratios are quite low, although they are in the range one would expect for developing countries that have fol-

TABLE 1.—STRUCTURE OF THE ECONOMY IN THE BASE SOLUTION

		1	2	3	4	5	6	7	8	9
1.	Agriculture	21.5	71.5	3.2	1.6	8.6	52.0	3.0	2.0	1.6
2.	Mining	1.0	63.0	10.6	6.8	18.5	18.0	0.5	2.0	2.1
3.	Food	9.8	20.6	17.9	1.2	2.1	73.0	1.25	2.0	0.6
4.	Textiles	5.8	21.4	27.7	3.6	8.2	57.0	1.25	2.0	2.1
5.	Clothing	1.2	56.6	6.0	3.0	4.0	77.0	1.25	2.5	1.9
6.	Wood & Wood Products	1.2	41.9	0.4	0.6	3.6	38.0	1.25	2.5	1.9
7.	Paper & Printing	1.1	31.0	0.9	10.8	10.8	40.0	0.5	2.5	0.3
8.	Chemicals	2.3	35.3	3.8	47.7	31.0	39.0	0.5	2.5	0.2
9.	Rubber & Plastics	1.0	26.6	2.6	18.8	22.6	50.0	0.5	2.5	0.7
10.	Petroleum & Pet. Prod.	3.4	39.5	16.9	50.6	20.8	16.0	3.0	2.5	0.01
11.	Non-Met. Min. Prod.	1.5	38.8	7.5	7.6	10.5	40.0	0.5	2.5	0.6
12.	Basic Metals	3.2	22.6	5.2	24.0	20.6	0.0	0.5	2.5	0.3
13.	Metal Products	1.2	43.3	3.0	16.0	22.8	67.0	0.5	2.5	1.6
14.	Non-electrical Machinery	2.0	40.5	1.9	56.2	44.3	21.0	0.33	2.5	0.3
15.	Electrical Machinery	1.0	40.1	0.6	39.0	27.3	41.0	0.33	2.5	0.5
16.	Transp. Equipment	1.0	39.1	0.2	28.8	22.9	20.0	0.5	2.5	0.7
17.	Construction	6.5	51.3	—	—	17.0	1.0	—	—	1.4
18.	Infrastructure	12.9	67.9	10.1	1.8	16.3	70.0	0.33	1.25	0.2
19.	Services	22.5	80.9	7.2	1.5	4.4	66.0	0.33	1.25	1.4

Notes:
Column 1: Sectoral composition of gross output
2: Sectoral value-added as a percentage of domestic price
3: Ratio of exports to domestic output
4: Share of imports in aggregate composite expenditures
5: Share of imported intermediate inputs in total intermediate input
6: Ratio of private consumption to total composite output
7: Trade substitution elasticities
8: Export demand elasticities
9: Sectoral supply elasticities (see text for definition)

lowed an inward-looking development strategy. On the import side, a more typical picture emerges with regard to both the share of imports in aggregate composite expenditures (column 4) and the share of imported intermediate inputs in total intermediate inputs (column 5) (which indicates a sector's degree of trade dependence). With the exception of non-metallic mineral products, intermediates and capital goods are both import-oriented and import-dependent. Construction is the only pure non-traded sector in the economy, yet 17% of its intermediate inputs are imported. Finally, column 6 indicates the share of final demand consumption and therefore gives an approximation of the price elasticity of demand, ϵ^d.

The last three columns give the important elasticities for determining the resource-pull effects of changes in tariffs and subsidies. The sectoral variation in trade substitution elasticities (column 7) roughly captures the extent of product differentiation due to differences in quality and degree of product homogeneity.[6] Thus agricultural and petroleum products are viewed as the most homogeneous products, along with the more traditional non-durable consumer goods

which are assumed to be more substitutable in use than other manufactures. Export demand elasticities (column 8) correspond to values one might expect in the short to medium term. Finally, partial-equilibrium sectoral elasticities of supply (defined as the elasticity of substitution between capital and labor times the ratio of the labor share to the capital share in value-added) are given in column 9.

Trade Policy and the Domestic Price System

We are now in a position to investigate numerically the range of domestic price and output responses to single 50% tariffs and single 50% export subsidies. The nature of the experiment whereby only one tariff (or one subsidy) is imposed at a time makes the analysis of section II particularly relevant since general equilibrium repercussions should be minor so that the various partial equilibrium elasticities reported in table 1 can serve as indicators in determining the resulting change in domestic prices. This allows the discussion to be brief, the details being left to the reader.

The first two columns in table 2 show the percentage change in sectoral domestic prices and outputs when a 50% tariff is imposed on imports classified under that sector. Consider the percentage change in the domestic price. Primary

[6] For estimates of trade substitution elasticities that fall within the ranges found in table 1 see Armington (1969b), Hickman and Lau (1973), and Alaouze (1977).

TABLE 2.—RESOURCE PULLS FOR SINGLE TARIFFS AND SUBSIDIES
(% changes from base solution)

		Tariff		Subsidy	
		Domestic Price	Output	Domestic Price	Output
1.	Agriculture	0.6	0.0	3.6	0.0
2.	Mining	−0.7	0.5	3.2	9.7
3.	Food	0.2	0.0	6.4	10.6
4.	Textiles	−0.2	−1.9	5.1	23.0
5.	Clothing	0.5	0.4	3.1	6.8
6.	Wood and Wood Products	0.0	0.0	0.0	0.5
7.	Paper & Printing	1.1	0.0	0.5	1.8
8.	Chemicals	5.0	−0.7	5.6	3.2
9.	Rubber and Plastics	0.1	−0.1	1.2	3.5
10.	Petroleum and Pet. Prod.	28.0	0.3	15.9	0.3
11.	Non-Met. Min. Prod.	−0.1	0.1	5.5	7.7
12.	Basic Metals	10.7	2.5	7.8	6.8
13.	Metal Products	−0.4	−0.8	0.8	4.0
14.	Non-electrical Machinery	3.6	2.1	3.0	2.2
15.	Electrical Machinery	0.0	−1.7	0.3	1.1
16.	Transp. Equipment	5.5	2.6	0.0	0.4
17.	Construction	—	—	—	—
18.	Infrastructure	−0.7	0.1	5.5	1.4
19.	Services	0.1	0.0	4.9	0.0

goods and consumer goods which have low import shares and export a relatively large amount of their output show virtually no price increase at all. They behave either as non-tradables (e.g., wood) or as exportables (e.g., textiles and food). Intermediates, as a rule, behave as import substitutes since they generally have fairly large import shares. The exceptions are rubber and plastics and non-metallic mineral products, both of which have low import shares so that their domestic prices do not change much.

As an example, it is interesting to trace out the causes of the 28% increase in the domestic price of petroleum products which far exceeds any other price change. The reason for this result may be readily traced out with the information provided in table 1. It is due to the high import share, the low elasticity of final demand due to the fact that petroleum products are mostly used as intermediates and of course to the fact that these products are good substitutes in use. These factors, in conjunction with the extremely low elasticity of domestic supply, result in a dramatic rise in the domestic price of petroleum products. A similar but less dramatic combination of shares and elasticities underlies the large price increases registered for chemicals and basic metals.

Turning to an examination of the short-run output changes in column 2, one finds that they are quite small both because supply elasticities are low and because there is an inverse relation between price changes and supply elasticities captured in equations (12) and (13). Note, however, that it is supply elasticities and changes in net prices rather than gross prices that determine output response. To compare the resource shifts in column 2 with those that would obtain under a more traditional trade specification where domestic and foreign goods are perfect substitutes, multiply the supply elasticities in table 1 (column 9) by one half since in that case the domestic price would increase by the full amount of the tariff and $\hat{PD} = \hat{PM} = 0.5$. This would provide a rough estimate of the increase in sectoral outputs which could then be compared with the results in column 2. These resource pulls would still be larger than those which would be obtained in the very long run with product differentiation—but not by much. In that case, letting $\epsilon^s = \infty$, the output response to a change in

tariffs would be given by $\hat{X} = (\sigma - \epsilon) \theta_m \hat{PM}$, which turns out to be usually less than the short-run response with perfect substitution.[7]

While the effects of changes in tariffs on the domestic price system require careful interpretation because of the indirect effects caused by imperfect substitution, on the export side, the linkages are much easier to follow: the effect of an export subsidy on the domestic price system depends mostly on the sectoral elasticity of demand for exports. Moreover, this link is direct and, given that the pattern of export demand elasticities is fairly similar across sectors, one would expect the main determinant of the response of domestic prices to a change in subsidies to be the sectoral share of production that is exported. Thus the sectors whose prices rise the most following the imposition of a 50% subsidy are the export-oriented sectors. In table 2, the sectors that export over 5% of domestic production (namely, mining, food, textiles, clothing, petroleum products, non-metallic products, basic metals, infrastructure, and services) show the largest increase in prices (column 3). Since the increase in domestic prices is much greater than in the case of a similar change in tariff, the output response is also greater (column 4).

The magnitude of the export response in columns 3 and 4 confirms the greater sensitivity of the model to the specification of export demands than to the specification of import demands because the effects are direct. These results might provide a partial explanation as to why policy-makers in developing countries (where it is often argued that it is difficult to transform foreign resources into domestic ones because of bottlenecks or "gaps") provide much higher effective exchange rates of protection to imports than to exports.

Ranking Sectors by Resource Shifts:
Partial vs. General Equilibrium

The single tariff and export subsidy experiments with the general equilibrium model correspond closely to partial equilibrium assumptions in that only one parameter was changed at a time. It is also interesting to investigate how the economy responds to across-the-board changes in

---

[7] The expression for $\hat{X}$ is obtained from equations (8)–(10) after noting that $\epsilon^s = \infty$, $\hat{PD} = 0$ and hence $\hat{E} = 0$.

tariffs and subsidies. This is done by devising two experiments that might be viewed as extreme policy packages: an import-substitution strategy (IS) provided by a 120% tariff on imports across-the-board; and an export promotion strategy (EP) provided by 50% across-the-board subsidies.[8]

There are four important general equilibrium repercussions that must be taken into account in order to compare the resulting resource shifts with those from the single-change experiments. First, there are the effects on intermediate input costs. Other things equal, those sectors which are import-dependent will be adversely affected when there is an across-the-board change in tariffs. Second, there is a strong wage effect that will have a differential impact across sectors. In the case of an IS strategy, the industrial wage falls by 15% compared with its base value, whereas it rises by 9% with the EP strategy. This corroborates the often-made observation that developing countries' exports are labor-intensive so that an EP strategy would alleviate unemployment.

Third, there is an exchange rate effect. In the model, the exchange rate reflects the relative price of domestic and imported goods. Given the

normalization rule which fixes a weighted sum of domestic and imported prices, both experiments will result in an appreciation of the value of the exchange rate so as to maintain external balance. In the case of the IS strategy the exchange rate appreciates by 32% and in the case of the EP strategy it appreciates by 18%.

Fourth, there are income effects associated with changes in the international terms of trade. Thus the economy-wide change in tariff structure improves the terms-of-trade by 44% whereas the corresponding across-the-board change in subsidies leads to a deterioration in the terms-of-trade of 17%. Therefore one would expect that sectors which expand will expand more under an IS strategy because of the induced increase in demand for domestic goods caused by the increase in disposable income, and vice versa for the EP strategy.

These effects are reflected in table 3, which ranks sectors for single changes in trade policy and for across-the-board changes in trade policy. In each column the first number indicates the sector and the number in parentheses next to it indicates the percentage change in sectoral output from the level reached in the base solution. Thus 16(2.6) in column 1 means that domestic output in the transport equipment sector expands by 2.6% when the domestic currency price of imports of transport equipment increases by 50%, the domestic currency price of all other imports being held constant. From column 2, when the domestic currency price of all imports

[8] The selection of a 120% increase across-the-board is to insure that, after the revaluation of the exchange rate is taken into account (see discussion below), the domestic currency price of imports rises by 50% over the value in the base run, as in the case of a single 50% tariff change when the exchange rate change is usually negligible.

TABLE 3.—COMPARISON OF RANKINGS OF OUTPUT RESPONSES TO CHANGES IN TARIFFS AND SUBSIDIES

50% Tariff (One-by-One)	120% Tariff (Across-the-Board)	50% Subsidy (One-by-One)	50% Subsidy (Across-the-Board)
16(2.6)	5(6.0)	4(23.0)	4(10.7)
12(2.5)	16(5.2)	3(10.6)	3(3.3)
14(2.1)	6(4.6)	2(9.7)	2(1.9)
	17(3.5)	11(7.7)	14(1.1)
2(0.5)	12(2.7)	12(6.8)	11(0.9)
5(0.4)	7(1.0)	5(6.8)	12(0.7)
10(0.3)	10(0.4)	13(4.0)	8(0.5)
18(0.1)	18(0.3)	9(3.5)	10(−0.1)
11(0.1)	11(−1.1)	8(3.2)	15(−0.2)
3(0.0)	8(−1.2)	14(2.2)	9(−0.3)
6(0.0)	9(−1.8)	7(1.8)	13(−0.6)
7(0.0)	15(−1.9)	18(1.4)	18(−0.6)
9(−0.1)	13(−2.0)		17(−2.2)
8(−0.7)	2(−2.0)	15(1.1)	7(−2.4)
13(−0.8)	14(−3.2)	6(0.5)	16(−3.4)
15(−1.7)	3(−3.9)	16(0.4)	5(−3.8)
4(−1.9)	4(−14.1)	10(0.3)	6(−3.9)

Notes: Figures in parentheses are per cent output changes from the base solution. Sectors are referred to by numbers.

TRADE POLICY AND RESOURCE ALLOCATION   177

rises by 50% (i.e., when there is a 120% tariff across-the-board), the output expansion in the transport equipment sector is 5.2%.

It is interesting to note the substantial change in rankings among sectors indicated by the criss-crossing of lines joining sectors in columns 1 and 2 and in columns 3 and 4. As one might expect, they are more pronounced for changes in tariffs than for changes in subsidies because the links are more complicated on the import side. The results indicate the empirical importance of the general equilibrium repercussions discussed above.

V. Conclusions

We have argued that the empirical analysis of the price and resource-pull effects of trade policy, especially at a relatively high level of aggregation, is best done in the context of models that explicitly take account of product differentiation. The specification of imperfect substitutability provides a practical way of capturing product differentiation both in a partial equilibrium and in a general equilibrium model. However, results from the empirical general equilibrium model (sections III and IV) show that partial equilibrium based estimates are not likely to be robust when there are substantial policy changes that affect a number of sectors simultaneously.

REFERENCES

Alaouze, Chris, "Estimates of the Elasticity of Substitution between Imported and Domestically Produced Goods Classified at the Input-Output Level of Aggregation," Impact Working Paper No. 0-13, Industries Assistance Commission, Melbourne (1977).

Armington, Paul, "A Theory of Demand for Products Distinguished by Place of Production," *IMF Staff Papers* 16 (1) (1969a), 159–178.

———, "The Geographic Pattern of Trade and the Effects of Price Changes," *IMF Staff Papers* 16 (2) (1969b), 179–201.

Balassa, Bela, and Associates, *The Structure of Protection in Developing Countries* (Baltimore: Johns Hopkins University Press, 1971).

Balassa, Bela (ed.), *Development Strategies in Semi-Industrial Countries* (Baltimore: Johns Hopkins University Press, forthcoming, 1981).

Baldwin, Robert, Tracy Murray, and David Richardson, "Welfare Effects on the United States of a Significant Multilateral Tariff Reduction," mimeo, University of Wisconsin, Madison (1977).

Deardorff, Alan V., and Robert M. Stern, "A Disaggregated Model of World Production and Trade," mimeo, University of Michigan, Ann Arbor (1979).

Dervis, Kemal, Jaime de Melo, and Sherman Robinson, *General Equilibrium Models for Development Policy* (London: Cambridge University Press, forthcoming, 1981).

Dixon, Peter B., Brian R. Parmenter, George J. Ryland and John Sutton, *Orani, A General Equilibrium Model of the Australian Economy*, Vol. 2, Australian Government Publishing Service, Canberra (1977).

Evans, Peter B., *A General Equilibrium Analysis of Protection* (Amsterdam: North-Holland Publishing Company, 1972).

Grubel, Herbert, and Peter Lloyd, *Intra-Industry Trade: The Theory and Measurement of International Trade in Differentiated Products* (London: MacMillan and Halsted Press, 1975).

Hickman, Bert G., and Laurence J. Lau, "Elasticities of Substitution in a World Trade Model," *European Economic Review* 4 (1973), 347–380.

Isard, Peter, "How Far Can We Push the Law of One Price?" *American Economic Review* 67 (5) (1977), 942–948.

Melo, Jaime de, "Protection and Resource Allocation in a Walrasian Trade Model," *International Economic Review* 19 (1) (1978), 17–45.

Melo, Jaime de, and Sherman Robinson, "Tradability in Trade Theory," mimeo, World Bank, Washington, D.C. (1978).

Petri, Peter, "A Multilateral Model of Japanese-American Trade," in Jiri Skolka, Karen R. Polenske (eds.), *Advances in Input-Output Analysis* (Cambridge, MA: Ballinger Publishing Co., 1976).

Taylor, Lance, and Stephen Black, "Practical General Equilibrium Estimates of Resource Pulls Under Trade Liberalization," *Journal of International Economics* 4 (1) (1974), 37–58.

Whalley, John, "Discriminatory Features of Domestic Factor Tax Systems and Their Impact on World Trade: A General Equilibrium Approach," University of Western Ontario, London (1978).

5

An Evaluation of Neutral Trade Policy Incentives Under Increasing Returns to Scale

Jaime de Melo and David Roland-Holst

...in developing countries where protective barriers are high and there is bias against the exports of manufactured goods, the limitations of domestic markets generally permit only the construction of plants that are below optimum size. By contrast, the disadvantages of small national markets are surmounted in countries where low protective barriers and the lack of bias against exports permit efficient-scale operations through specialization according to comparative advantage....

Balassa (1971, 78-79)

New developments in the theory of international trade often suggest, implicitly or explicitly, that in an imperfectly competitive environment, government intervention may be needed to achieve optimality. The most celebrated example in this new literature is the profit-shifting argument of Brander and Spencer (1984). Another example, perhaps more widely applicable, is the argument developed by Krugman (1985) showing that protection can serve as an export promotion policy under certain circumstances. These arguments have fostered a literature on strategic trade theory, which deals with conditions of imperfect competition between international trading partners.[1] The trade and development literature, on the other hand, concentrates on the implications of imperfectly competitive domestic markets.

In the first of Balassa's (1971) comparative studies on trade policies in developing countries, he argued (in the passage quoted above) that the small size of domestic markets in developing countries was a hindrance to the exploitation of scale economies. He recommended policies to promote exports as a way to break this bottleneck. In his second comparative study of trade policies in semi-industrial countries (Balassa 1982), he ascribed the superior performance of the outward-oriented development strategies in East Asia to the provision of equal incentives to sales on the home and export markets, that is, to the avoidance of home-market bias. Further, in recognition of the learning effects and externalities that accompany the establishment of new industries, Balassa (1975) recommended temporary protection to new activities, which would be gradually scaled down to an across-the-board protection level of about 10 percent. In favoring market neutrality, Balassa is not only applying the principle of nondiscrimination, but he is also emphasizing trade policy rules or rules of thumb that have low administrative costs and do not depend on econometric evidence for their administration.

In this paper, we explore the robustness of these strategies in a setting that is representative of semi-industrial market structures and conduct. We recognize that production in some industrial sectors takes place under increasing returns to scale and that pricing in tradable sectors distinguishes between domestic and export markets. The home country is assumed to be a price-taker in both import and export markets. Thus terms of trade are fixed, and we rule out the possibility of strategic trade policy to exploit monopoly power in international trade, that is, the possibility of using trade policy to shift profits to domestic firms. (By contrast, the strategic trade literature assumes that oligopolistic interactions occur in international markets, so that trade policy affects the home country's terms of trade — circumstances that are more representative of developed countries than semi-industrial ones.) The purpose of the paper is to reexamine the merits of protection, with and without neutrality of domestic and foreign sales incentives, when some manufacturing sectors operate under increasing returns to scale and domestic firms behave oligopolistically.

We first derive analytically the comparative statics of tariff and subsidy policy in the setting described above, and then we derive criteria for optimal tariff-subsidy policies. Because of intermediate linkages, the welfare effects of trade policy changes are not generally determinate in this multisectoral, general equilibrium setting. This provides the motivation for our simulation analysis, which is prefaced by a summary of the model and a discussion of alternative specifications of oligopoly behavior. Next, we explore systematically the effects of tariffs and export subsidies on welfare with a computable general equilibrium (CGE) model of a representative semi-industrial economy with increasing returns and oligopoly behavior in selected manufacturing activities. Finally, we return to the issues of neutrality and optimal protection, comparing the welfare effects of trade policies that provide only import protection for sectors with scale economies with those of policies that combine tariffs and export subsidies.

Welfare Determinants of Trade Policy Under Increasing Returns

This section presents basic analytical results on the welfare effects of import tariffs and export subsidies. It extends the work of Dixit (1984) and Rodrik (1988) by encompassing export subsidies, the selling of sectoral output on different markets (domestic and export), and imperfect substitution between domestic and imported goods. These features are reproduced in the model structure of the empirical application in later sections. In this setting, we show that both import tariffs and export subsidies contribute to distortions in domestic demand. On the supply side, our results indicate that tariff protection alone may induce producers to divert output from exports to the domestic market rather than expanding production and realizing scale economies. When protection and export incentives are neutral, however, we show that scale economies can be realized that will offset or even

Jaime de Melo and David Roland-Holst

---

outweigh the welfare costs of distortions in demand. We conclude the section with the derivation of a general expression for the optimal tariff-subsidy combination. The expression takes explicit account of the linkages and cost externalities that arise under increasing returns in a general equilibrium context. The expression also shows how optimal trade policy necessitates a mixture of domestic market protection and export incentives to balance the relative profitability of sales in the two markets.

Notational conventions follow Dixit (1984). The economy has k sectors, each consisting of n_i identical firms ($i = 1,...,k$) producing output (z_i) for domestic use (y_i) and export (x_i). As in the numerical application below, firm output and sales allocation decisions are separable. Hence the allocation decision along a continuous transformation surface, $z_i = F_i(x_i,y_i)$, depends only on relative prices in the producer's domestic and export markets for output.[2] Each identical firm has a representative cost function $c_i(x_i,y_i)$. Domestic and world prices are k-vectors p and P, respectively, as are ad valorem import tariffs t and export subsidies s. Sectoral domestic prices are an inverse function $p(q)$ of domestic demands, $q_i = M_i + n_iY_i$, themselves an aggregate of imports and domestic output for domestic use.

To evaluate the welfare effect of import and export distortions, we consider all sectors simultaneously in a general equilibrium framework. In a situation in which the government makes only lump-sum transfers and commodity preferences are those of a single representative consumer, aggregate welfare can be decomposed into three components. The first of these is consumer surplus,

$$(1) \qquad g(q) = \int_0^q p(u)du - p(q)q,$$

or the area under sectoral demand curves, net of domestic sales revenues. The second component of domestic welfare is the sum of firm profits across sectors:

$$(2) \qquad n'\pi = n'[\hat{p}y + \hat{P}(I+\hat{s})x - c(x,y)],$$

where a caret expands the vector in question into a diagonal matrix and a prime denotes a transposition. This expression accounts for revenues from domestic and export sales (which may be subsidized) and total cost. The third component of domestic welfare is tariff revenue net of export subsidy outlays, $[t'\hat{P}M - s'\hat{P}\hat{n}x]$. It reflects the direct change in domestic income due to the imposition of trade-distorting measures when world prices are fixed.

The resulting domestic welfare function is then given by

$$(3) \qquad \begin{aligned} W &= g(q) + \hat{n}\pi + t'\hat{P}M - s'\hat{P}\hat{n}x \\ &= g(q) + \hat{n}[\hat{p}y + \hat{P}x - c(x,y)] + t'\hat{P}M. \end{aligned}$$

We are interested primarily in the welfare effects of trade policies in the form of tariffs and export subsidies. Total differentiation of expression 3 gives a decomposition of the welfare effects of trade policy changes:

$$(4) \qquad dW = t'q_p(p_t dt + p_s ds) + n'(I - c_z)\,[(y_p + x_p)p_t dt$$
$$+ (x_s + y_s)ds] - n'(\hat{a} - c_z)\,\hat{z}\hat{n}^{-1}dn.$$

Subscripts denote partial differentiation. So q_p is the Jacobian matrix of price derivatives for domestic demand, and y_p and x_s are matrices of direct supply responses in domestic and export markets. The Jacobian c_z is the marginal cost matrix for domestic production, including (off the diagonal) cost externalities that may be conferred by sectors with increasing returns. The vector $a = \hat{z}^{-1}c(x,y)$ contains sectoral average costs.

The first term on the right side of expression 4 measures the distortionary cost in consumption and is negative when the domestic demand curve slopes downward. We have assumed that imports and domestic goods are imperfect substitutes in use and that domestic goods are imperfect substitutes in domestic and export sales. These assumptions of product differentiation imply that domestic prices are endogenous and can be affected by either tariffs or export subsidies. So, under the assumption that the aggregate demand curve is downward sloping, the first term on the right side of expression 4 indicates welfare losses from consumption distortions due to a tariff (dt), an export subsidy (ds), or a combination of the two. This term corresponds to the standard welfare costs of protection in the case of constant returns to scale.

Scale efficiency effects, which are summarized in the second term on the right side of equation 4, are slightly more complex. Note first that, with normal demand behavior, benefits from protection can arise from expansion of total output in sectors with scale economies. Domestic supply can be expected to rise with domestic prices ($y_p > 0$) and exports with the subsidy rate ($x_s > 0$). However, the net effect of each of these direct supply responses on total sectoral output depends on the extent of intermarket diversion. Rising domestic prices may induce a diversion from exports to an increasingly lucrative domestic market ($x_p < 0$), while subsidies might induce diversion in the opposite direction ($y_s > 0$). The ultimate effect on output depends on the relative magnitudes of the supply and diversion effects ($z_p = y_p + x_p$ and $z_s = x_s + y_s$) and is ultimately an empirical question. What is clear from expression 4, however, is that tariffs and export subsidies can be beneficial if domestic firms' marginal costs are below world prices. Thus, with no firm entry or exit, tariffs and subsidies can be beneficial if the efficiency gains from scale expansion exceed the distortionary costs of protection.

The third term in expression 4 represents the effects on welfare of changes in the number of firms. The negative sign indicates that, where there are scale economies, firm entry is detrimental to welfare and that the magnitude of the welfare loss increases with the degree of unexploited scale economies.

Jaime de Melo and David Roland-Holst

We now pose the question: What would be an optimal choice of tariff and subsidy levels with respect to our domestic welfare function? Given the qualitative symmetry of tariff and subsidy effects, it is unlikely that any policy that implements one without the other could be optimal, but their interplay may be more subtle than simple rules of thumb such as neutrality (equal rates) would imply.

We now derive optimal tariff and subsidy rates in the context of the model already presented. To simplify discussion, we assume that there is no firm entry or exit.

To maximize domestic welfare, we form the Lagrangian expression

$$(5) \qquad L(t,s) = W(t,s) + \lambda[z - F(x,y)] ,$$

which leads to first-order conditions of the form

$$(6) \qquad W_t = t'q_p + n'(I - c_z)\,(y_p + x_p) = \lambda(Z_p - F_x x_p - F_y y_p)$$

and

$$(7) \qquad W_s = t'q_p p_s + n'(I - c_z)\,(x_s + y_s) = \lambda(Z_s - F_x x_s - F_y y_s) .$$

The last two equations can be solved for the vector of optimal tariffs:

$$(8) \qquad t = -\, n'(I - c_z)\, y_p\, q_p^{-1} .$$

This expression shows that the optimal tariff depends on the extent of unexploited scale economies and on the elasticities of supply and demand. Conditions for a nonzero optimal tariff are initial marginal costs below world prices or falling from that level, nonzero elasticity of domestic supply, and finite elasticity of domestic demand. Expression 8 also takes account of interactions across the economy and thus derives consistent optimal policy instruments for all sectors simultaneously.

An optimal tariff-subsidy combination will be one that equates the marginal rate of transformation (MRT) between domestic and export markets with their respective relative prices, that is, one where $MRT = F_x / F_y = p / (1+s)$ in the one-sector case. More generally, the optimal tariff-subsidy combination is given by

$$(9) \qquad (I + s')F_x = \hat{p} F_y.$$

Assuming that the Jacobians F_x and F_y are diagonal, then the optimal export subsidy would be that which exactly equalizes the value of marginal domestic product between the two markets. In the numerical exercises below, we compute the vector of optimal export subsidies for a selected vector of uniform import tariffs.

Modeling Oligopolistic Domestic Markets

Since the analytical results presented above are ambiguous with respect to the effects of trade policy on welfare, we use numerical analysis to reveal the relative importance of factors affecting overall welfare. First, we describe briefly the structure of the CGE model used for the simulation exercises in the remainder of the paper.

As was the case in the analytics of the previous section, the model specifies product differentiation between exports and domestic sales and between imports and domestically produced goods in domestic demand. Again, the country is small in international markets. A Leontief technology is specified for intermediate technology. Within sectors, however, domestic and imported inputs are imperfect substitutes. This assumption of product differentiation is also maintained for sectors with scale economies. In those sectors, goods are produced by n_i identical firms. Thus all goods produced for domestic sale in the same sector are perfect substitutes, allowing us to aggregate sectoral supply across firms. Consumption demand across sectors is described by a linear expenditure system with nonunitary income elasticities of demand. Finally, value added is produced by a constant elasticity of substitution technology for two primary factors of production, capital and labor (mobile across sectors), and there is a Leontief technology between aggregate value added and aggregate intermediates. All final demands arise from a representative consumer, who also receives net tax revenues as a lump-sum income transfer. As in Harris (1984), fixed costs include capital and labor (equal weight on each).

We contrast the case of constant returns to scale (where marginal cost pricing prevails) with two pricing hypotheses in sectors with increasing returns to scale.

In the first alternative, we specify an analogue to the case of perfect competition under constant returns to scale. We assume costless entry / exit, so that the threat of entry forces incumbent firms to price at average cost. In this contestable-market scenario (omitting sectoral subscripts),

$$(10) \qquad p_z = a,$$

for each sector with increasing returns to scale, where p_z is the unit price from the constant elasticity of transformation cost function associated with the transformation function describing sales allocation to the domestic and export markets. Here p_z is the weighted sum of unit sales prices on the domestic (p) and export ($1+s$) markets and a is average costs.

In the second alternative, we assume that each (identical) firm behaves in the domestic market as a monopolist facing a downward-sloping demand curve. In equilibrium, each firms equates marginal revenue with marginal costs (c_z), that is,

$$(11) \qquad \frac{p - c_z}{p} = \frac{\tilde{\Omega}}{n\varepsilon},$$

where ε is the endogenous elasticity of demand on domestic sales given by

$$(12) \qquad \varepsilon = \varepsilon^{F} S^{F} + \varepsilon^{v} S^{v},$$

where $F(v)$ denotes final (intermediate) demand and ε^{F} and ε^{v} are functions of the parameters describing substitution effects in intermediate and final demand. Because equation 12 is part of the system of equations that must be satisfied in equilibrium, ε is endogenous. The variable Ω is the representative firm's conjecture about the response of competitors to its output decision with respect to firm j. That is, if z_{-j} denotes the aggregate output of the remaining firms in its sectors, then $\Omega \equiv \Delta z_{-j} / \Delta z_{j}$. The value of Ω is obtained as follows. By choice of units, n is set equal to unity in expression 11. Since the value of ε is determined by the parameters and quantities in the model, if one takes p and c_{z} as data, then the value of Ω is determined by solving equation 11. We denote by $\tilde{\Omega}$ the value of the calibrated representative firm's conjecture.

We contrast two rules for determining firm entry / exit. Define

$$(13) \qquad \pi \equiv \pi_{y} + \pi_{x},$$

where π is profit per unit of sales and subscripts y and x denote sales to the domestic and export markets, respectively. In the first alternative, firm entry is determined to ensure that profit per unit of total sales is zero. This assumes that export subsidies allow firms to make a profit on export sales. However, since export subsidies are often justified as a way of defraying the cost of opening new markets, it is reasonable to consider the alternative case in which subsidies to export sales do not give rise to higher than normal profits. In this second alternative, firm entry is determined to give zero profit on domestic sales.

One would expect the degree of firm collusion to vary with the number of firms. The fewer the number of firms, the more collusive is behavior likely to be. To capture this effect, we add the following equation to determine conjectures:

$$(14) \qquad \tilde{\Omega} = n^{-1},$$

which completes the description of the model.

A Comparison of Trade Policies Under Constant and Increasing Returns to Scale

We now turn to illustrative numerical calculations based on the model outlined above. All simulations refer to the effects of a departure from free trade in an archetypal semi-industrial economy.[3]

The structure of the economy in the hypothetical free trade solution is described in table 5.1. Of the seven sectors, one is nontradables. The data on sectoral structure indicate an open economy with high trade shares in GDP. Sectoral value

Table 5.1   Sectoral Features of the Semi-Industrial Economy

Sector	Share in gross output (%)	Exports/ output (%)	Imports/ domestic sales (%)	Elasticity of substitution in production	Export supply elasticity[a]	Import elasticity of demand[a]	Cost dis- advantage ratio[b]	Domestic price elasticity of demand
Primary	8.9	4.9	40.4	2.5	0.75	1.8	--	--
Food products	9.6	2.5	6.5	1.5	1.5	2.5	--	--
Consumer goods	14.4	32.5	14.2	1.0	1.5	2.4	0.1	1.6
Producer goods	20.1	16.6	19.2	0.9	1.5	2.2	0.1	1.3
Heavy industry	7.7	31.9	41.0	0.9	1.5	1.9	0.1	1.4
Traded services	13.2	24.4	7.5	1.5	1.5	2.0	--	--
Nontraded services	26.1	--	--	0.9	--	--	--	--

a. Expenditure-compensated price elasticities. For imports (exports), expenditures (sales) on constant elasticity of substitution (transformation) aggregate of domestic and import (export) goods held constant.

b. The cost disadvantage ratio (difference between average and marginal costs divided by average cost) is a measure of unrealized economies of scale.

added ratios are quite low, indicating the strong interindustry linkages observed in a semi-industrial economy. The three sectors with increasing returns to scale account for 42 percent of gross output, 73 percent of export sales, and 51 percent of import expenses. For the simulations in this section, we assume a low and uniform cost-disadvantage ratio of 10 percent in sectors with economies of scale.[4]

Table 5.2 gives the results of simulations comparing the effects of tariff protection and export subsidization. All simulations refer to 10-percent tariff and 10-percent export subsidy rates. We contrast four scenarios: constant returns to scale (CRTS) across all sectors, contestable-market pricing for the three sectors with increasing returns to scale, and Cournot competition with total profit or domestic profit determining firm entry. The results presented in table 5.2 are for protection or export subsidization of (1) sectors with constant returns to scale only (primary, food processing, and traded services); (2) sectors with increasing returns only (consumer goods, producer goods, and heavy industry); or (3) all traded sectors.

Two measures of the welfare effects of changes in trade policy are reported in table 5.2. The equivalent variation measure is derived from the indirect utility function associated with the Stone-Geary utility function assumed for final demand. It is an aggregate measure of efficiency gains and losses in production and of efficiency losses in consumption. Equivalent variation measures how much the representative consumer would have to be compensated at the new set of prices to be indifferent to the bundle of goods now available at the initial set of prices. The second measure is the scale efficiency gain or loss from moving along average cost curves.[5] Like equivalent variation, scale efficiency evaluates the new output level at old prices, so that the measure controls for shifts in the average cost curve induced by changes in factor and product prices.

Now let us examine the results presented in table 5.2. Consider first the results under constant returns to scale in the first three columns. In the case of tariff protection, there is a welfare loss from protection regardless of which group of sectors is protected. As expected, the welfare cost of protection increases with the number of sectors being protected. Note that the corresponding welfare loss estimates for export subsidization yield very similar orders of magnitude, with the differences depending on trade volumes and substitution elasticities.

Turn now to the case of contestable-market pricing, which assumes increasing returns to scale for the consumer goods, producer goods, and heavy industry sectors. Now protection of sectors with constant returns to scale is much more costly because of scale efficiency losses when resources are pulled out of sectors with scale economies. The loss of scale efficiency occurs because firms are forced to produce higher up on their average cost curves. By contrast, protection of sectors with increasing returns to scale is much less costly because of the scale efficiency gain. Note, however, that even though protection is provided across the board for sectors with increasing returns to scale, there is a scale efficiency loss in one sector. Finally, protecting all sectors results in a larger welfare loss than under the scenario of constant returns to scale in all sectors because of scale efficiency losses.

Table 5.2 Comparison of the Welfare Effects of Tariffs and Export Subsidies under Different Pricing Conditions

Sector	CRTS			Contestable[a]			Cournot (total profit)[b]			Cournot (domestic profit)[c]		
	CRTS	IRTS	All	CRTS	IRTS	All	CRTS	IRTS	All	CRTS	IRTS	All
Ten-percent tariff												
Equivalent variation	-7	-9	-12	-50	-2	-46	12	60	78	-33	-30	-57
Scale efficiency (total)				-42	6	-34	19	69	88	-27	-22	-47
Producer goods				-14	-8	-21	9	33	42	-7	-8	-14
Consumer goods				-24	15	-8	8	15	23	-3	-6	-8
Heavy industry				-4	-1	-5	2	21	23	-3	-6	-8
Firm entry (+) / exit (-)												
Producer goods							-5	-9	-14	-1	2	1
Consumer goods							-5	-1	-5	-1	4	4
Heavy industry							-2	-1	-12	0	4	4
Ten-percent export subsidy												
Equivalent variation	-6	-19	-13	-45	52	27	52	-168	-108	18	15	36
Scale efficiency (total)				-39	74	42	57	-155	-97	24	25	46
Producer goods				-14	38	26	23	-69	-46	8	7	14
Consumer goods				-15	22	10	21	-48	-27	12	14	24
Heavy industry				-10	14	6	13	-38	-24	4	4	8
Firm entry(+) / exit (-)												
Producer goods							-8	23	15	-4	2	-1
Consumer goods							-6	11	6	-4	0	-4
Heavy industry							-9	22	13	-5	1	-4

Note: CRTS = constant returns to scale; IRTS = increasing returns to scale. All figures are basis points. Figures for equivalent variation and scale efficiency are basis points of GDP (e.g., -168 is 1.68% of GDP); figures for entry/exit are basis points of initial number of firms.

a. Pricing according to equation 10.

b. Pricing according to equation 11, with firm entry / exit determined by total profits, so that $\pi = 0$.

c. Same as note b but with firm entry determined by profits on domestic sales, so that $\pi_y = 0$.

Jaime de Melo and David Roland-Holst

Now, compare these results with those for export subsidization in the bottom half of the table. The subsidization results corroborate Balassa's assertion that specialization according to comparative advantage enables the disadvantages of small national markets to be surmounted in sectors with unexploited economies of scale. As before, the benefits are greatest when trade policy is confined to sectors with increasing returns to scale. The export subsidization effects dominate the tariff protection effects because of the difficulty of substituting away from imports when incentives are provided to domestic producers, and the ease of expanding sales in international markets when market share is small.

When contestable market pricing is replaced by Cournot competition, the welfare effects of trade policy are affected by three additional adjustment mechanisms: firm entry / exit (the mechanism that achieves zero profits in long-run equilibrium), the endogeneity of firm collusion, and — generally less significant — the anticompetitive effect of protection, which lowers the elasticity of domestic demand, ε.[6]

The most important of these mechanisms influencing the welfare effects of trade policy under Cournot competition is the pattern of firm entry or exit. Take the case of tariff protection, which raises the profitability of domestic sales and lowers the profitability of export sales because of induced appreciation in the real exchange rate. If firm entry or exit depends on the joint profitability of sales in both markets, then there is firm exit because sectors with increasing returns to scale happen to have high export shares in our numerical example. Firm exit allows the remaining firms to move down their average cost curves, thereby reaping the benefits of more efficient scale. If, however, one assumes that firm entry is governed by profits from sales in the domestic market alone, then there is firm entry and protection results in a welfare loss because of the loss in scale efficiency.

By symmetry, a policy of subsidizing exports has opposite effects. Export subsidization leads to crowding-in if the decision to enter depends on total profits because export subsidies lead to large profits on export sales. For the case of export subsidization of sectors with increasing returns to scale, the welfare loss amounts to 1.7 percent of GDP. If, on the other hand, one assumes that export subsidies do not give rise to abnormal profits but rather contribute to defraying the costs (and risks) of selling in new markets, there is a small welfare gain. Interestingly, in the case of export subsidization in sectors with scale economies there is a scale efficiency gain despite some firm entry.

The results presented in table 5.2 clearly show that if Cournot competition is a reasonable representation of behavior in sectors with increasing returns to scale, firm entry and exit are crucial in determining the sign and magnitude of the effects of trade policy interventions. For the illustrative trade policy interventions reported in table 5.2, one could argue that entry behavior based on total profits is the more reasonable assumption. However, one can interpret a policy of protection more broadly as one that produces home-market bias because it usually involves quotas and nontariff barriers that create barriers to entry as competition from abroad is suppressed. Then a sheltered domestic market is likely to lead to excessive firm entry because of high profits.[7]

On the other hand, the experience of successful East Asian exporters suggests that it was the provision of export incentives that put domestic producers on an equal footing with their foreign competitors. As argued by Frischtak et al. (1989, 10-11), exporters need support to make the commitment to riskier activities that have a long lead time and sunk costs for identifying suitable markets and setting up distribution channels. Under this interpretation of the costs of establishing successful export activities, subsidies (or incentives that increase the relative profitability of exports) are not likely to give rise to abnormally high profits and hence to induce excessive entry.

An alternative interpretation would emphasize that the appropriate policy in a setting of increasing returns to scale is to promote competition in domestic markets. This logic recognizes that imperfect competition in domestic markets can act as an export barrier by increasing the relative profitability of domestic operations. Ideally, industrial policy would be coordinated with trade policy to encourage the exploitation of efficient scale, promoting exports while avoiding excessive entry.[8]

Evaluation of Protection in Sectors with Scale Economies

We return to the issues raised in the introduction: Are there welfare gains from protecting sectors with increasing returns to scale, and how does import protection compare with neutral incentives (for example, with tariffs and export subsidies at equal rates)? To answer these questions, we report on simulations in which we contrast across-the-board tariffs of 15 percent with across-the-board export subsidies of 15 percent, both in sectors with scale economies. Protection and export subsidies are confined to the consumer, producer, and capital goods sectors. Now we assume a cost-disadvantage ratio of 20 percent, a value more in line with the unexploited economies of scale in the manufacturing sector of a typical semi-industrial country. The results of these simulations appear in table 5.3. In the constant-returns-to-scale benchmark case, there is, as before, a welfare loss from protection alone or from export subsidization alone. Neutrality, however, is less costly because the distortion introduced by the export subsidy partly offsets the distortion introduced by the tariff.

The same pattern of welfare estimates emerges under the assumption of contestable markets. However, because we have assumed a greater degree of unexploited economies of scale, the magnitudes are larger than in table 5.2. There is a welfare gain of 2.7 percent of base year GDP to be reaped from subsidizing export sales of sectors with increasing returns to scale. Note the superiority of export subsidization over import protection, which springs from our assumption that exporters face a perfectly elastic foreign demand whereas domestically produced goods face a downward sloping domestic demand curve. Hence the incentives created by export subsidization are more direct than those created by

Jaime de Melo and David Roland-Holst

Table 5.3 Protection and Subsidization of Sectors with Increasing Returns to Scale
(cost-disadvantage ratio of 20 percent)

Protection/subsidy	*CRTS*	*Contestable* [a]	*Cournot (domestic profit)* [b]
15-percent tariff			
Equivalent variation	-18	12	-106
Scale efficiency	0	31	-88
15-percent export subsidy			
Equivalent variation	-42	274	86
Scale efficiency	0	336	110
15-percent tariff and export subsidy			
Equivalent variation	-31	281	4
Scale efficiency	0	322	27

Note: CRTS is constant returns to scale. All figures are basis points of GDP (e.g., -106 is -1.06 percent of GDP).
a. Pricing according to equation 10.
b. Pricing according to equation 11, with firm entry and exit determined by profits on domestic sales, so that $\pi_y = 0$.

protection for domestic sales. While the export demand specification deserves further scrutiny, it appears to correspond to the experience of countries that have followed an export-led development strategy.

In the contestable-market scenario, neutrality produces the largest welfare gains from trade incentives to sectors with increasing returns to scale and sustains the recommendations of Balassa (1975, 1989). In the case of Cournot competition, under the assumptions about firm entry, subsidization of exports dominates the alternative of providing equal incentives to domestic and export sales. This occurs because we have assumed that subsidies to exports do not give rise to profits (and hence do not induce firm entry) whereas protection on the domestic market gives rise to profits and induces firm entry. As we saw above, firm entry results in scale efficiency losses, an effect that comes out clearly in the case of protection to domestic sales. In that case, tariff protection results in a welfare loss that exceeds 1 percent of GDP.

It is obvious that the results under Cournot competition are quite sensitive to the determinants of the number of firms — about which little is known. In the simulations reported here, we have attempted to portray the stylized facts suggested by the comparative studies of foreign trade regimes in developing countries. These studies reveal that countries that have followed import-substitution industrialization strategies have often tended to provide made-to-measure protection for all domestic activities. This protection has, in turn, tended to create excess profit opportunities from domestic sales. When pushed to the extreme, excessive across-the-board protection of industrial activities has been shown to result in excessive firm entry.

We conclude by comparing neutrality of incentives with optimal trade policy. The "optimal" trade policy package is obtained by maximizing the value of the utility function for the representative consumer, taking tariffs as given and export subsidies as endogenous policy instruments. To facilitate the comparison with the results in table 5.2, we fix all import tariffs at 10 percent for all sectors.

The results of the calculation of these "optimal" trade policy packages appear in table 5.4. Note first that under the assumption of constant returns to scale in all sectors, the numerical calculations confirm the well-known results predicted by Lerner (1936), namely that across-the-board tariff and export subsidies at the same rates are equivalent to free trade.[9] Note also that the equivalent variation measure achieves a maximum of zero in this case because departure from free trade cannot be beneficial under constant returns to scale.

Table 5.4 Optimal Export Subsidies for a Given Ten-Percent Import Tariff on All Tradables
(cost-disadvantage ratio of 10 percent)

	CTRS	Contestable	Cournot (domestic profit)[a]
Equivalent variation	0	66 (58)[b]	55 (-6)[b]
Scale efficiency (total)		128	102
Producer goods		54	32
Consumer goods		49	52
Heavy industry		24	18
Firm entry			
Producer goods			-4
Consumer goods			-12
Heavy industry			-11
Export subsidy			
Primary products	10	-6	62
Food processing	10	-1	36
Producer goods	10	24	33
Consumer goods	10	27	25
Heavy industry	10	25	41
Traded services	10	-1	41

Note: The subsidy is in percentage points. Other figures are in basis points.
a. Pricing according to equation 11, with firm entry determined by profits on domestic sales, so that $\pi_y = 0$.
b. Corresponding equivalent variation figure under neutrality, that is, from combining a 10-percent import tariff with a 10-percent export subsidy in sectors with increasing returns to scale.

Jaime de Melo and David Roland-Holst

Under increasing returns to scale, Lerner symmetry still holds: across-the-board tariffs and export subsidies at the same rate are equivalent to free trade. But, as the pattern of export subsidy figures shows, neutrality is no longer optimal. Two results stand out in the contestable-market case. First, as expected, optimality requires that greater incentives be provided to sectors with increasing returns to scale. Second, the difference in welfare benefits is small between optimal trade policy and the rules of thumb advocated by Balassa (1975, 1989) — across-the-board protection (with equal incentives to exports) for manufacturing activities. Here, optimality dominates the rule of thumb of incentive neutrality by less than 10 basis points. Given the notorious lack of the precise elasticity estimates needed to calculate optimal incentives, the illustrative calculations here do not support a departure from the rule of thumb advocated by Balassa.

In the case of Cournot competition, however, the optimal pattern of export subsidies departs further from neutrality. Under this scenario, an optimal policy would encourage firm exit to reap scale economies. As the figures in the last column of table 5.4 indicate, firm exit would be achieved by providing higher export subsidies to sectors with constant returns to scale.[10] Now departure from a simple rule of thumb yields larger welfare benefits. However, the discussion of table 5.2 suggested that the results under Cournot competition are very sensitive to the determinants of firm entry, so these results should be interpreted with care.

Conclusion

This paper set out to test the robustness of Balassa's recommendation of neutral incentives to domestic and export sales in a setting where some sectors have domestic market power. We have shown analytically that the welfare effects of trade policy are more complex than they are in a setting of across-the-board constant returns to scale. In particular, we have shown, analytically and numerically, that the standard distortionary costs of protection emphasized under conditions of constant returns to scale must be amended to accommodate, among other things, the welfare effects of changes in scale efficiency. Illustrative numerical calculations also show that the magnitude of the welfare gains or losses from trade policy intervention are sensitive to the determinants of firm entry and exit.

Calculations comparing trade policies that achieve neutrality of incentives between sales to domestic and those to foreign markets found such policies to be generally superior to policies creating non-neutral incentives. Numerical results also suggest that export promotion is likely to be more beneficial than protection for sectors with increasing returns to scale. Finally, illustrative calculations of optimal trade policy packages suggest that the benefits of departing from the principle of neutrality, or nondiscrimination between domestic and export sales, may be insufficient to justify their higher administrative costs.

Notes

The research reported here is part of the World Bank research project "Industrial Competition, Productive Efficiency and Their Relation to Trade Regimes" (RPO 674-46). The numerical work is based on a model developed in de Melo and Tarr (forthcoming). The views expressed here are those of the authors and should not be attributed to their affiliated institutions.

1. See Harris (1989) and Helpman and Krugman (1989) for surveys of this work.
2. Imperfect substitutability in the allocation of sales implies that F_{xi} / F_{yi} varies along a convex transformation frontier. Lower-case letters indicate partial derivatives.
3. The archetypal economy was obtained from the free trade solution of a seven-sector CGE model calibrated to the Korean economy for the year 1982. For a description of the data set and parameters values, see de Melo and Roland-Holst (forthcoming).
4. The cost-disadvantage ratio is the difference between average and marginal costs, divided by average costs. It is a measure of unrealized economies of scale.
5. The aggregate scale efficiency measure is calculated by using current outputs as weights. For further discussion, see de Melo and Roland-Holst (forthcoming).
6. The magnitude of this effect is small for the functional forms specified here and is not reported. For a discussion of its magnitude, see de Melo and Roland-Holst (forthcoming). Also, see Devarajan and Rodrik (1989).
7. Frischtak et al. (1989) document the pervasive barriers to competition in the manufacturing sectors of developing countries. Eastman and Stykolt (1962) is an early example of a model in which protection leads to firm entry. The typical example is the automobile industry in Latin America (see Baranson 1968).
8. In this regard, the Korean experience during the 1970s is instructive. An activist industrial policy was successful in promoting the growth of large conglomerates and reaping the benefits of scale economies. While exports benefited from this policy, oligopolistic markets developed, and a vigorous antitrust policy was established in the early 1980s to promote greater competition in domestic markets. For further discussion, see Lee, Urata, and Choi (1988) and World Bank (1987).
9. Since there is no guarantee that the optimal vector of subsidies is unique, numerical verification of Lerner symmetry is a useful computational check.
10. While the results of these optimal calculations appear reasonable, there is no guarantee that the computed optima are global optima rather than local optima. Hence these results should be viewed as suggestive and subject to further scrutiny.

References

Balassa, B. 1975. "Reforming the System of Incentives in Developing Countries." *World Development* 3 (June): 365-81.

Balassa, B. 1989. *Tariff Policy and Taxation in Developing Countries.* PPR Working Paper No. 281. Washington, D.C.: World Bank.

Balassa, B., and Associates. 1971. *The Structure of Protection in Developing Countries.* Baltimore, Md.: Johns Hopkins University Press.

Balassa, B., and Associates. 1982. *Development Strategies for Semi-Industrial Countries.* Baltimore, Md.: Johns Hopkins University Press.

Baranson, J. 1968. *The Automotive Industry in Latin America.* Praeger: New York.

Bergsman, J. 1974. "Commercial Policy, Allocative Efficiency and X-Efficiency." *Quarterly Journal of Economics* 88: 409-33.

Jaime de Melo and David Roland-Holst

Brander, J., and B. Spencer. 1984. "Tariff Protection and Imperfect Competition." In H. Kierzkowski, ed., *Monopolistic Competition in International Trade.* Oxford: Oxford University Press.

Chenery, H. 1975. "The Structuralist Approach to Development Policy." *American Economic Review* 65: 310-16.

Corden, M. 1967. "Monopoly, Tariffs and Subsidies." *Economica* 34: 50-8.

Devarajan, S., and D. Rodrik. 1989. "Pro-competitive Effects of Tariff Reform." Working Paper, J.F. Kennedy School of Government, Harvard University, Cambridge, Mass.

Dixit, A.K. 1984. "International Trade Policy for Oligopoly Industries." *Economic Journal* 94: 1-16.

Eastman, H., and S. Stykolt. 1962. "A Model for the Study of Protected Industries." *Economic Journal* 70: 336-47.

Frischtak, C., with B. Hadjimichael and U. Zachan. 1989. *Competition Policies for Industrializing Countries.* Policy and Research Series No. 7. Washington, D.C.: World Bank.

Harris, R.G. 1984. "Applied General Equilibrium Analyses of Small Open Economies with Scale Economies and Imperfect Competition." *American Economic Review* 74: 1016-33.

Harris, R.G. 1989. "The New Protectionism Revisited." *Canadian Journal of Economics* 24: 751-78.

Helpman, E., and P. Krugman. 1989. *Trade Policy and Market Structure.* Cambridge, Mass.: MIT Press.

Horstmann, I., and J. Markusen. 1986. "Up the Average Cost Curve: Inefficient Entry and the New Protectionism." *Journal of International Economics* 20: 225-48.

Krugman, P. 1984. "Import Protection as Export Promotion." In H. Kierzkowski, ed., *Monopolistic Competition in International Trade.* Oxford: Oxford University Press.

Lee, K., S. Urata, and I. Choi. 1988. "Recent Developments in Industrial Organization in Korea." World Bank, Washington, D.C.

Lerner, A. 1936. "The Symmetry Between Import and Export Taxes." *Economica* 3: 306-13.

Melo, J. de, and D.W. Roland-Holst. Forthcoming. "Industrial Organization and Trade Liberalization: Evidence from Korea." In R.E. Baldwin, ed., *Empirical Studies of Commercial Policy.* Chicago: University of Chicago Press.

Melo, J. de, and D. Tarr. Forthcoming. *A General Equilibrium Analysis of U.S. Foreign Trade Policy.* Cambridge, Mass.: MIT Press.

Rodrik, D. 1988. "Imperfect Competition, Scale Economies, and Trade Policy in Developing Countries." In R.E. Baldwin, ed., *Trade Policy Issues and Empirical Analysis.* Chicago: University of Chicago Press.

Venables, A. 1985. "Trade and Trade Policy with Imperfect Competition: The Case of Identical Products and Free Entry." *Journal of International Economics* 19: 1-19.

World Bank. 1987. *Korea: Managing the Industrial Transition.* Washington, D.C.

10

Industrial Organization and Trade Liberalization: Evidence from Korea

Jaime de Melo and David Roland-Holst

10.1 Introduction

The theory of industrial organization has exerted a strong influence on trade theory and commercial policy in recent years. At a theoretical level, the welfare implications of trade policy in the presence of unexploited economies of scale, exit and entry barriers, and oligopolistic markets are now better understood. Concurrent with the flow of new theoretical contributions,[1] a number of case studies, mostly partial equilibrium, have sought to evaluate the welfare and resource allocation effects of trade liberalization in sectors like autos where the above characteristics are an important feature of industrial organization.[2] Most case studies have been for developed countries, yet it is in developing countries, particularly the emerging so-called semi-industrial countries, that the interaction of unexploited economies of scale and oligopolistic market structures is likely to be greatest.[3]

A case in point is the Republic of Korea. Following a drive to develop heavy and chemical industries in the mid-1970s, Korea found itself with an

Jaime de Melo is an economist at the World Bank, teaches at the University of Geneva, and is a fellow of the CEPR. David Roland-Holst teaches at Mills College and was visiting at the U.S. International Trade Commission when this paper was written.

This paper draws on joint work with David Tarr. We thank Robert Baldwin, Drusilla Brown, Dani Rodrik, and Marie Thursby for comments on an earlier draft, and Maria Ameal for logistic support. This paper is part of a research project, "Industrial Competition, Productive Efficiency, and Their Relation to Trade Regimes," funded by the World Bank (RPO 674-46). The views expressed here are those of the authors, not their affiliated institutions.

1. Early contributions include Corden (1967) and Snape (1977). Major contributions in the new literature are surveyed in Helpman and Krugman (1985, 1989), and in the edited volumes by Kierkowski (1984) and Krugman (1988). For a recent survey, see Harris (1989).

2. See, for example, Dixit (1988) and Smith and Venables (1988).

3. Developing country case studies include Bergsman (1974), Rodrik (1988), Gunasekera and Tyers (1988), Devarajan and Rodrik (1989a, 1989b), and Condon and de Melo (1991).

287

288   Jaime de Melo and David Roland-Holst

---

extremely concentrated domestic industrial structure in the early 1980s, when it embarked on cautious trade liberalization. Government policies had not only erected entry barriers into those sectors in the hands of conglomerates but also conferred a high level of protection from import competition. In many ways Korea resembles the ideal case so often referred to in the recent research on trade policy in imperfectly competitive environments. Indeed the evidence we review in this paper indicates that protection in sectors with unexploited economies of scale erected entry barriers, which in turn allowed firms to exploit market power. What then would be the effects of an across-the-board trade liberalization in this environment?

In this paper, we apply a computable general equilibrium (CGE) model developed in de Melo and Tarr (forthcoming) to assess the welfare and resource allocation effects of trade liberalization in Korea. A CGE model is particularly relevant for such an exercise because of the relatively high and dispersed protection in the Korean economy and because of the importance of economies of scale in several sectors. Our calculations are derived from a seven-sector model calibrated to 1982, a year that has especially good protection estimates. Three sectors—consumer goods, producer goods, and heavy industry—are calibrated to increasing returns to scale (IRTS). In some simulations, in line with the empirical evidence, we allow these sectors to earn supernormal profits when protected. To anticipate our results, the welfare gains from a move to free trade reach up to 10 percent of GDP, an estimate tenfold larger than the corresponding gains under constant returns to scale (CRTS). Even if, when protected, these sectors cannot earn above normal profits, our estimates of the welfare gains reach up to 5 percent of GDP.

Our results stand in sharp contrast to other estimates of the costs of protection, one exception being the work of Harris (1984) on Canada. To judge the plausibility of these results, one must question whether our model of the Korean industrial organization structure is a reasonable one. Therefore, in section 10.2 we go into some detail on recent Korean industrial organization and industrial policies, as we believe they provide good support for our modeling of trade policy in the Korean environment. Section 10.3 discusses our modeling of imperfectly competitive markets and how we calibrated the model to 1982 data. Results are in section 10.4 and conclusions follow in section 10.5.

10.2   Trade Policies, Industrial Structure, and Industrial Organization Policies in Korea

Until the move to a sectoral development strategy focusing on heavy and chemical industries (HCIs) between 1973 and 1979, Korea's outward-oriented strategy was predicated on superior organizational ability and emphasis in development of labor-intensive activities. During this early phase (prior to 1973), Korea's innovative policies included a rationalized exchange rate regime, strong export incentives, selective import liberalization, directed credit, and a host of finely tuned export promotion instruments. A key feature of that phase was high protection of the domestic market in industries in which Korea did not face favorable international prospects, combined with low protection in industries where Korean products were competitive. As a result, unlike many other countries following an active industrialization strategy, Korea offered little incentive for industries producing exportables to keep them at home. Examples of heavily protected sectors (effective protection rates for 1968 in parenthesis) were transport equipment (163 percent), durable construction (64 percent), and machinery (44 percent).

The shift toward HCIs was achieved by directing to these sectors up to four-fifths of manufacturing investment credit, usually at preferential rates, by providing protection, and by encouraging the development of conglomerates ("Jaebol"). These policies recognized that most industries favored by the HCI drive have large economies of scale and hence that efficient production implied capacities well beyond the scale of the domestic market. However, this shift from a broad, export-led strategy toward a more typical sector orientation had some undesirable side effects, including underutilized capacity and a sharp decline in the incremental output-capital ratio, effects that eventually led to a return toward greater industrial neutrality and cautious import liberalization starting in 1979. Nonetheless, it should be recognized that the HCI drive achieved many objectives, including the target of 50 percent of export sales for the HCIs and the successful transition to an economy fully based on modern technology by a leapfrog strategy with respect to technological requirements during the HCI drive.[4]

A legacy of the HCI drive, however, has been an extremely concentrated industrial structure by international standards (see table 10.1, panel A). For example, in 1982, the top fifty Korean firms accounted for 37 percent of total sales, while the corresponding figure for Japan is 27 percent for the top one hundred firms and for Taiwan 16 percent for the top fifty firms. Furthermore, the percentage of sales classified as "competitive" (three-firm concentration ratio less than 60 percent), which has been relatively low since 1970, declined as a result of the HCI drive.[5]

Various factors led to accelerated economic concentration. The introduction of mass production techniques into a small domestic market at a relatively early stage of development allowed conglomerates to accumulate stocks of superior human and physical capital while they were protected from domestic and international competition by various institutional barriers erected to limit new entry into the market. In addition, sometimes the government's economic policy intensified concentration. During the HCI drive, overlapping investment was prevented in the most important industrial branches. Furthermore, Lee, Urata, and Choi (1988) conclude that the protection and incentive poli-

---

4. For further discussion of the HCI drive see World Bank (1987).
5. The market share of the twenty leading Jaebol continued to rise until the early 1980s.

290　　Jaime de Melo and David Roland-Holst

Table 10.1　　　Commodity Market Structure and Performance in Korean Manufacturing

---

A. Commodity Market Structure, 1982[a]

	Monopoly	Duopoly	Oligopoly	Competitive	Total
Number of	533	251	1,071	405	2260
commodities	(23.6)	(11.1)	(47.4)	(17.9)	(100)
Sales	5,649	3,275	24,967	15,481	49,372
(billion won)	(11.4)	(6.6)	(50.6)	(31.4)	(100)

B. Performance of Different Market Structures (average of 1978 and 1983)

	Monopoly/ Oligopoly	Competitive	Protected	Less Protected	High Export Share	Low Export Share
Price cost margin[b] (mean)	29.0	26.0	34.0	24.0	25.0	29.0

Note: Monopoly if $CR1 > 80$ percent, $S1/S2 < 10$; duopoly if $CR2 > 80$ percent, $S1/S2 < 5$, $S3 < 5$ percent; oligopoly if $CR3 > 60$ percent (monopoly and duopoly excluded); competitive if $CR3 > 60$ percent, where CRi inicates i-firm concentration ratio, and Si indicates area of largest ith firm.

Source: K. Lee, S. Urata, and I. Choi, "Recent Developments in industrial organization in Korea," World Bank Working Paper (Washington, D.C., 1988), tables 3 and 8.

[a]Numbers in parentheses are percentages; totals sum to 100.

[b]Percent; PCM is calculated as value of sales less labor costs divided by value of sales ($\times$ 100).

cies, including taxation, banking, and commercial policy measures, operated almost exclusively to the advantage of the conglomerates.

Many observers of Korea agree that conglomerates exercise market power on domestic sales. However, the data in table 10.1, panel B, suggest that sectors competing in international markets (i.e., sectors with high export shares and/or low rates of protection) price more competitively.[6] One way of finding out if this is so is by cross-section regressions linking performance with structure. Such regressions, traditionally carried out by industrial organization economists, attempt to isolate the effects of industry structure on sectoral average price-cost margin (PCMs) after controlling for other factors affecting the PCM, such as differences in technology across sectors. In the Korean case, estimates by Lee, Urata, and Choi (1988) for sixty-five manufacturing sectors for 1983 show that, after controlling for capital intensity, R&D expenditures (and other factors), the PCM is positively (and significantly) related to concentration.[7] More interestingly, they also find a statisti-

---

6. Mean price-cost margins (PCMs) for protected sectors were a third higher than for less protected sectors in 1982.

7. The positive correlation between PCM and concentration does not necessarily support the "structuralist view" that sees in this relationship rent-seeking behavior by oligopolistic firms. It

291   Industrial Organization and Trade Liberalization

---

cally significant negative correlation between PCMs and import shares in domestic sales, suggesting that imports exert a discipline on the pricing of domestic firms.[8] These authors also note that the pace of import liberalization was accelerated in markets dominated by a few firms.

Perhaps the most telling indication that regulation of market structure became a major concern for Korean industrial policy comes from the vigorous enforcement of the Monopoly Regulation Act of 1981. About 10 percent of firms designated by the government as dominating their respective markets were accused of having their market position. Administrative recommendations and orders were issued to trade associations that had clauses permitting undue concerting activities in their articles of incorporation. Over two hundred cases in violation of the provisions against unfair trade practices were leveled between 1981 and 1985. Moreover, 35 percent of the 2,600 applications for international agreements during this period were judged to contain provisions restricting competition or involving unfair trade practices and had to be revised.

Two stylized facts emerge from this discussion and from the data in table 10.1. First, Korea appears to have achieved a very concentrated industrial structure by the early 1980s, as a legacy of the HCI drive when industrial policy discouraged firm entry. Second, the evidence suggests that, after controlling for other factors, highly protected sectors were earning above normal profits. By creating barriers to entry, protection allowed conglomerates to exercise market power. These stylized facts are incorporated in the model outlined below.

10.3.   Modeling Imperfectly Competitive Domestic Markets[9]

On the basis of the evidence discussed above, we concentrate on modeling the implications of imperfectly competitive behavior in domestic markets in sectors with IRTS. At the same time, in the absence of evidence to the contrary, we assume that Korean exports are sold in competitive world markets. We also assume that Korea is a small economy in the markets in which it trades. This implies that there are no induced terms-of-trade effects from changes in trade policy. While this small-country assumption may be debatable for a few export markets in which Korea competes, it has the great advantage of simplifying the interpretation of welfare calculations and, in any case, could be relaxed without difficulty as in de Melo and Tarr (forthcoming).

---

could also reflect the superior performance of large firms according to the "efficiency-based view." However, in the case of Korea, evidence indicates that the efficiency of small and medium-sized firms had caught up with that of large firms by the end of the 1970s. See Kim (1985).

8. This result is known in the industrial organization literature as the "import discipline" hypothesis. See the symposia led by Caves (1980) and Geroski and Jacquemin (1981).

9. For a fuller description of the model, see de Melo and Tarr (forthcoming).

Apart from the treatment of imperfect competition discussed below, the CGE model is quite standard. In this application two primary factors, labor and capital, are in fixed supply but mobile between sectors. Intersectoral mobility leads to equal rewards across sectors for each type of factor. Domestic demand includes two components, final and intermediate. The government collects (and distributes in lump sum) revenues from tariff collection.

Substitution possibilities in production and demand are summarized in figure 10.1. Production possibilities are parametrized by assuming CES functions for value-added and Leontief functions between intermediates (as a whole) and value added, as well as within intermediates. However, within each sector, intermediate demand is a CES function between the domestically produced intermediate and the competing foreign intermediate. To give an example, no substitution in purchases is allowed between consumer goods and producer goods, but substitution in purchases is allowed between domestically produced consumer goods and foreign-produced consumer goods when their relative prices change as a result of a change in trade policy. Likewise in consumption demand, the demand system derived from the Stone-Geary utility indicator allows for nonunitary income elasticities of demand and nonzero cross-price elasticities of demand between domestically produced and foreign-produced consumption good.

Traded goods are imperfect substitutes by country of origin (CES assumption). In each sector, goods produced domestically are imperfect substitutes for imports. As in the case analyzed by Snape (1977), changes in trade policy will shift the demand curve of domestic firms. Likewise, goods supplied on the domestic market are imperfect substitutes for goods supplied for export (CET assumption). The implications of this treatment of foreign trade with production differentiation on the import and export sides is analyzed in greater detail in de Melo and Robinson (1989), where it is shown that the domestic country's foreign offer curve has the usual shape.

For sectors with IRTS, goods are produced by N_i identical firms. All goods produced for domestic sales in the same sector are perfect substitutes, allowing us to aggregate sectoral demand and supplies. The assumption that product differentiation is modeled at the national level rather than at the firm level has three implications for the welfare estimates reported below. First, because all domestic firms are identical and supply a homogeneous product, one cannot capture product variety and hence we may underestimate the benefits of trade liberalization as additional product variety occurs. Second, the assumption of national product differentiation implies that the domestic firms' perceived elasticity of demand (defined below in eq. [3]) only depends on the number of competing domestic firms rather than on the total number of competing firms in the world. Our numerical results, however, show that the value of the perceived elasticity of demand is quite insensitive to firm entry/exit. Third, the assumption of national product differentiation implies that adjustment to achieve zero profits occurs by firm entry/exit. In the case of firm entry,

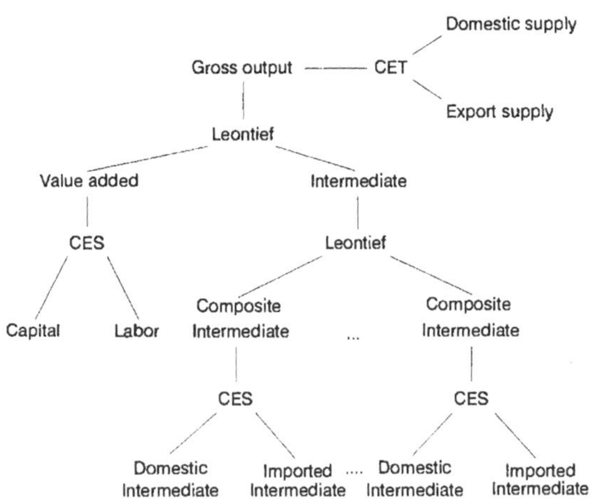

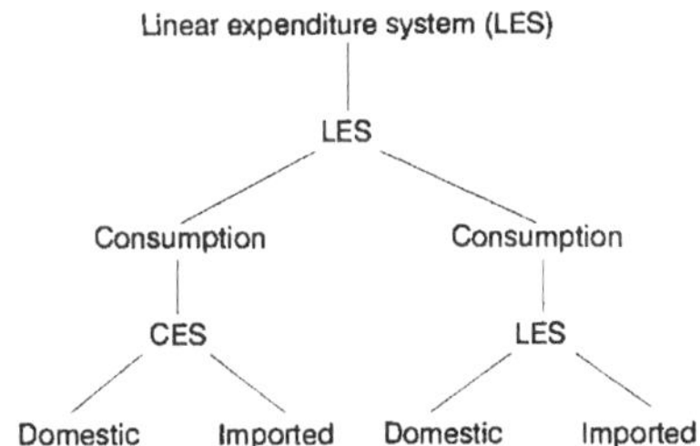

Fig. 10.1   Model structure

one gets market fragmentation that may overstate scale inefficiency.[10] If Korean firms are indeed "small" in the market in which they compete, an increase in the number of Korean firms would have little effect on their demand. Hence adjustment to zero profits would occur by an alternative mechanism. One possible adjustment is that which occurs when incumbent firms price competitively, just covering average costs.

In view of these implications of the national product differentiation assumption, we shall contrast two pricing hypotheses in IRTS sectors against the alternative of CRTS where marginal cost pricing prevails. Furthermore, we

---

10. For an approach that relies on product differentiation at the firm level see Brown and Stern (1989).

shall consider for each pricing hypothesis the possibility that protection, by creating barriers to entry, allows for supernormal profits.

10.3.1   Contestable Market Pricing

In the first alternative, we specify an analogue to the case of perfect competition under CRTS. We assume costless entry/exit, so that the threat of entry forces incumbent firms to price at average cost. We shall refer to this hypothesis as the *contestable market* pricing rule. Omitting sectoral subscripts:

$$(1) \qquad\qquad\qquad PX = AC$$

for each sector with IRTS, where PX is the weighted sum of the unit sales prices on the domestic *(PD)* and export *(PE)* markets (recall that in the export market the unit sales price in domestic currency is determined by the exogenously given price in foreign currency times the exchange rate) and AC is average costs. As shown below, this pricing rule represents only a small departure from competitive pricing and has the advantage of isolating the role of market structure from that of market conduct.

10.3.2   Monopolistic Competition

In the second alternative, we assume that each identical firm behaves in the domestic market as a monopolist facing a downward-sloping demand curve. In equilibrium, each firm equates marginal revenue with marginal costs, that is,

$$(2) \qquad\qquad \frac{PD - MC}{PD} = \frac{1 + \Omega}{N\epsilon},$$

where MC is marginal cost, PD is the unit price on domestic sales, and ϵ is the representative firm's conjecture about the response of competitors to its output decision with respect to firm j. That is, if Q_{-j} denotes the aggregate output of the remaining firms in its sector, then $\Omega \equiv \Delta Q_{-j}/\Delta Q_j$. We refer to this specification as the *monopolistic competition* or *exogenous conjectures* case (to distinguish it from the variant below where conjectures are endogenous).

For the functional forms selected to represent import demand and export supply, de Melo and Tarr (forthcoming) show that the perceived elasticity of demand facing each firm is given by

$$(3) \qquad\qquad\qquad \epsilon = \epsilon^F S^F + \epsilon^V S^V,$$

where S^F and S^V denote the shares of final and intermediate goods in total demand, respectively, and ϵ^F and ϵ^V are functions of the parameters describing substitution effects in intermediate and final demand.

Expression (3), which is obtained by differentiating the first-order conditions describing demand for domestic and imported goods, indicates that the perceived elasticity of demand is a share-weighted average of the price elastic-

295   Industrial Organization and Trade Liberalization

---

ities of demand for final (ϵ^F) and intermediate (ϵ^V) goods. Because the shares depend on quantities demanded that are themselves price-responsive, the perceived elasticity of demand is itself endogenous and will increase in response to trade liberalization. This implies that there is a "pro-competitive" effect of trade liberalization in the monopolistic competition model.

Whereas the threat of entry insures zero profits in the contestable market alternative, in the conjectural variation case we have to make assumptions about entry and exit. In one closure, we assume no entry/exit. One can think of this alternative as the *short-run monopolistic competition* case. In the other, which is more representative of a long-run equilibrium, entry/exit ensures zero profits. Then the model also includes explicitly the zero profit condition

$$(4) \qquad\qquad \pi = 0,$$

where π is the profit rate.

One might expect the degree of firm collusion to vary with the number of firms. The fewer the number of firms, the more collusive behavior is likely to be. Indeed, if N represents the number of firms, one would expect that $\Omega \to 0$ as $N \to \infty$ so that firms behave competitively as N becomes large. In our case, N is an arbitrary number normalized to unity in the calibration. To capture the idea that firms' conjectures depend on the number of firms, and, more important, to account for the fact that firm entry implies the availability of a larger number of varieties, we add the following equation to determine conjectures:

$$(5) \qquad\qquad \Omega = \Delta Q_{-j}/\Delta Q_j = N^{-1}.$$

We refer to this variant as the *endogenous conjectures* case. This means that, as firms enter (exit), incumbents adapt their conjectures and price more (less) competitively. Equation (5) can be viewed as a shortcut to account for product variety and the influence of the number of firms on behavior.[11]

10.3.3   Supernormal Profits

In light of the evidence in section 10.2, we present a variant of the model in which protection allows for supernormal profit because of barriers to entry. Supernormal profits exist because of protection. This variant is applied to both pricing rules described above. In the presence of supernormal profits, firms sell in the domestic market at a price $\tilde{P}D > PD$. The rate of supernormal profit, ψ, per unit of domestic sales, is an exogenous parameter. Then, in the contestable market case, equation (1) is replaced by

$$(1') \qquad\qquad PX\,(\tilde{P}D,\ PE) = AC\,(1 + \psi),$$

which is contestable for $\psi = 0$. In the conjectural variation case, equation (4) is replaced by

---

11. While the conjectural variation approach is a convenient way of parametrizing oligopolistic behavior and suitable for a static simulation exercise, it is inadequate to study detailed interactions under dynamic oligopoly. For a critique of the conjectural variation approach see Shapiro (1989).

$$(4') \qquad\qquad\qquad \pi = \psi,$$

which sets the profit rate to its exogenously determined value. In the experiments reported below, we assume that liberalization eliminates the market power of domestic firms in the domestic market. Therefore removing protection entails concurrently setting $\psi = 0$ in equation $(1')$ or $(4')$. To control for the effect of entry/exit in the monopolistic competition case, we also run this specification with no entry/exit under both profitability scenarios.

10.3.4 Data and Calibration

In the application, we remove protection in a model where the economy is disaggregated into seven sectors. Table 10.2 gives the aggregation and structure of production and final demand. The base case against which we contrast our various pricing rules assumes constant returns to scale (CRTS) for all sectors. When we assume IRTS, three sectors have increasing returns: consumer goods, producer goods, and heavy industry. Together, these three sectors account for 42 percent of value added. Each of the three pricing hypotheses requires a different calibration so as to replicate quantities and values contained in base data.

In the case of normal initial profits ($\psi = 0$), to incorporate fixed costs while replicating observed prices and quantities in the CRTS case, we reduce the primary variable cost component to total costs by the amount of fixed costs. In the case of monopolistic competition, equation (2) is also solved to yield the value of the conjecture Ω. This implies that the conjecture is in fact calibrated.[12] Hence we denote the calibrated conjecture by $\bar{\Omega}$. The calibrated values of $\bar{\Omega}$ appear in table 10.4 below.

In the presence of supernormal profits, we allocate fixed costs as before and then, given the profit rate ψ and all quantities and foreign prices, we solve for the domestic price vector $\bar{P}D$ which satisfies the firm's profitability constraint.[13] As before, the value of $\bar{\Omega}$ is obtained from equation (2) but with the new set of domestic prices.

For the seven sectors in the present aggregation, table 10.2 gives the composition of sectoral output, exports and imports. Also included are estimates for (1) elasticity of capital/labor substitution; (2) import price elasticities of demand; (3) export supply price elasticities. The last column of table 10.2 gives the value of the calibrated price elasticity of demand, ϵ.

---

12. An equivalent approach is to read in Cournot conjectures and calibrate for N_i, the Cournot-equivalent number of firms. An alternative (but in our view less appealing) approach is to solve for marginal costs or demand elasticities, both of which are likely to be more reliable information than conjectures. In any case, the system of eqs. (2) and (3) can only deliver two of the three variables Ω, N, and ϵ.

13. Because of interindustry relationships, this calibration involves solving simultaneously for the vector of domestic prices, $\bar{P}D$.

Table 10.2   **Structure of Production, Trade, and Elasticity Values**

	Share in Gross Output (X) (1)	Exports/ Output (E/X) (2)	Imports/ Domestic Sales (M/D) (3)	Elasticity of Substitution in Production (σp) (4)	Export Supply Elasticity[a] (σt) (5)	Import Elasticity of Demand[a] (σv) (6)	Nominal Tariff Rate[b] (tm) (7)	Price Elasticity of Demand for Domestic Sales (ε) (8)
Primary	8.9%	4.9%	64.4%	2.5	0.75	1.8	59.7	—
Food processing	9.6	2.5	6.7	1.5	1.5	2.5	18.4	—
Consumer goods	14.4	32.5	11.2	1.0	1.5	2.4	15.7	1.49
Producer goods	20.1	16.6	19.7	0.9	1.5	2.2	17.6	1.30
Heavy industry	7.7	31.9	47.3	0.9	1.5	1.9	28.3	1.31
Traded services	13.2	24.4	6.1	1.5	1.5	2.0	0.0	—
Nontraded services	26.1	—	—	0.9	—	0.4	—	—

[a]Income compensated price elasticity of export supply (import demand).

[b]Nominal tariff rate includes an estimate of tariff equivalent protection conferred by existing nontariff barriers.

298   Jaime de Melo and David Roland-Holst

10.4   Simulation Results

The simulations consist of the abolition of the import protection Korea had in 1982, the year for the most recent input-output table. Column (7) in table 10.2 gives the nominal tariff structure of Korea in that year. The protection rates reported here are based on direct comparisons of domestic and international prices. Hence they include tariff equivalent protection by existing nontariff measures, and are as reliable an estimate of protection as one is likely to obtain. The most notable feature of the tariff structure displayed in column (4) is the high protection conferred on the primary sector. This reflects Korea's tradition of protecting its agricultural sector.

Tables 10.3 and 10.4 report the welfare and sectoral resource pull effects of removing protection under the pricing alternatives described above. To facilitate interpretation of results, we compare them with those obtained under CRTS. Recall that for the cases with IRTS, the three sectors with increasing returns are consumer goods, producer goods, and heavy industry. Simulations are for two sets of parameter values describing unexploited economies of scale in the base solution. For the case of low economies of scale, we assume for all three sectors a cost-disadvantage ratio (CDR) of 0.10, which is thought to be a conservative value for Korean manufacturing. For the case of medium/high economies of scale, a cost-disadvantage ratio of 0.20 is assumed. Each set of CDRs is applied to the three pricing rules described earlier. For profits, we also assume two alternatives. In the first, normal profits ($\pi = 0$) are as-

Table 10.3   **Aggregate Welfare Effects of Trade Liberalization**

	CRTS	Contestable Market		Monopolistic Competition			
				No Entry/Exit		Entry/Exit	
	(1)	(2)	(3)	(4)	(5)	(6)	(7)
Cost Disadvantage Ratio[a]	0.0	0.10	0.20	0.10	0.20	0.10	0.20
			% of Base-Year National Income				
Equivalent variation (EV)[b]	1.1						
$\pi = 0$		2.6	5.3	2.1	4.7	−0.6	2.8
$\pi = 10\%$		4.9	10.2	2.5	5.2	1.6	6.0
Scale efficiency gain (SE)[c]	0.0						
$\pi = 0$		1.3	3.4	0.8	3.0	−1.4	1.5
$\pi = 10\%$		2.0	5.8	0.7	2.5	−0.4	2.9

[a]CDR = $1 - MC/AC$.

[b]EV = $C\,[\text{IU}\,(P_J,\,Y_1)P_1] - C[\text{IU}\,(P_0,Y_0)]$, where C is the cost function associated with the indirect utility function (IU) corresponding to the LES utility function describing consumer choice.

[c]SE = $[TC\,(P_0,\,X_0) - TC\,(P_0,\,X_1)]/\text{GDP}_0$ is a vector of product and factor prices, and GDP_0 is real GDP prior to the removal of protection.

299   Industrial Organization and Trade Liberalization

Table 10.4   **Sectoral Results (CDR = 0.1)**
                      (percentage changes)

| | | Contestable Market | | Monopolistic Competition | | | |
| | | | | No Entry/Exit | | Entry/Exit | |
	CRTS (1)	$\pi=0$ (2)	$\pi=10$ (3)	$\pi=0$ (4)	$\pi=10$ (5)	$\pi=0$ (6)	$\pi=10$ (7)
Consumer goods:							
X	12.4	19.0	31.7	10.0	9.4	6.9	22.7
E	25.1	34.9	57.9	20.7	21.3	17.4	45.3
SE		1.6	1.9	0.3	0.3	−1.8	−0.1
ε				0.9	0.9	0.8	1.4
Ω						0.2	0.4
N						25.8	23.8
Producer goods:							
X	12.9	17.2	26.5	12.9	10.9	10.1	18.8
E	40.1	48.2	69.9	39.9	37.8	36.6	55.8
SE		1.6	2.0	0.6	0.4	−1.1	−0.4
ε				0.2	0.3	0.2	0.2
Ω						0.2	0.3
N						21.6	24.1
Heavy industry:							
X	−1.7	−5.1	8.4	−3.3	−1.7	−5.5	4.3
E	9.7	2.8	23.8	6.9	10.3	4.6	19.5
SE		−0.6	0.7	−0.1	0.0	−1.8	−1.0
ε				2.6	2.6	2.5	3.1
Ω						0.2	0.3
N						10.7	17.0

Note: X = gross output; E = exports; SE = scale efficiency measure (see table 10.3) expressed as a percentage of sectoral sales at current prices; ε = elasticity of demand (defined in eq. [3]); Ω = calibrated conjecture; N = number of firms (initially set equal to 1).

sumed, regardless of whether there is protection. In the second case, in line with the pattern of PCM values described in section 10.2, we assume that a supernormal profit rate of 10 percent ($\pi = 10$) is achievable under protection because of the barriers to entry from restricted foreign competition.

Two measures of the gains/losses from removing protection are reported in table 10.3. The equivalent variation (EV) measure is derived from the indirect utility (IU) function associated with the Stone-Geary utility function assumed for final demand. EV is an aggregate measure of both efficiency gains in production and in consumption. It measures how much the representative consumer would have to be compensated, at the new set of prices, to be indifferent to the bundle of goods now available at the initial set of prices. The second measure is the scale efficiency gain/loss (SE) from moving along the average cost curve. Like EV, SE evaluates the new output level at old prices, so that the measure controls for shifts in the average cost curve induced by changes in factor and product prices.

Figure 10.2 illustrates the measure of scale efficiency change used in table 10.3. Prior to removing protection, the observed cost output combination is (C_0, X_0). As a result of the removal of protection, relative product and factor prices change, leading to a shift in the cost curve. Consider two cases. In figure 10.2, panel A, there is output expansion, leading to an estimated scale efficiency gain indicated by the shaded area. In contrast, in panel B there is output contraction and, therefore, a scale efficiency loss, again indicated by the shaded area. In both cases, the scale efficiency change is measured by evaluating the cost function at the initial vector of product and factor prices. The measure (SE) reported in table 10.3 is the sum of the sectoral gains and losses.

Table 10.3 expresses both EV and SE as a percentage of initial national income (GDP). In the reference case of CRTS, liberalization yields a 1.1 percent increase in welfare (col. 1). Because there are no scale efficiency effects, the welfare gain under CRTS is the sum of the traditional producer and consumer surplus gains from removing distortions.

Now compare this result with the corresponding estimate under contestable market pricing. In this specification there is no firm entry, so scale efficiency gains/losses vary directly with sectoral output. Sectors that expand (contract) will achieve scale economy gains (losses). In the case of no initial supernormal profits, welfare gains are higher than under CRTS because, on average, sectors with IRTS expand as a result of removing protection. This is so because resources are pulled out of the heavily protected primary sector into industry, where three out of the five sectors have IRTS.

As expected, welfare gains are greater the greater the degree of unrealized scale economies. Doubling the value of CDR approximately doubles the overall welfare gain, although it almost triples the associated scale efficiency gains. Note also that the EV measure under IRTS is greater than the sum of the EV measure under CRTS and the corresponding SE measure. This is so because there is a further gain as average cost pricing comes closer to marginal cost pricing.

When trade liberalization eliminates supernormal profits ($\pi = 10$ percent), welfare and scale efficiency gains increase substantially. This is one aspect of the pro-competitive effect of trade liberalization (the other appears in the form of a higher elasticity of demand in the monopolistic competition model; see table 10.4). For example, with the combination (CDR $= 10$ percent, $\pi = 10$ percent), EV $= 4.9$ percent of GDP. Compared with the case of no initial profits (EV $= 2.6$ percent of GDP), the greater welfare gain can be decomposed into two components: the first is the scale efficiency gain (2.0 percent versus 1.1 percent) as firms expand more because they can no longer price restrictively. The second component is again due to the welfare gains of pricing closer to marginal costs. This effect is about $1.8 = 4.9 - (1.1 + 2.0)$ percent of initial GDP. In the not implausible combination

301   Industrial Organization and Trade Liberalization

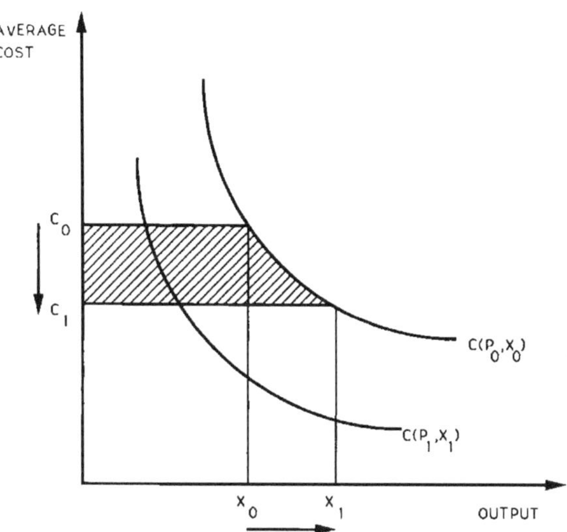

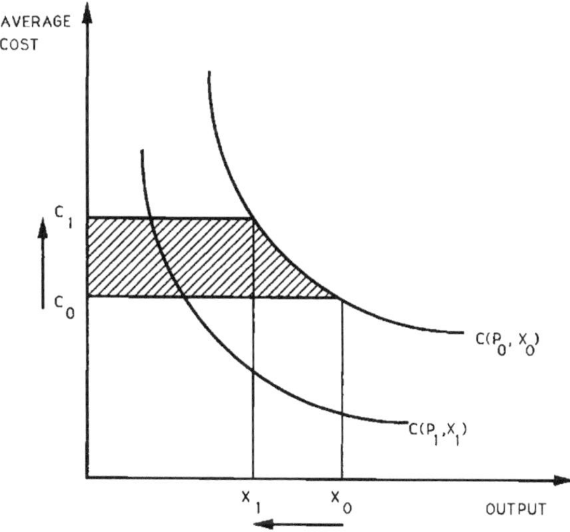

Fig. 10.2   Efficiency effects on aggregate welfare

302   Jaime de Melo and David Roland-Holst

(CDR = 20 percent, π = 10 percent), welfare gains from trade liberalization are estimated at 10.2 percent of GDP.

The monopolistic competition case is more complicated, since there are three additional adjustment mechanisms that affect the calculated welfare gain measure. First, there may be firm entry/exit to attain exogenously specified profit rates. A second factor is the endogeneity of oligopoly behavior, an effect we consider later. As firms enter (exit), incumbents adapt their conjectures and price less (more) competitively. Third, but apparently less significant, is the pro-competitive effect that is due to trade liberalization raising the elasticity of sectoral domestic demand, ϵ (see table 10.4).[14]

Compare contestable market pricing and monopolistic competition with no entry/exit (cols. 4 and 5). In the contestable market case, scale efficiency gains are higher because firms expand output to maintain or to achieve zero profits. On the other hand, in the monopolistic competition case, with no entry/exit, firms may make profits, realizing lower scale efficiency gains. At the same time, profits reduce welfare gains as prices diverge further from marginal costs. These two factors explain why welfare gains are larger under contestable market pricing. The larger difference in welfare gains for the specification with positive profits in the base results from substantially greater output expansion to achieve the necessary price reductions after the removal of protection.

Now consider firm entry, which exerts a crowding effect that diminishes the overall scale efficiency gain (this is the effect analyzed in Horstmann and Markusen 1986). In the case of CDR = 0.10, this effect dominates the positive output effect of liberalization on scale efficiency, so that overall scale efficiency is reduced.[15] By contrast, with CDR = 0.20, average sectoral output expands more than the firm population and scale efficiency is increased. In the case of zero initial profits, the scale efficiency loss is large enough to offset the other welfare gains from trade liberalization.

When there are profits in the initial situation, as before, there is a gain from moving closer to marginal cost pricing with trade liberalization. However, two other effects are also at work. On the one hand, more firm entry is required to eliminate excess profits, with its deleterious effect on scale efficiency. However, there is a counterbalancing effect as firm entry leads to more competitive behavior. The net result is that scale efficiency improves more and that the overall welfare gain is greater than in the zero initial profit scenario. Since we have not taken direct account of increased product variety on welfare, these results may understate the benefits of increased competition.

Table 10.4 summarizes the microeconomic results from removing protection for the sectors with IRTS and a CDR value of 0.10. The table also dis-

---

14. This effect is also discussed by Devarajan and Rodrik (1989b).

15. The reduction in scale efficiency obtained here also occurs for certain parameter configurations in the theoretical models of Krugman (1984), Snape (1977), and Venables (1985).

303   Industrial Organization and Trade Liberalization

plays the value of $\tilde{\Omega}$, which suggests that all three sectors are more competitive than Cournot. For each of the three sectors with IRTS, exports expand, even though under most scenarios output contracts for heavy industry (the most protected sector after agriculture). The reasons for export expansion despite output contraction is that removing protection leads to a real exchange rate depreciation, a general equilibrium effect.

Consumer and producer goods follow similar patterns: with $\pi = 0$, expansion is greatest under contestable mark-up pricing and least under monopolistic competition with CRTS in the middle. The reason for a stronger expansion under contestable market pricing is the absence of firm entry that impedes the realization of economies of scale. Interestingly, the scale efficiency loss caused by firm entry (the number of firms increases by between 21 and 25 percent) can dampen output expansion below that achieved under CRTS when $\pi = 0$. Compare columns (6) and (1) in the case of consumer goods, where firm entry is greatest and scale efficiency loss greatest. Output expansion under monopolistic competition is only half that achieved under CRTS. There are two reasons for this smaller output expansion. First, the higher price for domestic sales resulting from less efficient scale means less demand for domestic consumer goods (and greater demand for imported consumer goods). Second, because of interindustry linkages, under monopolistic competition production costs go up in sectors that are intensive purchasers of producer goods and heavy industry.

When protection alters market structure by allowing for supernormal profits (cols. 3 and 5), removing protection leads to a magnification effect on resource pulls. The magnification effect is stronger under monopolistic competition for consumer and producer goods than under contestable market pricing. For heavy industry, the (exogenous) pro-competitive effect of eliminating profits is sufficient to compensate for the negative resource pull effect of eliminating protection. This example illustrates the possibility that sectors that would be predicted to contract because of liberalization expand instead because they become more competitive. Even in this highly aggregated model, a ranking of sectors in ascending order of effective protection would thus not be an accurate ranking of comparative advantage.

The other pro-competitive effect of trade liberalization comes from the greater elasticity of demand facing firms after protection is eliminated. For the functional forms specified here, the results in table 10.4 indicate that this effect is small. However, one cannot judge the likely importance of this effect from the simulations reported here, since constant substitution elasticities are maintained throughout. Changes in the values of ϵ are entirely accounted for by changes in import (and domestic) shares in final and intermediate demand.

So far, all the results for the monopolistic competition case are with exogenous conjecture. We have seen that firm entry to eliminate profits reduces the welfare gains of trade liberalization because of less scale efficiency gain. Moving to the assumption of endogenous conjecture (eq. [5]) increases scale

304   Jaime de Melo and David Roland-Holst

efficiency because incumbent firms price more competitively as new firms enter. As a result, welfare gains under the monopolistic competition scenario with endogenous conjectures (not reported here) are between those obtained under contestable market pricing and those obtained under monopolistic competition with exogenous conjectures.

10.5   Conclusions

This paper has developed a simulation model to evaluate the welfare effects of trade liberalization. In contrast with previous general equilibrium simulation exercises, this paper decomposes the welfare effects of trade policy changes into its various components. Although the calibrated simulation exercise for Korea relies on judgmental parameter values to represent demand and supply elasticities, evidence on the links between trade policies, industrial structure, and industrial organization policies in Korea provides good support for the alternative modeling approaches adopted here. The estimated gains from trade liberalization were found to be quite sensitive to the specification of firm pricing behavior in the three manufacturing sectors with IRTS.

In the benchmark case of across-the-board CRTS, elimination of protection yields a welfare gain of 1.1 percent of GDP. This gain represents the traditional production and consumption costs of protection. Under IRTS and no firm entry, net scale efficiency gains (scale efficiency gains in consumer goods and producer goods coupled with scale efficiency losses in heavy industry) give an additional gain between 1.3 and 3.4 percent of GDP, depending on the extent of unrealized economies of scale. If it is recognized, as the evidence suggests, that protection allowed Korean conglomerates to act collusively in their sales on the domestic market, one would obtain an additional welfare gain of between 1.3 and 4.9 percent of GDP, thereby yielding a total gain of between 5 percent of GDP if unexploited economies of scale are small and 10 percent of GDP if they are in a range commonly attributed to them in this country (a cost disadvantage ratio of 20 percent).

Welfare gain estimates are, however, much lower if the contestable market scenario is replaced by one with the assumption of monopolistic competition, even if one recognizes that firm entry/exit may occur. Under the monopolistic competition scenario where liberalization is accompanied by firm entry, the number of firms increases by between 10 and 25 percent in sectors with IRTS. Trade liberalization results in scale efficiency losses. In some cases there is sufficient entry to yield a net aggregate welfare loss if firms are not allowed to make excess profits under protection. If firms are allowed to earn supernormal profits under protection, aggregate welfare gains are between 1.6 and 6.0 percent of GDP.

In the Korean example, trade liberalization would favor industry since agriculture is the most heavily protected sector. In many other semi-industrial countries, elimination of protection would involve a resource shift out of man-

305   Industrial Organization and Trade Liberalization

ufacturing. A case in point is Chile, where trade liberalization involved a relative expansion of agriculture. In this case, scale efficiency gains would only be achieved if the elimination of protection were accompanied by firm exit, and the scale efficiency gains of trade liberalization would be greater in a world of monopolistic competition than in one of contestable market pricing. However, the competitive effects of trade liberalization could be even greater than those estimated here.

It should be apparent from this summary description of the results that the welfare cost estimates of protection are quite sensitive to the specification of market structure and conduct and, in particular, to the firm entry/exit patterns accompanying trade liberalization. In the Korean case, estimates of the gains from trade liberalization are much larger under IRTS than under CRTS, if inefficient firm entry is forestalled while the competitive discipline imposed by greater import competition is maintained on the domestic market.

References

Bergsman, J. 1974. Commercial policy, allocative efficiency and X-efficiency. *Quarterly Journal of Economics* 88: 409–33.

Brown, D., and R. M. Stern. 1989. US-Canada bilateral tariff elimination: The role of product differentiation and market structure. In *Trade Policies for International Competitiveness*, ed. R. Feenstra. Chicago: University of Chicago Press.

Caves, R. 1980. Introduction to the symposium on trade and industrial organization. *Journal of Industrial Economics* 29(2): 11–28.

Condon, T., and J. de Melo. 1991. Industrial organization implications of QR trade regimes: Evidence and welfare costs. *Empirical Economics* 16:139–53.

Corden, M. 1967. Monopoly, tariffs, and subsidies. *Economica* 34: 50–58.

Devarajan, S., and D. Rodrik. 1989a. Trade liberalization in developing countries: Do imperfect competition and economies of scale matter? *American Economic Review* 79, no. 2 (May):283–87.

———. 1989b. Pro-competitive effects of trade reform: Results from a CGE model for Cameroon. Working Paper, J. F. Kennedy School of Government, Harvard University.

Dixit, A. 1989. Comparative statics for oligopoly. *International Economic Review* 27: 107–22.

———. 1988. Optimal trade and industrial policies for the US automobile industry. In *Empirical Methods for International Trade*, ed. R. Feenstra. Cambridge: MIT Press.

Geroski, P., and A. Jacquemin. 1981. Imports as competitive discipline. In Symposium on industrial organization and international trade, ed. P. Geroski and A. Jacquemin. *Recherches economiques de Louvain* 47: 197–208.

Gunasekera, D. B. H., and R. Tyers. 1988. Imperfect competition and returns to scale in a newly industrializing economy: A general equilibrium analysis of Korean trade policy. National Centre for Development Studies, Australian National University, Canberra. Manuscript.

Harris, R. G. 1984. Applied general equilibrium analysis of small open economies

306   Jaime de Melo and David Roland-Holst

with scale economies and imperfect competition. *American Economic Review* 74(5): 1017–32.

———. 1989. The new protection revisited. *Canadian Journal of Economics* 24(4): 751–78.

Helpman, E., and P. Krugman. 1985. *Market Structure and Foreign Trade.* Cambridge, Mass.: MIT Press.

———. 1989. *Trade Policy and Market Structure.* Cambridge, Mass.: MIT Press.

Horstmann, I., and J. Markusen. 1986. Up your average cost curve: Inefficient entry and the new protectionism. *Journal of International Economics* 20: 225–48.

Kierkowski, H. (ed.). 1984. *Monopolistic Competition and International Trade.* Oxford: Oxford University Press.

Kim, J. W. 1985. The rate of TFP changes in small and medium industries and economic development: The case of Korea's manufacturing. Working Paper No. 85-01. Seoul: Korean Development Institute.

Krugman, P. 1984. Import protection as export promotion: International competition in the presence of oligopoly and economies of scale. In *Monopolistic Competition and International Trade,* ed. H. Kierzkowski. Oxford: Oxford University Press.

———. (ed.). 1988. *Strategic Trade Policy and the New International Economics.* Cambridge, Mass.: MIT Press.

Lee, K., S. Urata, and I. Choi. 1988. Recent developments in industrial organization in Korea. World Bank Working Paper, Washington, D.C.

Melo, J. de, and S. Robinson. 1989. Product differentiation and the treatment of foreign trade in computable general equilibrium models. *Journal of International Economics* 27: 47–67.

Melo, J. de, and D. Tarr. Forthcoming. *A General Equilibrium Analysis of U.S. Trade Policy.* Cambridge, Mass.: MIT Press.

Rodrik, D. 1988. Imperfect competition, scale economies, and trade policy in developing countries. In *Trade Policy Issues and Empirical Analysis,* ed. R. E. Baldwin. Chicago: University of Chicago Press.

Shapiro, C. 1989. Theories of oligopoly behavior. In *Handbook of Industrial Organization,* ed. R. Schmalensee and R. Willig. Amsterdam: North-Holland.

Smith, A., and A. Venables. 1988. Completing the internal market in European community: Some industry simulations. *European Economic Review* 32(7): 1501–25.

Snape, R. 1977. Trade policy in the presence of economics of scale and product variety. *Economic Record* 53(144): 525–33.

Venables, A. 1985. Trade and trade policy with imperfect competition: The case of identical products and free entry. *Journal of International Economics* 19: 1–19.

World Bank. 1987. *Korea: Managing the Industrial Transition.* Washington, D.C.: World Bank.

empec (1991) 16: 139–153

Industrial Organization Implications of QR Trade Regimes: Evidence and Welfare Costs

By T. Condon and J. de Melo[1]

Abstract: Evidence of the relationship between trade regimes, concentration and profitability in semi-industrial countries' manufacturing sectors is reviewed. This evidence is used to justify the formulation and simulation of a three sector general equilibrium model in which the manufacturing sector's behavior is linked to the degree of restrictiveness of the QR regime. Simulations are conducted with several variants of the model to ascertain separately the effects of introducing economies of scale, firm entry/exit, departures from competitive pricing, and interactions between entry and pricing rules. Numerical results suggest that a 20 percent rationing rate of intermediates and consumption goods can have welfare costs of about 2.0 percent of national income in the absence of economies of scale and industrial organization interactions with the trade regime. When industrial organization features are included, the costs of the same 20 percent rationing quadruples.

1 Introduction

Quantitative restriction (QRs) are the most common form of protection in many developing countries. Often this type of protection emerges during balance of payments crises but, once in place, is not removed. Students of developing countries' foreign exchange regimes have long noted that QRs have deleterious effects beyond those that would emerge from calculations relying strictly on the "tariff equivalent" of quotas. So far most analysis has concentrated on quantifying the cost of rent-seeking activities which allegedly accompany QRs.[2] The purpose of this paper is to extend this analysis by parametrizing two stylized observations that have often been noted about the manufacturing sector of QR-ridden foreign trade regimes: (1) unrealized economies of scale; (2) lack of competition among domestic firms. The first arises because of the small size of

---

[1] Timothy Condon and J. de Melo, The World Bank 1818 H Street, N.W. Room N10–031 Washington, D.C. 20433.

[2] Krueger (1974) first drew attention to the potential costs of rent-seeking activities in restrictive trade regimes. For illustrative quantitative estimates of the costs of rent-seeking see Mohammad and Whalley (1984), and Grais, de Melo and Urata (1986).

140   T. Condon and J. de Melo

the domestic market; the second arises because of the made-to-measure protection of QR trade regimes. In sum, the paper builds on the stylized observation that in most QR regimes too many firms operate at too small a scale and often making above normal profits.

The interaction between trade policies and industrial organization has received theoretical and empirical attention in industrial organization studies of structure-couduct-performance in developed countries where it is known as the "import-discipline" hypothesis: the threat of entry by foreign competitors constrains domestic firms to adopt entry-forestalling prices that more closely approximate competitive prices. In addition to receiving empirical support in cross-section econometric analyses of structure-performance relationships, the import-discipline hypothesis has also been recently included in general equilibrium calculations of the costs of protection in Canada (Harris 1985, Cox and Harris 1985).[3] The analysis here is also in a general equilibrium setting where the interactions between trade policies and industrial organization issues give rise to welfare costs not recognized in the more traditional applied general equilibrium trade models where constant returns to scale prevail. The mechanisms incorporated in the model are in the spirit of Harris, though because of QRs, the modelling of trade policies and of the linkages between pricing behavior and barriers to entry are different.

The remainder of the paper is organized as follows. Section 2 reviews evidence on linkages between firm behavior, firm size and restrictiveness of the trade regime in semi-industrial developing countries that lend support to our stylized modelling strategy. Section 3 outlines the model. Section 4 reports on simulations from a three sector model that explores the sensitivity of numerical estimates to the parameters describing foreign trade and firm behavior under increasing returns to scale.

2 Profitability, and Firm Behavior in Manufacturing Under Different Trade Regimes: Evidence and Modelling Issues

Evidence about the extent to which restrictive foreign trade regimes in developing countries give rise to oligopolistic behavior and suboptimal scale is scant. This is so because few countries have drastically liberalized QRs. One exception is Chile where evidence on firm profitability and concentration during a regime ridden by tariff and non-tariff barriers (1967) can be compared with firm profitability and

---

[3] Theoretical and empirical studies of the import discipline hypothesis for developed countries are covered in two symposia edited Caves (1980) and Geroski and Jacquemin (1981). For developing countries see de Melo and Urata (1986), Rodrik (1988), Frischtak et al. (1989), Roberts and Tybout (forthcoming), and citations therein.

concentration during a quasi-free-trade regime (1979). Another example is Korea where many observers agree that conglomerates exercised market power on domestic sales (see World Bank 1987). The evidence from the manufacturing sectors in these two countries is summarized in table 1.

Table 1.   Profitability and exposure to foreign trade

(1a) Chilean manufacturing

Year	Mean tariff	Mean price-cost margin	4-firm concentration ratio	Exports/ output	Import share in apparent consumption
1967	74%	48%	49.0	4.0%	20.0%
1979	11%	32%	61.6	13.0%	29.0%

(1b) Korean manufacturing
Performance of different market structures (Average of 1978 and 1983)

	Monopoly/ Oligopoly	Competetive	More protected	Less protected	High export share	Low export share
Mean price cost margin	29%	26%	34%	24%	25%	29%

Sources:
(1a)   de Melo and Urata (1986, table 1).
(1b)   Lee, Urata, and Choi (1988, tables 3 and 8)

Table 1a compares summary statistics from the Chilean manufacturing censuses of 1967 and 1979. The figures indicate that during the restrictive quota-ridden trade regime of 1967, price-cost margins were large compared with the liberalized trade regime of 1979. The increase in concentration (and decline in the number of firms not shown here) between the two census years is dramatic given that the manufacturing sector was of roughly the same size in 1967 and in 1979. Full adjustment to the new trade regime was not complete, however, since the uniform tariff structure of 10% with no QRs had just been achieved in June 1979 when census data were gathered. It is noteworthy that increased concentration was accompanied by *lower* price cost margins (PCMs), which is consistent with the removal of protection forcing more competitive pricing because firms face a more elastic demand.

In Korea, the legacy of Korea's development strategy between 1973 and 1979 focussing on heavy and chemical industries has been an extremely concentrated industrial structure by international standards. For example, in 1982, the top 50 Korean firms accounted for 37 percent of total sales while in Japan the top 100 firms accounted for 27 percent of total sales. The figures in table (1b) show higher PCMs in the more concentrated sectors. Furthermore, mean PCMs are higher in the highly protected sectors. Also PCMs are lower for sectors with higher export shares. Both results suggest that sectors that compete in international markets price more competitively.

Further evidence taking into account factors other than protection (e.g. differences in capital/labor intensity across sectors) support the conclusions drawn from table 1. For Chile, structural change tests by de Melo and Urata, (1986) based on a cross-sectoral simultaneous equations model of structure and performance applied to the two census years for 41 industrial sectors confirmed these observations and provided further support for the import discipline hypothesis after controlling for other factors. Likewise, in Korea, after controlling for other factors, results from a cross-sectoral simultaneous equations model of structure and performance (similar to the one fitted for Chile) indicated lower profitability for sectors with higher import penetration shares. But statistical tests revealed no significant structural change in the way the import share affected profitability in different years, a result that is not surprising since trade liberalization was much less in Korea than in Chile.[4]

In sum, these comparisons provide support for the import-discipline hypothesis, namely that protection, by creating barriers to entry, allows existing firms to collude and earn above normal profits. Unfortunately the evidence does not provide direct support for Bhagwati's (1965) insight that QRs create more demestic power than tariffs. However, the Chilean evidence can be viewed as indirect support for his proposition since QRs were very high in 1967 (See Behrman 1976) and average manufacturing-wide profitability was almost 50 percent higher than in 1979.

The Chilean trade liberalization was also accompanied by an increase in intra-industry trade and a reduction in the number of firms (see de Melo and Urata 1986, table 1). This outcome is consistent with recent models of international trade featuring economies of scale with free-entry and a noncooperative equilibrium among firms in Chamberlinian monopolistic competition. A prediction of these models is that a reduction in protection leads to intraindustry specialization and more intraindustry trade.[5] And the exit of firms in response to a major trade liberalization is consistent with the proposition that protection creates

---

[4] Further tests for Korea provide support for the "structuralist view" (rather than the "efficiency view") interpretation of a positive correlation between concentration and profitability. The two views are contrasted in Clarke, Davies and Waterson (1984).

[5] Increased intraindustry specialization was also accomplished by a reduction in the number of products at the plant level. See Corbo and de Melo (1985, chp. 1) for a summary of firm-level interviews that indicate product rationalization, and Harris (1985) for modelling of this effect in the Canadian context.

Industrial Organization Implications of QR Trade Regimes   143

excessive entry. This observation, known as the *inefficient entry* problem, implies that the number of firms permitted by economies of scale is small enough to allow effective collusive behavior that raises profits which in turn attracts new firms into the industry until sufficient entry eliminates profits by driving scale down and average costs up.[6]

In the absence of information about foreign firm behavior during trade liberalization, we assume perfectly competitive behavior on the part of foreign suppliers.[7] Then the question is whether protection, which raises profitability even in the absence of collusion, will not reduce the penalty for cheating on a collusive agreement. This suggests that a variable price-fixing agreement should set prices low enough to make cheating unappealing (see Rotemberg and Saloner (1988)). Below we recognize this possibility by allowing for collusive behavior to diminish via entry.

A final issue not recognized in the trade and industrial organization literature but common to many foreign trade regimes in developing countries is that, in foreign-exchange-scarce economies, nearly all imports are essential, that is they are intermediates not produced domestically. One would then expect that the proliferation of inefficient firms engendered by the QR regime would eventually cease when quotas become very binding. In our modeling, we explore this possibility by analyzing a case where firm entry depends negatively on how binding QRs are.

We approach the modelling of the welfare costs of QR regimes in a sequential manner to isolate the effects of changes in scale efficiency, entry/exit and departure from average cost pricing. The pricing rules for the most part are ad-hoc, since they are intended to represent situations where firms can coexist while earning above normal profits. The next section presents the different variants of a model which includes economies of scale with variable collusive behavior, and firm entry/exit in response to changes in the degree of restrictiveness of QRs.

3 A Stylized CGE Model with QR and Industrial Organization Focus

The model developed here is a static one-period CGE model. (For the illustrative welfare calculation reported in section 4, the representative semiindustrial eco-

---

[6] Note however that inefficient entry may also occur in the Cournot model with free entry. See Eastman and Stykolt (1960) and Dixit and Norman (1980).

[7] Corbo and de Melo (1985) note the effect of barriers to entry in the commerce sector during the trade liberalizations in the Southern Cone. Several cases of "indirect" cooperation between domestic producers and foreign firms were revealed by interviews: producers turned themselves into importers and entered a profit sharing agreement with foreign firms and maintained high retail prices. This suggests that the assumption of perfectly competitive behavior on the part of foreign suppliers may not be appropriate.

nomy is aggregated into three sectors: agriculture, manufacturing, and services.) In addition to its focus on industrial organization issues, the model differs from companion formulations (e.g. Devarajan and Rodrik (1989) and de Melo and Roland-Holst (forthcoming)) because of its treatment of oligopolistic behavior. Here we focus on exploring the effect of alternative oligopolistic pricing rules. The model has a simple structure. There is no government sector and one single consumer to simplify the disposition of rents under binding QRs. Final demand excludes investment demand, and thus consists of intermediate demand, consumption demand, and imports and exports.

The specification of foreign trade combines the small country assumption with symmetric national product differentiation for imports and exports.[8] For private consumption, we specify an LES demand system. For intermediate demand, domestic and imported intermediate imports of a same category are imperfect substitutes in use. For example, technology does not allow for substitution between steel and chemicals as inputs, but substitution is allowed between domestic and imported steel, and domestic and imported steel need not combine in use in the same proportions across users. Two primary factors, capital and labor, mobile across sectors, combine to produce value-added.

Our treatment of firm pricing behavior relies on the observation that domestic industrial policy coupled with import rationing usually provides an environment in which there are *barriers to entry*. This allows firms to depart from average cost procing and to maintain above normal profits in long-run equilibrium under QRs. Barriers to entry come from the presence of QRs, and domestic barriers to entry come from various incentives (investment, credit, etc.), which are appropriated by incumbent firms (for evidence see Frischtak et al. 1989).

Since the model only includes barriers to entry from imports, we start with our modelling assumptions about QRs. We model QR-ridden trade regimes by rationing (separately or jointly) intermediates and consumer goods. Since there is only one representative consumer, rents from consumption and intermediate demand rationing are returned in lump-sum to the representative consumer. For future reference denote by RC_i and RV_i the rents arising from rationing import consumption and intermediate goods. Our proxy for the extent of barriers to entry to sector i will be $B_i = (RC_i + RV_i)/X_i$ i.e. the value of rents per unit of domestic output. The proxy is coarse, but it is the most natural one in this kind of model and it captures the idea that barriers to entry increase as quotas become more binding.

---

8 This treatment differs from Harris (1985) and is viewed as more appropriate since it controls for trade-reform-induced terms-of-trade effects which may influence heavily welfare calculations. The offer curve implications of this formulation are treated qualitatively in de Melo and Robinson (1989).

So far we have said nothing about firm entry-exit, and firm behavior. We will consider five model variants, ranging from constant returns to scale (CRTS) to increasing returns to scale (IRTS) with collusive behavior.

Start with the traditional case where all firms have CRTS production functions (i.e. no fixed costs). This is the base case (*variant* 1) and the typical firm pricing rule is:

$$PX_i = TC_i / X_i \tag{1}$$

In equation (1), PX_i is unit price (a weighted sum of export sale price and domestic sale price); TC_i is total costs; VC_i is variable costs; and; X_i is firm output. Under CRTS, $TC_i = VC_i$ so that firms price at marginal costs. Therefore, in variant 1, the welfare costs of rationing are the traditional production and consumption costs emphasized in the literature on the costs of protection.

Next consider the introduction of fixed costs. Denote the number of firms in the industry by $\bar{N}_i$ where a bar denotes that the number of firms is fixed for now. As in Harris (1985) we have:

$$TC_i = VC_i + FC_i \tag{2}$$

where FC_i is fixed costs defined by:

$$FC_i = (W\overline{FL}_i + R\overline{FK}_i)\bar{N}_i \tag{3}$$

and $\overline{FL}_i$ and $\overline{FK}_i$ are the labor and machines necessary to keep the plant open. Throughout, we maintain the assumption that variable costs, VC_i, are independent of scale. However, variable costs will shift up with a QR because firms have to pay the premium-inclusive price for imported intermediates. The parameter we use to calibrate economies of scale is the cost disadvantage ratio (CDR), defined as $CDR_i = FC_i/TC_i$. This is *variant* 2. In this variant, firms use the pricing rule described in equation (1) so that there are zero profits. With this variant, we assess the impact of IRTS on scale efficiency. The calibration of the model to the representative data set assumes that economies of scale are only operative when QRs are binding.

Next come several variants which we discuss together since they involve the treatment of entry and pricing and the interaction between the two. From Section 2, we assume that firm entry is an increasing function of profits, π_i, that result from collusive behavior. By choice of units, assume one firm prior to rationing. Then firm entry is given by:

$$N_i = 1 + S_i(\pi_i)^{\gamma_i} \qquad S_i \quad = 1 \text{ if } FC_i > 0$$
$$= 0 \text{ otherwise} \tag{4}$$

where $\gamma_i \geq 0$ is a parameter.

To examine the problem of inefficient entry separately from collusive pricing, we combine the average cost pricing rule of equation (1) with equation (3) in which π_i is replaced by B_i, the rents accruing from QRs in sector i. This is *variant* 3 (inefficient entry, no collusive pricing).

Now consider collusive behavior. For firm pricing, we assume that departure from competitive pricing is greater the more quotas are binding but that firm entry may dampen collusive behavior. Firm pricing is given by:

$$PX_i = TC_i \, / \, X_i + a_i B_i^{\alpha_i} \, / \, N_i^{\beta_i} \tag{5}$$

where a_i, α_i, $\beta_i \geq 0$ are again parameters.

As mentioned earlier, this representation of pricing behavior has no specific theoretical foundation and is essentially ad-hoc, but it is convenient to explore parametrically a wide range of interactions. In the experiments of Section 4 we report two combinations. In *variant 4*, we consider collusive pricing but no entry ($a_i > 0$, $\beta_i = \gamma_i = 0$). This is the polar case to Cox and Harris and de Melo and Roland-Holst where collusive pricing is the cause of entry which continues until $\pi_i = 0$ in the new long-run equilibrium. In *variant 5* we introduce simultaneously entry and the negative effect that entry has on collusive behavior (a_i, β_i, $\gamma_i > 0$). Other variants are possible, including the case in which entry leads again to zero long-run profits, but we do not report experiments with these variants here since evidence seems to suggest that QR trade regimes are accompanied by higher long-run equilibrium profits than other foreign trade regimes.

Even though the options included here allow us to consider a fairly broad set of interactions between trade policy and industrial organization, the range is still limited. For example, it is quite possible that the excessive entry problem that appears to characterize QR trade regimes in developing countries would be better modelled by having two groups of firms: large and small with a leader-follower model where entry would be restricted to small (and perhaps less efficient) firms.

4   Illustrative Simulations of the Welfare Costs of Protection Under QR Trade Regimes

We now report results from simulations with a three-sector representative model of a semi-industrial economy. The sectors are agriculture, manufacturing and services. Economies of scale, when operative, are restricted to manufacturing. Services are nontradable. The equilibrium values resulting from calibrating the model are given in the Appendix. Initial national income (against which welfare losses are measures) is 594 and, by choice of units: Exports = imports = 250 (in domestic currency units) with the following breakdown for imports: intermediates

Industrial Organization Implications of QR Trade Regimes 147

(177) and consumer goods (73). This initial situation thus depicts an open semi-industrialized economy like Korea in the middle seventies (see Kubo, et. al. 1986). Consequently the welfare costs reported below may be viewed as an upper bound, and one may accordingly wish to scale down the estimates to have a more representative initial starting point. However, we would argue that the alternative to which a QR-ridden trade regime should be evaluated is precisely a relatively undistorted economy, i.e., the case chosen here.

We start by reporting results of sensitivity analysis. In table 2, we vary the price elasticities of import demand and export supply in a CRTS model. We show that the welfare costs of imposing QRs are higher, the less price responsive are import demands and export supplies. In table 3, we vary the extent of economies of scale in the version of the model with zero profits. We show that across-the-board rationing of imports results in a welfare loss and that the welfare loss is greater, the more there are unexploited economies of scale.

Table 2.   Welfare costs of rationing (Variant 1)

Rationing rate a/	Consumer imports	Consumer and intermediate Imports	
		High trade b/ elasticities (1.5)	Low trade b/ elasticities (0.5)
Column	1	2	3
.9	0.0	0.4	1.0
.8	0.4	1.7	4.9
.7	0.8	4.1	11.9
.6	1.6	7.7	NS
.5	2.7	13.0	NS

Notes: Variant 1 assumes CRTS across all sectors. Welfare costs measured by the equivalent variation expressed as a percentage of pre-rationing national income (e.g. 1.0 is one percent of national income).

NS: No solution (the algorithm failed to converge).
a/   Expresses constraint imports as proportion of unrationed import levels.
b/   High (low) trade elasticities assume across-the-board price elasticities of import demand and export supply of 1.5 (0.5).

Table 2 measures the costs (expressed as percentage of national income) of increasingly binding quotas. All welfare results are obtained from the equivalent variation measure applied to the indirect utility function associated with the Cobb-Douglas utility function describing consumer choice. Column 2 shows that restricting consumer goods imports alone has a relatively small cost, reaching only 2.7 percent of base national income when they are restricted to 50 percent of their initial level. This is so both because of the calibrated price elasticities of final demand (unitary price elasticities) and because consumer goods are typically a small fraction of total imports. When intermediates are included, welfare costs reach 13 percent. Usually, rationing of imported intermediates will not exceed 20 percent in restrictive QR regimes. If consumer rationing comes first and is carried out to 50 percent, welfare costs could still be in the range of 7 to 13 percent, depending on the extent of elasticity optimism. From now on, we consider only high trade elasticities, which may be more representative of a semi-industrial economy where substitution possibilities are greater than in a less industrialized economy.

Table 3.   Welfare costs of rationing (Variant 2) to scale in manufacturing *a/*

Rationing rate *a/*	.9	.8	.7	.6	.5
CDR = 0.07	5.3	6.1	8.1	11.2	16.0
Scale elasticity *b/*	(.925)				(.956)
CDR = 0.035	2.7	3.8	5.9	9.4	14.4
Scale elasticity *b/*	(.965)				(.979)

Notes: CDR, the cost disadventage ratio, is defined as the ratio of fixed costs to total costs.

a/   See table 2 for definition. Rationing is for both consumer and intermediate goods.

b/   The scale elasticity for solutions with rationing rates of .9 and .5 respectively are reported in parentheses. Scale elasticities are computed as the ratio of narginal to average costs costs at the solution values.

Table 3 introduces economies of scale (variant 2). Results from Table 3 should be compared with the results in Table 2, Column 2. Calibration for scale economies in manufacturing was done to take into account that even in a medium-size developing country only a fraction of manufacturing sectors have economies of scale. Somewhat arbitrarily, the cost disadvantage ratio (CDR) parameter is set at a value that produces a scale elasticity of about one-half the average used by Cox and Harris for Canada (CDR = 0.07). If anything, we would argue that this estimate of unexploited economies of scale is on the low side because we have not included the costs of idle capacity that is said to be prevalent among manufacturing firms in highly restricted QR trade regimes.

Table 4. A comparison of the welfare costs of rationing alternative market structures

	Rationing Rate a/	*Variant 1* CRTS	*Variant 2* IRTS; no entry, no collusive behavior	*Variant 3* IRTS; entry, no collusive behavior	*Variant 4* IRTS; no entry collusive behavior	*Variant 5* IRTS; entry, collusive behavior
Welfare costs						
(% of base	.8	1.7	6.1	6.5	6.5	6.7
national income)	.5	13.0	16.0	16.7	17.1	17.3
Price cost margin (π_i)b/	.8	0	0	0	6.0	6.1
	.5	0	0	0	25.7	21.3
Number of firms	.8	1	1	1.07	1	1.06
(Ratio to base)	.5	1	1	1.24	1	1.18

Notes: Model variants refer to variants described in section 3. Parameter values for all results are: High trade elasticies (1.5), and CDR = 0.07.

a/   See table 2 for definition. Rationing is for both intermediates and consumption goods.

b/   The price cost margin is measured by the profit rate.

When compared with the results in table 2, the welfare costs of rationing are higher under IRTS than under CRTS. This is so, even though increasing rationing (where lower imports are accompanied by lower exports through the balance of trade constraint) leads to a slight increase in scale efficiency reflected in higher values of the scale elasticity as the rationing rate increases. The reason is similar to the results in table 2. With fixed costs, the economy is less able to adjust to rationing. Therefore the flexibility to adjust is lower, the higher is the share of fixed costs in total costs. The results in table 3 suggest that this latter effect dominates the scale effect. Cutting in half the value of CDR only has an impact on the computed value of the local economies of scale when rationing is small. When rationing is severe, the upward shift in variable costs dominates, and the computed welfare costs are quite insensitive to variations in CDR. From now on, we set CDR = 0.07.

We now come to the more controversial aspects of the links between QR regimes and industrial organization as we introduce excessive entry (variant 3), collusive behavior (variant 4), and excessive entry cum collusive behavior (variant 5). The results of these alternative formulations are reported in Table 4 for across-the-board rationing rates of 20 percent and 50 percent. Because parameterizing is even more difficult in these cases, we opted to approximate the Chilean firm exit rate when we introduce excessive entry (variant 3) and the rationing rate is 50 percent. The same procedure is adopted when we parameterize collusive behavior (variant 4): we approximate the decline in PCM observed in Chile between 1967 and 1979. The parameters for variants 3 and 4 remain unchanged in variant 5.

Under this parameterization, the welfare costs of a 50 percent rationing rate continue to be dominated by the upward shift in variable costs caused by the higher costs of imported intermediate inputs. Therefore, we concentrate on the results for a 20 percent rationing rate of consumer and intermediate imports. The major difference in estimates is accounted for by the introduction of scale economies. Across-the-board rationing has a welfare cost that is three times higher under IRTS than under CRTS. Clearly, a less costly alternative would be to constrain rationing to sectors with IRTS so that resources would be drawn into these sectors and scale efficiency would be raised.

Contrasting the welfare costs of collusive behavior with no entry (variant 4) with excessive entry and no collusive behavior (variant 3), one finds that welfare costs are the same for this parameterization. When the two variants interact (variant 5), welfare costs of rationing are marginally higher. The results from these simulations suggest that there is a trade-off between excessive entry and collusive behavior. Collusive behavior facilitates the exploitation of scale economies but adds a welfare cost because pricing exceeds average costs. Entry to eliminate above normal profits leads to scale inefficiency.

Industrial Organization Implications of QR Trade Regimes   151

5 Conclusions

The empirical evidence reviewed in this paper suggests that QR trade regimes in developing countries are characterized by above normal profits and excessive entry (in the sense of too many firms operating at suboptimal scale) in manufacturing. Cross-sectional econometric evidence, in which factors contributing to differences in profitability across sectors are taken into account, further support the view that imports create a discipline on the behavior of domestic firms in the sense that firms in sectors with high import shares adopt pricing rules that more closely approximate competitive behavior.

This evidence serves as a basis for building a three sector simulation model to examine the welfare effects of an increase in QRs where some sectors have increasing returns to scale. Several model variants are introduced separately to ascertain the effects of introducing economies of scale, firm entry/exit, departure from competitive pricing, and interactions between entry and pricing rules.

Numerical simulations are then performed on a representative three-sector semi-industrial economy with the simulations consisting of progressively tightening QRs starting from a regime with no QRs. Numerical simulations suggest as a rough order of magnitude that the traditional welfare cost calculations for moderate rationing could be tripled if the manufacturing sector has increasing returns to scale. Further experimentation with alternative formulations including entry until profits are eliminated and oligopolistic pricing with no entry indicate a trade-off between scale efficiency loss caused by firm entry to eliminate profits and departures from average cost pricing under collusive arrangements.

Appendix

The simulations reported in the text are derived from a three sector representative semi-industrial economy. The initial solution was calibrated to reproduce the following initial equilibrium values (with all prices set equal to one by choice of units):

	Agriculture	Manufacturing	Services
Gross output			
(XO)	300	400	500
Exports	100	150	
Domestic Consumption	65	111	345

152   T. Condon and J. de Melo

	Agriculture	Manufacturing	Services
Imported Consumption	28	45	
Imported Intermediates	46	115	16
Domestic Intermediates	135	139	155
National income 594			

The model also includes tariffs and subsidies which are not altered. Production functions are Cobb-Douglas and the parameters of the LES system are such that all subsistence minima are set to zero.

References

Behrman J (1976) Foreign Trade Regimes and Economic Development: Chile, Columbia University Press, New York

Bhagwati, J (1965) "On the Equivalence of Tariffs and Quotas", in Trade, Growth and the Balance of Payments, (ed Baldwin R), Amsterdam, North-Holland

Caves, R (1980), "Introduction" Symposium on Trade and Industrial Organization, Journal of Industrial Economics, vol. 29: 11–28

Clarke R, Davies S, Waterson M (1984) "The Profitability Concentration Relation: Market Power or Efficiency", Journal of Industrial Economics, Vol. 32: 435–50

Corbo V, de Melo J eds. (1985) "Scrambling for Survival: How Firms Adjusted to the Southern Cone Reforms", World Bank Staff Working Papers Series No. 704

Cox D, Harris R (1985) "Trade Liberalization and Industrial Organization: Some Estimates for Canada", Journal of Political Economy, Vol 93, No. 1: 115–45

Devarajan S, Rodrik D (1989) "Pro-Competitive Effects of Trade Reform: Results from a CGE Model for Cameroon". Working Paper. J F Kennedy School of Government, Harvard University, Cambridge

Dixit A K, Norman V (1980) Theory of International Trade, Cambridge University Press

Eastman H, Stykolt S (1960) "A Model for the Study of Protected Oligopolies", Economic Journal, Vol. 70: 336–47

Frischtak C, Hadjimichael B, Zachau U (1989) "Competition Policies for Industrializing Countries", Policy Research Series No. 7, Washington, DC, The World Bank

Grais W, de Melo J, Urata S (1986) "A General Equilibrium Estimation of the Effects of Reductions in Tariffs and Quantitative Restrictions in Turkey in 1978", in Srinivasan T N, Whalley J (eds) General Equilibrium Trade Policy Modelling, MIT Press: 61–88

Geroski P, Jacquemin A (1981) "Imports as Competitive Discipline", in Geroski P, Jacquemin A (eds) Symposium on Industrial Organization and International Trade", Recherches Economiques de Louvain: 209–42

Industrial Organization Implications of QR Trade Regimes 153

Harris R. (1985) "Applied General Equilibrium Analysis of Small Open Economies with Scale Economies and Imperfect Competition", American Economic Review, Vol. 74, No. 5: 1017–1032

Helpman E, Krugman P (1989) Trade Policy and Market Structure, Cambridge: MIT Press

Horstmann I, Markusen J (1986) "Up the Average Cost Curve: Inefficient Entry and the New Protectionism", Journal of International Economics, vol. 24, 225–48.

Krueger A (1974) "The Political Economy of the Rent-Seeking Society", American Economic Review, vol. 64: 291–303

Kubo Y, de Melo J, Robinson S (1986) "Trade Strategies and Growth Episodes" in Chenery H et al, (eds) Industrialization and Growth: A Comparative Study, Oxford University Press: 148–87

Lee K, Urata S, Choi I (1986) "Recent Developments in Industrial Organizational Issues in Korea", (mimeo) World Bank

Melo J. de, Robinson S (1989) "The Treatment of Foreign Trade in Computable General Equilibrium Model of Small Economies", Journal of International Economics, vol. 27: 47–67

Melo J de, and Urata S (1986) "The Influence of Increased Foreign Competition on Industrial Concentration and Profitability", International Journal of Industrial Organization: 287–304

Melo J de, Roland-Holst D (forthcoming) "Industrial Organization and Trade Liberalization: Evidence from Korea", in Baldwin R (ed) Empirical Studies of Commercial Policy, University of Chicago Press

Mohammad S, Whalley J (1984) "Rent-Seeking in India: Its Cost and Policy Significance", Kyklos, Vol. 37, No. 3: 387–413.

Roberts M, Tybout J (forthcoming) "Rationalizing and Trade Exposure in Developing Countries", in Baldwin R ed, Empirical Studies of Commercial Policy. Chicago: University of Chicago Press

Rodrik D (1988) "Imperfect Competition, Scale Economies, and Trade Policy in Developing Countries", in Baldwin R (ed), Trade Policy Issues and Empirical Analysis, University of Chicago Press and NBER, Chicago and Cambridge

Rotemberg J, Saloner D (1988) "Tariffs vs. Quotas with Implicit Collusion", Canadian Journal of Agricultural Economics, vol. 22: 237–44.

World Bank (1987) Korea: Managing the Industrial Transition. Washington, DC: the World Bank.

Market Access and Welfare under Free Trade Agreements: Textiles under NAFTA

Olivier Cadot, Céline Carrère, Jaime de Melo,
and Alberto Portugal-Pérez

The effective market access granted to textiles and apparel under the North American Free Trade Agreement (NAFTA) is estimated, taking into account the presence of rules of origin. First, estimates are provided of the effect of tariff preferences combined with rules of origin on the border prices of Mexican final goods exported to the United States and of U.S. intermediate goods exported to Mexico, based on eight-digit Harmonized System tariff-line data. A third of the estimated rise in the border price of Mexican apparel products is found to compensate for the cost of complying with NAFTA's rules of origin, and NAFTA is found to have raised the price of U.S. intermediate goods exported to Mexico by around 12 percent, with downstream rules of origin accounting for a third of that increase. Second, simulations are used to estimate welfare gains for Mexican exporters from preferential market access under NAFTA. The presence of rules of origin is found to approximately halve these gains.

Improved market access may not have been the main reason that Mexico entered the North American Free Trade Agreement (NAFTA), but it was certainly among the anticipated benefits at the negotiations. By 2002, NAFTA preferences in goods markets should have given Mexican exporters a 4 percent

Olivier Cadot is a professor of economics at Ecole des Hautes Etudes Commerciales, University of Lausanne, and he is associated with the Centre of Economic Policy Research (CEPR) and the Center for Studies and Research in International Development (CERDI); his email address is olivier.cadot@unil.ch. Céline Carrère is an assistant professor of economics at Ecole des Hautes Etudes Commerciales, University of Lausanne, and she is associated with CERDI; her email address is celine.carrere@unil.ch. Jaime de Melo is a professor of economics, Department of Political Economy, University of Geneva, and he is associated with CEPR and CERDI; his email address is demelo@ecopo.unige.ch. Alberto Portugal-Pérez is a PhD candidate in economics at the University of Geneva; his email address is alberto.portugal@ecopo.unige.ch. The authors thank Patrick Conway, Marcelo Olarreaga, seminar participants at CERDI and Groupement de Recherche en Economie Quantitative d'Aix Marseille, and two anonymous referees for comments on an earlier draft. All editorial matters were handled by Luis Serven. The findings, interpretations, and conclusions expressed in it are entirely those of the authors and do not necessarily reflect the views of the World Bank, its executive directors, or the countries they represent. An earlier version with some appendix material is available in Cadot and others (2005a). Supplementary data can be found at wber.oxfordjournals.org.

THE WORLD BANK ECONOMIC REVIEW, VOL. 19, NO. 3, pp. 379–405   doi:10.1093/wber/lhi019
Advance Access publication December 29, 2005

379

average price margin over competitors in U.S. markets. On the basis of the tariff data, the average tariff preference for textiles and apparel was close to 8 percent.

Were it not for rules of origin that must be satisfied to sell in the United States at the tariff-inclusive price, market access would be expected to result in substantial rents for Mexican exporters to the United States. However, NAFTA negotiations reveal the importance of rules of origin in preferential trading arrangements. Krueger (1993) notes that the November 1992 draft chapter on rules of origin was 193 pages long and that the United States supported more stringent rules of origin, while Canada and Mexico preferred a low regional value-added content rule. She also notes that the interesting case to analyze was that in which the "US had a significant cost advantage relative to Mexico, but a cost disadvantage vis-à-vis the rest of the world" (p. 11). This is almost the exact case for trade in textiles (i.e., intermediate goods) between Mexico and the United States.

Krishna (2005) summarizes several contributions since Krueger's study, and more empirical research is starting to appear (see Cadot and others 2005b). As a result of this work, rules of origin are being increasingly recognized as the primary causes of the disappointing trade expansion effects of preferential trading arrangements. Rules of origin constrain the sourcing policies of final good producers, generating higher input and administrative compliance costs. Recent studies that rely on utilization rates of preferences to assess the effects of rules of origin on the benefits of trade preferences (Estevadeordal 2000; Anson and others 2005; Cadot and others 2005; Carrère and de Melo 2005) have found evidence of non-negligible compliance costs.

Trade flows, however, offer no information on the distribution of the rents generated by trade preferences, which is necessary to determine the likely welfare effects of preferential market access combined with rules of origin. To make further progress and assess the welfare effects of market access under free trade agreements, the effects of preferences on prices rather than on quantities or utilization rates must be estimated. This implies estimating the pass-through effects of tariff preferences on consumer prices (i.e., the extent to which tariff preferences translate into a corresponding increase in foreign producer prices)— an exercise similar to estimating exchange rate pass-through—which is carried out in section I. These estimates are then used in a simulation model to quantify the likely welfare effects for Mexican producers of preferential access in textiles and apparel under rules of origin in the United States.

Two recent studies estimate the effects of trade preferences on member-country prices in agreements between developed and developing countries using the textiles and apparel sector, where preferences are typically substantial. Olarreaga and Özden (2005) looked at the effect the Africa Growth and Opportunity Act had on the unit values of U.S. apparel imports from Africa, and Özden and Sharma (2004) explore rent capture by apparel producers from the Caribbean Basin Initiative. Their research shows that preferences translate into higher border prices for preferred exporters and that pass-through of the tariff reductions is also substantial (between a third and a half).

However, the premise that higher border prices imply higher rents for producers is not necessarily true. First, as Olarreaga and Özden (2005) note, part of the increase in the border price may be captured by intermediaries in the exporting country, which may in fact be large companies based in the importing country. Second, as Özden and Sharma (2004) note, part of the border price increase may simply cover the additional cost of complying with rules of origin (higher input prices and other administrative costs).[1]

Cadot, Estevadeordal, and Suwa-Eisenmann (2005) suggest that rules of origin under NAFTA have the political function of creating a captive market for U.S. intermediate goods. In this case, the price of U.S. intermediate goods should be sensitive to rules of origin and tariff preferences downstream. This hypothesis is tested by regressing the border price of U.S. intermediate goods exported to Mexico (relative to the border price of those same goods when exported to nonpreferential destinations) on rules of origin and tariff preferences applied by the United States on downstream (re-exported) Mexican goods. Vertical links are captured using an input–output table.

This article contributes to the literature in three ways. First, it estimates pass-through effects in the presence of rules of origin from intermediate good producers to final good producers in partner countries (in this case, from textile producers in the United States to Mexican apparel producers). Second, it links pass-through estimates directly to rules of origin through the use of proxies. This is the first time that estimates of the pass-through effects of tariff preferences directly take into account the effects of rules of origin. Third, it sets up a partial equilibrium simulation model that gives the order of magnitude of these estimated effects on welfare.

When rules of origin are not controlled for, the elasticity of the border price of Mexican exports to U.S. tariff preference margins is close to 80 percent.[2] After rules of origin are controlled for, however, Mexican apparel producers retain only about half the preference margin. Rules of origin and tariff preferences downstream indeed affect U.S. intermediate good prices in a statistically significant way, contributing over half of the predicted price rise of U.S. exports

---

1. The approach in this research is extended in the following ways. As in Olarreaga and Özden (2005), border prices for preferential and most-favored-nation apparel shipments are compared using unit values calculated from International Trade Commission trade data at the eight-digit level of the Harmonized System (HS). As in Özden and Sharma (2004), these border price differences are regressed on tariff preference margins and control variables. But instead of quantity variables, a vector of dummy variables for rules of origin are included using a database compiled by Estevadeordal (2000). In a second step, on the basis of those estimates, simulation techniques are used to calculate the likely market access improvement for Mexican exporters of apparel to the United States under NAFTA.

2. That is, a reduction of NAFTA tariffs below most-favored-nation tariffs by x percentage points translates into an increase in Mexican producer prices by $0.8x$ percentage points, and so a decrease in U.S. consumer prices by $0.2x$ percentage points or a 20 percent pass-through.

382   THE WORLD BANK ECONOMIC REVIEW, VOL. 19, NO. 3

that is attributable to NAFTA (30 percent for rules of origin alone), and U.S. intermediate good producers are able to retain a sizable share of the rents generated by Mexican preferential tariffs. Inspired by these reduced-form econometric estimates, a partial equilibrium structural model is then simulated to calculate the orders of magnitude of the reduced welfare gain for Mexican exporters to the United States that is due to the presence of rules of origin.

I. MODELING PREFERENCE PASS-THROUGH UNDER RULES OF ORIGIN

Table 1 describes the data used in section II to estimate the pass-through effects under NAFTA. The 865 tariff lines (at the eight-digit level of the Harmonized System, HS) of the data set are spread across the 11 textiles and apparel chapters. Exports are concentrated in two sectors, knitted apparel (HS-61) and nonknitted apparel (HS-62), both final sectors according to the Broad Economic Categories classification used here. On average, utilization rates for exports of Mexican textiles and apparel that entered the U.S. market under NAFTA are fairly high, although they are lower for final goods (around 70 percent) than for intermediate goods. The preference margins were just about equal to the U.S. most favored nation tariff rates in 2002. Because the statistical work is carried out at the HS eight-digit level, tariffs and utilization rates are weighted by import shares (to prevent giving undue weight to tariff lines with marginal trade flows).

The cumulative density function confirms that utilization rates are higher for intermediate goods than for final goods, though the majority of Mexican exports to the United States are in the final goods category (figure 1). This heterogeneity in utilization rates at the HS eight-digit level reflects a combination of heterogeneity in firm cost characteristics and possibly of heterogeneity in product characteristics.[3]

As in most preferential trade agreements, preferential rules of origin in textiles and apparel under NAFTA include a change of tariff classification that can be applied at either the chapter level (HS two-digit level) or the heading level (HS four-digit level).[4] This requires the Mexican final product shipped to

---

3. Carrère and de Melo (2005) develop a simple model in which heterogeneity in compliance costs across firms leads to utilization rates in the range $(0 < u_i < 1)$ and exploit this heterogeneity to come up with an estimate of the breakdown of compliance costs associated with RoO into a (fixed) administrative component and a distortionary component.

4. In addition to the product-specific rules described in table 1, rules of origin also include regime-wide rules. In the case of NAFTA, these include a *do minimis* (or tolerance) criterion, which stipulates a 7 percent maximum share of nonoriginating materials that can be used without affecting the origin of the final product; bilateral cumulation, which stipulates that producers in Mexico can use inputs from the United States (and Canada) without affecting the final good's originating status provided that the inputs are themselves originating (i.e., provided that they themselves satisfy the area's rules of origin); roll-up, which states that nonoriginating materials (which have acquired origin by meeting specific processing requirements) maintain this origin when used as inputs in a subsequent transformation (i.e., the non-originating materials are no longer taken into account in calculating value added; and a self-certification method. In the case of NAFTA, duty-drawbacks are not allowed. For more details, see Cadot and others (forthcoming), table 2.

TABLE 1. Mexican Exports of Textiles and Apparel to the United States and Description of Rules of Order under North American Free Trade Agreement

| | | | | | | Rules of origin (percent of HS eight-digit tariff lines) | | | | |
| | | | | | | Change in tariff classification | | Technical requirement and change in tariff classification | | |
	Number of HS eight-digit tariff lines	Share of total (percent)	Share of Mexican exports to United States (percent)	Mean utilization rate[a] (percent)	Mean tariff preference margin[a] (percent)	At heading level (HS four-digit)	At chapter level (HS two-digit)	At heading level (HS four-digit)	At chapter level (HS two-digit)	Final goods
Section 11: Textiles and textile articles	865	100	100	80.70 (77.93)	9.97 (6.63)	15.84	34.2	0.69	49.25	53.53
Chapter										
50: Silk	1	0.12	0.01	—	—	100	0	0	0	0
51: Wool, fine, or coarse animal hair; horsehair yarn and woven fabric	24	2.77	0.33	98.85 (99.86)	12.82 (17.45)	91.67	8.33	0	0	4.17
52: Cotton	90	10.4	1.96	92.60 (97.95)	8.36 (8.15)	68.89	27.78	3.33	0	3.33
53: Other vegetable textile fibers; paper yarn and woven fabrics of paper yarn	13	1.5	0.02	83.65 (83.69)	1.67 (3.09)	53.85	46.15	0	0	0
54: Man-made filaments	67	7.75	2.61	94.3 (99.81)	11.86 (19.78)	0	98.51	0	1.49	5.97
55: Man-made staple fibers	68	7.86	1.79	90.34 (98.81)	11.31 (9.44)	57.35	38.24	1.47	2.94	5.88
56: Wadding, felt, and nonwovens; special yarns; twine, cordage, ropes, and cables and articles thereof	52	6.01	1.32	71.89 (81.63)	7.34 (6.97)	0	98.078	0	1.92	1.92
57: Carpets and other textile floor coverings	27	3.12	0.18	95.96 (97.58)	3.07 (3.71)	0	100	0	0	100
58: Special woven fabrics; tufted textile fabrics; lace; tapestries; trimmings; embroidery	45	5.2	0.47	87.48 (97.09)	7.04 (8.49)	0	100	0	0	4.44

(Continued)

TABLE 1. Continued

	Number of HS eight-digit tariff lines	Share of total (percent)	Share of Mexican exports to United States (percent)	Mean utilization rate[a] (percent)	Mean tariff preference margin[a] (percent)	Rules of origin (percent of HS eight-digit tariff lines)				Final goods
						Change in tariff classification		Technical requirement and change in tariff classification		
						At heading level (HS four-digit)	At chapter level (HS two-digit)	At heading level (HS four-digit)	At chapter level (HS two-digit)	
59: Impregnated, coated, covered or laminated textile fabrics, textiles articles of a kind suitable for industrial use	42	4.86	0.79	87.68 (95.98)	4.53 (5.05)	7.14	90.48	0	2.38	0
60: Knitted or crocheted fabrics	4	0.46	0.01	99.77 (99.76)	18.02 (17.71)	0	100	0	0	0
61: Articles of apparel and clothing accessories, knitted or crocheted	145	16.76	33.85	69.41 (62.16)	13.13 (6.40)	1.38	2.069	0	96.55	100
62: Articles of apparel and clothing accessories, not knitted or crocheted	205	23.7	48.74	71.03 (82.91)	11.11 (6.03)	0	0.49	0	99.51	100
63: Other made-up textile articles; sets; worn clothing and worn textile articles rags	82	9.48	7.91	88.10 (92.80)	7.85 (5.59)	1.22	2.44	2.44	93.9	86.59

—, not available.

[a]Figure in parentheses is the weighted average, which reflects the importance of each tariff line in total Mexican exports to the United States.

Note: Exceptions to change in tariff classification (generally prohibiting the use of nonoriginating materials from a certain subheading, heading, or chapter) also exist but are not mentioned since they concern 99 percent of the tariff lines in section 11. The sample period is 2002; sample data are from the textiles and apparel sector (HS eight-digit level, section 11).

Source: Authors' analysis based on data described in the text.

FIGURE 1. Cumulative Density Function of Utilization Rates by Mexican Exporters under NAFTA in Textiles and Apparel Sector 2002

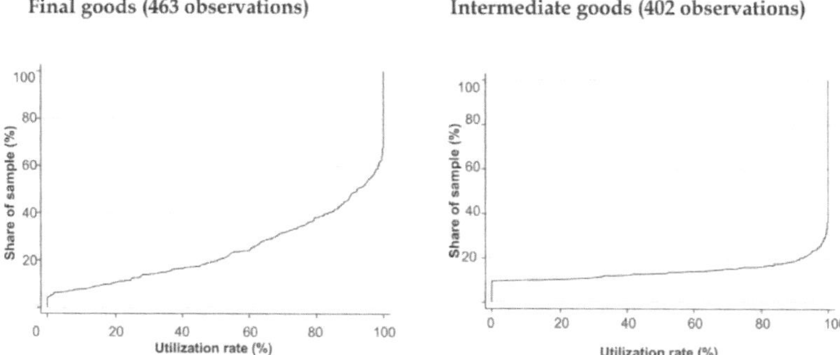

Source: Authors' analysis based on data described in the text.

the United States to be classified in a chapter (or heading) of the HS different from its imported intermediate components. Clearly, a change of chapter is more restrictive than a change of heading. Most sectors subject to a change in heading or chapter are classified as intermediate. Except carpets (chapter 57), final goods not only include a change of tariff classification but also rely on a technical requirement imposed on the final good's production process to confer origin. Changes of tariff classification and technical requirements are not the only criteria applied. In the case of textiles and apparel, 99 percent of the tariff lines also include an exception (not included in table 1). Exceptions lead to considerable complication for customs officials in determining origin in preferential agreements.[5]

The textiles and apparel sector has several characteristics that merit attention here. First, there is product differentiation, which suggests that there might be price interaction between member and nonmember countries. If so, modeling this interaction might be useful (as in Chang and Winters 2002), rather than assuming perfect competition (as in Özden and Sharma 2004).

Second, virtually all nonpreferential trade in textiles and apparel products is governed by the Agreement on Textiles and Clothing, the successor to the Multi-Fibre Arrangement. Under the Agreement on Textiles and Clothing agreed on as part of the Uruguay Round, quotas on garments were to be progressively enlarged until final phaseout in January 2005. But importing

---

5. Since an exception applies to virtually all tariff lines in textiles and apparel, it cannot be included in the statistical analysis here, which relies on the use of dummy variables. Furthermore, exceptions can be positive (the criterion does not apply) or negative (a further criterion must apply). Exceptions usually require a further criterion, beyond a change of tariff classification, to be met. A particularly vivid example in the case of NAFTA is the case of men's overcoat made of wool (HS-62011). Establishing origin requires in most instances a change in chapter with the restriction that the visible lining must be produced from yarn and finished in either party (see the detailed description in Brenton and Imawaga 2005).

386   THE WORLD BANK ECONOMIC REVIEW, VOL. 19, NO. 3

countries backloaded the enlargement of binding quotas until the very end of the transition phase—the end of 2004 (Spinanger 1998). Thus, during the sample period (2000–02), most of the world's nonpreferential trade in garments was still affected by binding quotas. Intra-NAFTA trade in textiles and apparel, by contrast, has been governed by annex 300B of NAFTA, which superseded the Multi-Fibre Arrangement and the Agreement on Textiles and Clothing and mandated an immediate elimination of quotas on "originating" Mexican goods (those that comply with the stipulated rules of origin) and a gradual elimination of quotas for "nonoriginating" Mexican goods (those that do not comply with the stipulated rules of origin).[6] Under a regime of binding quantitative restrictions on nonpreferred exporters, price interaction did not exist between Mexican producers and non-NAFTA exporters because Mexicans were operating along a residual demand curve, whose elasticity was unaffected by the pricing decisions of quota-constrained competitors. These observations justify the monopolistic competition modeling framework below with product differentiation.

Modeling Pass-Through: A Monopolistic Competition Framework

The model outlined here features monopolistic competition with Dixit–Stiglitz preferences on the final good market but disregards price competition between suppliers. This allows an expression of the pass-through that depends on the presence of rules of origin to be derived.[7]

Suppose then that n different Mexican final goods, indexed by j, are sold on the U.S. market in competition with goods imported from the rest of the world. Let x_j be the quantity of Mexican goods sold and x_j^* the quantity of foreign goods sold (i.e., imports from the rest of the world). There is no U.S. production of final goods. And let X_0 be an aggregate of other goods consumed by U.S. households. Preferences are

$$(1) \qquad U(\cdot) = X_0 + \sum_{j=1}^{n} \ln X_j$$

where

$$(2) \qquad X_j = \left[x_j^{\rho_j} + \left(x_j^* \right)^{\rho_j} \right]^{1/\rho_j}.$$

---

6. The NAFTA Treaty, annex 300B, section 1, §2.

7. A similar framework with product differentiation (the so-called "Armington framework") but without monopolistic competition across suppliers is also adopted in the simulation exercise of section III. This slightly different framework is largely equivalent since it also implies less than full rent capture by Mexican exporters even without rules of origin on intermediate goods and obviates the need to make assumptions about economies of scale that is typical in the monopolistic competition framework. To shorten the presentation of the simulation model in section III, all instances in this section where the simulation model departs from the structure presented here are noted.

The quasi-linearity of U ensures that the marginal utility of income is constant and equal to 1, while the log form of the second term ensures that an interior budget allocation holds between the n Mexican goods and other goods. This means that tariff changes have no income effects, an assumption maintained in the simulations of section III. Additivity of preferences implies strong separability, so two-stage budgeting holds, confining the price effects of tariff preferences to apparel products. The elasticity of substitution between Mexican and foreign brands of good j is

$$(3) \qquad \sigma_j = \frac{1}{(1 - \rho_j)}$$

where p_j is the border price of Mexican goods and p_j^* the border price of foreign goods. When q_j is the internal price of Mexican goods, q_j^* the internal price for foreign goods, and t_j the ad valorem tariff,

$$(4) \qquad q_j = (1 + t_j)p_j.$$

An equation that accounts for the difference between most-favored-nation and NAFTA tariffs will be introduced shortly.

Let

$$(5) \qquad Q_j \equiv q_j^{1-\sigma_j} + (q_j^*)^{1-\sigma_j}.$$

The U.S. demand for the Mexican brand of good j is then

$$(6) \qquad x_j = \left(\frac{q_j^{-\sigma_j}}{Q_j} \right) E_j$$

where

$$(7) \qquad E_j = q_j x_j + q_j^* x_j^*$$

is the subexpenditure on good j. The own-price elasticity of U.S. demand for Mexican final good j is

$$(8) \qquad \varepsilon_j = \sigma_j + \frac{(1 - \sigma_j)q_j^{1-\sigma_j}}{Q_j}.$$

The equations for the foreign good are similar.

Mexican final goods are produced by combining value-added with m different intermediate goods indexed by i under a Leontief technology with input–output coefficient a_{ij}. Each intermediate good can come from either the United States or the rest of the world, because the goods are perfect substitutes.[8] Let $\bar{z}_{ij}$ denote the

---

8. In the simulations below, intermediate goods by origin enter into production according to a constant elasticity of substitution aggregator function.

quantity of "composite" (U.S and foreign) intermediate good i used in the production of final good j; that is, $\bar{z}_{ij} = z_{ij} + z_{ij}^*$. Then,

$$(9) \qquad x_j = \min\left\{ F_j(K_j, L_j); \frac{\bar{z}_{1j}}{a_{1j}}; \cdots; \frac{\bar{z}_{mj}}{a_{mj}} \right\}.$$

In the absence of rules of origin, perfect substitutability means that Mexican choice of intermediate goods (U.S. or foreign) would be bang–bang. If U.S. intermediate goods were all more expensive than foreign ones, for instance, they would not be used at all. However, with rules specifying a minimum content r_j (expressed here for simplicity as a proportion of total intermediate use), Mexican exporters have to use U.S. intermediate goods in proportion r_j and foreign intermediate goods in proportion $1 - r_j$.[9]

Let $C_j(x_j)$ be the cost function dual to F_j and $\phi_j(p_j) \equiv C_j[x_j(p_j)]/x_j(p_j)$ the corresponding unit-cost function, and suppose that $\phi_j' > 0$. If p_i is the price of U.S. intermediate good i and p_i^* the price of its foreign substitute, the marginal cost of Mexican final good j is

$$
(10) \qquad
\begin{aligned}
\Phi_j &= \phi_j + \sum_{i=1}^{m} a_{ij}\left[r_j p_i + (1 - r_j)(1 + t_i)p_i^* \right] \\
&= \phi_j + \sum_{i=1}^{m} a_{ij}\bar{p}_i
\end{aligned}
$$

where

$$(11) \qquad \bar{p}_i = r_j p_i + (1 - r_j)q_i^*$$

and

$$(12) \qquad q_i^* = (1 + t_i)p_i^*.$$

A similar expression holds for the functional forms adopted in section III, where binding rules of origin raise final good unit costs.

Optimal pricing by Mexican final good exporters implies

$$(13) \qquad \left(1 - \frac{1}{\varepsilon_j}\right)q_j = (1 + t_j)\left(\phi_j + \sum_{i=1}^{m} a_{ij}\bar{p}_i \right).$$

9. As summarized in table 1, there is actually no regional value content in the textiles and apparel sector, the most common rules of origin requiring changes of tariff classification. Exceptions apply to 99 percent of textiles and apparel tariff lines, and technical requirements apply to 50 percent of them. Given the large increase in Mexican intermediate purchases from the United States since NAFTA, it can be safely assumed that these requirements were designed to raise the regional value content of Mexican production. Several papers collected in Cadot and others (forthcoming) document how NAFTA's exceptions, changes of tariff classification, and technical requirements have been calibrated to make U.S. sourcing the only option.

Because $\bar{p}_i$ is an increasing function of r_j whenever $p_i > q_i^*$, the supply price of the Mexican final good in the United States is itself an increasing function of the local content requirement r_j.[10]

MEXICAN PASS-THROUGH. Mexican pass-through is addressed here first, then a slightly different version of the model is used to study U.S. pass-through. Assume first that the price of U.S. intermediate goods is fixed. Let p_j^N stand for NAFTA producer prices, p_j^M for most-favored-nation producer prices, t_j^N for NAFTA tariffs, and t_j^M for most-favored-nation tariffs. And let $\Delta p_j \equiv p_j^N - p_j^M$ and $\Delta t_j \equiv t_j^M - t_j^N$. Differentiating equation 13 and linearizing show that

$$(14) \qquad \frac{\Delta p_j}{p_j^M} \simeq \psi_j \frac{\Delta t_j}{1 + t_j^M} + \Theta_j r_j$$

where $\Theta_j > 0$ and $\psi_j > 0$ are expressions given in full in supplemental appendix 1 (available at http://wber.oxfordjournals.org). The first term captures the impact of NAFTA tariff preferences on Mexican producer prices, so $1 - \psi_j$ measures the pass-through effect (i.e., the impact on U.S. consumer prices) resulting from preferential market access. The second term, which depends on input–output relationships, the price of U.S. intermediate goods, and the elasticity of demand for the final Mexican good in the United States, measures the impact on Mexican border prices of increases in the price of the intermediate good "exported" from the United States and induced by rules of origin.

In this model, both preferential rates and rules of origin are assumed to be exogenous. In general (and certainly in the case of NAFTA, as explained by Estevadeordal 2000), negotiations can be viewed as a game played by three parties in which negotiation is over two instruments: speed of preferential tariffs phaseout and rules of origin criteria. Thus, there is a potential for multicollinearity between r_j and $\Delta t_j/(1 + t_j^M)$ in equation 14. However, this article uses the most recent trade data (2000–02), covering a period when the phaseout was virtually complete, and nearly all tariff preferences were equal to most-favored-nation tariffs.[11] The U.S. most-favored-nation tariff can be considered free from endogeneity to NAFTA's rules of origin.[12] But a more ambitious assessment of rules of origin would rely on a political economy approach, as in Cadot, Estevadeordal, and Suwa-Eisenmann (2005).

---

10. If $p_i \leq q_i^*$, the local content requirement is not binding.

11. For example, on the Mexican method sample below for 2000–02, the preference margin for Mexican imports was equal to the U.S. most-favored-nation tariff for 1,176 of 1,304 tariff lines—that is, 90 percent of the HS eight-digit tariff lines.

12. In the context of the debate on the relation between preferential trade arrangements and multilateral trade liberalization, Limão (forthcoming) finds evidence that the U.S. most-favored-nation tariffs could be endogenous because U.S. preferential trade arrangements led to less subsequential multilateral trade liberalization.

390   THE WORLD BANK ECONOMIC REVIEW, VOL. 19, NO. 3

U.S. PASS-THROUGH. To consider the market for U.S. intermediate good i, the assumption that its price is fixed is relaxed. Let $z_i\,(p_i)$ be its U.S. supply; if it is exhausted by Mexican demand, the market-clearing condition is

$$(15) \qquad \sum_{j=1}^{n} a_{ij} x_j(p_j) = z_i(p_i).$$

Differentiating equation 15 and letting ε_i^s be the supply elasticity of intermediate goods and ε_j^s the supply elasticity of final goods result in:

$$(16) \qquad \frac{\Delta p_i}{p_i^M} \simeq \frac{z_i}{p_i^2 \varepsilon_i^s} \sum_{j=1}^{n} a_{ij} x_j \varepsilon_j^s \frac{\Delta p_j}{p_j^M},$$

which is similar in form to equation 14 but depends on downstream final good prices.[13]

II. PASS-THROUGH ESTIMATION AND RESULTS

In equation 14, rules of origin took the form of a regional value content. This is not the case in the textiles and apparel sector, though exceptions and technical requirements have similar effects. Dummy variables are used to capture the effects of the current rules, with each representing a specific legal form of rules of origin. CC_j is equal to 1 if a change of chapter on good j is required, and $TECH_j$ is equal to 1 if a technical requirement is imposed.[14] The equation to be estimated for the Mexican pass-through is thus

$$(17) \qquad \frac{\Delta p_j}{p_j^M} = \alpha_0 + \alpha_1 \frac{\Delta t_j}{1 + t_j^M} + \alpha_2 CC_j + \alpha_3 TECH_j + u_j.$$

All parameter estimates are expected to be positive, and $1 - \alpha_1$ measures the Mexican pass-through.

13. This may raise an endogeneity issue. As in equation 14, $\Delta p_i/p_i^M$ depends on a weighted sum of $\Delta p_i/p_i^M$ in which the weights are the input–output coefficients b_{ij}. In equation 14, $\Delta p_i/p_i^M$ can be similarly shown to depend on a weighted sum of $\Delta p_i/p_i^M$ through Θ_j (see supplemental appendix 1). Thus, the link between the regressor and the error term in equation 14 is through two nested weighted sums and is thus, although linear, very indirect.

14. As an alternative, Estevadeordal (2000) index could have been used as a proxy for the effect of rules of origin. Such an approach would not be appropriate for the textiles and apparel sector. First, besides the ubiquitous exceptions, only three types of rules of origin are used: change in tariff classification at the heading level, change in tariff classification at the chapter level, and a technical requirement. Thus, for textiles and apparel, Estevadeordal's index takes only three different values (out of seven). Given that, changes in headings and changes in chapters are perfectly collinear (i.e., a tariff line without a change in chapter systematically has a chapter heading and vice versa), using Estevadeordal's index does not add more variability to the rules of origin indicator than the dummies CC and $TECH$. Moreover, the specification used here does not impose an a priori ranking between the different combinations of rules of origin.

The equation to be estimated for the U.S. pass-through is

$$\frac{\Delta p_i}{p_i^M} = \beta_0 + \beta_1 \frac{\Delta t_i}{1 + t_i^M} + \beta_2 CC_i + \beta_3 TECH_i + \beta_4 \sum_j b_{ij} \frac{\Delta t_j}{\left(1 + t_j^M\right)}$$
$$+ \beta_5 \sum_j b_{ij} CC_j + \beta_6 \sum_j b_{ij} TECH_j + \varepsilon_i$$

(18)

The U.S. pass-through of Mexican tariff preferences, measured by $1 - \beta_1$, is estimated after controlling for two types of effects relevant to the determination of U.S. intermediate good prices. The first type, measured by coefficients β_2 and β_3, is the effect of rules of origin applying to U.S. intermediate goods themselves. To avoid unnecessarily complicating the calculations, this effect is not considered when intermediate goods are not assumed to be produced with imported intermediate goods, but it does occur in the simulation in section III where Mexican final goods use imported intermediate goods.

The second type is demand effects, which are measured by coefficients β_4 (effect of downstream U.S. preferences on Mexican goods using intermediate i filtered by input–output coefficients a_{ij}), β_5, and β_6 (the same effect for downstream rules of origin). These effects are instruments for the prices of downstream final goods, which are endogenous, as argued above. Intuitively, a higher U.S. preference on downstream Mexican goods raises the induced demand for intermediate goods and thus their price. Likewise, stiffer rules of origin downstream pick up the "captive market" effect discussed in the introduction. Thus, all coefficients are expected to be positive, and the null hypothesis for β_5 and β_6 is that there is no captive market effect.

Equation 16 is estimated with panel data using the weighted least squares estimator, which performs better than ordinary least squares on the sample because it modulates the importance of each observation in the final solution (details are supplied in supplemental appendix 4). This method assigns each tariff line a weight that reflects its importance in total Mexican exports to the United States (NAFTA and most-favored-nation regimes combined). In the same way, equation 17 is estimated on cross-section data using the weighted least squares estimator with a weight that reflects the importance of each line in total U.S. exports to Mexico.[15] (Input–output data are available for only 1 year.)

Data

Unit values and tariff preference margins are compiled at the HS eight-digit level from U.S. Department of Commerce, Department of Treasury, and International

---

15. It could be that unobserved commodity characteristics affect the difference between NAFTA and most-favored-nation export prices, even at the HS-8 level. In principle, this could be corrected by the use of difference-in-difference estimation (comparing before and after NAFTA). However, the difference between NAFTA and most-favored-nation export prices cannot be computed before NAFTA, so this method is unusable here.

Trade Commission data, as detailed in supplemental appendixes 2 and 3.[16] For equation 17, the sample includes all HS eight-digit lines of section 11 (textiles and textile articles as defined in the HS trade classification; see supplemental appendix 2) for 2000–02. Only tariff lines with positive U.S. imports of Mexican products and strictly positive U.S. imports from Mexico under NAFTA are included—that is, only tariff lines with positive rates of utilization u_{jt} of NAFTA's preferential regime, since when $u_{jt} = 0$, there is no rent to share.[17]

Two methods are used to compute $\Delta p_j / p_j^M$, the dependent variable in the estimation of the Mexican pass-through in equation 17. The first method, called the Mexican method because it compares the unit value of the same Mexican good imported under NAFTA and most-favored-nation tariff rates, has the advantage of using two unit values that are strictly comparable in the calculation, but it reduces the size of the sample by excluding tariff lines with 100 percent utilization rates (nearly half the observations). The second method, called the rest of the world (ROW) method, includes all observations but measures the relative price $\Delta p_j / p_j^M$ as the percentage difference between the border price (unit value) of a good imported from Mexico under NAFTA and the border price of the same good imported from all U.S. import sources including Mexico under the most-favored-nation regime. In contrast to the Mexican method, the ROW method introduces some product heterogeneity.

The sample used for the estimation of equation 18 includes all intermediate goods used in manufacturing Mexican textiles and apparel products for export to the United States under the same conditions as before—that is, positive Mexican imports from the United States under NAFTA with utilization rates of 0–100 percent. Tariff preference is now computed on Mexico's imports of U.S. intermediate good i, while the rules of origin are the same as before (because the same rules apply to all of NAFTA's signatories). In addition to tariff preferences and rules of origin on imports of U.S. intermediate goods i, the regression includes tariff preferences and rules of origin on downstream

---

16. Unit values are calculated by dividing import values by volumes. This method yields notoriously noisy proxies for the true prices at which goods are sold, as customs records of physical volumes are typically less reliable than their records of values, and both are affected by composition problems. Composition problems are somewhat mitigated at deep levels of disaggregation, but then the quantities involved tend to be smaller, and aberrant numbers are encountered more frequently. The HS eight-digit level is arguably the best compromise in this regard. U.S. tariffs are calculated by taking the ratio of collected duties to custom value at the tariff-line level in order to take into account any special subregime or partial exemption.

17. There may be no rent to capture from those lines because of very stringent rules of origin. This would indicate a sample selection problem. However, the lines with $u_{jt} = 0$ account for only 6.7 percent of the total HS-8 tariff lines, and there is no evidence that rules of origin are more restrictive for those lines (for instance, only 37 percent of lines with $u_{jt} = 0$ have to satisfy a technical requirement compared with 68 percent for lines with $0 < u_{jt} < 100$). Nevertheless, with a selection bias, the cost of rules of origin for Mexican exporters is underestimated (based on the assumption that if complying with rules of origin is costly enough, and if tariff preferences do not compensate for these larger costs, the utilization rate would be 0), which reinforces the argument defended in the article.

TABLE 2. Descriptive Statistics, Mexican Pass-Through (percent)

	Mexican method		ROW method	
Good j	All goods	Only final goods	All goods	Only final goods
Number of observations	1,304	913	2,497	1,324
u_{jt} [a]	73.24	69.58	75.68	71.78
$\frac{\Delta p_{jt}}{p_{jt}^M}$ [a]	4.58	4.87	3.99	4.55
$\frac{\Delta t_{jt}}{1+t_{jt}^M}$ [a]	6.07	5.87	6.22	5.79
CC_j [b]	91.87	92.36	82.66	92.56
$TECH_j$ [b]	65.57	80.36	48.34	88.60
Intermediate goods	29.98	—	46.98	—
Final goods	70.02	—	53.02	—

—, not applicable.

[a] Weighted averages (reflecting the importance of each tariff line j in total Mexican exports to the United States).

[b] Share of HS eight-digit level tariff lines.

Note: The sample period is 2000–02. Sample data are from the textiles and apparel sector (HS eight-digit level, section 11).

Source: Authors' analysis based on data described in the text.

good j weighted by input–output coefficients b_{ij}.[18] Table 2 reports descriptive statistics for the variables used in equation 16 and table 3 for the variables in equation 18.

A change of chapter because of rules of origin together with bilateral cumulation implies that when nonoriginating (rest of the world) inputs are used, the transformation in Mexico must be substantial enough for the final good to belong to a chapter that is not identical to that of its nonoriginating components. This amounts to an implicit regional value content for value-added and originating inputs, taken together, relative to the value of nonoriginating inputs. Such a requirement is more complicated that in the simple model of section I but has essentially the same effect—and is modeled as a regional value content in the simulation in section III. Cadot, Estevadeordal, and Suwa-Eisenmann (2005) document how technical requirements tend to be fine-tuned to suit special interests, with equivalent cost-raising effects.

Under the Mexican method, 91.9 percent of tariff lines at the HS eight-digit level had to satisfy a change of classification at the chapter levels, and 65.6

18. Because of lack of data, these "input–output" coefficients are computed from the U.S. input–output table for 2000 converted from U.S. input–output codes (approximately 300 lines) to the HS eight-digit level, the degree of disaggregation at which unit values are measured. "Blowing up" of aggregate coefficients into HS eight-digit level disaggregation was done by attributing to each HS eight-digit line a value of intermediate good sales equal to the inverse of the number of HS eight-digit lines falling in its U.S. input–output code category.

TABLE 3. Descriptive Statistics, U.S. Pass-Through (percent)

Good i	All goods	Only intermediate goods
Number of observations	837	473
$\dfrac{\Delta p_i}{p_i^M}$ [a]	12.16	13.33
$\dfrac{\Delta t_i}{\left(1+t_i^M\right)}$ [a]	12.32	13.76
CC_i [b]	82.32	68.92
$TECH_i$ [b]	42.29	7.61
$\sum_j a_{ij} \dfrac{\Delta t_j}{\left(1+t_j^M\right)}$ [a]	5.71	5.72
$\sum_j a_{ij} CC_j$ [a]	34.01	42.33
$\sum_j a_{ij} TECH_j$ [a]	68.80	67.24

[a]Weighted averages (reflecting the share of each U.S. intermediate sales of line i to Mexican textiles and apparel sector).
[b]Percentage of HS eight-digit tariff lines.
Note: The sample period is 2000. Sample data are from the textiles and apparel sector (HS eight-digit level, section 11).
Source: Authors' analysis based on data described in the text.

percent had technical requirements on the product or process (see table 2). The share of tariff lines affected by technical requirements strongly increases if the sample is restricted to final goods.

Results

Table 4 reports the Mexican pass-through estimates using the Mexican method. (Results obtained using the ROW method, which were almost identical, are in table S5.1.) The first set of estimates includes only the tariff preference margin (and time effects) as explanatory variables. Coefficients for the rate of tariff preference are always significant at the 5 percent level and robust to the choice of method, suggesting that Mexican producers retain about 80 percent of the preference margin. The null hypothesis of no pass-through (no change in U.S. consumer price or border price increase equal to 100 percent of the tariff preference) cannot be rejected at the 5 percent level, indicating that Mexican producers retained a fairly large share of the rents created by trade preference. The extent of pass-through is consistent with a differentiated product model with a relatively high elasticity of substitution between suppliers to the United States. Furthermore, because the effects of tariff changes in a period with no rules of origin are not estimated here, it is unknown whether these effects reflect some of the cost-increasing effects for Mexican producers that result from applying rules of origin.

However, when dummy variables for the presence of rules of origin are included, the picture changes. Part of the border price increase now compensates Mexican producers for the cost of complying with NAFTA's rules of origin,

TABLE 4. Regression Results, Mexican Pass-Through, Mexican Method

$\frac{\Delta p_{jt}}{P_{jt}^M}$	All goods		Only final goods		All goods		Only final goods	
	Coefficient	t-statistics	Coefficient	t-statistics	Coefficient	t-statistics	Coefficient	t-statistics
$\frac{\Delta t_{jt}}{1+t_{jt}^M}$	0.784**	3.29	0.799**	3.33	0.501**	2.98	0.474**	3.04
CC_j	—	—	—	—	0.998*	1.97	1.054**	2.73
$TECH_j$	—	—	—	—	1.674**	3.75	1.989**	4.51
Number of observations	1,304		913		1,304		913	
Adjusted R^2	0.51		0.51		0.55		0.56	

—, not applicable;
*, significant at the 10 percent level;
**, significant at the 5 percent level.
Note: Constant and time effects are included but not reported. The sample period is 2000–02. Sample data are from the textiles and apparel sector (HS eight-digit level, section 11). The estimator used is weighted least squares.
Source: Authors' analysis based on data described in the text.

whose coefficients are large, positive, and significant.[19] The coefficient on the tariff preference falls from 0.784 to 0.501, meaning that Mexican producers retain only about half the tariff preference margin. This suggests that previous estimates of the share of rents retained by producers were significantly overestimated.

The coefficients on rules of origin variables also suggest that these requirements have a significant effect on price and therefore—presumably—on production costs.[20] This is consistent with Carrère and de Melo's (2005) research on the relative costs of various types of rules of origin under NAFTA. As intuition suggests, the effect of rules of origin is also stronger and more precisely estimated when the sample is restricted to final goods (as defined in the Broad Economic Categories classification).

If such a significant share of the preferences granted to Mexican producers is lost, where do they go? On one hand, rules of origin may well be dissipative barriers (like discriminatory product standards), raising production costs without directly creating offsetting rents elsewhere. On the other hand, they may generate rents upstream in the value chain. To explore this hypothesis, the pass-through of Mexican preferences by U.S. exporters of intermediate goods is now analyzed.

Mexico's tariff preference has a highly significant and quantitatively large effect, with a pass-through of only 38 percent over the whole sample and no pass-through at all when the sample is restricted to intermediate goods (table 5). This suggests that U.S. intermediate good suppliers may have substantial market power relative to Mexican final good assemblers. Since the United States sells mostly intermediate textile products to Mexico, it would appear that U.S. producers retain 93 percent of the price increase available to U.S. suppliers from not having to pay the Mexican tariff.

The effect of rules of origin on the price of U.S. exports to Mexico is not significant, suggesting, as expected, that rules of origin affect final good

19. Because dummy variables serve as proxies for rules of origin and the dependent variable is measured in percentage points, the coefficients give the estimated price increase, measured in percentage points, attributable to the presence of rules of origin.

20. By 2000–02, quantitative restrictions on all Mexican textiles and apparel exports had been phased out. A few residual quotas remained on nonoriginating Mexican goods in peculiar cases (for example, upon use of NAFTA's safeguard clause; see U.S. Customs Service 1998). As for quantitative restrictions on most-favored-nation producers under the Agreement on Textiles and Clothing, they contributed to create a rent for Mexican producers that is not taken into account in the equation here. If those rents were positively correlated with the presence of rules of origin, the estimates here might attribute to the presence of rules of origin the effect of the rent from quantitative restrictions and then overestimate the rules of origin coefficient, though the coefficient on the price term would still be consistent (provided that the rents would be uncorrelated with the price term). The authors are grateful to a referee for pointing this out.

TABLE 5. Regression Results, U.S. Pass-Through

$\frac{\Delta p_i}{p_i^M}$	All goods		Only intermediate goods	
	Coefficient	*t*-statistics	Coefficient	*t*-statistics
$\frac{\Delta t_i}{1+t_i^M}$	0.620**	6.54	0.928**	6.76
CC_i	−1.516	−1.31	1.405	0.72
$TECH_i$	2.319	1.11	1.983	1.51
$\sum_j a_{ij} \frac{\Delta t_j}{1+t_j^M}$	0.689**	3.86	0.637**	2.07
$\Sigma_j a_{ij} CC_j$	0.037*	1.86	0.022	0.54
$\Sigma_j a_{ij} TECH_j$	0.053**	2.01	0.119**	2.39
Cst	−3.848*	−1.67	−9.898**	−2.28
Number of observations	837		473	
Adjusted R^2	0.54		0.51	

—, not applicable;
*, significant at the 10 percent level;
**, significant at the 5 percent level.
Note: Constant and time effects are included but not reported. The sample period is 2000–02. Sample data are from the textiles and apparel sector (HS eight-digit level, section 11). The estimator used is weighted least squares.
Source: Authors' analysis based on data described in the text.

assemblers in Mexico more than intermediate good producers in the United States. By contrast, U.S. tariff preferences on downstream final goods have a large and significant effect on the price of U.S. intermediate goods used to fabricate them. The strength of the effect (with a pass-through of only 31–36 percent) is indeed a surprise, given how imperfectly the input–output links are measured. More important here, rules of origin downstream matter, although their effect is quantitatively small (unsurprising, given that the effect is filtered by input–output coefficients). For the entire sample, changes of chapter and technical requirements are significant, confirming anecdotal evidence that technical requirements are often manipulated by upstream interests to distort the input choices of downstream industries.

The estimates in table 5 lead to a decomposition of the sources of the price increase of U.S. intermediate (textile) exports of textiles and apparel to Mexico of 12.16 percent, computed from the raw data in table 3. The predicted rise in the price of U.S. exports to Mexico for all exports computed from the estimated coefficients in table 5 at the sample mean is 12.6 percent, which is close to the observed value of 12.2 percent (see table 3). Similar decomposition results hold when only exports of intermediate goods are considered. The predicted price rise attributable to the combination of tariff preferences and rules of origin can be decomposed as follows: 46 percent is due to the Mexican tariff preference $[\Delta t_i/(1+t_i^M)]$, 24 percent to U.S. preferences downstream $\sum_j b_{ij}[\Delta t_j/(1+t_j^M)]$, and 30 percent to rules of origin downstream

$(\sum_j b_{ij} CC_j + \sum_j b_{ij} TECH_j)$. The last two effects are felt upstream through input–output coefficients.[21]

In sum, on the basis of the results for Mexican exports of final goods to the United States and for U.S. exports of intermediate goods to Mexico, only half the price increase from selling in the United States without having to pay the U.S. tariff is retained by Mexican exporters, while U.S. exporters retain over 90 percent of the price increase from being able to sell in the Mexican market without having to pay the tariff. Rules of origin contribute significantly to the lower pass-through for Mexican exporters but not for U.S. exporters. Finally, U.S. exporters of intermediate goods appear to derive market power from the increase in demand for their products from downstream Mexican producers of final apparel goods. These results are captured in the stylized simulations reported below.

III. NAFTA Welfare Effects for Mexican Producers: Some Simulations

Taken together, the econometric evidence seems to suggest that Mexican producers of final goods may have hardly increased their sales to the United States, while U.S. producers of intermediate goods substantially increased their sales to Mexico. If so, the welfare benefits from earning higher rents from sales in the U.S. market since the signing of NAFTA should be less than in the absence of rules of origin.

The data confirm these predictions. NAFTA resulted in a sharp increase of 24 percent in the ratio of intermediate good (textiles) purchases by Mexico from the United States relative to purchases from the rest of the world since NAFTA, while the corresponding ratio of sales of final goods to the United States relative to the rest of the world increased only 2 percent. Likewise, NAFTA has been accompanied by a pattern of vertical exchange of the offshore assembly type whereby the United States ships semifinished goods for assembly in Mexico and then reimports them as finished products.[22] Taken together, these quantity

---

21. It may be tempting to interpret the negative value for the constant as evidence of strategic price cuts in response to a decrease in the prices charged by either U.S. producers or nonpreferred ones, as documented by Winters and Chang (2000) in the context of Spain's accession to the European Union and by Chang and Winters (2002) in the context of Mercosur. However, this interpretation of the constant would be dubious in our context: strategic price cuts ought to be systematically related to the depth of tariff preferences and thus should not be picked up by the constant.

22. Let R^Z denote the 2-year average value of the ratio of Mexican intermediate good purchases from the United States to those from the rest of the world, and let R^F denote the 2-year average value of the ratio of Mexican sales of final goods to the United States to those to the rest of the world. Likewise let V, the ratio of specialization in intermediate purchases in the United States over final sales to the United States be an indicator of the extent of vertical trade between Mexico and the United States. Let 1998–2000 averages be representative of NAFTA and 1992–94 be representative of pre-NAFTA averages. The figure cited in the text refers to the increase in these indicator values following the implementation of NAFTA. See Anson and others (2005) for a further description of these results.

developments suggest poor Mexican access to the U.S. market and a shift to a vertical pattern of Mexican–U.S. trade, as predicted by the exante analysis of Krueger (1993). Along with the econometric results, these quantity developments suggest the fruitfulness of carrying out illustrative simulations that help capture the likely welfare effects of the presence of rules of origin revealed in the pass-through estimates.

Model Sketch

To calculate orders of magnitude of the effects of NAFTA on Mexican exporters, simulations are carried out with a partial equilibrium structural model (see supplemental appendix 6) inspired from the model presented in section I and calibrated to take into account the results in tables 4 and 5. Suppose that Mexican apparel producers sell all their output abroad, either to the United States under NAFTA, X^{US}, or to the rest of the world, X^{ROW}. (No domestic sales simplifies the welfare analysis, but it results in an overestimate of the welfare gains from NAFTA preferences because higher prices for Mexican consumers are not taken into account.) They direct their sales to each market depending on relative profits per unit, according to a constant elasticity of transformation function with elasticity Ω.

Likewise, to simplify the evaluation, Mexican producers purchase all their intermediate goods abroad, either from the United States, Z^{US}, or from the rest of the world, Z^{ROW}. A Leontief technology links value-added and aggregate intermediate demand, a_z. Assume an upward-sloping supply curve for value added in the Mexican textiles and apparel industry (if value-added has an infinitely elastic supply, there would be no opportunity costs for capital and labor, and welfare effects of NAFTA would be 0). And let ε_X be this elasticity of supply and P_X^{US} the unit producer price of Mexican apparel exported to the U.S. market. The unrestricted unit cost under nonbinding rules of origin is C_z, and the restricted cost under binding rules of origin is C_Z^R. To capture the market power to U.S. producers of the rules of origin negotiated under NAFTA (the captive market effect), it is assumed that under NAFTA, only Mexican producers purchase U.S. intermediate goods at increasing cost—that is, they face a finite supply elasticity of U.S. intermediate goods ($\varepsilon_Z^{US} < \infty$). Finally, let λ be the administrative cost component of complying with rules of origin, assumed to be fixed per unit of apparel sold to the United States. In line with the econometric evidence in table 5, U.S. producers of intermediate goods are not penalized by the presence of rules of origin negotiated under NAFTA.

Mexican apparel producers sell most of their apparel to the United States (80 percent in the illustrative simulations in table 6) and are assumed to be price-takers when they sell their apparel to the rest of the world. U.S. demand for apparel is represented by a Marshallian demand curve with elasticity ε, and, as in section I, income effects are omitted. U.S. consumers choose between apparel from Mexico and the rest of the world according to a constant elasticity of substitution function with elasticity σ_Q.

TABLE 6. Simulation Results

Percent	1	2	3	4	5	6	7
ε_Z^{US}	8	8	8	8	5	5	5
λ	0	0	2	2	2	2	2
$\Delta t_X \equiv \left(t_X^M - t_X^N\right)$	10	10	10	10	10	10	10
$\Delta t_Z \equiv \left(t_Z^M - t_Z^N\right)$	0	10	10	10	10	10	10
$\left(\frac{Z}{X}\right)$	40	40	40	40	40	60	60
$\left[\frac{z^{US}}{Z^{US}+Z^{ROW}}\right]_0$	30	30	30	30	30	30	40
$\left(\frac{z^{US}}{Z^{US}+Z^{ROW}}\right)_1^{(R)}$	30	32	32	(38)[a]	(38)[a]	(38)[a]	(52)[a]
Results	Percent change from corresponding base values						
X^{US}	11.0	15.5	13.2	9.8	8.7	10.9	9.5
P_X^{US}	7.2	6.1	4.6	5.5	5.7	5.2	5.5
P_Z^{US}	0.0	0.0	0.0	0.0	6.7	7.1	7.7
$C_Z\left(C_Z^R\right)$	0.0	−9.1	−9.1	(−2.1)	(0.2)	(0.4)	(1.9)
W_P	20.1	30.4	20.6	18.2	15.6	20.6	17.4
G	9.6	−22.3	−23.6	−31.7	−32.4	−31.0	−46.5
W_T	19.5	27.2	22.9	15.0	12.6	13.9	9.1

$Z(X)$, intermediate good; λ, administrative costs (percent of unit cost); G, government tariff revenue; W_P (= $P_{VA}X$), private welfare [see also equation 19 in the text; W_T (= $G + W_P$) is total welfare].

[a]Corresponds to a binding regional value content.

Note: All simulations, assume $\varepsilon = 1$, $\varepsilon_X = 1$, $\sigma = 1$, $\sigma_Q = 5$, $\Omega = 1$. $ES_0 = \left[X^{US}/\left(X^{US} + X^{ROW}\right)\right] = 80$ percent. See equation 22 in the text for definition of variables.

Source: Authors' estimates.

For a small NAFTA preference margin $(\Delta t \equiv t^M - t^N < 0)$, the percentage increase in producer surplus from preferential market access $\hat{W}_p$[23] (here equal to the private welfare benefit under the assumption of no domestic demand) is

$$(19) \qquad \hat{W}_p = \left(1 + \hat{P}_{VA}\right)^{1+\varepsilon_X} - 1 \approx (1 + \varepsilon_X)\hat{P}_{VA}.$$

Nothing prevents $\hat{W}_p$ from being negative, in which case Mexican apparel producers would not export under NAFTA.

As in section I, the distortionary cost of rules of origin is black boxed through a regional value content equivalent. If subscript 0 denotes profit maximizing per unit use of U.S. intermediate goods before NAFTA and subscript 1 denotes the corresponding use by the representative competitive Mexican firm when it faces binding rules of origin and preferential access, on the cost side

$$(20) \qquad z^R \equiv \frac{Z_1^{US}}{Z_1^{ROW}} > z^0 \equiv \frac{Z_0^{US}}{Z_0^{ROW}}$$

23. Let hats (ˆ) denote a percentage change in the variables.

which gives the restricted cost function for intermediate goods

$$(21) \qquad C_Z^R = P_Z^R\big(z^R, P_z^{ROW}; \sigma\big)$$

where P_z^{ROW} is the price of intermediate goods purchased outside NAFTA and σ the elasticity of substitution in use between intermediate goods from the United States and the rest of the world. Thus, $C_Z^R > C_Z$ in the presence of binding rules of origin, and equation 18 captures the distortionary costs associated with rules of origin.

Equilibrium in the U.S. market for Mexican apparel requires U.S. demand for Mexican goods, Q_{US}^{Mex}, to equal Mexican supply to the United States, X^{US}, as reflected in equation 22. NAFTA has effects on the demand and supply sides. On the demand side, the preference margin, Δt, reduces the consumer price of Mexican apparel, P_Q^{Mex}, sold in the United States. On the supply side, rules of origin (r, λ) raise the unit cost of sales to the United States, $P_X^{US}(r, \lambda)$. Likewise, when U.S. producers of intermediate goods have market power, Mexican production costs are raised. Equilibrium under NAFTA in the Mexican apparel industry is achieved by adjusting the unit price of Mexican apparel exports to the United States until $P_Q^{Mex} = P_X^{US}$. The reduced-form expression corresponding to the underlying structural model (see supplemental appendix 6) for equilibrium in the Mexican apparel sector can then be written in terms of demand and supply elasticities, and share parameters describing the sector before NAFTA can be written as:

$$(22) \qquad Q_{US}^{Mex}\Big[P_Q^{Mex}(\Delta t); \varepsilon, \Omega, \sigma_Q\Big] = X^{US}\Big[P_X^{US}(r, \lambda); \varepsilon_X, a_Z, \varepsilon_Z^{US}, \sigma\Big]$$

where ε is the U.S. apparel price elasticity of import demand and σ_Q the elasticity of substitution between apparel from Mexico and the rest of the world in U.S. apparel demand.

Welfare Estimates

Table 6 describes the results of illustrative simulations with calibration inspired from the pre-NAFTA shares given above and the pass-through estimates reported in section II. Because no econometric estimates of the various elasticities are available, they are all assumed to be equal to unity (i.e., $\varepsilon = \sigma = \Omega = \varepsilon_X = 1$), except for those influencing Mexican and U.S. pass-through, that is, σ_Q and ε_Z^{US}.[24] The simulations start in a pre-NAFTA situation where Mexican apparel producers benefit from a 10 percent tariff preference in the United States and U.S. producers of intermediate goods benefit from a 10 percent tariff preference when they sell in Mexico. These starting values are roughly in line with the

---

24. Assuming $\sigma_Q = 5$ gives a value of the pass-through of approximately 0.7, which is close to the econometric estimates in table 4. Likewise, $\varepsilon_Z^{US} = 5$ yields an estimated pass-through of close to 0.7, also in line with the results in table 5.

aggregate data in tables 2 and 3 if factoring in that Mexican producers of apparel probably had a margin of preference in excess of the most-favored-nation tariff (6 percent) because of binding quotas under the Agreement on Textiles and Clothing. Moreover, assuming symmetry in preferences helps to further isolate the determinants of NAFTA's welfare effects under asymmetric rules of origin. Except in column 7, the unrestricted share of intermediate textile imports from the United States is assumed to be 30 percent, and, in line with the data, Mexicans initially export 80 percent of their apparel products to the United States. All these assumptions are described in the top part of table 6, where the corresponding row indicates the assumed values for the parameters leading to the results in the corresponding column. To ease interpretation, simulations are additive for the first five columns (the last two columns report on sensitivity analysis on the results given in column 5) so that the results of any given column are directly comparable to the results in the preceding column.

Simulations are intended to give orders of magnitude of sequentially adding the NAFTA effects detected above. Start then with the results in column 1. Giving a 10 percent preference to Mexican exporters of apparel to the United States allows them to retain 7.2 percent of the price preference, and exports to the United States increase 11 percent. Private welfare goes up by 20.1 percent, and government revenue increases by 9.6 percent. In column 2, the 10 percent tariff on the purchase of intermediate goods from the United States is eliminated. Because rules of origin have not yet been introduced, Mexican producers benefit from paying a lower price for their purchases of intermediate goods from the United States. Since they minimize costs, they also increase their share of U.S. intermediate good purchases to 32 percent, and unit costs fall 9.1 percent. Lower intermediate costs are reflected in a slightly lower increase in the unit sale price to the United States (and also to the rest of the world), and total welfare goes up even more despite the tariff revenue loss, thanks to the gains from removing a distortion.

The effects of rules of origin are added successively in columns 3, 4, and 5. In column 3, a 2 percent per unit cost is added to account for the administrative costs associated with compliance with rules of origin. This estimate is borrowed from the nonparametric estimates reported in Carrère and de Melo (2005). Not surprisingly, benefits from NAFTA for Mexican exporters decrease markedly. In column 4, the regional value content scheme is introduced. It forces Mexican producers to increase their purchase of U.S. intermediate goods 25 percent (the observed increase mentioned above). This regional value content serves as a proxy for the costs associated with exceptions and the various technical requirements that have to be met to obtain originating status. For the chosen parameter configuration and assumed preferential access, unit costs still fall, but export sales increase by only 9.8 percent, and welfare gains are almost halved from what they would be in the absence of rules of origin. Finally, in column 5, the market power and pass-through effects for U.S. producers of intermediate goods are added. Mexican firms can no longer assume a fixed price $(\varepsilon_Z^{US} = \infty)$ to purchase U.S. intermediate goods; instead, they face an upward-sloping U.S. supply of intermediate goods, with unit costs up by 6.7 percent. Welfare gains are further reduced to less than half their estimated value in the absence of rules of origin. Arguably, this is a conservative estimate, since the data indicate that despite NAFTA, the ratio of Mexican exports of textiles and apparel to the United States barely increased 2 percent.

The last two columns give results of NAFTA, factoring in all the rules of origin effects, but starting from different parameter values. In column 6, the share of intermediate goods in apparel is increased from 40 to 60 percent. Two opposite effects—a gain from tariff reduction and a loss from paying a higher price for U.S. intermediate goods—almost cancel each other out, so that the overall effect is small. In column 7, the 25 percent increase in the share of purchases of U.S. intermediate goods is assumed to start at 40 percent (instead of 30 percent). The regional value content is more constraining, and gains from NAFTA implementation are down to a third of their estimated values in the absence of rules of origin.

IV. Concluding Remarks

This article studied Mexican access to the U.S. market under NAFTA in the textiles and apparel sector and shows that only about half the tariff preference (of about 8 percent) was retained by Mexican producers. The induced upstream effect on the price of U.S. intermediate (textile) goods used in the production of Mexican final (apparel) goods is found to be significant and rather large. The price of U.S. intermediate goods sold to Mexico is, on average, 12–13 percent higher than the price of the same goods for export to other (nonpreferential) destinations. The elimination of the tariff on imports of U.S. intermediate goods by Mexican producers thus did not result in lower intermediate goods costs. Technical requirements (a particular form of rules of origin that is prevalent in the textiles and apparel sector) alone account for a full third, or about 4 percentage points, of that price increase—a strong signal in otherwise noisy data.

On the basis of these estimates, simulations were conducted in a stripped-down model of the Mexican textiles and apparel sector, in which Mexican apparel producers can sell to the rest of the world with no conditions or to the United States under NAFTA with the condition that they increase their purchases of U.S. textile intermediate goods. The results confirm that preferential margins of the magnitude granted under NAFTA severely reduced the gains from NAFTA for Mexican exporters. Arguably, plausible parameter estimates suggest that welfare gains were easily reduced by half because of the rules associated with proving the goods' origin.

Beyond the specifics of the textiles and apparel sector under NAFTA, these results inform the debate on the usefulness of trade preferences as a development tool. Because preference margins are limited to the level of most-favored-nation tariffs, which for industrial countries are fairly low (with apparel among the few exceptions), preferences absorbed in half by a combination of higher costs and pass-through to buyers are likely to be of limited value to developing country partners. Taken together, the results support the suspicion that rules of origin are less a development policy tool to prevent screwdriver assembly (a potentially worthy objective) and more a circuitous way of raising the profits of upstream producers by creating a captive market for them in partner countries. This is likely to be especially important in preferential trade arrangements between developed and developing countries where vertical trade (capital-intensive component manufacturing in developed countries, labor-intensive assembly in developing countries) is prevalent. The flurry of regional trade agreements may then well be a costly diversion that distracts from necessary reforms to improve the functioning of the world trading system.

Supplementary Data

Supplementary data can be found at www.wber.oxfordjournals.org.

References

Anson, José, Olivier Cadot, Antoni Estevadeordal, Akiko Suwa-Eisenmann, Jaime de Melo, and Boloorma Tumurchudur. 2005. "Rules of Origin in North-South Preferential Trading Arrangements with an Application to NAFTA." *Review of International Economics* 13(2):501–17.

Brenton, Paul. 2003. "Integrating the Least Developed Countries into the World Trading System: The Current Impact of EU Preferences under Everything But Arms." *Journal of World Trade* 37(3):623–46.

Brenton, P., and H. Imagawa. 2005. "Rules of Origin, Trade and Customs." In Luc de Wulf and José Sokol, eds., *Customs Modernization: A Handbook*. Washington, D.C.: World Bank.

Brenton, Paul, and Miriam Manchin. 2003. "Making EU Trade Agreements Work: The Role of Rules of Origin." *World Economy* 26(5):755–69.

Cadot, Olivier, Antoni Estevadeordal, and Akiko Suwa-Eisenmann. 2005. "Rules of Origin as Export Subsidies." Discussion Paper 4999. London: Centre for Economic Policy Research.

Cadot, Olivier, Céline Carrère, Jaime de Melo, and Alberto Portugal-Pérez. 2005a. "How Much Market Access Under FTAs? Textiles Under NAFTA." Discussion Paper 5262. London: Centre for Economic Policy Research.

Cadot, Olivier, Antoni Estevadeordal, Akiko Suwa-Eisenmann, and Thierry Verdier (eds). 2005b. *The Origin of Goods: Rules of Origin in Regional Trade Agreements*. London: Oxford University Press.

Cadot, Olivier, Céline Carrère, Jaime de Melo, and Bolormaa Tumurchudur. Forthcoming. "Product Specific Rules of Origin in EU and US Preferential Trading Arrangements: An Assessment." *World Trade Review*.

Carrère, Céline, and Jaime de Melo. 2005. "Are Different Rules of Origin Equally Costly? Estimates from NAFTA." Discussion Paper 4437. London: Centre for Economic Policy Research.

Chang, Won, and Alan Winters. 2002. "How Regional Blocs Affect Excluded Countries: The Price Effects of Mercosur." *American Economic Review* 92(4):889–904.

Deardorff, Alan, James Levinsohn, and Robert Stern (eds). 1995. *New Directions in Trade Theory*. Ann Arbor, MI: University of Michigan Press.

Estevadeordal, Antoni. 2000. "Negotiating Preferential Market Access: The Case of the North American Free Trade Agreement." *Journal of World Trade* 34(1):141–66.

Feenstra, Robert. 1989. "Symmetric Pass-Through of Tariffs and Exchange Rates Under Imperfect Competition: An Empirical Test." *Journal of International Economics* 27(1–2):25–45.

Krishna, Kala. 2005. *Understanding Rules of Origin.* NBER Working Paper 11150. Cambridge, MA: National Bureau of Economic Research.

Krishna, Kala, and Anne Krueger. 1995. "Implementing Free Trade Areas: Rules of Origin and Hidden Protection." In Alan Deardorff, James Levinsohn, and Robert Stern, eds., *New Directions in Trade Theory.* Ann Arbor, MI: University of Michigan Press.

Krueger, Anne. 1993. *Free Trade Agreements as Protectionist Devices: Rules of Origin.* NBER Working Paper 4352. Cambridge, MA: National Bureau of Economic Research.

Limão, Nuno. Forthcoming. "Preferential Trade Agreements as Stumbling Blocs for Multilateral Trade Liberalization: Evidence for the U.S." *American Economic Review.*

Olarreaga, Marcelo, and Caglar Özden. 2005. "AGOA and Apparel: Who Captures the Tariff Rent in the Presence of Preferential Market Access?" *World Economy* 28(1):63–77.

Özden, Caglar, and Gunjan Sharma. 2004. "Price Effects of Preferential Market Access: Caribbean Basin Initiative and the Apparel Sector." Discussion Paper 3244. Washington, D.C.: World Bank.

Spinanger, Dean. 1998. *Textiles beyond the MFA Phase-Out.* Working Paper 13/98. University of Warwick, Coventry, U.K.: Centre for the Study of Globalisation and Regionalisation.

U.S. Customs Service. 1998. *A Guide to Customs Procedures under NAFTA.* Washington, D.C.

Winters, Alan, and Won Chang. 2000. "Regional Integration and the Rest of the World: An Empirical Investigation." *Journal of International Economics* 51(2):363–77.

Yeats, Alexander. 1998. "Does Mercosur's Trade Performance Raise Concerns about the Effects of Regional Trade Agreements?" *World Bank Economic Review* 12(10):1–28.

Part IV:

Estimating the Costs of US Foreign Trade Policy

WELFARE COSTS OF U.S. QUOTAS IN TEXTILES, STEEL AND AUTOS

Jaime de Melo and David Tarr*

Abstract—This paper quantifies the welfare effects and resource shifts that would occur if U.S. quantitative restrictions (QRs) in textiles, steel and autos were removed. Estimates are derived from a static ten-sector general equilibrium model of the U.S. economy. The welfare loss from the QRs is estimated at approximately U.S. $20 billion (1984 dollars). Due to the high rent transfer component of QRs (about 75%), the average across-the-board tariff equivalent of QRs (in terms of welfare costs) is estimated at about 20%, a rate which predates the early days of multilateral tariff reduction.

I. Introduction

RECENTLY, several studies have estimated the costs of U.S. special protection arrangements.[1] All these studies, using a partial equilibrium (PE) framework, provide a useful range of estimates of the costs of non-tariff protection. These studies are especially valuable when taken individually because then the assumptions of PE analysis provide an adequate approximation of reality. But, as we quantify below, when the costs of all restrictions are taken together, the underlying assumptions are much less tenable. In particular, the general equilibrium (GE) approach used here accounts for three effects omitted by PE estimates. First, the inclusion of a balance of trade constraint (expressed in world prices) removes an upward bias present in PE analysis. Second, the effects of income transfers to and from the rest of the world are properly accounted for so that, unlike in the PE analysis, capturing quota rents affects resource allocation. Third, economy-wide resource constraints and interindustry linkages provide a more accurate estimate of welfare and sectoral employment effects.

This paper deals with the problems of PE analysis by presenting estimates from a static ten-sector computable general equilibrium (CGE) model of the U.S. economy calibrated to the year 1984 when quantitative restrictions (QRs) in textiles and autos were in effect, and those on steel were in negotiation. To our knowledge, the treatment of QR-associated effects here is more satisfactory than in previous CGE applications. While the U.S.-negotiated voluntary export restraint (VER) on automobiles has expired, demand in the United States for protection through non-tariff barriers (NTBs) remains strong and may be on the rise. A new round of estimates of the costs of protection is therefore all the more welcome.

The remainder of the paper is organized as follows. Section II outlines the model. Section III details the sources of estimates of premia on preexisting QRs in 1984 and the sources for the parameters describing demand and supply elasticities. Estimates of the welfare and employment effects of QR removal are presented by industry and in the aggregate in sections IV and V. Conclusions follow in section VI.

Received for publication January 12, 1989. Revision accepted for publication November 16, 1989.

* The World Bank, University of Geneva, and CEPR; and the World Bank, respectively.

This is a revised and shortened version of de Melo and Tarr (1988) which extends an earlier study by Tarr (1989). We thank Morris Morkre and two referees for comments. The views are those of the authors, not those of the World Bank. We thank Julie Stanton for extremely valuable research assistance, Maria Ameal for logistic support and Soren Nielsen for computer support.

[1] Among the most widely known studies that provide estimates of the welfare costs of non-tariff barriers (NTBs) in the United States are individual sector studies for textiles (Morkre (1984); Tarr and Morkre (1984); Cline (1987); Keesing and Wolf (1980); for automobiles (Winston and Associates (1987); Tarr and Morkre (1984); Feenstra (1984, 1985, 1988); Dinopoulos and Kreinin (1988)); and for steel (Tarr and Morkre (1984)). Perhaps the most comprehensive recent estimates come from the 31 case studies of special protection by Hufbauer, Berliner and Elliott (1986).

II. Model Outline[2]

The simulation model is a static CGE model with assumptions that correspond closely to those followed by the partial equilibrium estimates cited above, namely, a neoclassical perfect-competition Walrasian model in which a representative consumer maximizes utility subject to a budget constraint, atomistic producers minimize costs, and the government redistributes tax revenues from trade policy in a lump sum. The economy has a fixed endowment of labor and capital and faces

[2] A full description of the model is contained in the appendix to de Melo and Tarr (1988) and is available from the authors upon request.

[489]

an exogenous balance of trade constraint expressed in world prices. Because we are interested in the static welfare costs of protection, we abstract from investment, thereby simplifying the welfare analysis. The components of demand, therefore, include only consumer and intermediate demand.

Under these assumptions, it is clear that the welfare changes due to a change in trade policy are the usual production and consumption costs of protection referred to in the literature on the costs of protection. Our measure of the welfare change due to a policy change is given by the equivalent variation (EV) measure associated with the Stone-Geary utility function describing the representative consumer's preferences, i.e.,

$$EV = C\left[IU(p^1, y^1), p^0\right] - C\left[IU(p^0, y^0), p^0\right]$$

where C is the cost function, IU is indirect utility which depends on prices and income, p is the vector of final goods prices, and superscripts 0 and 1 refer to the equilibrium before and after the counterfactual trade policy experiment. If EV is positive, the consumer is better off as a result of the policy shift.

The structure of the ten-sector model is as follows.[3] Commodities supplied (or purchased) abroad and domestic commodities sold on the domestic market are imperfect substitutes. This assumption of product differentiation is commonly used in applied general equilibrium analysis and is also adopted in most of the PE studies alluded to above. On the export side, the assumption of product differentiation is reflected in the constant elasticity of transformation (CET) function between domestic and foreign sales.[4] A symmetric functional form is specified for intermediate demand by sector (see below). The assumption of product differentiation allows for the cross-hauling observed in trade statistics.

Production possibilities are parametrized by assuming constant elasticity of substitution (CES) functions for value-added and Leontief functions between intermediates (as a whole) and value-added and across intermediates. However, within each sector, intermediate demand is a CES function between the domestically produced intermediate and the competing foreign intermediate. To give an example, no substitution is allowed between purchases of steel and other manufacturing intermediates, but substitution in purchases is allowed between domestically produced and foreign produced steel when their relative prices change as a result of a change in trade policy. Likewise, in consumption demand, the demand system derived from the Stone-Geary utility indicator allows for non-unitary income elasticities of demand and non-zero cross-price elasticities of demand between domestically produced and foreign produced consumer goods.

Finally, we note that in previous single-country partial equilibrium estimates, authors have invariably assumed that the United States is a small supplier and demander in world markets. In our preferred estimates, we retain this assumption except for the supply of auto imports and the demand for agricultural exports. However, because of the controversy about the importance of terms of trade effects reported in multi-country models (e.g., Whalley (1985), Deardorff and Stern (1986)), we report separately results under the assumption that the United States possesses generalized monopoly and monopsony power.

The description of the model is complete except for our treatment of QRs. In the United States, for the sectors considered here, there are no government controls or direct quota allocations with resale prohibition. Hence, unlike the case of many QR allocation schemes in developing countries, the U.S. system of QRs allows for market-clearing prices. Since in 1984 quotas were already in place in autos and textiles, we assume that observed purchases were at the premia-inclusive prices in that year. (The estimation of premia is discussed in section III.)[5]

III. Elasticity and Premia Estimates

Considerable effort was devoted to a "parameter search" for elasticities of demand and supply and to constructing premia estimates for existing

---

[3] The ten sectors are agriculture (1), food (2), mining (3), textiles and apparel (4), autos (5), steel (6), consumer goods (7), other manufacturing (8), traded services (9), and non-traded services (10). All sectors are traded with the exception of sector 10. See Tarr (1988) for details on aggregation.

[4] The CET was first introduced by Powell and Gruen (1967).

[5] Our calibration procedure assumes that the prices and quantities observed in 1984 correspond to an equilibrium of the U.S. economy with normal capacity utilization and in which the only distortions are the QRs and tariff on imports. This may be viewed as a strong assumption but it is implicit as well in most other estimates of the costs of protection.

WELFARE COSTS OF QUOTAS   491

TABLE 1.—ELASTICITY SPECIFICATION (CENTRAL CASE)

	Column Notes					Elasticity of Substitution Intermediates	Elasticity of Substitution Capital/Labor	Elasticity of Transformation Domestic/Export Sales	Price Elasticities of Final Demand		Premia Rates
									Domestic	Imports	
Sector	(1)	(2)	(3)	(4)	(5)	(1)	(2)	(3)	(4)	(5)	(6)
Agriculture	a	c	e	k	f	1.4	0.6	4.0	0.75	0.8	
Food	a	c	e	f	f	0.3	0.8	3.0	0.90	1.1	
Mining	b	b	e	j	f	0.5	0.8	3.0	0.50	1.0	
Iron and Steel	a	d	e	i	f	3.0	1.0	3.0	1.0	1.4	
Motor Vehicles	a	c	e	h	h	2.0	0.8	3.0	1.2	1.1	31.9%
Textiles and Apparel	a	c	e	l	f	2.6	1.0	3.0	0.4	3.9	40.5%
Other Manufactures	a	c	e	f	f	3.6	0.8	3.0	1.5	1.8	
Other Consumer	a	c	e	f	f	3.2	0.8	3.0	1.9	2.4	
Traded Services	b	c	e	g	g	2.0	0.8	0.7	0.5	0.6	
Non-traded Services		b		g			0.8		0.5		

Note: CES and CET functions imply that the corresponding elasticities of substitution (transformation) correspond to compensated import demand (export supply) elasticities.

All price elasticities of demand are defined as positive numbers. For premia estimates, see text. Column notes correspond to the sources from which estimates are interpolated. For interpolation details see Tarr (1988).

(a) Shiells, Stern and Deardorff (1986); (b) Dixon et al. (1982); (c) Caddy (1976); (d) Hekman (1978); (e) own estimates; (f) Stern, Francis and Schumacher (1976); (g) Houthakker and Taylor (1970); (h) Levinsohn (1988); (i) Crandall (1981); (j) Bohi and Russell (1978); (k) USDA (1984); (l) Hufbauer, Berliner and Elliott (1986).

QRs in textiles and autos. We discuss these briefly below. (Tarr (1989, chaps. 5 and 6) is devoted to a detailed discussion of how these estimates were derived.)

Table 1 presents all elasticities and our constructed estimates of pre-existing premia. These elasticities correspond to the "central" elasticities. (When we report in table 3 the likely range of the welfare effects of removing all trade restrictions, we are reporting results from the "low" and "high" elasticities that are derived from the "central" elasticities in table 1 by subtracting and adding, respectively, a standard deviation.[6]) Because much econometric work has been done to estimate the capital/labor substitution elasticities, we are fairly confident about the accuracy of these elasticities. We are also fairly confident of the import demand elasticities, for which a number of estimates are available. Less confidence can be placed on export supply elasticities. However, because these latter elasticities enter only indirectly into our estimations, we have found that our welfare estimates are quite insensitive to considerable changes in their values.[7]

For the premia rate estimates for apparel (expressed as a percentage of landed U.S. import price inclusive of tariffs), we have relied on Hamilton (1988). Hamilton's data are based on the sale of rights to export apparel products to the United States. His data give an estimate of the quota rents captured by Hong Kong. In order to understand the problem of premia rate estimation, it is crucial to recognize that the existing Multifiber Arrangement (MFA) allows a number of marginally inefficient foreign suppliers to sell in the United States. If the MFA were abolished, many of them would be squeezed out of the U.S. market by competition. The quota premium rate earned by these inefficient suppliers is less than the quota premium rate paid by U.S. consumers as a result of the MFA. Thus, we had to determine the marginal supplier to the United States if the MFA were abolished. Data in Hamilton (1988) allow us to determine that Hong Kong, which had a quota premium rate of 47% for apparel sold to the United States in 1984, or a supplier more

---

[6] As the sources for table 1 detail, the estimates were obtained from many studies. These studies generally provide standard errors of estimates. For those elasticities taken from Stern, Francis and Schumacher, the high and low estimates are generally the high and low estimates from their survey, which are not based on standard deviations. In a few cases the high and low estimates are obtained by doubling and halving the central estimate. See Tarr (1988, ch. 5) for details.

[7] For example, doubling (halving) the elasticity estimates in column (3) increases (decreases) our estimates of the welfare gains with the central elasticity estimates from US$22.0 billion (with infinite foreign trade elasticities) to $22.1 ($22.9) billion, respectively, or ±0.5%.

efficient than Hong Kong, would be the marginal supplier if quotas were removed.[8]

The United States is much more competitive in textiles than in apparel. Consequently, for textiles we take 5% as the premium rate, which is much more conservative than the 15% proposed by Cline (1987, p. 167). A positive rate is indicated, however, based on data in a study by the U.S. International Trade Commission (1987). For autos we relied on the quality-adjusted premia estimates of Feenstra (1988) for Japanese car imports by the United States. For European car imports, we relied on the quality-adjusted price increase of European cars sold in the United States estimated by Dinopoulos and Kreinin (1988). Our resulting premia estimates, which are weighted averages, are 41% for textiles and apparel and 32% for autos.[9]

IV. Welfare Cost Estimates

The costs of QRs reported in tables 2 and 3 below are based on estimates of the premia that accrue to the exporting countries rather than to the United States. One can therefore distinguish two components of the costs of the QRs: (1) the income or rent transfer to foreigners and (2) the distortionary cost due to the usual consumption and production costs of protection.[10] Table 2 summarizes these costs for each of the three industries: textiles and apparel, autos and steel. Since the restrictions on steel—which resulted in approximately a 15% reduction in imports of steel starting in early 1985—were not implemented until 1985, we obtain the estimates for steel by reducing intermediate and final consumption of imported steel products by 15% from the observed levels in 1984. This restriction results in a 7% premium on imported intermediate steel products. The employment figures in column 2 are only for the industry subject to quota removal; the total economy-wide relocation of workers is reported in column 3. This latter measure is a summary of interindustry effects (see Deardorff and Stern (1986)).

The figures in table 2 reveal that the largest welfare costs are due to the QRs in textiles and apparel. This may seem surprising since that sector is smaller than autos, and imports are three-fourths of auto imports in value (including premia). Also, the proportion of the total welfare costs due to distortionary costs are much higher in textiles and apparel than in autos even in the case of an infinite elasticity of import supply in autos. This is so because the premium rate is higher and because the price elasticity of demand for textiles and apparel is almost four times higher than the corresponding elasticity for autos. Furthermore, the relative homogeneity of domestic and imported steel reduces the production costs of distortion.[11]

Because elasticity estimates are not precise, we report in table 3 a range of welfare gains from removing all QRs simultaneously for the cases of low, central, and high elasticities. Because the marginal benefit to the economy of an income transfer is a decreasing function of demand and supply elasticities, the welfare gains from capturing rents from foreigners is higher in the low elasticity case than in the high elasticity case. Of course, these estimated welfare gains due to the

---

[8] We note that estimates of quota premia, in both textiles and automobiles, vary from year to year. We obtained estimates of quota premia for 1984, the year for which we benchmarked the model. Thus, our estimates apply to the conditions prevailing in that year. For other years, the premia rates and our cost estimates may differ.

[9] If the marginal supplier is more efficient than Hong Kong, our premium rate estimate is conservative and the associated welfare gain estimate is downward-biased. There is evidence that, during the quota era, U.S. dealers of Japanese autos captured about $550 per vehicle in rents above those rents captured by foreigners. This would correspond to a higher premium rate on autos of 43%, of which foreigners capture 80% of the rents. We shall provide separate estimates for this scenario.

[10] In the cases where there are terms of trade effects, the estimates of the distortionary costs of protection are reduced because the terms of trade effects partially offset the distortionary cost component of the QRs.

[11] The United States imposes QRs in other sectors in addition to textiles, autos and steel. For example, Hufbauer, Berliner and Elliott (1986) reported QRs in book manufacturing, motorcycles, shipbuilding and maritime industries, sugar and food products containing sugar, cheese and other dairy products, peanuts and meat. We have simulated the effects of removing all the QRs in the economy by assuming a high (low) premia rate (tariff equivalent) of the QRs (with rents going to the foreigners) of 5% (2.5%) in agriculture; 3% (1.5%) in other manufactures, other consumer goods and food; and zero in the remaining sectors. Given these premia rates, the welfare gain from removing all QRs, including those in textiles, autos and steel, is $27.6 billion in the high and $24.0 billion in the low premia rate cases. These estimates of the benefits of removing all QRs, however, can only be considered suggestive because, unlike the case of our estimates of the premia rates in textiles, autos and steel, we have not done a careful estimate of the premia rates in the remaining sectors of our model.

WELFARE COSTS OF QUOTAS

TABLE 2.—WELFARE COSTS AND EMPLOYMENT EFFECTS OF QRs:
INDIVIDUAL SECTORS

	Welfare[a] Gain	Employment Change in the Industry Losing Its QR[b]	Economy-Wide Employment Relocation[c]
Textiles and Apparel			
Remove QRs	11.92	−157.2	157.2 (0.15)
Capture Rents from Foreigners	6.05	−3.05	28.35 (0.03)
Autos			
Remove QRs	7.50 (9.10)	−1.2	1.3 (0.001)
Capture Rents from Foreigners	7.95[d] (7.92)	+1.3	37.2 (0.035)
Steel			
Remove QRs	0.86	−20.7	22.3 (0.021)
Capture Rents from Foreigners	0.74	−0.1	3.5 (0.003)

Note: Estimates based on central elasticities, with infinite foreign trade elasticities, except for $\epsilon_{auto}^{s} = 5$, and $\epsilon_{agr}^{d} = 4$, where ϵ_{auto}^{s} is the foreign elasticity of import supply of autos and ϵ_{agr}^{d} is the foreign elasticity of demand for exports of agriculture.

[a] Welfare is the EV measure expressed in billions of 1984 U.S. dollars. Numbers in parentheses are based on infinite foreign trade elasticities in all sectors.

[b] Employment is expressed in thousands of work-years.

[c] One-half of the sum of the absolute value of the employment changes expressed in thousand work-years. The numbers in parentheses are the percentage of employees in the economy who must relocate. For example, (0.15) means that fifteen-hundredths of 1% of the economy's employees must relocate.

[d] If U.S. dealers of Japanese autos capture additional rents (explained in footnote 9), the welfare gain from removing QRs is $9.87 billion with infinite foreign trade elasticities.

TABLE 3.—WELFARE COSTS OF QRs AND TARIFF PROTECTION

	Preferred Foreign Trade Elasticities			Strong Foreign Trade Elasticities
	Low Elasticity[a]	Central Elasticity[a b]	High Elasticity[a]	Central Elasticity[c]
Remove QRs	20.5	20.3 (22.0)	21.6	15.0
Capture Rents from Foreigners (retain QRs)	16.8	14.9 (14.8)	14.5	15.0
Eliminate Remaining Tariff Protection (after QR removal)	0.33	0.57 (0.94)	0.90	−4.3

Note: Welfare is the EV measure expressed in billions of 1984 U.S. dollars. Let ϵ_i^{d} = elasticity of demand for exports of sector i and ϵ_i^{s} = elasticity of supply of imports in sector i.

The central elasticity estimates are not between the high and low elasticity estimates, because we create a new base for comparison by imposing QRs on steel, and then estimate the effects of removing QRs in all 3 sectors.

[a] $\epsilon_{agr}^{d} = 4$; $\epsilon_{auto}^{s} = 5$. Small country assumption for all other export demand and import supply elasticities.

[b] Results in parentheses are the welfare estimates with infinite foreign trade elasticities.

[c] ϵ_i^{d} for exports = 3 and ϵ_i^{s} of supply of imports = 4 where i ranges over all traded sectors.

capturing of rents from foreigners are overestimates to the extent that rent-seeking activities dissipate them. For this reason, an auction quota mechanism is superior to a direct allocation of quota rights to imports. Thus our estimate of the annual cost of QRs in these three industries for 1985 protection levels is between $20 billion and $22 billion.

Insofar as removing QRs leads to increases in agricultural exports and auto imports, the U.S. terms of trade will decline and hence the welfare gain will be less. For the central elasticity case, the welfare gain is $20.3 billion, of which $5.4 billion is the distortionary cost component of QRs. Obtaining the quota rents is a pure income transfer from the rest of the world to the United

States, and its effect is a real appreciation of the dollar (about 1%) which is accompanied by a small improvement in the terms of trade.

It is conceivable that the United States would have monopoly and monopsony power in all sectors in which it trades. Although this seems unlikely because the U.S. market share is usually small in its main import and export markets, we have experimented with generalized terms of trade effects across all sectors for the central elasticity case. In column 4 of table 3, we assume constant import supply elasticities of 4 and constant export demand elasticities of 3 for all traded sectors. The gains from QR removal are smaller, but still substantial ($15.0 billion). However, in this case the terms of trade effects (from expanded trade volume at higher import prices and lower export prices) exactly offset the distortionary costs in total QR costs. Finally, adding unilateral tariff reduction now results in a welfare loss of $4.3 billion because of the dominating terms of trade effect, a result similar to those found in the global simulations mentioned above.

Evidence of pure profits in autos and of economies of scale in autos and, to a lesser extent, in steel raises the question of the extent to which our estimates would be affected by imperfect competition and economies of scale in autos and steel. We view the empirical effects of imperfect competition and economies of scale as offsetting. Due to the fact that costs will increase, QR removal will result in lower benefits than we have estimated to the extent that there are unrealized economies of scale in autos and steel. Following Krishna (1983), however, QRs should be viewed as a practice facilitating pricing above competitive levels. QR removal, therefore, will induce a reduction in oligopolistic pricing practices and lead to greater benefits (relative to our estimates) from a reduction in the distortion costs of these pricing practices. Thus, we do not know, a priori, the direction of the bias in our estimates due to imperfect competition and economies of scale. The issue, however, is clearly worthy of further investigation.

In the introduction, we said that PE estimates are upwardly biased because they fail to include the balance of trade constraint. An order of magnitude of the difference between PE and GE estimates due to this effect is obtained by solving the model with a fixed real exchange rate and hence an endogenous trade balance. This would correspond to what is typically done in PE estimates, which implicitly assume that the real exchange rate is unchanged as a result of QR removal and that resulting import increases need not be compensated by increased exports (or reduced imports from other sectors). For the central elasticity case, removing all QRs would lead to a trade balance deterioration of $12.1 billion and an EV estimate of $33.9 billion. This estimate is about one and two-thirds times the estimate obtained when the balance of trade constraint is properly taken into account. Economy-wide welfare costs estimates derived by adding up individual industry PE estimates are likely to be significantly upward-biased.

Our welfare cost estimates are significantly higher than previous GE estimates.[12] This is so for several reasons. First we properly account for the $14.9 billion transfer associated with the U.S. system of QRs.[13] Thus, even with generalized terms of trade effects which are stronger than we believe reasonable,[14] the QRs cost the U.S. economy $15 billion. Second, in comparison with most previous PE and GE estimates, we have benefited from the detailed work on premia estimates by Feenstra (1988), Hamilton (1988) and Dinopoulos and Kreinin (1988), which are higher than previous estimates.

V. Employment

Table 4 gives estimates of the employment effects of simultaneous removal of QRs in textiles, autos and steel for the central elasticity case. The simultaneous removal of QRs also points out the conflicting worker interests across the three industries subject to QRs. While the steel and textiles and apparel sectors would lose almost as many jobs when all QRs are removed

---

[12] For example, Whalley (1985, table 10.2) estimates welfare losses from unilateral U.S. removal of non-tariff barriers and tariffs. Deardorff and Stern (1986, table 4.6) obtain small welfare gains.

[13] Most previous GE studies of the costs of protection (e.g., Deardorff and Stern (1986) and Whalley (1985)) that have dealt with QRs have done so in the context of global models that treat QRs by their tariff equivalents without including the associated rent transfer that occurs with the U.S. QRs.

[14] In addition, Brown (1987) has shown that the structure of many previous GE models has required excessive estimates of terms of trade effects. See also de Melo (1986) and Deardorff and Stern (1986, p. 41).

as when they are removed in their sector alone, the auto sector gains 1,700 jobs when QRs on steel and textiles and apparel are removed concurrently with the VER on autos. This is so because steel, an important input into auto production, becomes cheaper and because the income elasticity of demand for autos is high. Both effects benefit the domestic auto industry which expands even when QR protection is removed.

Given that QR protection is obtained through the political process, one can argue that the U.S. Congress has decided to value a job in the protected sectors more highly than a job in other sectors. In our experiment, 172,000 jobs in textiles and steel were protected by the QRs on the three sectors at a cost of $20.3 billion. Hence, the annual cost per protected job is about $118,000, approximately 8 (3) times the average annual total compensation of workers in the textile (steel) industry.

If QRs are removed, displaced workers will incur search, relocation, and retraining costs (see Mussa (1978)). Net benefits from QR removal are obtained by subtracting these costs. A proxy for these costs is the discounted value of a displaced worker's earnings losses over a lifetime.[15] This measure allows us to estimate how much gainers will have left after compensating displaced workers for their earnings losses. Earnings losses for displaced workers last approximately six years.[16] A conservative estimate of net benefits, *NB*, is obtained as

$$NB = \sum_{t=0}^{5} \frac{[EV - C_t]}{(1 + r)^t}$$

where *EV* is the equivalent variation measure, C_t is estimated earnings losses in year t, and $r = 7\%$ is the discount rate. (This estimate is conservative since earnings losses are zero after six years, while yearly benefits do not decay.) *NB* is $104 billion, with an associated benefit/cost of 65.

TABLE 4.—EMPLOYMENT EFFECTS OF REMOVING QRs IN AUTOS, STEEL AND TEXTILES (CENTRAL ELASTICITY CASE)[a]
(thousand jobs)

Agriculture	6.4
Food	0.8
Mining	4.5
Textiles and Apparel	−156.4
Autos	1.7
Steel	−15.5
Consumer Goods	17.5
Other Manufacturing	87.1
Traded Services	35.4
Non-Traded Services	18.5

[a] Foreign trade elasticities defined in table 3.

That is, for every dollar of earnings losses saved, the economy loses $65.

VI. Conclusions

Perhaps the most striking result is the high cost of protection from NTBs relative to that from tariffs. While this is repeatedly mentioned in policy discussions, few relative estimates are available. The figures in table 3 suggest that the welfare cost of tariff protection is between 2% (low elasticity case) and 4% (high elasticity case) of the welfare cost of QRs in textiles, autos and steel. Since there are other QRs in the United States beyond those examined here, this estimate is a lower bound.

An alternative way to evaluate the costs of QRs is to ask what tariff structure would give the same welfare loss as existing QRs in the three sectors. In the central elasticity estimates (with infinite foreign trade elasticities), the total welfare cost is estimated at $22.0 billion (1984 dollars), of which $7.2 billion is the distortionary component. For that set of elasticities, moving from the actual tariff structure to a uniform tariff structure yielding the same (import weighted) average protection would represent a welfare gain of $0.70 billion. (Removing tariffs altogether would give a welfare gain of $0.94 billion.) Starting from the existing tariff dispersion, to get the distortionary cost element of QRs would require multiplying each tariff by 3.6 times its 1984 value, which would amount to an average (import weighted) nominal protection of 12.5%. Adding the loss due to rent transfers would require multiplying tariffs by 7.4 times their 1984 value,

[15] We call our estimate a proxy for these adjustment costs because we have not incorporated into our model an endogenous sector that moves resources, as suggested by the theoretical work by Mussa.

[16] See Jacobson (1978). To be conservative, we measure total compensation losses, which exceed earnings losses by the amount of fringe benefits. Morkre and Tarr (1980, chapter 3) discuss the merits of this measure and the alternative unemployment cost measure.

amounting to an average protection of 19.8%.[17] It is no exaggeration to say that, in terms of protection costs, QRs are taking us back to the early days of multilateral tariff negotiations, especially if one includes the rent transfer element.

REFERENCES

Baldwin, R. E., J. Mutti, and D. Richardson, "Welfare Effects on the United States of a Significant Multilateral Tariff Reduction," *Journal of International Economics* 10 (1980), 405–423.

Bohi, D., and M. Russell, *Limiting Oil Imports: An Economic History and Analysis* (Baltimore: Johns Hopkins University, 1978).

Brown, D. K., "Tariffs, the Terms of Trade and National Product Differentiation," *Journal of Policy Modelling* 9 (1987), 503–526.

Caddy, V., "Empirical Estimation of the Elasticity of Substitution: A Review," Preliminary Working Paper OP-09, IMPACT Project. IAC, Melbourne, Australia (1976).

Cline, W. *The Future of World Trade in Textiles and Apparel* (Washington, D.C.: Institute for International Economics, 1987).

Crandall, R., *The U.S. Steel Industry in Recurrent Crisis* (Washington, D.C.: Brookings Institution, 1981).

Deardorff, A., and R. Stern, *The Michigan Model of World Production and Trade* (Cambridge, MA: MIT Press, 1986).

Dinopoulos, E., and M. Kreinin, "Effects of the U.S. -Japan Auto VER on European Prices and U.S. Welfare," this REVIEW 70 (1988), 484–491. ·

Dixit, A., "Optimal Trade and Industrial Policies for the U.S. Automobile Industry," in R. Feenstra (ed.), *Empirical Methods for International Trade* (Cambridge, MA: MIT Press, 1988), 141–165.

Dixon, P., B. Parmenter, J. Sutton, and D. Vincent, *ORANI: A Multisectoral Model of the Australian Economy* (Amsterdam: North-Holland, 1982).

Elliott, K., J. Schott, and W. Takacs, *Auction Quotas and U.S. Trade Policy* (Washington, D.C.: Institute for International Economics, 1987).

Feenstra, R., "Voluntary Export Restraints in U.S. Autos, 1980–81: Quality, Employment and Welfare Effects," in R. Baldwin and A. Krueger (eds.), *The Structure and Evolution of Recent U.S. Trade Policy* (Chicago: University of Chicago Press for National Bureau of Economic Research, 1984).

——, "Automobile Prices and Protection: The U.S.–Japan Trade Restraint," *Journal of Policy Modelling* 7 (1985), 49–68.

——, "Quality Change Under Trade Restraints: Theory and Evidence from Japanese Autos," *Quarterly Journal of Economics* 103 (1988), 131–146.

Hamilton, C., "Restrictiveness and International Transmission of the 'New' Protectionism," in R. Baldwin, C. Hamilton, and A. Sapir (eds.), *Issues in US-EC Trade Relations* (Chicago: University of Chicago Press for National Bureau of Economic Research, 1988), 199–224.

Hekman, J., "An Analysis of the Changing Pattern of Iron and Steel Production in the Twentieth Century," *American Economic Review* 68 (1978), 123–133.

Houthakker, H., and L. Taylor, *Consumer Demand in the United States: Analyses and Projections* (Cambridge: Harvard University Press, 1970).

Hufbauer, G., D. Berliner, and K. Elliott, *Trade Protection in the United States: 31 Case Studies* (Washington, D.C.: Institute for International Economics, 1986).

Jacobson, L., "Earnings Losses of Workers Displaced from Manufacturing Industries." in W. Dewald (ed.), *The Impact of International Trade and Investment on Employment* (Washington, D.C.: U.S. Department of Labor, 1978), 87–98.

Johnson, H. G., "The Cost of Protection and the Scientific Tariff," *Journal of Political Economy* 68 (1960), 327–345.

Keesing, D., and M. Wolf, *Textile Quotas Against Developing Countries* (London: Trade Policy Research Centre, 1980).

Krishna, K., *Trade Restrictions as Facilitating Practices* Discussion paper Number 55 Princeton University (1983).

Levinsohn, J., "Empirics of Taxes on Differentiated Products: The Case of Tariffs in the U.S. Automobile Industry," in R. E. Baldwin (ed.), *Trade Policy Issues and Empirical Analysis* (Chicago: University of Chicago Press, 1988), 11–44.

Melo, J. de, "A Comparison of 50% Multilateral Tariff Reductions in Two Global Trade Models," in T. N. Srinivasan and J. Whalley (eds.), *General Equilibrium Trade Policy Modelling* (Cambridge, MA: MIT Press, 1986).

Melo, J. de, and D. Tarr, *Welfare Costs of US Quotas in Textiles, Steel and Autos*, PPR Working Paper No. 83, Washington D.C.: World Bank (1988).

Morkre, M., *Import Quotas on Textiles: The Welfare Effects of United States Restrictions on Hong Kong* (Washington, D.C.: Bureau of Economics Report to the U.S. Federal Trade Commission, 1984).

Morkre, M., and D. Tarr, *The Effects of Restrictions on U.S. Imports: Five Case Studies and Theory* (Washington, D.C.: Bureau of Economics Report to U.S. Federal Trade Commission, 1980).

Mussa, M., "Dynamic Adjustment in the Heckscher-Ohlin-Samuelson Model," *Journal of Political Economy* 86 (5), 775–791.

Powell, A., and F. Gruen, "The Constant Elasticity of Transformation Production Frontier and Linear Supply System," *International Economic Review* 8 (1967), 315–328.

Shiells, C., R. Stern and A. Deardorff, "Estimates of the Elasticities of Substitution between Imports and Home Goods for the United States," *Weltwirtschaftliches Archiv* 122 (3) (1986), 497–519.

Stern, R. M., J. Francis and B. Schumacher, *Price Elasticities in International Trade: An Annotated Bibliographer* (London: Macmillan Press, 1976).

---

[17] In that experiment we are increasing the variance of nominal protection by 3.6 and 7.4 times the variance prevailing in 1984. Since the distortionary cost of tariff protection is positively related to the average level of protection and to the variance of tariffs (see Johnson (1962)), another hypothetical calculation would consist of computing the average tariff under the assumption of no tariff dispersion across sectors. In that case, starting from a uniform tariff protection (3.5%) equivalent to the existing tariff protection in 1984, the distortionary cost element of QRs would require an average uniform protection of 24%. Adding the rent transfer loss would raise the average uniform protection to 50%. With linear, rather than constant elasticity demand and supply curves, welfare calculations would yield lower estimates as the corresponding elasticities would increase as one moves up the demand and supply curves.

Tarr, D., *A General Equilibrium Analysis of the Welfare and Employment Effects of US Quotas on Textiles, Autos, and Steel* (Washington, D.C.: U.S. Federal Trade Commission, 1989).

Tarr, D., and M. Morkre, *Aggregate Costs to the United States of Tariffs and Quotas on Imports: General Tariff Cuts and Removal of Quotas on Automobiles, Steel, Sugar, and Textiles* (Washington, D.C.: U.S. Federal Trade Commission, 1984).

U.S. Department of Agriculture, *Dairy: Background for the 1984 Farm Legislation* (Washington, D.C., 1984).

U.S. International Trade Commission, *US Global Competitiveness: the US Textile Mill Industry*, Publication No. 2048, Dec. 1987.

Whalley, J., *Trade Liberalization Among Major World Trading Areas* (Cambridge, MA: MIT Press, 1985).

Winston, C., and Associates, *Blind Intersection? Policy and the Automobile Industry* (Washington, D.C.: Brookings Institution, 1987).

ELSEVIER

Japan and the World Economy 8 (1996) 11–33

VERs under imperfect competition and foreign direct investment: A case study of the US–Japan auto VER

Jaime de Melo [a], David Tarr [b,*]

[a] *World Bank, University of Geneva, and CEPR*
[b] *The World Bank, 1818 H Street, N.W., Washington DC 20433, USA*

Received March 1994; accepted October 1994

Abstract

This paper first assesses the costs of the US–Japan auto VER in a general equilibrium constant returns to scale (CRTS) model at about $10 billion. It then sequentially introduces important features of the auto VER: endogenous rent premium determination, wage distortions in autos, the US capturing some of the rents of the VER, US monopsony power in autos, increasing returns to scale, pure profits and entry, foreign direct investment, and endogenous conjectures. In the preferred monopolistic competition, initial profit model, the estimated costs are about 10% less than under the assumption of CRTS, but costs remain high at over $200 000 per job protected in autos. Compared with exogenous rent determination, endogenous rent determination results in significantly lower estimated costs of the VER because domestic entry reduces the rent premium. Foreign direct investment with initial profits is shown to lower the costs of the VER if, and only if, the rent premium is endogenous.

Keywords: VERs, Imperfect competition; General equilibrium; Foreign direct investment

JEL classification: F12; F13; F14

---

1. Introduction

In 1981, the US induced the Japanese to agree to a voluntary export restraint (VER) on their exports of autos to the US. Among others, Baldwin (1982) has

---

*Corresponding author. Tel.: (202)473-7677. Fax: (202)676-1341. E-mail: dtarr@worldbank.org.

12   *J. de Melo, D. Tarr/Japan and the World Economy 8 (1996) 11–33*

noted that protection will generally have unintended effects, and the developments that followed the introduction of the auto VER demonstrate the complexity of the VER mechanism. Some have been studied by previous authors. These include: (1) the significant quality upgrading on the part of the Japanese auto producers (Feenstra, 1984, 1988); (2) a spillover effect on US demand for European autos which generated a premium on European autos after adjusting for quality upgrading (Dinopoulos and Kreinin, 1988); (3) the impact of the VER on imperfectly competitive pricing of the US auto producers (Dixit, 1988; Krishna et al., 1989); and (4) wage distortions in the auto industry may imply that additional labor employed in the auto industry has second-best benefits (Dixit, 1988; Krishna et al., 1989).[1] There are, however, several other aspects of the auto VER that have not yet been systematically investigated, which are the subject of this paper. These are: (5) US auto dealers captured some of the VER rents; (6) US monopsony power in autos will imply a positive optimal tariff, i.e., in the absence of retaliation, there are terms-of-trade gains that reduce the costs of the VER; (7) increasing returns to scale (IRTS) in the US auto industry implies that protection has an effect on scale efficiency; (8) the existence of pure profits (perhaps induced by the VER) in the domestic auto industry, which will induce entry that will also have scale efficiency effects; (9) massive entry into the US auto industry via foreign direct investment (FDI) by Japanese auto producers shortly after the VER went into effect; and (10) the proper evaluation of rent capture which implies an endogenous treatment of the rent premium.

This paper explores systematically the impact of these effects induced by the VER. We first estimate the effects of the VER under constant returns to scale (CRTS), without wage distortions and without US citizens capturing rents. We then sequentially introduce the elements mentioned above one by one. In this manner we isolate the impact of each of the effects on the welfare estimate of the effects of the VER, ultimately arriving at a representation of the auto industry which we believe yields a better estimate of the costs of the auto VER. The reader is thus able to readily assess the impact of each of the effects or industry attributes on the calculation of the costs of VER protection. Moreover, because our modelling recognizes IRTS and wage distortions, we also estimate separately the welfare gains from applying "optimal" trade and subsidy policy to take these features into account.

Interest in systematic calculations of the costs of the auto VER arises out of the interaction of several ambiguous effects. For example, as shown by Dixit (1986) and by Rodrik (1988), entry to eliminate pure profits will reduce monopolistic price distortion (a benefit), but will reduce scale efficiency (a cost). In addition, if entry occurs through foreign direct investment (FDI), Brecher and Diaz-

---

[1] Goto (1986) examined the impact of wage distortions in the auto industry. But he simulated a change from US autarky to integration into a single economy with Japan, rather than the effects of the VER in autos. de Melo and Tarr (1992) examined separately effects (1), (2), (4), (5) and (6).

J. de Melo, D. Tarr/Japan and the World Economy 8 (1996) 11–33   13

Alejandro (1977) have shown that the repatriation of the private returns to capital can be immiserizing if the private and social returns to capital are different due to distorted prices, such as would occur under a quota. In addition, increased entry with FDI imposes greater costs through reduced scale efficiency. But the costs of the VER are reduced through another channel. In a world of differentiated products, entry will reduce the price of domestic autos, which in turn will reduce the demand for and the price of imported autos. Since the rent premium on imported autos is endogenously determined as the difference between the price on the tariff-ridden demand curve at the rationed quantity of autos under the VER and the world price of autos inclusive of transport costs, entry will also reduce the rent premium earned by foreigners. Thus, entry has greater benefits when the rent premium is correctly determined endogenously than when the rent premium is treated exogenously.

We estimate the effects of the VER with a general equilibrium model because three of the items above (4, 6 and 9), are fundamentally general equilibrium effects. As a result, we estimate the combined effects of: (1) the effects of FDI in a second-best environment; (2) the second-best gain of labor reallocation when an industry with a wage premium receives protection; (3) the biases likely to occur in a partial equilibrium approach. Moreover, as mentioned above, our model structure analyzes a significantly greater variety of modelling features than previous models. This demonstrates that with modern software (GAMS in our case) thorough industry analysis is possible within a general equilibrium framework.

Our preferred representation of the US auto industry during the VER is one of monopolistic competition on the domestic market with above normal profits caused by the VER and a wage premium paid to auto workers. To anticipate our main results, we find that a perfect competition model which incorporates wage distortions and domestic rent capture results in an estimate of costs of the VER of about $10 billion, and almost $250 000 per job protected in autos at the expense of employment elsewhere. In the preferred monopolistic competition, initial profit model, the estimated costs are reduced by about 10% depending on the assumption made regarding oligopolistic conjectures. The ratio of the costs of the auto VER to the benefits (in saved adjustment costs) is between 14 and 26 to 1. Endogenous rent determination results in significantly lower estimated costs of the VER because domestic entry reduces the rent premium. The impact of FDI is to lower the costs of the VER if, and only if, the rent premium is determined endogenously. Then the greater entry into domestic auto manufacturing lowers the rent premium, which dominates scale efficiency loss and immiserizing effects of FDI.

The remainder of the paper is organized as follows. In Section 2, we review the main stylized facts of the US auto industry that are modelled in the remainder of the paper. Modelling specifications and calibration are discussed in Section 3. Section 4 reports on welfare cost calculations under the standard traditional assumption of a competitive market in the US auto industry. Estimates of the effects of wage distortions, partial domestic quota rent capture and endogenous

14   *J. de Melo, D. Tarr/Japan and the World Economy 8 (1996) 11–33*

terms-of-trade are provided. Corresponding calculations under various imperfectly competitive market structures are reported in Section 5. Optimal tariff and production subsidy calculations, which are rarely executed in computable general equilibrium exercises, are presented in Section 6. Conclusions follow in Section 7.

2. The US auto industry during the US–Japan VER

In the Spring of 1981, after negotiations with US government officials, the Japanese government announced that it would voluntarily restrain its exports to the US. The Japanese agreed to limit their exports of autos to the US to 1.68 million vehicles per year between 1 April 1981 and 31 March 1984. Between 1 April 1984 and 31 March 1985, Japanese auto exports to the US were limited to 1.85 million vehicles. This action was taken against a background of falling US production and employment in autos, and a number of legislative attempts to curb Japanese imports. After the US Administration failed to request an extension of the auto VER, the Japanese government continued to restrain its auto exports to the US, but at the less restrictive level of 2.3 million vehicles per year.[2] The Japanese action may have been motivated by fear of Congressional pressure to reintroduce a VER, or by their learning they had monopoly power they wished to continue to exploit.

After adjusting for the significant product upgrading that took place, Feenstra (1984, 1988) found that Japanese manufacturers earned premia on their US sales of over 17% in 1984 as a result of the VER. Dinopoulos and Kreinin (1988) also adjusted for product upgrading on European autos (which was less significant), and found a significant spillover effect on the price of European autos. These spillover effects could be explained by a variety of reasons including: (1) new found monopoly power because the VER restrained the Japanese (see Krishna, 1989 on quotas as a facilitating practice); (2) an upward sloping supply curve of a competitive industry; or (3) fear of restraint by the US Congress. As explained in de Melo and Tarr (1992), combining the estimates of Feenstra, and Dinopolous and Kreinin implies that the weighted average premium rate earned by European and Japanese auto exporters on their sales to the US in 1984 was 31.8%, yielding $7.87 billion of rents to foreign auto exporters.

In addition, there is evidence that during the VER period, Japanese manufacturers allowed their US dealers to capture part of the rents.[3] One explanation of

---

[2] These restraints continued into 1990. See General Agreement on Tariffs and Trade (1990, p. 221).

[3] Consumers Union, for example has reported that, when the quota was in effect, many dealers charged in excess of the sticker price, using such devices as charging high prices for decal stripes, rustproofing and undercoating. Its readers indicate that this was especially prevalent among Toyota, Honda and Mazda dealers. Consumer Reports, August 1983, 391. See also the statement by Senator Chafee, Congressional Record, 29 February 1984, S. 1966; Fortune, "Can Detroit Live without Quotas," 25 June 1984, 20; and Washington Post, "Car Dealer Markups Raise Questions," Washington Business, 19 November 1984, 1, 34, 35.

J. de Melo, D. Tarr/Japan and the World Economy 8 (1996) 11–33   15

this phenomenon is that this practice developed a strong US dealer network. Another is that it retained goodwill. A third is the allegation that US auto dealers of Japanese autos threatened collective antitrust action to void the VER if they did not receive a price from their suppliers that would allow them to capture some of the rents. Accordingly, we assume that US dealers of Japanese autos earned $500 of rents per vehicle due to the VER, but US dealers of European vehicles earned no rents. This implies that there were rents earned on the sale of Japanese autos during the VER period in addition to those estimated by Feenstra. Under this assumption, the weighted average premium paid on all imported autos was 36.4% (instead of 31.8%) and US residents captured 10% of the rents.[4]

After adjusting for human capital and demographic factors such as age, sex, education and race, Krueger and Summers (1988) have estimated that workers in certain industries earn wage premia; in particular, they estimated a 27% premium for workers in the transportation sector. This is the premium we apply to auto workers.[5] They, and Katz and Summers (1989), argue that efficiency wage theories generally explain these wage differences, but that in the case of autos, the premia appear to be explained by unionization. Assuming that workers in all industries are employed up to the point where the value of their marginal product equals their wage, this premium, so long as it is exogenous, implies that a reallocation of workers to autos should be efficiency-improving thereby reducing the welfare costs of protection. Since the welfare effect of reallocating labor from other sectors to the auto industry depends on the difference between the value of the marginal product of labor in autos and other sectors, a correct evaluation requires a general equilibrium model.

Should the US be regarded as a country which is unable to significantly influence the price at which foreigners supply autos, or does it possess monopsony power on world auto markets? The results of Dinopolous and Kreinin provide some indirect evidence in support of the latter view. Accordingly, we simulate two extreme alternatives: (1) the US is unable to influence the world price of autos (infinite import supply elasticity); and (2) an import supply elasticity of five. In the latter case, an elementary model would suggest an optimum tariff of about 20%.

All of the above effects can be analyzed in a CRTS model. However, Friedlaender et al. (1983) and Winston and Associates (1987) have estimated that the US auto industry operates under IRTS. Accordingly, we also evaluate the effects of the VER in a model where the auto sector has IRTS.

---

[4] See de Melo and Tarr (1992) for details of this calculation.

[5] Using a different methodology, de Melo and Tarr (1992); find a similar estimate of the premium earned by auto workers. On the other hand, the wage premium used by Dixit and by Krishna et al. is about double the actual wage premium because they did not adjust for the human capital differences between auto workers and the average manufacturing worker.

16   *J. de Melo, D. Tarr/Japan and the World Economy 8 (1996) 11–33*

Table 1 documents two important facts about the VER period not previously investigated. First, profits in the US auto industry were very high by historical standards from 1983 to 1986, declining, almost monotonically, after reaching their peak in 1984.[6] As mentioned above, the VER was in place until 31 March 1985, after which a Japanese VER remained in effect, apparently without US Administration request. Second, the data show that increased FDI followed the negotiation of the VER agreement and the appearance of high profits in the US auto industry. FDI peaked in 1986.

We believe these series are related and would argue that once the US recession of 1981 and 1982 ended, the VER allowed above normal profits in the US auto

Table 1
Profits and foreign direct investment in the US auto industry

	Profits[a]	Foreign direct investment[b]	
		Assembly	Parts
1979	4.7	200.0	N.A.
1980	− 5.0	200.0	N.A.
1981	− 1.1	500.0	N.A.
1982	− 0.8	65.0	4.0
1983	5.1	101.4	32.0
1984	9.9	487.5	48.0
1985	6.8	628.0	71.0
1986	2.2	850.8	234.8
1987	0.5	435.5	743.7
1988	2.4	419.5	830.8
1989	− 1.4	N.A.	N.A.

N.A.: Not available.

[a] Billion of current dollars.

Source: US Department of Commerce, *Survey of Current Business*, July, various issues.

[b] Millions of current dollars. Includes plant and other investment. Prior to 1982, data cover only FDI in assembly plants above $50 million.

Source: US Department of Commerce, *Foreign Direct Investment in the United States*, various issues and unpublished data of the Office of Trade Investment, US Department of Commerce.

---

[6] An alternate series for data on profits in motor vehicles and equipment is available from the Quarterly Financial Statistics, published by the US Federal Trade Commission until 1982 and the US Bureau of the Census for years after 1982. The Survey of Current Business and Quarterly Financial Statistics series differ mainly insofar as the former considers profits on US operations only, whereas the latter includes income from all sources including foreign operations. Both series would include profits of US subsidiaries of foreign corporations in their US operations, i.e., profits of companies like Honda USA earned on US sales are included in both; but only the Quarterly Financial Reports includes profits of Honda USA on its sales to Japan.

Between 1979 and 1984, both series are very close. From 1985 on, however, the Quarterly Financial Reports series show much higher profits. This principally reflects the increase in FDI (shown in Table 1) and the profits of US subsidiaries on their foreign sales. Since we are principally interested in the profits in the US market, we focus on the Survey of Current Business series. We thank Paul Zareth of the US Bureau of the Census for clarifying these distinctions.

J. de Melo, D. Tarr/Japan and the World Economy 8 (1996) 11–33   17

industry. The highly profitable US market could, however, be accessed by the Japanese through FDI in auto assembly facilities.[7] (Bhagwati (1987) has referred to this as VER-jumping.) If investment responds to profits with a lag, it is no surprise that the years of large investments began in 1984. The US "Big-Three" (GM, Ford and Chrysler), which had very little domestic competition following the exit of other US auto producers (e.g., Studebaker, Hudson, Packard), were suddenly facing stiff competition in the US. Between 1984 and 1987, seven Japanese firms (Honda, Toyota, Nissan, Mazda, Isuzu, Mitsubishi, and Fuji) established car assembly plants on US territory. As the Japanese followed their practice of vertical integration, FDI in parts continued to rise, even after FDI in assembly plants tapered off when the market became saturated with producers.[8] In sum, we believe that the VER generated pure profits in the US auto market which were then largely eliminated by Japanese entry. Consequently, we also estimate the effects of the VER under the assumption that it induced pure profits in 1984 that were eliminated by entry including FDI.

3. Modelling and auto industry

We now describe briefly how we model the auto industry under IRTS. Following Harris (1984) and Cox and Harris (1985), we assume that output is produced by N identical firms indexed over i so that sectoral output is $X = Nx_i$ where x_i is the output of the ith firm, and we have suppressed sector subscripts. We define total costs, TC, and average costs, AC, in terms of fixed costs, FC, and variable costs, VC, where fixed costs are defined by

$$FC \equiv (N/N_0)/(\overline{KF}\,R + \overline{LF}\,W), \tag{1}$$

where a bar over a variable indicates that it is exogenous, N_0 is the initial number of firms, $\overline{KF}$ and $\overline{LF}$ are the amount of capital and labor required to keep a firm open, and W and R are the prices (relative to the numeraire) of labor and capital respectively. (In the simulations reported here, the model is calibrated so that labor and capital shares in fixed costs are the same.) Unit variable costs are constant.

Each firm produces identical products which are differentiated from (identical) imports. This national product differentiation is also applied to export sales which are differentiated from domestic sales. This symmetric treatment of imports and exports is modelled by assuming CES and CET aggregation functions for imports and domestic output on the one hand, and domestic output and exports, on the other hand.

---

[7] FDI by Japanese firms outside of auto parts and assembly is ignored since it is not fundamental to the VER.

[8] Faced with domestic competitors who are more vertically integrated, the Big Three have begun to copy the Japanese practice of greater vertical integration among parts suppliers, suggesting some efficiency enhancing properties of the practice in the auto industry. See Lawrence (1990).

18   *J. de Melo, D. Tarr/Japan and the World Economy 8 (1996) 11–33*

For pricing, we assume that US auto firms price competitively in export markets because they face stiff foreign competition. The assumption is plausible, and not crucial empirically because exports accounted for less than 4% of total industry sales (see Table 2).

Our preferred pricing rule for domestic sales is to assume that each firm behaves in the domestic market as an oligopolist facing a downward sloping demand curve. Firms form conjectures regarding the output reactions of their domestic competitors. Denote by Ω_i^d, the ith firm's conjecture with respect to the change in domestic industry output when it changes its output by one unit. By symmetry, the marginal costs and conjectural variation parameters are equal for all firms in the industry. Profit maximization then implies that, at equilibrium, each firm sets marginal revenue equal to marginal costs, MC, so that:

$$(PD - MC)/PD = \Omega_d/(N\varepsilon^d), \tag{2}$$

Table 2
Production, demand structure and elasticities in the auto industry

Premium rate on imports	36.4%	(31.8%)
Rents accruing to foreigners [a]	7.87	(7.87)
Rents accruing to US citizens	0.87	(0.0)
Wage distortion in autos [b]	27.0%	
Production and demand [a]		
Gross output	124.2	
Domestic final demand sales	111.0	
Intermediate sales	8.3	
Exports	4.9	
Imports	32.6	
Intermediates	2.3	
Final demand	30.3	
Elasticities and Parameters [c]		
Capital–labor substitution	0.8	
Import–domestic substitution elasticity [d]	1.9	
Composite final demand	0.8	
Export–domestic transformation elasticity [d]	2.9	
Calibrated domestic conjecture (Ω^d)	0.72	
Derived price elasticity of demand (ε^d)	1.37	
Cost disadvantage ratio [e]	0.11	

Notes: Second column estimates assume no rent capture by US dealers of Japanese auto imports.
[a] 1984 US$ billion.
[b] Krueger and Summers (1988).
[c] Sources for demand and supply elasticities are detailed in de Melo and Tarr (1990).
[d] The selected CES (CET) functions imply that the corresponding substitution (transportation) elasticities are compensated import demand (export supply) elasticities.
[e] Friedlaender et al. (1983); and Winston and associates (1987).

J. de Melo, D. Tarr/Japan and the World Economy 8 (1996) 11–33   19

where ε^d is the market elasticity of demand. Note that in the simulations, the number of firms N and the market elasticity of demand are endogenous variables, where the latter is a share weighted average of the elasticities of demand for final and for intermediate sales implied by functional forms for consumer behavior and technology.

Eq. (2) defines the percentage markup over marginal costs in terms of N, Ω^d and ε^d. Given data on prices, costs and elasticities, only the ratio of Ω^d to N is identified. Given ε^d and N equal to 3 in 1984 (General Motors, Ford and Chrysler), we calibrate Ω^d at 0.72, i.e., pricing was more competitive than Cournot. An equivalent approach, followed by Dixit (1988) is to enter Cournot conjectures ($\Omega^d = 1$), and calibrate N, the "Cournot equivalent number of firms".[9] Dixit calibrated the Cournot equivalent number of firms in 1979, 1980 and 1983. If domestic firms are counted by corporation (rather than by division), then Dixit's results indicate that pricing was more competitive than Cournot in all three years he examined, and, of the three years, pricing was the most competitive in 1980 and least competitive in 1979.[10] In their estimates during the period 1979–1984, Krishna et al. (1989) found that pricing was the least competitive in 1984. They also find that pricing was more competitive than Cournot in all years they examined. We conclude that our calibrated conjecture is a reasonable estimate.

It is likely that conjectures will change as a result of firm entry. Intuitively, as the number of firms increases, in the limit, the industry becomes competitive and conjectures should approach competitive ($\Omega^d = 0$).[11] To capture this effect, in some simulations, we estimate the effect of additional competition by adding the following ad hoc equation:

$$\Omega^d = \Omega_0^d / [N/N_0], \tag{3}$$

where Ω_0^d is the conjecture in the initial calibrated equilibrium. When we use Eq. (3), we say that conjectures are endogenous.

The conjectural variation approach has been criticized because it involves applying a static concept to an inherently dynamic problem. It can, however, be

---

[9] Our approach is followed by Krugman (1987) and Krishna et al. (1989). Devarajan and Rodrik (1991) follow the approach of Dixit. Calibration procedures which differ substantively from ours are Smith and Venables (1988), who adjust elasticities to be consistent with Cournot conjectures, and the suggestion of Saloner (1989) that marginal cost data should be adjusted.

[10] Dixit calibrated $N = 13.9$ for 1983. If we choose $\Omega^d = 1$, we obtain $N = 4.2$. Since the industry is more competitive the higher the value of N, our calibration yields a less competitive auto industry than represented by Dixit.

[11] Of course, perfectly competitive conjectures are not possible in the presence of fixed costs and increasing returns to scale because firms will incur losses. Novshek (1980) notes that simply adding more firms drives Cournot output to zero in the limit. He shows, however, that if the minimum efficient scale becomes small in relation to demand as the number of firms goes to infinity, then Cournot equilibria with free entry exist and they approach perfect competition.

20   *J. de Melo, D. Tarr/Japan and the World Economy 8 (1996) 11–33*

defended as an equilibrium to a dynamic game, and, in any case it is used by most authors dealing with imperfect competition models in applied trade problems. We also assume that domestic firms form Cournot conjectures with respect to foreign rivals so that the output reaction of foreign firms does not appear in (2).

To isolate scale efficiency effects from entry effects, we also consider a contestable markets pricing rule, in which case the threat of entry forces incumbent firms to price at average costs:

$$PX = AC, \tag{4}$$

where PX is a weighted sum of domestic and export sales prices. Because of the evidence of entry, contestable markets is not our preferred pricing rule.

When we assume that the VER leads to pure profits, drawing on the data in Tables 1 and 2 and related data on profits, we assume pure profits in 1984 of $9.4 billion.[12] This yields a rate of profit of 8%.

As suggested by the evidence in Section 2, firm entry was the mechanism by which excess profits were eliminated. This implies that the following equation is added:

$$\text{PROFITS} = 0 \tag{5}$$

will determine the number of firms in the monopolistic competition case described above.

When there are initial profits, the calibration must be decomposed into two parts: (1) how much do average costs depart from marginal costs; and (2) what is the markup of price over average costs (due to imperfect competition). Independently of initial profits in autos, the amount of fixed costs is determined by the value of the cost-disadvantage ratio given in Table 2. To incorporate fixed costs while replicating observed prices and quantities in the CRTS case, the primary variable cost component of total cost is reduced by the amount of fixed costs.

When there are initial profits, in a first step we carry out the same allocation of total costs into fixed and variable components described above. In a second step, given the profit rate per unit of domestic sales and the quantities and foreign prices (expressed relative to the numeraire), we solve for the vector of prices that satisfies the constraint that the firm earn the rate of return given by the initial data.[13] As before, the calibration of Ω^d is obtained by solving (2) but with the newly calculated set of domestic prices.

---

[12] In addition to the estimate of Table 1, the Quarterly Financial Reports indicates that profits in motor vehicles and equipment were $10.8 billion in 1984 and the US International Trade Commission indicates that the industry's profits were $10.4 billion in that year. We assume any excess of profits over $9.4 billion were normal.

[13] Because of interindustry linkages, this step involves solving simultaneously for the entire vector of prices that satisfies firms' budget constraints in all sectors.

J. de Melo, D. Tarr/Japan and the World Economy 8 (1996) 11–33   21

Finally, is the issue of modelling capital mobility. We consider two polar cases. When capital is internationally immobile, the rental rate on capital is determined endogenously and the aggregate capital stock is fixed. When capital is internationally mobile, we assume perfect mobility. Then, the rental rate on capital is fixed in terms of the numeraire by an infinitely elastic supply of capital available on international markets and the capital stock is variable. When there is perfect capital mobility, the rental income from FDI accrues to the foreign owners of capital who repatriate the rental income. Capital inflow and outflow are treated symmetrically. Thus, the domestic economy achieves additional output from the use of foreign capital, but it loses the rentals. When capital flows into the auto sector it may go to an existing firm or a new firm may form. This is determined endogenously by the zero profit condition and other relevant model equations such as the endogenously determined markup of price over marginal costs and endogenously determined scale efficiency.

The remaining features of the model are standard to computable general equilibrium (CGE) models. The model includes two factors, capital and labor, mobile between sectors. Labor is always in fixed supply.[14] Domestic demand includes two components, final and intermediates. The government sector's role is limited to lump-sum redistributions to and from the representative consumer. In the simulations reported below, the auto sector is embedded in the static ten-sector model described in de Melo and Tarr (1992). In the calibration to 1984, tariffs are set at their levels in 1984 (an economy wide average of 3.5%) and the quotas in textiles and apparel resulting in a premium rate of 40.5% are also maintained at their base year level.

Table 2 describes the structure of the US auto industry in 1984. Imports represented 26% of domestic output, the bulk of which went to final demand. As mentioned above, exports were negligible. All elasticities are taken based on an extensive literature search of econometrically estimated elasticities. For example, price elasticities of demand are taken from Levinsohn (1988),[15] and estimates of the cost disadvantage ratio are taken from Friedlaender et al. (1983).[16] Subject to econometrically based estimates of elasticities, parameters (like the scalar in front of a CES production function) are chosen to insure that the initial observed data point is an equilibrium of the model. de Melo and Tarr (1990, 1992) elaborate details, but some information on the elasticities is provided in Table 2.

---

[14] As shown in de Melo and Tarr (1993), endogenous aggregate labor supply has a very small impact on the welfare costs of protection in our formulation.

[15] Unlike previous elasticity estimates, Levinsohn clusters autos into groups that take into account characteristics, prior to econometric estimation of the price elasticity of demand. Hence, the price elasticities of demand in this study are likely to be more accurate than previous estimates.

[16] The measure of scale economies captures the degree of multiproduct scale economies at the level of output achieved by General Motors, Ford and Chrysler in 1983.

22   *J. de Melo, D. Tarr/Japan and the World Economy 8 (1996) 11–33*

4. Welfare cost estimates under CRTS

We begin with the benchmark estimate of the auto VER under CRTS in Table 3. Welfare is evaluated by the Hicksian equivalent variation measure (column 2) and distortion costs (column 3).[17] We evaluate these components by estimating the total costs of the VER and separately estimating the benefits of capturing rents from foreigners. The distortion costs are defined as the difference between the two estimates.

The simulated estimate of the gain from rent capture is close to the initial exogenous estimate (see Table 2), but is slightly lower than the initial value of rents because capturing rents results in an income increase that will lead to an increase in demand for imported autos. This increase gets translated into a higher rent premium (now captured domestically) which increases the distortion costs of the VER.

Table 3
Welfare cost of auto VER under CRTS ($ 1984 billion)

	Total costs $1 = (2 + 3)$	Rent costs 2	distortion costs[a] 3	Employment change in autos[b] 4
1. Low elasticity[c]	8.92	7.71 (33.9)	1.21	−22.8
2. Central elasticity	9.82	7.80 (32.5)	2.02	−36.2
3. High elasticity[c]	10.84	7.83 (32.2)	3.01	−34.1
4. Central elasticity with US capturing some rents	10.28	7.77 (37.1)	2.51	−40.9
5. Central elasticity with US capturing some rents and exogenous wage distortions	10.08	7.77 (37.1)	2.31	−40.9
6. Central elasticity with US capturing some rents, exogenous wage distortions and endogenous terms of trade	7.27	7.77 (37.1)	−0.50	−30.7

[a] Distortion costs are calculated as the difference between total costs and rent costs.

[b] Thousand man years.

[c] Low (high) elasticity estimated are obtained by lowering (increasing) central elasticity values by one standard deviation.

---

[17] All results in the tables are reported with endogenous quota rent premium determination. See the appendix for results under exogenous quota rent premium determination.

J. de Melo, D. Tarr/Japan and the World Economy 8 (1996) 11–33   23

Although auctioning quota rights is often recommended as a device to capture quota rents (e.g., Bergsten et al. (1987)), in this instance quota right auction will likely be ineffective. First, since a significant portion of the rents were captured by Europeans, and there was no explicit VER or quota against the Europeans, it is doubtful that auctioning quota rights would have resulted in rent capture. In addition, to the extent that there is monopoly power in exporting, Krishna (1990) has shown that auctioning quota rights may not capture rents. This is because the price at which the exporters with monopoly power are willing to supply the market will increase with a binding quota, thereby reducing the value of a license to import. In this setting, a tariff at the rate of the quota premium from each region, would be the instrument best suited to capture rents.

Sensitivity of the welfare cost estimates to systematic variation in demand and supply elasticities in the first three rows indicates that the estimates of the distortion costs of the VER increase with demand and supply elasticities. This is because the price decrease from removing the VER induces a larger increase of auto purchases with larger elasticities, i.e, a larger deadweight loss triangle. On the other hand, rent cost estimates are insensitive to changes in elasticities. In the remainder of the paper, we report only simulations with central elasticity estimates.[18]

In row 4 (Table 3) we recognize that US dealers of Japanese autos captured some rents over and above the rents captured by the Japanese. The gain from removing the price wedge caused by the VER increases by about $500 million. This is because there is now a greater price wedge between the price paid by US consumers and the price at which imported autos are available on world markets.

In row 5, we add the effects of a 27% exogenous wage distortion in the auto industry. Now auto workers have a higher marginal product value than workers in other industries, so the reduction of auto employment when the VER is removed reduces the magnitude of the gain. The second best effect is, however, quite small since the estimated gains from removing the VER are only reduced by $200 million relative to row 4.

In row 6, we assume the US has monopsony power in autos with an elasticity of import supply of autos of 5. Now when the VER is removed, US importers pay a higher price. This terms-of-trade effect reduces the benefits of VER removal substantially. In fact, due to the terms of trade loss, the economy gains $500 million more from rent capture (which does not significantly affect import

---

[18]Employment loss in autos is less in the high elasticity case compared to the central elasticity because imported and domestic autos are not as close substitutes in the high elasticity case. This is because the extent to which imported and domestic autos are gross substitutes depends on the difference between two elasticities: (1) the elasticity of substitution between imported and domestic autos in the CES nest of composite autos; and (2) the elasticity of demand for composite autos. Although both elasticities increase in the high elasticity case, the relevant difference decreases. See de Melo and Tarr (1992) for an elaboration.

quantities or the terms of trade) than it does from removing the VER. We report this as a negative distortion "cost" of the VER.

5. Welfare cost estimates under IRTS and international capital mobility

So far, the more realistic estimate of the cost of the VER is the case in which US citizens capture some rents and there is a wage premium paid to US auto workers. It is reproduced as the reference case in row 0 of Table 4. Start with the contestable market pricing scenario (row 1) which isolates scale efficiency effects since there is no firm entry. Compared with the reference CRTS case, the distortionary cost estimate is cut by 48%. This is because removing the VER induces a reduction of domestic auto output. With contestable markets there is no firm exit which forces existing firms to operate at a lower scale. However, we have argued that monopolistic competition is the more realistic behavioral assumption for the auto industry. In that case (row 2), the reduction in demand for domestic autos induces firm exit which nearly compensates for the scale efficiency loss from reduced output, so that the distortionary cost component is larger than with contestable markets. Note, however, that the distortion cost with monopolistic competition is less than with CRTS. Thus, contrary to the result emphasized by Horstman and Markusen (1986), in this scenario, protection induces a slight movement down the average cost curve because the effect of protection removal on the reduction of demand for domestic output dominates the effect of inefficient firm entry. Despite a firm exit rate of 5.4%, average output of remaining firms decreases.

Now allow for the profits due to the VER. We model the VER as creating a profit that induces firm entry until profits are eliminated, but as long as the VER remains in effect, the traditional rent and distortion costs remain. Firm entry is required to eliminate profits. Consequently, we simulate the costs of the VER under this scenario by decomposing the costs into two components. First, we estimate the costs of firm entry to eliminate profits caused by the VER. Second, we estimate the remaining costs of the VER by removing the VER from this counterfactually created zero profit equilibrium. The total costs of the auto VER are then the sum of the two component costs with the second component disaggregated, as before, into a distortionary cost and a rent cost.[19]

In row 3, we allow for profits, but assume no international capital mobility and retain exogenous conjectures. Firm entry to eliminate profits results in estimated costs of $1.91 billion. The estimate is negative because the required firm entry –

---

[19] Analogously, in estimating the job protection in autos due to the VER, we add the jobs generated in the domestic auto industry due to entry and the jobs protected by the VER. That is, auto workers have jobs protected while the VER is in effect, plus additional jobs due to entry.

Table 4
Welfare cost of auto VERs under IRTS and international capital mobility (Exogenous wage distortions and partial rent capture by US in all simulations) ($ 1984 billion)

	Total costs $1 = -2 + 3 + 4$	Removal profits 2	Rent costs [f] 3	Distortion costs 4	Employment change in autos [a] 5	Entry/Exit (% change) (+) 6 [b]	(−) 7 [c]
0. CRTS reference case	10.08		7.77 (37.1)	2.31	−40.9		
1. Contestable market pricing	9.00		7.79 (37.1)	1.21	−24.5	—	—
2. Monopolistic competition	9.77		7.79 (37.1)	1.98	−22.1	—	−5.4
3. Monopolistic competition and initial profits (MCIP)	10.39	−1.91	7.00 (33.4)	1.48	−35.47	33.7	−6.0
4. MCIP and international capital mobility	10.23	−1.88 (157.1) [d]	6.85 (32.8)	1.50	−34.54 (−1.5) [e]	33.9	−5.9
5. MCIP and endogenous terms of trade	7.99	−1.91	7.00 (33.4)	−0.92	30.4	33.7	−4.5
6. MCIP and international capital mobility under endogenous terms of trade	7.86	−1.88 (157.1) [d]	6.85 (32.8)	−0.87	29.7 (−0.7) [e]	33.9	−4.4
7. MCIP with international capital mobility and endogenous conjectures	7.90	−0.06 (168.3) [d]	6.63 (31.9)	1.21	39.5 (−1.5) [e]	21.8	−3.5
8. MCIP with international capital mobility endogenous conjectures and endogenous terms of trade	5.66	−0.06 (168.3) [d]	6.63 (31.9)	−1.03	34.6 (−1.50)	21.8	−2.6

[a] Thousand man years. Employment change from removing the VER starting from solution with no initial profits plus the negative of the employment change from the simulation to eliminate initial profits.

[b] Remove profits.

[c] Remove QRs from zero profits solution.

[d] Net capital inflow from removing profits ($ million).

[e] Net capital inflow from removing QR starting from solution with initial profits ($ million).

[f] Figures in parentheses next to rent cost estimates are endogenous premia rates.

26   *J. de Melo, D. Tarr/Japan and the World Economy 8 (1996) 11–33*

33.7% in column 6 – results in a loss in scale efficiency, which dominates the two beneficial effects of a reduction in monopolistic price distortion and a reduction in the quota rent to foreigners.[20] Because of this reduction in the rent premium, when we estimate the costs of the VER from the counterfactually created zero profit equilibrium, we find that the rent costs are significantly reduced and now amount to 67% of the total costs. However, despite the reduction in rent costs, the total costs exceed the corresponding CTRS estimate because of the significant loss of scale efficiency, as emphasized by Hortsman and Markusen.

Now introduce the realistic assumption of international capital mobility (row 4). With perfectly mobile capital, the rental rate is fixed in terms of the numéraire and the returns from FDI are repatriated to foreign capital owners. Clearly removing profits involves firm entry so there will be net FDI into the US with the returns of that investment accruing to foreigners. Comparing rows 4 and 3, the costs of eliminating profits are $30 million *less* when there is international capital mobility. This is the result of three offsetting effects: reduction of rents to foreigners, loss of scale efficiency, and the Brecher and Diaz-Alejandro effect. The dominant effect is the reduction of rents caused by the slight increase in firm entry with international capital mobility (33.9% vs. 33.7% in rows 3 and 4 of Table 4). More entry occurs because the auto sector is relatively capital intensive. (Entry without international capital mobility raises the rental rate on capital, which reduces the profitability of capital intensive sectors such as autos thereby retarding entry.) More entry, because of no increase in the rental rate, raises domestic supply which lowers the demand for imported autos, thereby reducing the endogenously determined premium rate and hence, the rents to foreigners.

To further decompose these effects, we also estimated the effects of firm entry to eliminate profits, with and without international capital mobility under the assumption of exogenous quota rent premium. Then, the costs of firm entry are $120 million *more* with international capital mobility. This derives from two effects. First, greater entry reduces scale efficiency. Second, as shown by Brecher and Diaz-Alejandro (1977), FDI can be immiserizing if the marginal product of imported capital (valued at world prices, to reflect the value of the social marginal product) is less than the rental rate on capital, as would be expected to occur when a quota distorts upward the value of the private marginal product. Thus, while the scale efficiency and Brecher and Diaz-Alejandro effects from international capital mobility are immiserizing, they are dominated by the beneficial effect international capital mobility has on the reduction of the quota rent premium.

---

[20] To decompose these effects, we have simulated the effects of firm entry under the inappropriate (but normally employed) assumption that the rent premium is exogenously fixed at the initial level. In that case, the costs of firm entry to eliminate profits increase to $2.69 billion so that firm entry induces benefits of $0.7 billion due to the reduction in the rent premium, thereby partially defraying the loss of scale efficiency. The total cost of the VER with an exogenous rent premium is $11.96 billion. Thus, the assumption of an exogenous or endogenous rent premium has a very strong effect on the results.

J. de Melo, D. Tarr/Japan and the World Economy 8 (1996) 11–33   27

Also note that with capital mobility, distortion costs are slightly higher and rent costs are slightly lower. As explained above, capital mobility induces more firm entry, but it also increases the elasticity of domestic supply. Since entry reduces the endogenous rent premium, rent costs, which are estimated from the zero profit equilibrium, are lower. Estimated distortion costs are lower because removing the VER induces an inward shift of the demand curve for domestic autos which results in a smaller decrease in the domestic price with a more elastic domestic supply curve. In turn, the demand for imported autos shifts less inward. Consequently, the "triangle" of consumption distortion of imported autos is greater with capital mobility than without.[21] This is the result predicted by Neary (1988) and by Neary and Ruane (1988), namely that the benefits of eliminating tariff protection (in our case the tariff equivalent of a VER) are greater with international capital mobility than without.

The results of the simulations presented in rows 5 and 6 incorporate strong US monopsony power in autos and correspond to rows 3 and 4, respectively. We saw earlier in the CRTS case that endogenizing the terms-of-trade resulted in the total costs of the VER being less than the rent costs, i.e., there was an efficiency gain from the VER because the terms-of-trade costs were greater than the distortion costs of the VER by $500 million. In column 4, rows 5 and 6, we see that the efficiency gain from the VER is about $900 million, which is larger than under the CRTS case. This is because, as discussed above, with monopolistic competition there is a loss of scale efficiency when the VER is removed.

Finally, consider the effects of endogenous conjectures (row 7), so that firms price more (less) competitively as entry (exit) occurs. With endogenous conjectures, it takes less entry to eliminate profits (21.8% compared to 33.9% in row 4) because, as firms enter, the markup is reduced. Less entry implies less scale efficiency loss. Thus, the welfare costs of entry to eliminate profits results in losses of only 60 million from entry to eliminate profits. By inverse reasoning, when the VER is removed, there is less exit with endogenous conjectures. Hence the gain from VER removal is less.[22] Adding endogenous terms of trade (row 8), further lowers the estimated gain for reasons discussed above.

6. "Optimal" interventions for the auto industry

So far we have calculated the costs of the auto VER with Japan. However, as long as there is either IRTS or an unremovable distortion, e.g., a distortionary

---

[21]Graphical expositions of both this result and of the bias involved in using exogenous versus endogenous quota rent premia determinations are available, upon request, in an appendix. The appendix also replicates Tables 3 and 4 with exogenous rent premium determination.

[22]Another effect operating in all simulations with monopolistic competition is the increase in the value of the market elasticity of demand (ε^d in Eq. (2)) when protection is removed. The increase of about 3% contributes to lowering the markup rate, but is generally dominated by entry or exit in the markup determination.

wage differential under CRTS or IRTS, the question of optimal industrial policy arises. We now consider the potential welfare gains from industrial policy in a nonstrategic context. Although Bhagwati (1971) has shown that under perfect competition the optimal policy instrument is the one that acts directly on the relevant margin, no general theorem has been established under imperfect competition. Consequently, given the presence of IRTS and a wage distortion in the auto industry, it appears useful to examine the "optimal" use of either a tariff, a production subsidy or a wage subsidy. Due to the algorithmic difficulties and the possibility of multiple equilibria, efforts to calculate numerically the optimal values of policy instruments in applied general equilibrium are virtually nonexistent.[23] We maximize the utility function (noncentral Stone–Geary) underlying the final demand system of the model, using as instruments a combination of a tariff, a wage subsidy and a production subsidy in the auto sector. So that the results will not be dominated by second-best effects, we first counterfactually create an equilibrium that is distortion free, except for the wage distortion in autos. All welfare gain estimates are relative to this equilibrium.

The results are presented in Table 5. Consider first CRTS results. If only one instrument is available, the first best policy to counteract the exogenous wage distortion is the wage subsidy. If a wage subsidy is not available, then the second-best instrument is the production subsidy. The production subsidy is considerably inferior to the wage subsidy because it creates the by-product distortion of overuse of the nonlabor inputs in auto production. The third best policy is the tariff because it also creates a consumption distortion between domestic and imported autos. When the tariff and production subsidy instruments are available together, both the benefits as well as the tariff and subsidy rates are larger than when the instruments are used separately. This illustrates the principle stated by Corden (1974, p. 23): "If a second best policy is used to correct one divergence, hence creating a by-product distortion, it may create the need for a supplementary policy designed to correct, at least partially, the newly created distortion." Finally, note that when the available instruments are a wage and production subsidy, the algorithm verifies that the second-best policy instrument is redundant.

Consider now IRTS. There is now also the possibility of welfare gains from increasing scale efficiency or from reducing consumption distortion by narrowing the difference between price and marginal costs. Regardless of the combination of instruments, welfare gains are always larger under contestable markets than under monopolistic competition because there is no entry under contestable markets to reduce scale efficiency. When only one instrument is available, the

---

[23] We use the MINOS5 algorithm available in the GAMS programming language (see, Brooke et al. (1988)). An early example of optimal numerical solutions, which the authors characterized as illustrative because it was not a full numerical model of an actual economy, was that of Harris and MacKinnon (1979).

J. de Melo, D. Tarr/Japan and the World Economy 8 (1996) 11–33   29

Table 5
Optimal trade and industrial policies for the US auto industry [a]

Instrument\model	CRTS	Contestable market	Monopolistic competition
1. *Wage subsidy*			
Welfare gain	167.0	815.0	99.0
Relative wage in autos [b] (wage subsidy)	1.0 (27)	0.7 (57)	1.6 (−33)
			−5.9 [c]
2. *Production subsidy*			
Welfare gain	24.0	977.0	264.0
Production subsidy	1.8	10.0	5.4
			3.3 [c]
3. *Tariff*			
Welfare gain	4.0	182.0	30.0
Tariff	1.2	8.3	3.3
			0.6 [c]
4. *Wage and production subsidies*			
Welfare gain	167.0	1224.0	655.0
Relative wage in autos [b] (wage subsidy)	1.0 (27)	0.87 (40)	1.8 (−53)
Production subsidy	0.0	7.2	8.1
			−4.8 [c]
5. *Tariff and production subsidy*			
Welfare gain	36.0	1364.0	367.0
Production subsidy	2.1	11.0	6.2
Tariff	2.2	12.2	6.4
			5.0 [c]

[a] Welfare gain estimates are in millions of dollars. All subsidies and tariffs are in percent.

[b] Relative wage in autos under optimal wage subsidy or tax. Wage subsidy or tax in percentage in parentheses. A tax rate has a negative sign. All rates are calculated from an initial condition with a relative wage in autos of 1.27.

[c] Percentage change in the number of firms.

production subsidy yields the most benefits because scale efficiency benefits (which are most directly achieved with a production subsidy) dominate labor reallocation benefits with our parameters. When two instruments are available, by-product distortions are partially corrected by the second instrument, so the welfare gains are increased as in the CRTS case.

Note that under monopolistic competition the optimal wage policy is a tax. This is because the tax on auto employment induces exit of 5.9% from the auto sector, and the benefits this brings in terms of improved scale efficiency dominate the costs of additional labor misallocation. On the other hand, with contestable markets, because the wage subsidy does not induce entry, the optimal wage policy shifts from a 33% tax to a 57% subsidy. This is the type of result Eaton and Grossman (1986) derived, i.e., the optimal policy shifts from a subsidy to a tax depending on imperfect competition modelling assumptions (in our case entry

30   *J. de Melo, D. Tarr/Japan and the World Economy 8 (1996) 11–33*

conditions). These results confirm the need for caution before designing optimal industrial policies in imperfect competition.[24]

Moreover, government adoption of these "optimal" policies, may be counter-productive due to strategic considerations. If industries or unions perceive that the government's policy is to give subsidies or tariffs to counteract distortions, the distortions are likely to increase. For example, union wage demands will increase and management resistance will diminish. Moreover, retaliation by (or GATT required compensation to) foreign trade partners will likely eliminate the benefits of the policies.[25] Consequently, one should not conclude that these models are appropriate for the definition of optimal industrial policy.

7. Conclusions

How much is gained by a careful modelling of the US auto industry under the US–Japan auto VER? Of the previously unexamined features regarding the auto VER that were discussed in the opening paragraph, one of the most significant empirically is the endogenous determination of the quota rent premium; compared to calculations with exogenous premia rates, the estimated reduction in costs of the VER are up to $1.9 billion. This highlights the crucial and often dominant role that rents play in the welfare analysis of VERs. The impact of foreign direct investment is also to lower the costs of the VER, but for nonobvious reasons: the greater entry into domestic auto manufacturing results in a lower quota rent premium for foreign autos. We saw that "traditional" estimates based on a CRTS technology in autos yielded welfare costs of about $10 billion. In the most reasonable representation with IRTS, pure profits, internationally mobile capital and endogenous conjectures (between fixed and our particular assumption about endogenous conjectures) the estimate of the welfare costs of the VER are reduced by about $1 billion or 10%.

It is also instructive to note that the costs per job protected in the auto sector (at the expense of employment elsewhere) are very high, ranging from $164 000 to $296 000 per job per year. Alternatively, obtaining the ratio of the welfare benefit calculations to the adjustment costs, proxied by the present value of the lifetime

---

[24]Dixit (1988) and Krishna et al. investigated optimal policies in their models. They did not have a wage subsidy instrument available, but they found a similar pattern of results to Table 5 when production subsidies or tariffs are used alone in their scenarios with labor rent present. Dixit finds little use for a tariff when both a tariff and a production subsidy are available; but his model considers only distortion costs in autos. Krishna et al. find that the optimal policy is a subsidy to imports not a tariff when there is no labor rent, a result that led them to also call for caution in recommending optimal industrial policy.

[25]See Fernandez (1989) for additional strategic considerations which are likely to make the achievement of optimal industrial policies problematical. See Harrison and Rutstrom (1991) and Tower (1975) for an analysis of the impact of retaliation in a trade war.

J. de Melo, D. Tarr/Japan and the World Economy 8 (1996) 11–33   31

earnings losses of displaced auto workers displaced by VER removal, there are between 14 and 26 dollars of benefits for every dollar of worker adjustment costs saved.[26]

Finally we have illustrated the use of industrial policies to exploit scale economies and to counteract wage distortions. The results under IRTS call for caution regarding the use of industrial policy because the optimal policy may shift from a subsidy to a tax depending on behavioral assumptions.

Acknowledgements

We thank Bela Balassa, Kala Krishana and participants for comments on an earlier draft at a conference at Waterloo University. This paper is part of research on modelling the interaction between trade policy and industrial policies and their implications for industrial efficiency at the World Bank. We thank Mona Haddad and Rebecca Sugui for logistic support. The views are those of the authors, not necessarily those of the World Bank.

References

Baldwin, R.E., 1982, The inefficacy of trade policy, Frank D. Graham Memorial Lecture, Essays in International Finance no. 150, Princeton University.

Bergsten, C.F., K.A. Elliot, J.J. Schott and W. Takacs, 1987, Auction quotas and United States trade policy (Institute for International Economics, Washington, D.C.).

Bhagwati, J., 1987, VERs, quid pro quo DFIs and VIEs: Political economy theoretic analysis, International Economic Journal 1, 1–14.

Bhagwati, J., 1971, The generalized theory of distortions and welfare, in J. Bhagwati, ed., Trade, balance of payments, and growth: Papers in international economics in honor of Charles P. Kindleberger (North-Holland, Amsterdam).

Brecher, R.A. and C.F. Diaz-Alejandro, 1977, Tariffs, foreign capital, and immiserizing growth, Journal of International Economics 7, 317–322.

Brooke, A., D. Kendrick and A. Meeraus, 1988, GAMS: A user's guide, The Scientific Press, Palo Alto, CA.

Corden, W.M., 1974, Trade policy and economic welfare (Clarendon Press, Oxford).

Cox, D. and R. Harris, 1985, Trade liberalization and industrial organization: Some estimates for Canada, Journal of Political Economy 93, 115–145.

de Melo, J. and D. Tarr, 1990, The welfare costs of US quotas in textiles, autos, and steel, Review of Economics and Statistics 77, 489–497.

---

[26] In de Melo and Tarr (1993) we present data, based on Jacobson (1978), that indicate that the present value of the lifetime earnings losses of a displaced auto worker is about $57 thousand. Using this as a proxy for worker adjustment costs, 35 thousand displaced auto workers yield about $2 billion of adjustment costs. The benefits of quota removal (the avoidance of the quota costs) discounted conservatively over 6 years (at 7%), are between $29 billion (row 8) and $53 billion (row 4). See de Melo and Tarr (1992) for details on the methodology.

de Melo, J. and D. Tarr, 1992, A general equilibrium analysis of United States foreign trade policy (MIT Press, Cambridge, MA).

de Melo, J. and D. Tarr, 1993, Industrial policy in the presence of wage distortions: The case of the US auto and steel industries, International Economic Review 34, 833–851.

Devarajan, S. and D. Rodrik, 1991, Pro-competitive effects of trade reform: Results from a CGE model for Cameroon, European Economic Review 35, 1157–1184.

Dinopoulos, E. and M. Kreinin, 1988, Effects of the US-Japan auto VER on European prices and US welfare, Review of Economics and Statistics 70, 484–491.

Dixit, A., 1988, Optimal trade and industrial policies for the US automobile industry, in: R. Feenstra, ed., Empirical methods in international trade (MIT Press, Cambridge MA).

Dixit, A., 1986, Comparative statistics for oligopoly, International Economic Review 27, 107–122.

Eaton, J. and G. Grossman, 1986, Optimal trade and industrial policy under oligopoly, Quarterly Journal of Economics 101, 383–406.

Feenstra, R., 1984, Voluntary export restraints in US autos, 1980–1981: Quality, employment and welfare effects, in: R. Baldwin and A. Krueger, eds., The structure and evolution of recent US trade policy (University of Chicago Press for NBER, Chicago).

Feenstra, R., 1988, Quality change under trade restraints: Theory and evidence from Japanese autos, Quarterly Journal of Economics 102, 131–146.

Fernandez, R., 1989, Comment, in: R. Feenstra, ed., Trade policies for international competitiveness (University of Chicago Press, Chicago).

Friedlaender, A., C. Winston and K. Wang, 1983, Costs, technology and productivity in the US automobile industry, Bell Journal of Economics 14, 1–20.

General Agreement on Tariffs and Trade 1990, Trade Policy Review: United States (GATT, Geneva).

Goto, J., 1986, A general equilibrium analysis of international trade and imperfect competition in both product and labor markets – theory and evidence from the automobile trade, Ph.D Dissertation, Yale University.

Harris, R., 1984, Applied general equilibrium analysis of small open economies with scale economies and imperfect competition, American Economic Review 74(5), 1016–1032.

Harris, R. and J. G. MacKinnon, 1979, Computing optimal tax equilibria, Journal of Public Economics 11, 197–212.

Harrison, G. and E. Rutstrom, 1991, Trade wars, trade negotiations, and applied game theory, Economic Journal 101, 1–16.

Horstman, I. and J. Markusen, 1986, Up the average cost curve: Inefficient entry and the new protectionism, Journal of International Economics 20, 225–248.

Jacobson, L., 1978, Earnings losses of workers displaced from manufacturing industries, in: W. DeWald, ed., The impact of international trade and investment on employment (US Department of Labor, Washington, D.C.).

Katz, L. and L. Summers, 1989, Industry rents: Evidence and implications, Brookings Papers: Microeconomics, 209–290.

Krishna, K., 1990, The case of vanishing revenues: Auction quotas with oligopoly, American Economic Review 80, 828–836.

Krishna, K., 1989, Trade restrictions as facilitating practices, Journal of International Economics 26, 251–270.

Krishna, K., K. Hogan and P. Swagel, 1994, The non-optimality of optimal trade policies: The US automobile industry revisited, 1979–1985, in: P. Krugman and A. Smith, eds., Empirical studies of strategic trade policy (University of Chicago Press, Chicago), forthcoming.

Krueger, A.B. and L.H. Summers., 1988, Efficiency wages and the inter-industry wage structure, Econometrica 56, 259–293.

Krugman, P., 1987, Market access and competition in high technology industries, in: H. Kierzkowski, ed., Protection and competition in international trade (Basil Blackwell, Oxford).

J. de Melo, D. Tarr/Japan and the World Economy 8 (1996) 11–33   33

Lawrence, R., 1990, Comment on Fung, in: R.E. Baldwin, ed., Empirical studies of commercial policy (University of Chicago Press, Chicago).

Levinsohn, J., 1988, Empirics of taxes on differentiated products: The case of tariffs in the US automobile industry, in: R.E. Baldwin, ed., Trade policy issues and empirical analysis (University of Chicago Press, Chicago).

Neary, J.P., 1988, Tariffs, quotas, and voluntary export restraints with and without internationally mobile capital, Canadian Journal of Economics 11, 714–735.

Neary, J.P. and Ruane, F. 1988, International capital mobility, shadow prices, and the cost of protection, International Economic Review 29, 571–585.

Novshek, W., 1980, Cournot equilibrium with free entry, Review of Economic Studies 47, 473–486.

Rodrik, D., 1988, Imperfect competition, scale economies and trade policy in developing countries, in: R. Baldwin, ed., Trade policy issues and empirical analysis (University of Chicago Press, Chicago).

Saloner, G., 1994, Comments on Krishna et al., in: P. Krugman and A. Smith, eds., Empirical studies of strategic trade policy (University of Chicago Press, Chicago).

Smith, A. and A.J. Venables, 1988, Completing the internal market in the European Community: Some industry simulations, European Economic Review 32, 1501–1525.

Tower, E., 1975, The optimum quota and retaliation, Review of Economic Studies 432, 623–630.

Winston, C. and Associates, 1987, Blind intersection? Policy and the automobile industry (Brookings Institution, Washington, DC).

INTERNATIONAL ECONOMIC REVIEW
Vol. 34, No. 4, November 1993

INDUSTRIAL POLICY IN THE PRESENCE OF WAGE DISTORTIONS: THE CASE OF THE US AUTO AND STEEL INDUSTRIES*

By Jaime de Melo and David Tarr[1]

This paper examines the welfare effects of protection in two high wage premia sectors—autos and steel—to determine if protection is justified to correct for the labor misallocation due to the wage premia. If wage premia are exogenous, under most product market structures, labor misallocation is too small to justify protection. More importantly, due to union influence in autos and steel, the wage premium is endogenous. Then wage premia may even exacerbate the welfare costs of protection. With increasing returns to scale and firm entry optimal policies may be reversed, so further caution must be exercised.

1. INTRODUCTION

Recent empirical work, which has adjusted for sex, age, full time work, fringe benefits and other available worker characteristics, has estimated inter-industry wage differences in the United States (US). The conclusion is that it is difficult to account for remaining persistent inter-industry wage differentials on the basis of unobserved differences in ability or equalizing differences such as attractiveness of the work. Rather, it appears that workers in a number of industries earn rents (Krueger and Summers 1988, Katz and Summers 1989b). These wage differentials are often explained on the basis of "efficiency" wage theories,[2] and, in the cases more relevant to this paper, on the basis of union extraction of rents. Since firms presumably employ workers up to the point where the value of the workers' marginal product equals the industry wage, these data imply that the value of the marginal product of workers in wage premia industries exceeds the value of the marginal product of workers in industries without wage premia. It follows that labor

---

* Manuscript submitted November 1991; revised manuscript submitted August 1992.

[1] This paper is part of research on trade policy and industrial efficiency at the World Bank. An appendix describing the model is available from the authors on request. The views are those of the authors and should not be attributed to the World Bank or CEPR, which takes no institutional policy positions. We thank Tom Rutherford, Glenn Harrison, Shantayan Devarajan and Susan Vroman for helpful comments, and Ghislaine Bayard, Alex Pfaff, and Rebecca Sugui for excellent logistic support.

[2] Several "efficiency wages" theories, based on differences in technology across industries, explain these wage premia. Shapiro and Stiglitz (1984) suggest that in industries where shirking is difficult or costly to detect, it may be efficient for firms to pay premium wages. Similarly, an industry which faces relatively high costs from labor turnover will find it optimal to pay premium wages (Stiglitz 1985, Weiss 1980). Akerlof (1984) argues that if the firm is perceived as earning rents, productivity may suffer if workers do not also receive rents. A particularly appealing theory is developed by Thaler (1989) who argues that it may be desirable in some industries to pay high (nondistortionary) wages to attract highly qualified workers in particular skill categories. As a result, productivity of workers in skill categories where premia are not desirable to the firm may decline, unless they also receive a premium which is distortionary.

833

is misallocated in the economy, with too little labor employed in sectors that pay wage premia.

Some authors (e.g., Katz and Summers 1989a, 1989b) contend that these factors form the basis for a theory of industrial policy which is more relevant empirically than product market imperfections along the lines pioneered by Brander and Spencer (1983), (1984), i.e., there is little opportunity for international profit-shifting compared with situations where industrial policy can reallocate labor efficiently.[3] The argument is that, given the existence of wage distortions, we are in a second best world where the provision of an export subsidy or import tariff to a wage premium sector may be socially beneficial if the conventional production and consumption distortion costs of tariffs or subsidies are outweighed by the reduction of labor misallocation costs.[4] To date, however, the argument has not been subjected to any empirical test.[5]

Two industries where wage premia are among the highest and which have recently received import protection are autos and steel. In addition to the existence of wage premia and protection, these industries were chosen because of the existence of significant increasing returns to scale which implies that market structure issues may also be relevant to the conclusion. In this paper we investigate systematically the empirical validity of the wage distortion argument as a basis for protection with a general equilibrium model of the US economy in these industries. The model is calibrated to 1984, a year in which VERs on Japanese auto imports were binding and VERs on steel imports had just been negotiated. We estimate the costs of protection in autos and steel with and without wage premia under three different market structures: constant returns to scale (CRTS) and perfect competition, increasing returns to scale (IRTS) and contestable markets, and IRTS with oligopolistic interaction and free entry.

We show that if the wage premia are exogenous, the costs of protection are less than if there were no premia, but not significantly so. Under all market structures, the benefits of superior labor reallocation are far too small to justify the protection provided. However, we argue that wage distortions in autos and steel are more reasonably modelled as the result of union exploitation of monopoly power and therefore should be endogenous where the union has a tradeoff between employment and the wage premium. With endogenous wage premia, the imposition of protection will increase the wage distortion. This reduces the second best effect of labor misallocation, so under CRTS or IRTS with contestable markets the costs of protection are closer to the case of no wage premia. Moreover, if the union values

---

[3] Katz and Summers are careful to point out that the case for an activist industrial policy must be tempered by the fact that it is unlikely to be applied optimally in practice. Also see Section 5 below. Moreover, Brander and Spencer (1988) have argued that if there are opportunities for international profit shifting in an industry facing a union, the optimal subsidy will usually be larger because the union will capture some of the subsidy.

[4] This argument dates back to Hagen (1958) and was challenged by Bhagwati and Ramaswami (1963).

[5] Dixit (1988) has examined some aspects of this problem in a partial equilibrium framework. Our results may be expected to differ from those of Dixit because we model the demand for factors of production, allow for increasing returns to scale and, notably, model endogenous wage premia determination. Moreover, the assessment of the benefits of intersectoral labor reallocation is fundamentally a general equilibrium problem.

the wage premium highly relative to an increase in employment, the costs of protection may be greater than in the case with no wage distortions.[6]

Under IRTS and free entry, the costs of protection are lower the more the union values the wage premium relative to employment. This is because protection induces larger wage increases, the more wage oriented is the union, which in turn reduces entry and resulting scale efficiency. More strikingly, we find the "optimal" wage policy is a tax under IRTS with free entry. The reason again is that firm exit induces improved scale efficiency, and exit is encouraged by high wages. These results are analogous to those of Horstmann and Markusen (1986). They have shown that industrial policies such as tariffs and subsidies will, in a large class of cases, have negative welfare consequences when firm exit and entry is incorporated because of the adverse impact these policies have on the achievement of scale efficiency.

In sum, we show that once one recognizes the endogeneity of wage distortions, the case for industrial policy based on them all but vanishes; the costs of protection may be greater not less. If one adds IRTS with firm entry, optimal policies may be reversed, so further caution must be exercised.

In terms of modelling innovation, this paper is the first to model endogenous union-induced labor market distortions in applied general equilibrium. It is also the first to investigate systematically the impact of labor market distortions under different market structure assumptions. Also in line with our focus on the labor market and the interaction of employment and wage distortions, we incorporate labor-leisure choice in a more satisfactory manner than previous applied general equilibrium models.

The remainder of the paper is organized as follows. In Section 2, we describe how we model labor market distortions with and without labor union activity. We also describe how we model economies of scale and how we represent pricing practices. Section 3 describes the data and benchmarking for the counterfactual simulations and reports on the welfare costs of VERs under CRTS and no wage distortions. Section 4 evaluates the distortionary costs of protection created by the VERs both with and without labor market distortions and, with and without imperfectly competitive behavior. This step-by-step approach helps isolate the contribution of each distortionary component. Section 5 asks what would be the likely benefits of optimal wage and tariff policies in the auto and steel industries. Conclusions follow in Section 6.

2.   MODELLING LABOR AND PRODUCT MARKETS IN AUTOS AND STEEL[7]

The auto and steel sectors are among the sectors that pay the highest wages in US manufacturing. Steel worker (auto worker) compensation was 63 (53) percent above the compensation of the average US manufacturing worker in 1984. Using the 1984 Current Population Survey, Krueger and Summers (1988) estimate that,

---

[6] The latter result is similar to the result of Mezzeti and Dinopoulos (1991). They find that if there are opportunities for international profit shifting in an industry facing a union, if the union is wage rather than employment oriented, a tariff may result in a decline in employment, output and welfare. In our models, however, there are no profits.

after controlling for human capital and demographic factors such as sex, age, race, marital state and education, workers in the transport equipment sector earn a premium of 27 percent above the industrywide average, and workers of fabricated metal a premium of 26 percent. They also find that these statistically significant premia are stable across time and space. These wage premia are viewed as too large and persistent to be explained by compensating differentials such as attractiveness of work. Similar results were found by Katz and Summers (1989b).

In view of this (and other) evidence,[8] we assume that workers in auto and steel earn a premium. We model this premium in two different ways. In one variant, we assume that the premium is exogenous $\phi_i > 1$, i.e., $W_i = W\phi_i$, where W is the wage earned in sectors where workers do not receive rents. Workers in all industries receive the value of their marginal product at the wage rate $W\phi_i$. Since $\phi_i > 1$ is a premium, we choose $\phi = 1$ for all sectors other than autos and steel.[9] This places us in a typical second-best situation since the benefits of removing protection in autos and steel must now be balanced against the costs of taking labor out of these sectors where the value of the marginal product of labor is relatively high.

In the other variant, we model the determination of the wage premium. Katz and Summers (1989a) have noted that steel and autos are an exception to the pattern of high wage industries in that exports are not significant and that the high wages do not appear to be explained by efficiency wage theories. Rather, strong union behavior appears to explain the high wages. In this set-up, unions are viewed as an instrument of employees to generate (or extract) monopoly rents. These rents can exist due to regulation or imperfections in the product market. If the union can organize a sufficiently large percentage of workers in the industry, it can then restrict labor supply and collect these rents in classic monopoly fashion. When the conditions which led to the generation of the rents change, the premium earned by workers will change. Hence the premium earned by workers is endogenous with respect to a change in protection.[10]

In this variant, we assume that the union either unilaterally sets the wage rate or negotiates it with the firm, but that the firm unilaterally determines the level of

---

[7] This paper extends work presented in de Melo and Tarr (1992) by (1) integrating the modelling of labor market distortions and imperfect competition; (2) extending the analysis to include a discussion of "optimal" trade and industrial policies (see Section 5). A full description of the equations and data sources is available in de Melo and Tarr (1992).

[8] In de Melo and Tarr (1992), we show that although steel and auto workers in 16 other countries earn a premium above the average manufacturing worker in their own countries, that premium is much greater in the US.

[9] We utilize labor's quasi-share parameter in the CES cost function to calibrate to an arbitrary wage premia in autos and steel estimated by Krueger and Summers. Since observed wage rates of labor differ across sectors, our calibration of labor is equivalent to measuring labor in efficiency units (see de Melo and Tarr 1992). We choose ϕ_i for autos and steel to be 1.27 and 1.26, respectively, rather than 1.53 and 1.63, which are wage premia unadjusted for productivity differences.

[10] For example, deregulation in the airline and trucking industries led to a considerable reduction in rents captured by the unions in these industries. See Kahn (1980) and Levinson (1980). More generally, Freeman and Katz (1987) have found enough variation in changes in wages across industries in response to demand to trace out a "trade-off" curve between wages and employment. They find that wages respond more to sales in unionized than in nonunionized industries.

employment. It is well known (see McDonald and Solow 1981) that allowing unilateral determination of the employment level by the firm results in outcomes off the union-firm contact curve in wage-employment space. We choose our assumption, however, because the evidence indicates that firms and unions are not on their contact curve (Farber 1986).[11]

The union's utility function is given by (sector subscripts for autos and steel dropped)

$$(1) \qquad U = \bar{A}[W\phi - \bar{W}_o]^\gamma [L - \bar{L}_o]^\delta; \ \bar{A}, \ \gamma, \ \phi > 0$$

where W is the wage rate in the competitive labor market (i.e., in other sectors), γ, δ are parameters determining the weights attached to wages and employment, and $\bar{W}_o$, $\bar{L}_o$ are the minimum acceptable levels of the wage rate and employment. The formulation follows Farber (1986).[12] It is natural to take $\bar{W}_o = W$. For the CES technology for value-added assumed here, labor demand, L^d, is given by

$$(2) \qquad L^d = \left[\alpha \ \frac{PVC}{W\phi} \right]^\sigma (X/\bar{A})^{1-\sigma}$$

where $\bar{A}$ is a constant, PVC is primary variable cost, σ is the elasticity of substitution between capital and labor, α is a quasi-share parameter for labor from the CES value-added function, and X is output. The union maximizes (1) subject to (2), yielding the following expression for the endogenous wage differential:

$$(3) \qquad \frac{\phi - 1}{\phi} = \left[\frac{L^d - \bar{L}_o}{L^d} \right] \frac{\gamma}{\delta \sigma}.$$

Thus, since labor is a derived demand, the wage differential will be affected by changes in trade policy.

In this formulation, high (low) values for γ combined with low (high) values for δ correspond to cases where the union puts a high (low) weight on wages (employment). The evidence suggests that union behavior departs from the special cases of rent maximization or wage bill maximization (see Farber 1986 for a survey). Hence, we shall vary systematically the weights of the union's objective function to account for a range of plausible behavior.

By assuming a passive firm, we may be attributing the impact of a nonpassive firm (which would lower the wage and increase employment) to union preferences for more employment. For labor economists interested in explaining union behavior, the distinction between an active and a passive firm is crucial, but for our objective of approximating wage and employment levels in the steel and auto

---

[11] The union might accept a "low" wage in return for guarantees by the firm that it would employ more workers than given by its demand curve. But asymmetric information about product demand shifts (for which the firm must be permitted to adjust employment or it would not agree to the contract) will allow the firm to cheat on the agreement. Alternatively, an incentive-compatible contract which pays the union a lump-sum amount independent of employment in return for a "low" wage will present problems for the union in terms of being able to allocate the lump-sum payments to its members.

[12] See Oswald (1982) for a formulation that includes leisure in the union's utility function.

industries in response to a change in trade policy, this simplification is a natural one. This is because increasing the weight on employment in (1) is equivalent in terms of the wage-employment outcome to the firm nonpassively influencing the wage decision with a lower employment weight. What is crucial for the debate on trade and industrial policy is that this formulation allows for trade policy to influence the degree of distortion in the labor market. As an example, consider a decrease in the level of protection in the auto industry. This will induce an inward shift in the demand curve for labor as consumers shift towards imported autos. This inward shift, in turn, will induce the union to set a lower wage (i.e., to choose a lower ϕ).

Economywide labor supply is endogenous since the representative consumer-worker maximizes the extended nested Stone-Geary utility function:

$$(4) \qquad W = \prod_{i=0}^{n} (C_i - \lambda_i)^{\beta_i}$$

where $\sum_{i=0}^{n} \beta_i = 1$, $\beta_i > 0$, $(C_i - \lambda_i) > 0$, C_0 is leisure, $i = 1, \dots, n$ is an index over composite commodities. Utility maximization takes place in two stages. In the first stage, as in Abbott and Ashenfelter (1976), maximization of (4) subject to "full income" yields the labor supply equation:

$$(5) \qquad LS = \overline{\text{MAXHOURS}} - (\beta_o/W)\left(Y - \sum_{i=1}^{n} P_i\lambda_i\right)\Bigg/(1 - \beta_o),$$

where Y is income, W is the wage rate, $\overline{\text{MAXHOURS}}$ is a parameter denoting the maximum workforce, and P_i and λ_i may be interpreted as the price and minimum subsistence of the composite good of sector i, respectively. In the second stage, the consumer maximizes composite consumption C_i subject to income allocated to consumption of goods in sector i. This formulation of the utility function allows us to calibrate to exogenously given labor supply and commodity price elasticities.[13] Based on a review of the econometric evidence, we calibrate (5) to an elasticity of supply of labor to income of -0.12 and an elasticity of labor supply to the real wage of 0.055.[14]

The main focus of this paper is on the costs of trade restrictions in the presence of labor market distortions. Therefore, we consider first the effects of the costs of protection in both sectors under the assumption of perfect competition and a CRTS technology. However, there is evidence of unexploited economies of scale in both

---

[13] This is in contrast to Ballard et al. (1985) where own elasticities were all unity and where cross-substitution effects between composite commodities were not allowed. In addition, our formulation allows labor supply (including the parameter $\overline{\text{MAXHOURS}}$) to be written in terms of econometrically estimated elasticities rather than arbitrarily assuming a value for $\overline{\text{MAXHOURS}}$. Ballard et al., who chose the latter approach, noted that their results were heavily dependent on the assumed value for $\overline{\text{MAXHOURS}}$, for which there is little data.

[14] Elasticity estimates draw on Pencavel (1986) and especially Abbott and Ashenfelter (1976) for males and Killingsworth (1983), Killingsworth and Heckman (1986) and especially Mroz (1987) for females.

sectors.[15] Hence the alternative of an IRTS technology and the need to decide on the appropriate pricing rule.

For pricing, we assume that US steel and auto firms price competitively in export markets because they face close substitutes from stiff foreign competition. The assumption is plausible and, in any case, of little consequence for both industries where exports do not exceed 5 percent of total sales.

With respect to domestic sales, the evidence in steel strongly suggests the absence of monopolistic pricing practices in the last 30 years (see, e.g., Scherer 1980, Tarr 1990, US Federal Trade Commission 1977, Rippe 1970, or Mancke 1968). Hence we assume an analogue to marginal cost pricing under CRTS, namely contestable market pricing. Under this assumption, threat of entry (because of ease of entry) forces firms to price at average cost.

For autos, like Dixit (1988), we believe it is appropriate to model oligopolistic interaction. Therefore, for autos we contrast contestable market pricing with the alternative of oligopolistic interaction and free entry with a homogenous product. Denote then by ε^d the market elasticity of demand of the domestic variety for autos with respect to the domestic price (an endogenous variable that depends on elasticities and shares of all sectors—see de Melo and Tarr 1992). Then, in equilibrium, the price PD_i charged by each firm i for domestic sales is given by

$$(6) \qquad \frac{PD_i - MC_i}{PD_i} = \frac{\tilde{\Omega}}{N\varepsilon^d}$$

where N is the number of domestic firms and $\tilde{\Omega}$ is the output conjecture of the ith firm, i.e., the amount by which the ith firm assumes industry output will change in response to a small unit change in its own output. Equation (6) defines the percentage mark-up over marginal costs in terms of N, ε^d and $\tilde{\Omega}$. It can be rewritten to state that each (symmetric) firm sets marginal revenue equal to marginal costs MC_i. Given an initial value of ε^d, the ratio of $\tilde{\Omega}$ to N is calibrated from (6).[16] The value of ε^d appears in Table 1 along with other relevant information on the auto and steel sectors. In the simulations, the value of N is endogenously

---

[15] For steel we draw on Tarr (1984) and for autos on Winston and Associates (1987) and Friedlander, Winston and Wang (1983). The corresponding cost-disadvantage ratio (CDR) values are reported in Table 1.

[16] Given the zero profit condition, the cost disadvantage ratio defines the ratio in equation (6). Then given ε^d only the ratio of $\tilde{\Omega}$ to N is identified. Most often Cournot conjectures, i.e., $\tilde{\Omega} = 1$ are assumed and N, the number of firms, is calibrated from (6) and defined as the Cournot equivalent number of firms. This is the approach followed by Dixit (1988) who obtains the value of $N = 13.8$ for 1983. Our calibration yields a value of $N = 4.2$, indicating a less competitive industry in 1984. Nonetheless, since we assume there are three auto firms in 1984, this implies that competition remained more competitive than Cournot. Equivalently, if $N = 3$ in equation (6), $\tilde{\Omega} = 0.72$. An alternative—but in our view less appealing—approach is to solve for marginal costs or for the elasticity of demand given the values for $\tilde{\Omega}$, N and the zero profit condition. See Devarajan and Rodrik (1991) for another example along the lines followed by Dixit.

A natural extension is to recognize that conjectures are themselves dependent on the number of firms. Sensitivity simulations with this extended formulation yield slightly larger benefits from trade liberalization but similar results for the pattern of wage distortions and are available from the authors on request.

840   JAIME DE MELO AND DAVID TARR

TABLE 1

DISTORTIONS, PRODUCTION, DEMAND STRUCTURE, AND ELASTICITIES IN THE AUTO AND STEEL
INDUSTRIES

	Autos	Steel
Distortions		
Wage premium (ϕ)	27.0	26.0
Premium rate on imports	31.8	7.0[b]
Production and Demand[a]		
Gross output	124.2	57.5
Employment (1,000 man-years)	536.5	531.0
Domestic final demand sales	111.0	0.0
Intermediate sales	8.3	56.1
Exports	4.9	1.4
Imports		
Intermediates	2.3	12.7
Final demand	30.3	0.0
Elasticities and Parameters[c]		
Capital-labor substitution	0.8	1.0
Import-domestic substitution elasticity[d]	1.9	3.0
Composite final demand	0.8	n.a.
Export-domestic transformation elasticity[d]	2.9	2.9
Derived elasticity of demand (ε^d)	1.37	n.a.
Cost disadvantage ratio (CDR)	0.11	0.04

Notes: n.a. = not applicable.

[a] 1984 US$ billion.

[b] Premium rate resulting from rationing steel to 85 percent of the volume of steel imports in 1984.

[c] The sources for demand and supply price elasticities are detailed in de Melo and Tarr (1992).

[d] The selected CES (CET) functions imply that the corresponding substitution (transformation)
elasticities are compensated import demand (export supply) price elasticities.

determined so that the long-run zero profit condition is maintained by entry/exit.[17]

We assume perfect substitution across products for all firms' products within a
sector. To avoid specialization that would occur in response to changes in trade
policy if domestic and foreign goods were perfect substitutes, we assume national
production differentiation at the sector level. Foreign produced goods are imperfect
substitutes for domestically produced goods (the "Armington" assumption), and
goods sold abroad are imperfect substitutes with goods sold on the domestic
market. (Constant elasticities of substitution and transformation, respectively.)[18]
The alternative approach of firm level product differentiation (Dixit and Stiglitz
1977) would be a superior approach to modelling the auto industry. However, our
objective is to assess the impact of wage distortions, so it is preferable to maintain
a symmetric treatment of foreign trade across all sectors so as to isolate more
clearly the effects of different assumptions in the labor market.

The remaining features of the model are standard to computable general
equilibrium (CGE) models. The model includes two factors, capital and labor which

[17] Restricting N to integer values would allow a positive profit equilibrium due to fixed costs.
However, the numerical solution to the nonlinear system of equations defined by problems of this type
remains an unresolved problem.

[18] The specification of foreign trade is as in de Melo and Robinson (1989). National product
differentiation models and production were developed by Powell and Gruen (1968). We choose the small
country assumption. For an alternative large country formulation, see de Melo and Tarr (1990).

are mobile between sectors. To assess the impact of specific factors, some experiments are performed with sector specific capital. Total capital is in fixed supply. Domestic demand includes two components, final and intermediates. The government sector's role is limited to lump-sum redistributions to and from the representative consumer. In the simulations reported below, the static CGE model is disaggregated into 10 sectors, among which are autos and steel. The model is calibrated to 1984, a year when the VER on Japanese autos was particularly binding and the year in which the US Trade Representative negotiated VERs with foreign governments with the stated objective of inducing a reduction in the imports of carbon and alloy steel products to 18.5 percent of domestic apparent consumption down from the 26.4 percent level of 1984. In practice the VERs in steel were not so binding, so we assume they induced a 15 percent reduction in imports rather than the 30 percent reduction intended by the negotiations. All simulations maintain tariffs at their existing level in 1984 (an economywide average of 3.5 percent) as well as quotas in textiles and apparel negotiated under the Multi-Fiber Agreement (MFA).

3.   COSTS OF VERS UNDER CRTS AND NO WAGE DISTORTIONS

We start with a "traditional" welfare cost calculation of VERs in autos and steel. We assume perfect competition with a CRTS technology and a labor market where the auto and steel sectors do not pay a wage premium. We decompose the costs of protection into distortionary and rent components and check the sensitivity of results to the specification of labor supply. When we introduce product and labor market "imperfections" in Section 4, we shall concentrate mostly on the evaluation of the distortionary cost component. Also, in Section 4, all results will refer to the specification with endogenous aggregate labor supply.

Table 1 describes the structure of the auto and steel industries and the estimated distortions in both sectors. The source of the wage premia have been discussed above. The estimated premium rate on auto imports for 1984 is estimated at 31.8 percent. As discussed in de Melo and Tarr (1992), this rate combines the estimates by Feenstra (1988) (for Japanese premia) and Dinopoulos and Kreinin (1988) (for European premia). Both studies have used hedonic regressions to adjust for quality changes induced by the VER. The premia go predominantly to foreigners, in this case Japanese and European auto producers.[19] Simulating the costs of the VER on Japanese auto imports can therefore be decomposed into two components: a rent component that would arise if the US were to capture premia; and a distortionary cost component arising from the wedge created by the premium. For steel, the costs of protection also has the same two components, but the simulation is obtained by imposing quantitative restraints on steel imports rather than removing them as in

---

[19] We have also estimated the case where US auto dealers of Japanese vehicles captured some rents above the premia rate of Table 1. The costs of the VERs in this case exceed the estimates of Table 2 by about $1.3 billion (see de Melo and Tarr 1990).

TABLE 2
WELFARE COSTS OF VERS IN AUTOS AND STEEL: CRTS AND NO WAGE PREMIA
(IN BILLIONS OF 1984 DOLLARS)

	Fixed total labor supply		Endogenous total labor supply	
	Autos	Steel	Autos	Steel
Rent capture[a]	7.877	0.736	7.867	0.736
Distortionary costs[a]	1.939	0.128	1.998	0,128
Total costs[a]	9.816	0.864	9.815	0.864
Employment change[b]	36.22	20.80	36.24	20.80

Notes:

[a] Welfare costs given by the equivalent variation (EV) measure.

[b] Change in employment in the sector in thousand work-years.

autos; this yields a premium rate of 7 percent on steel imports.[20] Hence, there is asymmetry in the way the costs of protection are simulated in each sector. For simplicity, we report all welfare estimates (given by the Hicksian equivalent variation measure) as positive numbers.

Apart from these distortionary measures, Table 1 gives information on the production and demand structures in both sectors. Both sectors exported a very small share of total production and faced stiff competition from imports in 1984, at least as measured by import penetration ratios. Gross output of steel was about half that of autos and is the more labor-intensive of the two sectors. Elasticities of substitution in demand (between imports and domestic) are higher in steel than in autos, reflecting the characteristics of a more homogenous product.

Welfare and employment effects of the VERs are given in Table 2. To maintain symmetry in the table, we present all results as "costs" of VERs. In fact, since VERs are removed in autos (but imposed in steel) we are measuring benefits in the auto case. The welfare cost of VERs on autos is higher than on steel, because the import value of autos is about 2.5 times higher than the import value of steel products, and autos is the more distorted of the two sectors with a premium rate about 4.5 times that of steel.[21]

The welfare costs of protection are slightly less with variable labor supply. Removing protection increases income which is partly spent on leisure with endogenous labor supply; this implies a less elastic demand for imported autos and lower estimated benefits of quota removal. Also, the reduction in aggregate labor supply is distributed across all sectors including autos. Given our focus on the labor

---

[20] This implies that to obtain the joint costs of VERs in autos and steel one would remove the VERs from a solution where steel is rationed. Joint estimates are not reported here since the values are only very marginally less than the sum of the individual general equilibrium estimates.

[21] Sensitivity analysis to the assumed values of demand and supply elasticities with fixed labor supply are reported in de Melo and Tarr (1990). As explained there, the rent component is sensitive to assumed elasticities only in the steel case. As to the distortionary cost component, when low (high) elasticities are used, the cost is $1.09 billion ($2.96 billion) for autos and $0.27 billion ($0.10 billion) for steel. The asymmetry with respect to variation in elasticities comes from the fact that quota imposition in steel results in a larger price change the lower the set of elasticities. Quota removal in autos, however, is necessarily treated as the removal of the tariff equivalent of the quota and results in a greater quantity change the greater the elasticities. See de Melo and Tarr (1992).

market effects of protection, all remaining simulations assume an endogenous total labor supply. Also, most of our discussion will focus on the distortionary cost component of VERs.

4. DISTORTIONARY COSTS OF PROTECTION WITH LABOR AND PRODUCT MARKET IMPERFECTIONS

We now come to the central issue: are labor market imperfections sufficient to affect significantly the distortionary cost estimates reported above? We contrast the estimated value of the distortionary cost in two dimensions. First, under the assumption of CRTS, we compute distortionary costs under the assumption of an exogenous wage premium, then under the assumption of an endogenously determined wage premium affected by union activity. Because of uncertainty about the relative weight unions attach to wages and employment, we report results for three combinations of weights to wages and employment in the utility function: low weight on wages ($\gamma = 0.2$, $\delta = 0.8$); medium ($\gamma = \delta = 0.5$); high weight on wages ($\gamma = 0.8$; $\delta = 0.2$). Second, we examine the sensitivity of these results on labor market imperfections to assumptions about market structure. Results appear in Table 3.

Steel.   Start with CRTS. The distortionary costs of rationing steel when the steel sector pays an exogenous wage premium of 26 percent is only about one-fourth of the cost when there is no wage premium. This derives from the second best effect of superior reallocation of labor. Given the high rent transfer component of VERs, however, the total costs are reduced by only 11 percent. The distortionary cost estimate reflects the potential lower cost of protection if an "equivalent" tariff (or a quota that captured rents) were employed rather than the VER.

Now consider the role of union activity. Labor demand being a derived demand schedule, protection displaces to the right the labor demand schedule. Section 4 of Table 3 shows the percentage wage premium earned by steel workers after VERs in steel are imposed. The more weight the union attaches to wages (and the less weight it attaches to employment) the larger the induced increase in the wage premium and the lower the increase in employment. For the combination ($\gamma = 0.2$; $\delta = 0.8$), the wage premium barely increases and employment rises by almost as much as when the wage premium is exogenous. For the combination ($\gamma = 0.8$, $\delta = 0.2$), the wage premium reaches 33 percent and, as a result, there is only a small increase in employment of 5.9 thousand work-years. With a high weight on wages, the distortionary costs of protection are almost as high as in the absence of a wage premium. The increased wage premium raises distortion costs in the product market. This cost must be weighed against the improved allocation of labor. With a high weight on wages, the high wage premium and small labor reallocation results in an increase in product market distortions which almost exceeds the benefits of labor reallocation.

Note also that the rent costs of the VERs are sensitive to the weight the union places on wages (both under CRTS and contestable markets). This is because when VERs are imposed, there is an increase in demand for the domestic variety of the

TABLE 3
EFFECTS OF VERS IN STEEL AND AUTOS
(BILLIONS OF 1984 DOLLARS)

| | No wage distortion | | Exogenous wage distortion | | Endogenous wage distortion[a] | | | | | |
| | | | | | Union wage weight = .2 | | Union wage weight = .5 | | Union wage weight = .8 | |
	Steel	Autos	Steel	Autos	Steel	Autos	Steel	Autos	Steel	Autos
1. Distortionary costs of VERs[t]										
a. CRTS	0.128	1.95	0.033	1.78	0.036	1.79	0.069	1.84	0.113	1.88
b. Contestable markets	0.038	0.91	−0.048	0.82	−0.046	0.85	−0.015	0.98	0.027	1.08
c. Monopolistic competition[c]		1.63		1.49		1.48		1.43		1.38
		(.952)		(.952)		(.954)		(.966)		(.977)
2. Capture rents[b]										
a. CRTS	0.736	7.87	0.735	7.86	0.740	7.86	0.803	7.87	0.879	7.87
b. Contestable markets	0.716	7.87	0.715	7.86	0.721	7.86	0.784	7.87	0.862	7.87
c. Monopolistic competition		7.89		7.88		7.88		7.88		7.89
3. Total costs of VERs[b]										
a. CRTS	0.864	9.82	0.768	9.64	0.776	9.65	0.872	9.71	0.992	9.75
b. Contestable markets	0.754	8.79	0.667	9.68	0.675	8.71	0.769	8.84	0.889	8.96
c. Monopolistic competition		9.52		9.363		9.356		9.31		9.27
4. Percentage wage distortion										
a. CRTS	0.0	0.0	.260	0.27	.263	0.26	.293	0.21	.330	0.16
b. Contestable markets	0.0	0.0	.260	0.27	.263	0.26	.293	0.20	.331	0.14
c. Monopolistic competition		0.0		0.27		0.26		0.20		0.15
5. Change in employment[d]										
a. CRTS	20.8	−36.2	20.8	−36.2	20.2	−33.9	13.7	−21.2	5.9	−8.7
b. Contestable markets	18.9	−21.7	18.8	−21.7	18.3	−20.2	12.5	−12.5	5.4	−5.1
c. Monopolistic competition		−19.5		−19.5		−18.3		−11.6		−4.9

Notes:

All simulations are with endogenous economywide labor supply.

[a] Weight on wages is given by γ and in all cases $\gamma + \delta = 1.0$.

[b] EV measure in billions of 1984 dollars. The distortionary cost is calculated as the difference between the total costs of VERs and the rents.

[c] The number in parentheses is the proportion of firms which remain in the industry after firm exit due to VER removal.

[d] Change in employment in thousands of work-years.

DOMESTIC STEEL: **IMPORTED STEEL:**

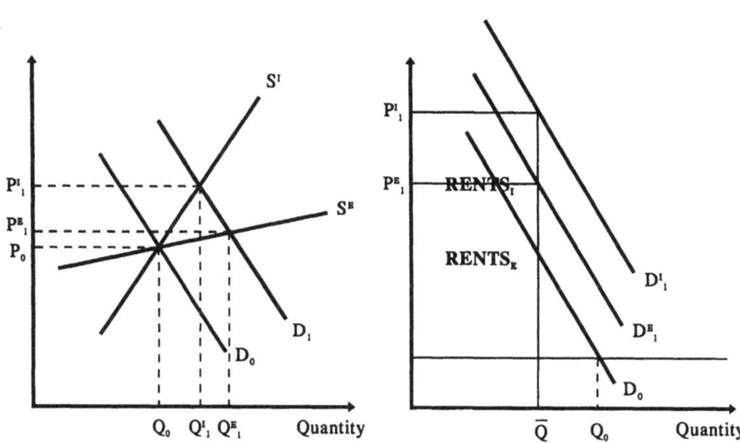

NOTE: Superscript E(I) denotes elastic(inelastic) scenario.

FIGURE 1

IMPACT OF DOMESTIC SUPPLY ELASTICITY ON VER RENTS

product which induces domestic firms to expand output. As firms expand output, however, they are faced with increased wage demands by the union. Thus, the greater the weight the union places on wages, the lower the elasticity of output supply of the domestic industry, and the higher the rent component cost of the VERs.

The impact of a relatively inelastic domestic supply on rents is illustrated in Figure 1, where the subscript 0 (1) indicates the initial (post-VER imposition) equilibrium. Imports and domestic steel are gross substitutes for each other so that an increase in the price of domestic steel increases the demand for imported steel. When the VER is imposed on imported steel, the increased demand for the domestic variety results in a larger increase in the price of the domestic variety of steel the more inelastic is domestic supply. A larger domestic price increase, in turn, induces a larger increase in the price of the foreign variety of steel and a larger rent earned on foreign steel. Thus, as a result of the impact of the wage premium on the rent component of the VER, the total costs of protection under CRTS with a high weight on wages exceed the estimate in the case of no wage premium.

Now consider the effects of VER imposition in steel with contestable markets. VER imposition results in increased demand for domestic steel and consequently greater exploitation of economies of scale. The improvement in scale efficiency lowers significantly the distortion costs of protection. With an exogenous wage distortion, the second best effects of superior labor reallocation are sufficient to result in efficiency gains (negative distortion costs) of $45 million. It is only with the high weight on wages that the distortion costs become positive. Finally because, as mentioned above, the rent effect also depends on the wage distortion, the total costs of VERs exceed the corresponding estimate with no wage distortion when the weight on wages is high.

Autos. Here the estimates of rents are virtually invariant. This is because, unlike steel, auto VERs existed in the base year, so we remove VERs rather than impose them as in steel. Since all models are calibrated to be consistent with the exogenous estimates of the premia rates and rents that existed in autos in 1984, results differ only due to the distortion costs of the VERs.[22] Now because protection is removed, the reduction in the derived demand for labor induces a larger reduction in the wage rate the higher the union's weight on wages. This pattern holds across all market structures.

First consider CRTS and competition. Moving labor out of autos represents a second best loss, and consequently lowers the estimated value of the benefits of liberalization. As before, distortion costs increase as the weight on wages increases because there is less labor reallocation. Distortion costs remain high in all cases.

With contestable markets, removing protection results in a decrease in scale efficiency, and hence lower benefits of protection removal. Exogenous wage distortions have the anticipated effect of lowering further the benefits of liberalization. With endogenous wage distortions, benefits can exceed those in the no wage distortion case. As explained above, this is because the reduction in the derived demand for labor induces a lower wage demand by the union. The lower wage demand, in turn, induces an increase in output, which reduces the difference between output price and marginal costs, i.e., reduces distortions in the product market.

Finally, consider oligopoly with free entry. First, observe that the distortion costs exceed those under contestable markets in all cases. This is because there is exit in response to trade liberalization, so greater realization of scale efficiency is achieved than with contestable markets. Second, contrary to all other cases, the distortion costs of protection decrease, the greater the union's weight on wages. The reason is the following. The decrease in the derived demand for labor which accompanies trade liberalization induces a relatively large wage decrease (with a high union weight on wages). This wage decrease lowers costs for firms which, in turn, retards exit. The effect of lesser scale efficiency dominates the effect of the lesser loss from reduced labor misallocation, so that the benefits of liberalization are smaller with a high union weight on wages.

Distributional consequences. Although labor is not a "specific" factor in the above mentioned models, it earns rents only in steel and autos. Therefore, an employment loss reported in Table 3 represents a loss of rents for the displaced workers. In addition, there is a rent loss for those workers who retain their jobs after VER removal, as reflected in the decline in the wage premium. The higher the union's weight on wages, the fewer the displaced workers, but the more rents lost among workers who retain auto employment.

To illustrate, we consider the impact of sector-specific capital (in all sectors) with

---

[22] Estimates of the benefits of capturing rents differ very slightly because the estimates depend on the income elasticity of demand for autos which is endogenous.

endogenous wage distortions in autos (union wage weight = .5) under CRTS and contestable markets. Under CRTS, after removing auto VERs, the rental rate on capital specific to autos declines by 16 percent. Moreover, since labor is the only variable primary factor, employment declines by 36.5 thousand work-years and the wage distortion declines to 16 percent (significantly larger declines than in the fungible capital case). The welfare gain of VER removal with sector-specific capital is $9.57 billion. This is slightly less than in the fungible capital case ($9.71 billion) due to the lower domestic elasticity of supply with fixed capital (Le Chatelier principle).[23] Analogous to the CRTS results, under contestable markets, specific capital serves to magnify distributional effects. However, with contestable markets the welfare benefit of VER removal is $9.22 billion (compared with $8.84 billion with fungible capital). This is because specific capital serves to mute output reduction and magnify price reduction. This leads to less scale efficiency loss and hence to greater benefits from VER removal. Summarizing these two cases, sector-specific capital considerably magnifies the distributional consequences of VER removal, but has an ambiguous impact on the welfare estimates.

Sensitivity Analysis.   How robust are the results in Table 3? To assess how sensitive results are to changes in the key wage distortion parameter, we have replicated all the simulations with a high and low estimate of the wage distortion, while leaving the value of all other parameters unchanged. For the high (low) simulations, we used Krueger and Summers' estimates of the wage distortion plus (minus) two times the standard error of their estimate of the wage distortion. After rounding, this yields wage distortion values of 33 and 19 percent in steel and 32 and 22 percent in autos. As expected, the second best effect of superior labor reallocation is increased (decreased) with higher (lower) assumed wage distortions. The change in the estimated welfare cost estimates with increased or decreased wage distortions is always less than $35 million in both autos and steel. For example, with CRTS in autos and exogenous wage distortions, the estimated distortion costs increase (decrease) from $1.78 billion to $1.81 ($1.75) in the high (low) wage distortion case. From Table 3, one can see that $35 million is less than two percent of the distortionary costs of the auto VERs; the changes in estimated welfare are also a small percentage of the total costs of the auto or steel VERs. Since the distortion costs of steel VERs are small or negative in some cases, an additional $25 to 35 billion of benefits from superior labor reallocation in the high wage distortion case is important in percentage terms. We conclude that, overall, the striking result is that even with high wage distortions, the benefits of labor reallocation are small relative to the costs of protection.[24]

5.   "OPTIMAL" POLICIES WITH WAGE DISTORTIONS

We now ask what are the gains from removing the wage premia and give illustrative calculations of the potential benefits from applying "optimal" policies

---

[23] See de Melo and Tarr (1992, section 6.4) for an elaboration of the impact of sector specific capital on welfare estimates.

[24] A similar pattern of results occurs when wage distortions are endogenous. A complete set of sensitivity results are in an appendix available from the authors on request.

848   JAIME DE MELO AND DAVID TARR

to counteract the distortions that arise from wage premia and/or market imperfections under IRTS. Start with the welfare gain of removing the wage premia in autos and steel under the assumption of CRTS and that QRs remain in autos and steel.[25] The gain from removing the wage premia in autos (steel) is \$0.18 (\$0.70) billion. The gain in steel is greater because the elasticity of labor demand is greater in steel than in autos. The wage distortion rates and number of employees are roughly the same in both sectors, but steel has a higher share of value added as wages and a higher elasticity of substitution of capital for labor.

Consider now the use of wage subsidies to achieve economies of scale and to counteract the effects of product market imperfections when there are IRTS in autos and steel. To isolate the effects of IRTS, all simulations start from a free trade undistorted equilibrium except for the effects of IRTS. The "optimal" policy then consists of choosing the wage subsidy rates in autos and steel which maximize utility of the representative consumer. We solve for these rates numerically. In the case where both industries use a contestable markets pricing rule, a welfare gain of \$1.045 billion would be achieved by wage subsidies of 5 percent in steel and 28 percent in autos. (The higher wage subsidy in autos reflects the higher cost-disadvantage ratio in that sector.) If more realistically one assumes that the auto industry is characterized by oligopolistic interaction, exploitation of scale economies will be achieved by firm exit. Then the optimal wage policy is a wage tax of 56 percent which reduces by 5 percent the number of firms in the auto industry. Combined with the gains of a 5 percent wage subsidy in steel, the overall welfare gain would be \$367 million. Thus, the optimal wage policy for the auto industry with IRTS reverses from a subsidy to a tax on labor depending on entry/exit conditions. This is explained by the Horstmann-Markusen result mentioned above.

Consider next applying optimal tariff policy in the presence of wage distortions. As before, we start from an undistorted equilibrium, except that now we include wage premia in autos and steel. The simulation exercise consists of maximizing utility using tariffs in autos and steel as instruments. As an illustration, we report the results of four sets of optimal tariff calculations: exogenous wage distortions with CRTS and IRTS, and endogenous wage distortions and high union weight on wages under CRTS and IRTS. In the case of CRTS, optimal tariff policy in both sectors with exogenous wage premia yields tariff rates of 5 (1) percent in steel (autos), for a total welfare gain of \$4 million. With endogenous wage premia, however, with a high weight on wages, the welfare gain is almost zero. The same pattern of lower benefits with endogenous wage distortions results if we assume IRTS with contestable markets in steel and oligopoly in autos. The corresponding magnitudes are \$145 million (with 10 (3) percent tariff rates in steel (autos)) with exogenous wage premia. With endogenous wage premia and high weight on wages the gains are reduced to \$7 million.[26]

---

[25] Bhagwati and Srinivasan (1983, Ch. 21) have shown that with CRTS and exogenous wage distortions, the optimal policy is a subsidy that offsets the wage distortion. A tariff would be a third best policy in this case.

[26] Our CRTS simulations are consistent with those of Dixit (1988). Dixit assumed CRTS and fixed input-output coefficients for labor and capital. He found a subsidy to the production of autos (which is equivalent to a wage subsidy with fixed coefficients) is a superior instrument to a tariff.

Due to strategic considerations, however, the gains from these optimal wage subsidy and tariff simulations may not be achievable. Wage subsidies to these industries to reduce distortions would be problematical if, as we have argued, wage distortions are the result of union activity. Unions would then find it to their advantage to increase wage demands resulting in increased government costs and taxation requirements with offsetting distortions. Similarly, the optimal tariff calculations are subject to the criticism that if the union believes that it can increase protection by its wage demands, then the benefits of optimal tariffs may not be achievable; and, of course, the optimal tariff would be significantly altered by retaliation.[27]

6. CONCLUSIONS

At the outset of this paper we asked whether acknowledging that both autos and steel pay among the highest wage premia in US manufacturing would be sufficient to justify protection for these sectors based on wage premia. If the wage premia can be considered exogenous, then the costs of protection will be lower than in the absence of wage premia, but not by much unless the wage premia interact with scale efficiency, and the latter is an important element of the product market structure. More importantly, we have argued that the more realistic representation of autos and steel is one in which unions set wages facing a tradeoff between employment and the wage premium. Then, through detailed modelling of the labor market and of its interactions with the product market, we find that the existence of wage premia may exacerbate the total costs of protection on two counts. First, if protection is by a VER, which is currently a frequent instrument of protection, then the rent loss component cost can be greater than if there are no wage premia. Second, if unions place a relatively high weight on wages, the distortionary costs of protection can be higher than if there were no wage premia. Our conclusion then is that, generally, the evidence does not support the case for an industrial policy in high wage industries. We also asked what would be the benefits of "optimal" wage and tariff policy in both industries to counteract prevailing wage premia. With endogenous wage distortions, our calculations suggest extremely small welfare gains from optimal tariff policy if such policies could be implemented in practice. Depending on market structure, the optimal wage policy may be a tax.

University of Geneve, Switzerland, and The World Bank, U.S.A.
The World Bank, U.S.A.

REFERENCES

ABBOTT, M. AND O. ASHENFELTER, "Labour Supply, Commodity Demand and the Allocation of Time," *Review of Economic Studies* 43 (1976), 389–411.

AKERLOF, G., "Gift Exchange and Efficiency–Wage Theory: Four Views," *American Economic Review*, Papers and Proceedings, 74 (1984), 79–83.

[27] See Fernandez (1989) for a discussion of other strategic issues that make the achievement of benefits from optimal policies in response to labor market distortions problematical.

850   JAIME DE MELO AND DAVID TARR

BALLARD, C., D. FULLERTON, J. SHOVEN AND J. WHALLEY, *A General Equilibrium Model for Tax Policy Evaluation* (Chicago: University of Chicago Press for NBER, 1985).

BHAGWATI, J. AND V. RAMASWAMI, "Domestic Distortions, Tariffs and the Theory of Optimum Subsidy," *Journal of Political Economy* 71 (1963), 44–50.

—— AND T. N. SRINIVASAN, *Lectures on International Trade* (Cambridge: MIT Press, 1983).

BRANDER, J. A. AND B. J. SPENCER, "International R & D Rivalry and Industrial Strategy," *Review of Economic Studies* 50 (1983), 707–722.

—— AND ——, "Tariff Protection and Imperfect Competition," in H. Kierkowski, ed., *Monopolistic Competition and International Trade* (Oxford: Oxford University Press, 1984), 194–206.

—— AND ——, "Unionized Oligopoly and International Trade Policy," *Journal of International Economics* 24 (1988), 217–234.

DEVARAJAN, S. AND D. RODRIK, "Pro-competitive Effects of Trade Reform: Results from a CGE Model for Cameroon," *European Economic Review* 35 (1991), 1157–1184.

DINOPOULOS, E. AND M. KREININ, "Effects of the US-Japan Auto VER on European Prices and US Welfare," *Review of Economics and Statistics* 70 (1988), 484–491.

DIXIT, A., "Optimal Trade and Industrial Policies for the US Automobile Industry," in R. Feenstra, ed., *Empirical Methods in International Trade* (Cambridge: MIT Press, 1988), 141–165.

—— AND J. STIGLITZ, "Monopolistic Competition and Optimum Product Diversity," *American Economic Review* 67 (1977), 297–308.

EATON, J. AND G. GROSSMAN, "Optimal Trade and Industrial Policy under Oligopoly," *Quarterly Journal of Economics* 101 (1986), 383–406.

FARBER, H., "The Analysis of Union Behavior," in O. Ashenfelter and R. Layard, eds., *Handbook of Labor Economics* (Amsterdam: North-Holland, 1986), 1039–1089.

FEENSTRA, R., "Quality Change under Trade Restraints: Theory and Evidence from Japanese Autos," *Quarterly Journal of Economics* 102 (1988), 131–146.

FERNANDEZ, R., "Comment," (On Katz and Summers), in R. Feenstra, ed., *Trade Policies for International Competitiveness* (Chicago: University of Chicago Press, 1989), 120–124.

FREEMAN, R. AND L. KATZ, "Industrial Wage and Employment Determination in an Open Economy," mimeo, paper presented at National Bureau of Economic Research Conference on Immigration, Trade, and Labor, 1987.

FRIEDLANDER, A., C. WINSTON AND K. WANG, "Costs, Technology, and Productivity in the US Automobile Industry," *Bell Journal of Economics* 14 (1983), 1–20.

HAGEN, E., "An Economic Justification of Protectionism," *Quarterly Journal of Economics* 72 (1958), 496–514.

HORSTMANN, I. AND J. MARKUSEN, "Up the Average Cost Curve: Inefficient Entry and the New Protectionism," *Journal of International Economics* 20 (1986), 225–247.

KAHN, M., "Airlines," in G. Somers, ed., *Collective Bargaining: Contemporary American Experience* (Wisconsin: Industrial Relations Research Association, 1980), 315–372.

KATZ, L. AND L. SUMMERS, "Can Interindustry Wage Differentials Justify Strategic Trade Policy," in R. Feenstra, ed., *Trade Policies for International Competitiveness* (Chicago: University of Chicago Press, 1989a), 85–119.

—— AND ——, "Industry Rents: Evidence and Implications," in *Brookings Papers on Economic Activity: Microeconomics* (Washington: Brookings Institution, 1989b), 209–290.

KILLINGSWORTH, M., *Labor Supply* (New York: Cambridge University Press, 1983).

—— AND J. HECKMAN, "Female Labor Supply: A Survey," in O. Ashenfelter and R. Layard, eds., *Handbook of Labor Economics* (New York: Elsevier Science Publishers, 1986), 103–204.

KRUEGER, A. AND L. SUMMERS, "Efficiency Wages and the Interindustry Wage Structure," *Econometrica* 56 (1988), 259–293.

LEVINSON, H., "Trucking," in G. Somers, ed., *Collective Bargaining: Contemporary American Experience* (Wisconsin: Industrial Relations Research Association, 1980), 99–150.

MANCKE, R., "The Determinants of Steel Prices in the US: 1947–65," *Journal of Industrial Economics* 16 (1968), 147–160.

MCDONALD, I. M. AND R. M. SOLOW, "Wage Bargaining and Employment," *American Economic Review* 71 (1981), 896–908.

MELO, J. DE AND S. ROBINSON, "Product Differentiation and the Treatment of Foreign Trade in

Computable General Equilibrium Models of Small Economies,'' *Journal of International Economics* 27 (1989), 47–67.

———— AND D. TARR, "Welfare Costs of US Quotas in Textiles, Steel and Autos," *Review of Economics and Statistics* 72 (1990), 489–497.

———— AND ————, *A General Equilibrium Analysis of US Foreign Trade Policy* (Cambridge: MIT Press, 1992).

MEZZETTI, C. AND E. DINOPOULOS, "Domestic Unionization and Import Competition," *Journal of International Economics* 31 (1991), 79–100.

MROZ, T., "The Sensitivity of an Empirical Model of Married Women's Hours of Work to Economic and Statistical Assumptions," *Econometrica* 55 (1987), 765–799.

OSWALD, A., "The Microeconomic Theory of the Trade Union," *Economic Journal* 92 (1982), 576–596.

PENCAVEL, J., "Labor Supply of Men: A Survey," in O. Ashenfelter and R. Layard, eds., *Handbook of Labor Economics* (New York: Elsevier Science Publishers, 1986), 3–102.

POWELL, A. AND F. GRUEN, "The Constant Elasticity of Transformation Production Frontier and Linear Supply System," *International Economic Review* 9 (1968), 315–328.

RIPPE, R., "Wages, Prices, and Imports in the American Steel Industry," *Review of Economics and Statistics* 47 (1970), 34–46.

SCHERER, F. M., *Industrial Market Structure and Economic Performance* (Boston: Rand McNally, 1980).

SHAPIRO, C. AND J. STIGLITZ, "Equilibrium Unemployment as a Worker Discipline Device," *American Economic Review* 74 (1984), 433–444.

STIGLITZ, J., "Equilibrium Wage Distribution," *Economic Journal* 95 (1985), 595–618.

TARR, D., "The Minimum Efficient Size Steel Plant," *The Atlantic Economic Journal* 12 (1984), 122.

————, "Steel: International Position and Mobilization Capabilities," in D. Losman and S. Liang, eds., *The Promise of American Industry* (New York: Quorum Books, 1990), 203–225.

THALER, R. H., "Anomalies: Interindustry Wage Differentials," *Journal of Economic Perspectives* 3 (1989), 181–193.

U.S. FEDERAL TRADE COMMISSION STAFF REPORT (D. TARR ET AL.), *The United States Steel Industry and Its International Rivals* (Washington: US Government Printing Office, 1977).

WEISS, A., "Job Queues and Layoffs in Labor Markets with Flexible Wages," *Journal of Political Economy* 88 (1980), 526–538.

WINSTON, C. AND ASSOCIATES, *Blind Intersection? Policy and the Automobile Industry* (Washington: Brookings Institution, 1987).

Revenue-Raising Taxes: General Equilibrium Evaluation of Alternative Taxation in U.S. Petroleum Industries

Jaime de Melo, Julie Stanton and David Tarr, *World Bank*

This paper assesses recent proposals to increase taxes and tariffs in the energy sector to reduce the U.S. federal deficit. The paper estimates the welfare, fiscal and employment effects of the most common proposals. The estimates are derived from a twelve-sector general equilibrium model of the U.S. economy calibrated to 1984. A proposed 25 percent import tariff on crude oil would raise $7.3 billion in government revenue, while a 15 percent excise tax on petroleum products would raise $35 billion. Each dollar of government revenue would come at a loss of 25 cents in welfare in the first case, but at only a one cent loss in welfare in the second.

The paper also estimates the least costly (in terms of welfare) combination of excise taxes and import tariffs on the two sectors to raise $20 billion in government revenue. The optimal tax structure is nonuniform, involving both taxes and import tariffs on oil, and a tariff and small subsidy on petroleum products to counteract the distortion induced by the taxation of oil—which is the most important input in the petroleum products sector.

1. INTRODUCTION

Several proposals have recently been made to increase taxes or tariffs in the energy sector. The most notable proposals have concentrated on: (1) an increase in tariffs on crude oil imports by $5 or $10 per barrel (roughly a tariff of 25 to 50 percent of the value of the imported oil);[1] (2) an increase in taxes on final petroleum products by between five and 25 cents per gallon (roughly between five and 25 percent of the value of a gallon of gasoline).[2] Domestic petroleum product refiners, however, have also sought an import tariff that is limited to imports of refined petro-

---

[1] See the U.S. General Accounting Office (1986) for a survey of these results.

[2] See Committee on Ways and Means (1987), Congressional Budget Office (1988), Alan Greenspan (1988) and the Department of Energy (1987).

Address correspondence to Jaime de Melo, The World Bank, 1818 H. Street, N.W., Washington, D.C. 20433.

This paper draws on a larger study by Tarr (1988) while he was at the U.S. Federal Trade Commission. We thank Bela Balassa for comments and Maria D. Ameal for excellent logistic support. The views are those of the authors, not those of the USFTC nor those of the World Bank.

Journal of Policy Modeling 11(3):425–449 (1989)

© Society for Policy Modeling, 1989

425

0161-8938/89/$3.50

leum products.[3] During the 1970s, proposals to increase the import tariffs on crude oil were commonly offered as devices to counteract the power of the OPEC cartel. In the late 1980s, however, the most prominent proposals to increase taxation in these sectors are being offered as a means of reducing the large U.S. federal budget deficit and its twin trade deficit. In addition, some argue that it will help the United States become energy independent,[4] and will be relatively painless due to the recent decline in energy prices. Opponents argue that these taxes would be very costly to the U.S. economy in terms of lost U.S. welfare and in terms of adverse impacts on other sectors.

Due to conflicting concerns, President Reagan asked the Department of Energy to study whether any policy changes were warranted due to the fall in the price of energy products. Without proposing specific policies, that study drew the vague conclusion that the challenge to policymakers is to utilize the market where possible and to otherwise find appropriate cost-effective action to the nation's energy problems (Department of Energy, 1987, p. 3). The purpose of this paper is to study explicitly cost-effective and welfare-effective methods of dealing with revenue generation through taxation of the crude oil and petroleum products sectors.

Previous quantitative studies have mostly been partial equilibrium exercises. Most made the unrealistic assumption that the demand for gasoline is perfectly inelastic in the short-run, and very inelastic in the long-run. Typically, the tax consequences were dealt with by adopting the rule of thumb that one billion dollars of revenue will be generated for the U.S. government for each one cent per gallon tax on gasoline and diesel fuel. Given that a tax on gasoline has strong economy-wide linkages, it is useful to obtain estimates based in a general equilibrium context where interactive effects are accounted for.[5]

It is only recently that two general equilibrium studies by Boyd and

---

[3] See Anderson and Metzger (1987).

[4] The energy independence issue is not an argument for taxation, since with an exhaustible resource such as oil, the faster it is utilized in the present, the less will be available in the future, if prices should rise. Moreover, applying the principle of using the most direct instrument for the noneconomic objective (see Bhagwati and Srinivasan (1969) and Bhagwati (1971)), stockpiling is a less costly alternative, if this argument is taken seriously. See Anderson and Metzger (1987) for further details.

[5] Policy issues relating to the energy sector have previously been addressed in a general equilibrium framework. These studies, however, are usually related to long-run alternatives to petroleum as an energy input. Examples of earlier efforts include Hudson and Jorgenson (1974), Manne (1976) and Borges and Goulder (1984). These studies, however, do not specifically address the issue of taxation. Manne (1984) provides a critical survey of these earlier studies.

REVENUE-RAISING TAXES 427

Uri (1988a, 1988b) address the issue of taxation and the fiscal deficit. They have analyzed the welfare and revenue implications of a $5 per barrel import tariff on crude oil, and a 15 cents per gallon excise tax on gasoline. Boyd and Uri (1988b) find that the rule of thumb of one billion dollars of revenue for every cent of gasoline tax is an overestimate by about 50 percent, that is, the government can be expected to realize about one-half of a billion dollars per one cent tax on gasoline. In addition, they estimate that U.S. welfare falls by about twice the amount of the gain in U.S. treasury revenues from a gasoline tax.

The purpose of this paper is to reexamine the welfare, fiscal, and employment implications of: (1) a 25 percent import tax on imported crude oil; and (2) a 15 percent excise tax on petroleum products. The estimates are derived from a 12-sector computable general equilibrium (CGE) model for the U.S. economy calibrated to 1984. Our estimates are derived under the assumption that the existing voluntary export restraints (VERs) prevailing in 1984 in the textiles and apparel and automobile sectors would remain in effect.[6] More importantly, we go beyond the existing literature by answering the question: what is the least costly combination (in terms of U.S. welfare) of taxes and tariffs on the crude oil and petroleum product sectors to generate a given amount ($20 billion) of U.S. government revenue?

The remainder of the paper is organized as follows. Section 2 presents the model and selected elasticity specifications. Section 3 reports on new welfare, revenue and trade balance estimates of the proposed tax rates mentioned above. Section 4 reports results on the set of least costly taxes in the crude oil and petroleum products sectors that would raise $20 billion in government revenue. Conclusions follow in section 5.

2. THE MODEL AND THE ELASTICITY SPECIFICATION

The simulation model is a neoclassical, perfect competition, static CGE Walrasian model, in which a representative consumer maximizes utility subject to a budget constraint, atomistic producers minimize costs, and the government redistributes, in a lump-sum manner, tax revenues. This stylized representation of government behavior is of course simplistic, but it adds great transparency to the estimation of the welfare costs of alternative taxation schemes designed to raise government revenue. The economy also has a fixed endowment of labor and capital, and faces an exogenous balance of trade expressed

---

[6]The welfare implications of U.S. VERs negotiated for autos, textiles and steel are examined in de Melo and Tarr (1988).

in foreign currency units, so as to help interpretation of the welfare effects of alternative taxation schemes. Our static representation of the economy allows us to abstract from investment, thereby further simplifying the welfare analysis. Thus the components of final demand only include consumer demand and intermediate demand.

2A. The Model

Before sketching the model formulated in Table 1, it should be noted that the simulations which apply to 1984 take as given the most important foreign trade restrictions then in existence, namely the U.S. VERs on Japanese autos and the quotas on U.S. textile and apparel imports.[7] We view these quotas as relatively important elements in our analysis since this implies that imports of these products are fixed, thereby adding a strong second best flavor to our estimates. Though less important quantitatively, we also assume that the existing tariff structure remains in place. To simplify the notation and presentation of the model, we do not list among the equations those that determine the rents ($RENT_k$ in equations 24 and 25) which accrue to foreigners, but the reader should be aware that the value of the transfer to foreigners implied by the U.S. system of quotas and VERs depends on the value of the real exchange rate, which is endogenous.

The following notation is adopted throughout. If double subscripts are employed, the first subscript denotes the sector of origin, the second the sector of destination. Upper case letters are reserved for endogenous variables, unless they have a bar, in which case they are exogenous variables or normalizing constants. Parameters and policy variables are denoted by Greek or lower case Latin letters. There are $i, j = 1, \ldots, n$ sectors of which $k = 1, \ldots 1$ are traded and the remainder, $m = 1 + 1, \ldots, n$ are non-traded. In the application $1 = 11$ and there is one non-traded sector.

The functional forms used throughout are the linear expenditure system (LES) to denote the preferences for the representative consumer, the constant elasticity of substitution (CES) function to represent capital-labor substitution and substitution between domestic and foreign intermediates, and the constant elasticity of transformation (CET) to model export supply. To save on notation, we note first that

---

[7]The welfare costs of these quotas are discussed in de Melo and Tarr (1988).

REVENUE-RAISING TAXES

429

Table 1. U.S. General Equilibrium Model

---

0. *Welfare Indicator*

$$W = \prod_{i,k} (CD_i - \lambda_i^d)^{\beta_i^d} (CM_k - \lambda_k^m)^{\beta_k^m}$$

1. *Unit Cost*

(1) $CV_i = CES_i (W, R; \alpha_i, \sigma_i, \overline{AD}_i) + \sum_{j=1}^{n} a_{ji} X_i PC_{ji}$

$$= \qquad PVC_i \qquad + \qquad INTC_i$$

2. *Factor Markets*

(2) $K_i^d = XD_i^{(1-\sigma_i)} \quad PVC_i^{\sigma_i} (R/(1-\alpha_i))^{-\sigma_i}$

(3) $L_i^d = XD_i^{(1-\sigma_i)} \quad PVC_i^{\sigma_i} (W/\alpha_i)^{-\sigma_i}$

(4) $\sum_i L_i^d = \overline{LS}; \sum_i K_i^d = \overline{KS}$

3. *Intermediate Products Demand*

(5) $V_{ji} = CES_i (VM_{ji}, VD_{ji}; \delta_j, \sigma c_j, \overline{AC}_{ji})$

(6) $VD_{ji}/VM_{ji} = ((1-\delta_j)/\delta_j)^{\sigma c_j} (PD_j/PM_j)^{-\sigma c_j}$

(7) $VM_{ji} = 0 \qquad j \in NT$

(8) $V_{ij} = a_{ij} XD_i$

4. *Output Allocation for Tradables*

(9) $XD_k = CET_k (E_k, D_k; \gamma_k, \sigma t_k, \overline{AT}_k)$

(10) $D_k/E_k = ((1-\gamma_k)/\gamma_k)^{-\sigma t_k} (PD_k/PE_k)^{\sigma t_k}$

5. *Cost Prices*

(11) $PX_k = CET_k (PE_k, PD_k; \gamma_k, \sigma t_k, \overline{AT}_k); PX_m = PD_m$

(12) $PC_{ij} = CES_j (PMI_{ij}, PD_i; \delta_i, \sigma c_i, \overline{AC}_{ji}); PC_{mj} = PD_m$

(13) $PN_i = PX_i - \sum_j a_{ji} PC_{ji}$

Table 1. *(continued)*

---

6. *Definition of Internal Prices of Traded Goods*

  (14) $PE_k = PWE_k\, ER$

  (15) $PD_i = \bar{P}D_i\,(1+tx_i)$; $tx_i > 0$; $i \in$ petroleum products and crude oil

  (16) $PM_k = PWM_k\,(1+tm_k)\,(1+prc_k)\,(1+tx_k)\,ER$; $prc_k > 0$ for autos and textiles

7. *Import Supply; Export Demand*

  (17) $PWE_k = \overline{PWE_k}$

  (18) $PWM_k = \overline{PWM_k}$ or $VTM_k = \overline{VTM_k}\,(PWM_k)^{\psi_k}$; $\psi_k > 0$; $\psi_k < \infty$ for crude oil

8. *Consumer and Intermediate Demands*

  (19) $CD_i = LES_i\,(PD_i,\ Y;\ \lambda_i^d,\ \beta_i^d)$

  (20) $CM_k = LES_k\,(PM_k,\ Y;\ \lambda_k^m,\ B_k^m)$

  (21) $VTD_i = \sum_j VD_{ij}$; $VTM_k = \sum_j VM_{kj}$

  (22) $D_i = VTD_i + C_i^d$

9. *Government Revenue (GR), Trade Balance Constraint ($\bar{B}$) and Income Definition (Y)*

  (23) $GR = \sum_k (PWM_k\, tm_k\,(CM_k + VTM_k)\,ER$

  $GR = \sum_i (\bar{P}D_iD_itx_i) + \sum_k PWM_k\, tx_k\,(1+tm_k)\,ER\,(VTM_k+CM_k)$

  (24) $\bar{B} = \sum_k (PWE_kE_k - PWM_k\,(CM_k + VTM_k)$

  $- \sum_k (RENT_k)/ER$

  (25) $Y = W\bar{L}S + R\bar{K}S + GR_1 + GR_2 + \sum_k (RENT_k) - \bar{B}\,ER$

CES and CET functions can be written analogously in the form $X = CES\,(X_1,\ X_2;\ \alpha_1,\ 1\text{-}\alpha_1,\ \rho,\ \bar{A})$ where $\sigma = \dfrac{1}{1-\rho}$; $\rho < 1$ in the CES case and $\sigma = \dfrac{1}{\rho - 1}$; $1 < \rho < \infty$ in the CET case. To further save on notation, we write the unit dual cost functions associated with the

---

Table 1. *(continued)*

---

10. *Market Equilibrium*

$$(26) \quad PX_i = CV_i$$

11. *Numeraire*

$$(27) \quad 1 = \sum_j PD_j\, XD_j^o / \Sigma\, PD_j^o\, XD_j^o$$

Endogenous Variables		*Number of Variables*
CV_i	= Unit costs	n
K_i^d	= Sectoral capital stocks	n
L_i^d	= Sectoral employment	n
V_{ji}	= Composite intermediate purchases	n^2
VD_{ji}	= Domestic intermediate purchases	n^2
VM_{ji}	= Imported intermediate purchases	$n(n-1)$
XD_i	= Gross output of sector i	n
D_i	= Supply for domestic sales	n
E_k	= Supply for export sales	m
PX_k	= Unit revenue of traded goods	m
PD_i	= Unit price of domestically sold goods	n
PC_{ij}	= Unit price of composite intermediates	n^2
PN_i	= value-added price of sector i	n
PE_k, PWE_k	= Domestic and border price of exports	m
$PM_k(PWM_k)$	= Domestic (border) price of imports of sector k	$2m$
$RENTC_k$	= Rents on imports subject to quotas	$2m$
VTD_i, VTM_k	= Total domestic and import intermediate demands	$2m+n$
CM_k, CD_i	= Consumer demand for imports and domestically produced goods	$m+n$
GR,Y,ER	= Government revenue from tariff collection, disposable income net of transfers and real exchange rate	3
W,R	= Wage, rental rates	2
	TOTAL	$3n^2 + n(n-1+9n+7m+5$

Note: Number of endogenous variables varies according to model closure. (See text).

CES (CET) functions as $PX = CES\,(CET)\,(PX_1, PX_2; \alpha\ \sigma)$ where PX is the price of X and PX_1 and PX_2 the prices of X_1 and X_2.

The equations describing the model appear in Table 1. The welfare function is the Stone-Geary utility function associated with the consumer demand equations described in equations (19)–(20). Our measure of the welfare cost of a policy change is given by the equivalent variation (*EV*) measure defined as:

432   J. de Melo et. al.

$$EV = C[IU(p^1, y^1), p^o] - C[IU(p^o, y^o), p^o]$$

where superscripts o and 1 refer to the equilibrium before and after
the counterfactual trade policy experiment, p is the tax inclusive vector
of final goods prices, IU is the indirect utility function, and C is the
cost or expenditure function.[8]

To best capture the trading possibilities at a relatively aggregated
level for an economy like the U.S., we have treated commodities
supplied (or purchased) abroad and domestic commodities sold on the
domestic market as imperfect substitutes. This assumption of product
differentiation, which has found considerable support at the disaggregate level, is commonly used in applied general equilibrium analysis
and is also adopted in many of the partial equilibrium estimates cited
in section 2. On the export side, the assumption of product differentiation is reflected in the constant elasticity of transformation (CET)
function between domestic and foreign sales. The choice of functional
forms implies that σc and σt are respectively the (compensated) price
elasticities of demand for imports and price elasticities of supply of
exports.

Table 1 shows that production possibilities are parameterized by
assuming CES functions for value-added and Leontief functions between intermediates (as a whole) and value-added, as well as within
intermediates. However, within each sector, intermediate demand is
a CES function between the domestically produced intermediate and
the competing foreign intermediate (Equations 5 and 6). To give an
example, no substitution is allowed between purchases of crude oil
and other manufacturing intermediates, but substitution in purchases
is allowed between domestic and foreign crude oil when their relative
prices change as a result of a change in trade policy. Likewise, in
consumption demand, we allow for nonunitary income elasticities of
demand and nonzero cross-price elasticities of demand between domestic and foreign produced consumer goods (Equations 19 and 20).

Apart from the existing quotas on textiles and autos, the only distortions are the existing tariffs on imports. Of course this is a simplification of the existing structure of distortions, but for the purpose of
studying the effects of taxation on crude oil and petroleum products,
this simplification makes results easier to interpret.

With respect to the petroleum industries, note that we allow for the
possibility of an upward sloping supply curve of imports for crude oil
which has been suggested by Anderson and Metzger (1987). Also note

---

[8]See Varian (1984) for a justification of this measure.

that positive excise taxes apply only to the two petroleum industries, oil and gas and petroleum products, and that the excise tax is imposed on top of the existing tariff rates (equal to 0.2 percent for oil and gas and 3.1 percent for petroleum products).

In the experiments reported in section 3, we take the domestic sales tax (tx_i) and tariffs on the oil and gas and petroleum products sectors as an exogenous policy instrument. We ask what are the revenue and welfare effects of imposing taxes and tariffs at the proposed levels. On the other hand, in the experiments reported in section 4, we ask what are the values of tx_i and tm_i, for the oil and gas and the petroleum products sectors which maximize welfare given by the Stone-Geary indicator subject to the constraint that we must increase government revenue by \$20 billion.

2B. Elasticity Specification for the Energy Sectors[9]

The model has twelve sectors: agriculture, mining, crude oil and natural gas, food, textiles and apparel, automobiles, steel, other manufacturing, other consumer goods, petroleum products, traded services, non-traded services. The classification provides for a disaggregation of mining and manufacturing so as to encompass five important policy sectors: automobiles, textiles and apparel, and steel on which VERs have recently been in effect; and crude oil and natural gas and petroleum products which are the subject of the policy experiments in this paper. Because the model is calibrated to 1984, we assume that existing import quotas on textiles and apparel and automobiles would remain in effect under the alternative taxation schemes analyzed here.

The structure of demand, the level of output and employment and the selected elasticities for the two energy sectors appear in Table 2. The structure of demand indicates that imports are a larger share of domestic supply in the oil and gas sector and the oil and gas sector is also the more labor intensive sector. All sales from the oil and gas sector are sales to other sectors. Thus, an increase in that sector's relative price will have a negative supply effect on sectors which use oil and gas intensively as an intermediate input, in particular, for the petroleum products sector where purchases from the oil and gas sector comprise 56.3 percent of its total costs.

Turning to the elasticity estimates in the bottom half of Table 2, we use Caddy's (1976) estimate of 0.8 for the elasticity of substitution between capital and labor for both sectors. Likewise, we use an iden-

---

[9]The elasticity specification for the other sectors is given in the appendix.

Table 2: Production, Demand Structure, and Elasticities in U.S. Petroleum Industry

	Oil + Gas	Petroleum products
Production and demand (1984 US$ billion)		
Gross Output (XD)	157.3	217.2 (56 3%)[a]
Employment (L)	619.0	204.0
Domestic final demand sales (CD)	0.07	45.7
Intermediate sales (VD)	156.4	167.3
Imports: Intermediates (VM)	43.6	16.6
Final demand (CM)	0.02	4.5
Price and substitution elasticities		
Capital-labor (σp)	0.8	0.8
Imports: Final demand (uncompensated)	-0.5	-0.9
Intermediates (σc)	2.4	2.4
Domestic: Final demand (uncompensated)	-0.5	-0.9
Export supply (σt)	2.9	2.9

[a]Percent of (direct) total costs attributable to intermediate purchases from the oil and gas sector.

tical estimate of 2.4 for the compensated price elasticity of demand for intermediate imports (Stern, Francis and Schumacher, 1976). A compensated price elasticity of supply of U.S. exports of three is assumed for both sectors. The insignificant value of exports in both sectors, and earlier experiments reported in de Melo and Tarr (1988), suggest that results are quite insensitive to a wide range of values for this parameter. The price elasticity of final demand for domestic and imported petroleum products is assumed to be -0.92 (an average of estimates of (-0.79) reported in Shiells, Deardorff and Stern (1986) and of (-0.96) reported in Stern, Francis and Schumacher (1976)). Finally, a price elasticity of final demand of -0.5 is assumed for crude oil (Bohi and Russell, 1978) and petroleum products.

In most simulations, we rely on the above values for elasticities which we refer to as the central elasticity case. However, to check on the sensitivity of results, we also carried out experiments for low elasticity and high elasticity cases. The low (high) elasticity case is obtained by reducing (augmenting) the values of the elasticities in Table 2 by one standard deviation. Finally, we also experiment with values of one and three for the foreign elasticity of supply of imported crude oil, which are in the range suggested by Anderson and Metzger (1987).

3. REVENUE AND WELFARE EFFECTS OF PROPOSED TAXATION OF US PETROLEUM INDUSTRIES

We report first in section 3A the revenue, welfare and employment effects of tariffs on imports of oil and gas products and of a domestic sales tax on petroleum products for the central elasticity case. Next, in section 3B, we establish the likely upper and lower bounds of the welfare costs per dollar of government revenue generated and also per additional percent of taxation.

3A. Revenue Employment and Welfare Estimates

Table 3 shows that above five times more revenue would be generated by the proposed excise tax on petroleum products than by the import tariff on oil and gas. This is to be expected since the excise tax applies to all domestic sales amounting to $234 billion, whereas the import tariff has a much smaller base of $43.6 billion. It is also noteworthy that the excise tax on petroleum products is much less distortionary than the import tariff on oil and gas products. Thus, an excise tax on petroleum products raises about five times more revenue than a tariff on imported oil and gas products at a welfare cost which is only 37 percent of the welfare cost of raising revenue by the import tariff. The reasons for this large discrepancy between the two revenue-raising instruments is that an excise tax applies to all sales and is therefore nondiscriminatory by source. We elaborate on this point below.

The employment effects of the import tariff on oil and gas products shows that this method of raising government revenue would have labor relocation effects across the entire economy. The last column of Table 3 is a measure of the total economy-wide relocation of workers. The value of that measure shows that interindustry effects are strong, since 153.6 thousand workers would be relocated but among these only 66.2 thousand would be relocating in the energy industries. The economy-wide relocation effect is even stronger for the proposed sales tax on petroleum products: only 11.3 thousand workers relocate within the energy industries, whereas 32.7 thousand relocate in nonenergy sectors. The relatively smaller effect on employment in the petroleum products sector compared with the tariff on oil and gas imports is due to the nondiscriminatory feature of an excise sales tax which applies to domestic as well as to import sales. Since 77 percent of petroleum products sales are to other sectors and we do not allow for substitution in intermediate inputs of a different sector of origin, purchasers of

Table 3: Revenue, Welfare and Employment Effects of Taxation on the U.S. Petroleum Industry

| Experiment | Increase in government revenue (billion $ 1984) | Change in welfare (billion $ 1984) | Employment Change | | Economy wide employment relocation (thousand work-years) |
| | | | Oil + Gas | Petroleum products | |
			(thousand work-years)		
25% import tariff on oil + gas (E–1)	7.29	−1.86	63.88	−2.32	153.64
15% excise tax on domestic sales of petroleum products (E–2)	34.99	−0.32	−7.01	−4.33	32.67
(E–1) + (E–2)	42.78	−2.34	56.12	−6.51	162.07

[a]One-half of the sum of the absolute value of the employment changes (expressed in thousand work years).

petroleum products cannot shift to other inputs. Such an assumption is of course a simplification which is only likely to hold for the short to medium run.

In interpreting the results in Table 3, one should bear in mind that the estimated figure on government revenue from the proposed excise tax is probably an upper-bound estimate. This is because an increase in the relative price of oil and gas or of petroleum products would induce users to shift to other sources of energy like coal. The possibility to substitute out of petroleum industries in response to an excise tax would both lower the welfare cost of the excise tax and the government revenue raised by the excise tax. Finally note that if the United States could be assumed to have monopsony power on oil and gas (an unrealistic assumption), there would be a welfare gain after imposition of the tariff, because of improved terms of trade.

3B. Relative Efficiency of Proposed Taxes

We now evaluate the relative efficiency of the proposed revenue-raising tax schemes relying on two indicators: (a) welfare cost per dollar of government revenue raised; and (b) billions of dollars of government revenue per additional one percent tax. These indicators appear in columns (3) and (4) of Table 4 for simulations under low and high elasticities. We also compare our result with previous estimates.

Low elasticities result in more government revenue and less welfare cost for each tax scheme. Why this is so is shown in Figure 1, which illustrates in partial equilibrium the effect of high and low elasticities on the welfare and revenue effect of a tariff on import demand. Initially, equilibrium is at (PM_0, VM_0) with infinitely elastic import supply of intermediates. Ignoring shifts in the (derived) demand for imported intermediates after the imposition of an import tariff, the new equilibrium shifts to (PM^L_1, VM_1) in the low elasticity case and to (PM, VM^H_1) in the high elasticity case. It is clear that the welfare costs, given by $W = \frac{1}{2} (PM_1 - PM_0) (VM_1 - VM_0)$, is greater in the high elasticity case, and the government revenue, given by $(PM_1 - PM_0) VM_1$, is higher in the low elasticity case. This observation corresponds to the prescription of Pigou (1947, p 105), based on partial equilibrium analysis:

the best way of raising a given revenue . . . is by a system of taxes, under which the rates become progressively higher as we pass from uses of very elastic demand or supply to uses where demand or supply are progressively less elastic.[10]

---

[10]See Atkinson and Stiglitz (1980, pp. 366–70) for a detailed discussion.

Table 4: Welfare Costs per Dollar of Tax Revenue (U.S.$ 1984 billion)

	Elasticity	Change in government revenue (1)	Change in welfare (2)	Welfare Revenue (2) ÷ (1)	Billion of revenue per additional percent tax (4)
25% import tariff on oil and gas	L	8.9	−1.0	−0.11	0.36
	H	4.9	−3.0	−0.61	0.20
25% import tariff on oil and gas: U.S. has monopsony power in oil and gas	L^a	8.2	4.4	+0.54	0.33
	H^a	7.8	1.7	+0.22	0.31
25% excise tax on domestic sales of oil and gas	L	49.7	−0.3	−0.01	1.99
	H	47.3	−1.1	−0.02	1.89
15% excise tax on domestic sales of petroleum products	L	35.3	−0.1	−0.00	2.35
	H	34.4	−0.7	−0.02	2.29

Note: the 25% import tariff is added to the existing 0.2% tariff.

^{a}Central elasticity case for all parameters except the import supply elasticity (ϵ_s^m) of oil-gas imports (L: $\epsilon_s^m = 1.0$; H: $\epsilon_s^m = 3.0$).

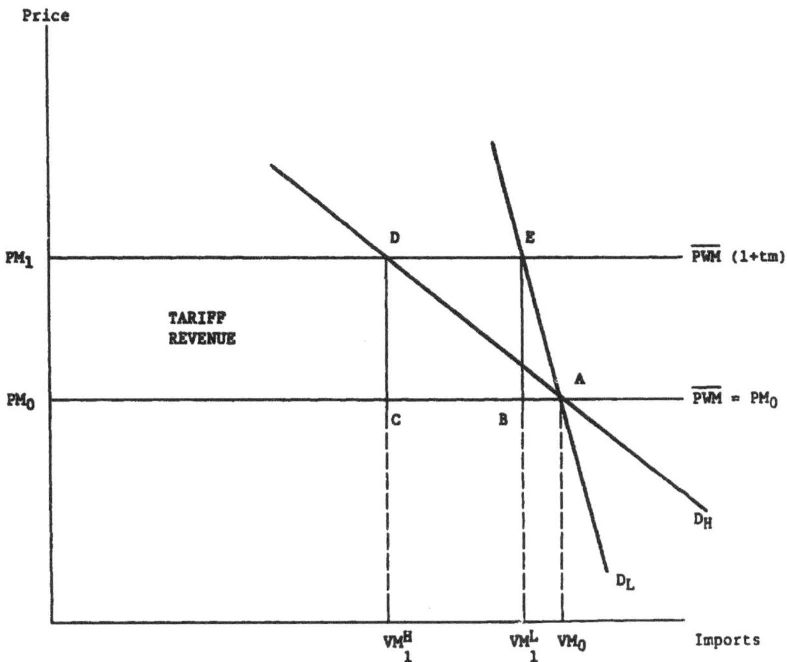

Figure 1. Import demand elasticity and welfare loss.

Note: ABE = Welfare loss (low elasticity).
ACD = Welfare loss (high elaticity).

Next, it is clear that raising revenue by taxes which do not discriminate by country of origin is more efficient. This is clearly seen by comparing the proposed import tariff on oil and gas with an excise tax on domestic sales of oil and gas. Not only does the excise tax raise far more revenue because it applies to all domestic sales, but it also generates revenue at a much lower welfare cost than an import tariff (see column 3).

3C. Comparison with Earlier Studies

In their partial equilibrium study for the U.S. Federal Trade Commission, Anderson and Metzger (1987) estimated that a $5 per barrel import tariff on both crude oil and petroleum products will generate $6.7 billion per year for the government, but at a cost of $3.8 billion in dead-weight losses. Since the bulk of the government revenues generated by tariffs in our model derive from the crude oil tariff, our estimate of the government revenue generated is within their range (see Table 4). Their implied estimate of the welfare costs per dollar of revenue generated (55 cents) is on the high side of those we present in Table 4, but within our range.[11]

Only Boyd and Uri have conducted general equilibrium experiments similar to those discussed in this section. They estimate (1988a) the effects of a $5 per barrel import fee on crude oil and the effects (in 1988b) of a 15 cents per gallon tax on gasoline. These taxes are about equal to our 25 percent import fee on crude oil and 15 percent tax on petroleum products. They estimate that the $5 per barrel import fee on crude oil will result in $3.4 billion of government revenue, and come at a cost of $208 million in lost social welfare. The welfare to government revenue ratio (6.1 percent) is about half the value of our low elasticity estimate (see Table 4).

In the case of a 15 cents per gallon excise tax on gasoline, Boyd and Uri (1988b) find that it will generate $8 billion in government revenue at a cost of $15 billion in welfare. Thus: (a) each dollar of government revenue comes at a cost of almost $2 in welfare (compared with less than two cents of welfare costs in our case); and (b) for each one cent (or percent) tax on gasoline, they find the government receives about one-half of a billion dollars in revenue (compared with about $2.3 billion in our case). Since Boyd and Uri apply the tax only on final demand for gasoline, not on intermediate demand, and our experiments apply the excise tax on both intermediate and final demand, we are applying the tax to a base 4.7 times larger. Adjusted for the size of the tax base, our results on dollars of revenue obtained per percent of tax are very close. We choose our formulation rather than theirs, since arbitrage would make it difficult, if not impossible, to tax

---

[11]Because it does not consider the effects on the real exchange rate, other things equal, partial equilibrium analysis will tend to overestimate the welfare costs of tariff increases. That is, in general equilibrium, a tariff increase will induce a reduction in imports. This will have the effect of appreciating the real exchange rate to bring about equilibrium in the balance of trade. In the new equilibrium, exports will be reduced. That reduction in exports is an addition to the consumption of domestic consumers, whose welfare is increased accordingly. Simulations with this model (see de Melo and Tarr, 1988), suggest about a 50 percent overestimate of the welfare costs of tariffs, when the impact on the real exchange rate is ignored.

Anderson and Metzger also consider the case of an upward sloping import supply curve for imported crude oil and for gasoline. Since they assume that a tariff on crude oil not only has the effect of lowering the import supply price of crude oil, but at the same time has the effect of raising the price of imported gasoline, they have competing terms-of-trade effects that neutralize each other

only final demand for gasoline, and because the proposals to apply a tax on gasoline do not envision excluding intermediate usage from taxation. However, we find it difficult to reconcile our estimate of the ratio of welfare costs per dollar of tax revenues raised from excise taxes with the unusually high estimate of Boyd and Uri.[12]

4. EFFICIENT TAXATION OF U.S. PETROLEUM INDUSTRIES

Partial equilibrium analysis suggests that the least burdensome way to impose excise taxes to raise a given amount of revenue is to levy a set of excise taxes that vary inversely with the elasticity of final demand of the sector. When general equilibrium interactions are taken into account, rules are more difficult to derive, and numerical calculations are computationally difficult to obtain. Consequently, there has been little empirical work on the subject. Two previous numerical exercises of optimal tax or tariff calculations are Harris and MacKinnon (1979) and Dahl, Devarajan and van Wijnbergen (1986). The former paper develops an algorithm for the calculation of optimal taxes and provides largely illustrative examples. The latter paper calculates optimal tariffs for Cameroon, and investigates the conditions under which departures from a uniform tariff structure are optimal. The latter study does not, however, numerically consider the interaction of taxes with tariffs.

We now ask what is the least costly way, in terms of foregone welfare, to raise a specified amount of government revenue. Computationally, we choose the tariff (tm) and the excise tax rate (tx) in the oil and gas and petroleum products industries which maximize welfare subject to the additional constraint that the application of these taxes raise government revenue by $20 billion. To simplify the computation and interpretation of results in this section, assume that VERs are not binding. However, we maintain the existing tariffs in other sectors. Computations are done with the MINOS5 algorithm available from Brooke, Kendrick and Meeraus (1988).

The results of the computation of optimal tax rates appear in Table 5. The calculations are labelled O (oil and gas) and O + P (oil and gas

---

Table 5: Optimal Taxes to Raise $20 Billion in Government Revenue (Central Elasticity Case)

Industry	Taxation	(0)	(P)	(O+P)	(O+P) $\epsilon_m^s = 3.0$
Oil + Gas	tm	2.4		2.7	36.3
	tx	9.6		10.6	4.9
Petroleum products	tm		2.0	8.9	5.2
	tx		8.7	−1.4	−0.3
Change in welfare (EV)		−0.12	−0.10	−0.07	÷2.4

+ petroleum products) to reflect which industries are being taxed to raise government revenue.

A number of results stand out from a comparison of the alternative least costly taxation schemes to raise $20 billion in government revenue. First, if taxation is allowed in both energy sectors, the welfare cost of raising $20 billion is less than when taxation is only allowed for one sector only. This is an illustration of the principle that a given revenue objective can be achieved at a lower cost with additional tax instruments, because the additional tax instruments can be used to reduce the size of the wedge created by the objective of raising the tax. That is, all the distortion does not fall on one sector causing resources to flow out of the sector. If all sectors could be taxed, distortion-induced resource movements would be minimized.

Second, when revenues are raised by taxing only one sector, then an excise tax is less costly than a tariff at the same rate because it is neutral as to source. Thus, the least costly combination of excise tax and import tariff rates will involve a higher excise tax rate than tariff rate. When both instruments can be used for one industry at a time, the optimal combination suggested by the results in columns (O) and (P) is that the excise tax rate should be set at a rate about four times higher than the import tariff rate.

The fact that the excise tax is the preferred instrument to a tariff is an illustration of the principle, shown by Dixit (1985), that domestic goods and factor taxes or subsidies are superior instruments to tariffs for the purpose of raising revenue. This is because a tariff induces domestic resources to flow into the industry when the product can be obtained at a lower relative price through international trade, but the excise tax does not discriminate as to source. The question that naturally arises then is that given that the excise tax is preferred to tariffs, why are there any tariffs (albeit small ones) in the optimum. The answer

REVENUE-RAISING TAXES   443

to this question is that we have limited the use of excise taxes to the two energy sectors, so that other sectors are untaxed. When the energy sectors are taxed, but others are not, resources flow out of the energy sectors and into the rest of the economy. This is a distortion that is reduced through the use of a tariff. This principle is discussed further below, illustrated in Figure 2, and derived by Dahl, Devarajan and van Wijnbergen (1986) for the case of zero cross elasticity of final demand.[13]

Third, when both sectors can be taxed simultaneously, the pattern of optimal taxation is strongly influenced by the interdependence between the two sectors. The results in columns labelled (O + P) are understood when one realizes that a tax on crude oil is, in effect, a tax on petroleum products. This results in a second best situation where the output of the petroleum sector is too low, because it is being taxed indirectly, and the nonenergy sectors are not being taxed. As above, we understand the reason for the tariffs by recognizing that the sectors that receive relatively high excise taxation require some tariff protection to reduce distortion-induced resource movement. In Figure 2, we illustrate the situation in partial equilibrium. A tax on crude oil shifts up the supply curve for the petroleum industry to $S(1 + tx)$, creating a distortion (equal to area ABC) in the market for domestic petroleum products. This results in a second best situation where output of the petroleum sector is too low, because the nonenergy sectors are not being taxed. A tariff, tm, on imported petroleum products or, for that matter, a subsidy for domestic producers of petroleum products will reduce this distortion. Figure 2 illustrates how the distortion is reduced by raising the tariff on petroleum products. An increase in the tariff on imported petroleum products will induce an increase in demand for its principal substitute, domestic petroleum products, from D^0 to D'. This will reduce the distortion costs in the domestic petroleum products industry (caused by the tax on crude oil) from ABC to ADE.

The results in column $(O+P)$ support this interpretation: rates of taxation in oil and gas are at about the same values as in the case where taxation is only on the oil and gas sector, but domestic petroleum production is subsidized by the combination of an import tariff and a small subsidy. Of course, the net effective subsidy on petroleum production is negative and about equal to -4.6 ($= 1.4 + [.563 * 10.6]$)

---

[13]In addition, the base data contains a nonuniform tariff structure. When we allow the tariffs in the energy sectors to seek optimal levels, the optimal values will partly offset the distortions of the base tariff structure.

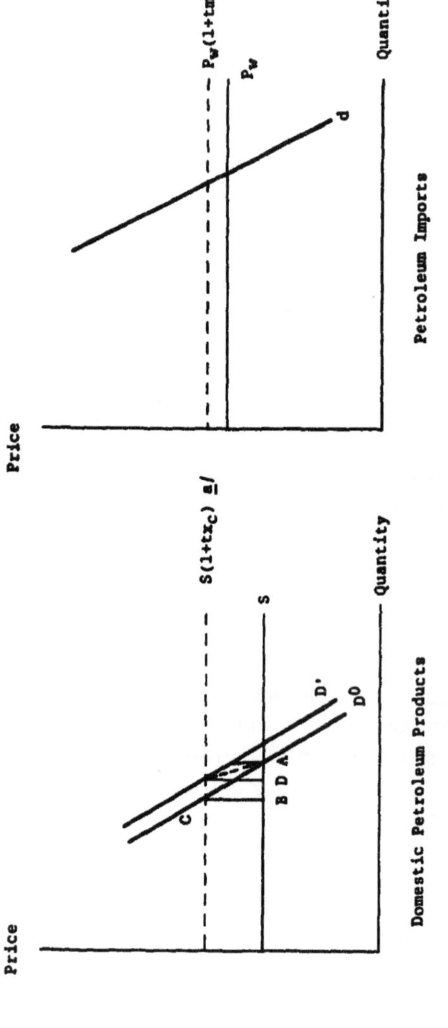

Figure 2. Welfare impact on domestic petroleum products of a tariff on imported petroleum products, given an excise tax on crude oil.

a/ tx_c is the excise tax on crude oil products.

REVENUE-RAISING TAXES   445

since purchases from the oil and gas sector comprise 56.3 percent of total costs of the petroleum products sector.

Fourth, note from the $(O + P)$ column, that the excise taxes and tariff rates are not uniform between the two sectors. It has been shown (see Atkinson and Stiglitz, 1980) that with perfectly inelastic labor supply, a uniform excise tax is optimal for revenue-raising purposes. Since a uniform tax on all goods is equivalent to a tax on labor alone, a uniform tax will minimize distortion induced resource movement if labor supply is perfectly inelastic.

With nonconstant labor supply, it is optimal to tax goods that are good substitutes with leisure at a lower rate to minimize distortion-induced consumption of leisure. A fully uniform tax is not possible in our case, because we have not allowed taxation of the nonenergy sectors. Analogous to the labor-leisure problem, we want to tax at a lower rate the good that is a better substitute for untaxed goods in the system. Since petroleum products are the better substitute for the other goods, it has the lower tax.

As a final illustration, the last column of Table 5 presents results where the United States is assumed to possess monopsony power on world oil markets. It considers the effect of an upward sloping supply curve of oil and gas imports on the selection of optimal taxation of both industries. Not surprisingly, the optimal taxation is now dominated by the optimal tariff on oil and gas imports which is set close to the rule of thumb welfare maximizing value $(1/(1 + \epsilon^s_m))$. Now the welfare gains from improved terms of trade dominate the calculations and welfare actually increases by $2.7 billion. Given the ability to raise revenue in a welfare enhancing manner through a tariff on crude oil, all other taxes (which are otherwise welfare reducing) are scaled down accordingly. Of course, this last simulation is only illustrative since it ignores both the possibility of retaliation and the case of a nonconstant import supply elasticity. Both considerations would lead to a lower optimal tariff rate than the one appearing in Table 5.

How much efficiency would be gained by the application of optimal tax rates instead of those proposed? We consider two experiments. First, recall from Table 4 that a 15 percent excise tax on petroleum products would raise $35 billion in government revenue. Allowing the optimal combination of import and excise taxes in petroleum products alone (2.4 percent and 15.1 percent, respectively) would reduce the welfare cost of raising $35 billion in revenue from $320 million to $300 million. In this case the welfare gains of optimal taxation are small, since the base experiment used only excise taxes and was close to the optimum. Second, recall from Table 3 that $42.8 billion is raised by the combination of a 25 percent import fee on crude oil and a 15 percent excise tax on petroleum. The welfare co~t of raising $42.8 billion by optimum taxation (with a set of rates proportional to those in column O+P of Table 5) falls from $2.34 billion to $276 million. Welfare gains of optimal taxation are much larger in this case because the baseline tax rates bear little relationship to the optimal taxation pattern for the two industries.

5. CONCLUSIONS

The estimates in this paper suggest that an import tariff on crude oil imports would be a very inefficient way to reduce the U.S. trade deficit. A tariff would cause much dislocation (an estimated 153 thousand workers would have to relocate) because sectors using crude oil would have to adjust to the 25 percent tariff on oil imports. Moreover, the welfare cost of such a proposed revenue-raising tax scheme would be large, resulting in an estimated welfare loss of 25 cents for every dollar of raised revenue. The paper shows that an excise tax would be a more efficient tax scheme to raise revenue, resulting in both a larger revenue per additional percent tax (because of a larger tax base) and a much lower welfare cost which we estimate in the neighborhood of one to two cents per dollar of raised revenue.

Besides being an inefficient instrument for raising revenue, an import tariff on crude oil would pose several problematic trade policy issues for the United States to begin with, because U.S. tariffs on crude oil are "bound" in the GATT, any rate increase would require compensation on other products. Futhermore, the GATT specifically prohibits the imposition of import fees for fiscal purposes (Article VIII:1(a)). Finally, an oil import fee would also complicate U.S. trade relations with Canada, Mexico, and Venezuela.

The paper also provides estimates of the least costly combination of excise tax and import tariffs in the crude oil and petroleum products sectors to raise a predetermined amount of government revenue. Because taxation is restricted to those two sectors only, and because of the linkages between the two sectors, the set of optimal taxes and tariffs is far from uniform. The least costly combination of tariffs and excise taxes in the energy sectors include taxation of crude oil (which has a lower elasticity of net demand than petroleum products and is hence a more efficient revenue-raiser)[14] combined with a tariff and a small subsidy on petroleum products to counteract the distortionary costs induced by the taxation of crude oil which accounts for nearly

REVENUE-RAISING TAXES   447

two-thirds of the value of intermediate purchases by the petroleum products sector.

APPENDIX: ELASTICITY SPECIFICATION

Table A1 describes the complete set of elasticities used in the model for the central elasticity calculations. The "low" and "high" elasticity elasticity results are derived by simulating the model with a set of elasticities derived from those in table A1 by subtracting (adding) one standard deviation.

REFERENCES

Anderson, K. and Metzger, M. (1987) A Critical Evaluation of Petroleum Import Tariffs. Analytical and Historical Perspectives. Washington, D.C., U.S. Federal Trade Commission.

Atkinson, and Stiglitz, J. (1980) *Public Economics*. New York: McGraw Hill.

Bhagwati, J. (1971) "The Generalized Theory of Distortions and Welfare," in *Trade, Balance of Payments and Growth*, ed. by J. Bhagwati et al., Amsterdam: North-Holland.

Bhagwati, J. and Srinivasan, T.N. (1969) Optimal Intervention to Achieve Non-Economic Objectives, *Review of Economic Studies* 36: 27–38.

Bohi, D. and Russell, M. (1978) *Limiting Oil Imports: An Economic History and Analysis*. Baltimore: Johns Hopkins University.

Borges, A.M. and Goulder, L.H. (1984) "Decomposing the Impact of Higher Energy Prices on Long-Term Growth," in *Applied General Equilibrium Analysis*, H.E. Scarf and J.B. Shoven (eds.). Cambridge: Cambridge University Press.

Boyd, R. and Uri, N. (1988a) Assessing the Impact of an Oil Import Fee, *Energy: the International Journal*, forthcoming.

Boyd, R. and Uri, N. (1988b) The Potential Benefits and Costs of an Increase in the Gasoline Tax, *Energy Policy*, forthcoming.

Brooke, A., Kendrick, D. and Meeraus, A. (1988) *GAMS: A User's Guide*. Redwood City, CA: The Scientific Press.

Caddy, V. (1976) Empirical Estimation of the Elasticity of Substitution: A Review. Preliminary Working Paper OP-09, IMPACT Project. IAC, Melbourne, Australia.

Committee on Ways and Means (June 25, 1987). Description of Possible Options to Increase Revenue. U.S. House of Representatives, U.S. Government Printing Office, Washington.

Congressional Budget Office (January 1987). Reducing the Deficit: Spending and Revenue Options. U.S. Government Printing Office, Washington.

Dahl, H., Devarajan, S. and van Wijnbergen, S. (1986) Revenue Neutral Tariff Reform: Theory and an Application to Cameroon. CPP Discussion Paper No. 1986-26. World Bank, Washington, D.C.

Department of Energy (1987) Energy Security. U.S. Department of Energy, Washington, D.C.

---

[14]Our selection of elasticities yield comparable substitution possibilities at the intermediate level, but crude oil is a pure intermediate product, so net elasticities of demand are different between the two sectors.

Table A1: Elasticity Specification (Central Case)

Sector	Column notes					Elasticity of substitution intermediates (+)	Elasticity of substitution capital/labor	Elasticity of transformation domestic/export sales	Price elasticities of final demand		Premia rates
	(1)	(2)	(3)	(4)	(5)	(1)	(2)	(3)	Domestic (4)	Imports (5)	(6)
Agriculture	a	c	e	k	f	1.4	0.6	4.0	0.75	0.8	
Food	a	c	e	f	f	0.3	0.8	3.0	0.90	1.1	
Mining	b	b	e	j	f	0.5	0.8	3.0	0.50	1.0	
Crude Oil and Natural Gas	f	c	e	j	a,f,e	2.4	0.8	3.0	.5	.9	
Iron and Steel	a	d	e	i	f	3.0	1.0	3.0	1.0	1.4	
Motor Vehicles	a	c	e	h	h	2.0	0.8	3.0	1.2	1.1	22.8%
Textiles and Apparel	a	c	e	l	f	2.6	?.0	3.0	0.4	3.9	40.5%
Other Manufactures	a	c	e	f	f	3.6	0.8	3.0	1.5	1.8	
Other Consumer	a	c	e	f	f	3.2	0.8	3.0	1.9	2.4	
Petroleum Products	f	c	e	j,e	a,f	2.4	0.8	3.0	.5	.9	
Traded Services	b	c	e	g	g	2.0	0.8	0.7	0.5	0.6	
Non-Traded Services		b		g			0.8		0.5		

(+) CES and CET functions imply that the corresponding elasticities of substitution (transformation) correspond to compensated import demand (export supply) elasticities.

All price elasticities of demand defined as positive numbers. For estimates, see de Melo and Tarr (1988). Column notes correspond to the sources from which estimates are interpolated. For interpolation details see Tarr (1988).

(a) Shiells, Deardorff and Stern (1986); (b) Dixon *et al.* (1982); (c) Caddy (1976); (d) Hekman; (e) own estimates; (f) Stern, Francis and Schumacher (1976); (g) Houthakker and Taylor (1970); (h) Levinsohn; (i) Crandall (1981); (j) Bohi and Russell (1978); (k) USDA (1984); (l) Hufbauer *et al.* (1986).

REVENUE-RAISING TAXES   449

Dixit, A. (1985) "Tax Policy in Open Economies," in A. Auerbach and M. Feldstein, eds., *Handbook of Public Economics,* Amsterdam: North-Holland.

Greenspan, A. (March 2, 1988). Testimony. Senate Budget Committee.

Harris, R. and MacKinnon, J.G. (1979) Computing Optimal Tax Equilibria, *Journal of Public Economics* 11: 197–212.

Hudson, E. and Jorgenson, D. (1974) US Energy Policy and Economic Growth 1975–2000. Discussion Paper No. 372, Harvard Institute of Economic Research, Cambridge, Mass.

Manne, A.S. (1976) ETA: A Model for Energy Technology Assessment, *Bell Journal of Economics and Management Science* 7: 379–406.

Manne, A.S. (1984) "Comments," in *Applied General Equilibrium Analysis,* H.E. Scarf and J.B. Shoven (eds.). Cambridge: Cambridge University Press.

Melo, J. de and Tarr, D. (1988) The Welfare Costs of U.S. Quotas in Textiles, Autos and Steel. World Bank, Washington, D.C., mimeo.

Pigou, A.C. (1947) *A Study in Public Finance.* 3rd ed. London: Macmillan.

Shiells, C., Stern, P. and Deardorff, A. (1986) Estimates of the Elasticities of Substitution Between Imports and Home Goods for the United States, *Weltwirtschaftliches Archiv,* pp. 497–519.

Stern, R.M., Francis, J. and Schumacher, B. (1976) *Price Elasticities in International Trade: An Annotated Bibliography.* London: Macmillan Press.

Tarr, D. (1988) A General Equilibrium Analysis of Quotas on U.S. Imports. US Federal Trade Commission, Washington, D.C.

U.S. General Accounting Office. (1986) Petroleum Products: Effects of Imports on US Oil Refineries and US Energy Security. Washington, D.C.

Varian, H. (1984) *Microeconomic Analysis.* New York: Norton.